JULIA WARD HOWE

1819–1910

IN TWO VOLUMES
VOLUME I

Julia Ward Howe.

Julia Ward Howe
1819-1910

By
Laura E. Richards
and Maude Howe Elliott

Assisted by
Florence Howe Hall

*With Portraits and other
Illustrations*

Volume I

Cherokee Publishing Company
Atlanta, Georgia
1990

Library of Congress Cataloging-in-Publication Data

Richards, Laura Elizabeth Howe, 1850-1943.
    Julia Ward Howe, 1819-1910 / by Laura E. Richards and
  Maude Howe Elliott : assisted by Florence Howe Hall
        p.   cm.
    Reprint. Originally published : Boston : Houghton Mifflin, 1915.
    Includes index.
    ISBN: 0-87797-196-X (cloth) : $39.95
    1. Howe, Julia Ward, 1819-1910--Biography.   2. Authors, American-
  -19th century--Biography.   3. Feminists--United States--Biography.
    I. Elliott, Maude Howe, 1854-1948.   II. Hall, Florence Howe, 1845-
  1922.   III. Title.
  PS2018.R5   1990
  811'.3--dc20
                                                                  90-47729
                                                                       CIP

This book is printed on acid-free paper which conforms to the American National
Standard Z39.48-1984 *Permanence of Paper for Printed Library Materials.* Paper
that conforms to this standard's requirements for pH, alkaline reserve and
freedom from groundwood is anticipated to last several hundred years without
significant deterioration under normal library use and storage conditions.

Manufactured in the United States of America

ISBN: 0-87797-196-X

94   93   92   91   90   10   9   8   7   6   5   4   3   2   1

Published by arrangement with Houghton Mifflin Company.

 Cherokee Publishing Company is an operating division of
The Larlin Corporation, P O Box 1730, Marietta, Ga 30061

TO
HENRY MARION HOWE

CONTENTS

ILLUSTRATIONS

JULIA WARD HOWE

JULIA WARD HOWE

CHAPTER I

ANCESTRAL

These are my people, quaint and ancient,
Gentlefolks with their prim old ways;
This, their leader come from England,
Governed a State in early days.

. . . .

I must vanish with my ancients,
But a golden web of love
Is around us and beneath us,
Binds us to our home above.

JULIA WARD HOWE.

OUR mother was once present at a meeting where
there was talk of ancestry and heredity. One of the
speakers dwelt largely upon the sins of the fathers.
He drew stern pictures of the vice, the barbarism, the
heathenism of the "good old times," and ended by
saying with emphasis that he felt himself "*bowed down
beneath the burden of the sins of his ancestors.*"

Our mother was on her feet in a flash.

"Mr. So-and-So," she said, "is bowed down by the
sins of his ancestors. I wish to say that all my life I
have been buoyed up and lifted on by the remembrance of the virtues of mine!"

These words are so characteristic of her, that in beginning the story of her life it seems proper to dwell
at some length on the ancestors whose memory she
cherished with such reverence.

The name of Ward occurs first on the roll of Battle
Abbey: "Seven hundred and ten distinguished persons" accompanied William of Normandy to England,
among them "Ward, one of the noble captains."

Her first known ancestor, John Ward, of Gloucester,
England, sometime cavalry officer in Cromwell's army,
came to this country after the Restoration and settled
at Newport in Rhode Island. His son Thomas married Amy Smith, a granddaughter of Roger Williams.
Thomas's son Richard became Governor of Rhode
Island and had fourteen children, among them Samuel,
who in turn became Governor of the Colony, and a
member of the Continental Congress. He was the only
Colonial governor who refused to take the oath to enforce the Stamp Act. In 1775, in the Continental Congress, he was made Chairman of the Committee of the
Whole, which from 1774 to 1776 sat daily, working
without intermission in the cause of independence.
But though one of the framers of the "Declaration,"
he was not destined to be a "signer." John Adams
says of him, "When he was seized with the smallpox
he said that if his vote and voice were necessary to
support the cause of his country, he should live; if not,
he should die. He died, and the cause of his country
was supported, but it lost one of its most sincere and
punctual advocates."

The correspondence between Governor Ward and
General Washington has been preserved. In one letter
the latter says: "I think, should occasion offer, I shall
be able to give you a good account of your son, as he
seems a sensible, well-informed young man."

This young man was Samuel Ward, Lieutenant-Colonel of the First Rhode Island Regiment, and our mother's grandfather.[1]

In Trumbull's painting of the Attack on Quebec in 1776, there is a portrait of Lieutenant-Colonel Ward, a young, active figure with sword uplifted. His life was full of stirring incident. In 1775 he received his commission as Captain, and was one of two hundred and fifty of the Rhode Island troops who volunteered to join Benedict Arnold's command of eleven hundred men, ordered to advance by way of the Kennebec River to reinforce General Montgomery at Quebec. In a letter to his family, dated Point-aux-Trembles, November 26, 1775, Captain Ward says: "We were thirty days in the wilderness, that none but savages ever attempted to pass. We marched a hundred miles upon shore with only three days' provisions, waded over three rapid rivers, marched through snow and ice barefoot, passed over the St. Lawrence where it was guarded by the enemy's frigates, and are now resting about twenty-four miles from the city to recruit our worn-out natures. General Montgomery intends to join us immediately, so that we have a winter's campaign before us. But I trust we shall have the glory of taking Quebec!"

The young soldier's hopes were vain. He was taken prisoner with many of his men while gallantly defending a difficult position, and spent a year in prison. On his release he rejoined the army of Washington and

[1] Born 1756, died 1832. He graduated in 1771 from Rhode Island College (now Brown University) with distinguished honors.

fought through the greater part of the Revolution,
rising to the rank of Lieutenant-Colonel. He was at
Peekskill, Valley Forge, and Red Bank, and wrote the
official account of the last-named battle, which may be
found in Washington's correspondence.

During the terrible winter at Valley Forge, Lieutenant-Colonel Ward obtained a month's furlough, wooed
and married his cousin, Phœbe Greene (daughter of
Governor William Greene, of Rhode Island, and of the
beautiful Catherine Ray,[1] of Block Island), and returned to the snows and starvation of the winter camp.
Our mother was very proud of her great-grandmother
Catherine's memory, treasured her rat-tail spoons and
her wedding stockings of orange silk, and was fond
of telling how Benjamin Franklin admired and corresponded with her. Some of Franklin's letters have
been preserved. He speaks of his wife as the "old
lady," but says he has got so used to her faults that
they are like his own — he does not recognize them
any more. In one letter he gives the following advice
to the lovely Catherine: "Kill no more Pigeons than
you can eat. Go constantly to meeting or to church —
till you get a good husband; then stay at home and
nurse the children and live like a Christian."

Some years after the Revolution, Colonel Ward was
in Paris on a business errand. He kept a record of his
stay there in a parchment pocket-book, where among
technical entries are found brief comments on matters
of general interest. One day the Colonel tells of a din-

---

[1] Granddaughter of Simon Ray, one of the original owners of the island.
He was "pressed in a cheese-press" on account of his religious opinions.

ner party where he met Vergniaud and other prominent revolutionists. He was surprised to find them such plain men; "yet were they exceeding warm." On December 29, 1792, he notes: "Dined with Gouverneur Morris. Served upon plate — good wines — his Kitchen neither french or English, but between both. Servants french, apartments good. . . . I have visited the halls of painting and sculpture at the Louvre. The peices [*sic*] are all called *chef d'œuvres* by connoisseurs. The oldest are thought the best, I cannot tell why, though some of the old peices are very good. Milo riving the oak is good. . . ."

He went to the theatre, and observed that the features which appeared to him most objectionable were specially applauded by the audience.

Briefly, amid items of the sale of land, he thus notes the execution of Louis XVI: —

"January 15th. The convention has this day decided upon two questions on the King; one that he was guilty, another that the question should not be sent to the people.

"January 17th. The convention up all night upon the question of the King's sentence. At eleven this night the question was determined — the sentence of death was pronounced. 366 death — 319 seclusion or banishment — 36 various — majority of 5 absolute — the King caused an appeal to be made to the people, which was not allowed; thus the convention have been the accusers, the judges, and will be the executors of their own sentence — this will cause a great degree of astonishment in America. . . .

"January 21st. Went to the Pont Royal to pass it at nine o'clock. Guards prevented me from going over. I had engaged to pass this day, which is one of horror, at Versailles, with Mr. Morris. The King was beheaded at eleven o'clock. Guards, at an early hour, took possession of the *Place Louis XV*, and were posted in each avenue. The most profound peace prevailed. Those who had feeling lamented in secret in their houses, or had left town. Others showed the same levity or barbarous indifference as on former occasions. Hichborn, Henderson, and Johnson went to see the execution, for which, as an American, I was sorry. The King desired to speak. He had only time to say he was innocent, and forgave his enemies. He behaved with the fortitude of a martyr. Santerre ordered the [executioner] to dispatch him. At twelve the streets were again all open."

There is a tradition that when Colonel Ward quitted Paris, with a party of friends, the carriage was driven by a disguised nobleman, who thus escaped the guillotine.

Our mother remembered him as a "gentleman advanced in years, with courtly manner and mild blue eyes, which were, in spite of their mildness, very observing."

She inherited many traits from the Wards, among them a force and integrity of purpose, a strength of character, and a certain business instinct which sometimes cropped up when least expected, and which caused some of her family to call her the "banker's daughter."

Those were also solid qualities which she inherited

from the Rhode Island Greenes. Greenes of Warwick, Greenes of East Greenwich; all through Colonial and Revolutionary history we find their names. Sturdy, active, patriotic men: Generals, Colonels, and Governors of "Rhode Island and Providence Plantations," chief among them Governor William Greene, the "War Governor," and General Nathanael Greene of glorious memory.

Our liveliest association with the name of Greene is the memory of Mrs. Nancy Greene, first cousin of our grandfather Ward and daughter-in-law of the General who died in Middletown, Rhode Island, in 1886, at the age of one hundred and two. This lady was dear to our mother as the one remaining link with her father's generation. A visit to "Cousin Nancy" was one of her great pleasures, and we children were happy if we were allowed to accompany her. The old lady sat erect and dignified in her straight-backed chair, and the two discoursed at length of days gone by. To Cousin Nancy "Julia" was always young, though the "Battle Hymn of the Republic" was already written when the old lady charged her to "cultivate a literary taste." On another occasion — it was one of the later visits — she said with emphasis, "Julia, do not allow yourself to grow old! When you feel that you *cannot* do a thing, *get up and do it!* " Julia never forgot this advice.

Cousin Nancy never read a novel in her life, as she announced with pride. She wished to read the "Annals of the Schönberg-Cotta Family," but, finding it to be a work of fiction, decided not to break her rule. She was

a fond and pious mother; when her son needed chas-
tisement, she would pray over him so long that he
would cry out, "Mother, it is time to begin whipping!"

If Julia Ward was part Ward and Greene, she was
quite as much Cutler and Marion; it is to this descent
that we must turn for the best explanation of her
many-sided character.

When she said of any relation, however distant, "He
is a Cutler!" it meant that she recognized in that person certain qualities — a warmth of temperament, a
personality glowing, sparkling, effervescent — akin to
her own. If in addition to these qualities the person
had red hair, she took him to her heart, and he could
do no wrong. All this, and a host of tender associations beside, the name of Cutler meant to her; yet it
may be questioned whether any of these characteristics would have appeared in the descendants of Johannes Demesmaker, worthy citizen of Holland, who,
coming to this country in 1674, changed his name to
Cutler for convenience' sake, had not one of these
descendants, Benjamin Clarke Cutler, married Sarah
(Mitchell) Hyrne, daughter of Thomas Mitchell and
Esther (or Hester) Marion.

To most people, the name of Marion suggests one
person only, — General Francis Marion of Revolutionary fame; yet it was the grandfather of the General,
Benjamin Marion, of La Rochelle, who was the first of
the name to settle in this country, coming hither when
the Revocation of the Edict of Nantes drove the
Huguenots into exile. Brigadier-General Peter Horry,[1]

---

[1] See Horry and Weems, *Life of Marion*. General Horry was a most

friend and biographer of General Marion, quotes the
letter which told Benjamin of his banishment: —

Your damnable heresy well deserves, even in this
life, that purgation by fire which awfully awaits it in
the next. But in consideration of your youth and worthy connections, our mercy has condescended to com-
mute your punishment to perpetual exile. You will,
therefore, instantly prepare to quit your country forever, for, if after ten days from the date hereof, you
should be found in any part of the kingdom, your miserable body shall be consumed by fire and your impious
ashes scattered on the winds of heaven.

(Signed) PÈRE ROCHELLE.

Within the ten days Benjamin Marion had wound
up his affairs, married his betrothed, Judith Baluet,
and was on his way to America to seek his fortune. He
bought a plantation on Goose Creek, near Charleston,
South Carolina, and here he and his Judith lived for
many peaceful years in content and prosperity, seeing
their children grow up around them.[1]

zealous and devoted friend; as a biographer his accuracy is questionable,
his picturesqueness never.

[1] We have not found the date of his death, but Horry gives the principal features of his will as he got them from the family. He calls Judith
Marion "Louisa," but that is his picturesque way. She may have been
"Judith Louisa"! Women's names were not of much consequence in those
days.

"After having, in the good old way, bequeathed 'his soul to God who
gave it,' and 'his body to the earth out of which it was taken,' he proceeds: —

"'In the first place, as to debts, thank God, I owe none, and therefore
shall give my executors but little trouble on that score.

"'Secondly, — As to the poor, I have always treated them as my brethren. My dear family will, I know, follow my example.

"'Thirdly, — As to the wealth with which God has been pleased to bless

Gabriel Marion, the eldest son of Benjamin, married
a young woman, also of Huguenot blood, Charlotte
Cordés or Corday, said to have been a relative of the
other Charlotte Corday, the heroine of the French
Revolution. To this couple were born six children, the
eldest being Esther, our mother's great-grandmother,
the youngest, Francis, who was to become the "Swamp
Fox" of Revolutionary days.

Esther Marion has been called the "Queen Bee" of
the Marion hive; she had fifteen children, and her descendants have multiplied and spread in every direction.
She was twice married, first to John Allston, of Georgetown, or Waccamaw, secondly to Thomas Mitchell,
of Georgetown. The only one of the fifteen children
with whom we have concern is Sarah Mitchell, the
"Grandma Cutler" of Julia Ward's childhood. This
lady was married at fourteen to Dr. Hyrne, an officer of
Washington's army. Julia well remembered her saying that after her engagement, she wept on being told
that she must give up her dolls.

me and my dear Louisa and children, lovingly have we labored together
for it — lovingly we have enjoyed it — and now, with a glad and grateful
heart do I leave it among them.

"'I give my beloved Louisa all my ready money — that she may never
be alarmed at a sudden call.

"'I give her all my fat calves and lambs, my pigs and poultry — that
she may always keep a good table.

"'I give her my new carriage and horses — that she may visit her
friends in comfort.

"'I give her my family Bible — that she may live above the ill-tempers
and sorrows of life.

"'I give my son Peter a hornbook — for I am afraid he will always be
a dunce.'"

General Horry goes on to say that Peter was so stunned by this squib
that he "instantly quit his raccoon hunting by night and betook himself
to reading, and soon became a very sensible and charming young man."

Dr. Hyrne lived but a short time, and four years after his death the twenty-year-old widow married Benjamin Clarke Cutler, then a widower, Sheriff of Norfolk County, Massachusetts, and third in descent from John Demesmaker,[1] before mentioned, sometime physician and surgeon.

Our mother was much attached to "Grandma Cutler," and speaks thus of her in a sketch entitled "The Elegant Literature of Sixty Years Ago": "Grandma will read Owen Feltham's 'Resolves,' albeit the print is too small for her eyes. She knows Pope and Crabbe by heart, admires Shenstone, and tells me which scenes are considered finest in this or that of Scott's novels. Calling one day upon a compeer of her own age, she was scandalized to find her occupied with a silly story called 'Jimmy Jessamy.'"

Mrs. Cutler had known General Washington, and was fond of telling how at a ball the Commander-in-Chief crossed the room to speak to her. Many of her letters have been preserved, and show a sprightliness which is well borne out by her portrait, that of a charming old lady in a turban, with bright eyes and a humorous mouth.

A word remains to be said about General Francis Marion himself. This hero of history, song, and romance was childless; our mother could claim as near relationship to him as could any of her generation. She was extremely proud of this kinship, and no one who

---

[1] On first coming to this country, Johannes Demesmaker settled in Hingham, Massachusetts. Later he moved to Boston, where he became known as Dr. John Cutler; married Mary Cowell, of Boston, and served as surgeon in King Philip's War.

knew her could doubt that from the Marions she inherited many vital qualities. One winter, toward the
end of her life, there was a meeting at the Old South
Church at which — as at the gathering described at the
beginning of this chapter — there was talk of ancestry
and kindred topics. The weather was stormy, our
mother well on in the eighties, but she was there. Being called on to speak, she made a brief address in the
course of which she alluded to her Southern descent,
and to General Francis Marion, her great-great-uncle.
As she spoke her eyes lightened with mirth, in the way
we all remember: "General Marion," she said, "was
known in his generation as the 'Swamp Fox'; and when
I succeed in eluding the care of my guardians, children and grandchildren, and coming to a meeting like
this, I think I may be said to have inherited some of
his characteristics!"

CHAPTER II

LITTLE JULIA WARD

1819–1835; *aet.* 1–16

FROM MY NURSERY: FORTY-SIX YEARS AGO

When I was a little child,
Said my passionate nurse, and wild:
"Wash you, children, clean and white;
God may call you any night."

Close my tender brother clung,
While I said with doubtful tongue:
"No, we cannot die so soon;
For you told, the other noon,

"Of those months in order fine
That should make the earth divine.
I've not seen, scarce five years old,
Months like those of which you told."

Softly, then, the woman's hand
Loosed my frock from silken bánd,
Tender smoothed the fiery head,
Often shamed for ringlets red.
Somewhat gently did she say,
"Child, those months are every day."

Still, methinks, I wait in fear,
For that wonder-glorious year —
For a spring without a storm,
Summer honey-dewed and warm,
Autumn of robuster strength,
Winter piled in crystal length.

I will wash me clean and white;
God may call me any night.
I must tell Him when I go
His great year is yet to know —
Year when working of the race
Shall match Creation's dial face;
Each hour be born of music's chime,
And Truth eternal told in Time.   J. W. H.

LIEUTENANT-COLONEL WARD had ten children, of
whom seven lived to grow up. The fifth child and

son was Samuel, our mother's father, born in Warwick, Rhode Island, May 1, 1786. When he was four
years old, the family moved to New York, where
the Colonel and his brother established themselves
as merchants under the firm name of Samuel Ward
& Brother.

The firm was only moderately successful; the children came fast. With his narrow income it was not
possible for the father to give his boy the college education he desired; so at fourteen, fresh from the common
schools, Samuel entered as a clerk the banking house
of Prime & King. While still a mere lad, an old friend
of the family asked him what he meant to be when he
came to man's estate.

"I mean to be one of the first bankers in the United
States!" replied Samuel.

At the age of twenty-two he became a partner in the
firm, which was thereafter known as Prime, Ward &
King.

In a memoir of our grandfather, the partner who
survived him, Mr. Charles King, says: —

"Money was the commodity in which Mr. Ward
dealt, and if, as is hardly to be disputed, money be the
root of all evil, it is also, in hands that know how to use
it worthily, the instrument of much good. There exist
undoubtedly, in regard to the trade in money, and
respecting those engaged in it, many and absurd prejudices, inherited in part from ancient error, and fo-
mented and kept alive by the jealousies of ignorance
and indigence. It is therefore no small triumph to have
lived down, as Mr. Ward did, this prejudice, and to

SAMUEL WARD

From a painting in the possession of his grandson
Henry Marion Howe

JULIA RUSH WARD

From a painting in the possession of her granddaughter
Mrs. Henry Richards

have forced upon the community in the midst of which he resided, and upon all brought into connexion with him, the conviction that commerce in money, like commerce in general, is, to a lofty spirit, lofty and ennobling, and is valued more for the power it confers, of promoting liberal and beneficent enterprises, and of conducing to the welfare and prosperity of society, than for the means of individual and selfish gratification or indulgence."

Mr. Ward's activities were not confined to financial affairs. He was founder and first president of the Bank of Commerce; one of the founders of the New York University and of the Stuyvesant Institute, etc., etc.

In 1812 he married Julia Rush Cutler, second daughter of Benjamin Clarke and Sarah Mitchell (Hyrne) Cutler. Julia Cutler was sixteen years old at the time of her marriage, lovely in character and beautiful in person. She had been a pupil of the saintly Isabella Graham, and her literary taste had been carefully cultivated in the style of the day. One of her poems, found in Griswold's "Female Poets of America," shows the deeply religious cast of her mind; yet she was full of gentle gayety, loved music, laughter, and pretty things.

During the first years of their married life, Mr. and Mrs. Ward lived in Marketfield Street, near the Battery. Here four children were born, Samuel and Henry, and the two Julias. She who was known as "the first little Julia" lived only four years. During her fatal illness her father was called away by urgent business. In great distress of mind, he arranged that certain tokens should inform him of the child's condition. A few days later, as he was riding homeward, a messenger came to meet him and silently laid in his hand a tiny shoe: the child was dead.

Not long after this, on May 27, 1819, a second daughter was born, and named Julia.

Julia Ward was very little when her parents moved to "a large house on the Bowling Green, a region of high fashion in those days." [1] Here were born three more children: Francis Marion, Louisa Cutler, and Ann Eliza. For some time before the birth of the last-named child, Mrs. Ward's health had been gradually failing, though every known measure had been used to restore it. There had been journeys to Niagara and up the Hudson, in the family coach, straw-color outside with linings and cushions of brilliant blue. Little Julia went with her mother on these journeys; the good elder sister, Eliza Cutler, was also of the party; and a physician, Dr. John Wakefield Francis, who was later to play an important part in the family life. Julia remembered many incidents of these journeys, though the latest of them took place when she was barely four years old. She sat in a little chair placed at the feet of her elders, and she used to tell us how, cramped with remaining in one position, she was constantly moving the chair, bringing its feet down on those of Dr. Francis, to his acute anguish. In spite of this, the good doctor would often read to her from a book of short tales and poems which had been brought for her amusement, and she always remembered his reading

[1] *Reminiscences,* p. 4.

of "Pity the sorrows of a poor old man," and how it
brought the tears to her eyes.

At Niagara Falls she asked Dr. Francis, "Who made
that great hole where the water came down?" and was
told "The great Maker of all!" This puzzled her, and
she inquired further, but when her friend said, "Do
you not know? Our Father who art in heaven!" she
"felt that she ought to have known, and went away
somewhat abashed." [1]

She remembered a visit to Red Jacket, the famous
Indian chief, at his encampment. Julia was given a
twist of tobacco tied with blue ribbon, which she was
to present to him. At sight of the tall, dignified savage, the child sprang forward and threw her arms
round his neck, to the great discomfiture of both; baby
as she was, Julia felt at once that her embrace was
unexpected and unwelcome.

Sometimes they went to the pleasant farm at
Jamaica, Long Island, where Lieutenant-Colonel Ward
was living at this time, with his unmarried sons, and
his two daughters, Phœbe and Anne.

Phœbe was an invalid saint. She lived in a darkened
room, and the plates and dishes from which she ate
were of brown china or crockery, as she fancied her
eyes could not bear white. Anne was equally pious, but
more normal. She it was who managed the farm, and
who would always bring the cheeses to New York herself for the market, lest any of the family grow proud
and belittle the dignity of honest work.

It is from Jamaica that Mrs. Ward writes to her

---

[1] *Reminiscences*, p. 4.

mother a letter which shows that though the tenderest
of mothers, she had been strictly imbued with the Old
Testament ideas of bringing up children.

DEAREST MOTHER, — . . . I find myself better since
I came hither. . . . Husband *more devoted than ever;*
children sweet tho' something of a drawback on my
recovery. . . . Thus in one page, you have the whole
history of my present life, reading and thinking only
excepted, which occupy by far the greatest portion of
my time. . . . I was obliged to whip Julia yesterday
afternoon, and have been sick ever since in consequence of the agitation it threw me into. . . . I felt
obliged to try Solomon's prescription, which had a
worse effect on me than on her. . . . I think it is the
last time, however, blow high or low, for she is as
nervous as her mama was at her age, at the sight
of a rod, and screamed herself almost to death; indeed her nerves were so affected that she cannot get
over it and has cried all today, trembling as violently
as if she had the ague all the time I whipped her and
could not eat.

Julia was to retain through life the memories of the
dear mother so early lost. She remembered her first
sewing-lesson; how being told to take the needle in one
hand she straightway placed the thimble on the other.
She remembered her first efforts to say "mother," and
how "muzzer" was all she could produce, till "the
dear parent presently said, 'if you cannot do better
than that, you will have to go back and call me

"mamma."' The shame of going back moved me to one last effort, and, summoning my utmost strength of tongue I succeeded in saying 'mother.'" [1]

All devices to restore the young mother's failing strength were in vain: soon after giving birth to the fourth daughter, Ann Eliza, she died.

Her life had been pure, happy, and unselfish; yet her last hours were full of anguish. Reared in the strictest tenets of Evangelical piety, she was oppressed with terror concerning the fate of her soul; the sorrows of death compassed her about, the pains of hell gat hold upon her. It is piteous to read of the sufferings of this innocent creature, as described by her mourning family; piteous, too, to realize, by the light of to-day, that she was almost literally *prayed to death*. She was twenty-seven years old when she died and had borne seven children.

Mr. Ward's grief at the death of this beloved wife was so extreme as to bring on a severe illness. For some time he could not bear to see the child who, he thought, had cost her mother's life; and though he gathered his other children tenderly around him, the little Annie was kept out of his sight.

By and by his father came to make him a visit and heard of this state of things. Going to the nursery, the old gentleman took the baby from its nurse, and carrying it into the room where his son sat desolate, laid it gently in his arms. From that moment the little youngest became almost his dearest care.

He could not live with his sorrow in the same dwell-

[1] *Reminiscences*, p. 8.

ing that had contained his joy. The beautiful house at
Bowling Green was sold, with the new furniture which
had lately been ordered to please his Julia, and which
the children never saw uncovered; and the family
removed to Bond Street, then at the upper end of
New York City.

"Mr. Ward," said his friends, "you are going out
of town!"

Bond Street in the twentieth century is an unlovely
thoroughfare, grimy, frowzy, given over largely to the
sale of feathers and artificial flowers; Bond Street in the
early part of the nineteenth century was a different
affair.

The first settler in the street was Jonas Minturn,
who about 1825 built No. 22. Mr. Ward came next.
The city was then so remote, one could hardly see the
houses to the south across the woods and fields.

The Ward children saw the street grow up around
them; saw the dignified houses, brick or freestone, built
and occupied by Kings, Halls, Morgans, Grinnells,
most of all by Wards. Mr. Ward was then at No. 16;
his father, the old Revolutionary soldier, soon came to
live at No. 7, with his daughter Anne; his brother
Henry was first at No. 14, then at No. 23; while his
brother John was to make No. 8 a dwelling beloved
by three generations.

Julia did not remember in what year her father
bought the tract of land at the corner of Bond Street
and Broadway. At first a large part of it was fenced in,
and used as a riding-ring by the Ward boys. There
was also, either here or at No. 16, something in the

"THE CORNER"

The house built by Mr. Ward in 1835 at the corner of Bond Street and Broadway

way of a garden, which she thus recalls in an address on horticulture, given in her later years: —

"My earliest horticultural recollections go back to an enclosure, usually called a yard, in the rear of my father's house in New York. When my little brother and I were turned out to play there, we might just as well have picked the bugs off the rosebushes as the buds, of which we made wicked havoc. Not knowing what to do with the flower border, we barbarized instead of cultivating it. Being of extremely inquiring minds, we picked the larkspurs and laburnums to pieces, but became nothing the wiser for the process. A little daily tuition might have transformed us into a miniature Adam and Eve, and might have taught us some things that these old friends of ours did not know. But tuition to us then meant six or eight daily hours passed in dry conversation with the family governess or French master. No one dreamed of turning the enamelled pages of the garden for us. We grew up consequently with the city measure of the universe — your own house, somebody else's, the trees in the park, a strip of blue sky overhead, and a great deal of talk about Nature read from the best authors. Much that is most beautiful in the works of all the poets was perfectly unintelligible to us, because we had never seen the phenomena referred to; or if we had seen them, we had not been taught to observe them. You will ask where we passed our summers? In travelling, or at the seashore, perhaps. But we took our city measure with us, and were never quite at home beyond its limits."

She adds: "I state these facts only to show how

much of the world's beauty and value may be shut out
from the eyes of a human being, by even a careful education! This loss cannot easily be remedied in later
years. I myself had reached mature life before I experienced the deep and calm enjoyments of country
life. The long, still summer days, the open, fragrant
fields, the shy wild blossoms, the song of birds; these
won me at last to delight in them — at first they
seemed to me only a void. It was a new gospel that the
meadows taught me, and my own little children were
its interpreters. I know now some country craft, and
could even trim fruit trees and weed garden beds. But
I have always regretted in this respect the lost time of
youth. When I made acquaintance with Nature, I was
too old to learn the skill of gardening. Year after year
in the savage island of Newport, where labor is hard to
hire, I have passed summers ungladdened by so much
as a hollyhock, and the garden I at last managed to
secure owes nothing to my skill or knowledge."

The truth is, people were afraid of the open air in
those days. Julia and her sisters sometimes went for a
drive in pleasant weather, dressed in blue pelisses and
yellow satin bonnets to match the chariot; they rarely
went out on foot; when they did, it was in cambric
dresses and kid slippers; the result was apt to be a cold
or a sore throat, proving conclusively to the minds
of their elders how much better off they were within
doors.

Julia's nursery recollections were chiefly of No. 16
Bond Street. Here the little Wards lived a happy but
somewhat sober life, under the watchful care of their

father, and their faithful Aunt Eliza, known in the family as "Auntie Francis."

The young mother, in dying, had commended her children specially to the care of this, her eldest sister, whose ability had been tried and proved from childhood. In 1810 her father, Benjamin Clarke Cutler, died suddenly under singular and painful circumstances. Her mother, crushed by this event, took to her bed, leaving the care of the family to Eliza, then fifteen years of age. Eliza took up the house-mother's burden without question; nursed her mother, husbanded the narrow resources of the household, brought up the four younger children with a strong hand. "There were giants in those days."

Nothing could daunt Eliza Cutler's spirits, which were a perpetual cordial to those around her. She was often "borrowed" by one member and another of the family; she threatened to hang a sign over her door with the inscription, "Cheering done here by the job by E. Cutler." Her tongue could be sharp as well as merry; witness many anecdotes.

The housekeeper of a certain millionnaire, calling upon her to ask the character of a servant, took occasion to enlarge upon the splendors of her employer's establishment. "Mr. So-and-So keeps this; Mr. So-and-So keeps that: —"

"Yes! yes!" said Mrs. Francis; "it is well known that Mr. So-and-So keeps everything, except the Ten Commandments!"

"Oh! Mrs. Francis, how *could* you?" cried the poor millionnaire when next they met.

In 1829 Eliza Cutler married Dr. John Wakefield
Francis, the historian of Old New York, the beloved
physician of a whole generation. He was already, as
has been seen, a member of the Ward household, friend
and resident physician. His tremendous vitality, his
quick sympathies, his amazing flow of vivid and picturesque language, made him the delight of the children. He called them by singular pet names, "Cream
Cheese from the Dairy of Heaven," "Pocket Edition of
Lives of the Saints," etc., etc. He sang to them odd
snatches of song which were to delight and exasperate
later generations: —

> "To a woodman's hut one evening there came
> A physician and a dancing-master:
> The wind did blow, io, io,
> And the rain poured faster and faster."

Edgar Allan Poe said of Dr. Francis that his conversation was "a sort of Roman punch, made up of tragedy, comedy, and the broadest of all possible farce."

In those days "The Raven," newly published, was
the talk of the town. Dr. Francis, meeting Poe, invited
him to come to his house on a certain evening, and
straightway forgot the matter. Poe came at the appointed time. The Doctor, summoned to the bedside
of a patient, left the drawing-room hastily, and in the
anteroom ran into a tall, cadaverous figure in black.
Seizing him in his arms, he carried him into the drawing-room and set him down before his wife. "Eliza,
my dear — the Raven!" and he departed, leaving
guest and hostess (the latter had never heard of "The
Raven"!) equally petrified.

Mrs. Francis adored her husband, yet he must sometimes have tried her patience sorely. One evening they had a dinner party, eighteen covers, a state occasion. Midway in the repast the Doctor rose, and begging the guests to excuse him and his wife for a moment, led her, speechless with amazement, into the next room. Here he proceeded to bleed her, removing twelve ounces of blood; replying to her piteous protestations, "Madam, I saw that you were on the point of apoplexy, and I judge it best to avert it."

In strong contrast with "Uncle Doctor" was "Uncle Ben," the Reverend Benjamin Clarke Cutler, for many years rector of St. Anne's Church, Brooklyn. This uncle was much less to Julia's taste: indeed, she was known to stamp her childish foot, and cry, "I don't care for old Ben Cutler!" Nevertheless he was a saintly and interesting person.

He was twelve years old at the time of his father's tragic death, and was deeply influenced by it. His youth was made unhappy by spiritual anguish, duty to his widowed mother and the call to the ministry fighting within him. The latter conquered. In his twenty-first year he drew up, signed, and sealed "An Instrument of Solemn Surrender of Myself, Soul and Body, to God!" This document was in the form of a testament, in which he solemnly ("with death, judgment and eternity in view") gave, covenanted, and made over himself, soul and body, all his faculties, all his influence in this world, all the worldly goods with which he might be endowed, into the hands of his Creator, Preserver, and Constant Benefactor, to be his forever, and at his disposal. He goes on to say: "Witness, ye holy angels! I am God's servant; witness, thou, Prince of Hell! I am thy enemy, thy implacable enemy, from this time forth and forevermore."

That this covenant was well kept, no one who reads his memoirs and the testimony of his contemporaries can doubt.

There are many anecdotes of Uncle Ben. Once, during his early ministry, he was riding in a crowded stage-coach. One of the passengers swore profusely and continuously, to the manifest annoyance of the others. Presently Dr. Cutler, leaning forward, addressed the swearer.

"Sir," he said, "you are fond of blasphemy; I am fond of prayer. This is a public conveyance, and for the remainder of our journey, as often as you swear aloud, I shall pray aloud, and we will see who comes off best." The swearing stopped!

In his later years, he met one day a parishioner clad in deep mourning for a near relative. The old clergyman laid his hand on the crape sleeve. "What!" he said sternly. "Heathen mourning for a Christian saint!"

But of all the uncles (and there were many) the beloved Uncle John Ward was always first. Of him, through many years Julia's devoted friend and chief adviser, we shall speak later on.

We have dwelt upon the generation preceding our mother's, because all these people, the beautiful mother so early lost, so long loved and mourned, the sternly devoted father, the vivacious aunts, the stalwart uncles, were strong influences in the life of Julia Ward.

The amusements of the little Wards were few, compared with those of children of to-day. As a child of seven, Julia was taken twice to the opera, and heard Malibran, then Signorina Garcia, a pleasure the memory of which remained with her through life. About this time Mr. Ward's views of religious duty deepened in stringency and in gloom. There was no more opera, nor did Julia ever attend a theatre until she was a grown woman. In Low Church circles at that time, the drama was considered distinctly of the devil. The burning of the first Bowery Theatre and of the great theatre at Richmond, Virginia, were spoken of as "judgments." Many an Evangelical pastor "improved" the occasions from the pulpit.

The child inherited a strong dramatic sense from the Marion Cutlers. She had barely learned to read when she found in an "Annual" a tale called "The Iroquois Bride," which she dramatized and presented to the nursery audience, with herself for the bride, her brother Marion for the lover, and a stool for the rock they ascended to stab each other. The performance was not approved by Authority, and the book was promptly taken away.

Her first written drama was composed at the age of nine, but even the name of it is lost.

Mr. Ward did not encourage intimacies with other children. He felt strongly that brothers and sisters were the true, and should be the only, intimates for one another; indeed, the six children were enough to make a pleasant little circle of their own, and there were merry games in the wide nursery. Sam, the eldest born, was master of the revels in childhood, as throughout his life. It was his delight, in the early morning, to wrap himself in a sheet, and bursting into the room where the little sisters slept, leap from bed to bed, announcing himself as a ghost come to haunt them; or, when the three ladies, Mrs. Mills, Mrs. Brown, and Mrs. Francis (otherwise known as Julia, Louisa, and Annie) were playing with their dolls, to whisper in their ears that they must on no account venture near the attic stairs, as an old man in red was sitting there. Of course the little Fatimas must needs peep, and the old man was always there, a terrible figure, his face hidden. In "Bro' Sam's" absence it was Marion who played the outlaw and descended like a whirlwind upon the unhappy ladies, who were journeying through dense and dreadful forests.

Mrs. Mills, Mrs. Brown, and Mrs. Francis were devoted mothers, and reared large families of dolls. They kept house in a wide bureau drawer, divided into three parts. Our Aunt Annie (Mrs. Adolphe Mailliard) writes: "Mrs. Mills' (Julia) dolls were always far more picturesquely dressed than ours, although I can say little for their neatness. Oh! to what numberless parties they went, and how tipsy they invariably got! I can see distinctly to-day the upset wagon (boxes, on spools for wheels), and the muddy dresses, for they always fell into mud puddles."

Marion was as pious as he was warlike. His morning sermons, delivered over the back of a chair, were fer-

JULIA, SAMUEL, AND HENRY WARD, *circa* 1825
From a miniature by Miss Anne Hall

vent and eloquent; he was only seven years old when
he wrote to his Cousin Henry Ward, who was ill with
some childish ailment: —

"Do not forget to say your prayers every morning
and evening. I hope that you trust in God; and, my
dear cousin, do not set your mind too much on Earthly
things! And my dear cousin, this is the prayer."

Follows the Lord's Prayer carefully written out. On
the next page of the same sheet, the eight-year-old
Julia adds her exhortation: —

"Dear Cousin, I hope that you will say the Prayer
which my Brother has written for you. I hear with
regret that you are sick, and it is as necessary as ever
that you should trust in God; love him, dear Henry,
and you will see Death approaching with joy. Oh,
what are earthly things, which we must all lose when
we die — to our immortal souls which never die! I
cannot bear the thought of anybody who is dying
without a knowledge of Christ. We may die before to-
morrow, and therefore we ought to be prepared for
death."

This was scarcely cheering for Henry, aged ten; as a
matter of fact, he was to have half a century in which
to make his preparations.

Some of the nursery recollections were the reverse of
merry. When Julia was still a little child, the old housekeeper died. The children loved her, and Auntie Francis did not wish them to be saddened by the funeral
preparations; she gave them a good dose of physic all
round and put them to bed for the day.

Julia was a beautiful child, but she had red hair,

which was then considered a sad drawback. She could remember visitors condoling with her mother on this misfortune, and the gentle lady deploring it also, and striving by the use of washes and leaden combs to darken the over-bright locks. Still, some impression of good looks must have reached the child's mind; for one day, desiring to know what she really was like, she scrambled up on a chair, then on a dressing-table, and took a good look in the mirror.

"*Is that all ?*" she cried, and scrambled down again, a sadly disappointed child.

Her first lessons were from governesses and masters; when she was nine years old, she was sent to a private school in the neighborhood. She was placed in a class with older girls, and learned by heart many pages of Paley's "Moral Philosophy"; memorizing from textbooks formed in those days a great part of the school curriculum. She did not care especially for Paley, and found chemistry (without experiments!) and geometry far more interesting; but history and languages were the studies she loved. She had learned in the nursery to speak French fluently; she soon began the study of Latin. Hearing a class reciting an Italian lesson, she was enchanted with the musical sound of the language; listened and marked, day after day, and presently handed to the amazed principal a note correctly written in Italian, begging permission to join the class.

At nine years old she was reading "Pilgrim's Progress," and seeking its characters in the people she met every day. She always counted it one of the books

which had most influenced her. Another was Gibbon's
"Decline and Fall of the Roman Empire," which she
read at seventeen.[1]

She began at an early age to write verse. A manuscript volume has been preserved in which some of
these early poems were copied for her father.

The title-page and dedication are here reproduced:—

Poems
Dedicated to
Samuel Ward esq
By His
affectionate daughter
Julia Ward.
LET ME BE THINE!
Regard not with a critic's eye.
New York   1831.

To Samuel Ward.

Beloved father,
               Expect not to find in these juvenile produc-
tions the delicacy and grace which pervaded the writings
of that dear parent who is now in glory. I am indeed conscious of the many faults they contain, but my object in
presenting you with these (original) poems, has been to give
you a little memorial of my early life, and I entreat you to
remember that they were written in the eleventh, twelfth,
and thirteenth years of my life.

Your loving daughter
JULIA.

The titles show the trend of the child's thought: "All
things shall pass away"; "We return no more"; "Invi-

---

[1] In later life she added to these the works of Spinoza, and of Theodore
Parker.

tation to Youth" (1831!); "To my dear Mother";
"Mine is the power to make thee whole"; "To an
infant's departing spirit"; "Redeeming Love"; "My
Heavenly Home," etc., etc.

At Newport, in 1831, she wrote the following: —

MORNING HYMN

Now I see the morning light,
Shining bright and gay.
God has kept me through the night;
He will, if He thinks it right,
Preserve me through this day.

Let thy holy Spirit send
Of heavenly light a ray;
Thy face, oh! Lord, I fain would seek,
But I am feeble, vain and weak;
Oh, guide me in thy way!

Let thy assistance, Lord, be given,
That when life's path I've trod,
And when the last frail tie is riven,
My spirit may ascend to heaven,
To dwell with thee, My God.

We cannot resist quoting a stanza from the effusion
entitled "Father's Birthday": —

Louisa brings a cushion rare,
Anne Eliza a toothpick bright and fair;
And O! accept the gift I bring,
It is a *daughter's* offering.

Julia's mind was not destined to remain in the evangelical mould which must have so rejoiced the heart
of her father. In 1834, at the ripe age of fifteen, she
describes her

"Vain Regrets
written on looking over a diary kept while I was under
serious impressions": —

> Oh! happy days, gone, never to return
> At which fond memory will ever burn,
> Oh, Joyous hours, with peace and gladness blest,
> When hope and joy dwelt in this careworn breast.

The next poem, "The Land of Peace," breaks off
abruptly at the third line, and when she again began to
write religious verse, it was from a widely different
standpoint.

It may have been about this time that she tried to
lead her sisters into the path of poesy.

Coming one day into the nursery, in serious mood,
she found the two little girls playing some childish
game. Miss Ward (she was always Miss Ward, even in
the nursery!) rebuked them for their frivolity; bade
them turn their thoughts to graver matters, and
write poetry.

Louisa refused point-blank, but little Annie, always
anxious to please, went dutifully to work, and produced the following lines: —

> He feeds the ravens when they call,
> And stands them in a pleasant hall.

"Mitter Ward" (to give him his nursery title) treasured these tokens of pious and literary promise. He
even responded in kind, as is shown by some verses
which are endorsed: —

> "From my dearest Father.
>   JULIA EUPHROSYNE WARD [sic]."

His letters are full of playful affection. He would fain be father and mother both to the children who were now his all. Under the austere exterior lay a tenderness which perhaps they hardly comprehended at the time. It was in fact this very anguish of solicitude, this passionate wish that they should not only have, but *be* everything desirable and lovely, that made him outwardly so stern. This sterner note impressed itself so deeply upon the minds of his children that the anecdotes familiar to our own generation echo it. We see the little Julia, weary with long riding in the family coach, suffering her knees to drop apart childwise, and we hear Mr. Ward say: "My daughter, if you cannot sit like a lady, we will stop at the next tailor's and have you measured for a pair of pantaloons!"

Or we hear the child at table, remarking innocently that the cheese is strong; and the deep voice replying, "It is no more so than the expression, Miss!"

The family was still at 16 Bond Street, when all the children had whooping-cough severely, and were confined to the house for many weeks. Mrs. Mailliard writes of this time: —

"I remember the screened-off corner of the diningroom, which was called the Bower, where we each retired when the spasms came on, and the promises which we vainly gave each other each morning to choke rather than cough whilst Uncle Doctor made his visit to the nursery; for the slightest sound from one of us provoked the general order of a dose all round."

It was after this illness that Julia Ward first went to Newport. A change of air was prescribed for the children, and they were packed off to the farmhouse of Jacob Bailey, two or three miles from the town of Newport. Here they spent a happy summer, to be followed by many others. They slept on mattresses stuffed with ground corncobs; the table was primitive; but there was plenty of cream and curds, eggs and butter, and there was the wonderful air. The children grew fat and hearty, and scampered all over the island with great delight.

(But when they went down to the beach, Julia must wear a thick green worsted veil to preserve her ivory-and-rose complexion.

"Little Julia has another freckle to-day!" a visitor was told. "It was not her fault, the nurse forgot her veil!")

Julia recalled Newport in 1832 as "a forsaken, mildewed place, a sort of intensified Salem, with houses of rich design, no longer richly inhabited." She was to watch through many years the growth of what was always one of the cities of her heart.

But we must return to Bond Street, and take one more look at No. 16. The Wards were soon to leave it for a statelier dwelling, but many associations would always cling about the old house. Here it was that the good old grandfather, Lieutenant-Colonel Samuel Ward, used to come from No. 7 to talk business with his son or to play with the children. Our mother had a vivid recollection of once, when still a little child, sitting down at the piano, placing an open music-book on the rack (though she could not yet read music), and beginning to pound and thump the keys with might and main. The Colonel was sitting by, book in hand, and endured the noise patiently for some time. Finally he said in his courtly way, "Is it so set down in the book, little lady?" "Yes, Grandpapa!" said naughty Julia, and went on banging; the Colonel, who indeed had little music, made no further comment. But when a game of "Tommy-come-tickle-me" was toward, the children must step in to No. 7 to share that excitement with their grandfather, since no cards were permitted under Mr. Ward's roof.

The year of the first Newport visit, 1832, was also the terrible "cholera year." Uncle Ben Cutler, at that time city missionary, writes in his diary: —

"The cholera is in Quebec and Montreal. This city is beginning to be alarmed; Christians are waking up. My soul, how stands the case with thee?"

And later: —

"I am now in the midst of the pestilence. The cholera, the universal plague, arrived in this city four weeks ago. It has caused the death of over nine hundred persons. This day the report of the Board of Health was three hundred new cases and one hundred and thirty deaths."

Many parts of the city were entirely deserted. Dr. Cutler retained through life the vivid recollection of riding down Broadway in full daylight, meeting no living soul, seeing only a face here and there at an upper window, peering at him as at a strange sight.

Newport took the alarm, and forbade steamboats from New York to land their passengers. This behavior was considered very cold-blooded, and gave rise to the conundrum: "Why is it impossible for Newporters to take the cholera? Answer: Because they have no bowels."

Grandma Cutler was at Newport with the Wards and Francises, and trembled for her only son. She implored him to "flee while it was yet day." "My most precious son," she cried, "oh, come out from thence! I entreat you; linger not within its walls, as Lot would have done, but for the friendly angels that drew him perforce from it!"

The missionary stood firm at his post, and though exhausted by his labors, came safe through the ordeal. But Colonel Ward, who had not thought fit to flee the enemy, — it was not his habit to flee enemies, — was stricken with the pestilence, and died in New York City, August 16. His death was a grievous blow to Mr. Ward. Not only had he lost a loving and beloved father, but he had no assurance of the orthodoxy of that father's religious opinions. The Colonel was thought in the family to be of a philosophizing, if not actually sceptical, turn of mind; it might be that he was not "safe"! Years after, Mr. Ward told Julia of the anguish he suffered from this uncertainty.

It is with No. 16 Bond Street that we chiefly associate the sprightly figure of "Grandma Cutler," who was a frequent visitor there. The affection between Mr. Ward and his mother-in-law was warm and lively. They had a "little language" of their own, and she was Lady Feltham (from her fondness for Feltham's "Resolves," a book little in demand in the twentieth century); and he was her "saucy Lark," or "Plato." Mrs. Cutler died in 1836.

CHAPTER III

"THE CORNER"

1835–1839; *aet.* 16–20

But well I thank my father's sober house
Where shallow judgment had no leave to be,
And hurrying years, that, stripping much beside,
Turned as they fled, and left me charity.

J. W. H.

THE house which Mr. Ward built on the corner of Bond Street and Broadway was still standing in the middle of the nineteenth century; a dignified mansion of brick, with columns and trimmings of white marble.

In her "Reminiscences," our mother recalls the spacious rooms, hung with red, blue, and yellow silk. The yellow drawing-room was reserved for high occasions, and for "Miss Ward's" desk and grand piano. This and the blue room were adorned by fine sculptured mantelpieces, the work of a young sculptor named Thomas Crawford, who was just coming into notice.

Behind the main house, stretching along Broadway, was the picture gallery, the first private one in New York, and Mr. Ward's special pride. The children might not mingle in frivolous gayety abroad, but they should have all that love, taste, and money could give them at home; he filled his gallery with the best pictures he could find. A friend (Mr. Prescott Hall), making a timely journey through Spain, bought for him

many valuable pictures, among them a Snyders, a
Nicolas Poussin, a reputed Velasquez and Rembrandt. It was for him that Thomas Cole painted the
four pictures representing "The Voyage of Life," engravings from which may still be found in old-fashioned
parlors.

Some years later, when the eldest son, Samuel, returned from Europe, bringing with him a fine collection
of books, Mr. Ward built a library specially for them.

This was the house into which the family moved in
1835, Julia being then sixteen years of age; this was
the house she loved, the memory of which was dear to
her through all the years of her life.

The family was at that time patriarchal in its dimen-
sions: Mr. Ward and his six children, Dr. and Mrs.
Francis and their four; often, too, "Grandma Cutler"
and other Cutlers, not to speak of Wards, Greenes, and
McAllisters. (Louisa, youngest of the Cutler sisters,
one of the most beautiful and enchanting women of
her time, was married to Matthew Hall McAllister.)
One and all were sure of a welcome at "The Corner";
one and all were received with cordial urbanity, first by
Johnson, the colored butler, later by Mr. Ward, the
soul of dignified hospitality.

Another inmate of the house during several years
was Christy Evangelides, a Greek boy, orphaned in a
Turkish massacre. Mr. Ward took the boy into his
family, gave him his education and a start in life.
Fifty years later Mr. Evangelides recalled those days
in a letter to his "sister Julia," and paid beautiful
tribute to his benefactor.

To all these should be added a host of servants and retainers; and masters of various kinds, coming to teach music, languages, even dancing, for the children were taught to dance even if they never (or very seldom) were allowed to go to dances. Many of these teachers were foreign patriots: those were the days when one French *émigré* of rank dressed the hair of fashionable New York, while another made its salads, the two going their rounds before every festivity.

Julia's musical education began early. Her first teacher was a French artist, so irritable that the terrified child could remember little that he taught her. He was succeeded in her tenth year by Mr. Boocock, a pupil of Cramer, to whom she always felt that she owed a great deal. Not only did he train her fingers so carefully that after eighty years they still retained their flexibility, but he also trained and developed her inborn taste for all that was best in music.

As she grew toward girlhood, the good master found that her voice promised to be a remarkable one, and recommended to her father Signor Cardini, formerly an intimate of the Garcia family, and thoroughly versed in the famous Garcia method. Under his care Julia's voice developed into a pure, clear mezzo-soprano, of uncommon range and exquisite quality. She felt all through her life the benefit of those early lessons.

When she was eighty years old she attended a meeting of the National Peace Society at Park Street Church, Boston. The church was packed with people. When her turn came to speak, the kindly chairman said: —

"Ladies and Gentlemen, we are now to have the great pleasure of listening to Mrs. Howe. I am going to ask you all to be very quiet, for though Mrs. Howe's voice is as sweet as ever, it is perhaps not quite so strong."

"*But it carries !*" said the pupil of old Cardini. The silver tone, though not loud, reached the farthest corner of the great building; the house "came down" in a thunder of applause. It was a beautiful moment for the proud daughter who sat beside her.

Music was one of the passions of her life. Indeed, she felt that it had sometimes influenced her even too much, and in recording the delight she took in the trios and quartets which Mr. Boocock arranged for her, she adds: "The reaction from this pleasure, however, was very painful, and induced at times a visitation of morbid melancholy, which threatened to upset my health."

She felt that "in the training of young persons, some regard should be had to the sensitiveness of youthful nerves, and to the overpowering response which they often make to the appeals of music. . . .

"The power and sweep of great orchestral performances, or even the suggestive charm of some beautiful voice, will sometimes so disturb the mental equilibrium of the hearer as to induce in him a listless melancholy, or, worse still, an unreasoning and unreasonable discontent." [1]

In a later chapter of her "Reminiscences," she says: "I left school at the age of sixteen, and began thereaf-

[1] *Reminiscences*, p. 43.

ter to study in good earnest. Until that time a certain over-romantic and imaginative turn of mind had interfered much with the progress of my studies. I indulged in day-dreams which appeared to me far higher in tone than the humdrum of my school recitations. When these were at an end, I began to feel the necessity of more strenuous application, and at once arranged for myself hours of study, relieved by the practice of vocal and instrumental music."

These hours of study were not all passed at home. In 1836 she was taking certain courses at the boarding and day school of Mrs. E. Smith, then in Fifth Avenue, "first house from Washington Square."

The Italian master was a son of the venerable Lorenzo da Ponte, who in his youth had written for Mozart the librettos of "Don Giovanni" and "Le Nozze di Figaro."

Four languages, English, French, German, and Italian, Julia learned thoroughly; she spoke and wrote them throughout her life correctly as well as fluently, with singularly pure accent and inflection, and seldom or never was at a loss for a word; nor was she less proficient in history. For mathematics she had no gift, and was wont to say that her knowledge of the science was limited to the fact that four quarts made a gallon: yet the higher mathematics had a mysterious attraction for her, as an unexplored region of wonder and romance.

She was always a student. When she began the study of German, she set herself a task each day; lest anything should interfere to distract her mind, she had herself securely *tied* to her armchair, giving orders that she

was on no account to be set free before the appointed
hour.

This was characteristic of her through life. The
chain of habit once formed was never broken, and
study was meat and drink to her. Her "precious time"
(which we children saucily abbreviated to "P.T.") was
as real a thing to us as sunrise: we were not to break in
upon it for anything short of a fire — or a cut finger!

Many years later, she laid down for the benefit of
the younger generation these rules: —

"If you have at your command three hours *per diem*,
you may study art, literature, and philosophy, not
as they are studied professionally, but in the degree
involved in general culture.

"If you have but one hour every day, read philosophy, or learn foreign languages, living or dead.

"If you can command only fifteen or twenty minutes, read the Bible with the best commentaries, and
daily a verse or two of the best poetry."

In the days when Julia was going round the corner to
Mrs. Smith's school, Sam was newly returned from a
long course of study and travel abroad, while Henry
and Marion were at Round Hill School under the care
of Dr. Joseph Greene Cogswell and Mr. George Bancroft. The former was a beloved friend of the Ward
family, and often visited them. We have pleasant
glimpses of the household at this time, when the lines
of paternal guidance, though still firmly, were somewhat less rigidly drawn.

Breakfast at "The Corner" was at eight in winter,
and at half past seven in summer, Mr. Ward reading

prayers before the meal, and again at bedtime. He would often wake his daughters in the morning by pelting them with stockings, crying, "Come, my rosebuds!"

The young people were apt to linger over the breakfast table in talk. If this were unduly prolonged, Mr. Ward would appear, "hatted and booted for the day," and say, "Young gentlemen, I am glad that you can afford to take life so easily. I am old, and must work for my living!"

Dinner was at four o'clock, supper at half past seven.

At table, Julia sat beside her father; he would often take her right hand in his left, half unconsciously, and hold it for some time, continuing the while to eat his dinner. Julia, her right hand imprisoned, would sit dinnerless, but never dreamed of remonstrating.

She had a habit of dropping her slippers off while at the table. Mr. Ward one day quietly secured an empty slipper with his foot, and then said: "My daughter, I have left my seals in my room. Will you be so good as to fetch them for me?" A moment's agonized search, and Julia went, "one shoe off and one shoe on," and brought the seals. Nothing was said on either side, but the habit was abandoned.

Mr. Ward's anxious care for his children's welfare extended to every branch of their conduct. One evening, walking with Julia, he met his sons, Henry and Marion, each with a cigar in his mouth. He was much troubled, and said: "Boys, you must give this up, and I will give it up too. From this time I forbid you to smoke, and I will join you in relinquishing the habit."

He never smoked again; nor did the boys — in his presence!

Three lads, young, handsome, brilliant, and eminently social as were the Wards, could not be kept out of society. They were popular, and would fain have had Julia, the only one of the three girls who was old enough, share in their pleasures; but this might not be. Mr. Ward had money and sympathy to spare for every benevolent enterprise, but he disliked and distrusted "society"; he would neither entertain it nor be entertained by it. Our mother quotes an argument between him and his eldest son on this point: —

"'Sir,' said my brother, 'you do not keep in view the importance of the social tie.'

"'The social what?' asked my father.

"'The social tie, sir.'

"'I make small account of that,' said the elder gentleman.

"'I will die in defence of it!' impetuously rejoined the younger.

"My father was so amused at this sally that he spoke of it to an intimate friend: 'He will die in defence of the social tie, indeed!'"

Julia's girlhood evenings were mostly spent at home, with books, needlework, and music, varied by an occasional lecture or concert, or a visit to some one of the uncles' houses in the street, which ought, one would think, to have been called "Ward Street," since at this time almost the whole family connection lived there.

Much as Julia loved her home, her books and music, she longed for some of the gayety which her brothers were enjoying. "I seemed to myself," she says, "like a young damsel of olden times, shut up within an enchanted castle. And I must say, that my dear father, with all his noble generosity and overweening affection, sometimes appeared to me as my jailer."

Once she expostulated with him, begging to be allowed more freedom in going out, and in receiving visits from the friends of her brothers. It may have been on the occasion when he refused to allow the late Louis Rutherford, of venerated memory, to be invited to the house, "because he belonged to the fashionable world."

Her father told her that he had early recognized in her a temperament and imagination over-sensitive to impressions from without, and that his wish had been to guard her from exciting influences until she should appear to him fully able to guard and guide herself.

Alas! the tender father meant to cherish a vestal flame in a vase of alabaster; in reality, he was trying to imprison the lightning in the cloud. When our mother wrote the words above quoted, on the power of music over sensitive natures, she was recalling these days, and perhaps remembering how, denied the society of her natural mates, her sixteen-year-old heart went out in sympathy and compassion to the young harper who came to take part in the trios and quartets, and who fell desperately in love with her and was summarily dismissed in consequence.

Yet who shall say that the father's austere régime did not after all meet a need of her nature deeper than she could possibly have realized at the time; that the

long, lonely hours, the study often to weariness, —
though never to satiety, — the very fires of longing
and of regret, were not necessary to give her mind that
temper which was to make it an instrument as strong
as it was keen?

The result of this system was not precisely what Mr.
Ward had expected. One evening (it was probably
after the marriage of his eldest son to Emily Astor,
when he joined perforce in the festivities of the time)
he did actually take Julia to an evening party. She did
not dance, but she was surrounded by eager youths all
the evening, and when her father summoned her to go
home, she was deep in talk with one of them. There
was no disobeying the summons; as she turned to take
her father's arm, Miss Julia made a little gesture of
farewell, fluttering the fingers of her right hand over
her shoulder, to cheer the disconsolate swain. Mr.
Ward appeared unconscious of this, but a day or two
later, on leaving the room where Julia was sitting, he
said: "My daughter, —" and fluttered his fingers over
his shoulder in precise mimicry of her gesture.

Another anecdote describes an occasion singularly
characteristic of both father and daughter.

Julia was nineteen years old, a woman grown, feeling
her womanhood in every vein. She had never been
allowed to choose the persons who should be invited to
the house: she had never had a *party of her own*. The
different strains in her blood were singularly diverse.
All through her life Saxon and Gaul kept house together as peaceably as they might, but sometimes the
French blood boiled over.

Calling her brothers in council, she told them that she was going to give a party; that she desired their help in making out lists, etc., but that the occasion and the responsibility were to be all her own. The brothers demurred, even Sam being somewhat appalled by the prospect; but finding her firm, they made out a list of desirable guests, of all ages. It was characteristic of her that the plan once made, the resolve taken, it became an obsession, a thing that must be done at whatever cost.

She asked her father if she might invite a few friends for a certain evening: he assented. She engaged the best caterer in New York; the most fashionable musicians; she even hired a splendid cut-glass chandelier to supplement the sober lighting of the yellow drawing-room.

The evening came: Mr. Ward, coming downstairs, found assembled as brilliant a gathering as could have been found in any other of the great houses of New York. He betrayed no surprise, but welcomed his guests with charming courtesy, as if they had come at his special desire; the music sounded, the young people danced, the evening passed off delightfully, to all save the young hostess. She, from the moment when the thing was inevitable, became as possessed with terror as she had been with desire. She could think of nothing but her father's displeasure, of the words he might speak, the glances he might cast upon her. During the whole evening, the cup of trembling was at her lips.

The moment the last guest had departed, the three

brothers gathered round her. "We will speak to him!" they cried. "Let us speak to him for you!"

"No!" said Julia, "I must go myself."

She went at once to the room where her father sat alone. For a moment she could find no words; but none were needed. Gravely but kindly Mr. Ward said he was surprised to find that her idea of "a few friends" differed so widely from his own; he was sorry she had not consulted him more freely, and begged that in the future she would do so. Then he kissed her good-night with his usual tenderness, and it was over. The matter was never mentioned again.

The Wards continued to pass the summers at Newport, but no longer at good Jacob Bailey's farmhouse. Mr. Ward had bought a house in town, which a later generation was to know as "The Ashurst Cottage," on the corner of Bellevue Avenue and Catherine Street.

Here the severity of his rule relaxed somewhat, and the pretty house became the centre of a sober hospitality. Indeed, Newport was a sober place in those days. There were one or two houses where dancing was allowed, but these were viewed askance by many people.

One evening, a dancing party was given by a couple on Bellevue Avenue. They had a manservant named Salathiel, a person of rigid piety. When supper-time came, Salathiel was not to be found. The other servants, being questioned, said that he had rushed suddenly out of the house, crying, "I won't stay to see those people dancing themselves to hell!"

Though Julia might not dance, except at home, she

might and did ride; first, with great contentment, on a Narragansett pacer, "Jeanie Deans," later on a thoroughbred mare, a golden bay named Cora. Cora was beautiful but "very pranky." After being several times run away with and once thrown off, it was observed by her sisters that Julia generally read her Bible and said her prayers before her ride: she has herself told us how, after being thrown off and obliged to make her way home on foot, she would creep in at the back door so that no one might see her.

She calls the "cottage" a "delightful house," and speaks with special pleasure of its garden planted with roses and gooseberry bushes by Billy Bottomore, a quaint old Newport sportsman, who took the boys shooting, and showed them where to find plover, woodcock, and snipe. Billy Bottomore passed for an adopted son of old Father Corné, another Newport "character" of those days. This gentleman had come from Naples to Boston, toward the end of the eighteenth century, as a decorative artist, and had made a modest fortune by painting the walls of the fine houses of Summer Street, Temple Place, and Beacon Hill. He chose Newport as his final home, because, as he told Mr. Ward, he had found that the climate was favorable to the growth of the tomato, "that most wholesome of vegetables." The Ward boys delighted in visiting Father Corné, and in hearing him sing his old songs, French and Italian, some of which are sung to-day by our grandchildren.

Father Corné lived to a great age. When past his ninetieth year, a friend asked him if he would not like to revisit Naples. "Ah, sir," replied the old man, "my father is dead!"

Our mother loved to linger over these old-time figures. The name of Billy Bottomore always brought a twinkle to her eye, and we never tired of hearing how he told her, "There is a single sister in Newport, a sempstress, to whom I have offered matrimony, but she says, 'No.'" The single sister finally yielded (perhaps when Billy inherited old Corné's money) and he became a proud and happy husband. "She keeps my house as neat as a nunnery!" he said. "When Miss E., the housekeeper, died, she nursed her and laid her out, and when Father Corné died, she nursed him and laid him out —"

"Yes, Billy," broke in our Aunt Annie, "and she'll lay you out too!" — which in due time she did.

He congratulated Julia on having girl-children only. "Give me daughters!" he cried. "As my good old Spanish grandfather used to say, give me daughters!"

"Of this Spanish ancestor," our mother says, "no one ever heard before. His descendant died, without daughter or son, of cholera in 185–."

We forget the name of another quaint personage, a retired sea-captain, who once gave a party to which she was allowed to go; but she remembered the party, and the unction with which the kindly host, rubbing his hands over the supper table, exclaimed: "Now, ladies and gentlemen, help yourselves *sang froidy!*"

The roses and gooseberry bushes of the Newport garden once witnessed a serio-comic scene. There was another sea-captain, Glover by name, who had busi-

ness connections with Prime, Ward & King, and who
came to the house sometimes on business, sometimes
for a friendly call. He was a worthy man of middle age
and unromantic appearance; probably the eighteen-
year-old Julia, dreamy and poetic, took no more notice
of him than civility required; but he took notice of her,
and one day asked her to walk out in the garden with
him. Wondering much, she went. After some desultory remarks, the Captain drew a visiting-card from
his pocket, wrote a few words upon it, and handed it
to his young hostess. She read: —

> *" Russell E. Glover's*
> heart is yours!"

CHAPTER IV

GIRLHOOD

1839-1843; *aet.* 20-23

The torch that lit these silent halls,
Has now extinguished been;
The windows of the soul are dark,
And all is gloom within.

But lo! it shines, a star in heav'n,
And through death's murky night,
The ruins of the stately pile
Gleam softly in its light.

And it shall be a beacon star
To cheer us, and to guide;
For we would live as thou hast lived,
And die as thou hast died.

JULIA WARD, on her father's death, 1839.

IN Julia's childhood her brother Sam was her ideal and her idol. She describes him as a "handsome youth, quick of wit and tender of heart, brilliant in promise, and with a great and versatile power of work in him." He had early shown special proficiency in mathematics, and to the end of his life rejoiced in being one of the few persons who clearly understood the function called "*Gamma*." His masters expected great things from him; but his brilliant and effervescent spirit was forced into the Wall Street mould, with kindly intent but disastrous effect. His life was checkered, sun and shadow; but from first to last, he remained the delight of all who knew him. Sam Ward; Uncle Sam to three generations, his was a name to conjure with: the soul of generosity, the essence of wit, the spirit of kindliness. No one ever looked in his face, ever met the kindling glance of his dark eyes, ever saw the sunshine break in his smile, without forgetting all else in love and admiration of one of the most enchanting personalities that ever brightened the world.

Sam Ward returned from Europe in 1835, and took up his residence under his father's roof. In 1838 he married Emily, daughter of William B. Astor. The wedding was a grand one. Julia was first bridesmaid, and wore a dress of white *moiré*, then a material of the newest fashion. Those were the days of the *ferronière*, an ornament then so popular that "evening dress was scarcely considered complete without it." [1] Julia begged for one, and her father gave her a charming string of pearls, which she wore with great contentment at the wedding.

The young couple took up their residence with the family at "The Corner," the Francises having by this time moved to a house of their own.

With all these changes, little by little, the discipline relaxed, the doors opened wider. The bridal pair, *fêted* everywhere, must, in their turn, entertain their friends; and in these entertainments the daughters of the house must have their share.

Julia Ward was now nineteen, in the fulness of her early bloom. Her red-gold hair was no longer regarded as a misfortune; her gray eyes were large and well opened; her complexion of dazzling purity. Her finely chiselled features, and the beauty of her hands and arms, made an *ensemble* which could not fail to impress

---

[1] *Reminiscences*, p. 65.

all who saw her Add to this her singing, her wit, and the charm which was all and always her own, and we have the *Diva Julia*, as she was called by some who loved her. Her sisters, also, were growing up, each exquisitely attractive in her way: they became known as the "Three Graces of Bond Street." Louisa was like a damask rose, Annie like a dark lily; dark, too, of eyes and hair were Sam and Marion, while Henry was fair and blue-eyed.

At this distance of time, it may not be unpardonable to touch briefly on another aspect of our mother's youth; indeed, it would hardly be candid to avoid it. From the first she seems to have stirred the hearts of men. Her masters, old and young, fell in love with her almost as a matter of course. Gilded youth and sober middle-age fared no better; her girlhood passed to the sound of sighing.

"My dear," said an intimate friend of the three, speaking of these days, "Louisa had her admirers, and Annie had hers; but when the men saw your mother, they just *flopped !*"

Among her papers we have found many relics of these days, from the faded epistle addressed, "*à Julie, la respectée, la choisie, l'aimée, la chérie,*" to the stern letter in which Mr. Ward "desires not to conceal from the Rev. Mr. —— the deliberate and dispassionate opinion, that a gentleman whose sacred office commanded ready access to his roof, might well have earlier ascertained the views of a widow'd Father on a subject so involving the happiness of his child."

The unhappy suitor's note to Miss Julia is enclosed,

and Mr. Ward trusts that "the return will be considered by the Rev. Mr. —— as finally terminating the matter therein referred to."

Julia had for her suitors a tender and compassionate sympathy. She could not love them, she would not marry them, but she was very sorry for them, and — it must be admitted — she liked to be adored. So she sang duets with one, read German with another, Anglo-Saxon with a third; for all, perhaps, she may have had something the feeling of her "*Coquette et Tendre*" in "Passion Flowers."

> Ere I knew life's sober meaning,
>   Nature taught me simple wiles,
> Gave this color, rising, waning,
>   Gave these shadows, deepening smiles.
>
> More she taught me, sighing, singing,
>   Taught me free to think and move,
> Taught this fond instinctive clinging
>   To the helpful arm of love.

The suitors called her "*Diva*," but in the family circle she was "Jules," or "Jolie Julie." The family letters of this period are full of affectionate cheerfulness.

When "Jolie Julie" is away on a visit, the others send her a composite letter. Louisa threatens to shut her up on her return with nothing to read but her Anglo-Saxon grammar and "Beowulf." ("If that does not give you a distaste for all wolves," she says, "not excepting those *Long fellows*,[1] I do not know what will!")

[1] Longfellow had lent her "Beowulf."

Annie tells of opening the window in Julia's room
and of all the poetical ideas flying out and away.

Emily, her brother's wife, describes Mr. Ward sighing, "Where is my beauty?" as he sits at the table; and
the letter closes with a lively picture of the books in the
library "heaving their dusty sides in sorrow for her
absence."

In describing life at "The Corner," we must not forget the evenings at No. 23, Colonel Henry Ward's
house. Uncle Henry and his namesake son (the boy
who was to "see death approaching with joy"!) were
musical. When Mr. Ward permitted (in his later and
more lenient days) an informal dance at "The Corner,"
the three girls sent for Uncle Henry as naturally as
they sent for the hair-dressing and salad-making *émi-
grés ;* and the stately, handsome gentleman came, and
played waltzes and polkas with cheerful patience all
the evening.

On Sunday the whole family from "The Corner"
took tea with Uncle Henry, and music was the order of
the evening. Mr. Ward delighted in these occasions,
and was never ready to go home. When Uncle Henry
thought it was bedtime, he would go to the piano and
play the "Rogue's March."

> (Twice flogged for stealing a sheep,
> Thrice flogged for de*s*artion!
> If ever I go for a soldier again,
> The devil may be my portion!

We hear the fife shrill through the lively air!)

"No! no, Colonel!" Mr. Ward would cry. "We
won't march yet; give us half an hour more!" And

in affectionate mischief he would stay the half-hour through before marshalling his flock back to "The Corner."

A stern period was put to all this innocent gayety by the death of Mr. Ward, at the age of fifty-three. His life, always laborious, had been doubly so since the death of his wife. Stunned at first by the blow, his strong sense of duty soon roused him to resume his daily responsibilities — with a difference, however. Religion had always been a powerful factor in his life; henceforth it was to be his main inspiration, and he found his chief comfort in works of public and private beneficence.

An earnest patriot, he was no politician; but when his services were needed by city, state, or country, they were always forthcoming. Throughout the series of financial disasters beginning with Andrew Jackson's refusal to renew the charter of the Bank of the United States, and culminating in the panic of 1837, Mr. Ward acted with vigor, decision, and sagacity. His denunciation of the removal of the public deposits from the Bank of the United States by the famous Specie Circular as "an act so lawless, violent, and fraught with disaster, that it would and must eventually overthrow the men and the party that resorted to it," was justified, literally and entirely.

The crisis of 1836–37 called for all the strength, wisdom, and public spirit that the men of the country could show. Mr. Ward labored day and night to prevent the dishonor of the banks of New York.

"Individual effort, however, was vain, and the

10th of May saw all the banks reduced to suspend specie payments; and upon no man did that disastrous day close with deeper mortification than upon him. Personally, and in his business relations, this event affected Mr. Ward as little possibly as any one at all connected with affairs; but, in his estimation, it vitally wounded the commercial honor and character of the city. He was not, however, a man to waste, in unavailing regrets, hours that might be more advantageously employed to repair the evil, and he therefore at once set about the arrangement of measures for inducing and enabling the banks to resume at the earliest possible moment." [1]

This was accomplished within the year. About the same time the Bank of England sent to Prime, Ward & King a loan of nearly five million dollars in gold. Mr. King says, "This extraordinary mark of confidence, this well-earned tribute to the prudence and integrity of the house, Mr. Ward did not affect to undervalue, and confirming, as it did, the sagacity of his own views, and the results which he had so confidently foretold, it was not lost upon the community in the midst of which he lived."

Our mother never forgot the afternoon when Brother Sam came into her study on his return from Wall Street and cried out to her: —

"Julia, men have been going up and down the office stairs all day long, carrying little wooden kegs of gold on their backs, marked 'Prime, Ward & King' and filled with English gold!"

[1] *The Late Samuel Ward*, by Mr. Charles King.

That English gold saved the honor of the Empire State, and the fact that her father procured the loan was the greatest asset in her inheritance from the old firm.

Mr. Ward did not see the kegs, for he was in bed, prostrated by a severe fit of sickness brought on by his labors for the public honor. The few years that remained to him were a very martyrdom, his old enemy, rheumatic gout, attacking him more and more fiercely; but his spirit was indomitable. He labored almost single-handed to establish the Bank of Commerce, and became its first president, stipulating that he should receive no compensation. What he did receive was his death-warrant. The dampness of the freshly plastered walls of the new building brought on in the spring of 1839 two successive attacks so severe that he could not rally from them. Still he toiled on, giving all his energies to perfect and consolidate the enterprise which he believed would be of lasting benefit to his beloved city.

In October of the same year came another financial crisis. The banks of Philadelphia and the Southern States suspended specie payments, and every effort was made to induce the New York banks to follow suit. Mr. Ward was ill at Newport, but hearing the news he hurried back and threw himself into the conflict, exhorting, sustaining, encouraging.

A friend protested, warning him of the peril to his enfeebled health of such exertions. "I should esteem life itself not unworthily sacrificed," said Mr. Ward, "if by word or deed, I could aid the banks in adhering faithfully to their duty."

For nearly two weeks he labored, till the work was done, his city's honor and fair fame secure; then he went home literally to die, departing this life, November 27, 1839.

Julia was with him when he died, his hand in hers. The beauty of his countenance in death was such that Anne Hall, the well-known miniature painter, begged permission to paint it, and his descendants may still gaze on the majestic features in their serene repose.

Our mother writes of this time: "I cannot, even now, bear to dwell upon the desolate hush which fell upon our house when its stately head lay, silent and cold, in the midst of weeping friends and children." [1]

Her love for her father was to cease only with her life. She never failed to record his birthday in her diary, with some word of tender remembrance.

Shortly before Mr. Ward's death, Sam and his wife had moved to a house of their own. The five unmarried children would have been desolate, indeed, if left to themselves in the great house: but to the joy and comfort of all, their bachelor uncle, John Ward, left his own house and came to live with them. From this time until his death in 1866, he was a second father to them.

Uncle John! The words call up memories of our own childhood. We see a tall, stalwart figure, clad in loose-fitting garments; a noble head crowned by a small brown scratch wig; a countenance beaming with kindliness and humor. A Manila cheroot is between his lips — the fragrance of one never fails to call up his image — and he caresses an unamiable little dog which he

[1] *Reminiscences*, p. 53.

fondly loves. He offers a grand-niece a silk dress if she will make it up herself. This was the "Uncle John" of No. 8 Bond Street, one of the worthies of Wall Street, and uncle, by courtesy, to half New York.

In his youth he had received an injury which deprived him of speech for more than a year. It was feared that he would never speak again; one day his mother, trying to help him in some small matter, and not succeeding to her mind, cried, "I am a poor, awkward, old woman!"

"*No, you are not!*" exclaimed John Ward; and the trouble was over.

His devotion to his orphan nieces and nephews was constant and beautiful. He desired ardently that the three girls should be good housekeepers, and grudged the amount of time which one of them at least devoted to books and music. To them also he was fond of giving dress-materials, with the proviso that they should make them up for themselves. This they managed to do, "with a good deal of help from the family seamstress."

When Julia published her first literary venture, a translation of Lamartine's "Jocelyne," Uncle John showed her a favorable notice of it in a newspaper, saying: "This is my little girl who knows about books, and writes an article and has it printed, but I wish she knew more about housekeeping."

"A sentiment," she adds, "which in after years I had occasion to echo with fervor."

While Sam was her ideal of youthful manhood, Henry was her mate, the nearest to her in age and in sympathy. The bond between them was close and tender; and when in October, 1840, he died of typhoid fever, the blow fell on her with crushing severity.

"When he closed his eyes," she says, "I would gladly, oh, so gladly have died with him!" And again, "I remember the time as one without light or comfort."

She turned to seek consolation in religion, and — naturally — in that aspect of religion which had been presented to her childish mind as the true and only one. At this time a great Calvinistic revival was going on in New York, and a zealous friend persuaded Julia to attend some of the meetings. In her anguish of grief, the gloomy doctrines of natural depravity, of an angry and vengeful Deity, of a salvation possible only through certain strictly defined channels, came home to her with terrible force. Her deeply religious nature sought the Divine under however portentous an aspect it was presented; her poet's imagination clung to the uplifted Cross; these were days of emotion, of fervor, of exaltation alternating with abasement; *thought* was to come later.

While under these influences, Julia, now at the head of the household, enforced her Calvinistic principles with rigor. The family were allowed only cold meat on Sunday, to their great discomfort; the rather uninviting midday dinner was named by Uncle John "Sentiment"; but at six o'clock they were given hot tea, and this he called "Bliss." Pious exhortations, sisterly admonitions, were the order of the day. "The Old Bird" — this *nom de tendresse* had now superseded "Jolie Julie," and was to be hers while her sisters and brothers lived — hovered over the younger ones with maternal anxiety. In the poems and letters of this period, she adopts unconsciously the phraseology of the day.

Being away on a visit, she writes to her sisters: "Believe me, it is better to set aside, untasted, the cup of human enjoyment, than to drink it to the bitter dregs, and then seek for something better, which may not be granted to us. The *manna* fell from heaven early in the morning, those who then neglected to gather it were left without nourishment; it is early in life's morning that we must gather the heavenly food, which can alone support us through the burden and heat of the day."

The emotional fervor of this time was heightened by a complication which arose from it. A young clergyman of brilliant powers and passionate nature fell deeply in love with Julia, and pressed his suit with such ardor that she consented to a semi-engagement. Fortunately, a visit to Boston gave her time to examine her feelings. Relieved from the pressure of a twofold excitement, breathing a calmer and a freer air, she realized that there could be no true union between her and the Rev. Mr. ——, and the connection was broken off.

The course of Julia's studies had for some years been leading her into wider fields of thought.

In her brother's library she found George Sand and Balzac, and read such books as he selected for her. In German she became familiar with Goethe, Jean Paul, and Matthias Claudius. She describes the sense of intellectual freedom derived from these studies as "half delightful, half alarming."

Mr. Ward one day had undertaken to read an English translation of "Faust" and came to her in great alarm. "My daughter," he said, "I hope that you have not read this wicked book!" She had read it, and "Wilhelm Meister," too (though in later life she thought the latter "not altogether good reading for the youth of our country"). Shelley was forbidden, and Byron allowed only in small and carefully selected doses.

The twofold bereavement which weighed so heavily upon her checked for a time the development of her thought, throwing her back on the ideas which her childhood had received without question; but her buoyant spirit could not remain long submerged, and as the poignancy of grief abated, her mind sought eagerly for clearer vision.

In the quiet of her own room, the bounds of thought and of faith stretched wide and wider. Vision often came in a flash: witness the moment when the question of Matthias Claudius, "And is He not also the God of the Japanese?" changed from a shocking suggestion to an eternal truth. Witness also the moment when, after reading "Paradise Lost," she saw "the picture of an eternal evil, of Satan and his ministers subjugated, indeed, by God, but not conquered, and able to maintain against Him an opposition as eternal as his goodness. This appeared to me impossible, and I threw away, once and forever, the thought of the terrible hell which till then had always formed part of my belief. In its place I cherished the persuasion that the victory of goodness must consist in mak-

JULIA WARD, AET. 22
From the bust by Clevenger now in the Boston Public Library

ing everything good, and that Satan himself could have no shield strong enough to resist permanently the divine power of the divine spirit."

New vistas were opening everywhere before her. She made acquaintance with Margaret Fuller, who read her poems, and urged her to publish them. Of one of these poems, Miss Fuller writes: —

"It is the record of days of genuine inspiration, — of days when the soul lay in the light, when the spiritual harmonies were clearly apprehended and great religious symbols reanimated with their original meaning. Its numbers have the fulness and sweetness of young love, young life. Its gifts were great and demand the service of a long day's work to *requite* and to interpret them. I can hardly realize that the Julia Ward I have seen has lived this life. It has not yet pervaded her whole being, though I can recall something of it in the steady light of her eye. May she become all attempered and ennobled by this music. I saw in her taste, the capacity for genius, and the utmost delicacy of passionate feeling, but caught no glimpse at the time of this higher mood. . . . If she publishes, I would not have her omit the lines about the 'lonely room.' The personal interest with which they stamp that part is slight and delicate. . . .

"S. MARGARET FULLER.

"I know of many persons in my own circle to whom I think the poem would be especially grateful."[1]

On every hand she met people, who like herself were

[1] This manuscript poem was lost, together with many others of the period, a loss always regretted by our mother.

pressing forward, seeking new light. She heard Channing preach, heard him say that God loves bad men as well as good; another window opened in her soul. Again, on a journey to Boston, she met Ralph Waldo Emerson. The train being delayed at a wayside station, she saw the Transcendentalist, whom she had pictured as hardly human, carrying on his shoulder the child of a poor and weary woman; her heart warmed to him, and they soon made acquaintance. She, with the ardor of youth, gave him at some length the religious views which she still held in the main, and with which she felt he would not agree. She enlarged upon the personal presence of Satan on this earth, on his power over man. Mr. Emerson replied with gentle courtesy, "Surely the Angel must be stronger than the Demon!" She never forgot these words; another window opened, and a wide one.

Julia Ward had come a long way from old Ascension Church, where Peter Stuyvesant, in a full brown wig, carried round the plate, and the Reverend Manton (afterwards Bishop) Eastburn preached sermons "remarked for their good English"; and where communicants were not expected to go to balls or theatres.

The years of mourning over, the Ward sisters took up the pursuits natural to their age and position. Louisa was now eighteen, very beautiful, already showing the rare social gift which distinguished her through life. The two sisters began a season of visiting, dancing, and all manner of gayeties.

The following letter illustrates this period of her girlhood: —

To her sisters

BOSTON (1842),
Friday, that's all I know about to-day.

MY DEAREST CHICKS, —

Though I have a right to be tired, having talked and danced for the two last nights, yet my enjoyment is most imperfect until I have shared it with you, so I must needs write to you, and tell you what a very nice time I am having. Last night I went to a party at Miss Shaw's, given to *Boz and me*, at least, I was invited before he came here, so think that I will only give him an equal share of the honor. I danced a good deal, with some very agreeable partners, and talked as usual with Sumner, Hillard,[1] Longo,[2] etc. I was quite pleased that Boz recognized Fanny Appleton and myself, and gave us a smile and bow *en passant*. He could do no more, being almost torn to pieces by the crowd which throngs his footsteps, wherever he goes. I like to look at him, he has a bright and most speaking countenance, and his face is all wrinkled with the lines, not of care, but of laughter. His manners are very free and cordial, and he seems to be as capital a fellow as one would suppose from his writings. He circulates as universally as small change, and understands the art of gratifying others without troubling himself, of letting himself be seen without displaying himself — now this speaks for his real good taste, and shows that if not a gentleman born and bred, he is at least a man, every inch of him.

. . . I have had hardly the least dash of Transcen-

---

[1] George S. Hillard. [2] Longfellow.

dentalism, and that of the very best description, a lecture and a visit from Emerson, in both of which he said beautiful things, and to-morrow (don't be shocked!) a conversation at Miss Fuller's, which I shall treasure up for your amusement and instruction. I have also heard (don't go into hysterics!) Dr. Channing once. It was a rare chance, as he does not now preach once in a year. His discourse was very beautiful — and oh, such a sermon as I heard from Father Taylor! I was almost disposed to say, "surely never man spake like this man." And now good-bye. I must shut up the budget, and keep some for a rainy day. God bless my darling sisters. Love to dear Sam and Uncle. Your

DUDIE.

In these days also she first met her future husband. Samuel Gridley Howe was at this time (1842) forty-one years of age; his life had been a stirring and adventurous one. After passing through Brown University, and the Harvard Medical School, in 1824 he threw in his lot with the people of Greece, then engaged in their War of Independence, and for six years shared their labor and hardships in the field, and on shipboard, being surgeon-in-chief first to the Greek army, then to the fleet. It was noted by a companion in arms, that "the only fault found with him was that he always would be in the fight, and was only a surgeon when the battle was over." He eventually found, however, that his work was to be constructive, not destructive.

The people were perishing for lack of food; he returned to America, preached a crusade, and took back to Greece a shipload of food and clothing for the starving women and children. Having fed them, he set them to work; built a hospital and a mole (which stands to this day in Ægina), founded a colony, and turned the half-naked peasants into farmers. These matters have been fully related elsewhere.[1]

Returning to this country in 1831, he took up the education of the blind, which was to be chief among the multifarious labors of his life.

When Julia Ward first met him, he had been for nine years Director of the Perkins Institution for the Blind, and was known throughout the civilized world as the man who had first taught language to a blind deaf mute (Laura Bridgman).

Up to this time a person thus afflicted was classed with idiots, "because," as Blackstone says, "his mind cannot be reached." This dictum had been recently reaffirmed by a body of learned men. Dr. Howe thought otherwise. Briefly, he invented a new science. "He carefully reasoned out every step of the way, and made a full and clear record of the methods which he invented, not for his pupils alone, but for the whole afflicted class for which he opened the way to human fellowship. . . . His methods have been employed in all subsequent cases, and after seventy years of trial remain the standard."[2]

Hand in hand with Dorothea Dix, he was beginning the great fight for helping and uplifting the insane; was already, with Horace Mann, considering the con-

---

[1] *Letters and Journals of Samuel Gridley Howe.*
[2] *Memoir of Dr. Samuel G. Howe*, by Julia Ward Howe.

dition of the common schools, and forging the weapons for other fights which laid the foundations of the school system of Massachusetts. Later, he was to take up the cause of the feeble-minded, the deaf mute, the prisoner, the slave; throughout his life, no one in "trouble, sorrow, need, sickness, or any other adversity" was ever to call on him in vain.

His friends called him the "Chevalier"; partly because the King of Greece had made him a Knight of St. George, but more because they saw in him a good knight without fear and without reproach. Charles Sumner was his *alter ego*, the brother of his heart; others of his intimates at that time were Longfellow, George Hillard, Cornelius Felton, Henry Cleveland. This little knot of friends called themselves "The Five of Clubs," and met often to make merry and to discuss the things of life.

The summer of 1842 was spent by Julia Ward and her sisters at a cottage in the neighborhood of Boston, in company with their friend Mary Ward.[1] Here Longfellow and Sumner often visited them, and here Julia first heard of the Chevalier and his wonderful achievement in educating Laura Bridgman. Deeply interested, she gladly accepted the offer of the two friends to drive her and her sisters over to the Perkins Institution. She has described how "Mr. Sumner, looking out of a window, said, 'Oh! here comes Howe on his black horse.' I looked out also, and beheld a noble rider on a noble steed."

[1] Afterward Mrs. Charles H. Dorr. This lady was of no kin to them. She had been betrothed to their brother Henry, and was the lifelong friend of all three sisters.

SAMUEL G. HOWE IN DRESS OF A GREEK SOLDIER

From a drawing by John Elliott

The slender, military figure, the jet-black hair, keen blue eyes, and brilliant complexion, above all the vivid presence, like the flash of a sword — all these could not fail to impress the young girl deeply; the Chevalier, on his part, saw and recognized the *Diva Julia* of his friends' description. She has told us "how acquaintance ripened into good-will" between the two.

The Chevalier, eager to push the acquaintance further, went to New York to call on the Diva and her family. In a private journal of the time we find the following glimpse of the pair: —

"Walked down Broadway with all the fashion and met the pretty blue-stocking, Miss Julia Ward, with her admirer, Dr. Howe, just home from Europe. She had on a blue satin cloak and a white muslin dress. I looked to see if she had on blue stockings, but I think not. I suspect that her stockings were pink, and she wore low slippers, as Grandmamma does. They say she dreams in Italian and quotes French verses. She sang very prettily at a party last evening, and accompanied herself on the piano. I noticed how white her hands were."

During a subsequent visit to Boston in the winter of 1842–43, Julia Ward and Dr. Howe became engaged. The engagement was warmly welcomed by the friends of both.

Charles Sumner writes to Julia: —

"Howe has told me, with eyes flashing with joy, that you have received his love. May God make you happy in his heart, as I know he will be happy in yours! A truer heart was never offered to woman. I know him well. I know the depth, strength, and constancy of his affections, as the whole world knows the beauty of his life and character. And oh! how I rejoice that these are all to mingle in loving harmony with your great gifts of heart and mind. God bless you! God bless you both! You will strengthen each other for the duties of life; and the most beautiful happiness shall be yours — that derived from inextinguishable mutual love, and from the consciousness of duty done.

"You have accepted my dear Howe as your lover; pray let me ever be

"Your most affectionate friend,

"CHARLES SUMNER.

"P.S. Sir Huldbrand has subdued the restless Undine, and the soul has been inspired into her; and her 'wickedness' shall cease."

Longfellow's letter to Dr. Howe also has been preserved among the precious relics of the time.

MY DEAREST CHEVALIER, —

From the deepest dungeons of my heart, all the imprisoned sympathies and affections of my nature cry aloud to you, saying "All hail!" On my return from Portland this afternoon, I found your note, and before reading it I read in Sumner's eyes your happiness. The great riddle of life is no longer a riddle to you; the great mystery is solved. I need not say to you how very deeply and devoutly I rejoice with you; and no one more so, I assure you. Among all your friends, I am the oldest friend of your fair young bride; she is a beautiful spirit, a truth, which friendship has learned by heart in a few years. Love has taught you in as many hours!

Of course you seem to be transfigured and glorified. You walk above in the June air, while Sumner and I, like the poor (sprites) in "Faust," who were struggling far down in the cracks and fissures of the rocks, cry out to you, "O take us with you! take us with you!"

In fine, my dear Doctor, God bless you and yours. You know already how much I approve your choice. I went to your office this afternoon to tell you with my own lips; but you were not there. Take, therefore, this brief expression of my happiness at knowing you are so happy; and believe me

Ever sincerely your friend,

LONGFELLOW.

CAMBRIDGE, Feb. 20, 1843.

At the same time Diva writes to her brother Sam: —

"The Chevalier says truly — I am the captive of his bow and spear. His true devotion has won me from the world, and from myself. The past is already fading from my sight; already, I begin to live with him in the future, which shall be as calmly bright as true love can make it. I am perfectly satisfied to sacrifice to one so noble and earnest the day dreams of my youth. He will make life more beautiful to me than a dream. . . .

"The Chevalier is very presumptuous — says that he will not lose sight of me for one day, that I must stay here till he can return with me to New York. The Chevalier is very impertinent, speaks of two or three months, when I speak of two or three years, and seems determined to have his own way: but, dear Bunny, the Chevalier's way will be a very charming way, and is, henceforth, to be mine."

It was not to be supposed that the Chevalier would wait longer for his bride than was absolutely necessary. The wedding preparations were hurried on, most of them being made by Sisters Annie and Louisa, as Julia could not be brought down from the clouds sufficiently to give them much attention. It was hard even to make her choose her wedding dress; but this was finally decided upon, "a white embroidered muslin, exquisitely fine, to be worn over a satin 'slip.'"

The wedding, a quiet one, took place at Samuel Ward's house, on April 23, 1843, and four days later, Chevalier and Diva sailed together for Europe.

CHAPTER V

> . . . I have been
> In dangers of the sea and land, unscared;
> And from the narrow gates of childbed oft
> Have issued, bearing high my perilous prize
> (The germ of angel-hood, from chaos rescued),
> With steadfast hope and courage. . . .
>
> J. W. H.

IN the forties it was no uncommon thing for a sister or friend of the bride to form one of the wedding party when a journey was to be taken; accordingly Annie Ward went with the Howes and shared the pleasures of a notable year. She was at this time seventeen; it was said of her that "she looked so like a lily-of-the-valley that one expected to see two long green leaves spring up beside her as she walked."

Horace Mann and his bride (Mary Peabody, sister of Mrs. Nathaniel Hawthorne) sailed on the same steamer; the friends met afterward in London and elsewhere.

The first days at sea were rough and uncomfortable. Julia writes to her sister Louisa: —

"I have had two days of extreme suffering, and look like the Chevalier's grandmother. To-day I am on deck, able to eat soup and herring, with grog in small doses. Husband very kind, takes good care of me. I am good for nothing, but try to be courageous. Mr. and Mrs. Mann are very loving; she wears a monstrous sunbonnet; he lies down in his overcoat. . . . Brandy and water are consoling; Dr. won't give us much, though. . . . I could not get off my boots until last night, I was so ill; I slept all the time, and forgot that Annie was on board. . . . When you do get married, don't leave in four days for Europe. . . . Don't forget cake for my orphans. . . . Mrs. Mann wrote to me yesterday, and recommended lemonade. I wrote back to her, and recommended leeks and onions. . . ."

And again, several days later: —

"Although the ship is very tipsy, and makes my head and hand unsteady, I am anxious to write to you that you may see what a brave sailor I am become, for to write at sea one must be quite well. I am ashamed to have written you so sea-sick a letter near Halifax, but I was then just out of my berth, and very miserable. Since that time, I have not once laid by — we have had some rough days, but I have always held up my head, and eaten my dinner, 'helping myself *sang-froidy*' to all manner of good things. At first, I could not do without brandy and water, but in a little while I ceased to require it; now I go tumbling about all over the ship, singing at the top of my voice, teasing Chevalier, and comforting the sea-sick. . . . I live on deck, rain or shine. Annie stays too much in the cabin, which is strewn with sick ladies, and grannies of the other sex, and which ever resounds with cries of 'Mrs. Bean! Mrs. Bean! soda water! Mrs. Bean, soup! Mrs. Bean, gruel with brandy in it! Mrs. Bean, hold my head! Mrs. Bean, wag my jaws!' Mrs. Bean is the stewardess, and an angel. . . .

"*Saturday morning.* We are now in sight of land, and in smooth water. . . . Annie and I were getting very much used to the ship, and are just in fine trim for a long voyage. I even miss the rolling and pitching which we have had until to-day, and which made it necessary to walk with great circumspection. You would have laughed to have seen us, going about like tipsy witches. I have had various tumbles. I confess that when the ship rolled and I felt myself going, I generally made for the stoutest man in sight, and pitched into him, the result being various apologies on both sides, and great merriment on the part of the spectators — a little of the old mischief left, you see. The old cow began to smell the land yesterday, she reared and bellowed, and butted at the butcher when he went to milk her. This is her third voyage. I cannot tell you how good my husband is, how kind, how devoted. . . ."

Arriving in London, they took lodgings in upper Baker Street.

This first visit to London was one which our mother always loved to recall. Not only had the pair brought letters to many notabilities, but Dr. Howe's reputation had preceded him, and every reader of Dickens's "American Notes" was eager to meet the man who had brought a soul out of prison.

Julia writes to her sister Louisa (June 17): —

"I have said something, — I can hardly say enough, of the kindness we have received here. London seems already a home to us, and one surrounded by dear friends. Morpeth and his family, Rogers, Basil Montagu, and Sir R. H. Inglis have been our best friends.

Sydney Smith also has been kind to us; he calls Howe
'Prometheus,' and says that he gave a soul to an
inanimate body. For four mornings, we have not once
breakfasted at home. Milnes gave us one very nice
breakfast; among the guests was Charles Buller, celebrated here for his wit and various endowments. The
two handsomest women I have seen are Mrs. Norton
and the Duchess of Sutherland — the former of these
rather a haughty beauty, with flashing eye and swelling lip, and dress too low for our notions of propriety —
this is common enough here. . . ."

The Doctor was lame (the result of an accident on
shipboard), and the Reverend Sydney Smith, one of
their earliest visitors, insisted on lending him his own
crutches. The Doctor demurred; he was tall, while
Canon Smith was short and stout. The crutches were
sent, nevertheless. They could not be used, and were
returned with thanks; not so soon, however, but that
the kind and witty Canon made of the incident a peg
on which to hang a jest. He had lost money by American investments; in a letter published in a London
paper, after reflecting severely upon the failure of some
of the Western States to pay their debts, he added:
"And now an American doctor has deprived me of my
last means of support!"

Sydney Smith proved genuinely kind and solicitous.
He writes to the Doctor: —

"You know as well as I do, or better, that nature
charges one hundred per cent for a bad leg used before
the proper time, and that if you use it a day sooner
than you ought, it may molest you for a month longer

than you expect. This being; [*sic*] if your ladies will trust themselves to me any day, I shall have great pleasure in escorting them in their sight-seeing, and will call upon them with my carriage, if that be possible."

He did take them about a great deal; they dined with him, and passed more than one delightful evening at his house.

Another of their early visitors was Charles Dickens. Not only did he invite them to dine, but he took them to all manner of places unfamiliar to the ordinary tourist: to prisons, workhouses, and asylums, more interesting to the Chevalier than theatre or picture-gallery.

There were even expeditions to darker places, when Julia and Annie must stay at home. Dr. Howe's affair was with all sorts and conditions of men, and the creator of Joe and Oliver Twist, the child of the Marshalsea, could show him things that no one else could. The following note, in Dickens's unmistakable handwriting, shows how these expeditions were managed, and how he enjoyed them: —

MY DEAR HOWE, — Drive to-night to St. Giles's Church. Be there at half-past 11 — and wait. One of Tracey's people will put his head into the coach after a Venetian and mysterious fashion, and breathe your name. Follow that man. Trust him to the death.

So no more at present from

THE MASK.

Ninth June, 1843.

Horace Mann was of the party on most of these investigations.

Beside dinners and evening parties, there were break-
fasts, with Richard Monckton Milnes (afterward Lord
Houghton), with Samuel Rogers, — who gave them
plovers' eggs, — and with jovial Sir Robert Harry Inglis,
who cut the loaf at either end, giving the guests "a
slice or a hunch" at their desire.

This meal, our mother notes, was not "a luncheon
in disguise," but a genuine breakfast, at ten or even
half-past nine o'clock.

She writes to her sister Louisa: —

"People have been very kind to us — we have one
or two engagements for every day this week, and had
three dinners for one day, two of which we were, of
course, forced to decline. We had a pleasant dinner at
Dickens's, on Saturday — a very handsome entertainment, consisting of all manner of good things. Dickens
led me in to dinner — waxed quite genial over his wine,
and was more natural than I ever saw him — after
dinner we had coffee, conversation and music, to which
I lent my little wee voice! We did not get home until
half-past eleven. . . . Annie has doubtless told you
how we went to see Carlyle, and Mrs. was out, and I
poured tea for him, and he handed me the preserves
with: 'I do not know what thae little things are, perhaps you can eat them — I never touch them mysel'.'
This naturally made me laugh — we had a strange but
pleasant evening with him — he is about forty, looks
young for that, drinks powerful tea, and then goes it
strong upon all subjects, but without extravagance —
he has a fine head, an earnest face, a glowing eye. . . .
Furthermore, we have walked into the affections of the

Hon. Basil Montagu, and Mrs. Basil — furthermore, Annie and I did went alone to a rout at Mrs. Sydney Smith's, and were announced, 'Mrs. 'Owe hand Miss Vord' — did not know a soul, Annie frightened, I bored — got hold of some good people — made friends, drank execrable tea, finished the evening by a crack with Sir Sydney himself, and came off victorious, that is to say alive. Sir S. very like old Mrs. Prime, three chins, and such a corporosity! . . .

"*Saturday, June 2nd.* We have been too busy to write. We dined on Wednesday with Kenyon — present Dickens's wife, Fellows, Milnes and some others — Milnes a pert little prig, but pleasant. *À propos*, when he came to call upon us, our girl announced him as 'Mr. Miller' — our conversation ran upon literature, and I had the exquisite discrimination to tell him that except Wordsworth, there were no great poets in England now. Fortunately he soon took his departure, and thus prevented me from expressing the light estimation in which I hold his poetry. On Thursday Morpeth gave us a beautiful dinner — thirteen servants in the hall, powdered heads, Lady Carlisle very like Morpeth — Lady Mary Howard not pretty; Duchess of Sutherland, beautiful, but like Lizzie Hogg. They gave us strawberries, the first we have tasted, green peas, pines, peaches, apricots, grapes — all very expensive. We stayed until nearly twelve — they were very gracious — Annie and I are little people here — we are too young(?) to be noticed — we are very demure, and have learned humility. Chev receives a great deal of attention, ladies press forward to look at him, roll up their eyes, and exclaim, 'Oh! he is such a wonner!' I do not like that the pretty women should pay him so many compliments — it will turn his little head! He is now almost well, and so handsome! the wrinkles are almost gone — Yesterday, Sir Robert Inglis gin us a treat in the shape of a breakfast — it was very pleasant, albeit Sir R. is very pious, and a Tory to boot. We had afterward a charming visit from Carlyle — in the evening we went to Landsdowne House, to a concert given by the Marquis — heard Grisi, Lablache, Mario, Standigl, were much pleased — I was astonished, though, to find that our little trio at home was not bad, even in comparison with these stars. They have, of course, infinitely better voices, but hang me if they sing with half the enthusiasm and fire of our old Sam and Cousi, or even of poor Dudy. Grisi's voice is beautifully clear and flute-like — Mario sings *si-be-mol* and natural with perfect ease. I was most interested in the German Standigl, who sang the '*Wanderer*' with wonderful pathos. Lablache thundered away — I must see them on the stage before I shall be able to judge of them. After music we had supper. Willie Wad [1] was indefatigable in our service. 'Go, and bring us a great deal more lemonade!' these were our oft-repeated orders, and the good Geneseo trotted to the table for us, till, as he expressed it, 'he was ashamed to go any more.' Lansdowne is a devilish good fellow! ho! ho! He wears a blue belt across his diaphragm, and a silver star on his left breast — he jigs up and down the room, and makes himself at home in his own

[1] William Wadsworth, of Geneseo.

house. He is about sixty, with Marchioness to match; side dishes, I presume, but did not inquire. I have just been breakfasting at the Duke of Sutherland's superb palace. I will tell you next time about it. Lady Carlisle says I am nice and pretty, oh! how I love her! . . ."

In another letter she says: —

" I take some interest in everything I see — especially in all that throws light upon human prog. The Everetts [1] have given us a beautiful and most agreeable dinner: Dickens, Mrs. Norton, Moore, Landseer, and one or two others. Rogers says: 'I have three pleasures in the day: the first is, when I get up in the morning, and scratch myself with my hair mittens; the second is when I dress for dinner, and scratch myself with my hair mittens; the third is when I undress at night, and scratch myself with my hair mittens.' . . ."

Beside this feast of hospitality, there was the theatre, with Macready and Helen Faucit in the "Lady of Lyons," and the opera, with Grisi and Mario, Alboni and Persiani. Julia, who had been forbidden the theatre since her seventh year, enjoyed to the full both music and drama, but "the crowning ecstasy of all" she found in the ballet, of which Fanny Elssler and Cerito were the stars. The former was beginning to wane; the dancing which to Emerson and Margaret Fuller seemed "poetry and religion" had lost, perhaps, something of its magic; the latter was still in her early bloom and grace.

Years later, our mother suggested to Theodore Parker that "the best stage dancing gives the *classic, in a*

---

[1] Edward Everett was at that time American Minister to England.

fluent form, with the illumination of life and personality." She recalled nothing sensual or even sensuous in the dances she saw that season, only "the very ectasy and embodiment of grace." (But the Doctor thought Cerito ought to be sent to the House of Correction!)

Among the English friends, the one to whom our parents became most warmly attached was Lord Morpeth, afterwards Earl of Carlisle. This gentleman proved a devoted friend. Not only did he show the travellers every possible attention in London, but finding that they were planning a tour through Wales, Ireland, and Scotland, he made out with great care an itinerary for them, giving the roads by which they should travel and the points of interest they should visit.

Very reluctantly they left the London of so many delights, and started on the prescribed tour, following in the main the lines laid down by their kind friend.

To her sister Louisa

Sunday, July 2.

... We are in Dublin, among the Paddies, and funny enough they are. There are many beggars — you cannot get into the carriage without being surrounded with ragged women holding out their dirty hands, and clamouring for ha'pence — we have just returned from Edgeworthtown; on our way, we walked into some of the peasants' huts. I will tell you about one — it was thatched, built very miserably, had no floor except the native mud; there was a peat

fire, which filled the house with smoke — before the
fire lay the pig, grunting in concert with the chickens,
who were picking up scraps of the dinner, which consisted of potatoes and salt — three families live in it.
Two sets of little ragamuffins are sitting in the dirt.
Ch. bestows some pence: "God kape your honour —
God save ye, wherever ye go, and sure and it's a nice,
comfortable looking young woman you have got with
you, an uncommon pretty girl" (that is me). Don't
they understand the matter, eh? We passed three
delightful hours with Miss Edgeworth, in the library
in which she wrote all her works — she was surrounded
by a numerous and charming family, among others,
the last of her father's four wives, whom she calls
mother, although the lady must be some ten years her
junior. She is herself a most vivacious little lady, about
seventy-five years old, but gay and bright as a young
girl — she seemed quite delighted with Ch., and conversed with him on many topics in a very animated
manner. She has very clear and sound views of things,
and takes the liveliest interest in all that goes on
around her, and in the world. One of her younger
brothers (with a nice Spanish wife) has a nest of very
young children, in whom she delights as much as if she
had not helped to bring up three sets of brothers and
sisters. She said to me: "It is not only for Laura Bridgman that I wanted to see Dr. Howe, but I admire the
spirit of all his writings." She gave him some engravings, and wrote her name at the bottom. . . . At one
o'clock, we went to luncheon which was very nice,
consisting of meat, potatoes, and preserves. . . . She

made us laugh, and laughed herself. They were saying that American lard was quite superseding whale oil. "Yes," said she, "and in consequence, the whale cannot bear the sight of a pig." Her little nephew made a real bull. He was showing me his rat trap, "and," said he, "I shall kill the rat before I let him out, eh?" . . .

Dublin, Tuesday. Went to the Repeal meeting at the Corn Exchange. It was held in a small room in the third or fourth story. "A shilling, sir," said the man at the door to my husband. — "What!" replied he, "do ladies pay?" — "Not unless they'd like to become repealers." We passed up — the gentlemen went on to the floor of the room — we went to the ladies' gallery, a close confined place at one end — we were early, and had good seats, for a time at least — we separated, not anticipating the trouble we should have in finding each other again — for the ladies, comprising orangewomen, washerwomen, and I fear, all manner of women, poured in, without much regard to order, decency, and the rights of prior possession — and when O'Connell came in, which was in about three quarters of an hour, they pressed, and pushed, and squeezed, and scolded, as only Irishwomen can do. . . . The current of female patriotism bore down upon me in a most painful manner — a sort of triangular pressure seemed applied to my poor body which threatened to destroy, not only my centre of gravity, but my very personal identity. I was obliged, I regret to say, to defend myself as I have sometimes done in a quadrille or waltzing circle in New York — I was forced to push in my turn, though as moderately as I could. This was not

my only trouble — in the crowd, I had scraped acquaintance with a respectable Irishwoman, who, after
various questions, discovered that I was an American,
and imagined me at once to be a good Catholic and
repealer — so when O'Connell made some allusions to
the Americans, she said so as to be heard by several
people, who immediately began to look at me with
curious eyes — " You should n't disturb her, she's an
American," and they would for a time cease to molest
me. . . . O'Connell was not great on this occasion —
his remarks were rambling and superficial, distinguished chiefly by their familiarity, and by the extreme
ingenuity with which the cunning orator disguises the
tendencies of the sentiments he vindicates, and talks
treason, yet so that the law cannot lay a finger upon
him. He had begun his speech when Steele, a brother
repealer, entered. He stopped at once, held out his
hand to him, saying in a loud tone, "Tom Steele, how
d' ye do?" which drew forth bursts of applause. "And
is he a good man?" I asked of a lady repealer (whether
apple-woman or seller of ginger beer, I know not). "Oh,
Ma'am, he is the best *cratur*, the most charitable, the
most virtuous, the most religious man — sure, he goes
to the communion every Sunday, and never says no
to no one."

The visit to Scotland was all too hasty, the notes
are mere brief jottings; at the end she "remembered
but one thing, the grave of Scott. In return for all the
delight he had given me, I had nothing to give him but
my silent tears."

The end of July found the party once more in England. The following letter tells of the unlucky visit to Wordsworth which our mother (after forty-six years) describes from memory in her "Reminiscences" in slightly different terms.

To her sister Louisa

July 29.

. . . I am very glad to be out of Ireland and Scotland, where we had incessant rains — even the beautiful Loch Katrine would not show herself to us in sunshine. We crossed in an open boat, and had a pony ride of five miles, all in as abominable a drizzle as you would wish to see. The Cumberland Lakes, among which we sought the shrine of Wordsworth, were almost as unaccommodating — in driving to Windermere we got wetted to the skin, and dashed down the steep mountain road in a thick mist, with a pair of horses, so unruly that I supposed the miseries of wet garments would soon be cancelled by that of a broken neck. I prayed to Saint Crispin, Saint Nicholas, and the three kings of Köln, and got through the danger — in the evening we visited Wordsworth, a crabbed old sinner, who gave us a very indifferent muffin, and talked repudiation with Chev. As he had just lost a great deal of money by Mississippi bonds, you may imagine that he felt particularly disposed to be cordial to Americans — and not knowing, probably, that New York is not in the heart of Louisiana, he was inclined no doubt to cast part of the odium upon us. Accordingly Mrs. Wordsworth and her daughter sat at one end of the room, Annie and I at the other. Incensed at this unusual neglect, I made several interjections in a low tone for Annie's benefit (my husband allows me to swear once a week) — at length, good Townsend-on-Mesmerism came to my relief, and kindly talked with me for an hour or more — he is a charming person, and rides other people's horses as well as his own hobby. He dislikes England, and lives principally in Germany. Kind Heaven, at the termination of the evening, sent me an opportunity of imparting a small portion of the internal pepper and mustard which had been ripening in my heart during the whole evening. The mother and daughter beginning to whine to me about their losses, I told them that where one Englishman had suffered, twenty Americans were perhaps ruined. They replied, it was hard they should suffer for the misfortunes of another country. "And why," quoth I, "must you needs speculate in foreign stocks? Why did you not keep your money at home? It was safe enough in England — you knew there was risk in investing it so far from you — if we should speculate in yours, we should no doubt be ruined also." This explosion, from my meek self, took the company somewhat by surprise — they held their tongues, and we departed. . . .

From England the travellers had meant to go to Berlin, but the King of Prussia, who eleven years before had kept Dr. Howe in prison *au secret* for five weeks for carrying (at the request of General Lafayette) succor to certain Polish refugees, still regarded him as a dangerous person, and Prussia was closed to him and his. This greatly amused Horace Mann, who wrote to the Doctor, "I understand the King of Prussia has about 200,000 men constantly under arms, and if necessary he can increase his force to two millions. This shows the estimation in which he holds your single self!"

Years later, the King sent Dr. Howe a gold medal in consideration of his work for the blind: by a singular coincidence, its money value was found to equal the sum which the Doctor had been forced to pay for board and lodging in the prison of Berlin.

Making a détour, the party journeyed through Switzerland and the Austrian Tyrol, spent some weeks in Vienna, and a month in Milan, where they met Count Gonfalonieri, one of the prisoners of Spielberg. Julia had known two of these sufferers, Foresti and Albinola, in New York, where they lived for many years, beloved and respected. Hearing the talk of these men, and seeing Italy bound hand and foot in temporal and spiritual fetters, she was deeply impressed by the apparent hopelessness of the outlook for the Italian patriots. By what miracle, she asked herself long afterward, was the great structure overthrown? She adds, "The remembrance of this miracle forbids me to despair of any great deliverance, desired and delayed. He who maketh the wrath of men to serve Him, can make liberty blossom out of the very rod that the tyrant [wields]."

Southward still they journeyed, by *vettura*, in the old leisurely fashion, and came at last to Rome.

The thrill of wonder that Julia felt at the first sight of St. Peter's dome across the Campagna was one of the abiding impressions of her life; Rome was to be one of the cities of her heart; the charm was cast upon her in that first moment. Yet she says of that Rome of 1843, "A great gloom and silence hung over it."

The houses were cold, and there were few conveniences; but Christmas found the Howes established in the Via San Niccolo da Tolentino, as comfortably as might be. Here they were joined by Louisa Ward, and here they soon gathered round them a delightful circle of friends. Most of the *forestieri* of Rome in those days were artists; among those who came often to the house were Thomas Crawford, Luther Terry, Freeman the painter and his wife, and Törmer, who painted a portrait of Julia. The winter passed like a dream. There were balls as gorgeous as those of London, with the beautiful Princess Torlonia in place of the Duchess of Sutherland; musical parties, at which Diva sang to the admiration of all. There were visits to the galleries, where George Combe was of the party, and where he and the Chevalier studied the heads of statues and busts from the point of view of phrenology, a theory in which both were deeply interested. They were presented to the Pope, Gregory XVI, who wished to hear about Laura Bridgman. The Chevalier visited all the "public institutions, misnamed charitable," [1] and the schools, whose masters were amazed to find that he was an American, and asked how in that case it happened that he was not black!

[1] S. G. H. to Charles Sumner.

In her "Reminiscences" our mother records many
vivid impressions of these Roman days. She had forgotten, or did not care to recall, a certain languor and
depression of spirits which in some measure dimmed
for her the brightness of the picture, but which were
to give place to the highest joy she had yet known.
On March 12, her first child was born, and was christened Julia Romana.

There are neither journals nor letters of this period;
the only record of it — from her hand — lies in two
slender manuscript books of verse, marked respectively
"1843" and "1844." In these volumes we trace her
movements, sometimes by the title of a poem, as "Sailing," "The Ladies of Llangollen," "The Roman Beggar Boy," etc., sometimes by a single word written
after the poem, "Berne," "Milan."

From these poems we learn that she did not expect
to survive the birth of her child; yet with that birth
a new world opened before her.

> He gave the Mother's chastened heart,
> He gave the Mother's watchful eye,
> He bids me live but where thou art,
> And look with earnest prayer on high.
>
> .   .   .   .
>
> Then spake the angel of Mothers
> To me in gentle tone:
> "Be kind to the children of others
> And thus deserve thine own!"

When, in the spring of 1844, she left Rome with husband, sister, and baby, it seemed, she says, "like
returning to the living world after a long separation
from it."

Journeying by way of Naples, Marseilles, Avignon, they came at length to Paris.

Here Julia first saw Rachel, and Taglioni, the greatest of all dancers; here, too, she tried to persuade the Chevalier to wear his Greek decorations to Guizot's reception, but tried in vain, he considering such ornaments unfitting a republican.

The autumn found them again in England, this time to learn the delights of country visiting. Their first visit was to Atherstone, the seat of Charles Nolte Bracebridge, a descendant of Lady Godiva, a most cultivated and delightful man. He and his charming wife made the party welcome, and showed them everything of interest except the family ghost, which remained invisible.

Another interesting visit was to the Nightingales of Embley. Florence Nightingale was at this time a young woman of twenty-four. A warm friendship sprang up between her and our parents, and she felt moved to consult the Doctor on the matter which then chiefly occupied her thoughts. Would it, she asked, be unsuitable or unbecoming for a young Englishwoman to devote herself to works of charity, in hospitals and elsewhere, as the Catholic Sisters did?

The Doctor replied: "My dear Miss Florence, it would be unusual, and in England whatever is unusual is apt to be thought unsuitable; but I say to you, go forward, if you have a vocation for that way of life; act up to your inspiration, and you will find that there is never anything unbecoming or unladylike in doing your duty for the good of others. Choose your path, go on with it, wherever it may lead you, and God be with you!"

Among the people they met in the autumn of 1844 was Professor Fowler, the phrenologist. This gentleman examined Julia's head, and made the following pronunciamento: —

"You're a deep one! it takes a Yankee to find you out. The intellectual temperament predominates in your character. You will be a central character like Henry Clay and Silas Wright, and people will group themselves around you."

Now Julia could not abide Professor Fowler.

"Oh, yes!" she snapped out angrily. "They've always been my models!"

"The best things you do," he went on, "will be done on the spur of the moment. You have enough love of order to enjoy it, but you will not take the trouble to produce it. You have more religion than morality. You have genius, but no music in you by nature."

Fifty years later these words were fresh in her memory.

"I disliked Mr. Fowler extremely," she said, "and believed nothing of what he said; nevertheless, most of his predictions were verified. I had at the time no leading in any of the directions he indicated. I had been much shut up in personal and family life; was a person rather of antipathies than sympathies. His remarks made *no impression*. Yet," she added, "I always had a sense of *relation to the public*, but thought the connection would come through writing."

Apropos of Mr. Fowler's "more religion than morality," she said: "Morality is a thing of the will; we may
think differently of such matters at different times.
What he said may have been true."

Then the twinkle came into her eyes: "When Mr.
William Astor heard of my engagement, he said, 'Why,
Miss Julia, I am surprised! I thought you were too
intellectual to marry!' "

Another acquaintance of this autumn was the late
Arthur Mills, who was through life one of our parents'
most valued friends. He came to America with them;
in his honor, during the voyage, Julia composed
"The Milsiad," scribbling the lines day by day in a
little note-book, still carefully preserved in the Mills
family.

The first and last stanzas give an idea of this poem,
which, though never printed, was always a favorite
with its author.

> My heart fills
> With the bare thought of the illustrious Mills:
> That man of eyes and nose,
> Of legs and arms, of fingers and of toes.
>
> . . . .
>
> To lands devoid of tax
> Goeth he not, armed with axe?
> Trees shall he cut down,
> And forests ever?
> Tame cataracts with a frown?
> Grin all the fish from Mississippi River?
> (My style is grandiose,
> Quite in the tone of Mills's nose.)
>
> . . . .
>
> Harp of the West, through wind and foggy weather
> We've sung our passage to our native land,
> Now I have reached the terminus of tether,

And I must lay thee trembling from my hand.
That hand must ply the ignominious needle,
This mind brood o'er the salutary dish,
I must grow sober as a parish beadle,
And having fish to fry, must fry my fish.
Some happier muse than mine shall wake thy spell,
Harp of the West, oh Gemini! farewell!

CHAPTER VI

SOUTH BOSTON

1844–1851; *aet.* 25–32

THE ROUGH SKETCH

A great grieved heart, an iron will,
As fearless blood as ever ran;
A form elate with nervous strength
And fibrous vigor, — all a man.

A gallant rein, a restless spur,
The hand to wield a biting scourge;
Small patience for the tasks of Time,
Unmeasured power to speed and urge.

He rides the errands of the hour,
But sends no herald on his ways;
The world would thank the service done,
He cannot stay for gold or praise.

Not lavishly he casts abroad
The glances of an eye intense,
And did he smile but once a year,
It were a Christmas recompense.

I thank a poet for his name,
The "Down of Darkness," this should be;
A child, who knows no risk it runs,
Might stroke its roughness harmlessly.

One helpful gift the Gods forgot,
Due to the man of lion-mood;
A Woman's soul, to match with his
In high resolve and hardihood.

J. W. H.

The name of Laura Bridgman will long continue to suggest to the hearer one of the most brilliant exploits of philanthropy, modern or ancient. Much of the good that good men do soon passes out of the remembrance of busy generations, each succeeding to each, with its own special inheritance of labor and interest. But it will be long before the world shall forget the cour-

age and patience of the man who, in the very bloom of his manhood, sat
down to besiege this almost impenetrable fortress of darkness and isolation,
and, after months of labor, carried within its walls the divine conquest of
life and of thought.

J. W. H., *Memoir of Dr. Samuel G. Howe.*

In September, 1844, the travellers returned to America and took up their residence at the Perkins Institution, in South Boston, in the apartment known as the "Doctor's Wing."

At first, Laura Bridgman made one of the family, the Doctor considering her almost as an adopted child. His marriage had been something of a shock to her.

"Does Doctor love me like Julia?" she asked her teacher anxiously.

"No!"

"Does he love God like Julia?"

"Yes!"

A pause: then — "God was kind to give him his wife!"

She and Julia became much attached to each other, and were friends through life.

Julia was now to realize fully the great change that had come in her life. She had been the acknowledged queen of her home and circle in New York. Up to this time, she had known Boston as a gay visitor knows it.

She came now as the wife of a man who had neither leisure nor inclination for " *Society* "; a man of tenderest heart, but of dominant personality, accustomed to rule, and devoted to causes of which she knew only by hearsay; moreover, so absorbed in work for these causes, that he could only enjoy his home by snatches.

She herself says: " The romance of charity easily

interests the public. Its laborious details and duties
repel and weary the many, and find fitting ministers
only in a few spirits of rare and untiring benevolence.
Dr. Howe, after all the laurels and roses of victory,
had to deal with the thorny ways of a profession te-
dious, difficult, and exceptional. He was obliged to
create his own working machinery, to drill and instruct
his corps of teachers, himself first learning the secrets
of the desired instruction. He was also obliged to keep
the infant Institution fresh in the interest and good-
will of the public, and to give it a place among the
recognized benefactions of the Commonwealth."

From the bright little world of old New York, from
relatives and friends, music and laughter, fun and frolic,
she came to live in an Institution, a bleak, lofty house
set on a hill, four-square to all the winds that blew;
with high-studded rooms, cold halls paved with white
and gray marble, echoing galleries; where three fourths
of the inmates were blind, and the remaining fourth
were devoting their time and energies to the blind.
The Institution was two miles from Boston, where the
friends of her girlhood lived: an unattractive district
stretched between, traversed once in two hours by
omnibuses, the only means of transport.

Again, her life had been singularly free from responsibility. First her Aunt Francis, then her sister Louisa,
had "kept house" in Bond Street; Julia had been a
flower of the field, taking no thought for food or rai-
ment; her sisters chose and bought her clothes, had her
dresses made, and put them on her. Her studies, her
music, her dreams, her compositions — and, it must

be added, her suitors — made the world in which she lived. Now, life in its most concrete forms pressed upon her. The baby must be fed at regular intervals, and she must feed it; there must be three meals a day, and she must provide them; servants must be engaged, trained, directed, and all this she must do. Her thoughts soared heavenward; but now there was a string attached to them, and they must be pulled down to attend to the leg of mutton and the baby's cloak.

This is one side of the picture; the other is different, indeed.

Her girlhood had been shut in by locks and bars of Calvinistic piety; her friends and family were ready to laugh, to weep, to pray with her; they were not ready to think with her. It is true that surrounding this intimate circle was a wider one, where her mind found stimulus in certain directions. She studied German with Dr. Cogswell; she read Dante with Felice Foresti, the Italian patriot ; French, Latin, music, she had them all. Her mind expanded, but her spiritual growth dates from her early visits to Boston.

These visits had not been given wholly to gayety, even in the days when she wrote, after a ball: " I have been through the burning, fiery furnace, and it is Sadrake, Me-sick, and Abed-no-go!" The friends she made, both men and women, were people alive and awake, seeking new light, and finding it on every hand. Moreover, at her side was now one of the torch-bearers of humanity, a spirit burning with a clear flame of fervor and resolve, lighting the dark places of the earth. Her mind, under the stimulus of these influences,

opened like a flower; she too became one of the seekers
for light, and in her turn one of the light-bringers.

Among the poems of her early married life, none
is more illuminating than the portrait of Dr. Howe,
which heads this chapter. The concluding stanza gives
a hint of the depression which accompanied her first
realization of the driving power of his life, of the white-
hot metal of his nature. She was caught up as it were
in the wake of a comet, and whirled into new and
strange orbits: what wonder that for a time she was
bewildered? She had no thought, when writing "The
Rough Sketch," that a later day was to find her soul
indeed matched with his, "in high resolve and hardihood": that through her lips, as well as his, God was to
sound forth a trumpet that should never call retreat.

In her normal health she was a person of abounding
vitality, with a constitution of iron: as is common with
such temperaments, she felt a physical distaste to the
abnormal and defective. It required in those days all
the strength of her will to overcome her natural shrinking from the blind and the other defectives with whom
she was often thrown. There is no clearer evidence of
the development of her nature than the contrast between this mental attitude and the deep tenderness
which she felt in her later years for the blind. After
the Doctor's death, they became her cherished friends;
she could never do enough for them; with every year
her desire to visit the Perkins Institution, to talk with
the pupils, to give them all she had to give, grew
stronger and more lively.

Of the friends of this time, none had so deep and

lasting an influence over her as Theodore Parker, who
had long been a close friend of the Doctor's. She had
first heard of him in her girlhood, as an impious and
sacrilegious person, to be shunned by all good Christians.

In 1843 she met him in Rome, and found him "one
of the most sympathetic and delightful of men"; an
intimacy sprang up between the two families which
ended only with Parker's life. He baptized the baby
Julia; on returning to this country, she and the Doctor
went regularly to hear him preach. This she always
considered as among the great opportunities of her life.

"I cannot remember," she says, "that the interest
of his sermons ever varied for me. It was all one intense delight. . . . It was hard to go out from his presence, all aglow with the enthusiasm which he felt and
inspired, and to hear him spoken of as a teacher of
irreligion, a pest to the community."

These were the days when it was possible for a minister of a Christian church, hearing of Parker's dangerous illness, to pray that God might remove him from
the earth. To her, it seemed that "truly, he talked
with God, and took us with him into the divine presence."

Parker could play as well as preach; she loved to
"make fun" with him. Witness her "Philosoph-Mas-
ter and Poet-Aster" in "Passion Flowers." Parker's
own powers of merrymaking appear in his Latin epitaph on "the Doctor" (who survived him by many
years), which is printed in the "Letters and Journals
of Samuel Gridley Howe."

She used in later years to shake her head as she recalled a naughty *mot* of hers apropos of Parker's preaching: "I would rather," she said, "hear Theodore Parker preach than go to the theatre; I would rather go to the theatre than go to a party; I would rather go to a party than stay at home!"

A letter to her sister Annie shows the trend of her religious thought in these days.

Sunday evening, December 8, 1844.

DEAR ANNIE, —

Do not let the Bishop or Uncle or any one frighten you into any concessions — tell them, and all others that, even if you agree with them in doctrine, you think their notion of a religious life narrow, false, superficial. You owe it to truth, to them, to yourself, to say so. I think perfect and fearless frankness one of our highest duties to *man* as well as to God. Only see how one half the world pragmatically sets its foot down, and says to the other half, "Be converted, my opinion is truth! I must be right and you must be wrong," — while the other half timidly falters a reluctant acquiescence, or scarce audible expression of doubt, and continues troubled and afraid and discontented with itself and others. Let me never think of you as in this ignominious position, dear Annie. Do not think that I misapprehend you. I know you do not agree in doctrine with me, but I know too that you do not feel that you can abandon your life and conscience to the charge and guidance of such a man as Eastburn, or as Uncle Ben. Do not, therefore, be afraid of them, but let their censure be a very secondary thing with you — while your life is the true expression of your faith, whom can you fear? You are accountable to man for the performance of the duties which affect his welfare and well-being — for those which concern your own soul, you are accountable to God alone. A man, though with twenty surplices on his back and twenty prayer books in his hand, can no more condemn than he can save you. . . . There may be a hell and a heaven, and it may be good for most people, for you and me, too, if you choose to think that it is so. But there is a virtue which rises above such considerations — there are motives higher than personal fear or hope — the love of good because it is good, because it is God's and nature's law, because it is the secret of the beautiful order of things, because they are blessed by your virtuous deeds and pure thoughts — because every holy, every noble deed, word, or thought helps to build up the ruins of the world, and to elevate our degraded humanity. Those who propose to you hell and heaven as the great incentives to right, appeal merely to your natural love of personal advantage — those who hold up to you a God now frowning and indignant, now gracious and benignant, appeal simply to your natural cowardice, to your natural love of approbation. Does one love God for one's own advantage? One loves Him for His perfection, and if one loves Him, one keeps His commandments. Abandon, I pray you, the exploded formula of selfishness! . . . I think one should be capable of loving virtue, were one sure even that hell and not heaven would be its reward.

The benedictions of the Sermon on the Mount are very simple — no raptures, no ecstasies are promised. Blessed are all that seek the good of others and the knowledge of truth — blessed, simply that in so doing they obey the law of God, imitate His character, and coming nearer and nearer to Him shall find Him more and more in their hearts. One word about Unitarians. It is very wrong to say that they reject the Bible, simply because they interpret it in a different manner from the (so-called) orthodox, or that they reject Christ, because they understand him in one way, and you in another — while they emulate his wonderful life, while they acknowledge his divine mission, and the divine power of his words, why should they be said to despise him? . . .

During the years between 1843 and 1859, her life was from time to time shadowed by the approach of a great joy. Before the birth of each successive child she was oppressed by a deep and persistent melancholy. Present and future alike seemed dark to her; she wept for herself, but still more for the hapless infant which must come to birth in so sorrowful a world. With the birth of the child the cloud lifted and vanished. Sunshine and joy — and the baby — filled the world; the mother sang, laughed, and made merry.

In her letters to her sisters, and later in her journals, both these moods are abundantly evident. At first, these letters are full of the bustle of arrival and of settling in the Institution.

"I received the silver. . . . The soup-ladle is my delight, and I could almost take the dear old coffee-pot to bed with me. . . . But here is the most important thing.

"My tragedy is left behind! . . . My house . . . in great confusion, carpets not down, curtains not up, the devil to pay, and not a sofa to ask him to sit down upon. . . ."

She now felt sadly the need of training in matters which her girlhood had despised. (She could describe every room in her father's house save one — the kitchen!) The Doctor liked to give weekly dinners to his intimates, "The Five of Clubs," and others. These dinners were something of a nightmare to Julia, even with the aid of Miss Catherine Beecher's cookbook. She spent weeks in studying this volume and trying her hand on its recipes. This was not what her hand was made for; yet she learned to make puddings, and was proud of her preserves.

Speaking of the dinner parties, she tells of one for which she had taken special pains, and of which icecream, not then the food of every day, was to form the climax. The ice-cream did not come, and her pleasure was spoiled; she found it next morning in a snowbank outside the back door, where the messenger had "dumped" it without word or comment. "I should laugh at it now," she says, "but then I almost wept over it."

Everything in the new life interested her, even the most prosaic details. She writes to her sister Louisa: "Our house has been enlivened of late by two delightful visits. The first was from the soap-fat merchant, who gave me thirty-four pounds of good soap for my grease. I was quite beside myself with joy, capered about in the most enthusiastic manner, and was going to hug in turn the soap, the grease, and the man, had I not remembered my future ambassadress-ship, and reflected that it would not sound well in history. This morning came the rag-man, who takes rags and gives nice tin vessels in exchange. . . . Both of these were clever transactions. Oh, if you had seen me stand by the soap-fat man, and scrutinize minutely his weights and measures, telling him again and again that it was beautiful grease, and he must allow me a good price for it — truly, I am a mother in Israel."

Much as the Doctor loved the Perkins Institution, he longed for a home of his own, and in the spring of 1845 he found a place entirely to his mind.

A few steps from the Institution was a plot of land, facing the sun, sheltered from the north wind by the last remaining bit of "Washington Heights," the eminence on which Washington planted the batteries which drove the British out of Boston. Some six acres of fertile ground, an old house with low, broad, sunny rooms, two towering Balm of Gilead trees, and some ancient fruit trees: this was all in the beginning; but the Doctor saw at a glance the possibilities of the place. He bought it, added one or two rooms to the old house, planted fruit trees, laid out flower gardens, and in the summer of 1845 moved his little family thither.

The move was made on a lovely summer day. As

our mother drove into the green bower, half shade, half sunshine, silent save for the birds, she cried out, "Oh! this is green peace!" The name fitted and clung: "*Green Peace*" was known and loved as such so long as it existed.

This was the principal home of her married life, but it was not precisely an abiding one. The summers were spent elsewhere; moreover, the "Doctor's Wing" in the Institution was always ready for habitation, and it often happened that for one reason or another the family were taken back there for weeks or months. Two of the six children, Florence and Maud, were born at the Institution; the former just before the move to Green Peace. She was named Florence in honor of Miss Nightingale. The Doctor had ardently desired a son; finding the baby a girl, "I will forgive you," he cried, "if you will name her for Florence Nightingale!" Miss Nightingale became the child's godmother, sent a golden cup (now a precious heirloom), and wrote as follows: —

EMBLEY, December 26.

I cannot pretend to express, my dear kind friends, how touched and pleased I was by such a remembrance of me as that of your child's name. . . . If I could live to justify your opinion of me, it would have been enough to have lived for, and such thoughts, as that of your goodness, are great thoughts, "strong to consume small troubles" which should bear us up on the wings of the Eagle, like Guido's Ganymede, up to the feet of the God, there to take what work he has for us to do for him. I shall hope to see my little Florence

before long in this world, but if not, I trust there is a
tie formed between us, which shall continue in Eternity — if she is like you, I shall know her again there,
without her body on, perhaps the better for not having
known her here with it.

Letters to her sisters give glimpses of the life at
Green Peace during the years 1845-50.

To her sister Louisa

... I assure you it is a delightful but a terrible thing
to be a mother. The constant care, anxiety and thought
of some possible evil that may come to the little creature, too precious to be so frail, whose life and well-
being the mother feels God has almost placed in her
hands! If I did not think that angels watched over my
baby, I should be crazy about it.

To the same

My trouble has been Chev's illness. . . . He was
taken ill the night of his return, and established himself next morning on the sofa, to be coddled with Cologne, and dieted with peaches and grapes, when lo, in
an hour more, no coddling save that of (Dr.) Fisher,
no *diet* save ipecac and werry thin gruel — chills,
nausea, and blue devils. Bradford to watch by night,
Rosy and I by day; Fisher and I sympathizing deeply
in holding the head of a perfectabilian philanthropist. I making myself active in a variety of ways,
bathing Chev's eyes with cologne water by mistake instead of his brow, laying the pillow the wrong way, and

being banished at last in disgrace, to make room for Rosa.

Am I not the most unfortunate of human beings? Devil a bit! I enjoy all that I can — have I not milk for the baby, and the baby for milk? Cannot Julia make arrowroot pudding and cold custard? Can I not refresh myself by looking into Romana's sapphire eyes, with their deep dark fringe? Is there no balm in Gilead, is there no physician there? Yea, thou, oh Bradford, art the balm, thou, oh Fisher, art the physician! Food also is there for cachinnation, that chief duty of man — Quoth Chev this morning, lifting up his feeble voice and shaking his dizzy head: "Oh, oh, if I had fallen sick in New York, and old Francis had bled me, you would not have seen me again. . . ."

Florence's name is Florence Marion — pretty, *n'est-ce pas?* . . .

Farewell, my own darling. Your
JULES.

Well, life *am* strange! I am again cookless. I imprudently turned old Smith off and took a young girl, who left me in four days. Why? Her lover would not allow her to stay in a family where she did not sit at table with the lady. I had read of such things in Mrs. Trollope, and thought them quite impossible. In the place from which I took her, she had done all the cooking, washing and chamber work of the house — was, in fine the only servant, for the compensation of six dollars a month. But then, she sat at table!!! oh, ho!

To the same

SOUTH BOSTON, April 21, 1845.

... The weather here is so gloomy, that one really deserves credit for not hanging oneself! ... I passed last evening with ——. Chev was going to a " 'versary," left me there at about seven, and did not come for me until after ten. Consequence was, I got heartily tired of the whole family, and concluded that bright people without hearts were in the long run less agreeable than good gentle people without wits — glory on my soul, likewise also on my baby's soul, which I am!

To the same[1]

SOUTH BOSTON, November, 1845.

MY DARLING WEVIE, —

The children have been so very obliging as to go to sleep, and having worried over them all day, and part of the evening, I will endeavor to give you what is left of it. When you become the mother of two children you will understand the value of time as you never understood it before. My days and nights are pretty much divided between Julia and Florence. I sleep with the baby, nurse her all night, get up, hurry through my breakfast, take care of her while Emily gets hers, then wash and dress her, put her to sleep, drag her out in the wagon, amuse Dudie, kiss, love and scold her, etc., etc. ... Oh, my dear Wevie, for one good squeeze in your loving arms, for one kiss, and one smile from you, what would I not

[1] Louisa Ward married Thomas Crawford in 1844, and lived thereafter in Rome.

give? Anything, even my box of Paris finery, which I have just opened, with great edification. Oh, what headdresses! what silks! what a bonnet, what a mantelet! I clapped my hands and cried glory for the space of half an hour, then danced a few Polkas around the study table, then sat down and felt happy, then remembered that I had now nothing to do save to grow old and ugly, and so turned a misanthropic look upon the Marie Stuart garland, etc., etc. You have certainly chosen my things with your own perfect taste. The flowers and dresses are alike exquisite, and so are all the things, not forgetting Dudie's little darling bonnet. But I fear that even this beautiful toilette will hardly tempt me from my nursery fireside where my presence is, in these days, indispensable. I have not been ten minutes this whole day, without holding one or other of the children. I have to sit with Fo-fo on one knee and Dudie on the other, trotting them alternately, and singing, "Jim along Josie," till I can't Jim along any further possibly. Well, life is peculiar anyhow. Dudie does n't go alone yet — heaven only knows when she will. *Sunday evening.* I wore the new bonnet and mantelet to church, to-day: — frightened the sexton, made the minister squint, and the congregation stare. It looked rather like a green clam shell, some folks thought. I did not. I cocked it as high as ever I could, but somehow it did plague me a little. I shall soon get used to it. Sumner has been dining with us, and he and Chev have been pitying unmarried women. Oh, my dear friends, thought I, if you could only have one baby, you would change your tune. . . . Heaven grant that your dear little child may arrive safely, and gladden your heart with its sweet face. What a new world will its birth open to you, an ocean of love unfathomed even by your loving heart. I cannot tell you the comfort I have in my little ones, troublesome as they sometimes are. However weary I may be at night, it is sweet to feel that I have devoted the day to them. I am become quite an adept in washing and dressing, and curl my little Fo-fo's hair beautifully. Tell Donald that I can even wash out the little crease in her back, without rubbing the skin off. . . .

To her sister Annie [1]

1846.

My poor dear little Ante-nuptial, I will write to you, and I will come to you, though I can do you no good — sentiment and sympathy I have none, but such insipidity as I have give I unto thee. . . . Dear Annie, your marriage is to me a grave and solemn matter. I hardly allow myself to think about it. God give you all happiness, dearest child. Some sufferings and trials I fear you must have, for after all, the entering into single combat, hand to hand, with the realities of life, will be strange and painful to one who has hitherto lived, enjoyed, and suffered, *en l'air*, as you have done. . . . To be happily married seems to me the best thing for a woman. Oh! my sweet Annie, may you be happy — your maidenhood has been pure, sinless, loving, beautiful — you have no remorses, no anxious thought about the past. You have lived to make the earth

[1] Before the marriage of the latter to Adolphe Mailliard.

more beautiful and bright — may your married life
be as holy and harmless — may it be more complete,
and more acceptable to God than your single life could
possibly have been. Marriage, like death, is a debt we
owe to nature, and though it costs us something to pay
it, yet are we more content and better *established* in
peace, when we have paid it. A young girl is a loose
flower or flower seed, blown about by the wind, it may
be cruelly battered, may be utterly blighted and lost to
this world, but the matron is the same flower or seed
planted, springing up and bearing fruit unto eternal
life. What a comfort would Wevie now be to you —
she is so much more *loving* than I, but thee knows I
try. I have been better lately, the quiet nights seem
to speak to me again, and to quicken my dead soul.
What I feel is a premature *old age*, caused by the strong
passions and conflicts of my early life. It is the languor and indifference of old age, without its wisdom,
or its well-earned right to repose. Sweetie, was n't the
bonnet letter hideous? I sent it that you might see
how *naughty I could be. . . .*

The Doctor's health had been affected by the hardships and exposures of his service in the Greek Revolution, and his arduous labors now gave him little time
for rest or recuperation. He was subject to agonizing
headaches, each of which was a brief but distressing
illness. In the summer of 1846 he resolved to try the
water cure, then considered by many a sovereign remedy for all human ailments, and he and our mother
spent some delightful weeks at Brattleboro, Vermont.

To her sister Louisa

August 4, 1846.

DEAREST WEVIE, —

. . . We left dear old Brattleboro on Sunday afternoon, at five o'clock, serenely packed in our little carriage; the good old boarding-house woman kissed me, and presented me with a bundle, containing cake, biscuits, and whortleberries. . . . Two calico bags, one big and one little, contained our baggage for the journey. Chev and I felt well and happy, the children were good, the horses went like birds, and showed themselves horses of good mettle, by carrying us over a distance of one hundred miles in something less than two days, for we arrived here at three o'clock to-day, so that the second 24 hours was not completed. Very pleasant was our little journey. We started very early each morning, and went ten or twelve miles to becassim; [1] the country inns were clean, quiet and funny. We had custards, pickles, and pies for breakfast, and tea at dinner. Oh, it was a good time! At Athol, I found a piano, and sat down to sing negro songs for the children. A charming audience, comprising cook, ostler, and waiter, collected around the parlour door, and encouraged me with a broom and a pitchfork. Well, it was pleasant to arrive at our dear Green Peace, or Villa Julia, as they call it. We found everything in beautiful order, the green corn grown as high as our heads, and ripe enough to eat, the turkey sitting on eleven eggs, the peahen on four, six young turkeys already growing up, and two broods of young chickens.

[1] Breakfast.

Peas, tomatoes, beans, squashes and potatoes, all
flourishing. Our garden entirely supplies us with vegetables, and we shall have many apples and pears. Immediately upon my arrival, I found the box and little
parcel from you. You may imagine the pleasure it gave
me to receive, at this distance, things which your taste-
ful little fingers had worked. . . . I am rather ashamed
to see how beautiful your work is, when mine is as
coarse as possible. In truth, I am a clumsy seamstress,
but I make good puddings, and the little things I make
do well enough here in the country. . . . *August 15th.*
I have passed eleven quiet and peaceful days since I
got so far with my letter. My chicks have been good,
and my husband well. My household affairs go on
very pleasantly and easily nowadays. My good stout
German girl takes care of the chicks and helps a little
with the chamber work. My little Lizzie does the cooking, all but the puddings which I always make myself,
so I keep but two house servants. The man takes care
of the horses, drives and keeps the garden in excellent
order. I make my bed and put my room in order as
well as I can. I generally wipe the dishes when Lizzie
has washed them, so you see that I am quite an industrious flea. I have made very nice raspberry jam and
currant jelly with my own hands. . . . Felton came to
tea last evening. He was pleasant and bright. He will
be married some time in November. Hillard, too, has
been to see me. Yesterday was made famous by the
purchase of a very beautiful piano of Chickering's
manufacture. The value of it was $450, but the kind
Chick sold it to us at wholesale price. It arrived at

Green Peace to-day, and has already gladdened the children's hearts by some gay tunes, the rags of my antiquated musical repertory. You will be glad, I am sure, to know that I have one at last, for I have been many months without any instrument, so that I have almost forgotten how to touch one. . . . My mourning [for a sister-in-law] has been quite an inconvenience to me, this summer. I had just spent all the money I could afford for my summer clothes, and was forced to spend $30 more for black dresses. . . . The black clothes, however, seem to me very idle things, and I shall leave word in my will that no one shall wear them for me. . . .

To the same

BORDENTOWN, August, 1846.

. . . Sumner and Chev came hither with us, and passed two days and nights here. Chev is well and good. Sumner is as usual, funny but very good and kind. Philanthropy goes ahead, and slavery will be abolished, and so shall we. New York is full of engagements in which I feel no interest. John Astor and Augusta Gibbs are engaged, and are, I think, fairly well matched. One can only say that each is good enough for the other.

These were the days when Julia sang in her nursery:

> " Rero, rero, riddlety rad,
> This morning my baby caught sight of her Dad,
> Quoth she, 'Oh, Daddy, where have you been?'
> 'With Mann and Sumner a-putting down sin!'"

To her sister Annie

August 17, 1846.

MY DEAR DARLING ANNIE, —

. . . After seeing the frugal manner in which country people live, and after deriving great benefit from hydropathic diet, Chev and I thought we could get along with one servant less, and so we have no cook. Lizzie[1] cooks, I make the pudding, we have no tea, and live principally upon vegetables from our own garden, hasty pudding, etc. I make the beds and do the rooms, as well as I can. We get along quite comfortably, and I like it very much — the fewer servants one has, the more comfort, I think. . . . I have plenty of occupation for my fingers. My heart will be much taken up with my babies; as for my soul, that part of me which thinks and believes and imagines, I shall leave it alone till the next world, for I see it has little to do in this. . . .   Good-bye. Your own, own

DUDIE.

To her sister Louisa

BOSTON, December 1, 1846.

Dearest old absurdity that you are, am I to write to you again? Is not my life full enough of business, of flannel petticoats, aprons, and the wiping of dirty little noses? Must I sew and trot babies and sing songs, and tell Mother Goose stories, and still be expected to know how to write? My fingers are becoming less and less familiar with the pen, my thoughts grow daily more insignificant and commonplace. What earthly good

[1] The nurserymaid.

can my letters do to anyone? What interesting information can I impart to anyone? Not that I am not happy, very happy, but then I have quite lost the power of contributing to the amusement of others. . . .

To her sister Annie

1845 or 1846.

. . . I visited my Mother Otis [1] on Thursday evening, and had a pleasant time. I went alone, Chev being philanthropically engaged — party being over, I called for him at Mr. Mann's, but they were so happy over their report that they concluded to make a night of it, and I came home alone. Chev returned at one, quite intoxicated with benevolence. . . .

Finding that the isolation of South Boston was telling seriously upon her health and spirits, the Doctor decided on a change, and the winter of 1846 was spent at the Winthrop House in Boston.

To the same

Monday morning, 1846.

MY DEAREST, SWEETEST ANNIE, —

. . . I have neglected you sadly this winter, and my heart reproaches me for it. . . . It has been strange to me, to return to life and to feel that I have any sympathy with living beings. . . . I have been singing and writing poetry, so you may know that I have been happy. Alas! am I not a selfish creature to prize these enjoyments as I do, above *almost* everything else in the

[1] Mrs. Harrison Gray Otis.

world? God forgive me if I do wrong in following with
ardor the strongest instincts of my nature, but I have
been doing wrong all my life, in some way or other. I
have been giving a succession of little musical parties
on Saturday evenings, and I assure you they have been
quite successful. I have to be sure only my little parlour in the Winthrop House, but even that is larger
than the grand saloon at S. Niccolo da Tolentino
which managed to hold so much fun on Friday evenings. I have found some musical friends to sing with
me — Lizzie Cary, Mrs. Felton, Mr. Pelosos and William Story, of whom more anon. . . . Agassiz, the
learned and charming Frenchman, is also one of my
habitués on Saturday evenings, and Count Pourtalés, a
Swiss nobleman of good family, who has accompanied
Agassiz to this country! I illuminate my room with a
chandelier and some candles, draw out the piano into
the room, and order some ice from Mrs. Mayer's — so
that the reception gives me very little trouble. My
friends come at half-past eight and stay until eleven.
I do not usually have more than twenty people, but
once I have had nearly sixty, and those of the best
people in Boston. Chev is very desirous of having a
house in town, and is far more pleased with my success than I am. My next party will be on the coming Saturday. It is for Lizzie Rice and Sam Guild
who are just married. Am I not an enterprising little
woman? . . . Dear Annie, I am anxious to be with
you, that I may really know how you are, and talk
over all the little matters with you. . . . I always feel
that this suffering must be some expiation for all the

follies of one's life, whereupon I will improvise a coup-
let upon the subject.

> Woman, being of all critters the darn'dest,
> Is made to suffer the consarn'dest.

To her sister Louisa

May 17, 1847.

MY SWEETEST BEAUTIFULLEST WEVIE, —

... I have not written because I have been in a studious, meditative, and most uncommunicative frame of
mind, and have very few words to throw at many dogs.
It is quite delightful to take to study again, and to feel
that old and stupid as one may be, there is still in one's
mind a little power of improvement. ... The longer I
live the more do I feel my utter childlike helplessness
about all practical affairs. Certainly a creature with
such useless hands was never before seen. I seem to need
a dry nurse quite as much as my children. What useful
thing can I possibly teach these poor little monkeys?
For everything that is not soul I am an ass, that I am.
I have now been at Green Peace some six weeks, and it
is very pleasant and quiet, but oh! the season is so backward; it is the 17th of May, and the trees are only beginning to blossom. Every day comes a cold east wind
to nip off my nose, and the devil a bit of anything else
comes to Green Peace. I am thin and languid. I have
never entirely recovered from my fever,[1] but my mind
is clearer than it has ever been since my marriage. I
am able to think, to study and to pray, things which I
cannot accomplish when my brain is oppressed. ...

[1] She had had a severe attack of scarlet fever during the winter.

Boston has been greatly enlivened during the past month by a really fine opera, the troupe from Havana, much better than the N. Y. troupe, with a fine orchestra and chorus, all Italians. The Prima Donna is an artist of the first order, and has an exquisite voice. I have had season tickets, and have been nearly every night. This is a great indulgence, as it is very expensive, and I have one of the best boxes in the house, but Chev is the most indulgent of husbands. I never knew anything like it. Think of all he allows me, a house and garden, a delicious carriage and pair of horses, etc., etc., etc. My children are coming on famously. Julia, or as she calls herself, Romana, is really a fine creature, full of sensibility and of talent. She learns very readily, and reasons about things with great gravity. She remembers every tune that she hears, and can sing a great many songs. She is very full of fun, and so is my sweet Flossy, my little flaxen-haired wax doll. I play for them on the piano, Lizzie beats the tambourine, and the two babies take hold of hands and dance. "Is not your heart fully satisfied with such a sight?" you will ask me. I reply, dear Wevie, that the soul whose desires are not fixed upon the unattainable is dead even while it liveth, and that I am glad, in the midst of all my comforts, to feel myself still a pilgrim in pursuit of something that is neither house nor lands, nor children, nor health. What that something is I scarce know. Sometimes it seems to me one thing and sometimes another. Oh, immortality, thou art to us but a painful rapture, an ecstatic burthen in this earthly life. God teach me to bear thee until thou shalt bear me!

MRS. HOWE IN 1847
From a painting by Joseph Ames

The arms of the cross will one day turn into angels' wings, and lift us up to heaven. Don't think from this rhapsody that I am undergoing a fit of pietistic exaltation. I am not, but as I grow older, many things become clearer to me, and I feel at once the difficulty and the necessity of holding fast to one's soul and to its divine relationships, lest the world should cheat us of it utterly.

To her sister Annie

June 19 [1847], GREEN PEACE.

MY DEAREST LITTLE ANNIE, —

... Boston has been in great excitement at the public debates of the Prison Discipline Society, which have been intensely interesting. Chev and Sumner have each spoken twice, in behalf of the Philadelphia system, and against the course of the Society. They have been furiously attacked by the opposite party. Chev's second speech drew tears from many eyes, and was very beautiful. Both of Sumner's have been fine, but the last, delivered last evening, was *masterly*. I never listened to anything with more intense interest, — he held the audience breathless for two hours and a half. I have attended all the debates save one — there have been seven.

To her sister Louisa

July 1, 1847.

MY DEAREST OLD WEVIE, —

I should have written you yesterday but that I was obliged to entertain the whole Club [1] at dinner, prior

---

[1] The Five of Clubs. See *ante*.

to Hillard's departure. I gave them a neat little dinner, soup, salmon, sweetbreads, roast lamb and pigeon,
with green peas, potatoes *au maitre d'hotel*, spinach
and salad. Then came a delicious pudding and blanc-
mange, then strawberries, pineapple, and ice-cream,
then coffee, etc. We had a pleasant time upon the
whole. That is, they had; for myself it is easy to find
companions more congenial than the Club. Still, I like
them very well. I had last week a little meeting of
the *mutual correction* club, which was far pleasanter to
me. This society is organized as follows: Julia Howe,
grand universal philosopher; Jane Belknap, charitable
censor; Mary Ward, moderator; Sarah Hale, optimist.
I had them all to dinner and we were jolly, I do assure
you. My children looked so lovely yesterday, in muslin
dresses of bright pink plaid, made very full and reaching only to the knee, with pink ribbands in their
sleeves. . . .

How I do wish for you this summer. My little place
is so green, my flowers so sweet, my strawberries so
delicious — the garden produces six quarts or more a
day. The cow gives delicious cream. I even make a
sort of cream cheese which is not by any means to be
despised. Do you eat *ricotta* nowadays? Chev gave me
a little French dessert set yesterday, which made my
table look so pretty. White with very rich blue and
gold. Oh, but it was bunkum! Dear old Wevie, you
must give me one summer, and then I will give you a
winter — is n't that fair? Chev promises to take me
abroad in five years, if we should sell Green Peace well.
They talk of moving the Institution, in which case

I should have to leave my pretty Green Peace in two years more, but I should be sad to leave it, for it is very lovely. I don't know any news at all to communicate. The President [1] has just made a visit here; he was coolly but civilly received. His whole course has been very unpopular in Massachusetts, and nobody wanted to see the man who had brought this cursed Mexican War upon us. He was received by the Mayor with a brief but polite address, lodgings were provided for him, and a dinner given him by the city. But there was no crowd to welcome him, no shouts, no waving of handkerchiefs. The people quietly looked at him and said, "This is our chief magistrate, is it? Well, he is *très peu de chose*." I of course did not trouble myself to go and see him. . . . I send you an extract from a daily paper. Can you tell me who is the authoress? It has been much admired. Uncle John was very much tickled to see *somebody* in print. Try it again, Blue Jacket.

. . . .

The wayward moods shown in these letters sometimes found other expression. In those days her wit was wayward too: its arrows were always winged, and sometimes over-sharp. In later life, when Boston and everything connected with it was unspeakably dear to her, she would not recall the day when, passing on Charles Street the Charitable Eye and Ear Infirmary, she read the name aloud and exclaimed, "Oh! I did not know there was a charitable eye or ear in Boston!" Or that other day, when having dined with the Ticknors, a family of monumental dignity, she said to a

[1] James K. Polk.

friend afterward, "Oh! I am so cold! I have been dining with the *Tête Noir*, the *Mer(e) de Glace*, and the
Jungfrau!"

It may have been in these days that an incident occurred which she thus describes in "A Plea for Hu-
mour": "I once wrote to an intimate friend a very
high-flown and ridiculous letter of reproof for her frivolity. I presently heard of her as ill in bed, in consequence of my unkindness. I immediately wrote, 'Did
not you see that the whole thing was intended to be a
burlesque?' After a while she wrote back, 'I am just
beginning to see the fun of it, but the next time you
intend to make a joke, pray give me a fortnight's
notice.' It was now my turn to take to my bed."

In September, 1847, a heavy sorrow came to her in
the death of her brother Marion, "a gallant, gracious
boy, a true, upright and useful man." She writes to
her sister Louisa: "Let us thank Him that Marion's
life gave us as much joy as his death has given us pain.
. . . Our children will grow up in love and beauty,
and one of us will have a sweet boy who shall bear
the dear name of Marion and make it doubly dear
to us."

This prophecy was fulfilled first by the birth, on
March 2, 1848, of Henry Marion Howe (named for
the two lost brothers), and again in 1854 by that of
Francis Marion Crawford.

The winter of 1847–48 was also spent in Boston, at
No. 74 Mount Vernon Street; here the first son was
born. The Doctor, recording his birth in the Family
Bible, wrote after the name, "*Dieu donné!*" And, his

mind full of the Revolution of 1848 in France, added, "*Liberté, Egalité, Fraternité!*"

On April 18 she writes: "My boy will be seven weeks old to-morrow, and . . . such a darling little child was never seen in this world before. . . . I shall have some fears lest his temperament partake of the melancholy which oppressed me during the period of his *creation*, but so far he is so placid and gentle, that we call him the little saint. . . . I have seen little of the world since his birth, and thought still less. I shall try to pursue my studies as I have through this last year, for I am good for nothing without them. I will rather give up the world and cut out Beacon Street, but an hour or two for the cultivation of my poor little soul I must and will have. . . ."

To her sister Annie

[1848.]

DEAREST ANNIE, —

. . . My literary reputation is growing apace. Mr. Buchanan Read has written to me from Philadelphia to beg some poetry for a book he is about to publish, and I am going to hunt up some trash for him in the course of the week. I find that my name has been advertised in relation to Griswold's book [1] — people come to ask Chev if *that* Mrs. Howe is his wife. I feel as if I should make a horribly shabby appearance. Do tell me if Griswold liked the poems. . . .

[1] *Female Poets of America.*

To the same

Sunday, December 15, 1849.

. . . I do want to see you, best Annie, and to have a
few long talks with you about theology, the soul, the
heart, life, matrimony, and the points of resemblance
between the patriarch Noah and Sir Tipsy Squinteye.
Those talks, madam, are not to be had, so instead of
the rich *crême fouettée* of our conversation, we will take
an insipid water-ice of a letter together, the two spoons
being ourselves, the sugar, ice and lemon representing
our three husbands, all mixed up together, the whole
to be considered good when one can't get anything
better. I will be hanged, however, if you shall make
me say which is which.

I pass my life after a singular manner, Annie. I am
in the old room, in the old house, even in the old dress-
ing-gown, which is of some value, inasmuch as it fur-
nishes my *rent*. I am in the old place, but the old Dudie
is not in me; in her stead is a spirit of crossness and
dullness, insensible to all the gentler influences of life,
knowing no music, poetry, wit, or devotion, intent
mainly upon holding on to the ropes, and upon getting
through the present without too much consciousness of
it. . . . All society has been paralyzed by the shocking
murder of Dr. Parkman. There has perhaps never been
in Boston so horrible and atrocious an affair. The
details of the crime are too heart-sickening to be dwelt
upon. There can scarcely be a doubt of the guilt of
Dr. Webster — the jury of inquest have returned a
verdict of guilty, but he has still a chance for his life,
as his trial in court does not come on for some months.

The wisest people say that he will be convicted and hanged. I saw Dr. Parkman two or three days before he was missing—he was an old friend of Chev's. . . . I have not been able to see much company, yet we have had a few pleasant people at the house, now and then. Among these, a Mr. Twisleton, brother of Lord Saye and Sele, the most agreeable John Bull I have seen this many a day, or indeed ever. . . .

The winter of 1849–50 was also spent at No. 74 Mount Vernon Street. Here, in February, 1850, a third daughter was born, and named Laura for Laura Bridgman. In the spring, our parents made a second voyage to Europe, taking with them the two youngest children, Julia Romana and Florence being left in the household of Dr. Edward Jarvis.

They spent some weeks in England, renewing the friendships made seven years before; thence they journeyed to Paris, and from there to Boppart, where the Doctor took the water cure. Julia seems to have been too busy for letter-writing during this year; the Doctor writes to Charles Sumner of the beauty of Boppart, and adds: "Julia and I have been enjoying walks upon the banks of the Rhine, and rambles upon the hillside, and musings among the ruins, and jaunts upon the waters as we have enjoyed nothing since we left home."

He had but six months' leave of absence; it was felt by both that Julia needed a longer time of rest and refreshment; accordingly when he returned she, with the two little children, joined her sisters, both now

married, and the three proceeded to Rome, where they
spent the winter.

Mrs. Crawford was living at Villa Negroni, where
Mrs. Mailliard became her companion; Julia found a
comfortable apartment in Via Capo le Case, with the
Edward Freemans on the floor above, and Mrs. David
Dudley Field on that below.

These were pleasant neighbors. Mrs. Freeman was
Julia's companion in many delightful walks and excursions; when Mrs. Field had a party, she borrowed Mrs.
Howe's large lamp, and was ready to lend her tea-cups
in return. There was a Christmas tree — the first
ever seen in Rome! — at Villa Negroni; "an occasional
ball, a box at the opera, a drive on the Campagna."

Julia found a learned Rabbi from the Ghetto, and
resumed the study of Hebrew, which she had begun
the year before in South Boston. This accomplished
man was obliged to wear the distinctive dress then
imposed upon the Jews of Rome, and to be within the
walls of the Ghetto by six in the evening. There were
private theatricals, too, she appearing as "Tilburina"
in "The Critic."

Among the friends of this Roman winter none was
so beloved as Horace Binney Wallace. He was a Phila-
delphian, a *rosso*. He held that "the highest effort of
nature is to produce a *rosso*"; he was always in search
of the favored tint either in pictures or in living beings.
Together the two *rossi* explored the ancient city, with
mutual pleasure and profit.

Some years later, on hearing of his death, she recalled these days of companionship in a poem called

"Via Felice," [1] which she sang to an air of her own composition. The poem appeared in "Words for the Hour," and is one of the tenderest of her personal tributes: —

> For Death's eternal city
> Has yet some happy street;
> 'T is in the Via Felice
> My friend and I shall meet.

In the summer of 1851 she turned her face westward. The call of husband, children, home, was imperative; yet so deep was the spell which Rome had laid upon her that the parting was fraught with "pain, amounting almost to anguish." She was oppressed by the thought that she might never again see all that had grown so dear. Looking back upon this time, she says, "I have indeed seen Rome and its wonders more than once since that time, but never as I saw them then."

The homeward voyage was made in a sailing-vessel, in company with Mr. and Mrs. Mailliard. They were a month at sea. In the long quiet mornings Julia read Swedenborg's "Divine Love and Wisdom"; in the afternoons Eugène Sue's "*Mystères de Paris*," borrowed from a steerage passenger. There was whist in the evening; when her companions had gone to rest she would sit alone, thinking over the six months, weaving into song their pleasures and their pains. The actual record of this second Roman winter is found in "Passion Flowers."

[1] Formerly part of the Via Sistina.

CHAPTER VII

"PASSION FLOWERS"

1852–1858; *aet.* 33–39

ROUGE GAGNE

The wheel is turned, the cards are laid;
The circle's drawn, the bets are made:
I stake my gold upon the red.

The rubies of the bosom mine,
The river of life, so swift divine,
In red all radiantly shine.

Upon the cards, like gouts of blood,
Lie dinted hearts, and diamonds good,
The red for faith and hardihood.

In red the sacred blushes start
On errand from a virgin heart,
To win its glorious counterpart.

The rose that makes the summer fair,
The velvet robe that sovereigns wear,
The red revealment could not spare.

And men who conquer deadly odds
By fields of ice, and raging floods,
Take the red passion from the gods.

Now, Love is red, and Wisdom pale,
But human hearts are faint and frail
Till Love meets Love, and bids it hail.

I see the chasm, yawning dread;
I see the flaming arch o'erhead:
I stake my life upon the red.

J. W. H.

WE have seen that from her earliest childhood
Julia Ward's need of expressing herself in verse was
imperative. Every emotion, deep or trivial, must

take metrical shape; she laughed, wept, prayed — even stormed, in verse.

Walking with her one day, her sister Annie, always half angel, half sprite, pointed to an object in the road. "Dudie dear," she said; "squashed frog! little verse, dear?"

We may laugh with the two sisters, but under the laughter lies a deep sense of the poet's nature.

As in her dreamy girlhood she prayed —

> "Oh! give me back my golden lyre!" —

so in later life she was to pray —

> "On the Matron's time-worn mantle
> Let the Poet's wreath be laid."

The tide of song had been checked for a time; after the second visit to Rome, it flowed more freely than ever. By the winter of 1853–54, a volume was ready (the poems chosen and arranged with the help of James T. Fields), and was published by Ticknor and Fields under the title of "Passion Flowers."

No name appeared on the title-page; she had thought to keep her *incognito*, but she was recognized at once as the author, and the book became the literary sensation of the hour. It passed rapidly through three editions; was, she says, "much praised, much blamed, and much called in question."

She writes to her sister Annie: —

"The history of all these days, belovèd, is comprised in one phrase, the miseries of proof-reading. Oh, the endless, endless plague of looking over these proof-sheets — the doubts about phrases, rhymes, and expressions, the perplexity of names, especially, in which I have not been fortunate. To-morrow I get my last proof. Then a fortnight must be allowed for drying and binding. Then I shall be out, fairly out, do you hear? So far my secret has been pretty well kept. My book is to bear a simple title without my name, according to Longfellow's advice. Longfellow has been reading a part of the volume in sheets. He says it will make a sensation. . . . I feel much excited, quite unsettled, sometimes a little frantic. If I succeed, I feel that I shall be humbled by my happiness, devoutly thankful to God. Now, I will not write any more about it."

The warmest praise came from the poets, — the "high, impassioned few" of her "Salutatory." Whittier wrote: —

AMESBURY, 29th, 12 mo. 53.

MY DEAR FR'D, —

A thousand thanks for thy volume! I rec'd it some days ago, but was too ill to read it. I glanced at "Rome," "Newport and Rome," and they excited me like a war-trumpet. To-day, with the wild storm drifting without, my sister and I have been busy with thy book, and basking in the warm atmosphere of its flowers of passion. It is a great book — it has placed thee at the head of us all. I like its noble aims, its scorn and hate of priestcraft and Slavery. It speaks out bravely, beautifully all I have *felt*, but could not express, when contemplating the condition of Europe. God bless thee for it!

I owe an apology to Dr. Howe, if not to thyself,

for putting into verse [1] an incident of his early life which a friend related to me. When I saw his name connected with it, in some of the papers that copied it, I felt fearful that I had wounded, perhaps, the feelings of one I love and honor beyond almost any other man, by the liberty I have taken. I can only say I could not well help it — a sort of necessity was before me, to say what I did.

I wish I *could* tell thee how glad thy volume has made me. I have marked it all over with notes of admiration. I dare say it has faults enough, but thee need not fear on that account. It has beauty enough to save thy "slender neck" from the axe of the critical headsman. The veriest "de'il" — as Burns says — "wad look into thy face and swear he could na wrang thee."

With love to the Doctor and thy lovely little folk,
I am   Very sincerely thy friend,
                                      JOHN G. WHITTIER.

Emerson wrote: —

                              CONCORD, MASS., 30 Dec., 1853.
DEAR MRS. HOWE, —

I am just leaving home with much ado of happy preparation for an absence of five weeks, but must take a few moments to thank you for the happiness your gift brings me. It was very kind in you to send it to me, who have forfeited all apparent claims to such favor, by breaking all the laws of good neighborhood in these years. But you were entirely right in

[1] "The Hero." See Whittier's *Poems.*

sending it, because, I fancy, that among all your friends, few had so earnest a desire to know your thoughts, and, I may say, so much regret at never seeing you, as I. And the book, as I read in it, meets this curiosity of mine, by its poems of character and confidence, private lyrics, whose air and words [are] all your own. I have not gone so far in them as to have any criticism to offer you, and like better the pure pleasure I find in a new book of poetry so warm with life. Perhaps, when I have finished the book, I shall ask the privilege of saying something further. At present I content myself with thanking you.

With great regard,
R. W. EMERSON.

Oliver Wendell Holmes, always generous in his welcome to younger writers, sent the following poem, never before printed: —

> If I were one, O Minstrel wild,
>   That held "the golden cup"
> Not unto thee, Art's stolen child,
>   My hand should yield it up;
>
> Why should I waste its gold on one
>   That holds a guerdon bright —
> A chalice, flashing in the sun
>   Of perfect chrysolite.
>
> And shaped on such a swelling sphere
>   As if some God had pressed
> Its flowing crystal, soft and clear
>   On Hebe's virgin breast?
>
> What though the bitter grapes of earth
>   Have mingled in its wine?

The stolen fruits of heavenly birth
Have made its hue divine.

Oh, Lady, there are charms that win
Their way to magic bowers,
And they that weave them enter in
In spite of mortal powers;

And hearts that seek the chapel's floor
Will throb the long aisle through,
Though none are waiting at the door
To sprinkle holy dew!

I, sitting in the portal gray
Of Art's cathedral dim,
Can see thee, passing in to pray
And sing thy first-born hymn; —

Hold out thy hand! these scanty drops
Come from a hallowed stream,
Its sands, a poet's crumbling hopes,
Its mists, his fading dream.

Pass on. Around the inmost shrine
A few faint tapers burn;
This altar, Priestess, shall be thine
To light and watch in turn;

Above it smiles the Mother Maid,
It leans on Love and Art,
And in its glowing depth is laid
The first true woman's heart!

O. W. H.

Boston, Jan. 1, 1854.

This tribute from the beloved Autocrat touched her
deeply, the more so that in the "Commonwealth"[1]

[1] The *Commonwealth* was a daily newspaper published in the Anti-
Slavery interest. Dr. Howe was one of its organizers, and for some time
its editor-in-chief. She says, "Its immediate object was to reach the body
politic which distrusted rhetoric and oratory, but which sooner or later
gives heed to dispassionate argument and the advocacy of plain issues."
She helped the Doctor in his editorial work, and enjoyed it greatly, writing
literary and critical articles, while he furnished the political part.

she had recently reviewed some of his own work rather
severely. She made her acknowledgment in a poem
entitled "A Vision of Montgomery Place," [1] in which
she pictures herself as a sheeted penitent knocking at
Dr. Holmes's door.

> I was the saucy Commonwealth:
> Oh! help me to repent.
>
> . . . .
>
> Behind my embrasure well-braced,
> With every chance to hit,
> I made your banner, waving wide,
> A mark for wayward wit.
>
> 'T was now my turn to walk the street,
> In dangerous singleness,
> And run, as bravely as I might,
> The gauntlet of the press.
>
> And when I passed your balcony
> Expecting only blows,
> From height or vantage-ground, you stooped
> To whelm me with a rose.
>
> A rose, intense with crimson life
> And hidden perfume sweet —
> Call out your friends, and see me do
> My penance in the street.
>
> . . . .

She writes her sister Annie: —

"My book came out, darling, on Friday last. You
have it, I hope, ere this time. The simple title, ' Passion Flowers,' was invented by Scherb [2] and approved
by Longfellow. Its success became certain at once.
Hundreds of copies have already been sold, and every
one likes it. Fields foretells a second edition — it is

[1] Printed in *Words for the Hour*, 1857.
[2] A German scholar, at this time an *habitué* of the house.

sure to pay for itself. It has done more for me, in point of consideration here, than a fortune of a hundred thousand dollars. Parker quoted some of my verses in his Christmas sermon, and this I considered as the greatest of honors. I sat there and heard them, glowing all over. The authorship is, of course, no secret now. . . ."

Speaking of the volume long after, she says, "It was a timid performance upon a slender reed."

Three years later a second volume of verse was published by Ticknor and Fields under the title of "Words for the Hour." Of this, George William Curtis wrote, "It is a better book than its predecessor, but will probably not meet with the same success."

She had written plays ever since she was nine years old. In 1857, the same year which saw the publication of "Words for the Hour," she produced her first serious dramatic work, a five-act drama entitled "The World's Own." It was performed in New York at Wallack's Theatre, and in Boston with Matilda Heron and the elder Sothern in the leading parts. She notes that one critic pronounced the play "full of literary merits and of dramatic defects"; and she adds, "It did not, as they say, 'keep the stage.'"

Yet her brother Sam writes to her from New York: "Lenore still draws the best houses; there was hardly standing room on Friday night"; and again: "Mr. Russell went last night, a second time, bought the libretto, which I send you by this mail — declares that there is not a grander play in our language. He says that it is full of dramatic vigor, that the interest

never flags — but that unhappily Miss H., with the
soul and self-abandonment of a great actress, lacks
those graces of elocution, which should set forth the
beauties of your verses."

Some of the critics blamed the author severely for
her choice of a subject — the betrayal and abandon-
ment of an innocent girl by a villain; they thought it
unfeminine, not to say indelicate, for a woman to
write of such matters.

At that time nothing could be farther from her
thoughts than to be classed with the advocates of
Women's Rights as they then appeared; yet in "The
World's Own" are passages which show that already
her heart cherished the high ideal of her sex, for which
her later voice was to be uplifted: —

> I think we call them Women, who uphold
> Faint hearts and strong, with angel countenance;
> Who stand for all that's high in Faith's resolve,
> Or great in Hope's first promise.
> .   .   .   .
> Ev'n the frail creature with a moment's bloom,
> That pays your pleasure with her sacrifice,
> And, having first a marketable price,
> Grows thenceforth valueless, — ev'n such an one,
> Lifted a little from the mire, and purged
> By hands severely kind, will give to view
> The germ of all we honor, in the form
> Of all that we abhor. You fling a jewel
> Where wild feet tramp, and crushing wheels go by;
> You cannot tread the splendor from its dust;
> So, in the shattered relics, shimmers yet
> Through tears and grime, the pride of womanhood.
> .   .   .   .

We must not forget the Comic Muse. Comparatively

little of her humorous verse is preserved; she seldom
thought it important enough to make two copies, and
the first draft was often lost or given away. The
following was written in the fifties, when Wulf Fries
was a young and much-admired musician in Boston.
Miss Mary Bigelow had invited her to her house " at
nine o'clock" to hear him play, meaning nine in the
morning. She took this for nine in the evening; the
rest explains itself : —

> Miss Mary Big'low, you who seem
> So debonair and kind,
> Pray, what the devil do you mean
> (If I may speak my mind)
>
> By asking me to come and hear
> That Wulf of yours a-Friesing,
> Then leaving me to cool my heels
> In manner so unpleasing?
> . . . .
> With Mrs. Dr. Susan you
> That eve, forsooth, were tea-ing:
> Confess you knew that I should come,
> And from my wrath were fleeing!
>
> To Mrs. Dr. Susan's I
> Had not invited been:
> So when the maid said, "Best go there!"
> I answered, "Not so green!"
>
> Within the darksome carriage hid
> I bottled up my beauty,
> And, rather foolish, hurried home
> To fireside and duty.
>
> It's very pleasant, *you* may think,
> On winter nights to roam;
> But when you next invite abroad,
> *This* wolf will freeze at home!

While she was pouring out her heart in poem and
play, and the Doctor was riding the errands of the
hour and binding up the wounds of Humanity, what,
it may be asked, — it *was* asked by anxious friends,
— was becoming of the little Howes? Why, the little
Howes (there were now five, Maud having been born
in November, 1854) were having perhaps the most
wonderful childhood that ever children had. Spite of
the occasional winters spent in town, our memories
centre round Green Peace; — there Paradise blossomed for us. Climbing the cherry trees, picnicking
on the terrace behind the house, playing in the bowling-
alley, tumbling into the fishpond, — we see ourselves
here and there, always merry, always vigorous and
robust. We were also studying, sometimes at school,
sometimes with our mother, who gave us the earliest
lessons in French and music; more often, in those
years, under various masters and governesses. The
former were apt to be political exiles, the Doctor always having many such on hand, some learned, all
impecunious, all seeking employment. We recall a
Pole, a Dane, two Germans, one Frenchman. The
last, poor man, was married to a Smyrniote woman
with a bad temper; neither spoke the other's language,
and when they quarrelled they came to the Doctor,
demanding his services as interpreter.

Through successive additions, the house had grown
to a goodly size; the new part, with large, high-studded
rooms, towering above the ancient farmhouse, which
nevertheless seemed always the heart of the place. Between the two was a conservatory, a posy of all sweet

flowers: the large greenhouse was down in the garden, under the same roof as the bowling-alley.

The pears and peaches and strawberries of Green Peace were like no others that ever ripened; we see ourselves tagging at our father's heels, watching his pruning and grafting with an absorption equalling his own, learning from him that there must be honor in gardens as elsewhere, and that fruit taken from his hand was sweet, while stolen fruit would be bitter.

We see ourselves gathered in the great dining-room, where the grand piano was, and the Gobelin carpet with the strange beasts and fishes, bought at the sale of the ex-King Joseph Bonaparte's furniture at Bordentown, and the Snyders' Boar Hunt, which one of us could never pass without a shiver; see ourselves dancing to our mother's playing, — wonderful dances, invented by Flossy, who was always *première danseuse*, and whose "Lady Macbeth" dagger dance was a thing to remember.

Then perhaps the door would open, and in would come "Papa" as a bear, in his fur overcoat, growling horribly, and chase the dancers into corners, they shrieking terrified delight.

Again, we see ourselves clustered round the piano while our mother sang to us; songs of all nations, from the Polish drinking-songs that Uncle Sam had learned in his student days in Germany, down to the Negro melodies which were very near our hearts.

Best of all, however, we loved her own songs: cradle-songs and nursery nonsense made for our very selves —

"(Sleep, my little child.
So gentle, sweet and mild!
The little lamb has gone to rest,
The little bird is in its nest, —"

"Put in the donkey!" cries Laura. The golden voice
goes on without a pause —

"The little donkey in the stable
Sleeps as sound as he is able;
All things now their rest pursue,
You are sleepy too!)"

Again, she would sing passionate songs of love or battle, or hymns of lofty faith and aspiration. One and
all, we listened eagerly; one and all, we too began to
see visions and dream dreams.

Now and then, the Muse and Humanity had to
stand aside and wait while the children had a party;
such a party as no other children ever had. What
wonder, when both parents turned the full current
of their power into this channel?

Our mother writes of one such festival: —

"My guests arrived in omnibus loads at four o'clock.
My notes to parents concluded with the following P.S.:
'Return-omnibus provided, with insurance against
plum-cake and other accidents.' A donkey carriage
afforded great amusement out of doors, together with
swing, bowling-alley, and the Great Junk. While all
this was going on, the H.'s, J. S., and I prepared a
theatrical exhibition, of which I had made a hasty
outline. It was the story of 'Blue Beard.' We had curtains which drew back and forth, and regular foot-
lights. You can't think how good it was! There were
four scenes. My antique cabinet was the 'Blue Beard'

cabinet; we yelled in delightful chorus when the door was opened, and the children stretched their necks to the last degree to see the horrible sight. The curtain closed upon a fainting-fit done by four women. In the third scene we were scrubbing the fatal key, when I cried out, 'Try the "Mustang Liniment"! It's the liniment for us, for you know we *must hang* if we don't succeed!' This, which was made on the spur of the moment, overcame the whole audience with laughter, and I myself shook so that I had to go down into the tub in which we were scrubbing the key. Well, to make a long story short, our play was very successful, and immediately afterward came supper. There were four long tables for the children; twenty sat at each. Ice-cream, cake, blanc-mange, and delicious sugar-plums, oranges, etc., were served up 'in style.' We had our supper a little later. Three omnibus loads went from my door; the last — the grown people — at nine o'clock."

And again:—

"I have written a play for our doll-theatre, and performed it yesterday afternoon with great success. It occupied nearly an hour. I had alternately to grunt and squeak the parts, while Chev played the puppets. The effect was really extremely good. The spectators were in a dark room, and the little theatre, lighted by a lamp from the top, looked very pretty."

It was one of these parties of which the Doctor wrote to Charles Sumner: "Altogether it was a good affair, a religious affair; I say religious, for there is nothing which so calls forth my love and gratitude to God as the sight of the happiness for which He has given the capacity and furnished the means; and this happiness is nowhere more striking than in the frolics of the young."

Among the plays given at Green Peace were the "Three Bears," the Doctor appearing as the Great Big Huge Bear; and the "Rose and the Ring," in which he played Kutasoff Hedzoff and our mother Countess Gruffanuff, while John A. Andrew, not yet Governor, made an unforgettable Prince Bulbo.

It was a matter of course to us children, that "Papa and Mamma" should play with us, sing to us, tell us stories, bathe our bumps, and accompany us to the dentist; these were things that papas and mammas did! Looking back now, with some realization of all the other things they did, we wonder how they managed it. For one thing, both were rapid workers; for another, both had the power of leading and inspiring others to work; for a third, so far as we can see, neither ever wasted a moment; for a fourth, neither ever reached the point where there was not some other task ahead, to be begun as soon as might be.

Life with a Comet-Apostle was not always easy. Some one once expressed to "Auntie Francis" wonder at the patience with which she endured all the troublesome traits of her much-loved husband. "My dear," she replied, "I shipped as Captain's mate, for the voyage!"

Our mother, quoting this, says, "I cannot imagine a more useful motto for married life."

During the thirty-four years of her own married

life the Doctor was captain, beyond dispute; yet sometimes the mate felt that she must take her own way, and took it quietly. She was fond of quoting the words of Thomas Garrett,[1] whose house was for years a station of the Underground Railway, and who helped many slaves to freedom. "How did you manage it?" she asked him. His reply sank deep into her mind.

"It was borne in upon me at an early period, that if I told no one what I intended to do, I should be enabled to do it."

The bond between our mother and father was not to be entirely broken even by death. She survived him by thirty-four years; but she never discussed with any one of us a question of deep import, or national consideration, without saying, "Your father would think thus, say thus!" It has been told elsewhere [2] how she once, being in Newport and waked from sleep by some noise, called to him; and how he, in Boston, heard her, and asked, when next they met, "Why did you call me?" To the end of her life, if startled or alarmed, she never failed to cry aloud, "Chev!"

Children were not the only guests at Green Peace. Some of us remember Kossuth's visit; our mother often told of the day when John Brown knocked at the door, and she opened it herself. To all of us, Charles Sumner and his brothers, Albert and George, Hillard, Agassiz, Andrew, Parker were familiar figures, and fit naturally into the background of Green Peace.

[1] Of Wilmington, Delaware.
[2] *Letters and Journals of Samuel Gridley Howe.*

Of these Charles Sumner, always the Doctor's closest and best-beloved friend, is most familiarly remembered. We called him "the harmless giant"; and one of us was in the habit of using his stately figure as a rule of measurement. Knowing that he was just six feet tall, she would say that a thing was so much higher or lower than Mr. Sumner. His deep musical voice, his rare but kindly smile, are not to be forgotten.

We do not remember Nathaniel Hawthorne's coming to the house, but his shy disposition is illustrated by the record of a visit made by our parents to his house at Concord. While they were in the parlor, talking with Mrs. Hawthorne, they saw a tall, slim man come down the stairs, and Mrs. Hawthorne called out, "Husband! Husband! Dr. Howe and Mrs. Howe are here!" Hawthorne bolted across the hall and out through the door without even looking into the parlor.

Of Whittier our mother says: —

"I shall always be glad that I saw the poet Whittier in his youth and mine. I was staying in Boston during the winter of 1847, a young mother with two dear girl babies, when Sumner, I think, brought Whittier to our rooms and introduced him to me. His appearance then was most striking. His eyes glowed like black diamonds — his hair was of the same hue, brushed back from his forehead. Several were present on this occasion who knew him familiarly, and one of these persons bantered him a little on his bachelor state. Mr. Whittier said in reply: 'The world's people have

taken so many of our Quaker girls that there is none
left for me.' A year or two later, my husband invited
him to dine, but was detained so late that I had a
tête-à-tête of half an hour with Mr. Whittier. We sat
near the fire, rather shy and silent, both of us. Whenever I spoke to Whittier, he hitched his chair nearer
to the fire. At last Dr. Howe came in. I said to him
afterwards, 'My dear, if you had been a little later,
Mr. Whittier would have gone up the chimney.'"

The most welcome visitor of all was Uncle Sam
Ward. He came into the house like light: we warmed
our hands at his fire and were glad. It was not because he brought us peaches and gold bracelets, Virginia hams (to be boiled after his own recipe, with a
bottle of champagne, a wisp of new-mown hay and
— we forget what else!), and fine editions of Horace:
it was because he brought himself.

"I disagree with Sam Ward," said Charles Sumner,
"on almost every known topic: but when I have talked
with him five minutes I forget everything save that
he is the most delightful companion in the world!"

A volume might be filled with Uncle Sam's *mots*
and jests; but print would do him cold justice, lacking
the kindling of his eyes and smile, the mellow music
of his laugh. Memory pictures rise up, showing him
and our mother together in every variety of scene. We
see them coming out of church together after a long
and dull sermon, and hear him whisper to her, "*Ce
pauvre Dieu!*"

Again, we see them driving together after some
function at which the address of one Potts had roused

Uncle Sam to anger; hear him pouring out a torrent of eloquent vituperation, forgetting all else in the joy of freeing his mind. Pausing to draw breath, he glanced round, and, seeing an unfamiliar landscape, exclaimed, "Where are we?" "At Potsdam, I think!" said our mother quietly.

Hardly less dear to us than Green Peace, and far dearer to her, was the summer home at Lawton's Valley, in Portsmouth,[1] Rhode Island. Here, as at South Boston, the Doctor's genius for "construction and repairs" wrought a lovely miracle. He found a tiny farmhouse, sheltered from the seawinds by a rugged hillock; near at hand, a rocky gorge, through which tumbled a wild little stream, checked here and there by a rude dam; in one place turning the wheel of a mill, where the neighboring farmers brought corn to grind. His quick eye caught the possibilities of the situation. He bought the place and proceeded to make of it a second earthly paradise. The house was enlarged, trees were felled here, planted there; a garden appeared as if by magic; in the Valley itself the turbulent stream was curbed by stone embankments; the open space became an emerald lawn, set at intervals with Norway spruces; under the great ash tree that towered in the centre rustic seats and tables were placed. Here, through many years, the "Mistress of the Valley" was to pass her happiest hours; to the Valley and its healing balm of quiet she owed the inspiration of much of her best work.

The following letters fill in the picture of a time to

---

[1] Near Newport, of which it is really a suburb.

which in her later years she looked back as one of the happiest of her life.

Yet she was often unhappy, sometimes suffering. Humanity, her husband's faithful taskmistress, had not yet set her to work, and the long hours of his service left her lonely, and — the babies once in bed — at a loss.

Her eyes, injured in Rome, in 1843, by the throwing of *confetti* (made, in those days, of lime), gave her much trouble, often exquisite pain. She rarely, in our memory, used them in the evening. Yet, in later life, all the miseries, little and big, were dismissed with a smile and a sigh and a shake of the head. "I was very naughty in those days!" she would say.

To her sister Louisa

GREEN PEACE, Feb. 18, 1853.

MY DEAREST LOUISA, —

I have kept a long silence with you, but I suppose that it is too evident before this time that letter-writing is not my *forte*, to need any further explanation of such a fact. Let me say, however, once for all, that I do not stand upon my reputation as a letter-writer. About my poetry and my music, I may be touchy and exacting — about my talents for drawing, correspondence, and housekeeping, I can only say that my pretensions are as small as my merits. With such humility, Justice herself must be satisfied. It is Modesty with her pink lining (commonly mistaken for blushes) turned outside. Are you surprised, my love, at the new style of my writing, and do you think

I must have been taking lessons of Mr. Bristow? Learn that my eyes do not allow me to look attentively at my writing, and that I give a glance and a scribble, in a truly frantic and indiscriminate manner. Having ruined my own eyes, you see, I am doing my utmost to ruin the eyes of my friends. This is human nature — all evil seeks thus to propagate itself, while good is satisfied with itself, and stays where it is. When I think of this, I ask myself, does not the devil, then, send missionaries? You will agree with me that he at least sends ambassadors. I have passed, so far, a very studious winter. Never, since my youth, have I lived so much in reading and writing — hence these eyes! Of course, you exclaim, what madness! but, indeed, I should have a worse madness if I did not cram myself with books. The bareness and emptiness of life were then insupportable. . . .

Of the nearly eighteen months since my return to America, I have passed fourteen at South Boston. Last winter I was fresh from my travels, and had still strength enough to keep up my relation with society, and to invite people a good deal to my house. But this year I am more worn down, my health quite impaired, and the exertion of going out or receiving at home is too much for me. . . .

I have made acquaintance with the Russell Lowells, but we are too far apart to profit much by it. I cannot swim about in this frozen ocean of Boston life in search of friends. I feel as if I had struggled enough with it, as if I could now fold my arms and go down. . . .

To the same

S. BOSTON, Dec. 20, 1853.

MY DEAR SISTER WEVIE, —

I have been of late a shamefully bad correspondent, and am as much ashamed of it as I ought to be. But, indeed, it hurts my eyes so dreadfully to write, and *that* you may find it difficult to believe, for perhaps you find writing less trying to the eyes than reading. Most people do, but with me the contrary is the case. I can read with tolerable comfort, but cannot write a single page, without positive pain. Well, that is enough about my eyes; now for other things. You say that you tremble to know the result of the Lace purchase. Well you may, wretched woman. Don't be satisfied with trembling; shake! shiver! shrink into nothing at all! Do you know, Madam, that my cursed bill from Hooker amounted to over $130? The rascal charged me ten per cent, which you and he probably divided together, or had a miscellaneous spree upon. You sent no specification of items. Madam, to this day, I do not know whether the earrings or the lace cost the most. People ask me the price of bertha, flounces and earrings, I can only reply that Mrs. Crawford drew upon me for an enormous sum of money, but that I have no idea how she spent it. Moreover, my poor little means (a favorite expression of Annie Mailliard's) have been entirely exhausted by you and Hooker. My purse is in a dangerous state of collapse — my credit all gone long ago. I want a coat, a bonnet, stockings, and pkthdkfs, but when for want of these things I am cold and snuffly, I go and take out the flounces, look at them, turn them over, and say: "Well, they are *very* warming for the price, are n't they?" Besides, you send me a bill, and don't send Aunt Lou McAllister any. Who paid for her Malachites? I have a great mind to say that I did, and pocket the money, which she is anxious to pay, if she could only get her account settled, which please to attend to at once, you lymphatic, agreeable monster! About the mosaics, straw for Bonnets, and worsted work, you were right in supposing that I would not be very angry. It was undoubtedly a liberty, your sending them, but it is one which I can make up my mind to overlook, especially as you will not be likely to do it again for some time.

Now, if you really want to know about the lace, I will tell you that I found it perfectly magnificent, and that every one who sees it admires it prodigiously. If this is the case now, before I have worn it, how much more will it be so when it shall show itself abroad heightened by the charms of my person! Admiration will then know no bounds. Newspaper paragraphs will begin thus: "The lovely wearer of the lace is about thirty-four years of age, but looks much older — in fact, nearly as antique as her own flounces," etc., etc. The ornaments are not less beautiful, in their kind. I wear them on distinguished occasions, and at sight of them, people who have closely adhered to the Decalogue all their lives incontinently violate the Tenth Commandment, and then excuse it by saying that Mrs. Howe does not happen to be their neighbor, living as she does beyond the reach of everything but Omnibuses

and Charity. So you see that I consider the investment a most successful one, and may in future honor
you with more commissions. I even justify it to myself on the ground that the Brooch and earrings will
make charming pins for my three girls, while the lace,
Mrs. Cary says, is as good as Real Estate. So set your
kind heart completely at rest, you *could* not have done
better for me, or if you could, I don't know it. As to
my being without pocket handkerchiefs, you will be the
first to reply that *that* is nothing new. Now for your
charming presents; I was greatly delighted at them.
The Mosaics are perfectly exquisite, the most beautiful I ever saw. The straw is very handsome, and will
make me the envy of Newport, next summer. The
worsted work appears to me rich and quaint, and shall
be made up as soon as circumstances shall allow. For
each and all accept my hearty thanks. . . .

*(No year. Probably from Portsmouth, Rhode Island, to
her sister Annie)*

Sunday, August 5.

. . . I went in town [Newport] the other day, and dined
with Fanny Longfellow. The L.'s, Curtis,[1] Tommo,[2] and
Kensett are all living together, but seem to make out
tolerably. After dinner Fanny took me to drive on the
Beach in her Barouche. I looked fine, wore my grey
grapery with my drapery, and spread myself out as
much as possible. Curtis took Julia in his one-horse
affair on the Beach. Julia wore a pink silk dress, a
white drawn bonnet with pink ribbons, and a little

[1] George William Curtis.   [2] Thomas Gold Appleton.

white shawl. Oh, she did look lovely. Mamma was not at all proud, oh, no! Well, thereafter, I dined elsewhere and did not want to tell Dudie where. So when she asked, "Where did you dine yesterday?" I replied: "I dined, dear, with Mrs. Jimfarlan, and her pig was at table. Now, before we sat down, Mrs. J. said to me, 'Mrs. Howe, if you do not love my pig, you cannot dine with me,' and I replied, 'Mrs. Jimfarlan, I adore your pig,' so down we sat." "Oh, yes, Mamma," says Julia, "and I know the rest. When you had got through dinner, and had had all you wanted, you rose, and told the lady that you had something to tell her in the greatest confidence. Then she went into the entry with you, and you whispered in her ear, 'Mrs. Jimfarlan, I *hate* your pig!' and then rushed out of the house." . . . I have had one grand tea-party — the Longos, Curtis, etc., etc. We had tea out of doors and read Tennyson in the valley. It was very pleasant. . . . The children spent Tuesday with the Hazards. I went over to tea. You remember the old beautiful place.[1] We have now a donkey tandem, which is the joy of the Island. The children go out with it, and every one who meets them is seized with cramps in the region of the diaphragm, they double up and are relieved by a hearty laugh.

To her sister Annie

October, 1854.

I will tell you how I have been living since my return from Newport. I get up at seven or a little before,

[1] Vaucluse, at Portsmouth.

and am always down at half-past for breakfast. After breakfast I despatch the chicks to school and clear off the table; then walk in the garden or around the house; then consult with the cook and order dinner, and see as far as I can to all sewing and other work. I get to my own room between ten and eleven, where I study and write until two P.M. Dinner is at half-past two. After that I take all the children in my room. I read to them and fix worsted work for them. I get half an hour's reading for myself sometimes, but not often, the days being so short. Then I walk with dear Julia, the dearest little friend in the world. The others often join us, and sometimes we have the donkey for a ride. I then go in and sing for the children, or play for them to dance, until tea-time. At a quarter past eight I go to put Dudie and Flossy to bed. I prolong this last pleasure and occupation of the day. When I come down I sit with idle fingers, unable, as you know, to do the least thing. Chev reads the papers to me. At ten I am thankful to retire. I do not suppose that this life is more monotonous than yours in Bordentown, is it? . . .

Oct. 19th. I was not able to finish this at one sitting, my best darling. I cannot write long without great pain. I had to go in town on Monday and Tuesday, and yesterday, for a wonder, Baby [Laura] was ill. She had severe rheumatic pains in both knees, and could not be moved all day. We sent for a physician, who prescribed various doses, and told us we should have a siege of it. To-day she is almost well, though we gave her no medicine. She is the funniest little soul in the world. You should hear her admonishing her father not to "worry so about everything." He is obliged to laugh in spite of himself. . . . I am very poor just now. I furnished my Newport house with the money for my book ["Passion Flowers"]. It was very little — about $200.

Spite of the troublesome eyes, and the various "pribbles and prabbles," she was in those days editor-in-chief of "The Listener," a "Weekly Publication." Julia Romana was sub-editor, and furnished most of the material, stories, plays, and poems pouring with astonishing ease from her ten-year-old pen; but there was an Editor's Table, sometimes dictated by the chief editor, often written in her own hand.

The first number of "The Listener" appeared in October, 1854. The sub-editor avows frankly that "The first number of our little paper will not be very interesting, as we have not had time to give notice to those who we expect to write for it."

This is followed by "Select Poetry, Mrs. Howe"; "The Lost Suitor" (to be continued), and "Seaside Thoughts." The "Editor's Table" reads: —

"It is often said that Listeners hear no good of themselves, and it often proves to be true. But we shall hope to hear, at least, no harm of our modest little paper. We intend to listen only to good things, and not to have ears for any unkind words about ourselves or others. Little people of our age are expected to listen to those who are older, having so many things to learn. We will promise, too, to listen as much as we

can to all the entertaining news about town, and to
give accounts of the newest fashions, the parties in
high life (nurseries are generally three stories *high*)
and many other particulars. So, we venture to hope
that 'The Listener' will find favour with our friends
and Miss Stephenson's select public."

This was Miss Hannah Stephenson's school for
girls, which Julia and Florence were attending. "The
Listener" gives pleasant glimpses of life at Green
Peace, the Nursery Fair, the dancing-school, the new
baby, and so forth.

Sometimes the "Table" is a rhyming one: —

> What shall we do for an Editor's table?
> To make one really we are not able.
> Our Editorial head is aching,
> Our lily white hand is rather shaking.
> Our baby cries both day and night,
> And puts our "intelligence" all to flight.
> Yet, for the gentle Julia's sake,
> Some little effort we must make.
> We did n't go vote for the know-nothing Mayor,
> A know-nothing's what we cannot bear,
> We know our lessons, that's well for us,
> Or the school would be in a terrible fuss.
> .   .   .   .
> That's all for the present, we make our best bow,
> And are your affectionate
>
> *Editor Howe.*

On January 14, 1855, we read: —

"Last evening began the opera season. Now, as all
the Somebodies were there, we would not like to have
you suppose, dear reader, that we were not, although
perhaps you did not see us, with our little squeezed-up
hat slipping off of our head, and we screwing up our

eyebrows to keep it on. There was a moment when we thought we felt it going down the back of our neck, but a dexterous twitch of the left ear restored the natural order of things. Well, to show you that we were there, we'll tell you of what the Opera was composed. There was love of course, and misery, and plenty of both. The slim man married the lady in white, and then ran away with another woman. She tore her hair, and went mad. One of the stout gentlemen doubled his fists, the other spread out his hands and looked pitiful. The mad lady sang occasionally, and retained wonderful command of her voice. They all felt dreadfully, and went thro' a great deal, singing all the time. The thing came right at last, but we have no room to explain how."

In May, 1855, the paper died a natural death.

To her sister Annie

SOUTH BOSTON, Jan. 19, 1855.

MY SWEET MEATEST, —

. . . First of all you wish to know about the Bonnet, of course. I am happy to say that it is entirely successful, cheap, handsome, and becoming. Boston can show nothing like it. As to the green and lilac, I all but sleep in it. I never wear it, glory on my soul, without attracting notice. Those who don't know me, at lectures and sich, seem to say: "Good heavens, who is that lovely creature?" Those who do know me seem to be whispering to each other, "I never saw Julia Howe look so well!" So much for the green bonnet. As for the white one, since I took out the pinch behind, it fits and flatters — to the Opera, I will incontinently wear it. I have been there and still would go. Every woman seen in front, seems to have a cap with a great frill, like that of an old-fashioned night-cap; it is only when she turns sideways that you can see the little hat behind. . . .

Did I write you that I have been to the Assembly? Chev went to the first without me, with his niece, the pretty one, of course, much to my vexation, so I spunked up, and determined to go to the second. A white silk dress was a necessary tho' unprofitable investment. Turnbull had, fortunately for me, made a failure, and was selling very cheap. I got a pretty silk for $17, and had it made by a Boston fashionable dressmaker, with three pinked flounces — it looked unkimmon. Next I caused my hair to be dressed by Pauline, the wife of Canegally. "Will you have it in the newest fashion?" asked she; "the very newest," answered I. She put in front two horrid hair cushions and, combing the hair over them, made a sort of turban of hair, in which I was, may I say? captivating. I was proud of my hair, and frequented rooms with looking-glasses in them, the rest of the afternoon. At the Ass-embly, Chev and I entered somewhat timidly, but soon took courage, and parted company. Little B—— (your neighbor of Bond St.) was there, wiggy and smiley, but oh! so youthful!! Life is short, they say, but I don't think so when I see little B—— trying to look down upon me from beneath, and doing the patronizing. There was something very nice about her, however, that is, her pearl necklace with a diamond

clasp two inches long, and one and a half broad. . . .
Oculist said weakness was the disease, and rest the
remedy — oculist recommended veratrine ointment,
frequent refreshing of eyes with wet cloth, cleared his
throat every minute, and was an old humbug.

They are playing at the Boston Museum a piece,
probably a farce, called "A Blighted Being." When
I see the handbills posted up in the streets it is like
reading one's own name. I must now bid you farewell
and am ever with dearest love,

Your affectionate sister and

A Blighted Being!!!!

To the same

South Boston, June 1, 1855.

. . . Well, my darling, it is a very uninteresting time
with me. I am alive, and so are my five children. I
made a vow, when dear Laura was so ill, to complain
never more of dulness or ennui. So I won't, but you
understand if I had n't made such a vow, I could under
present circumstances indulge in the howling in which
my soul delighteth. I don't know how I keep alive.
The five children seem always waiting, morally, to
pick my bones, and are always quarrelling over their
savage feast. . . . The stairs as aforesaid kill me. The
Baby keeps me awake, and keeps me down in strength.
Were it not for beer, I were little better than a dead
woman, but, blessed be the infusion of hops, I can still
wink my left eye and look knowing with my right,
which is more, God be praised, than could have been

expected after eight months of Institution. I have
seen Opera of "Trovatore" — in bonnet trimmed with
grapes I went, bonnet baptized with "oh d-Cologne,"
but Alexander McDonald was my escort, Chev feeling very ill just at Opera time, but making himself
strangely comfortable after my departure with easy-
chair, foot-stool, and unlimited pile of papers. Well,
dear, you know they would be better if they could,
but somehow they can't — it is n't in them. . . .

To the same

South Boston, Nov. 27, 1855.

I have been having a wow-wow time of late, or you
should have heard from me. As it is, I shall scribble a
hasty sheet of Hieroglyphics, and put in it as much of
myself as I can. Mme. Kossuth (Kossuth's sister di-
vorced from former husband) has been here for ten days
past; as she is much worn and depressed I have had a
good deal of comforting up to do — very little time and
much trouble. She is a *lady*, and has many interesting qualities, but you can imagine how I long for the
sanctity of home. Still, my heart aches that this
woman, as well bred as any one of ourselves, should
go back to live in two miserable rooms, with three
of her four children, cooking, and washing everything
with her own hands, and sitting up half the night to
earn a pittance by sewing or fancy work. Her eldest
son has been employed as engineer on the Saratoga
and Sacketts Harbor railroad for two years, but has
not been paid a cent — the R.R. being nearly or quite
bankrupt. He is earning $5 a week in a Bank, and

this is all they have to depend upon. She wants to hire a small farm somewhere in New Jersey and live upon it with her children. . . .

To her sisters

Thursday, 29, 1856.

. . . We have been in the most painful state of excitement relative to Kansas matters and dear Charles Sumner, whose condition gives great anxiety.[1] Chev is as you might expect under such circumstances; he has had much to do with meetings here, etc., etc. New England spunk seems to be pretty well up, but what will be done is uncertain as yet. One thing we have got: the Massachusetts Legislature has passed the "personal liberty bill," which will effectually prevent the rendition of any more fugitive slaves from Massachusetts. Another thing, the Tract Society here (orthodox) has put out old Dr. Adams, who published a book in favor of slavery; a third thing, the Connecticut legislature has withdrawn its invitation to Mr. Everett to deliver his oration before them, in consequence of his having declined to speak at the Sumner meeting in Faneuil Hall. . . .

To her sister Annie

CINCINNATI, May 26, 1857.
CASA GREENIS.

DEAREST ANNIE, *Fiancée de marbre et Femme de glace,*—
Heaven knows what I have not been through with since I saw you — dust, dirt, dyspepsia, hotels, rail-

---

[1] In consequence of the assault upon him in the Senate Chamber by Preston Brooks of South Carolina.

roads, prairies, Western steamboats, Western people, more prairies, tobacco juice, captains of boats, pilots of ditto, long days of jolting in the cars, with stoppages of ten minutes for dinner, and the devil take the hindmost. There ought to be no chickens this year, so many eggs have we eaten. Flossy was quite ill for two days at St. Louis. Chev is too rapid and restless a traveller for pleasure. Still, I think I shall be glad to have made the journey when it is all over — I must be stronger than I was, for I bear fatigue very well now and at first I could not bear it at all. We went from Philadelphia to Baltimore, thence to Wheeling, thence to see the Manns at Antioch — they almost ate us up, so glad were they to see us. Thence to Cincinnati, where two days with Kitty Rölker, a party at Larz Anderson's — Longworth's wine-cellar, pleasant attentions from a gentleman by the name of King, who took me about in a carriage and proposed everything but marriage. After passing the morning with me, he asked if I was English. I told him no. When we met in the evening, he had thought matters over, and exclaimed, "You must be Miss Ward!" "And you," I cried, "must be the nephew of my father's old partner. Do you happen to have a strawberry mark or anything of that kind about you?" "No." "Then you are my long-lost Rufus!" And so we rushed into each other's confidence and swore, like troopers, eternal friendship. Thence to Louisville, dear, a beastly place, where I saw the Negro jail, and the criminal court in session, trying a man for the harmless pleasantry of murdering his wife. Thence

to St. Louis, where Chev left us and went to Kansas,
and Fwotty and I boated it back here and went to a
hotel, and the William Greenes they came and took
us, and that's all for the present. . . .

To the same

GARRET PLATFORM,
LAWTON'S VALLEY, July 13, 1857.

. . . Charlotte Brontë is deeply interesting, but I
think she and I would not have liked each other,
while still I see points of resemblance — many indeed
— between us. Her life, on the whole, a very serious
and instructive page in literary history. God rest
her! she was as faithful and earnest as she was clever
— she suffered much.

. . . Theodore Parker and wife came here last night,
to stay a week if they like it (have just had a fight
with a bumble-bee, in avoiding which I banged my
head considerably against a door, in the narrow limits
of my garret platform); so you see I am still a few
squashes ("some pumpkins" is vulgar, and I is n't) . . .

To her sisters

S. BOSTON, April 4, 1858.

. . . I am perfectly worn out in mind, body and
estate. The Fair [1] lasted five days and five evenings.
I was there every day, and nearly all day, and at the
end of it I dropped like a dead person. Never did I
experience such fatigue — the crowd of faces, the bad

---

[1] This Fair was got up by Mr. Robert C. Winthrop for the benefit of
the poor.

air, the responsibility of selling and the difficulty of
suiting everybody, was almost too much for me. On
the other hand, it was an entirely new experience,
and a very amusing one. My table was one of the
prettiest, and, as I took care to have some young and
pretty assistants, it proved one of the most attractive.
I cleared $426.00, which was doing pretty well, as I
had very little given me. . . . For a week after the Fair
I could do nothing but lie on a sofa or in an easy-chair,
. . . but by the end of the week I revived, and it
pleased the Devil to suggest to me that this was the
moment to give a long promised party to the Governor
and his wife. All hands set to work, therefore, writing
notes. With the assistance of three Amanuenses I
scoured the whole surface of Boston society. . . . Un-
luckily I had fixed upon an evening when there were
to be two other parties, and of course the cream of
the cream was already engaged. I believe in my soul
that I invited 300 people — every day everybody sent
word they could not come. I was full of anxiety, got
the house well arranged though, engaged a colored
man, and got a splendid supper. Miss Hunt, who is
writing for me, smacks her lips at the remembrance
of the same, I mean the supper, not the black man.
Well! the evening came, and with it all the odds and
ends of half a dozen sets of people, including some of
the most primitive and some of the most fashionable.
I had the greatest pleasure in introducing a dowdy
high neck, got up for the occasion, with short sleeves
and a bow behind, to the most elaborate of French ball-
dresses with head-dress to match, and leaving them to

take care of each other the best way they could. As
for the Governor [Nathaniel P. Banks], I introduced
him right and left to people who had never voted
for him and never will. The pious were permitted
to enjoy Theodore Parker, and Julia's schoolmaster
sat on a sofa and talked about Carlyle. I did not care
— the colored man made it all right. Imagine my
astonishment at hearing the party then and after
pronounced one of the most brilliant and successful
ever given in Boston. The people all said, "It is such
a relief to see new faces — we always meet the same
people at city parties." Well, darlings, the pickings of
the supper was very good for near a week afterwards,
and, having got through with my party, I have nearly
killed myself with going to hear Mr. Booth, whose
playing is beautiful exceedingly. Having for once in
my life had play enough and a great deal too much,
I am going to work to-morrow like an old Trojan
building a new city. I am too poor to come to New
York this spring; still it is not impossible. Farewell,
Beloveds, it is church time, and this edifying critter
is uncommon punctual in her devotions. So farewell,
love much, and so far as human weakness allows imitate the noble example of

Your sister,
JULIA.

CHAPTER VIII

LITTLE SAMMY: THE CIVIL WAR

1859-1863; *aet.* 40-44

There came indeed an hour of fate
By bitter war made desolate
When, reading portents in the sky,
All in a dream I leapt on high
To pin my rhyme to my country's gown.
'T is my one verse that will not down.
Stars have grown out of mortal crown.

J. W. H.

I honour the author of the "Battle Hymn," and of "The Flag." She was born in the city of New York. I could well wish she were a native of Massachusetts. We have had no such poetess in New England.

EMERSON's *Journals.*

IN the winter of 1859 the Doctor's health became so much impaired by overwork that a change of air and scene was imperative. At the same time Theodore Parker, already stricken with a mortal disease, was ordered to Cuba in the hope that a mild climate might check the progress of the consumption. He begged the Howes to join him and his wife, and in February the four sailed for Havana. This expedition is described in "A Trip to Cuba."

The opening chapter presents three of the little party during the rough and stormy voyage: —

"The Philanthropist has lost the movement of the age, — keeled up in an upper berth, convulsively embracing a blanket, what conservative more immovable than he? The Great Man of the party refrains from his large theories, which, like the circles made by the

stone thrown into the water, begin somewhere and
end nowhere. As we have said, he expounds himself
no more, the significant forefinger is down, the eye
no longer imprisons yours. But if you ask him how he
does, he shakes himself as if, like Farinata, —

'*avesse l'inferno in gran dispetto*,' —

he had a very contemptible opinion of hell."

Several "portraits" follow, among them her own.

"A woman, said to be of a literary turn of mind, in
the miserablest condition imaginable. Her clothes,
flung at her by the Stewardess, seem to have hit in
some places and missed in others. Her listless hands
occasionally make an attempt to keep her draperies
together, and to pull her hat on her head; but though
the intention is evident, she accomplishes little by her
motion. She is being perpetually lugged about by a
stout steward, who knocks her head against both
sides of the vessel, folds her up in the gangway, spreads
her out on the deck, and takes her upstairs, downstairs,
and in my lady's chamber, where, report says, he
feeds her with a spoon, and comforts her with such
philosophy as he is master of. N.B. This woman, upon
the first change of weather, rose like a cork, dressed
like a Christian, and toddled about the deck in the
easiest manner, sipping her grog, and cutting sly
jokes upon her late companions in misery; — is supposed by some to have been an impostor, and, when
ill-treated, announced intentions of writing a book.

"No. 4, my last, is only a sketch; — circumstances
allowed no more. Can Grande,[1] the great dog, has

---

[1] Her pet name for Theodore Parker. *Vide* Dante's *Inferno*.

SAMUEL G. HOWE, *circa* 1859
From a photograph by Black

been got up out of the pit, where he has worried the Stewardess and snapped at the friend who tried to pat him on the head. Everybody asks where he is. Don't you see that heap of shawls yonder, lying in the sun, and heated up to about 212° Fahrenheit? That slouched hat on top marks the spot where his head should lie, — by treading cautiously in the opposite direction you may discover his feet. All between is perfectly passive and harmless. His chief food is pickles, — his only desire is rest. After all these years of controversy, after all these battles, bravely fought and nobly won, you might write with truth upon this moveless mound of woollens the pathetic words from Père La Chaise: *Implora Pace.*"

The trip to Cuba was only the beginning of a long voyage for the Parkers, who were bound for Italy. The parting between the friends was sad. All felt that they were to meet no more. Parker died in Florence fifteen months later.

"A pleasant row brought us to the side of the steamer. It was dusk already as we ascended her steep gangway, and from that to darkness there is, at this season, but the interval of a breath. Dusk too were our thoughts, at parting from Can Grande, the mighty, the vehement, the great fighter. How were we to miss his deep music, here and at home! With his assistance we had made a very respectable band; now we were to be only a wandering drum and fife, — the fife particularly shrill, and the drum particularly solemn. . . . And now came silence, and tears, and last embraces; we slipped down the gangway into our little craft, and looking up, saw bending above us, between the slouched hat and the silver beard, the eyes that we can never forget, that seemed to drop back in the darkness with the solemnity of a last farewell. We went home, and the drum hung himself gloomily on his peg, and the little fife *shut up* for the remainder of the evening."

"A Trip to Cuba" appeared first serially in the "Atlantic Monthly," then in book form. Years after, a friend, visiting Cuba, took with her a copy of the little volume; it was seized at Havana by the customs house officers, and confiscated as dangerous and incendiary material.

On her return, our mother was asked to write regularly for the New York "Tribune," describing the season at Newport. This was the beginning of a correspondence which lasted well into the time of the Civil War. She says of it: —

"My letters dealt somewhat with social doings in Newport and in Boston, but more with the great events of the time. To me the experience was valuable in that I found myself brought nearer in sympathy to the general public, and helped to a better understanding of its needs and demands."

To her sister Annie

Sunday, November 6, 1859.

The potatoes arrived long since and were most jolly, as indeed they continue to be. Did n't acknowledge them 'cause knew other people did, and thought it best to be unlike the common herd. Have just been to church and heard Clarke preach about John Brown, whom God bless, and will bless! I am much too dull to write anything good about him, but shall say something at the end of my book on Cuba, whereof I am at present correcting the proof-sheets. I went to see his poor wife, who passed through here some days since. We shed tears together and embraced at parting, poor soul! Folks say that the last number of my Cuba is the best thing I ever did, in prose or verse. Even Emerson wrote me about it from Concord. I tell you this in case you should not find out of your own accord that it is good. I have had rather an unsettled autumn — have been very infirm and inactive, but have kept up as well as possible — going to church, also to Opera, also to hear dear Edwin Booth, who is playing better than ever. My children are all well and delightful. . . .

I have finished Tacitus' history, also his Germans. . . . Chev is not at all annoyed by the newspapers, but has been greatly overdone by anxiety and labor for Brown. Much has come upon his shoulders, getting money, paying counsel, and so on. Of course all the stories about the Northern Abolitionists are the merest stuff. No one knew of Brown's intentions but Brown himself and his handful of men. The attempt I must judge insane but the spirit *heroic*. I should be glad to be as sure of heaven as that old man may be, following right in the spirit and footsteps of the old martyrs, girding on his sword for the weak and oppressed. His death will be holy and glorious — the gallows cannot dishonor him — he will hallow it. . . .

On Christmas Day, 1859, she gave birth to a second
son, who was named Samuel Gridley. This latest and
perhaps dearest child was for three short years to fill
his parents' life with a joy which came and went with
him. His little life was all beautiful, all bright. We
associate him specially with the years we spent at
No. 13 Chestnut Street, Boston, a spacious and cheerful house which we remember with real affection. The
other children were at school; little Sam was the
dear companion of our mother's walks, the delight of
our father's few leisure hours. For him new songs
were made, new games invented: both parents looked
forward to fresh youth and vigor in his sweet companionship. This was not to be. "In short measures,
life may perfect be": little Sam died of diphtheritic
croup, May 17, 1863.

This heavy sorrow for a time crushed both these
tender parents to the earth. Our father became seriously ill from grief; our mother, younger and more
resilient, found some relief in nursing him and caring
for the other children; but this was not enough. She
could not banish from her mind the terrible memory
of her little boy's suffering, the anguish of parting with
him. While her soul lifted its eyes to the hills, her
heart sought some way to keep his image constantly
before her. Her sad thoughts must be recorded, and
she took up, for the first time since 1843, the habit of
keeping a journal.

The first journal is a slender Diary and Memo-
randum Book. On May 13, the first note of alarm is
sounded. Sammy "did not seem quite right." From

that date the record goes on, the agonizing details briefly described, the loss spoken of in words which no one could read unmoved. But even this was not enough: grief must find further expression, yet must be repressed, so far as might be, in the presence of others, lest her sorrow make theirs heavier. This need of expression took a singular form. She wrote a letter to the child himself, telling the story of his life and death; wrote it with care and precision, omitting no smallest detail, gathering, as it were a handful of pearls, every slightest memory of the brief time.

A few extracts show the tenor of this letter: —

"MY DEAREST LITTLE SAMMY, —

"It is four weeks to-day since I saw your sweet face for the last time on earth. It did not look like your little face, my dear pet, it was so still, and sad, and quiet. But Death had changed it, and I had to submit, and was thankful to have even so much of you as that still face, for some days. Everybody grieved to part from you, dear little soul, but I suppose that I grieved most of all, because you belonged most to me. You were always with me, from the time you began to exist at all. The time of your birth was a sad one. It was the time of the imprisonment and death of John Brown, a very noble man, who should be in one of the many mansions of which Christ tells us, and in which I hope, dear, that you are nearer to Him than any of us can be. . . .

"You arrived, I think, at three in the morning, very red in the face, and making a great time about it. You

were a fine large Baby, weighing twelve pounds. . . .
I have some of your baby dresses left, and shall
hunt them up and lay them with the clothes you have
worn lately. . . . I gave you milk myself. . . . I used
to lay you across my breast when you cried, and you
liked this so well that you often insisted upon sleeping
in that position after you were grown quite large. It
hurt me so much that I finally managed to break you
of the habit, but not until you were more than a year
old. . . . I had a nice crimson merino cloak made for
you, trimmed with velvet, and lined with white silk.
I bought also a very nice crochet cap, of white and
crimson worsted, and in these you were taken to drive
with me. . . .

"During this first year of your life I had some
troubles, and your Baby ways were my greatest comfort. I used to think: this Baby will grow up to be a
man, and will protect me when I am old. For I thought,
dear, that you should have outlived me many years.
But you are removed from us to grow in another
world, of which I know nothing but what Christ has
told me. . . .

"You used to keep me awake a good deal at night,
and this sometimes made me nervous and fretful,
though I was usually very happy with you. I would
give a good deal for one of those bad nights now, though
at the time they were pretty hard upon me. . . .

". . . Your second summer brings me to the winter
that followed. It was quite a gay winter for us at old
South Boston. Marie, the German cook, made very
nice dishes, and I had many people to dine, and one

or two pleasant evening parties. You still slept in my room, and when I was going to a party in the evening, Annie [1] used to bring my nice dress and my ornaments softly out of the room, that I might dress in the nursery, and not disturb your slumbers. I was always glad to get home and undress, and it was always sweet to come to the bed, and find you in it, sound asleep, and lying right across. . . . I learned to sleep on a very little bit of the bed, you wanted so much of it. This winter, I bought you a pair of snow-boots, of which you were very proud. . . .

"We all got along happily, dear, till early in April (1863), when your father desired me to make a journey with Julia, who needed change of scene a little. So I had to go and leave you, my sweet of sweets. . . .

"We were glad enough to see each other again, you and I, and I felt as if I could never part with you again. But I was only to have you for a few days, my darling. . . .

"Thursday I sat up in your nursery, in the afternoon, as I usually did, with my book — you having your toys. When I had finished reading, I built houses with blocks for you, and rolled the balls and dumb-bells across the floor to you. You rolled them back to me and this amused you very much. I go to sit up in your nursery in the afternoon now, with my book — the light shines in now as it used to do, and I hear the hand-organ and children's voices in the street. It seems to bring you a little nearer to me, my dear lost one, but not near enough for comfort."

[1] The child's faithful nurse.

The child's illness and death are described minutely, every symptom, every remedy, every anguish noted. Then follows: —

"It gives me dreadful pain to recall these things and write them down, my dearest. I don't do it to make myself miserable, but in order that I may have some lasting record of how you lived and died. You left little by which you might be remembered, save the love of kindred and friendly hearts, but in my heart, dear, your precious image is deeply sculptured. All my life will be full of grief for you, dearest Boy, and I think that I shall hardly live as long as I should have lived, if I had had you to make me happy. Perhaps it seems very foolish that I should write all this, and talk to you in it as if you could know what I write. But, my little darling, it comforts me to think that your sweet soul lives, and that you do know something about me. Christ said, 'This day thou shalt be with me in Paradise': and he knew that this was no vain promise. So, believing the dear Christ, I am led along to have faith in immortal life, of which, dear, I know nothing of myself.

"Your little funeral, dear, was bitter and agonizing. The good God does not send affliction without comfort, but the weeping eyes and breaking heart must struggle through much anguish before they can reach it. . . ."

There was no hearse at this little funeral. The small white casket was placed on the front seat in the carriage in which she rode.

"We came near the gate of Mount Auburn, when I began to realize that the parting was very near. I now opened the casket, took your dear little cold hand in mine, and began to take silent farewell of you. And here, dearest child, I must stop. The remembrance of those last moments so cuts me to the heart, that I cannot say one word more about them, and not much about the life of loneliness and desolation which now began for me, and of which I do not see the end. God knows why I lost you, and how I suffer for you, and He knows how and when I shall see you again, as I hope to do, my dearest, because Christ says we are to live again after this life, and I know that if I am immortal, God will not inflict upon me the pain of an eternal separation from you. So, we shall meet again, sweet Angel Sammy. God grant that the rest of my life may be worthy of this hope, more dear than life itself. . . .

"I must finish these words by saying that I am happy in believing that my dear Child lives, in a broader land, with better teaching and higher joys than I could have given him. I hope that the years to come will brighten, not efface, my mind's picture of him, and that among these, the cipher of one blessed year is already written, in which the picture will become reality, and the present sorrow the foundation of an eternal joy."

The following stanzas are chosen from among many poems on little Sammy's life and death: —

REMEMBRANCE

. . . .
So thou art hid again, and wilt not come
For any knockings at the veilèd door;

Nor mother-pangs, nor nature, can restore
The heart's delight and blossom of thy home.

And I with others, in the outer court,
Must sadly follow the excluding will,
In painful admiration, of the skill
Of God, who speaks his sweetest sentence short.

At this time she writes to her sister Annie: —

"I cannot yet write of what has come to me. Chev and I feel that we are baptized into a new order of suffering — those who have lost children, loving them, can never be like those who have not. It makes a new heaven and a new earth. The new heaven I have not yet — the blow is too rough and recent. But the new earth, sown with tears, with the beauty and glory gone out of it, the spring itself, that should have made us happy together, grown tasteless and almost hateful. All the relish of life seems gone with him. I have no patience to make phrases about it — for the moment it seems utterness of doubt and of loss.

"No doubt about him. 'This night shalt thou be with me in Paradise' was said by one who knew what he promised. My precious Baby is with the Beautiful One who was so tender with the children. But I am alone, still fighting over the dark battle of his death, still questioning whether there is any forgiveness for such a death. Something must have been wrong somewhere — to find it out, I have tortured myself almost out of sanity. Now I must only say, it is, and look and wait for divine lessons which follow our bitter afflictions.

"God bless you all, darling. Ask dear Cogswell to write me a few lines — tell him that this deep cut

makes all my previous life seem shallow and superficial. Tell him to think of me a little in my great
sorrow.

"Your loving
"JULIA."

She had by now definitely joined the Unitarian
Church, in whose doctrines her mind found full and
lasting rest; throughout this sorrowful time the Reverend James Freeman Clarke was one of her kindest
helpers. Several years before this, she had unwillingly
left Theodore Parker's congregation at our father's
request. She records in the "Reminiscences" his
views on this subject: —

"'The children (our two oldest girls) are now of an
age at which they should receive impressions of reverence. They should, therefore, see nothing at the
Sunday service which militates against that feeling. At
Parker's meeting individuals read the newspapers before the exercises begin. A good many persons come
in after the prayer, and some go out before the conclusion of the sermon. These irregularities offend my
sense of decorum, and appear to me undesirable in the
religious education of my family.'"

It was a grievous thing to her to make this sacrifice;
she said to Horace Mann that to give up Parker's
ministry for any other would be like going to the synagogue when Paul was preaching near at hand; yet,
once made, it was the source of a lifelong joy and
comfort.

Mr. Clarke was then preaching at Williams Hall;

hearing Parker speak of him warmly, she determined
to attend his services. She found his preaching "as
unlike as possible to that of Theodore Parker. He
had not the philosophic and militant genius of Parker,
but he had a genius of his own, poetical, harmonizing.
In after years I esteemed myself fortunate in having
passed from the drastic discipline of the one to the
tender and reconciling ministry of the other."

She has much to say in the "Reminiscences" about
the dear "Saint James," as his friends loved to call
him. The relation between them was close and affectionate: the Church of the Disciples became her spiritual home.

These were the days of the Civil War; we must turn
back to its opening year to record an episode of importance to her and to others.

In the autumn of 1861 she went to Washington in
company with Governor and Mrs. Andrew, Mr. Clarke
and the Doctor, who was one of the pioneers of the
Sanitary Commission, carrying his restless energy and
indomitable will from camp to hospital, from battle-
field to bureau. She longed to help in some way, but
felt that there was nothing she could do — except
make lint, which we were all doing.

"I could not leave my nursery to follow the march
of our armies, neither had I the practical deftness
which the preparing and packing of sanitary stores
demanded. Something seemed to say to me, 'You
would be glad to serve, but you cannot help anyone:
you have nothing to give, and there is nothing for
you to do.' Yet, because of my sincere desire, a word

MRS. HOWE, *circa* 1861

was given me to say, which did strengthen the hearts of those who fought in the field and of those who languished in the prison."

Returning from a review of troops near Washington, her carriage was surrounded and delayed by the marching regiments: she and her companions sang, to beguile the tedium of the way, the war songs which every one was singing in those days; among them —

> "John Brown's body lies a-mouldering in the grave.
> His soul is marching on!"

The soldiers liked this, cried, "Good for you!" and took up the chorus with its rhythmic swing.

"Mrs. Howe," said Mr. Clarke, "why do you not write some good words for that stirring tune?"

"I have often wished to do so!" she replied.

Waking in the gray of the next morning, as she lay waiting for the dawn, the word came to her.

> "Mine eyes have seen the glory of the coming of the Lord —"

She lay perfectly still. Line by line, stanza by stanza, the words came sweeping on with the rhythm of marching feet, pauseless, resistless. She saw the long lines swinging into place before her eyes, heard the voice of the nation speaking through her lips. She waited till the voice was silent, till the last line was ended; then sprang from bed, and groping for pen and paper, scrawled in the gray twilight the "Battle Hymn of the Republic." She was used to writing thus; verses often came to her at night, and must be scribbled in the dark for fear of waking the baby; she crept back to bed, and as she fell asleep she said to herself, "I like this better than most things I have written." In the morning, while recalling the incident, she found she had forgotten the words.

The poem was published in the "Atlantic Monthly" for February, 1862. "It was somewhat praised," she says, "on its appearance, but the vicissitudes of the war so engrossed public attention that small heed was taken of literary matters. . . . I knew and was content to know, that the poem soon found its way to the camps, as I heard from time to time of its being sung in chorus by the soldiers."

She did not, however, realize how rapidly the hymn made its way, nor how strong a hold it took upon the people. It was "sung, chanted, recited, and used in exhortation and prayer on the eve of battle." It was printed in newspapers, in army hymn-books, on broadsides; it was the word of the hour, and the Union armies marched to its swing.

Among the singers of the "Battle Hymn" was Chaplain McCabe, the fighting chaplain of the 122d Ohio Volunteer Infantry. He read the poem in the "Atlantic," and was so struck with it that he committed it to memory before rising from his chair. He took it with him to the front, and in due time to Libby Prison, whither he was sent after being captured at Winchester. Here, in the great bare room where hundreds of Northern soldiers were herded together, came one night a rumor of disaster to the Union arms. A great battle, their jailers told them; a great Confederate victory. Sadly the Northern men gathered together in groups, sitting or lying on the floor, talking in low tones, wondering how, where, why. Suddenly, one of

the negroes who brought food for the prisoners stooped
in passing and whispered to one of the sorrowful
groups. The news was false: there had, indeed, been a
great battle, but the Union army had won, the Con-
federates were defeated and scattered. Like a flame
the word flashed through the prison. Men leaped to
their feet, shouted, embraced one another in a frenzy
of joy and triumph; and Chaplain McCabe, standing
in the middle of the room, lifted up his great voice and
sang aloud, —

"Mine eyes have seen the glory of the coming of the Lord !"
Every voice took up the chorus, and Libby Prison rang
with the shout of "Glory, glory, hallelujah!"

The victory was that of Gettysburg. When, some
time after, McCabe was released from prison, he told
in Washington, before a great audience of loyal people,
the story of his war-time experiences; and when he
came to that night in Libby Prison, he sang the "Battle
Hymn" once more. The effect was magical: people
shouted, wept, and sang, all together; and when the
song was ended, above the tumult of applause was
heard the voice of Abraham Lincoln, exclaiming, while
the tears rolled down his cheeks, —

"Sing it again!"

(Our mother met Lincoln in 1861, and was presented
to him by Governor Andrew. After greeting the party,
the President "seated himself so near the famous portrait of Washington by Gilbert Stuart as naturally
to suggest some comparison between the two figures.
On the canvas we saw the calm presence, the serene
assurance of the man who had successfully accom-

plished a great undertaking, a vision of health and of peace. In the chair beside it sat a tall, bony figure, devoid of grace, a countenance almost redeemed from plainness by two kindly blue eyes, but overshadowed by the dark problems of the moment. . . .

"When we had left the presence, one of our number exclaimed, 'Helpless Honesty!' As if Honesty could ever be helpless.")

The "Battle Hymn of the Republic" has been translated into Italian, Spanish, and Armenian. Written in the dark on a scrap of Sanitary Commission paper, it has been printed in every imaginable form, from the beautiful parchment edition presented to the author on her seventieth birthday by the New England Woman's Club, down to the cover of a tiny brochure advertising a cure for consumption. It has also been set to music many times, but never successfully. It is inseparably wedded to the air for which it was written, an air simple, martial, and dignified: no attempt to divorce the two could ever succeed.

From the time of writing it to that of her death, she was constantly besieged by requests for autograph copies of part or the whole of the hymn. Sometimes the petitioners realized what they asked, as when Edmund Clarence Stedman wrote: —

"I can well understand what a Frankenstein's monster such a creation grows to be — such a poem as the 'Battle Hymn,' when it has become the sacred scroll of millions, each one of whom would fain obtain a copy of it."

Reasonable or unreasonable, she tried to meet every

such request; no one can ever know how many times she copied the hymn, but if a record had been kept, some one with a turn for multiplication might tell us whether the lines put together made up a mile, or more, or less.

She wrote many other poems of the war, among them "The Flag," which is to be found in many anthologies. As the "Battle Hymn" was the voice of the nation's, so this was the expression of her own ardent patriotism: —

> There's a flag hangs over my threshold
> Whose folds are more dear to me
> Than the blood that thrills in my bosom
> Its earnest of liberty.
>
> And dear are the stars it harbors
> In its sunny field of blue,
> As the hope of a further Heaven
> That lights all our dim lives through.

This was no figure of speech, but the truth. The war and its mighty issues filled her heart and mind; she poured out song after song, all breathing the spirit of the time, the spirit of hope, resolve, aspiration. Everything she saw connected itself in some way with the great struggle. Seeing her daughters among their young friends, gay as youth must be gay, even in wartime, she cries out, —

> Weave no more silks, ye Lyons looms,
> To deck our girls for gay delights!
> The crimson flower of battle blooms,
> And solemn marches fill the night.
>
> Weave but the flag whose bars to-day
> Drooped heavy o'er our early dead,

And homely garments, coarse and gray,
For orphans that must earn their bread! [1]

"The Jeweller's Shop in War-Time," "The Battle Eucharist," "The Harvard Student's Song," all reveal the deep feeling of her heart; we remember her singing of "Left Behind" (set to her own music, a wild, mournful chant) as something so thrilling that it catches the breath as we think of it.

Being again in Washington in the spring of 1863, she visited the Army of the Potomac, in company with the wife of General Francis Barlow, and wrote on her return a sketch of the expedition. She carried "a fine Horace, which repeatedly annoyed me by tumbling in the dirt, a volume of Sully's Memoirs, and a little fag end of Spinoza, being his *Tractat* upon the Old Testament."

She saw the working of the Sanitary Commission; saw "Fighting Joe" Hooker, who looked like "the man who can tell nineteen secrets and keep the twentieth, which will be the only one worth knowing"; and William H. Seward, "looking singularly like a man who has balanced a chip on the fence, and who congratulates himself upon its remaining there"; saw, too, from the heights above Fredericksburg (within the danger line!), an artillery skirmish.

Departing, she writes: —

"Farewell, bristling heights! farewell, sad Fredericksburg! farewell, river of sorrows; farewell, soldiers death-determined, upon whose mournful sacrifice we must shut unwilling eyes. Would it were all at end! the

[1] "Our Orders."

dead wept and buried, the living justified before God. For the deep and terrible secret of the divine idea still lies buried in the burning bosom of the contest. Suspected by the few, shunned by the many, it has not as yet leapt to light in the sight of all. This direful tragedy, in whose third dreary act we are, hangs all upon a great thought. To interpret this, through waste and woe, is the first moral obligation of the situation. ... This terrible development of moral causes and effects will enchain the wonder of the world until the crisis of poetical justice which must end it shall have won the acquiescence of mankind, carrying its irresistible lesson into the mind of the critics, into the heart of the multitude."

CHAPTER IX

NO. 13 CHESTNUT STREET, BOSTON

1864; *aet.* 45

PHILOSOPHY

Naked and poor thou goest, Philosophy!
Thy robe of serge hath lain beneath the stars;
Thy weight of tresses, ponderously free,
Of iron hue, no golden circlet bars.

Thy pale page, Study, by thy side doth hold,
As by Cyprigna's her persuasive boy:
Twin sacks thou bear'st; one doth thy gifts infold,
Whose modest tendering proves immortal joy.

The other at thy patient back doth hang
To keep the boons thou'rt wonted to receive:
Reproof therein doth hide her venomed fang,
And hard barbaric arts, that mock and grieve.

Here is a stab, and here a mortal thrust;
Here galley service brought the age to loss;
Here lies thy virgin forehead rolled in dust
Beside the martyr stake of hero cross.

They who besmirched thy whiteness with their pitch,
Thy gallery of glories did complete;
They who accepted of thee so grew rich,
Men could not count their treasures in the street.

Thy hollow cheek, and eye of distant light,
Won from the chief of men their noblest love;
Olympian feasts thy temperance requite,
And thy worn weeds a priceless dowry prove.

I know not if I've caught the matchless mood
In which impassioned Petrarch sang of thee;
But this I know, — the world its plenitude
May keep, so I may share thy beggary.   J. W. H.

AFTER the two real homes, Green Peace and Lawton's Valley, the Chestnut Street house was nearest

to our hearts; this, though we were there only three
years, and though it was there that we children first
saw the face of sorrow. It was an heroic time. The
Doctor was in constant touch with the events of the
war. He was sent by Governor Andrew to examine
conditions of camps and hospitals, in Massachusetts and at the seat of war; he worked as hard on
the Sanitary Commission, to which he had been appointed by President Lincoln, as on any other of
his multifarious labors: his knowledge of practical
warfare and his grasp of situations gave him a foresight of coming events which seemed well-nigh miraculous. When he entered the house, we all felt the
electric touch, found ourselves in the circuit of the
great current.

So, these three years were notable for us all, especially for our mother; for beside these vital interests,
she was entering upon another phase of development.
Heretofore her life had been domestic, studious, social;
her chief relation with the public had been through her
pen. She now felt the need of personal contact with
her audience; felt that she must speak her message.
She says in her "Reminiscences": "In the days of
which I now write, it was borne in upon me (as the
Friends say) that I had much to say to my day and
generation which could not and should not be com-
municated in rhyme, or even in rhythm."

The character of the message, too, was changing.
In the anguish of bereavement she sought relief in
study, her lifelong resource. Religion and philosophy
went hand in hand with her. She read Spinoza eagerly:

read Fichte, Hegel, Schelling; finally, found in Immanuel Kant a prophet and a friend. But it was not enough for her to receive; she must also give out: her nature was radiant. She must formulate a philosophy of her own, and must at least offer it to the world.

In September, 1863, she writes to her sister Louisa, "My Ethics are now the joke of my family, and Flossy or any child, wishing a second helping, will say: 'Is it ethical, Mamma?' Too much of my life, indeed, runs in this channel. I can only hope that the things I write may do good to somebody, how much or how little we ourselves are unable to measure."

Yet she could make fun of her philosophers: *vide* the following passage from one of her "Tribune" letters: —

"We like to make a clean cut occasionally, and distinguish ourselves from our surroundings. Else, we and they get so wedded that we scarcely know ourselves apart. Do I own these four walls, or do they own me, and detain me here for their pleasure and preservation? Do I want these books, or do their ghostly authors seize me wandering near the shelves, impanel me by the button-hole, and insist upon pouring their bottled-up wisdom into my passive mind? I once read a terrible treatise of Fichte upon the *me and not me*, in which he gave so many reasons why I could not be the washstand, nor the washstand I, that I began after a while to doubt the fact. Had I read further, I think I should never have known myself from house-furniture again. Let me here remark that many of

these gymnastics of German metaphysics seem to have
no other office than that of harmlessly emptying the
brain of all its electricity. Their battery strikes no
hammer, turns no wheel. Fichte, having decided that
he was not the washstand, smoked, took beer, and
walked out to meet some philosophic friend, who, view-
ing himself *inclusive*, as the Germans say, thought he
might be that among other things. Fatherland meantime going to the Devil — strong hands wanted, clear,
practical brains, — infinitesimal oppression to be un-
dermined, the century helped on. 'I am not the washstand,' says Fichte; 'I am everything,' says Hegel.
Fatherland, take care of yourself. Yet who shall say
that it is not a vital point to know our real selves from
the factitious personalities imposed upon us, and to
distinguish between the symptoms of our fancy and
the valid phenomena of our lives?"

The Journal says: —

"At 11.53 [September 24] finished my Essay on Religion, for the power to produce which I thank God.
I believe that I have in this built up a greater coher-
ence between things natural and things divine than I
have seen or heard made out after this sort by anyone
else. I therefore rejoice over my work, . . . hoping it
may be of service to others, as it has certainly been
to me."

Two days later she adds, "I leave this record of my
opinion of my work, but on reading it aloud to Paddock,[1] I found the execution of the task to have fallen

[1] Miss Mary Paddock, our father's devoted amanuensis: one of the
earliest and best-loved teachers at the Perkins Institution; often our
mother's good helper; the faithful and lifelong friend of us all.

far short of my conception of it. I shall try to rewrite much of the Essay."

The Journal of 1864 is a quarto volume, with a full page for every day. There are many blank pages, but the record is much fuller than heretofore.

"*January 15.* Worked all the afternoon at my Essay on Distinction between Philosophy and Religion. Got a bad feeling from fatigue. A sort of trembling agony in my back and left side."

Yet she went to the opera in the evening, and saw "Faust," a "composition with more faults than merits." She concludes the entry with "*Dilige et relinque* is a good motto for some things."

"*Sunday, January 17.* It was announced from the pulpit that an Essay on the Soul and Body would be read by a friend at Wednesday evening meeting. That friend was myself, that essay my Lecture on Duality. This would be an honor, but for my ill-deserts. Be witness, O God! that this is no imaginary or sentimental exclamation, but a feeling too well founded on fact."

After the lecture she writes: "Mr. Clarke introduced me charmingly. I wore my white cap, not wishing to read in my thick bonnet. I had quite a full audience. ... I consider this opportunity a great honor and privilege conferred upon me."

"*January 28.* At a quarter before 2 P.M. finished my Essay on Philosophy and Religion. I thank God for this, for many infirmities, some physical, some moral, have threatened to interrupt my work. It is done, and if it is all I am to do, I am ready to die,

since life now means work of my best sort, and I value
little else, except the comfort of my family. Now for a
little rest!"

The "rest" of the following day consisted in paying
eight visits between twelve and two o'clock and going
to the opera in the evening.

She now began to read her philosophical essays aloud
to a chosen circle of friends gathered in the parlor of
No. 13 Chestnut Street. After one of these occasions
she says: "Professor Rogers took me up sharply (not
in temper), on my first statement and definition of
Polarity. I suffered in this, but was bound to take it
in good part. A thoroughbred dog can bear to be
lifted by the ear without squealing. Endurance is a
test of breeding. . . ."

"*May 27, 1864.* My birthday; forty-five years old.
This year, begun in intolerable distress, has been, I
think, the most valuable one of my life. Paralyzed
at first by Sammy's death, I soon found my only refuge from grief in increased activity after my kind.
When he died I had written two-thirds of 'Proteus.'
As soon as I was able, I wrote the remaining portion
which treats of affection. At Newport I wrote my
Introductory Lecture on 'How *Not* to Teach Ethics,'
then 'Duality of Character,' then my first Lecture
on Religion. Returned from Newport, I wrote my
second and third essays on Religion. I read the six
essays of my first course to a large circle of friends at
my own house, not asking any payment. This done,
I began to write a long essay on Polarity which is only
partially completed, intending also to write on Limita-

tions and the three degrees, should it be given to me to do so. I have read and re-read Spinoza's Ethics within the last thirteen months. His method in the arrangement of thought and motive has been of great use to me, but I think that I have been able to give them an extended application and some practical illustrations which did not lie within his scope."

The next day she writes: "Dreamed of dearest Sammy. Thought that he was in the bed, and that I was trying to nurse him in the dark as I have so often done. I thought that when his little lips had found my breast, something said in my ear, 'My life's life — the glory of the world.' Quoting from my lines on Mary Booth. This woke me with a sudden impression, *Thus Nature remembers*."

She decided this spring to read some of her essays in Washington. There were various difficulties in the way, and she was uncertain of the outcome of the enterprise. She writes: —

"I leave Bordentown [the home of her sister Annie] with a resolute, not a sanguine heart. I have no one to stand for me there, Sumner against me, Channing almost unknown to me, everyone else indifferent. I go in obedience to a deep and strong impulse which I do not understand nor explain, but whose bidding I cannot neglect. The satisfaction of having at last obeyed this interior guide is all that keeps me up, for no one, so far as I know, altogether approves of my going."

Spite of these doubts and fears, the enterprise was successful. Perhaps people were glad to shut their ears for a moment to the sound of cannon and the

crying of "Latest news from the front!" and listen to
the quiet words of philosophic thought and suggestion.

Side by side with work, as usual, went play. In
January she records the first meeting of the new club,
the "Ladies' Social," at the home of Mrs. Josiah
Quincy. This club of clever people, familiarly known
as the "Brain Club," was for many years one of her
great pleasures. Mrs. Quincy was its first president.
It may have been at this meeting that our mother,
being asked to present in a few words the nature and
object of the club, addressed the company as follows:
"Ladies and Gentlemen; this club has been formed
for the purpose of carrying on" — she paused, and
began to twinkle — "for the purpose of *carrying on!*"

She describes briefly a meeting of the club at 13
Chestnut Street: —

"Entertained my Club with two charades. *Pan-
demon-ium* was the first, *Catastrophe* the second. For
Pan I recited some verses of Mrs. Browning's 'Dead
Pan,' with the gods she mentions in the background,
my own boy as Hermes. For 'Demon' I had a female
Faust and a female Satan. Was aided by Fanny Mc-
Gregor, Alice Howe, Hamilton Wilde, Charles Carroll,
and James C. Davis, with my Flossy, who looked
beautifully. The entertainment was voted an entire
success."

We remember these charades well. The words

> "Aphrodite, dead and driven
> As thy native foam thou art . . . "

call up the vision of Fanny McGregor, white and beautiful, lying on a white couch in an attitude of perfect grace.

We hear our mother's voice reciting the stately verses. We see her as the "female Faust," first bending over her book, then listening entranced to the promises of Mephistopheles, finally vanishing behind a curtain from which the next instant sprang Florence (the one child who resembled her) in all the gayety of her bright youth.

The next day she was, "Very weary all day. Put things to rights as well as I could. Read in Spinoza, Cotta, and Livy."

It was for the Brain Club that she wrote "The Socio-Maniac," a cantata caricaturing fashionable society. She set the words to music, and sang with much solemnity the "Mad Song" of the heroine whose brain had been turned by too much gayety: —

> "Her mother was a Shaw,
>   And her father was a Tompkins;
> Her sister was a bore,
>   And her brother was a bumpkin;
>   Oh! Soci— oh! Soci—
>   Oh! Soci—e—ty!

> "Her flounces were of gold,
>   And her slippers were of ermine;
> And she looked a little bold
>   When she rose to lead the Ger*min*;
>   Oh! Soci—oh! Soci—
>   Oh! Soci—e—ty!

> "For my part I never saw
>   Where she kept her fascination;
> But I thought she had an aw-
>   Ful conceit and affectation;
>   Oh! Soci— oh! Soci—
>   Oh! Soci—e—ty!"

New interests were constantly arising. In these days Edwin Booth made his first appearance in Boston. Our mother and father went to the Boston Theatre one rainy evening, "expecting to see nothing more than an ordinary performance. The play was 'Richelieu,' and we had seen but little of Mr. Booth's part in it before we turned to each other and said, 'This is the real thing!'"

Then they saw him in "Hamlet" and realized even more fully that a star had risen. He seemed

> ... beautiful as dreams of maidenhood,
>   That doubt defy,
> Young Hamlet, with his forehead grief-subdued,
>   And visioning eye.[1]

Mr. Booth's manager asked her to write a play for the young tragedian. She gladly consented; Booth himself came to see her; she found him "modest, intelligent, and above all genuine, — the man as worthy of admiration as the artist."

In all the range of classic fiction, to which her mind naturally turned, no character seemed to fit him so well as that of Hippolytus; his austere beauty, his reserve and shyness, all seemed to her the personification of the hunter-prince, beloved of Artemis, and she chose this theme for her play.

The writing of "Hippolytus" was accomplished under difficulties. She says of it: —

"I had at this time and for many years afterward a superstition about a north light. My eyes had given me some trouble, and I felt obliged to follow my literary work under circumstances most favorable for

[1] "Hamlet at the Boston," *Later Lyrics*, 1866.

their use. The exposure of our little farmhouse [at Lawton's Valley] was south and west, and its only north light was derived from a window at the top of the attic stairs. Here was a platform just large enough to give room for a table two feet square. The stairs were shut off from the rest of the house by a stout door. And here, through the summer heats, and in spite of many wasps, I wrote my five-act drama, dreaming of the fine emphasis which Mr. Booth would give to its best passages and of the beautiful appearance he would make in classic costume. He, meanwhile, was growing into great fame and favor with the public, and was called hither and thither by numerous engagements. The period of his courtship and marriage[1] intervened, and a number of years elapsed between the completion of the play and his first reading of it."

At last the time seemed ripe for the production of the play. E. L. Davenport, the actor manager of the Howard Athenæum, agreed to produce it: Charlotte Cushman was to play Phædra to Booth's Hippolytus. Rehearsals began, the author's dream seemed close upon fulfilment. Then came a slip never fully explained: the manager suddenly discovered that the subject of the play was a painful one; other reasons were given, but none that appeared sufficient to author or actors.

"My dear," said Miss Cushman, "if Edwin Booth and I had done nothing more than stand upon the stage and say 'good evening' to each other, the house would have been filled."

[1] To Mary Devlin, an actress of great charm.

Briefly, the play was withdrawn. Our mother says: "This was, I think, the greatest 'let down' that I ever experienced. It affected me seriously for some days, after which I determined to attempt nothing more for the stage."

She never forgot the play nor her bitter disappointment.

Many memories cluster about the gracious figure of Edwin Booth. He came often — for so shy and retiring a man — to the Chestnut Street house. We children all worshipped at his shrine; the elder girls worked his initials on the under side of the chair in which he once sat, which was thereafter like no other chair; the younger ones gazed in round-eyed admiration, but the great man had eyes for one only of us all. We gave a party for him, and Beacon Street came in force to meet the brilliant young actor. Alas! the brilliant young actor, after the briefest and shyest of greetings to the company, retired into a corner with eight-year-old Maud, where he sat on the floor making dolls and rabbits out of his pocket handkerchief!

This recalls an oft-quoted anecdote of the time. Our mother wished Charles Sumner to see and know Booth. One evening when the Senator was at the house, she told him of her wish. The next day she writes in her Journal: "Sumner to tea. Made a rude speech on being asked to meet Booth. Said: 'I don't know that I should care to meet him. I have outlived my interest in individuals.' Fortunately, God Almighty had not, by last accounts, got so far."

Sumner was told of this in her presence. "What a

strange sort of book," he exclaimed, "your diary must
be! You ought to strike that out immediately."

She admired Charles Sumner heartily, but they dis-
agreed on many points. He disapproved of women's
speaking in public (as did the Doctor), and — with
wholly kind intentions — did what he could to prevent her giving the above-mentioned readings in
Washington. She notes this in her Journal.

"I wrote him a very warm letter, but with no inju-
rious phrase, as I felt only grief and indignation, not
dis-esteem, towards him. Yet the fact of having written
the letter became extremely painful to me, when it
was once beyond recall. I could not help writing a
second on the day following, to apologize for the roughness of the first. This was a diplomatic fault, I think,
but one inseparable from my character. C. S.'s reply,
which I dreaded to read, was very kind. While I
clearly saw his misapprehension of the whole matter,
I saw also the thorough kindliness and sincerity of his
nature. So we disagree, but I love him."

Mr. Sumner did not attend the readings, but he came
to see her, and was, as always, kind and friendly. After
seeing him in the Senate she writes: "Sumner looks
up and smiles. That smile seems to illuminate the
Senate."

Another passage in the Journal of March, 1864,
is in a different note: "Maggie ill and company to
dinner. I washed breakfast things, cleared the table,
walked, read Spinoza a little, then had to 'fly round,'
as my dinner was an early one. Picked a grouse, and
saw to various matters. Company came, a little early.

The room was cold. Hedge, Palfrey, and Alger to dinner. Conversation pleasant, but dinner late, and not well served. Palfrey and Hedge read Parker's Latin epitaph on Chev, amazed at the bad Latinity."

In June, 1864, a Russian squadron, sent to show Russia's good-will toward the United States, dropped anchor in Boston Harbor, and hospitable Boston rose up in haste to receive the strangers. Dr. Holmes wrote a song beginning, —

> "Seabirds of Muscovy,
> Rest in our waters," —

which was sung to the Russian national air at a public reception.

Our mother for once made no "little verse," but she saw a good deal of the Russian officers; gave parties for them, and attended various functions and festivities on board the ships. On Sunday, June 22, she writes: —

"To mass on board the Oslaba. . . . The service was like the Armenian Easter I saw in Rome. . . . It is a sacrifice to God instead of a lesson from Him, which after all makes the difference between the old religions and the true Christian. For even Judaism is heathen compared with Christianity. Yet I found this very consoling, as filling out the verities of religious development. I seemed to hear in the responses a great harmony in which the first man had the extreme bass and the last born babe the extreme treble. Theo. Parker and my dear Sammy were blended in it."

Soon after this the "seabirds of Muscovy" departed; then came the flitting to Newport, and a summer of steady work.

"Read Paul in the Valley. Thought of writing a review of his first two epistles from the point of view of the common understanding. The clumsy Western mind has made such literal and material interpretations of the Oriental finesses of the New Testament, that the present coarse and monstrous beliefs, so far behind the philosophical, æsthetic, and natural culture of the age, is imposed by the authority of the few upon the ignorance of the many, and stands a monument of the stupidity of all.

"Paul's views of the natural man are, inevitably, much colored by the current bestiality of the period. To apply his expressions to the innocent and inevitable course of Nature is coarse, unjust, and demoralizing, because confusing to the moral sense."

"I came to the conclusion to-day that an heroic intention is not to be kept in sight without much endeavor. Now that I have finished at least one portion of my Ethics and Dynamics, I find myself thinking how to get just credit for it, rather than how to make my work most useful to others. The latter must, however, be my object, and shall be. Did not Chev so discourage it, I should feel bound to give these lectures publicly, being, as they are, a work for the public. I do not as yet decide what to do with them."

Returning to 13 Chestnut Street, she found a multiplicity of work awaiting her. Ethics had to stand aside and make way for Poetry and Philanthropy. New

York was to celebrate the seventieth birthday of William Cullen Bryant; she was asked to write a poem for the occasion. This she did joyfully, composing and arranging the stanzas mostly in the train between Newport and Boston.

On the day of the celebration, she took an early train for New York: Dr. Oliver Wendell Holmes was on the train. "I will sit by you, Mrs. Howe," he said, "but I must not talk! I am going to read a poem at the Bryant celebration, and must save my voice."

"By all means let us keep silent," she replied. "I also have a poem to read at the Bryant Celebration."

Describing this scene she says, "The dear Doctor, always my friend, overestimated his power of abstinence from the interchange of thought which was so congenial to him. He at once launched forth in his own brilliant vein, and we were within a few miles of our destination when we suddenly remembered that we had not taken time to eat our luncheon."

George Bancroft met them at the station, carried her trunk himself ("a small one!"), and put her into his own carriage. The reception was in the Century Building. She entered on Mr. Bryant's arm, and sat between him and Mr. Bancroft on the platform. The Journal tells us: —

"After Mr. Emerson's remarks my poem was announced. I stepped to the middle of the platform, and read my poem. I was full of it, and read it well, I think, as every one heard me, and the large room was crammed. The last two verses — not the best — were applauded. . . . This was, I suppose, the greatest public honor of my life. I record it for my grandchildren."

The November pages of the Journal are blank, but on that for November 21 is pasted a significant note. It is from the secretary of the National Sailors' Fair, and conveys the thanks of the Board of Managers to Mrs. Howe "for her great industry and labor in editing the 'Boatswain's Whistle.'"

Neither Journal nor "Reminiscences" has one word to say about fair or paper; yet both were notable. The great war-time fairs were far more than a device for raising money. They were festivals of patriotism; people bought and sold with a kind of sacred ardor. This fair was Boston's contribution toward the National Sailors' Home. It was held in the Boston Theatre, which for a week was transformed into a wonderful hive of varicolored bees, all "workers," all humming and hurrying. The "Boatswain's Whistle" was the organ of the fair. There were ten numbers of the paper: it lies before us now, a small folio volume of eighty pages.

Title and management are indicated at the top of the first column: —

THE BOATSWAIN'S WHISTLE.

Editorial Council.

Edward Everett.	A. P. Peabody.
John G. Whittier.	J. R. Lowell.
O. W. Holmes.	E. P. Whipple.

Editor.

Julia Ward Howe.

Each member of the Council made at least one contribution to the paper; but the burden fell on the Editor's shoulders. She worked day and night; no wonder that the pages of the Journal are blank. Beside the editorials and many other unsigned articles, she wrote a serial story, "The Journal of a Fancy Fair," which brings back vividly the scene it describes. In those days the raffle was not discredited. Few people realized that it was a crude form of gambling; clergy and laity alike raffled merrily. Our mother, however, in her story speaks through the lips of her hero a pungent word on the subject: —

"The raffle business is, I suppose, the great humbug of occasions of this kind. It seems to me very much like taking a front tooth from a certain number of persons in order to make up a set of teeth for a party who wants it and who does not want to pay for it."

We should like to linger over the pages of the "Boatswain's Whistle"; to quote from James Freeman Clarke's witty dialogues, Edward Everett's stately periods, Dr. Holmes's sparkling verse; to describe General Grant, the prize ox, white as driven snow and weighing 3900 pounds, presented by the owner to President Lincoln and by him to the fair. Did we not see him drawn in triumph through Boston streets on an open car, and realize in an instant — fresh from our "Wonder-Book" — what Europa's bull looked like?

But of all the treasures of the little paper. we must content ourselves with this dispatch: —

Allow me to wish you a great success. With the old fame of the navy made bright by the present war, you cannot fail. I name none lest I wrong others by omission. To all, from Rear Admiral to honest Jack, I tender the nation's admiration and gratitude.

A. LINCOLN.

CHAPTER X

THE WIDER OUTLOOK

1865; *aet.* 46

THE WORD

Had I one of thy words, my Master,
　With a spirit and tone of thine,
I would run to the farthest Indies
　To scatter the joy divine.

I would waken the frozen ocean
　With a billowy burst of joy:
Stir the ships at their grim ice-moorings
　The summer passes by.

I would enter court and hovel,
　Forgetful of mien or dress,
With a treasure that all should ask for,
　An errand that all should bless.

I seek for thy words, my Master,
　With a spelling vexed and slow:
With scanty illuminations
　In an alphabet of woe.

But while I am searching, scanning
　A lesson none ask to hear,
My life writeth out thy sentence
　Divinely just and dear.

　　　　　　　　　　　　　　J. W. H.

THE war was nearly over, and all hearts were with
Grant and Lee in their long duel before Richmond.
Patriotism and philosophy together ruled our mother's
life in these days; the former more apparent in her
daily walk among us, the latter in the quiet hours with
her Journal.

The Journal for 1865 is much fuller than that of

1864; the record of events is more regular, and we find more and more reflection, meditation, and speculation. The influence of Kant is apparent; the entries become largely notes of study, to take final shape in lectures and essays.

"A morning visit received in study hours is a sickness from which the day does not recover. I can neither afford to be idle, nor to have friends who are so."

"Man is impelled by inward force, regulated by outward circumstance. He is inspired from within, moralized from without. . . . A man may be devout in himself, but he can be moral only in his relation with other men. . . ."

"Early to Mary Dorr's, to consult about the Charade. Read Kant and wrote as usual. Spent the afternoon in getting up my costumes for the Charade. The word was Au-thor-ship. . . . Authorship was expressed by my appearing as a great composer, Jerry Abbott performing my Oratorio — a very comical thing, indeed. The whole was a success."

No one who saw the "Oratorio" can forget it. Mr. Abbott, our neighbor in Chestnut Street, was a comedian who would have adorned any stage. The "book" of the Oratorio was a simple rhyme of Boston authorship.

"Abigail Lord,
  Of her own accord,
  Went down to see her sister,
  When Jason Lee,
  As brisk as a flea,
  He hopped right up and kissed her."

With these words, an umbrella, and a chair held be-

fore him like a violoncello, Mr. Abbott gave a truly
Handelian performance. Fugue and counterpoint, first
violin and bass tuba, solo and full chorus, all were ren-
dered with a *verve* and spirit which sent the audience
into convulsions of laughter. — This was one of the
"carryings-on" of the Brain Club. After another such
occasion our mother writes: —

"Very weary and aching a little. I must keep out of
these tomfooleries, though they have their uses. They
are much better than some other social entertainments,
as after all they present some æsthetic points of interest. They are better than scandal, gluttony, or wild
dancing. But the artists and I have still better things
to do."

"*January 23.* It is always legitimate to wish to rise
above one's self, never above others. In this, however,
as in other things, we must remember the maxim:
'*Natura nil facit per saltum.*' All true rising must be
gradual and laborious, in such wise that the men of to-
morrow shall look down almost imperceptibly upon the
men of to-day. All sudden elevations are either imaginary or factitious. If you had not a kingly mind before
your coronation, no crown will make a king of you. The
true king is somewhere, starving or hiding, very like.
For the true value which the counterfeit represents
exists somewhere. The world has much dodging about
to produce the real value and escape the false one."

Throughout the Journal, we find a revelation of the
conflict in this strangely dual nature. Her study was,
she thought, her true home; yet no one who saw her in
society would have dreamed that she was making an

effort: *nor was she!* She gave herself up entirely to the work or the play of the hour. She was a many-sided crystal: every aspect of life met its answering flash. The glow of human intercourse kindled her to flame; but when the flame had cooled, the need of solitude and study lay on her with twofold poignancy. She went through life in double harness, thought and feeling abreast; though often torn between the two, in the main she gave free rein to both, trusting the issue to God.

The winter of 1864–65 was an arduous one. She was writing new philosophical essays, and reading them before various circles of friends. The larger audience which she craved was not for the moment attainable. She was studying deeply, reading Latin by way of relaxation, going somewhat into society (Julia and Florence being now of the dancing age), and entertaining a good deal in a quiet way. In February she writes: "Much tormented by interruptions. Could not get five quiet minutes at a time. Everybody torments me with every smallest errand. And I am trying to study philosophy!"

Probably we were troublesome children and made more noise than we should. Her accurate ear for music was often a source of distress to her, as one of us can witness, an indolent child who neglected her practising. As this child drummed over her scales, the door of the upstairs study would open, and a clear voice come ringing down, "*B flat*, dear, *not* B natural!"

It seemed to the child a miracle; she, with the book before her, could not get it right: "Mamma," studying

Kant upstairs behind closed doors, knew what the note should be.

"Few of us consider the wide and laborious significance of the simplest formulas we employ. 'I love you!' opens out a long vista of labor and endeavor; otherwise it means: 'I love myself and need you.' . . ."

"Played all last evening for Laura's company to dance. My heart flutters to-day. It is a feeling unknown to me until lately."

Now, Laura would have gone barefoot in snow to save her mother pain or fatigue; yet she has no recollection of ever questioning the inevitability of "Mamma's" playing for all youthful dancing. Grown-up parties were different; for them there were hired musicians, who made inferior music; but for the frolics of the early 'teens, who *should* play except "Mamma"?

On March 10, she writes: "I have now been too long in my study. I must break out into real life, and learn some more of its lessons."

Two days later a lesson began: "I stay from church to-day to take care of Maud, who is quite unwell. This is a sacrifice, although I am bound and glad to make it. But I shall miss the church all the week."

The child became so ill that "all pursuits had to be given up in the care of her." The Journal gives a minute account of this illness, and of the remedies used, among them "long-continued and gentle friction with the hand." The words bring back the touch of her hand, which was like no other. There were no trained nurses in our nursery, rarely any doctor save "Papa," but "Mamma" rubbed us, and that was a whole pharmacopœia in itself.

At this time she gave her first public lecture before the Parker Fraternity. This was an important event to her; she had earnestly desired yet greatly dreaded it. She found the hall pleasant, the audience attentive. "When I came to read the lecture," she says, "I felt that it had a value."

"All these things in my mind point one way, viz.: towards the adoption of a profession of Ethical exposition, after my sort."

She had been asked to give a lecture at Tufts College, and says of this: "The difficulties are great, the question is to me one of simple duty. If I am sent for, and have the word to say, I should say it."

And again: "I determine that I can only be good in fulfilling my highest function — all else implies waste of power, leading to demoralization."

She declined the invitation, "feeling unable to decide in favor of accepting it."

"But I was sorry," she says, "and I remembered the words: 'He that hath put his hand to the plough and looketh back is not fit for the kingdom of heaven.' God keep me from so looking back!"

The Journal of this spring is largely devoted to philosophic speculations and commentaries on Kant, whose theories she finds more and more luminous and convincing; now and then comes a note of her own: —

"'I am God!' says the fool. 'I see God!' says the wise man. For while you are your own supreme, you are your own God, and self-worship is true atheism."

"It is better to use a bad man by his better side than a good man by his worse side."

"Christ said that he was older than Abraham. I think that he used this expression as a measure of value. His thoughts were further back in the primal Ideal necessity. He did not speak of any personal life antedating his own existence. . . . In his own sense, Christ was also newer than we are, for his doctrine is still beyond the attainment of all and the appreciation of most of us."

"There is no essential religious element in negation."

"Saw Booth in 'Hamlet' — still first-rate, I think, although he has played it one hundred nights in New York. 'Hamlet' is an æsthetic Evangel. I know of no direct ethical work which contains such powerful moral illustration and instruction."

"James Freeman [Clarke] does not think much of Sam's book, probably not as well as it deserves. But the knowledge of Sam's personality is the light behind the transparency in all that he does." [1]

These were the closing months of the Civil War. All hearts were lifted up in thankfulness that the end was near. She speaks of it seldom, but her few words are significant.

"*Monday, April 3.* . . . Richmond was taken this morning. *Laus Deo!*"

On April 10, after "Maud's boots, $3.00, Vegetables, .12, Bread, .04," we read, "Ribbons for victory, .40. To-day we have the news of Lee's surrender with the

[1] *Lyrical Ventures*, by Samuel Ward.

whole remnant of his army. The city is alive with
people. All flags hung out — shop windows decorated
— processions in the street. All friends meet and
shake hands. On the newspaper bulletins such plac-
ards as 'Gloria in excelsis Deo,' 'Thanks be to God!'
We all call it the greatest day of our lives.

"Apples, half-peck, .50."

That week was one of joy and thankfulness for all.
Thursday was Fast Day; she "went to church to
fatigue Satan. Afterwards made a visit to Mrs. ——
who did not seem to have tired her devil out."

The joy bells were soon to be silenced. Saturday,
April 15, was

"A black day in history, though outwardly most
fair. President Lincoln was assassinated in his box
at the theatre, last evening, by J. Wilkes Booth. This
atrocious act, which was consummated in a very theatrical manner, is enough to ruin not the Booth family
alone, but the theatrical profession. Since my Sammy's
death, nothing has happened that has given me so
much personal pain as this event. The city is paralyzed. But we can only work on, and trust in
God."

Our father's face of tragedy, the anguish in his voice,
as he called us down to hear the news, come vividly
before us to-day, one of the clearest impressions of
our youth. Our mother went with him next day to
hear Governor Andrew's official announcement of the
murder to the Legislature, and heard with deep emotion his quotation from "Macbeth": —

"Besides, this Duncan
Hath borne his faculties so meek, hath been
So clear in his great office, that his virtues
Will plead like angels, trumpet-tongued, against
The deep damnation of his taking-off," etc.

Wednesday, April 19, was: —

"The day of President Lincoln's funeral. A sad, disconnected day. I could not work, but strolled around to see the houses, variously draped in black and white. Went to Bartol's church, not knowing of a service at our own. Bartol's remarks were tender and pathetic. I was pleased to have heard them.

"Wrote some verses about the President — pretty good, perhaps, — scratching the last nearly in the dark, just before bedtime."

This is the poem called "Parricide." It begins: —

O'er the warrior gauntlet grim
Late the silken glove we drew,
Bade the watch-fires slacken dim
In the dawn's auspicious hue.
Staid the armèd heel;
Still the clanging steel;
Joys unwonted thrilled the silence through.

On April 27 she "heard of Wilkes Booth's death — shot on refusing to give himself up — the best thing that could have happened to himself and his family"; and wrote a second poem entitled "Pardon," embodying her second and permanent thought on the subject:

Pains the sharp sentence the heart in whose wrath it was uttered,
Now thou art cold;
Vengeance, the headlong, and Justice, with purpose close muttered,
Loosen their hold, etc.

Brief entries note the closing events of the war.

"*May 13.* Worked much on Essay. . . . In the evening said to Laura: 'Jeff Davis will be taken to-morrow.' Was so strongly impressed with the thought that I wanted to say it to Chev, but thought it was too silly."

"*May 14.* The first thing I heard in the morning was the news of the capture of Jeff Davis. This made me think of my preluding the night before. . . ."

Other things beside essays demanded work in these days. The great struggle was now over, and with it the long strain on heart and nerve, culminating in the tragic emotion of the past weeks. The inevitable re-action set in. Her whole nature cried out for play, and play meant work.

"Working all day for the Girls' Party, to-morrow evening. Got only a very short reading of Kant, and of Tyndall. Tea with the Bartols. Talk with [E. P.] Whipple, who furiously attacked Tacitus. Bartol and I, who know a good deal more about him, made a strong fight in his behalf."

"Working all day for the Party. The lists of men and women accepting and declining were balanced by my daughter F. with amusing anxiety. . . . The two sexes are now neck and neck. Dear little Maud was in high glee over every male acceptance. Out of all this hubbub got a precious forty-five minutes with Kant. . . ."

The party proved "very gay and pleasant."

Now came a more important event: the Musical Festival celebrating the close of the war, which was given by the Handel and Haydn Society, at its semi-centennial, in May, 1865. Our mother sang alto in the chorus. The Journal records daily, sometimes semi-daily, rehearsals and performances, Kant squeezed to the wall, and getting with difficulty his daily hour or half-hour. Mendelssohn's "Hymn of Praise" and "Elijah"; Haydn's "Creation," Handel's "Messiah" and "Israel in Egypt"; she sang in them all.

Here is a sample Festival day: —

"Attended morning rehearsal, afternoon concert, and sang in the evening. We gave 'Israel in Egypt' and Mendelssohn's 'Hymn of Praise.' I got a short reading of Kant, which helped me through the day. But so much music is more than human nerves can respond to with pleasure. This confirms my belief in the limited power of our sensibilities in the direction of pure enjoyment. The singing in the choruses fatigues me less than hearing so many things."

After describing the glorious final performance of the "Messiah," she writes: —

"So farewell, delightful Festival! I little thought what a week of youth was in store for me. For these things carried me back to my early years, and their passion for music. I remembered the wholeness with which I used to give myself up to the concerts and oratorios in New York, and the intense reaction of melancholy which always followed these occasions."

And the next day: —

"Still mourning the Festival a little. If I had kept up my music as I intended, in my early youth, I should never have done what I have done — should never have studied philosophy, nor written what I have written. My life would have been more natural and passionate, but I think less valuable. Yet I cannot but regret the privation of this element in which I have lived for years. But I do believe that music is the most expensive of the fine arts. It uses up the whole man more than the other arts do, and builds him up less. It is more passional, less intellectual, than the other arts. Its mastery is simple and absolute, while that of the other arts is so complex as to involve a larger sphere of thought and reflection. I have observed the faces of this orchestra just disbanded. Their average is considerably above the ordinary one. But they have probably more talent than thought."

On May 31 we find a significant entry. The evening before she had attended the Unitarian Convention, and "heard much tolerable speaking, but nothing of any special value or importance." She now writes: —

"I really suffered last evening from the crowd of things which I wished to say, and which, at one word of command, would have flashed into life and, I think, into eloquence. It is by a fine use of natural logic that the Quaker denomination allows women to speak, under the pressure of religious conviction. 'In Christ Jesus there is neither male nor female,' is a good sentence. Paul did not carry this out in his church discipline, yet, one sees, he felt it in his religious contemplation. I feel that a woman's whole moral responsibility is lowered by the fact that she must never obey a transcendent command of conscience.

Man can give her nothing to take the place of this. It is the *divine* right of the human soul."

The fatigue and excitement of the Festival had to be paid for: the inevitable reaction set in. "*June 3.* Decidedly I have spleen in these days. Throughout my whole body, I feel a mingled restlessness and feebleness, as if the nerves were irritated, and the muscles powerless. I feel puzzled, too, about the worth of what I have been doing for nearly three years past. There is no one to help me in these matters. I determine still to work on and hope on. Much of the work of every life is done in the dark."

Again: "Spleen to-day, and utter discouragement. The wind is east, and this gives me the strange feeling, described before, of restlessness and powerlessness. My literary affairs are in a very confused state. I have no market. This troubles me. . . . God keep me from falling away from my purpose, to do only what seems to me necessary and called for in my vocation, and not to produce for money, praise, or amusement."

"Was melancholy and Godless all day, having taken my volume of Kant back to the Athenæum for the yearly rearrangement. Could not interest myself in anything. . . . Visited old Mrs. Sumner,[1] whose chariot and horses are nearly ready."

At this time there was some question of selling Lawton's Valley for economic reasons. The exigency passed, but the following words show the depth of her feeling on the subject: "If I have any true philosophy, any sincere religion, these must support me under the

[1] The mother of Charles Sumner.

privation of the Valley. I feel this, and resolve to do well, but nature will suffer. That place has been my confidante, — my bosom friend, — intimate to me as no human being ever will be — dear and comforting also to my children. . . ."

"*June 11*. . . .Thought of a good text for a sermon, 'In the world ye shall have tribulation,' the scope being to show that our tribulation, if we try to do well, is in the world, our refuge and comfort in the church. Thought of starting a society in Newport for the practice of sacred music, availing ourselves of the summer musicians and the possible aid of such ladies as Miss Reed, etc., for solos. Such an enterprise would be humanizing, and would supply a better object than the empty reunions of fashion. . . ."

"*Wednesday, June 21.* Attended the meeting at Faneuil Hall, for the consideration of reconstruction of the Southern States. Dana made a statement to the effect that voting was a civic, not a natural, right, and built up the propriety of negro suffrage on the basis first of military right, then of duty to the negro, this being the only mode of enabling him to protect himself against his late master. His treatment was intended to be exhaustive, and was able, though cold and conceited. Beecher tumbled up on the platform immediately after, not having heard him, knocked the whole question to pieces with his great democratic power, his humor, his passion, and his magnetism. It was Nature after Art, and his nature is much greater than Dana's art."

A few days after this she writes: ". . . Sumner in

the evening — a long and pleasant visit. He is a very sweet-hearted man, and does not grow old."

The Musical Festival had not yet exacted full arrears of payment; she was too weary even to enjoy the Valley at first; but after a few days of its beloved seclusion she shook off fatigue and was herself again, reading Kant and Livy, teaching the children, and gathering mussels on the beach.

She flits up to town to see the new statue of Horace Mann, "in order to criticise it for Chev's pamphlet"; [1] meets William Hunt, who praises its simplicity and parental character; and Charles Sumner, who tells her it looks better on a nearer view.

The day after — "we abode in the Valley, when three detachments of company tumbled in upon us, to wit, Colonel Higginson and Mrs. McKay, the Tweedys and John Field, and the Gulstons. All were friendly. Only on my speaking of the rudeness occasionally shown me by a certain lady, Mrs. Tweedy said: 'But that was in the presence of your superiors, was it not?' I replied: 'I do not know that I was ever in Mrs. X.'s company under those circumstances!' After which we all laughed."

She was at this time sitting to Miss Margaret Foley for a portrait medallion and was writing philosophy and poetry. Family and household matters also claimed their share of attention.

"Finished reading over 'Polarity' [her essay]. Reading to the children, 'Foxes have holes, and birds of the air have nests, but the Son of Man hath not where

---

[1] Dr. Howe raised the money for this statue.

to lay his head' — my little Maud's eyes filled with
tears."

"Much worried by want of preparedness for to-
day's picnic. Managed to get up three chickens killed
on short notice, a pan of excellent gingerbread, two
cans of peaches, and a little bread and butter. Went
in the express wagon. . . . At the picnic I repeated my
Cambridge poem, . . . and read 'Amanda's Inventory'
and my long poem on Lincoln's death. . . . Duty depends on an objective, happiness upon a subjective,
sense. The first is capable of a general and particular
definition, the second is not."

"In the afternoon mended Harry's shirt, finished
Maud's skirt, read Livy and Tyndall, and played
croquet, which made me very cross."

"Exhumed my French story and began its termination. Mended a sheet badly torn."

After a long list of purchases —
"Worked like a dog all day. Went in town, running
about to pick up all the articles above mentioned. . . .
Came home — cut bread and butter and spread sandwiches till just within time to slip off one dress and
slip on another. My company was most pleasant,
and more numerous than I had anticipated. . . ."

"Legal right is the universal compulsion which se-
cures universal liberty."

"I feel quite disheartened when I compare this summer with the last. I was so happy and hopeful in
writing my three Essays and thought they should open
such a vista of usefulness to me, and of good to others.
But the opposition of my family has made it almost

impossible for me to make the use intended of them.
My health has not allowed me to continue to produce
so much. I feel saddened and doubtful of the value of
what I have done or can do. . . ."

"*August 23.* . . . Rights and duties are inseparable
in human beings. God has rights without duties. Men
have rights and duties. If a slave have not rights, he
also has not duties. . . ."

"With the girls to a matinée at Bellevue Hall. They
danced and I was happy."

"My croquet party kept me busy all day. It was
pleasant enough. . . ."

". . . 'My peace I give unto you' is a wonderful
saying. What peace have most of us to give each other?
But Christ has given peace to the world, peace at
least as an ideal object, to be ever sought, though
never fully attained."

"*September 10.* . . . Read Kant on state rights.
According to him, wars of conquest are allowable only
in a state of nature, not in a state of peace (which is
not to be attained without a compact whose necessity
is supreme and whose obligations are sacred). So
Napoleon's crusade against the constituted authority
of the European republic was without logical justification, — which accounts for the speedy downfall of
his empire. What he accomplished had only the subjective justification of his genius and his ambition.
His work was of great indirect use in sweeping away
certain barriers of usage and of superstition. He drew a
picture of government on a large scale and thus set a
pattern which inevitably enlarged the procedures of his

successors, who lost through him the prestige of divine
right and of absolute power. But the inadequacy of
his object showed itself through the affluence of his
genius. The universal dominion of the Napoleon family was not to be desired or endured by the civilized
world at large. The tortoise in the end overtook the
hare, and slow, plodding Justice, with her loyal hack,
distanced splendid Ambition mounted on first-rate
ability, once and forever. . . ."

"To Zion church, to hear —— preach. Text, 'Son,
remember that thou in thy lifetime receivedst thy
good things.' Sermon as far removed from it as
possible, weak, sentimental, and illiterate. He left
out the 'd' in 'receivedst,' and committed other errors
in pronunciation. But to sit with the two aunts [1] in
the old church, so familiar to my childhood, was touching and impressive. Hither my father was careful to
bring us. Imperfect as his doctrine now appears to
me, he looks down upon me from the height of a better life than mine, and still appears to me as my
superior."

"A little nervous about my reading. Reached Mrs.
[Richard] Hunt's at twelve. Saw the sweet little
boy. Mrs. Hunt very kind and cordial. At one Mr.
Hunt led me to the studio which I found well filled,
my two aunts in the front row, to my great surprise;
Bancroft, too, quite near me. I shortened the essay
somewhat. It was well heard and received. Afterwards I read my poem called 'Philosophy,' and was
urged to recite my 'Battle Hymn,' which I did. I was

---

[1] Mrs. Francis and Mrs. McAllister.

much gratified by the kind reception I met with and the sight of many friends of my youth. A most pleasant lunch afterwards at Mrs. Hunt's, with Tweedys, Tuckermans, and Laura."

"I see no outlook before me. So many fields for activity, but for passivity, which seems incumbent upon me, only uselessness, obscurity, deterioration. Some effort I must make."

Many efforts were impending, though not precisely in the direction contemplated. First, a new abode must be found for the winter, as the owners of 13 Chestnut Street claimed it for themselves. She and the Doctor added house-hunting to their other burdens, and found it a heavy one. On October 6 she writes: —

"Much excited about plans and prospects. Chev has bought the house in Boylston Place.[1] God grant it may be for the best. Determine to have classes in philosophy, and to ask a reasonable price for my tickets. . . .

"The Sunday's devotion without the week's thought and use is a spire without a meeting-house. It leaps upward, but crowns and covers nothing.

"I have too often set down the moral weight I have to carry, and frisked around it. But the voice now tells me that I must bear it to the end, or lose it forever."

The move to Boylston Place was in November. Early in the month a "frisking" took place, with amusing results. Our mother went with Governor and Mrs. Andrew and a gay party to Barnstable for the

[1] No. 19.

annual festival and ball. The Ancient and Honorable
Artillery Company acted as escort, and — according
to custom — the band of the Company furnished the
music. For some reason — the townspeople thought
because the pretty girls were all engaged beforehand
for the dance — the officer in command stopped the
music at twelve o'clock, to the great distress of the
Barnstable people who had ordered their carriages
at two or later. The party broke up in disorder far
from "admired," and our mother crystallized the
general feeling in the following verses, which the
Barnstableites promptly printed in a "broadside,"
and sang to the then popular tune of "Lanigan's
Ball": —

THE BARNSTABLE BALL

A LYRIC

(Appointed to be sung in all Social Meetings on the Cape)

March away with your old artillery;
　　Don't come back till we give you a call.
Put your Colonel into the pillory;
　　He broke up the Barnstable Ball.

Country folks don't go a-pleasuring
　　Every day, as it doth befall;
They with deepest scorn are measuring
　　Him who broke up the Barnstable Ball.

He came down with his motley company,
　　Stalking round the 'cultural hall;
Could n't find a partner to jump any,
　　So broke up the Barnstable Ball.

Warn't it enough with their smoking and thundering,
　　Sweeping about like leaves in a squall,
But they must take to theft and plundering, —
　　Steal the half of the Barnstable Ball?

Put the music into their pocket,
  Order the figure-man not to bawl,
Twenty jigs were still on the docket,
  When they adjourned the Barnstable Ball.

Gov'nor A. won't hang for homicide,
  That's a point that bothers us all;
He must banish ever from his side
  Such as murdered the Barnstable Ball.

When they're old and draw'd with rheumatiz,
  Let them say to their grandbabes small,
"Deary me, what a shadow of gloom it is
  To remember the Barnstable Ball!"

This autumn saw the preparation of a new volume of poems, "Later Lyrics." Years had passed since the appearance of "Words for the Hour," and our mother had a great accumulation of poems, the arrangement of which proved a heavy task.

"The labor of looking over the manuscript nearly made me ill. . . . Had a new bad feeling of intense pressure in the right temple."

And again: —

"Nearly disabled by headaches. . . . Determine to push on with my volume."

"Almost distracted with work of various sorts — my book — the new house — this one full of company, and a small party in the evening."

"All these days much hurried by proofs. Went in the evening to the opening of the new wards in the Women's Hospital — read two short poems, according to promise. These were kindly received. . . ."

The next day she went with a party of friends to the Boys' Reform School at Westboro. "In the yard where the boys were collected, the guests were introduced. Quite a number crowded to see the Author of the 'Battle Hymn.' Two or three said to me: 'Are you the woman that wrote that "Battle Hymn"?' When I told them that I was, they seemed much pleased. This I felt to be a great honor."

The next day again she is harassed with correcting proofs and furnishing copy. "Ran to Bartol for a little help, which he gave me."

The Reverend C. A. Bartol was our next-door neighbor in Chestnut Street, a most kind and friendly one. His venerable figure, wrapped in a wide cloak, walking always in the middle of the road (we never knew why he eschewed the sidewalk), is one of the pleasant memories of Chestnut Street. We were now to leave that beloved street; a sorrowful flitting it was.

"*Friday, November 3.* Moving all day. This is my last writing in this dear house, No. 13 Chestnut Street, where I have had three years of good work, social and family enjoyment. Here I enjoyed my dear Sammy for six happy months — here I mourned long and bitterly for him. Here I read my six lectures on Practical Ethics. Some of my best days have been passed in this house. God be thanked for the same!"

CHAPTER XI

1866; *aet.* 47

IN MY VALLEY

From the hurried city fleeing,
From the dusty men and ways,
In my golden sheltered valley,
Count I yet some sunny days.

Golden, for the ripened Autumn
Kindles there its yellow blaze;
And the fiery sunshine haunts it
Like a ghost of summer days.

Walking where the running water
Twines its silvery caprice,
Treading soft the leaf-spread carpet,
I encounter thoughts like these: —

"Keep but heart, and healthful courage,
Keep the ship against the sea,
Thou shalt pass the dangerous quicksands
That ensnare Futurity;

"Thou shalt live for song and story,
For the service of the pen;
Shalt survive till children's children
Bring thee mother-joys again.

"Thou hast many years to gather;
And these falling years shall bring
The benignant fruits of Autumn,
Answering to the hopes of Spring.

"Passing where the shades that darken
Grow transfigured to thy mind,
Thou shalt go with soul untroubled
To the mysteries behind;

"Pass unmoved the silent portal
Where beatitude begins,
With an equal balance bearing
Thy misfortunes and thy sins."

Treading soft the leaf-spread carpet,
Thus the Spirits talked with me;
And I left my valley, musing
On their gracious prophecy.

To my fiery youth's ambition
Such a boon were scarcely dear;
"Thou shalt live to be a grandame,
Work and die, devoid of fear."

"Now, as utmost grace it steads me,
Add but this thereto," I said:
"On the matron's time-worn mantle
Let the Poet's wreath be laid."   J. W. H.

"MY first writing in the new house, where may God help and bless us all. May no dark action shade our record in this house, and if possible, no surpassing sorrow."

After the wide sunny spaces of No. 13 Chestnut Street, the new house seemed small and dark; nor was Boylston Place even in those days a specially cheerful *cul de sac;* yet we remember it pleasantly enough as the home of much work and much play.

"*November 19.* Had the comforts of faith from dear James Freeman [Clarke] to-day. Felt restored to something like the peace I enjoyed before these two tasks of printing and moving broke up all leisure and all study. Determined to hold on with both hands to the largeness of philosophical pursuit and study, and to do my utmost to be useful in this connection and path of life. . . ."

"Comforting myself with Hedge's book. Determined to pass no more godless days. . . ."

She began to read Grote's Plato, and the Journal contains much comment on the Platonic philosophy. Another interest which came to her this autumn was

MRS. HOWE IN LAWTON'S VALLEY, *circa* 1865
From a painting

that of singing with the Handel and Haydn Society.
She and Florence joined the altos, while "Harry,"
then in college (Harvard, 1869), sang bass. We find
her also, in early December, rehearsing with a small
chorus the Christmas music for the Church of the
Disciples, and writing and rehearsing a charade for
the Club.

"*December 12.* Saw my new book at Tilton's. It
looks very well, but I am not sanguine about its
fate."

"Later Lyrics" made less impression than either of
the earlier volumes. It has been long out of print; our
mother does not mention it in her "Reminiscences";
even in the Journal, the book once published, there are
few allusions to it, and those in a sad note: "Discouraged about my book," and so forth; yet it contains
much of her best work.

"*December 16.* Sarah Clarke[1] and Foley[2] are to dine
with me at 5.30. Went out at 10 A.M. to take Foley to
see [William] Hunt, whom we found in his studio in
a queer knitted coat. He showed an unfinished head
of General Grant, in which it struck me that the eyes
looked like the two scales of a balance in which men
and events could be weighed."

The Journal for 1866 opens with a Latin aspiration:
"*Quod bonus, felix, faustusque sit hic annus mihi et
meis amicis dilectis et generi humano!*"
February finds her in New York, going to a "family

[1] Sister of James Freeman Clarke. An artist of some note and a beloved
friend of our mother.
[2] Margaret Foley, the sculptor.

party at Aunt Maria's.[1] Uncle John came. He was
the eldest, my Harry the youngest member. I made
a charade, *Shoddy*, in which Mary [Ward] and Flossy
took part. Mary did very well. Flossy always does
well. I enjoyed this family gathering more than anything since leaving home. It is so rare a pleasure
for me. Family occasions are useful in bringing people
together on the disinterested ground of natural affection, without any purpose of show or self-advancement.
Relations should meet on more substantial ground than
that of fashion and personal ambition. Nature and
self-respect here have the predominance. In my youth
I had no notion of this, though I always clung to those
of my own blood."

From New York she went to Washington, where she
gave a series of philosophical readings. Here, while
staying at the house of Mrs. Eames, she had a violent attack of malarial fever, but struggled up again
with her usual buoyancy.

"*February 19.* Weather rainy, so stayed at home;
eyes weak, so could do little but lie in my easy-chair,
avoid cold, and hang on to conversation. To-day the
President[2] vetoed the bill for the Freedmen's Bureau.
The reading of the veto was received by the Senate
with intense, though suppressed, excitement. Governor
Andrew read it to us. It was specious, and ingeniously
overstated the scope and powers demanded for the
Bureau, in order to make its withholdment appear a
liberal and democratic measure. Montgomery Blair
is supposed to have written this veto."

[1] The widow of her uncle, William G. Ward.   [2] Andrew Johnson.

At her first reading, she had "an excellent audience. The rooms were well filled and there were many men of note there. . . . Governor Andrew brought me in. Sam Hooper was there. I read 'The Fact Accomplished.' They received it very well. I was well pleased with my reception."

The next day she was so weary that she fell asleep while the Marquis de Chambrun was talking to her.

"*February 23.* To-day we learned the particulars of President Johnson's disgraceful speech, which awakens but one roar of indignation. To the Senate at 11.30. When the business hour is over, Fessenden moves the consideration of the House Resolution proposing the delay in the admission of members for the Southern States until the whole South shall be in a state for readmission. Sherman, of Ohio, moves the postponement of the question, alleging the present excitement as a reason for this. (He probably does this in the Copperhead interest.) At this Fessenden shows his teeth and shakes the Ohio puppy pretty well. Howe of Wisconsin also speaks for the immediate discussion of the question. Doolittle, of ——, speaking against it, Trumbull calls him to order. Reverdy Johnson pitches in a little. The Ayes and Noes are called for and the immediate consideration receives a good majority. Fessenden now makes his speech, reads the passage from the President's speech, calling the committee of fifteen a directory, — comments fully on the powers of Congress, the injustice of the President and his defiant attitude. . . . He has force as

debater, but no grasp of thought. . . . In the evening
I read the first half of 'Limitations' to a very small
circle. A Republican caucus took all the members
of Congress. Garrison also lectured. I was sorry,
but did my best and said, 'God's will be done.' But I
ought to have worked harder to get an audience."

"*February 25.* . . . Rode with Lieber [1] as far as Baltimore. He heard Hegel in his youth and thinks him,
as I do, decidedly inferior to Kant, morally as well as
philosophically. . . .

"The laws and duties of society rest upon a supposed compact, but this compact cannot deprive any
set of men of rights and limit them to duties, for if
you refuse them all rights, you deprive them even of
the power to become a party to this compact, which
rests upon their right to do so. Our slaves had no
rights. Women have few."

After leaving Washington, she spent several days
with her sister Annie in Bordentown, and there
and in New York gave readings which seem to have
been much more successful than those in Washington.
After the New York reading she is "glad and thankful."

The visits in Bordentown were always a delight and
refreshment to her. She and her "little Hitter"
frolicked, once more two girls together: e.g., the following incident: —

The Reverend —— Bishop was the Mailliards'
pastor; a kindly gentleman, who could frolic as well as

[1] Dr. Francis Lieber, the eminent German-American publicist.

another. One day our Aunt Annie, wishing to ask him to dine, sat down at her desk and wrote: —

"My dear Mr. Bishop,
    To-day we shall dish up
    At one and a half
    The hind leg of a calf —"

At this point she was called away on household business. Our mother sat down and wrote: —

"Now B., if he's civil,
    May join in our revel;
    But if he is not,
    He may go to the devil!"

During the days that followed, Kant and charades divided her time pretty evenly.

"Kant's 'Anthropologia' is rather trifling, after his great works. I read it to find out what Anthropology is."

. . . .

"Good is a direction; virtue is a habit."

. . . .

"Wearied by endless running about to find help for my charade, —— having disappointed me. Determine to undertake nothing more of the kind."

. . . .

The charade (*Belabor*), which came off the following evening, was marked by a comic "To be or not to be," composed and recited by her in a "Hamlet costume, consisting of a narrow, rather short black skirt, a long black cloak and a black velvet toque, splendid lace ruff, amethyst necklace. It was very effective, and the verses gave reasonable pleasure."

"*March 15.* ... Went to the Masonic Banquet, which was preceded by a long ceremony, the consecration of three new banners. The forms were curious, the music good, the occasion unique. The association appeared to me a pale ghost of knighthood, and the solemnities a compromise between high mass and dress parade. The institution now means nothing more than a military and religious toy."

In this year she met with a serious loss in the death of her uncle, John Ward. He had been a second father to her and her sisters; his kindly welcome always made No. 8 Bond Street a family home.

"*April 4.* The contents of uncle's will are known to-day. He had made a new one, changing the disposition of his property made in a previous will which would have made my sisters and me much richer. This one gives equally to my cousins, Uncle William's four sons, and to us; largely to Uncle Richard, and most kindly to Brother Sam and Wardie. We know not why this change was made, but once made, it must be acquiesced in, like other events past remedy. My cousins are wealthy already — this makes little difference to them, but much to us. God's will be done, however. I must remember my own doctrine, and build upon 'The Fact Accomplished.'"

This passage explains the financial worries which, from now on, often oppressed her. She was brought up in wealth and luxury; sober wealth, unostentatious luxury, but enough of both to make it needless for her ever to consider questions of ways and means. Her whole family, from the adoring father down to the loving youngest sister, felt that she must be shielded from every sordid care or anxiety; she was tended like an orchid, lest any rough wind check her perfect blossoming.

Her father left a large fortune, much of which was invested in blocks of real estate in what is now the heart of New York. Uncle John, best and kindest of men, had no knowledge of real estate and none of the foresight which characterized his elder brother. After Mr. Ward's death, he made the mistake of selling out the Manhattan real estate, and investing the proceeds in stocks and bonds. Later, realizing his grave error, he resolved to mitigate the loss to his three nieces by dividing among them the bulk of his property.

This failing, the disappointment could not but be a sensible one, even to the least money-loving of women. The Doctor's salary was never a large one: the children must be given every possible advantage of education and society; no door that was open to her own youth should be closed to them; again, to entertain their friends (albeit in simple fashion), to respond to every call of need or distress, was matter of necessity to both our parents: small wonder that they were often pressed for money. All through the Journals we find this note of financial anxiety: not for herself, but for her children, and later for her grandchildren. She accepted the restricted means; she triumphed over them, and taught us to hold such matters of little account compared with the real things of life; but they never ceased to bewilder her.

Yet to-day, realizing of what vital importance this seeming misfortune was to her; how but for this, her life and other lives might have lacked "the rich flavor of hope and toil"; how but for this she might have failed to lock hands with humanity in a bond as close as it was permanent, who can seriously regret Uncle John's devastating yet fruitful mistake?

In April again she writes: —

"Dull, sad and perplexed. My uncle not having made me a rich woman, I feel more than ever impelled to make some great effort to realize the value of my mental capacities and acquisitions. I am as well entitled to an efficient literary position as any woman in this country — perhaps better than any other. Still I hang by the way, picking up ten dollars here and there with great difficulty. I pray God to help me to an occasion or sphere in which I may do my utmost. I had as lief die as live unless I can be satisfied that I have delivered the whole value of my literary cargo — all at least that was invoiced for this world. Hear me, great Heaven! Guide and assist me. No mortal can."

The next day's entry is more cheerful.

"Feel better to-day. Made the acquaintance of Aldrich and Howells and their wives, at Alger's last evening. I enjoyed the evening more than usual. Aldrich has a very refined face. Howells [1] is odd-look-

---

[1] Mr. Howells, in his *Literary Boston Thirty Years Ago*, thus speaks of her (1895): "I should not be just to a vivid phase if I failed to speak of Mrs. Julia Ward Howe and the impulse of reform which she personified. I did not sympathize with this then so much as I do now, but I could appreciate it on the intellectual side. Once, many years later, I heard Mrs. Howe speak in public, and it seemed to me that she made one of the best speeches I had ever heard. It gave me for the first time a notion of what

ing, but sympathetic and intelligent. Alger was in all his glory."

"*April 11.* . . . Between a man governed by inner and one governed by outer control, there is the difference which we find between a reptile in a shell and a vertebrate. The one has his vertebræ within to support him, the other has them without to contain him."

"*April 19.* Very busy all day. Ran about too much, and was very tired. Had friends, in the evening, to meet young Perabo. I did not wish to give a party, on account of Uncle's death, but could not help getting together quite a lovely company of friends. Aldrich and wife were here, Alger, Bartol, Professor Youmans, Perabo, Dresel, Louisa D. Hunt, and others. It was a good time. . . . Saw my last cent go — nothing now till May, unless I can earn something."

"*April 20.* Began to work over and correct my poem for the Church Festival, which must be licked into shape, for the Gods will give me none other. So I must hammer at it slowly, and a good deal. . . . To write purely for money is to beg, first telling a story."

In these days the Doctor was very weary through excess of work. He longed for a change, and would

women might do in that sort if they entered public life; but when we met in those earlier days I was interested in her as perhaps our chief poetess. I believe she did not care to speak much of literature; she was alert for other meanings in life, and I remember how she once brought to book a youthful matron who had perhaps unduly lamented the hardships of house-keeping, with the sharp demand, 'Child, where is your *religion?*' After the many years of an acquaintance which had not nearly so many meetings as years, it was pleasant to find her, not long ago, as strenuous as ever for the faith or work, and as eager to aid Stepniak as John Brown. In her beautiful old age she survives a certain literary impulse of Boston, but a still higher impulse of Boston she will not survive, for that will last while the city endures."

have been glad to receive the mission to Greece, of
which some prospect had been held out to him. She
writes: "Chev full of the Greek mission, which I
think he cannot get. I wish he might, because he
wishes it. Surely a man so modest and meritorious
in his public career might claim so small an acknowledgment as this. But as we are, he represents Charity, I the study of Philosophy — we cannot be more
honored than by standing for these things."

It was thought that she might have some influence
in obtaining the mission: accordingly she went to
Washington, anxious to help if she might. She saw the
President of the Senate, who promised support. While
there she writes: "Governor Andrew took me to General Grant's, where I saw the General, with great satisfaction. Prayed at bedtime that I might not become a
superficial sham and humbug."

Hearing that Charles Sumner had sought her at the
house of Mrs. Eames, she sent a message to him by a
common friend. She writes: "Sumner cannot make
a visit at the hotel, but will see me at the Capitol. I
know of nothing which exempts a man in public life
from the duty of having, in private, some *human*
qualities." Mr. Sumner did come to see her later,
when she was staying with Mrs. Eames. She saw Secretary Seward, who was very ungracious to her; and
President Johnson, whom she found "not one inclined to much speech." Before the latter interview her
prayer was: "Let me be neither unskilful nor mean!"

The visit to Mrs. Eames was a sad one, being at the
time of the death of Count Gurowski, a singular man

whom she has described in her "Reminiscences"; but she met many notable persons, and had much interesting conversation with her host and hostess. She records one or two bits of talk.

"Mr. Eames saying that Mrs. X. was an intelligent but not an original woman, I said: 'She is not a silkworm, but a silk-wearer!' Nine women out of ten would rather be the latter than the former."

"Mr. Eames saying that he often talked because he could not make the effort to be silent, I said: 'Yes, sir; we know that the *vis inertiæ* often shows itself in motion.'

"I record these sayings," she adds, "because they interested me, opening to myself little shades of thought not perceived before."

"*May 27.* Boston. My birthday. Forty-seven years old. J. F. C. preached on 'The seed is the word,' and gave a significant statement of the seminal power of Christianity. They sang also a psalm tune which I like, so that the day (a rainy one) seems to me auspicious. I have little to show for the past year's work, having produced no work of any length and read but little in public. The doctrine of the *seed* does, however, encourage us to continue our small efforts. The most effectual quickening of society is through that small influence which creeps like the leaven through the dough. . . ."

". . . Roman piety was the duteous care of one's relatives. It follows from this that the disregard of parents and elders common in America is in itself an irreligious trait, and one which education should sedulously correct."

On May 29 she attended the Unitarian Festival. She recalls the fact that at the last festival she was "tormented by the desire to speak. But I am now grown more patient, knowing that silence also is valuable. . . ."

The Chevalier was not to receive the only reward he had ever sought for his labors. On May 31 she writes: "To-day the blow fell. A kind letter from Vice-President Foster informed me that Charles T. Tuckerman had been nominated for the Greek mission. This gave me an unhappy hour. Chev was a good deal overcome by it for a time, but rallied and bears up bravely. The girls are rather glad. I am content, but I do not see what can take the place of this cherished object to Chev. . . ."

The following verses embody her thoughts on this matter: —

To S. G. H.

On his failure to receive the Grecian mission which he had been led to think might be offered to him. 1866.

> The Grecian olives vanish from thy sight,
> The wondrous hills, the old historic soil;
> The elastic air, that freshened with delight
> Thy youthful temples, flushed with soldier toil.
>
> O noble soul! thy laurel early wreathed
> Gathers the Christian rose and lilies fair,
> For civic virtues when the sword was sheathed,
> And perfect faith that learns from every snare.
>
> Let, then, the modern embassy float by,
> Nor one regret in thy high bosom lurk:
> God's mission called thy youth to that soft sky;
> Wait God's dismissal where thou build'st His work!

"*Divide et impera* is an old maxim of despotism which does not look as if States' rights pointed in the direction of true freedom."

"It is only in the natural order that the living dog is better than the dead lion. Will any one say that the living thief is better than the dead hero? No one, save perhaps the thief himself, who is no judge."

The Journal is now largely concerned with Kant, and with Maine's work on "Ancient Law," from which she quotes freely. Here and there are touches of her own.

"Epicureans are to Stoics as circumference to centre."

"I think Hegel more difficult than important. Many people suppose that the difficulty of a study is a sure indication of its importance."

In these years the Doctor and our sister Julia were in summer time rather visitors than members of the family. The former was, as Governor Bullock said of him, "driving all the Charities of Massachusetts abreast," and could enjoy the Valley only by snatches, flying down for a day or a week as he could. Julia, from her early girlhood, had interested herself deeply in all that concerned the blind, and had become more and more the Doctor's companion and workfellow at the Perkins Institution, where much of his time was necessarily spent. She had classes in various branches of study, and in school and out gave herself freely to her blind pupils. A friend said to her mother, many years later, "It was one of the sights of Boston in the days of the Harvard Musical concerts to see your Julia's

radiant face as she would come into Music Hall, leading a blind pupil in either hand."

Early in this summer of 1866 Julia accompanied the
Doctor on a visit to the State Almshouse at Monson,
and saw there a little orphan boy, some three years
old, who attracted her so strongly that she begged to be
allowed to take him home with her. Accordingly she
brought him to the Valley, a sturdy, blue-eyed Irish
lad. Julia, child of study and poetry, had no nursery
adaptability, and little "Tukey" was soon turned over
to our mother, who gladly took charge of him. He was
nearly of the age of her little Sammy: something in his
countenance reminded her of the lost child, and she
found delight in playing with him. She would have
been glad to adopt him, but this was not thought prac-
ticable. Julia had already tired of him; the Doctor for
many reasons advised against it.

She grieved all summer for the child; but was afterward made happy by his adoption into a cheerful and
prosperous home.

This was a summer of arduous work. The "Tribune"
demanded more letters; Kant and Maine could not be
neglected, and soon Fichte was added to them.

Moreover, the children must have every pleasure
that she could give them.

"Worked hard all the morning for the croquet party
in the afternoon, which was very pleasant and successful.

"Took Julia to the party on board the Rhode Island.
She looked charmingly, and danced. I was quite happy
because she enjoyed it."

Early August found her in Northampton, reporting for the "Tribune" the Convention of the American Academy of Science. The Doctor and Julia joined her, and she had "very busy days," attending the sessions and writing her reports.

"Read over several times my crabbed essay on the 'Two Necessities,' which I determine to read in the evening. I have with me also the essay on 'Limitations,' far more amusing and popular. But for a scientific occasion, I will choose a treatise which aims at least at a scientific treatment of a great question. This essay asserts the distinctness of the Ideal Order and its legitimate supremacy in human processes of thought. I make a great effort to get its points thoroughly in my mind. Go late to the Barnards'. The scientifics arrive very late, Agassiz gets there at 9. I begin to read soon after. The ladies of our party are all there. I feel a certain enthusiasm in my work and subject, but do not communicate it to the audience, which seemed fatigued and cold; all at least but Pierce, Agassiz, and Davis. Had I done well or ill to read it? . . . Some soul may have carried away a seed-grain of thought."

"*August 11.* . . . To Mount Holyoke in the afternoon. The ascent was frightful, the view sublime. In the evening went to read to the insane people at the asylum; had not 'Later Lyrics,' but 'Passion Flowers.' Read from this and recited from the other. Had great pleasure in doing this, albeit under difficulties. Finished second 'Tribune' letter and sent it."

Back at the Valley, she plunges once more into

Fichte; long hours of study, varied by picnics and sailing parties.

"To church at St. Mary's. X. preached. The beginning of his sermon was liberal, — the latter half sentimental and sensational. 'The love of Christ constraineth us,' but he dwelt far too much on the supposition of a personal and emotional relation between the soul and Christ. It is Christian doctrine interpreted by human sympathy that reclaims us. Christ lives in his doctrine, influences us through that, and his historical personality. All else is myth and miracle. What Christ is to-day ideally we may be able to state, of what he is really, Mr. X. knows no more than I do, and I know nothing.

"Stayed to Communion, which was partly pleasant. But the Episcopal Communion struck me as dismal, compared to our own. It is too literal and cannibalistic; — the symbolism of the eating and drinking is too little made out. Our Unitarian Communion is a feast of joy. The blessedness of Christ's accomplishment swallows up the sorrow of his sacrifice. We have been commemorating the greatest act and fact of human history, the initiation of the gentler morals of the purer faith. We are glad, — not trivially, but solemnly, and our dear Master is glad with us, but not as if he aimed a direct personal influence at each one of us. This is too human and small a mode of operation.

"He is there for us as the sun is there and the brightness of his deed and doctrine penetrates the recesses of our mind and consciousness. But that he knows each one of us cannot and need not be affirmed.

'The moon looks
On many brooks:
The brook can see no moon but this.'

So that we see him, it matters not whether he sees us or no.

"Spinoza's great word; — if we love God, we shall not trouble ourselves about his loving us."

"I yesterday spoke to Joseph Coggeshall, offering to give a reading at the schoolhouse, in order to start a library fund. He appeared pleased with the idea. I proposed to ask .50 for each ticket."

"Chev suggests Europe. '*Je suis content du palazzo Pitti.*'"

"I cannot study Fichte for more than forty-five minutes at a time. Reading him is not so bad as translating, which utterly overpowers my brain, although I find it useful in comprehending him."

"I begin to doubt the availability of Fichte's methods for me. I become each day more dispirited over him. With the purest intention he is much less of an ethicist than Kant. These endless refinements in *rationale* of the *ego* confuse rather than enlighten the moral sense. Where the study of metaphysics becomes de-energizing, it becomes demoralizing. Subtlety used in a certain way unravels confusion, in a certain other way produces it. Kant unwinds the silkworm's web, but Fichte tangles the skein of silk, — at least so it seems to me.

"Spent most of the afternoon in preparing for a tea party, cutting peaches and preparing bread and butter."

"Read 11th and 12th chapters of Mark in the Valley. At some moments one gets a clearer and nearer perception of the thought and personality of Christ than that which we commonly carry with us."

Early in October came the move "home to Boylston Place, leaving the Valley with great regret, but feeling more the importance of being with the children, as I draw nearer to them."

Our mother had remained after the rest of us, to close the house. In Boston she had the great pleasure of welcoming to this country her nephew, Francis Marion Crawford, then a boy of twelve years. Born and bred in Rome, a beautiful and petted child, he was now to learn to be an American schoolboy. She took him herself to St. Paul's School in Concord, New Hampshire; and for a year or two he spent most of his holidays with us, to the delight of us all.

In this autumn of 1866 she undertook a new task, of which the first mention in the Journal reads: "I will here put the names of some writers of stories whom I may employ for the magazine."

A list of writers follows: and the next day she writes: "I saw J. R. Gilmour and agreed with him to do editorial service for thirty dollars per week for three months."

This magazine was the "Northern Lights." The first number appeared in January, 1867. It contained two articles by Mrs. Howe: the "Salutation" and a thoughtful poem called "The Two R's" (Rachel and Ristori). Later, we find her in the "Sittings of the Owl Club," making game of the studies she loved.

This owl went to Germany,
This owl stayed at home;
This owl read Kant and Fichte,
This owl read none.
This owl said To-whit! I can't understand
the dogmatic categorical! "

The "Northern Lights" gleam fitfully in the Journal.

"*October 26.* To write Henry James for story, Charles T. Brooks for sketches of travel. Saw and talked with Gilmour, who confuses my mind."

"*October 29.* Chev went with me to Ristori's *début*, which was in Medea."

"*November 3.* All of these days have been busy and interrupted. Maggi [1] has been reading Ristori's plays in my parlor every day this week and my presence has been compulsory. I have kept on with Fichte whose '*Sittenlehre*' I have nearly finished. Have copied one or two poems, written various letters in behalf of the magazine, have seen Ristori thrice on the stage and once in private."

"*November 10.* Finished copying and correcting my editorial for the first number of my weekly. Finished also Fichte's '*Sittenlehre*' for whose delightful reading I thank God, praying never to act quite unworthily of its maxims."

"*November 11.* Called on Mrs. Charles Sumner, and saw both parties, who were very cordial and seemed very happy."

"*November 15.* Crackers, .25, eggs, .43, rosewater for Frank Crawford, .48. Very weary and overdone.

[1] Count Alberto Maggi, an Italian *littérateur*.

The twelve apostles shall judge the twelve tribes in
that the Christian doctrine judges the Jews.

"I lead a weary life of hurry and interruption."

"*November 18.* Weary hearts must, I think, be idle
hearts, for it is cheery even to be overworked. My
studies and experience have combined to show me the
difficulty of moral attainment, but both have made me
feel that with every average human being there is a
certain possible conjunction of conviction, affection,
and personality which, being effected, the individual
will see the reality of the ethical aspects of life and the
necessary following of happiness upon a good will and
its strenuous prosecution.

"I began Fichte's '*Wissenschaftslehre*' two or three
days ago.

"Gave a small party to Baron Osten Sacken. . . .
Peaceably if we can, forcibly if we must, makes the
difference between the beggar and the thief."

"*November 26.* Very unwell; a good day's work,
nevertheless."

"*November 27.* Better. Last week was too fatiguing
for a woman of my age. I cannot remember my forty-
seven years, and run about too much. The oratorio
should, I fear, be given up."

"*December 8.* I came in from Lexington last night
after the reading[1] in an open buggy with a strange
driver, a boy of eighteen, who when we were well under
way showed me a pistol, — a revolver, I think, — and
said that he never travelled at night without one. As
the boy's very face was unknown to me, the whole

[1] At the Lexington Lyceum for the Monument Fund.

adventure seemed bizarre. He brought me home to my own house. . . . Am writing on 'Representation.' . . . Man asks nothing so much as to be helped to self-control."

"*December 9.* Heard J. F. C. as usual. 'She hath done what she could' — a good text for me at this moment. Independently of ambition, vanity, pride, — all of which prompt all of us, I feel that I must do what my hand finds to do, taking my dictation and my reward from sources quite above human will and approbation."

"*December 19.* . . . Vicomte de Chabreuil came. We had a long, and to me splendid, conversation. Were I young this person would occupy my thoughts somewhat. Very intelligent, simple, and perfectly bred, also a *rosso*, — a rare feature in a Frenchman."

"*December 27.* Let me live until to-morrow, and not be ridiculous! I have a dinner party and an evening party to-day and night, and knowing myself to be a fool for my pains, am fain to desire that others may not find it out and reproach me as they discover it.

"Got hold of Fichte a little which rested my weary brain.

"My party proved very pleasant and friendly."

"*December 29.* . . . I read last night at the Club a poem, 'The Rich Man's Library,' which contrasts material and mental wealth, much to the disparagement of the former. I felt as if I ought to read it, having inwardly resolved never again to disregard that inner prompting which leaves us no doubt as to the authority of certain acts which present themselves to us for accomplishment. Having read the poem, however, I felt doubtful whether after all I had done well to read it in that company. I will hope, however, that it may prove not to have been utterly useless. The imperfection of that which we try to do well sometimes reacts severely upon us and discourages us from further effort. It should not."

"*December 31.* Ran about all day, but studied and wrote also.

"Farewell, old Diary, farewell, old Year! Good, happy and auspicious to me and mine, and to mankind, I prayed that you might be, and such I think you have been. To me you have brought valued experience and renewed study. You have introduced me to Fichte, you have given me the honor of a new responsibility, you have made me acquainted with some excellent personages, among them Baron McKaye, a youth of high and noble nature; Perabo, an artist of real genius. . . . You have taught me new lessons of the true meaning and discipline of life, — the which should make me more patient in all endurance, more strenuous in all endeavor. You have shown me more clearly the line of demarcation between different talents, pursuits, and characters. So I thank and bless your good days, looking to the Supreme from whom we receive all things. The most noticeable events of the year just passed, so far as I am concerned, are the following: the invitation received by me to read at the Century Club in New York. This reading was hindered by the death of my brother-in-law, J. N. Howe. The death of dear Uncle John. My journey to Washington to get Chev the

Greek appointment. Gurowski's death. Attendance at the American Academy of Science at Northampton in August. The editorship of the new weekly. My study of Fichte's '*Sittenlehre*' and the appearance of my essay on the 'Ideal State' in the 'Christian Examiner.' My reading at Lexington for the Monument Association. My being appointed a delegate from the Indiana Place Church to the Boston Conference of Unitarian and other Christian Churches. My readings at Northampton, Washington, and elsewhere are all set down in their place. The bitter opposition of my family renders this service a very difficult and painful one for me. I do not, therefore, seek occasions of performing it, not being quite clear as to the extent to which they ought to limit my efficiency; but when the word and the time come together I always try to give the one to the other and always shall. God instruct whichever of us is in the wrong about this. And may God keep mean and personal passions far removed from me in the coming years. The teaching of life has of late done much to wean me from them, but the true human requires culture and the false human suppression every day of our lives and as long as we live."

CHAPTER XII

GREECE AND OTHER LANDS

1867; *aet.* 48

OUR COUNTRY

On primal rocks she wrote her name,
Her towers were reared on holy graves;
The golden seed that bore her came
Swift-winged with prayer o'er ocean waves.

The Forest bowed his solemn crest,
And open flung his sylvan doors;
Meek Rivers led the appointed Guest
To clasp the wide-embracing shores;

Till, fold by fold, the broidered Land
To swell her virgin vestments grew,
While Sages, strong in heart and hand,
Her virtue's fiery girdle drew.

O Exile of the wrath of Kings!
O Pilgrim Ark of Liberty!
The refuge of divinest things,
Their record must abide in thee.

First in the glories of thy front
Let the crown jewel Truth be found;
Thy right hand fling with generous wont
Love's happy chain to farthest bound.

Let Justice with the faultless scales
Hold fast the worship of thy sons,
Thy commerce spread her shining sails
Where no dark tide of rapine runs.

So link thy ways to those of God,
So follow firm the heavenly laws,
That stars may greet thee, warrior-browed,
And storm-sped angels hail thy cause.

O Land, the measure of our prayers,
Hope of the world, in grief and wrong!
Be thine the blessing of the years,
The gift of faith, the crown of song.   J. W. H.

IN January, 1867, a new note is sounded.
"In the evening attended meeting in behalf of Crete,

at which Chev presided and spoke. Excellent as to matter, but always with a defective elocution, not sending his voice out. He was much and deservedly glorified by other speakers, and, indeed, his appearance on this occasion was most touching and interesting. Phillips was very fine; Huntington was careful, polished, and interesting. Andrew read the resolutions, with a splendid compliment to Chev."

Some months before this, in August, 1866, the Cretans had risen against their Turkish oppressors, and made a valiant struggle for freedom. From the first the Doctor had been deeply interested in the insurrection: now, as reports came of the sufferings of the brave mountaineers, and of their women and children, who had been sent to the mainland for safety, he felt impelled to help them as he had helped their fathers forty years before.

He was sixty-six years old, but looked much younger. When, at the first meeting called by him, he rose and said, "Forty-five years ago I was much interested in the Greek Revolution," the audience was amazed. His hair was but lightly touched with silver; his eyes were as bright, his figure as erect and martial, as when, in 1826, he had fought and marched under the Greek banner, and slept under the Greek stars, wrapped in his shaggy capote.

His appeal in behalf of Crete roused the ever-generous heart of Boston. Committees were formed, and other meetings were held, among them that just described. Governor Andrew's "splendid compliment" to him was given thus: —

"I venture, Mr. Chairman, to make one single suggestion — that if all of us were dumb to-night, if the eloquent voices which have stimulated our blood and inspired our hearts had been silent as the tomb, your presence, sir, would have been more eloquent than a thousand orations; when we remember that after the life-time of a whole generation of men, he who forty years ago bared his arm to seize the Suliote blade, speaks again with the voice of his age in defence of the cause of his youth."

Thirty-seven thousand dollars were raised for Crete, and in March, 1867, Dr. Howe sailed again for Greece on an errand of mercy. The Journal gives an outline of the busy winter: —

"The post is the poor man's valet. . . ."

"*January 12.* A busy and studious day; had the neighbors in after tea. Want clamors for relief, but calls for cure, which begins in discipline. . . ."

"*January 24.* N. P. Willis's funeral. Chev came home quite suddenly and asked me to go with him to the church, St. Paul's. The pallbearers were Longfellow and Lowell, Drs. Holmes and Howe, Whipple and Fields, T. B. Aldrich and I don't know who. Coffin covered with flowers. Appearance of the family interesting: the widow bowed and closely shrouded. Thus ends a man of perhaps first-rate genius, ruined by the adoption of an utterly frivolous standard of labor and of life. George IV and Bulwer have to answer for some of these failures.

"My tea party was delightful, friendly, not fashionable. We had a good talk, and a lovely, familiar time.

"Heard J. F. C. Took my dear Francesco [Marion Crawford] at his request, with great pleasure, feeling that he would find there a living Jesus immortal in influence, instead of the perfumed and embalmed mummy of orthodoxy. . . .

"Of that which is not clear one cannot have a clear idea. My reading in Fichte to-day is of the most confused."

"*February 7.* Chev came dancing in to tell me that Flossy is engaged to David Hall. His delight knew no bounds. I am also pleased, for David is of excellent character and excellent blood, the Halls being first-rate people and with no family infirmity (insanity or blindness). My only regret is that it must prove a long engagement, David being a very young lawyer."

"*February 14.* All's up, as I feared, with 'Northern Lights' in its present form. Gilmour proposes to go to New York and to change its form and character to that of a weekly newspaper. I of course retire from it and, indeed, despite my title of editor, have been only a reader of manuscripts and contributor — nothing more. I have not had power of any sort to make engagements."

The tenth number of "Northern Lights" was also the last, and we hear no more of the ill-fated magazine.

The Journal says nothing of the proposed trip to Greece, until February 15: —

"I had rather die, it seems to me, than decide wrongly about going to Europe and leaving the children. And yet I am almost sure I shall do so. Chev clearly wishes me to go. . . . Whether I go or stay, God help me to make the best of it. My desire to help Julia is a strong point in favor of the journey. It would be, I think, a turning-point for her."

Later she writes: —

"Chev has taken our passage in the Asia, which sails on the 13th proximo. So we have the note of preparation, and the prospect of change and separation makes us feel how happy we have been, in passing this whole winter together."

The remaining days were full of work of every kind. She gave readings here and there in aid of the Cretans.

"Ran about much: saw Miss Rogers's deaf pupils at Mrs. Lamson's, very interesting. . . . For the first time in three days got a peep at Fichte. Finished Jesse's 'George the Third.'

"Went to Roxbury to read at Mrs. Harrington's for the benefit of the Cretans. It was a literary and musical entertainment. Tickets, one dollar. We made one hundred dollars. My poems were very kindly received. Afterwards, in great haste, to Sophia Whitwell's,[1] where I received a great ovation, all members greeting me most affectionately. Presently Mr. [Josiah] Quincy, with some very pleasant and complimentary remarks on Dr. Howe and myself, introduced Mrs. Silsbee's farewell verses to me, which were cordial and feeling. Afterwards I read my valedictory verses, strung together in a very headlong fashion, but just as well liked as though I had bestowed more care upon them. A bouquet of flowers crowned the whole, really a very gratifying occasion."

[1] This was evidently a meeting of the " Brain Club."

"*March 13.* Departure auspicious. Dear Maud, Harry, and Flossy on board to say farewell, with J. S. Dwight, H. P. Warner, and other near friends. Many flowers; the best first day at sea I ever passed."

Julia and Laura were the happy two chosen to join this expedition, the other children staying with relatives and friends. From first to last the journey was one of deepest interest. The Journal keeps a faithful record of sight-seeing, which afterward took shape in a volume, "From the Oak to the Olive," published in 1868, and dedicated "To S. G. H., the strenuous champion of Greek liberty and of human rights."

It is written in the light vein of "A Trip to Cuba." In the first chapter she says: "The less we know about a thing, the easier it is to write about it. To give quite an assured and fluent account of a country, we should lose no time on our first arrival. The first impression is the strongest. Familiarity constantly wears off the edge of observation. The face of the new country astonishes us once, and once only."

Though much that she saw during this trip was already familiar to her, there is no lack of strength in the impression. She sees things with new eyes; the presence of "the neophytes," as she calls the daughters, gives an atmosphere of "first sight" to the whole.

In London she finds "the old delightful account reopened, the friendly visits frequent, and the luxurious invitations to dinner occupy every evening of our short week."

"*London.* Lunch with the Benzons, whose palatial

residence moved me not to envy. This seems an idle word, but I like to record my satisfaction in a simple, unencumbered life, without state of any kind, save my pleasant relations and my good position in my own country. Mrs. Benzon asked me to come alone to dinner in the evening. First, however, I called upon Arthur Mills at Hyde Park Gardens; then upon Mrs. Ambassadress Adams, who was quite cordial; then in frantic hurry home to dress. At Benzon's I met Robert Browning, a dear and sacred personage, dear for his own and his wife's sake. He sat next me at table and by and by spoke very kindly of my foolish verses [1] about himself and E. B. B. I mean he spoke of them with magnanimity. Of course my *present* self would not publish, nor I hope write, anything of the kind, but I launched the arrow in the easy petulance of those days, more occupied with its force and polish than with its direction."

"To Lady Stanley's 5 o'clock tea, where I met her daughter Lady Amberley and Sir Samuel Baker, the explorer of the sources of the Nile. Dined with the Benzons, meeting Browning again."

"Tea with Miss Cobbe. Met the Lyells. Dined with Males family, Greek, — a most friendly occasion. Afterwards went for a short time to Mrs. ——, a very wealthy Greek widow, who received us very ill. Heard there Mr. Ap Thomas, a Welsh harper who plays exceedingly well. The pleasure of hearing him scarcely compensated for Mrs. ——'s want of politeness, which was probably not intentional. Saw there Sir Samuel

[1] "Kenyon's Legacy," printed in *Later Lyrics*.

and Lady Baker, the latter wore an amber satin tunic over a white dress, and a necklace of lion's teeth."

"*April 5.* Breakfast with Mr. Charles Dalrymple at 2 Clarges Street, where we met Mr. Grant Duff, Baron McKaye, and others. Tea at Lady Trevelyan's, where I was introduced to Dean Stanley of Westminster . . . and young Milman, son of the Reverend H. M. Lady Stanley was Lady Augusta Bruce, a great favorite of the Queen. Dined at Argyll Lodge, found the Duchess serene and friendly; the Duke seemed hard and sensible, Lord Lorne, the eldest son, very pleasant, and Hon. Charles Howard and son most amiable, with more breeding, I should say, than the Duke. Chev was the hero of this occasion; the Duchess always liked him."

During this brief week, the Doctor had been in close communication with the Greeks of London, who one and all were eager to welcome him, and to bid him Godspeed on his errand. His business transacted, he felt that he must hurry on toward Greece. Some stay must be made in Rome, where our Aunt Louisa (now Mrs. Luther Terry) was anxiously expecting the party; but even this tie of affection and friendship could not keep the Doctor long from his quest. On May 1 he and Julia went to Greece, the others remaining for some weeks in Italy.

Sixteen years had passed since our mother's last visit to Rome. She found some changes in the city, but more vital ones in herself.

"I left Rome," she says, "after those days, with entire determination, but with infinite reluctance. America seemed the place of exile, Rome the home of sympathy and comfort. . . . And now I must confess that, after so many intense and vivid pages of life, this visit to Rome, once a theme of fervent and solemn desire, becomes a mere page of embellishment in a serious and instructive volume."

Here follows a disquisition on "the Roman problem for the American thinker"; the last passage gives her conclusion: —

"A word to my countrymen and countrywomen, who, lingering on the edge of the vase, are lured by its sweets, and fall into its imprisonment. It is a false, false superiority to which you are striving to join yourself. A prince of puppets is not a prince, but a puppet; a superfluous duke is no dux; a titular count does not count. Dresses, jewels, and equipages of tasteless extravagance; the sickly smile of disdain for simple people; the clinging together, by turns eager and haughty, of a clique that becomes daily smaller in intention, and whose true decline consists in its numerical increase — do not dream that these lift you in any true way — in any true sense. For Italians to believe that it does, is natural; for Englishmen to believe it, is discreditable; for Americans, disgraceful."

The Terrys were at this time living in Palazzo Odescalchi. Our mother observes that "the whole of my modest house in Boylston Place would easily, as to solid contents, lodge in the largest of those lofty rooms. The Place itself would equally lodge in the palace. I regard my re-found friends with wonder, and expect to see them execute some large and stately manœuvre, indicating their possession of all this space."

It was Holy Week when they arrived in Rome, and she was anxious that the "neophytes" should see as much as possible of its impressive ceremonies. She took them to St. Peter's to see the washing of the pilgrims' feet by noble Roman ladies, and to hear the "Miserere" in the Sistine Chapel. These functions are briefly chronicled in the Journal and more fully in "From the Oak to the Olive."

"Solid fact as the performance of the *functions* remains, for us it assumes a forcible unreality, through the impeding intervention of black dresses and veils, with what should be women under them. But as these creatures push like battering-rams, and caper like he-goats, we shall prefer to adjourn the question of their humanity, and to give it the benefit of a doubt. We must except, however, our countrywomen from dear Boston, who were not seen otherwise than decently and in order."

A vivid description follows of the ceremonies of Good Friday and Easter Sunday, ending with the illumination of St. Peter's.

"A magical and unique spectacle it certainly is, with the well-known change from the paper lanterns to the flaring *lampions*. Costly is it of human labor, and perilous to human life. And when I remembered that those employed in it receive the sacrament beforehand, in order that imminent death may not find them out of a state of grace, I thought that its beauty did not so much signify."

In the Journal she writes, April 19: "It is the golden calf of old which has developed into the papal bull."

At a concert she saw the Abbé Liszt, "whose vanity and desire to attract attention were most apparent."

Though the sober light of middle age showed Rome less magical than of old, yet the days were full of delight.

"In these scarce three weeks," she cries, "how much have we seen, how little recorded and described! So sweet has been the fable, that the intended moral has passed like an act in a dream — a thing of illusion and intention, not of fact. Impotent am I, indeed, to describe the riches of this Roman world, — its treasures, its pleasures, its flatteries, its lessons. Of so much that one receives, one can give again but the smallest shred, — a leaf of each flower, a scrap of each garment, a proverb for a sermon, a stave for a song. So be it; so, perhaps, it is best."

"Last Sunday I attended a Tombola at Piazza Navona. . . . I know the Piazza of old. Sixteen years since I made many a pilgrimage thither, in search of Roman trash. I was not then past the poor amusement of spending money for the sake of spending it. The foolish things I brought home moved the laughter of my little Roman public. I appeared in public with some forlorn brooch or dilapidated earring; the giddy laughed outright, and the polite gazed quietly. My rooms were the refuge of all broken-down vases and halting candelabra. I lived on the third floor of a modest lodging, and all the wrecks of art that neither first, second, nor fourth would buy, found their way into my parlor, and stayed there at my expense. I recall some of these adornments to-day. Two heroes, in painted wood, stood in my dark little entry. A gouty Cupid in bas-relief encumbered my mantelpiece. Two forlorn figures in black and white glass recalled the auction whose unlucky prize they had been. And Horace Wallace, coming to talk of art and poetry, on my red sofa, sometimes saluted me with a paroxysm of merriment, provoked by the sight of my last purchase. Those days are not now. Of their accumulations I retain but a fragment or two. Of their delights remain a tender memory, a childish wonder at my own childishness. To-day, in heathen Rome, I can find better amusement than those shards and rags were ever able to represent."

On May 26 she writes in her Journal: —

"I remembered the confusion of my mind when I was here sixteen years ago and recognized how far more than equivalent for the vivacity of youth, now gone, is the gain of a steadfast standard of good and happiness. To desire supremely ends which are incompatible with no one's happiness and which promote the good of all — this even as an ideal is a great gain from the small and eager covetousness of personal desires. Religion gives this steadfast standard whose pursuit is happiness. Therefore let him who seeks religion be glad that he seeks the only true good of which, indeed, we constantly fail, and yet in seeking it are constantly renewed. . . . Studios of Mozier and of Rogers — the former quite full. Both have considerable skill, neither has genius. The statues of Miss Hosmer are marble silences — they have nothing to say."

Greece was before her. On June 17 the Journal
says: —

"Acroceraunian mountains, shore of Albania. Nothing strikes me — I have been struck till I am stricken
down. *Sirocco* and head wind — vessel laboring with
the sea, I with Guizot's 'Meditations,' which also have
some head wind in them. They seem to me inconclu-
sive in statement and commonplace in thought, yet
presenting some facts of interest. A little before 2 P.M.
we passed Fano, the island on which Calypso could not
console herself, and no wonder. At 2 we enter the
channel of Corfù."

At Corfù a Turkish pacha came on board with his
harem, to our lively interest. The Journal gives every
observable detail of the somewhat squalid *ménage*,
from the pacha's lilac trousers down to the dress of
his son and heir, a singularly dirty baby. She remarks
that "An Irish servant's child in Boston, got up for
Sunday, looks far cleaner and better."

The pacha looked indolent and good-natured, and
sent coffee to her before she disembarked at Syra. Here
she was met by Mr. Evangelides, the "Christy" of her
childhood, the Greek boy befriended by her father.
He was now a prosperous man in middle life, full of
affectionate remembrance of the family at 16 Bond
Street, and of gratitude to "dear Mr. Ward." He welcomed her most cordially, and introduced her not only
to the beauties of Syra, but to its principal inhabitants,
the governor of the Cyclades, the archbishop, and Doctor Hahn, the scientist and antiquary. She conversed
with the archbishop in German.

"He deplored the absence of a state religion in America. I told him that the progress of religion in our country seemed to establish the fact that society attains the best religious culture through the greatest religious liberty. He replied that the members should all be united under one head. 'Yes,' said I, 'but the Head is invisible'; and he repeated after me, 'Indeed, the Head is invisible.' I will here remark that nothing could have been more refreshing to the New England mind than this immediate introduction to the theological opinions of the East."

A few hours later his Grace returned the visit, seeking in his turn, it would appear, the refreshment of a new point of view.

"We resumed our conversation of the morning, and the celibacy of the clerical hierarchy came next in order in our discussion. The father was in something of a strait between the Christian dignification of marriage and its ascetic depreciation. The arrival of other visitors forced us to part, with this interesting point still unsettled."

Arrived in Athens, the travellers found the "veteran" (as the Doctor is called throughout her book) in full tide of work. The apartment in the pleasant hotel swarmed with dark-eyed patriots, with Cretan refugees, with old men who had known "Xaos" in the brave days of old, with young men eager to see and greet the old Philhellene. Among the latter came Michael Anagnostopoulos, who was to become his secretary, and later his son-in-law and his successor at the Perkins Institution for the Blind. The ladies of

Athens came too, full of hospitable feeling. There were visits, deputations, committee meetings, all day long, and in the evening parties and receptions.

Spite of all this, her first impression of Athens was melancholy. She was oppressed and depressed at sight of the havoc wrought by Time and war upon monuments that should have been sacred. Speaking of the Parthenon, she exclaims: —

"And Pericles caused it to be built; and this, his marble utterance, is now a lame sentence, with half its sense left out. . . .

"Here is the Temple of Victory. Within are the bas-reliefs of the Victories arriving in the hurry of their glorious errands. Something so they tumbled in upon us when Sherman conquered the Carolinas, and Sheridan the Valley of the Shenandoah, when Lee surrendered, and the glad President went to Richmond. One of these Victories is untying her sandal, in token of permanent abiding. Yet all of them have trooped away long since, scared by the hideous havoc of barbarians. And the bas-reliefs, their marble shadows, have all been battered and mutilated into the saddest mockery of their original tradition. The statue of Wingless Victory, that stood in the little temple, has long been absent and unaccounted for. But the only Victory that the Parthenon now can seize or desire is this very Wingless Victory, the triumph of a power that retreats not — the power of Truth.

"I give heed to all that is told me in a dreary and desolate manner. It is true, no doubt, — this was, and this, and this; but what I see is, none the less, empti-

ness, — the broken eggshell of a civilization which
Time has hatched and devoured. And this incapacity
to reconstruct the past goes with me through most of
my days in Athens. The city is so modern, and its
circle so small! The trumpeters who shriek around the
Theseum in the morning, the café-keeper who taxes
you for a chair beneath the shadow of the Olympian
columns, the *custode* who hangs about to see that you
do not break the broken marbles further, or carry off
their piteous fragments, all of these are significant of
modern Greece; but the ruins have nothing to do with it.

"Poor as these relics are, in comparison with what
one would wish them to be, they are still priceless. This
Greek marble is the noblest in descent; it needs no
eulogy. These forms have given the models for a hundred familiar and commonplace works, which caught a
little gleam of their glory, squaring to shapeliness some
town-house of the West, or Southern bank or church.
So well do we know them in the prose of modern design
that we are startled at seeing them transfigured in the
poetry of their own conception. Poor old age! poor old
columns!"

There was a colony of Cretan refugees at Nauplia,
another at Argos, both in dire need of food and clothing. The Doctor asked the Government for a steamer,
and received the Parados, in which he promptly embarked with wife, daughters, and supplies, and sailed
for Nauplia.

The travelling library of this expedition was reduced
to "a copy of Machiavelli's '*Principe*,' a volume of
Muir's 'Greece,' and a Greek phrase-book on Ollen-

dorff's principle." Our mother also took some worsted work, but she suffered such lively torment from the bites of mosquitoes and sand-fleas on her hands and wrists that she could make little use of this. To one recalling the anguish of this visitation, it seems amazing that she could even write in her Journal; indeed, the entries, though tolerably regular, are brief and condensed.

"*June 24.* . . . We arrived in the harbor of Nauplia by 7 P.M. . . . Crowd in the street. Bandit's head just cut off and brought in. We go to the prefect's house, . . . he offers us his roof — sends out for mattresses. . . . I mad with my mosquito bites. Mattresses on the floor. We women lie down four in a row, very thankfully. . . ."

At the fortress of Nauplia, she was deeply touched by the sight of a band of prisoners waiting, in an inner court, for the death to which they had been condemned.

"'Do not pity them, madam!' said the major; 'they have all done deeds worthy of death.'

"But how not to pity them," she cries, "when they and we are made of the same fragile human stuff, that corrupts so easily to crime, and is always redeemable, if society would only afford the costly process of redemption!

"As I looked at them, I was struck by a feeling of their helplessness. What is there in the world so helpless as a disarmed criminal? No inner armor has he to beat back the rude visiting of society; no secure soul-citadel, where scorn and anger cannot reach him. He has thrown away the jewel of his manhood; human law crushes its empty case. But the final Possessor and Creditor is unseen."

After Nauplia came Argos, where the Cretan refugees were gathered in force. Here the travellers had the great pleasure of helping to clothe the half-naked women and children. Many of the garments had been made by Florence and her young friends in their sewing circle; the book recalls "how the little maidens took off their feathery bonnets and dainty gloves, wielding the heavy implements of cutting, and eagerly adjusting the arms and legs, the gores and gathers! With patient pride the mother trotted off to the bakery, that a few buns might sustain these strenuous little cutters and sewers, whose tongues, however active over the charitable work, talked, we may be sure, no empty nonsense nor unkind gossip. For charity begins indeed at home, in the heart, and, descending to the fingers, rules also the rebellious member whose mischief is often done before it is meditated. At sight of these well-made garments a little swelling of the heart seized us, with the love and pride of remembrance so dear."

The Journal describes briefly the distribution among the Cretans, "some extremely bare and ragged, with suffering little children. Our calico skirts and sacks made a creditable appearance. We gave with as much judgment as the short time permitted. Each name was called by a list, and as they came in we hastily selected garments: the dresses, however, gave out before we had quite finished. . . . Ungrateful old woman, who wanted a gown and would hardly take a chemise.

Meddlesome lady of the neighborhood bringing in her favorites out of order."

Generous as the supplies from America were, they did not begin to meet the demand. After visiting Crete (in spite — perhaps partly because — of the fact that a high price was set on his head) and the various colonies of refugees, the Doctor felt that further aid must be obtained. Accordingly, the journeyings of the little party after leaving Greece were for the most part only less hurried than the earlier ones, the exception being a week of enchantment spent in Venice, awaiting the Doctor, who had been called back to Athens at the moment of departure.

The Journal tells of Verona, Innsbrück, Munich. Then came flying glimpses of Switzerland, with a few days' rest at Geneva, where she had the happiness of meeting her sister once more; finally, Paris and the Exposition of 1867.

After a visit to Napoleon's tomb, she writes: "Spent much of the afternoon in beginning a piece of tapestry after a Pompeiian pattern copied by me on the spot."

Worsted work was an unfailing accompaniment of her journeyings in those days; indeed, until age and weariness came upon her, she never failed to have some piece of work on hand. When her eyes could no longer compass cross-stitch embroidery, she amused herself with knitting, or with "hooking" small rugs.

Her sketchbook was another resource while travelling. She had no special talent for drawing, but took great pleasure in it, and was constantly making pencil sketches of persons and things that interested her. We even find patterns of Pompeiian mosaic or of historic needlework reproduced in the Journal.

From Paris the travellers hurried to Belgium, and after a glance at Brussels, spent several days in Antwerp with great contentment. Both here and in Brussels she had been much interested in the beautiful lace displayed on every hand. She made several modest purchases, not without visitings of conscience.

"I went to the Cathedral. . . . I saw to-day the Elevation of the Cross [Rubens] to special advantage. As I stood before it, I felt lifted for a moment above the mean and foolish pleasures of shopping, etc., on which I have of late dwelt so largely. The heroic face before me said, 'You cannot have those and these, cannot have Christian elevation with heathen triviality.' That moment showed me what a picture can do. I hope I shall remember it, though I do plead guilty of late to an extraordinary desire for finery of all sorts. It is as if I were going home to play the part of Princess in some great drama, which is not at all likely to be the case."

Yet the same day she went to the beguinage and bought "Flossy's wedding hdkf, 22 frc — lace scarf, 3 fr., piece of edging, 4 fr."

Among the notabilities of Antwerp in those days was Charles Félu, the armless painter. He was to be seen every day in the Museum, copying the great masters with skill and fidelity. He interested the Doctor greatly, and the whole party made acquaintance with him. A letter from one of them describes the meeting with this singular man: —

"As we were looking round at the pictures, I noticed a curious painting arrangement. There was a platform raised about a foot above the floor, with two stools, one in front of the other, and an easel. Presently the artist entered. The first thing he did, on stepping on the platform, was to kick off his shoes. He then seated himself (Heaven knows how) on one stool and placed his feet in front of him on the other, close before the easel. I was surprised to see that his stockings had no toes to them. But my surprise was much greater when I saw him take the palette in one foot and the brush in the other, and begin to paint. The nicety with which he picked out his brushes, rubbed the paints, erased with his great toe, etc., was a mystery to me. . . . In a few minutes he put his foot into his pocket, drew out a paper from which he took his card, and *footed* it politely to papa. . . . He shaves himself, plays billiards (and well, too), cards, and dominoes, cuts up his meat and feeds himself, etc."

"*October 1.* By accident went to the same hotel [in Bruges] to which I went twenty-four years ago, a bride. I recognized a staircase with a balustrade of swans each holding a stiff bulrush in its mouth. . . . Made a little verse thereupon."

From Belgium the way led to London; thence, after a brief and delightful visit to the Bracebridges at Atherstone, to Liverpool, where the China awaited her passengers. The voyage was long and stormy, thirteen days: the Journal speaks chiefly of its discomforts; but on the second Sunday we read: "X. preached a horrible sermon — stood up and mocked at philosophy in good

English and bad Christianity. He failed alike of satire and of sense, and talked like a small Pharisee of two thousand years ago. 'Not much like the Sermon on the Mount,' quoth I; not theology enough to stand examination at Andover. Bluejackets in a row, unedified, as were most of us."

On October 25 the travellers landed in Boston, thankful to be again on firm land, and to see the family unit once more complete.

"The dear children came on board to greet us — all well, and very happy at our return."

Thus ends the story, seven months of wonder and of delight.

At her Club, soon after, she gave the following epitome of the trip, singing the doggerel lines to an improvised tune which matched them in absurdity: —

Oh! who were the people you saw, Mrs. Howe,
When you went where the Cretans were making a row?
Kalopathaki — Rodocanachi —
Paparipopoulos — Anagnostopoulos —
Nicolaïdes — Paraskevaïdes —
These were the people that saw Mrs. Howe
When she went where the Cretans were making a row.

Oh! what were the projects you made, Mrs. Howe,
When you went where the Cretans were making a row?
Emancipation — civilization — redintegration of a great nation,
Paying no taxes, grinding no axes —
Flinging the Ministers over the banisters.
These were the projects of good Mrs. Howe
When she went where the Cretans were making a row.

.   .   .   .

Oh! give us a specimen, dear Mrs. Howe,
Of the Greek that you learned and are mistress of now.
Potichomania — Mesopotamia.
Tatterdemalion — episcopalian —

Megalotherium — monster inferium —
Scoulevon — auctrion — infant phenomenon.
Kyrie ticamete — what's your calamity?
Pallas Athenae Aun,
Favors no Fenian.
Such is the language that learned Mrs. Howe,
In the speech of the Gods she is mistress of now.

CHAPTER XIII

CONCERNING CLUBS

1867–1871; *aet.* 48–52

"Behold," he said, "Life's great impersonate,
Nourished by labor!
Thy gods are gone with old-time faith and fate;
Here is thy Neighbor."

J. W. H., "A New Sculptor."

AFTER such a rush of impression and emotion, the return to everyday life could not fail to bring about a corresponding drop in our mother's mental barometer. Vexations awaited her. The Boylston Place house had been let for a year, and — Green Peace being also let on a long lease — the reunited family took refuge for the winter in the "Doctor's Wing" of the Perkins Institution.

Again, an extremely unfavorable critique of "Later Lyrics" in a prominent review distressed her greatly; her health was more or less disturbed; above all, the sudden death of John A. Andrew, the beloved and honored friend of many years, saddened both her and the Doctor deeply.

All these things affected her spirits to some extent, so that the Journal for the remainder of 1867 is in a minor key.

". . . In despair about the house. . . ."

On hearing of the separation of Charles Sumner from his wife: —

"For men and women to come together is nature —

for them to live together is art — to live well, high
art."

"*November 21.* Melancholy, thinking that I did but
poorly last evening [at a reading from her 'Notes on
Travel' at the Church of the Disciples]. . . . At the
afternoon concert felt a savage and tearful melancholy,
a profound friendlessness. In the whole large assembly
I saw no one who would help me to do anything
worthy of my powers and life-ideal. I have so dreamed
of high use that I cannot decline to a life of amusement
or of small occupation."

". . . I believe in God, but am utterly weary of man."

After a disappointment: —

". . . To church, where my mental condition speedily
improved. Sermon on the Good Samaritan. Hymns
and prayers all congenial and consoling. Felt much
consoled and uplifted out of all petty discords and disappointments. A disappointment should be digested
in patience, not vomited in spleen. Bitter morsels
nourish the soul, not less perhaps than sweet. Thought
of the following: Moral philosophy begins with the
fact of accepting human life."

In November came a new interest which was to
mean much to her.

"Early in town to attend the Free Religious Club.
Weiss's essay was well written, but encumbered with
illustrations rarely pertinent. It was neither religion,
philosophy, nor cosmology, but a confusion of all three,
showing the encyclopædic aim of his culture. It advocated the natural to the exclusion of the supernatural.
Being invited to speak, I suggested real and ideal as a

better antithesis for thought than natural and supernatural. Weiss did all that his method would allow. He is a man of parts. I cannot determine how much, but the Parkerian standard, or a similar one, has deformed his reasoning powers. He seeks something better than Christianity without having half penetrated the inner significance of that religion.

"Alcott spoke in the idealistic direction. Also Wasson very well. Lucretia Mott exceptionally well, a little rambling, but with true womanly intuitions of taste and of morality."

This association of thinkers was afterwards known as the "Boston Radical Club." She has much to say about it in her "Reminiscences."

"I did, indeed," she says, "hear at these meetings much that pained and even irritated me. The disposition to seek outside the limits of Christianity for all that is noble and inspiring in religious culture, and to recognize especially within these limits the superstition and intolerance which have been the bane of all religions — this disposition, which was frequently manifested both in the essays presented and in their discussion, offended not only my affections, but also my sense of justice. . . .

"Setting this one point aside, I can but speak of the Club as a high congress of souls, in which many noble thoughts were uttered. Nobler than any special view or presentation was the general sense of the dignity of human character and of its affinity with things divine, which always gave the master tone to the discussions."

She says elsewhere of the Radical Club: —

"The really radical feature in it was the fact that the thoughts presented at its meetings had a root; were in that sense radical. . . . Here I have heard Wendell Phillips, and Oliver Wendell Holmes, John Weiss and James Freeman Clarke, Athanase Coquerel, the noble French Protestant preacher; William Henry Channing, worthy nephew of his great uncle; Colonel Higginson, Doctor Bartol, and many others. Extravagant things were sometimes said, no doubt, and the equilibrium of ordinary persuasion was not infrequently disturbed for a time. But the satisfaction of those present when a sound basis of thought was vindicated and established is indeed pleasant in remembrance. . . ."

"To Dickens's second reading, which I enjoyed very much. The 'wreck' in 'David Copperfield' was finely given. His appearance is against success; the face is rather commonplace, seen at a distance, and very red if seen through a glass: the voice worn and *blasé*."

". . . Club in the evening, at which my nonsense made people laugh, as I wished. . . ."

"A little intoxicated with the pleasure of having made people laugh. A fool, however, can often do this better than a wise man. I look earnestly for a higher task. Yet innocent, intelligent laughter is not to be despised."

"Was taken with verses in church. They did not prove nearly as good as I had hoped. . . ."

"Made three beds, to help Bridget, who had the washing alone. Read a difficult chapter in Fichte."

"Studied and worried as usual, — Fichte and Greek. . . ."

"Have not been strenuous enough about the Cretan Fair. . . ."

Any lack of strenuousness about the Cretan Fair was amply atoned for.

An "Appeal" was published, written by her and signed by Julia Ward Howe, Emily Talbot, Sarah E. Lawrence, Caroline A. Mudge, and Abby W. May.

"What shall we say? They are a great way off, but they are starving and perishing, as none in our midst can starve and perish, and we Americans are among the few persons to whom they can look for help."

In this cry for aid we hear the voice of both parents. The response was cordial and generous. The fair was held in Easter Week, at the Boston Music Hall, and recalled on a smaller scale the glories of the war-time fairs. Of the great labor of preparation, the Journal gives a lively impression; and "speaking for Crete" was added to the other burdens borne by her and the Doctor.

She could not give up her studies; the entries for the winter of 1867–68 are a curious mingling of Fichte and committees, with here and there a prayer for spiritual help and guidance, which shows her over-wrought condition.

Another interest had come to her from the visit to Greece: the study of ancient Greek. Latin had been her lifelong friend, but she had always longed for the sister classic; now the time was ripe for it. She made a beginning in Athens, not only picking up a good deal

of modern Greek, but attacking the ancient language
with the aid of primer and phrase-book. A valuable
teacher was at hand in Michael Anagnos,[1] who
was aiding the Doctor as secretary, and preparing
himself for the principal work of his life. Anagnos
encouraged and assisted her in the new study, which
became one of her greatest delights. She looked forward to a Greek lesson as girls do to a ball; in later life
she was wont to say, "My Greek is my diamond necklace!"

"*January 1, 1868.* May I this year have energy,
patience, good-will and good faith. May I be guilty
of no treason against duty and my best self. May I
acquire more system, order, and wisdom in the use
of things. May I, if God wills, carry out some of my
plans for making my studies useful to others. This is
much to ask, but not too much of Him who giveth
all." 288

"*January 24.* A dreadfully busy day. Meeting of
General Committee on Cretan Fair. . . . Felt overcome with fatigue, and nervous and fretful, but I am
quite sure that I do not rave as I used to do. . . ."

"*January 26.* Some mental troubles have ended
in a determination to hold fast till death the liberty
wherewith Christ has made me free. The joyous belief
that his doctrine of influences can keep me from all
that I should most greatly dread, lifts me up like a pair
of strong wings. 'I shall run and not be weary. I shall

---

[1] Formerly Anagnostopoulos. He dropped the last three syllables soon
after coming to this country.

walk and not faint.' At church the first hymn contained this line: —

"'Her fathers' God before her moved' —

which quite impressed me, for my father's piety and the excellence of other departed relatives have always of late years been a support and pledge to me of my own good behavior."

. . . .

"The thief's heart, the wanton's brow, may accompany high talent and geniality of temperament; but thanks be to God they *need* not."

". . . Wished I could make a fine poetic picture of Paul preaching at Mars Hill. On the one side, the glittering statues and brilliant mythology — on the other, the simplicity of the Christian life and doctrine. But to-day no pictures came."

. . . .

"Got Anagnos to help me read two odes of Anacreon. This was a great pleasure."

. . . .

"Much business — no Greek lesson. I was feeble in mind and body, and brooded over the loss of the lesson in a silly manner. Habit is to me not second, but first nature, and I easily become mechanical and fixed in my routine. . . . I confess that to lay down Greek now would be to die, like Moses, in sight of the promised land. All my life I have longed for this language. . . ."

"All of these days are mixed of satisfaction and dissatisfaction. I am pretty well content with my work, not as well with myself. I feel the need of earnest prayer and divine help. . . ."

"I had been invited to read the essay to the Radical Religious Club on this day at 10 A.M. I asked leave for Anagnos and took him with me. My dæmon [Socratic] had told me to read 'Doubt and Belief,' so I chose this and read it. I find my dæmon justified. It seemed to have a certain fitness in calling forth discussion. Mr. Emerson first spoke very beautifully, then Mr. Alcott, these two sympathizing in my view. Wasson followed, a little off, but with a very friendly contrast. . . . Much of this talk was very interesting. It was all marked by power and sincerity, but Emerson and Alcott understood my essay better than the others except J. F. C. I introduced Anagnos to Emerson. I told him that he had seen the Olympus of New England. Thought of my dear lost son, dead in this house [13 Chestnut Street, where the meeting was held]. Anagnos is a dear son to me. I brought him home to dinner, and count this a happy day."

·   ·   ·   ·   ·   ·   ·   ·

"I have heard the true word of God to-day from Frederick Hedge — a sermon on Love as the true bond of society, which lifted my weak soul as on the strong wings of a cherub. The immortal truths easily lost sight of in our everyday weakness and passion stood out to-day so strong and clear that I felt their healing power as if Christ had stood and touched my blinded eyes with his divine finger. So be it always! *Esto perpetua!*"

On April 13 the fair opened; a breathless week followed. She was much exhausted after it, but in a few days "began to rehearse for Festival." [1]

---

[1] The Handel and Haydn Festival.

"After extreme depression, I begin to take heart a little. Almighty God help me!

"Greek lesson — rehearsal in the evening — choral symphony and *Lobgesang*."

During the summer of 1868 she had great pleasure in reading some of her essays at Newport, in the Unitarian Church. She notes in her "Reminiscences" that one lady kissed her after the reading, saying, "This is the way I want to hear women speak"; and that Mrs. P—— S——, on hearing the words, "If God works, madam, you can afford to work also!" rose and went out, saying, "I won't listen to such stuff as this!"

The parlor readings brought her name into wider prominence. She began to receive invitations to read and speak in public.

Mr. Emerson wrote to her concerning her philosophical readings: "The scheme is excellent — to read thus — so new and rare, yet so grateful to all parties. It costs genius to invent our simplest pleasures."

The winter of 1867–68 saw the birth of another institution which was to be of lifelong interest to her: the New England Woman's Club. This, one of the earliest of women's clubs, was organized on February 16, 1868, with Mrs. Caroline M. Severance, in whose mind the idea had first taken shape, as president. Its constitution announces the objects of the association as "primarily, to furnish a quiet, central resting-place, and place of meeting in Boston, for the comfort and convenience of its members: and ultimately to become an organized social centre for united thought and action."

How far the second clause has outdone and outshone the first, is known to all who know anything of the history of women's clubs. From the New England Woman's Club and its cousin Sorosis, founded a month later in New York, has grown the great network of clubs which, like a beneficent railway system of thought and good-will, penetrates every nook and corner of this country.

Our mother was one of the first vice-presidents of the Club, and from 1871 to her death in 1910, with two brief intervals, its president. Among all the many associations with which she was connected this was perhaps the nearest to her heart. "My dear Club!" no other organization brought such a tender ring to her voice. She never willingly missed a meeting; the monthly teas were among her great delights. The Journal has much to say about the Club: "a good meeting"; "a thoughtful, earnest meeting," are frequent entries. "Why!" she cried once, "we may be living in the Millennium without knowing it!"

In her "Reminiscences," after telling how she attended the initial meeting, and "gave a languid assent to the measure proposed," she adds: —

"Out of this small beginning was gradually developed the plan of the New England Woman's Club, a strong and stately association, destined, I believe, to last for many years, and having behind it, at this time of my writing, a record of three decades of happy and acceptable service."

The Club movement was henceforth to be one of her widest interests. To thousands of elder women in the late sixties and early seventies it came like a new gospel of activity and service. They had reared their children and seen them take flight; moreover, they had fought through the war, their hearts in the field, their fingers plying needle and thread. They had been active in committees and commissions the country over; had learned to work with and beside men, finding joy and companionship and inspiration in such work. How could they go back to the chimney-corner life of the fifties? In answer to their question — an answer from Heaven, it seemed — came the women's clubs, with their opportunities for self-culture and for public service.

At first Society looked askance at the movement. What? Women's clubs? They would take women away from the Home, which was their Sphere! Shocking! Besides, it might make them Strong-Minded! Horrible! ("But," said J. W. H., "I would rather be strong-minded than weak-minded!")

Possibly influenced in some measure by such plaints as these, the early clubs devoted themselves for the most part to study, and their range of activities was strictly limited and defined. This, however, could not last. The Doctor used to say, "You may as well refuse to let out the growing boy's trousers as refuse larger and larger liberty to his growing individuality!" Even so the club petticoats had to be lengthened and amplified.

Our mother, with all her love of study, realized that no individual or group of individuals must neglect the present with its living issues for any past, however

beautiful. She threw her energies into widening the
club horizon. "Don't tie too many *nots* in your constitution!" she would say to a young club; and then
she would tell how Florence Nightingale cut the
Gordian knots of red tape in the Crimea.

Did the constitution enforce such and such limits?
Ah! but committees were not thus limited; let a committee be appointed, to do what the club could not!
(This was what the Doctor called "whipping the devil
round the stump!")

Many and many a reform had its beginning in one
of those quiet Park Street rooms of the "N. E. W. C."
"When I want anything in Boston remedied," said
Edward Everett Hale, "I go down to the New England
Woman's Club!"

When the General Federation of Women's Clubs
was formed in 1892, our mother served on the board
of directors for four years, and was then made an
honorary vice-president. She was also president of
the Massachusetts State Federation from 1893 to
1898, and thereafter honorary president

Dr. Holmes once said to her, "Mrs. Howe, I consider
you eminently clubable"; and he added that he himself was not. He told us why, when he adopted the
title of "Autocrat of the Breakfast-Table." The most
brilliant of talkers, he did not care to listen, as a good
club member must. Now, she too loved talking, but
perhaps she loved listening even more. No one who
knew her in her later years can forget how intently she
listened, how joyously she received information of
any and every kind. She never was tired; she always

wanted more. All human experience thrilled her; the choreman, the dressmaker, the postman, the caller; one and all, she hung on their words. After a half-hour with her, seeing her face alight with sympathy, her delicate lips often actually forming the words as he spoke them, the dullest person might go away on air, feeling himself a born *raconteur*. What she said once of Mr. Emerson, "He always came into a room as if he expected to receive more than he gave!" was true of herself.

To return to the clubs! At a biennial meeting of the General Federation in Philadelphia, she said: "What did the club life give me? Understanding of my own sex; faith in its moral and intellectual growth. Like so many others, I saw the cruel wrongs and vexed problems of our social life, but I did not know that hidden away in its own midst was a reserve force destined to give precious aid in the righting of wrongs, and in the solution of discords. In the women's clubs I found the immense power which sympathy exercises in bringing out the best aspirations of the woman nature. . . . To guard against dangers, we must do our utmost to uphold and keep in view the high object which has, in the first instance, called us together; and let this be no mere party catchword or cry, as East against West, or North against South. We can afford to meet as citizens of one common country, and to love and serve the whole as one."

She believed firmly in maintaining the privacy of club life. "The club is a larger home," she said, "and we wish to have the immunities and defences of home;

therefore we do not wish the public present, even by its attorney, the reporter."

The three following years were important ones to the Howe family.

Lawton's Valley was sold, to our great and lasting grief: and — after a summer spent at Stevens Cottage near Newport — the Doctor bought the place now known as "Oak Glen," scarce half a mile from the Valley; a place to become only less dear to the family. No. 19 Boylston Place was also sold, and he bought No. 32 Mount Vernon Street, a sunny, pleasant house whose spacious rooms and tall windows recalled the Chestnut Street house, always regretted.

Here life circled ever faster and faster, fuller and fuller. Our father, though beginning to feel the weight of years, had not yet begun to "take in sail," but continued to pile labor on labor, adding the new while never abandoning the old. For our mother clubs, societies, studies were multiplying, while for both family cares and interests were becoming more and more complicated. The children were now mostly grown. To the mother's constant thought and anxiety about their teeth, their hair, their eyes, their music, their dancing — to say nothing of the weightier matters of the law — was added the consideration of their ball dresses, their party slippers, their partners. She went with the daughters to ball and assembly; if they danced, she was happy; if not, there was grief behind the cheerful smile, and a sigh was confided to the Journal next day.

Romance hovered over No. 32 Mount Vernon Street.

THE CHILDREN OF SAMUEL G. AND JULIA WARD HOWE, 1869-1874

Maud   Laura Elizabeth

Henry Marion

Julia Romana   Florence Marion

The Greek lessons which were to mean so much to Julia and Laura were brought to a sudden end by the engagement of Julia to the Greek teacher, Michael Anagnos. Florence (who was now housekeeper, lightening our mother's cares greatly) was already engaged to David Prescott Hall; while Laura's engagement to Henry Richards was announced shortly after Julia's.

The three marriages followed at intervals of a few months. Meantime Harry, whose youthful pranks had been the terror of both parents, had graduated from Harvard, and was now, after two years [1] at the Massachusetts Institute of Technology, beginning his chosen work as a metallurgist.

She wrote of this beloved son: —

> God gave my son a palace,
> And a kingdom to control;
> The palace of his body,
> The kingdom of his soul.

In childhood and boyhood this "palace" was inhabited by a tricksy sprite. At two years Harry was pulling the tails of the little dogs on the Roman Pincio; at eighteen he was filling the breasts of the college authorities with the same emotions inspired by his father in the previous generation.

"Howe," said the old President of Brown University, when the Chevalier called to pay his respects on his return from Greece, "I am afraid of you now! There may be a fire-cracker under my chair at this moment!"

[1] 1869–1871. He took the course of geology and mining engineering, graduating at the head of his class.

Once out of college, it fared with the son as with the father. The current of restless energy hitherto devoted to "monkey shines" (as the Doctor called them) was now turned into another channel. Work, hardly less arduous and unremitting than his father's, became the habit of his life. Science claimed him, and her he served with the same singleness of purpose, the same intensity of devotion with which his parents served the causes that claimed them. He married, in 1874, Fannie, daughter of Willard Gay, of Troy, New York.

We love to recall the time at this house on Beacon Hill. We remember it as a cheerful house, ringing with song and laughter, yet with a steady undercurrent of work and thought; the "precious time," not to be interrupted; the coming and going of grave men and earnest women, all bent on high and hopeful errands, all seeking our two Wise Ones for counsel, aid, sympathy; the coming and going also of a steady stream of "lame ducks" of both sexes and all nationalities, all requiring help, most of them getting it; yet, as ever, the father leaving State Charities and Reforms, the mother flying from Fichte or Xenophon, at any real or fancied need of any child. It is thus that we love to think of No. 32 Mount Vernon Street, the last of the many homes in which we were all together.

CHAPTER XIV

THE PEACE CRUSADE

1870–1872; *aet.* 51–53

ENDEAVOR

"What hast thou for thy scattered seed,
    O Sower of the plain?
Where are the many gathered sheaves
    Thy hope should bring again?"
"The only record of my work
    Lies in the buried grain."

"O Conqueror of a thousand fields!
    In dinted armor dight,
What growths of purple amaranth
    Shall crown thy brow of might?"
"Only the blossom of my life
    Flung widely in the fight."

"What is the harvest of thy saints,
    O God! who dost abide?
Where grow the garlands of thy chiefs
    In blood and sorrow dyed?
What have thy servants for their pains?"
"This only, — to have tried."

J. W. H.

WHEN a branch is cut from a vigorous tree, Nature at once sets to work to adjust matters. New juices flow, new tissues form, the wound is scarfed over, and after a time is seen only as a scar. Not here, but elsewhere, does the new growth take place, the fresh green shoots appear, more vigorous for the pruning.

Thus it was with our mother's life, as one change after another came across it. Little Sam died, and her heart withered with him: then religion and study came to her aid, and through them she reached an-

other blossoming time of thought and accomplishment
Now, with the marriage and departure of the children, still another notable change was wrought, rather
joyful than sorrowful, but none the less marking an
epoch.

Up to this time (1871) the wide, sunny rooms of
the house on Beacon Hill had been filled with young,
active life. The five children, their friends, their music, their parties, their talk and laughter, kept youth
and gayety at full tide: the green branches grew and
blossomed.

For all five she had been from their cradle not only
mistress of the revels and chief musician, but spur and
beacon of mind and soul.

Now four of the five were transplanted to other
ground. Many women, confronting changes like these,
say to themselves, "It is over. For me there is no more
active life; instead, the shelf and the chimney corner."
This woman, lifting her eyes from the empty spaces,
saw Opportunity beckoning from new heights, and
moved gladly to meet her. Now, as ever, she "staked
her life upon the red."

The empty spaces must be filled. Study no longer
sufficed: the need of serving humanity actively, hand
and foot, pen and voice, was now urgent.

Her first work under this new impulse was for peace.
The Franco-Prussian War of 1870 made a deep and
painful impression upon her. She had felt a bitter dis-
like for Louis Napoleon ever since the day when he
"stabbed France in her sleep" by the *Coup d'État* of
December, 1851; but she loved France and the French

people; the overwhelming defeat, the bitter humiliation suffered by them filled her with sorrow and indignation. In a lecture on Paris she says: "The great Exposition of 1867 had drawn together an immense crowd from all parts of the world. Among its marvels, my recollection dwells most upon the gallery of French paintings, in which I stood more than once before a full-length portrait of the then Emperor.[1] I looked into the face which seemed to say: 'I have succeeded. What has any one to say about it?' And I pondered the slow movements of that heavenly Justice whose infallible decrees are not to be evaded."

Her "Reminiscences" say: "As I was revolving these matters in my mind, while the war was still in progress, I was visited by a sudden feeling of the cruel and unnecessary character of the contest. It seemed to me a return to barbarism, the issue having been one which might easily have been settled without bloodshed. The question forced itself upon me, 'Why do not the mothers of mankind interfere in these matters, to prevent the waste of that human life of which they alone bear and know the cost?' I had never thought of this before. The august dignity of motherhood and its terrible responsibilities now appeared to me in a new aspect, and I could think of no better way of expressing my sense of these than that of sending forth an appeal to womanhood throughout the world, which I then and there composed."

This appeal is dated Boston, September, 1870.

[1] Napoleon III.

APPEAL TO WOMANHOOD THROUGHOUT THE WORLD

Again, in the sight of the Christian world, have the skill
and power of two great nations exhausted themselves in
mutual murder. Again have the sacred questions of international justice been committed to the fatal mediation of military weapons. In this day of progress, in this century of
light, the ambition of rulers has been allowed to barter the
dear interests of domestic life for the bloody exchanges of
the battle-field. Thus men have done. Thus men will do.
But women need no longer be made a party to proceedings
which fill the globe with grief and horror. Despite the
assumptions of physical force, the mother has a sacred and
commanding word to say to the sons who owe their life to
her suffering. That word should now be heard, and answered
to as never before.

Arise, then, Christian women of this day! Arise, all
women who have hearts, whether your baptism be that of
water or of tears! Say firmly: "We will not have great questions decided by irrelevant agencies. Our husbands shall not
come to us, reeking with carnage, for caresses and applause.
Our sons shall not be taken from us to unlearn all that we
have been able to teach them of charity, mercy and patience.
We, women of one country, will be too tender of those of
another country, to allow our sons to be trained to injure
theirs." From the bosom of the devastated earth a voice
goes up with our own. It says: "Disarm, disarm! The sword
of murder is not the balance of justice." Blood does not
wipe out dishonor, nor violence indicate possession. As men
have often forsaken the plough and the anvil at the summons of war, let women now leave all that may be left of
home for a great and earnest day of counsel.

Let them meet first, as women, to bewail and commemorate the dead. Let them then solemnly take counsel with
each other as to the means whereby the great human family
can live in peace, man as the brother of man, each bearing

after his own kind the sacred impress, not of Cæsar, but of
God.

In the name of womanhood and of humanity, I earnestly
ask that a general congress of women, without limit of
nationality, may be appointed and held at some place
deemed most convenient, and at the earliest period consist-
ent with its objects, to promote the alliance of the different
nationalities, the amicable settlement of international questions, the great and general interests of peace.

The appeal was translated into French, Spanish,
Italian, German, and Swedish, and sent broadcast far
and wide.

In October our mother wrote to Aaron Powell, president of the American Peace Society: "The issue is one
which will unite virtually the whole sex. God gave us,
I think, the word to say, but it ought to be followed by
immediate and organizing action. . . . Now, you, my
dear sir, are bound, as a Friend and as an Advocate of
Peace, to take especial interest in this matter, so I call
upon you a little confidently, hoping that you will help
my unbusinesslike and unskilful hands to go on with
this good work. I wish to avoid occasioning any confusion in the different meetings and organizations of
the Woman Suffrage Movement. But I should wish
to move for various meetings in which the matter of
my appeal, the direct intervention of Woman in the
Pacification of the World, should be discussed, and the
final move of a general Congress promoted. Please
take hold a little now and help me. I have wings but
no feet nor hands — rather, only a voice, '*vox et prae-
terea nihil.*'"

The next step was to call together those persons supposedly interested in such a movement. In December, 1870, it was announced that a meeting "for the purpose of considering and arranging the steps necessary to be taken for calling a World's Congress of Women in behalf of International Peace" would be held in Union League Hall, Madison Avenue and Twenty-sixth Street, New York, on Friday, December 23. The announcement, which sets forth the need for and objects of such a congress, is signed by Julia Ward Howe, William Cullen Bryant, and Mary F. Davis.

The meeting was an important one: there were addresses by Lucretia Mott, Octavius Frothingham, and Alfred Love, the Peace prophet of Philadelphia; letters from John Stuart Mill, Harriet Beecher Stowe, and William Howard Furness, who adjures peace-lovers to "labor for the establishment of a Supreme Court to which all differences between nations shall be referred for settlement."

Mrs. Howe made the opening address, from which we quote these words: —

"So I repeat my call and cry to women. Let it pierce through dirt and rags — let it pierce through velvet and cashmere. It is the call of humanity. It says: 'Help others, and you help yourselves.'

.   .   .   .

"Let the woman seize and bear about the prophetic word of the hour, and that word becomes flesh, and dwells among men. This rapturous task of hope, this perpetual evangel of good news, is the woman's special business, if she only knew it.

"Patience and passivity are sometimes in place for

women — not always. I think of this when I go to women, intelligent and charming, who warn me off with white hands, unaccustomed to any graver labor than that of gesticulation. 'Don't ask me to work,' they say; 'I cannot do it. God always raises up a set of people to do these things, like the Anti-Slavery people, and they set to work to do them.' And then I want to say to these friends: 'God can raise you up too, and I hope He will.'

"As for what one can or cannot do, remember that, active or passive, we must work to live. If we have not real labor, we must have simulated exercise. If we have not real objects, we must have fanciful caprices. A little less exertion than keeps us in the padded chair would take us out of it, and send us to try whether nature has made any special exemption in our cases, and whether the paralysis of our life need be traced further outward than our self-centred heart. . . .

"Would that I were still young, as are many of you; would at least that I had followed the angel of my youth as gravely and steadfastly as he invited me; but the world taught, applauded in another direction, and I was at fault. But from this assembly a will might go forth, an earnest will, quick with love, and heavy with meaning. And this will might say to our sisters all over the world, 'Trifle no more.' If women did not waste life in frivolity, men would not waste it in murder. For the tenderness of the one class is set by God to restrain the violence of the other."

The New York meeting was followed by one in Boston. In the spring of 1871 the friends of peace met in the rooms of the New England Woman's Club, and formed an American Branch of the Women's International Peace Association: Julia Ward Howe, president. It took five meetings to accomplish this; the minutes of these meetings are curious and interesting. Mr. Moncure D. Conway wrote objecting strongly to the movement being announced as Christian: his objections were courteously considered.

.   .   .   .

"Mrs. Howe gave her reasons for making her Appeal in the name of Christianity. She found the doctrine of peace and forgiveness of injuries the most fundamental of the Christian doctrines. She thought it proper to say so, but did not by this prevent the believers in other religions from asserting the same doctrine, if considered as existing in those religions."

Mr. Conway's objection was overruled.

The object of the association was "to promote peace, by the study and culture of its conditions." A "notice" appended to the constitution announced, "This Association proposes to hold a World's Congress of Women, in London, in the summer of 1872, in which undertaking the coöperation of all persons is earnestly invited."

Before continuing the story of this peace crusade, we return to the Journal. The volume for 1871 is fragmentary, the entries mostly brief and far apart. Written and blank pages are alike significant of the movement going on in her mind, the steadily growing desire and resolve to dedicate her life, as her husband had dedicated his, to the highest needs of humanity.

"*January 20.* Have been ill all these days. Had a

divine glimpse this day, between daylight and dusk,
of something like this — a beautiful person splendidly
dressed entering a theatre as I have often done with
entire delight and forgetfulness of everything else, and
the restraining hand of Christ holding me back in the
outer darkness — the want and woe of the world, and
saying, 'The true drama of life is *here*.' Oh! that
restraining hand had in it the true touch, communicat-
ing knowledge of human sorrow and zeal for human
service. Never may I escape it to my grave![2]

. . . .

"I confess that I value more those processes of
thought which explain history than those which arraign
it. I would not therefore in my advocacy of peace strip
one laurel leaf from the graves so dear and tender in our
recollection. Our brave men did and dared the best
which the time allowed. The sorrow for their loss was
none the less brought upon us by those who believed in
the military method. It is not in injustice to them that
I listen while the Angel of Charity says: 'Behold, I
show you a more excellent way.' Again, 'Come now,
let us reason together, saith the Lord. Though your
sins be as scarlet, they shall be as wool.' This treat-
ing of injuries from the high ground of magnanimity
is the action that shall save the world."

. . . .

"The special faults of women are those incidental to a
class that has never been allowed to work out its ideal."

. . . .

"Must work to earn some money, but will not sacrifice greater ends to this one."

. . . .

"Hear that the Greek mission is given to an editor in Troy, New York. Sad for Greece and for Chev, who longs so to help her."

.   .   .   .

"Civil liberty is that which the one cannot have without the many, or the many without the one. The liberty of the State, like its solvency, concerns and affects all its citizens. Equal sacredness of rights is its political side, equal stringency of duties its moral side. The virtue of single individuals will not give them civil liberty in a despotic state, but the only safeguard of civil liberty to all is the virtue of each individual."

.   .   .   .

"You men by your vice and selfishness have created for women a hideous profession, whose ranks you recruit from the unprotected, the innocent, the ignorant. This is the only profession, so far as I know, that man has created for women.

"We will create professions for ourselves if you will allow us opportunity and deal as fairly with the female infant as with the male. Where, even in this respect, do we find your gratitude? We instruct your early years. You keep instruction from our later ones.

"French popular authors have satirized American women freely. Let them remember that French literature has done much to corrupt American women. Unhappy Paris has corrupted the world. She is now swept from the face of the earth."

France was constantly in her thoughts.

"The *morale* of the *Commune*, that which has commended it to good people, has undoubtedly been a supposed resistance to the return of absolutism, which the Versailles Government was supposed covertly to represent. . . . No matter what advantage of reason the *Commune* may have had over the Versailles Government, the *Commune* committed a civil crime in attempting military enforcement of its political opinions. Such was the crime which our South committed and which we resisted as one defends one's own life. No overt military act of ours gave them the advantage of a *casus belli*. They differed from us and determined to coerce us forcibly. In that weltering mass of ruin and corruption which was Paris, what lessons lie of the utter folly and futility of mutual murder! What hearts of brothers estranged which time would have harmonized! What hecatombs of weltering corpses poisoning the earth which industry should make wholesome! What women demonized by passion, forgetting all their woman's lore and skill, the appointed givers of life speeding death and reaping the bitter fruit themselves! With this terrible picture before us, let no civilized nation from henceforth and forever admit or recognize the instrumentality of war as worthy of Christian society. Let the fact of human brotherhood be taught to the babe in his cradle, let it be taught to the despot on his throne. Let it be the basis and foundation of education and legislation, the bond of high and low, of rich and poor. . . ."

"*May 27.* I am fifty-two years old this day and must regard this year as in some sense the best of my life. The great joy of the Peace Idea has unfolded itself to me. . . . I have got at better methods of working in the practical matters at which I do work, and believe more than ever in patience, labor, and sticking to one's own idea of work. Study, book-work, and solitary thinking and writing show us only one side of what we study. Practical life and intercourse with others supply the other side. If I may sit at work on this day next year, I hope that my peace matter will have assumed a practical and useful form, and that I may have worked out my conception worthily. . . . I pray that neither Louis Napoleon nor the Bourbons may return to feed upon France, but that merciful measures, surely of God's appointing, may heal her deadly wounds and uplift her prostrate heart. She must learn that the doctrine of self is irreligious. The *Commune* surely knew this just as little as did Louis Napoleon. I want to keep eyesight enough to read Greek and German, and my teeth for clear speaking and good digestion."

.   .   .   .

"Paul says: 'Ye that are strong ought to bear the infirmities of the weak,' but now we that are weak bear the infirmities of the strong."

.   .   .   .

"Peace meeting at the Club. Read in Greek first part of the eighth chapter of Matthew; the account given of the centurion seems very striking in the Greek. The contrast of his Western mind with the Eastern subtleties of Jew and Greek seems to have struck Christ. He supposed Christ's power over unseen things to be like his own control over things committed to his authority. Then Christ began, perhaps, to see that the other nations of the world would profit by his work and doctrine before his Jewish brethren."

. . . .

"My first presidency at the New England Woman's Club. . . . I do not shine in presiding over a business meeting and some others can do much better than I. Still I think it best to fulfil all expected functions of ordinary occasions, living and learning."

". . . Negro Christianity. It is something of a very definite and touching character — all forgiving, all believing, making a decided religious impression of its own — the heart so ripe, the intellectual part so little made out, like a fruit which might be all pulp and no fibre."

. . . .

"On Sunday we bring back the worn and dim currency of our active life to be redeemed by the pure gold of the Supreme Wisdom. I bring to church my coppers and small pieces and take away a shining gold piece. Self is the talent buried in the napkin no matter with how much of culture and natural capacity. Till we get out of self we are in the napkin. Hospitable entertainment of other people's opinions, brotherly promotions of their interests — these acts make our five talents ten in use to others and in enjoyment and profit to ourselves. . . ."

"Christ's teaching about marriage. Its tender and sacred reciprocity. Adultery among the Jews was only recognized as crime when committed by a woman. The right of concubinage was too extensive to bring condemnation for unchastity. The man might not steal another man's wife, but any woman's husband might have intercourse with other women. Christ showed how men did offend against this same law which worked so absolutely and partially against women. An unchaste thought in the breast of the man infringed the high law of purity. This teaching of the tender mutual obligations of married life was probably new to many of his hearers.

"The present style of woman has really been fashioned by man, and is only *quasi* feminine.

"Peace meeting at Mystic, Connecticut. Spoke morning and afternoon, best in the morning. The natural unfolding of reform. 'His purposes will ripen fast' — Watts's verse. Providence does not plant so as to gather all its crops in one day. First the flowers, then the fruits, then the golden grain.

"John Fiske's lecture, first in the course on the theory of Evolution. . . . Did not think the lecture a very profitable one, yet we must be willing that our opposites should think and speak out their belief."

In the spring of 1872 she went to England, hoping to hold a Woman's Peace Congress in London. She also hoped to found and foster "a Woman's Apostolate of Peace." These hopes were not then to be fulfilled: yet she always felt that this visit, with all its labors and its disappointments, was well worth while, and that much solid good came of it, to herself and to others.

We have seen her in London as a bride, enjoying to the full its gayeties and hospitality, as bright a vision as any that met her eyes, with a companion to whom all doors opened eagerly. This was the picture of 1843; that of 1872 is different, indeed.

A woman of middle age, quiet in dress and manner, with a serene and constant dignity; a face in which the lines of thought and study were deepening year by year; eyes now flashing with mirth, now tender with sympathy, always bright with the "high resolve and hardihood" for which, but a few years before, she had been sighing: this was the woman who came to London in 1872, alone and unaided; who, standing before the Dark Tower of established Order and Precedent, might say with Childe Roland, —

> "Dauntless the slug horn to my lips I set,
> And blew."

She spoke at the banquet of the Unitarian Association. "The occasion was to me a memorable one." She hired the Freemasons' Tavern and preached there on five or six successive Sundays.

"My procedure was very simple, — a prayer, the reading of a hymn, and a discourse from a Scripture text. . . . The attendance was very good throughout, and I cherished the hope that I had sown some seed which would bear fruit hereafter."

She was asked to address meetings in various parts of England, speaking in Birmingham, Manchester, Leeds, Bristol, Carlisle, with good acceptance. In Cambridge she talked with Professor J. R. Seeley, whom she found most sympathetic. She was everywhere welcomed by thoughtful people, old friends and new, whether or no they sympathized with her quest.

"*June 9.* My first preaching in London. Worked pretty much all day at sermon, intending, not to read, but to talk it — for me, a difficult procedure. At 4.30 P.M. left off, but brain so tired that nothing in it. Subject, the kingdom of heaven. . . . Got a bad cup of tea — dressed (in my well-worn black silk) and went to the Drawing-Room at Freemasons' Tavern. God knows how I felt. 'Cast down but not forsaken.' . . . I got through better than I feared I might. Felt the method to be the right one, speaking face to face and heart to heart."

"*June 10.* Small beer going out of fashion leaves women one occupation the less. Fools are still an institution; and will remain such." [1]

"*June 16.* . . . A good attendance in spite of the heat. . . . Agonized over my failure to come up to what I had designed to do in the discourse."

"*June 18.* . . . Saw the last of my dear friend E. Twisleton, who took me to the National Gallery, where we saw many precious gems of art. . . . At parting, he said: 'The good Father above does not often give so great a pleasure as I have had in these meetings with you.' Let me enshrine this charming and sincere word in my most precious recollection, from the man of sixty-three to the woman of fifty-three."

"*June 27.* Left Leeds at 7 A.M., rising at 4.30. . . . To Miss [Frances Power] Cobbe's, where met Lady Lyall, Miss Clough, Mrs. Gorton, Jacob Bright, *et al.* Then to dinner with the dear Seeleys. An unceremonious and delightful meal. Heart of calf. Then to John

---

[1] "To suckle fools and chronicle small beer." *Othello.*

Ridley's. . . . Home late, almost dead — to bed, having been on foot twenty hours."

"*July 4.* . . . Saw a sight of misery, a little crumb of a boy, barefoot, tugging after a hand-organ man, also very shabby. Gave the little one a ha'penny, all the copper I had. But in the heartache he gave me, I resolved, God helping me, that my luxury shall henceforth be to minister to human misery, and to redeem much time and money spent on my own fancies, as I may. . . ."

She had been asked to attend two important meetings as American delegate: a peace congress in Paris, and a great prison reform meeting in London.

The French meeting came first. She crossed the Channel, reaching Paris in time to attend the principal *séance* of the congress. She presented her credentials, asked leave to speak, and was told "with some embarrassment" that she might speak to the officers of the society, when the public meeting should be adjourned! She makes no comment on this proceeding, but says, "I accordingly met a dozen or more of these gentlemen in a side room, where I simply spoke of my endeavors to enlist the sympathies and efforts of women in behalf of the world's peace."

Returning to London, she had "the privilege of attending as a delegate one of the great Prison Reform meetings of our day."

In 1843, Julia the bride would not have considered it a privilege to attend a meeting for prison reform. She would have shrugged her shoulders, would perhaps have pouted because the Chevalier cared more for these things than for the opera, with Grisi, Mario, and Lablache: she might even have written some funny verses about the windmill-tilting of her Don Quixote. Now, she stood in the place that failing health forbade him to fill, with a depth of interest, an earnestness of purpose, equal to his own. She, too, now heard the sorrowful sighing of the prisoners.

At one of the meetings of this congress, a jailer of the old school spoke in defence of the system of flogging refractory prisoners, and described in brutal fashion a brutal incident. Her blood was on fire: she asked leave to speak.

"It is related," she said, "of the famous Beau Brummel that a gentleman who called upon him one morning met a valet carrying away a tray of neck-cloths, more or less disordered. 'What are these?' asked the visitor; and the servant replied, 'These are our failures!' When I see the dark coach which in our country carries the criminal to his place of detention, I say, 'Society, here are your failures.'"

Her words were loudly applauded, and the punishment was voted down.

The Journal gives her further speech on this occasion: "Spoke of justice to women. They had talked of fallen women. I prayed them to leave that hopeless phrase. Every fallen woman represents a man as guilty as herself, who escapes human detection, but whose soul lies open before God. Speak of vicious, dissolute women, but don't speak of fallen women unless you recognize the fall of man, the old doctrine."

Two days before this she had preached her last ser-

mon in London. The Journal says: "All Sunday at
work upon my sermon, the last in London. 'Neither
height nor depth, nor any other creature.' The sermon
of high and low, and the great unity beyond all dimen-
sions. A good and to me a most happy delivery of
opinions and faith which I deeply hold. . . . So ended
my happy ministration in London, begun in fear and
anxiety, ended in certainty and renewed faith, which
God continue to me."

August found her back at Oak Glen, exhausted in
body and mind. She is almost too tired to write in the
Journal, and such entries as there are only accentuate
her fatigue.

"I am here at my table with books and papers, but
feel very languid. My arms feel as if there were no
marrow in their bones. I suppose this is reaction after
so much work, but unless I can get up strength somehow I shall not accomplish anything. Weakness in all
my limbs. Have had my Greek lesson and begun to
read the Maccabees and the Apocrypha. I shall probably come up after a few days, but feel at present
utterly incapable of exertion. I must help Maud —
have helped her with music to-day. . . ."

"Walked about with dear Chev, whose talk is
always instructive. Every break in our long-continued
habits shows us something to amend in our past lives.
What do I see in mine after this long break? That I
must endeavor to have more real life and more religion.
The passive and contemplative following of thought,
my own or other people's, must not de-energize my
sympathies and my will. I must daily consult the

divine will and standard which can help us to mould
our lives aright without running from one extreme to
another. My heart's wish would now be to devote
myself to some sort of religious ministration. God can
open a way for this in which the spirit of my desire may
receive the form of his will. I must lecture this winter
to earn some money and spread, I hope, some good
doctrine. . . ."

Such was the beginning of her work for peace, which
was to end only with her life. Disappointed in her hope
of a world congress, she turned the current of her effort
in a new direction. She would have a festival, a day
which should be called Mothers' Day, and be devoted to the advocacy of peace doctrines. She chose
the second day of June; for many years she and her
friends and followers kept this day religiously, with
sweet and tender observances which were unspeakably
dear to her.

In 1876 there was a great peace meeting in Philadelphia. The occasion is thus described by the Reverend Ada C. Bowles: "There were delegates from
France, Italy, and Germany, each with a burning desire
to be heard, and all worth hearing, but none able to
speak English. The audience looked to the anxious
face of the President with sympathy; then a voice was
heard, 'Call for Mrs. Howe.' Those present will never
forget how her presence changed the meeting from a
threatened failure to a noble success. The German,
Frenchman, and Italian stood in turn by her side. At
the proper moment she lifted a finger, and then gave in

her perfect English each speech in full to the delight of the delegates and the admiration of all."

The last celebration of her Mothers' Day was held in Riverton, New Jersey, on June 1, 1912, by the Pennsylvania Peace Society, in conjunction with the Universal Peace Union. On the printed invitation to this festival we read

"Aid it, paper, aid it, pen,
Aid it, hearts of earnest men.
Julia Ward Howe, 1874."

And further on, "Thirty-nine years ago Julia Ward Howe instituted this festival for peace, — a time for the women and children to come together; to meet in the country, invite the public, and recite, speak, sing and pray for 'those things that make for peace.'"

CHAPTER XV

SANTO DOMINGO

1872–1874; *aet. 53–56*

A PARABLE

"I sent a child of mine to-day;
    I hope you used him well."
"Now, Lord, no visitor of yours
    Has waited at my bell.

"The children of the Millionnaire
    Run up and down our street;
I glory in their well-combed hair,
    Their dress and trim complete.

"But yours would in a chariot come
    With thoroughbreds so gay;
And little merry maids and men
    To cheer him on his way."

"Stood, then, no child before your door?"
    The Lord, persistent, said.
"Only a ragged beggar-boy,
    With rough and frowzy head.

"The dirt was crusted on his skin,
    His muddy feet were bare;
The cook gave victuals from within;
    I cursed his coming there."

What sorrow, silvered with a smile,
    Slides o'er the face divine?
What tenderest whisper thrills rebuke?
    "The beggar-boy was mine!"

J. W. H.

WE must go back a little to tell another story.

In the winter of 1870–71 the Republic of Santo Domingo sent through its president an urgent request for annexation to the United States. President Grant appointed a commission to visit this island republic, to inquire into its conditions and report upon the question. Of this commission Dr. Howe was one, the others being Messrs. Benjamin Wade and Andrew D. White. The commissioners sailed on the government steamer Tennessee. At parting the Doctor said, "Remember that you cannot hear from us under a month; so do not be frightened at our long silence."

A week later came reports of a severe storm in the Southern seas. A large steamer had been seen struggling with wind and wave, apparently at their mercy. Some newspaper thought it might be the Tennessee. All the newspapers took up the cry: it probably *was* the Tennessee; most likely she had foundered and gone down with all on board.

Mindful of the Doctor's warning, our mother tried to disregard these voices of terror. She went quietly about her work as usual, but none the less the days of suspense that followed were "dark indeed and hard to live through." [1]

We remember these days well, the resolute cheerfulness, the avoidance of outward sign of anxiety, the sudden lifting of the cloud when the good news came of the steamer's safe arrival.

The prayer of Santo Domingo was not to be answered, spite of the favorable report of the commission: but the Doctor had been so delighted with the island that when, a year later, he was asked to visit it in the interests of the Samana Bay Company, he gladly accepted the commission.

---

[1] *Reminiscences*, p. 346.

This time our mother went with him, together with Maud and a party of friends. She had been loth to go, for she had already planned her peace crusade in England, but finding how much he desired it, she compromised on part of the time.

They sailed from New York early in February, 1872, in the steamer Tybee. The voyage was rough and stormy. The companion daughter of the time remembers how the wretched little Tybee pitched and heaved; even more vividly she recalls the way in which our mother from the first made society out of the strangely assorted company on board. She was the magnet, and drew them all to her: the group of conventional ladies who had never before been at sea, the knot of naval officers going to join their ship, — among them George W. De Long, the hero of the ill-fated Jeannette expedition; a colonel, and a judge, the former interested in the Samana Bay Company. She made out of this odd company and the gruff old captain a sort of court which she ruled in a curious way. She did not seem to compel their admiration so much as to compel each to give his best.

The Tybee cast anchor in the harbor of Puerto Plata, and the voyagers saw Mont Isabel towering above them, its foot in the clear beryl water where the palms grew down to the very edge of the yellow sea sand, its head wrapped in the clouds. The Doctor came to the stateroom, crying, "Come up and see the great glory!"

Our mother's delight can be imagined when they sailed into the harbor of Santo Domingo and landed near an immense and immemorial tree, where, they were told, Columbus had landed.

The party lodged in a fine old Spanish *palacio*, built round a courtyard. It had been originally a convent. The nuns were gone, and their place was now taken by the gay company of American ladies, who possibly gave the sleepy little city more new ideas than it had ever received in so short a space of time. President Baez put the palace at the Doctor's disposal; he was an important person to the President and to the Dominicans, for at that time the hope of annexation had not died out. All the party were treated with extraordinary courtesy. Not only were they given the presidential palace to live in, but a guard of honor was kept in the courtyard. Their horses were lodged, Spanish fashion, on the ground floor. The trampling, the neighing, and the fleas made them rather uncomfortable neighbors. Our mother soon found out that the only way she could see the country, or enjoy its life, was by riding. At first she was a little nervous, but she soon regained her courage and her seat. This was her first riding since the days of Cora, the wicked little mare, when she read her Bible and said her prayers before every ride. She thus describes it: —

"In Santo Domingo, nothing is more charming than the afternoon ride. It is, of course, the great event of the neighborhood. Our cavalcade usually numbers four or five ladies. Sometimes we cross the river in a flat-bottomed boat, which is pulled over by a rope stretched and made fast at either end. We then visit the little village of Pajarita, and trot along under the shade of heavy mango trees. Or we explore the country on this side the river. The great thing to guard against is the danger of rain. This we encountered one afternoon in some severity. Suddenly one of the party cried '*Llava!*' and down came the waters. We were somewhat heated with our ride, and the penetrating rain fell chill upon us. A large tree gave us shelter for a few moments, but we were soon forced to seek more effectual protection. This we found, after some delay, in a *boio*, or hut, into which horses and riders were dragged pell-mell. The night was closing in, the Chief at home, and presumably anxious, the rain unabating. Which of the tropical spasms would end our far-spent life? Would it be lockjaw, a common result of severe chill in these regions? Would it be a burning, delirious fever with a touch of yellow; or should we get off with croup and diphtheria?

"The rain presently stopped, and we returned to the saddle, and then, by easy stages, to the city. On reaching home, we were advised to bathe the chilled surfaces with rum, not the wicked New England article, but the milder product of the country. Of all the evil consequences spoken of as sure to follow such an exposure, fever, lockjaw, and sore throat, we have so far not seen the earliest symptom."

It was Carnival. All the cabinet officers and their wives devoted themselves to the entertainment of the party. The Minister of War, Señor Curiel, a little twinkling fiery man, devoted himself especially to our mother, and was her right hand in the many expeditions she arranged. The Secretary of State, Señor

Gautier, a grave person with more culture than most of the Dominicans, was the Doctor's chosen friend. To return the many attentions showered upon them, a ball in the old convent was arranged. The Doctor once said to her, "If you were on a desert island with nobody there but one old darkey, you would give a party." (But it was from Cuba that he wrote, "Julia knows three words of Spanish, and is constantly engaged in active conversation.")

To find herself at Carnival, the leader of a gay party, living in a spacious palace, supported by the guns and the officers of an American warship (the Narragansett, with De Long and other officers on board), was an opportunity not to be missed. She thus describes the entertainment: —

"*Hans Breitmann gife a barty.*

"So did we. To see Santo Domingo was little, without seeing the Dominicans also. Some diplomatic overtures were made. Would the first families come and pass an evening with us at the *Palacio?* Yes, they would. Which *were* the first families? That would have been for us a point very difficult to determine. The family of the President and those of the heads of departments would certainly stand in that prominence. For the necessary beaux we were referred to a society recently established here, calling itself '*La Juventad,*' 'the young people.' This body of philanthropists, being appealed to, consented to undertake the management of our party. The occasion was announced as a *bailecita*, 'little ball.' We asked them to provide such refreshments as are customary in this place. Thirty

dollars' worth of sweet cake and a bottled ocean of
weak beer formed the principal items of the bill, as
brought to us. The friends came at 5 P.M., to decorate
the room with flowers, also to arrange two tables, on
one of which *las dulces* were arrayed, while the other
was made to display a suspicious-looking group of
glasses. A band, we were told, would be indispensable.
We demurred at this, having intended to musicate
upon our own grand piano. Hearing, however, that
the band could be had for the sum of twelve dollars,
we gave in on this point.

"One long room runs the whole length of one side of
the palace, and serves us at once for dining and reception room. A long corridor encounters this room at
right angles, entirely open to the weather, on one side.
These two spaces constitute all our resources for receiving company. We lit them with Downer's best [kero-
sene] and ranged rows of rocking-chairs, opposite to
each other, after the manner of this country, and also
of Cuba.

"The company began to arrive at 8 P.M. The young
ladies were mostly attired in colored tarlatans, prettily
trimmed with lace and flowers. Some of them were not
over fourteen years of age. All were quite youthful
in their appearance, and unaffected in their manners.
The young men, mostly employed in the various shops
of the city, were well-dressed and polite. The band
was somewhat barbaric in its aspect. A violin, a 'cello,
a tambourine, and a clarinet. The clarinet-player was
of uncommon size, with wild, dark eyes, which seemed
to dilate as he played. . . .

"The dancing continued with little interruption until nearly 2 A.M. We were told that it is often continued till daylight. From time to time an attack was made upon the two tables. But the enjoyment of the good things provided was quite moderate compared with the cramming of a first-class party in Boston or New York. The guests were of many shades, as to color, although the greater number would have passed for white people, anywhere. Some of the handsomest among them were very dark. One young man reminded us of Edwin Booth in "Othello." . . . None of these people look like the mulattoes in the North. The features and the fibre appear finer, and the jet-black hair often suggests an admixture of Indian blood. The difference of social position shows itself in the manners of these people. The cruel colorphobia has never proscribed them. They have no artificial sense of inferiority, but take themselves as God made them, and think that if He is content with their complexions, mankind at large may be so.

"We were much pleased with our party, and with the simple and unaffected gayety of our guests. It was really a party in the open air, one whole side of our ballroom being unenclosed, save by the infrequent colonnade. We looked from the dancers to the stars, and back again to the dancers. It was all fairylike and dreamlike. The favorite 'dansa' much resembles, not a ballet, but a stage dance, such as is introduced in the course of the drama. The beer flowed, and the couples flew. One innovation we introduced, a Virginia reel, which the clever clarinet-player caught and accom-

panied. The figures much amazed the natives. The
dénouement of Mr. Leland's classic ballad was wanting.
No

> " 'Gompany fited mit daple lecks
> Till de coonshtable made em shtop';

yet we may quote further from that high source: —

> " 'Hans Breitmann gife a barty,
> Where ish that barty now?
> . . . .
> All goned afay mit der lager pier,
> Afay in der Ewigkeit!' "

The Journal gives pleasant glimpses of the Santo
Domingo days.

"M. Marne, a Frenchman ninety-seven years old,
paid us a visit. Had been secretary of Joseph Buona-
parte in Madrid — praised him much. Talked very
copiously and not ill. Enjoys full mental and physical
activity. Lives at a small village in sight of our windows, but on the other side of the river. Talked much
of the Roi Cristophe."

The mention of this old gentleman recalls her visit
to a Dominican *padre*, himself in extreme age, who told
her that he had known a negress who lived to the age
of one hundred and forty-three; he had confessed and
buried her. "She had her teeth and her hair still."

"Not to market to-day, but breakfast early — then
all hands to the cathedral to see the high mass performed — to-day in honor of the independence of the
island. . . .

"Baez' face, cunning, pretty strong, *enjoué*, as if he
must be, or seem, a *bon enfant*. . . . The noise at the

elevation of the Host a perfect Babel. Music, 'Ernani,' 'Fra Diavolo,' with some similar things. A single trumpet shrieked at some high moments. The bells rang like a thousand tin pans. Orchestra and chorus not together and both out of tune. The ceremony otherwise perhaps as well as usual. A priest made a brief address in Spanish, praising the day and complimenting the President. . . ."

"Studied Baur, Aristophanes, and *'Etudes sur la Bible.'* Music lesson to Maud. O'Sullivan to dine. . . . Baez sent word that he would visit us between 5 and 6 P.M. We accordingly put things in the best order possible under the circumstances. *Ung puo de tualetta* for the ladies seemed proper. At dinner received Baez' card with a great dish of fine sapotes. Baez arrived. He speaks French quite tolerably, is affable, and has an intelligent face; in fact looks like a person of marked talent. We talked of things in the United States. He has made fourteen voyages to Europe. . . . I sang *'Una Barchetta'* for him. He came with one servant, who stayed outside — no ceremony and no escort. . . ."

After the beauty of the place — indeed possibly before it — she valued the opportunity that came to her of preaching. On the voyage to Santo Domingo she had learned of a shepherdless flock of colored Protestants, their minister dead, their "elder" disabled by lameness. Here was an opportunity not to be lost. She engaged to hold Sunday evening services in their church, a small wooden building with a mud floor and a mahogany pulpit. The "Reminiscences" describe these services; the tattered hymn-books whose leaves

were turned mechanically while the congregation (few
of whom could read) sang with a will the hymns they
knew by heart; the humble, devout people with their
attentive faces.

When Holy Week came, the congregation begged her
to hold special services. They wished their young people to understand that these sacred days meant as
much to them as to the surrounding Catholics. Accordingly she and her companion "dressed the little
church with flowers. It looked charmingly. Flowers
all along the railing [here follows in the Journal a pen-
and-ink sketch], flowers in the pulpit over my head.
Church was crowded. Many people outside and at the
windows."

She always remembered with pleasure one feature
of her Easter sermon, her attempt to describe Dante's
vision of a great cross in the heavens, formed of star
clusters, each cluster bearing the name of Christ. "The
thought," she says, "that the mighty poet of the four-
teenth century should have something to impart to
these illiterate negroes was very dear to me."

One of the party has an undying impression of this
Easter service: the shabby little chapel crowded with
dark faces, and the preacher, standing touched by a
ray of sunlight, speaking to that congregation of simple black people. In her notes she speaks of these
services.

"A pastoral charge bringing me near to the hearts
and sympathies of the people. I have preached five
times in the little church, including Good Friday and
Easter Monday. This service, which has not been with-

out its difficulties, is so much better to me in remembrance than anything else I have done here that I must make a little break and pause before I speak of other things.

"In this pause I remember my prayer at Puerto Plata, that I and mine might come to this new region with a reverent and teachable spirit. That prayer was an earnest one to me. I hope it has, as all prayers should, accomplished its own fulfilment. I have been here among dear people. I find all the human varieties in this society, not digested and harmonized by noble culture, but existing and asking for the centralizing and discriminating agencies which in civilization sort out the different tastes, characters, and capacities, and assign to each its task, giving devotion its wings and crime its treadmill. This little population in a great country, a country in which Nature allows no one to starve, has lived and so shown its right to live and maintain itself. It has accomplished its political division from a state antipathetic to it, having its dark face turned fixedly towards barbarism [Hayti].

"I stood in a little church in the city and island of Santo Domingo, to preach the glad tidings of the gospel of Peace. It was a humble little temple, with a mud floor, and plastered walls, and a roof which scarcely kept out the rain, but it was a place full of comfort to me and to others. The seats and spaces were all filled, for it had no aisles. The small windows and doors were cushioned, so to speak, with human countenances, wearing an expression of curiosity or attention. The way to the church was lined on both sides with the

simple people, who held their service at night because
the poverty of their attire made them ashamed to hold
it by day. And this crowd came together, Sunday after
Sunday, because a woman from a distant country stood
in that little church to tell them what a woman can tell
about the kingdom of heaven."

Loth as she had been to go to Santo Domingo, she
was far more loth to leave it; but the time appointed
for her peace crusade in London was at hand, and she
could tarry no longer. On April 5 she writes: —

"Ah! my time is nearly out. Dear Santo Domingo,
how I do love you, with your childish life, and your
ancestral streets — a grandam and a babe! To-day I
read my last in Baur and Greek for some time, probably, as must pack to-morrow. As at present advised,
God grant that we may come here again."

"*April 6.* Here to-day and gone to-morrow, literally. Mostly packed — have left out my books for a
last sweet morsel. . . . Did not get that sweet morsel.
Was busy all day — farewell calls from friends, little
talks, and the fear of sitting down and forgetting my
preparations in my books. In the evening the Gauti-
ers came and I played for them to dance. So, one last
little gayety in common."

"*Sunday, April 7.* Got up at 4 A.M. Dressed and got
off pretty easily. . . . The parting from Maud was very
hard. Oh! when the line was drawn in, and my darling
and I were fairly sundered, my old heart gave way, and
I cried bitterly. . . .

"Henry Blackwell is a dear, comforting man, most
kind and companionable. A woman on board with a

wretched baby of six months, he in a muslin gown and
nothing else, crying with cold. I got out a cotton flannel dressing-sack, and wrapped him up in it and tended
him a good deal. . . .

"May the purpose for which I undertake this painful and solitary journey be ever strong enough in my
thoughts to render every step of it pure, blameless and
worthy. Great God, do not let me desert thee! For
that is the trouble. Thou dost not desert us. I dread
unspeakably these dark days of suffering and confusion. To go is like being hanged. . . ."

"Captain said something about my preaching on
Sunday, so I have been laying out some points for a
sermon. . . . But it is not very likely that the Captain
will really ask me to hold service.

"Talk with purser about Homer. He has a vivacious
mind, and might easily learn Greek, or anything else he
would have a mind to."

"*Sunday.* It turned out that the Captain and passengers did wish me to hold a little service to-day, so
at 10.30 A.M. I met them in the dining-saloon. I had a
Bible, from which I read the 116th Psalm — a prayer
followed — then the missionary hymn, 'From Green-
land's icy mountains' — then my little sermon, of
which I have the headings. I am so very glad to have
been able and enabled to do this.

"Began to teach the purser to read from notes with
a leaf of music out of some periodical. Copied Baur a
little — talked and heard much talk."

"*April 17.* . . . Expect to get in to-morrow, not very
late, unless another contrary gale. Frigate birds and

petrels yesterday — to-day, whales, blackfish, and an immense number of porpoises. Revelation cannot go beyond human consciousness.

"The Western mind has taken Christ's metaphorical illustrations literally, and his literal moral precepts metaphorically."

"*April 18.* . . . Very thankful to have got through so well so far."

As at the beginning of this chapter we took a step backward, so we must now take one forward and speak briefly of the second visit to Santo Domingo in 1874.

The Doctor's health was failing; he had suffered from the winter's cold, and longed for the warm sunshine of the beloved island. Would she go with him? he asked. She should preach to her colored folks as much as she liked.

They sailed together in the Tybee in March. After a brief visit to the capital (where Revolution had been before them, expelling the friendly Baez, and putting in his place a man opposed to the Samana Bay Company), they took up their quarters at Samana, in a little hillside cottage about a mile from the town.

Our mother writes in her Journal: —

"*March 20.* In Santo Domingo as glad as a child. . . . Went to Garcia's and foolishly bargained for the gold necklace and emerald ring I fancied the last time I was here. The necklace is for Maud."

The love of jewelry was one of the "little passions" of her whole life. Speaking once of this as her "besetting sin," she said: "It is rather respectable to have a besetting sin, as it shows one must have had an ancestor from whom it was inherited!" She enjoyed a jewel as she did a flower or a song: she loved to deck her dear ones and herself with trinkets; a jeweller's window was a thing of delight to her, not to be passed without the tribute of a pause and a glance at its treasures. Yet a purchase of this kind seldom failed to bring its retributive pang the day after.

"Was sorry to have made so foolish a use of the money. Resolve never to do so again, unless some new light should make it seem right. God will not have my mind occupied with such nonsense. . . . Have written my sermon for to-morrow evening."

They spent two months in Samana in almost absolute retirement. The Doctor read "Don Quixote" in Spanish, she Aristotle in Greek and Baur in German. The former "was early and late in the saddle, and dashed up and down the steep hillsides of Samana with all his old fearlessness." The latter followed as she might, "in perils and dangers, in terrors often."

"I had never been a bold rider, and I must confess that I suffered agonies of fear in following him on these expeditions. If I lagged behind, he would cry, 'Come on! it's as bad as going to a funeral to ride with you.' And so, I suppose, it was. I remember one day when a great palm branch had fallen across our path. I thought that my horse would certainly slip on it, sending me to the depths below. That very day, while Dr. Howe took his siesta, I went to the place where this impediment lay, and with a great effort threw it over the steep mountain-side. The whole neighborhood of Samana is very mountainous, and I sometimes found it impossible to obey the word of command. One day my husband spurred his horse and made a gallant dash at a very steep ascent, ordering me to follow him. I tried my best, but only got far enough to find myself awkwardly at a standstill, and unable to go either backward or forward. The Doctor was obliged to dismount and to lead my horse down to the level ground. This, he assured me, was a severe mortification for him." [1]

In spite of the permission given, she spoke only a few times in Samana. She tells of an open-air service in which she took part. She arrived late, and found a zealous elder holding forth and "reading" from a Bible held upside down. At sight of her he said, "And now dat de lady hab come, I will obdunk from de place!"

One day she spoke to the pupils of a little school kept by an English carpenter, who studied Greek in order to understand the New Testament, yet allowed his pupils to use the small i for the personal pronoun. The schoolhouse was perched on a hill so steep that she was thankful to mount astride on a huge white steer furnished with a straw saddle, and be led up by a friendly neighbor.

In these days the ill-fated Samana Bay Company, of which the Doctor and many others had had high hopes, came to an end, and the Dominican Government insisted that its flag should be officially withdrawn. Our mother describes the incident: —

"To town early to be present at the taking down of the Samana Company's flag by the commission sent on

---

[1] *Reminiscences*, p. 362.

board the Dominican war schooner. I went in the boat and found Chev in the custom-house with the commission seated around. A good many of our people present. Chev read his protest, which was strong and simple. . . . We then went out of the building; the *employés* of our Company marched up in their best clothes, their hats stuck full of roses, and stood in order on either side the flagstaff. The man ordered by the commission lowered the flag. Just before, Chev got our people to stand in a circle around him, made a lovely little address. The old Crusader never appeared nobler or better than on this occasion, when his beautiful chivalry stood in the greatest contrast to the barbarism and ingratitude which dictated this act. My mind was full of cursing rather than blessing. Yet finding myself presently alone with the superseded flag I laid my hand upon it and prayed that if I had power to bless anything, my prayers might bless the good effort which has been made here."

On April 2 she adds: "The blacks here say that the taking down of our flag was like the crucifixion of our Lord. We are assured that they would have offered forcible resistance, if we had authorized their so doing."

"*May 9*. The last day of our last week in Samana. . . . God knows when I shall have so much restful leisure again. My rides on horseback, too, are ended for the present, though I may mount once more to-day or to-morrow. All these pleasures have been mixed with pains — my fear on horseback . . . but far more than all, my anxiety about the dearest ones at home. The affairs of the Company, too, have given me many sad thoughts, but in spite of all this the time has been a blessed one. I have improved in mind and body, if not in estate — have had sweet leisure for thought and study, opportunity to preach the gospel (three times), and most invigorating air and exercise. Over the door of the little parlor here hangs a motto: 'God bless our Home.' I think, indeed, He has blessed this little home, though, at first, when I looked at the motto, I always thought of my own home."

The next day they saw the "last of beautiful Samana for the present," and ten days later found them in New York. Her final word on this brief and lovely episode is given in the Journal for May 24: "My heart sinks whenever Chev says he will never go to Samana again. 'There are my young barbarians all at play.'"

CHAPTER XVI

THE LAST OF GREEN PEACE

1872-1876; *aet.* 53-57

He who launched thee a bolt of fire
Strong in courage and in desire
Takes thee again a weapon true
In heaven's armory ever new.

Still shall the masterful fight go on,
Still shall the battle of Right be won
And He who fixed thee in upper air
Shall carry thy prowess otherwhere.

J. W. H.

As our father's health failed more and more, his heart turned to the home he had made. He longed for Green Peace; and — the lease falling in about this time — in the spring of 1872 he and our mother and Maud moved thither, and took up their quarters in the "new part," while Laura and her husband came to occupy the old. Here the first grandchild (Alice Maud Richards) was born; here and at Oak Glen the next four years were mainly passed.

The Doctor's ardent spirit longed for new fields of work, new causes to help; the earthly part could not follow. How he struggled, toiling, suffering, fighting the good fight to his last breath, has been told elsewhere:[1] suffice it to say that these years were grave ones for the household, spite of new joys that dawned for all.

[1] *Letters and Journals of Samuel Gridley Howe.*

The grandchildren opened a new world for both our parents: a world which one was to enjoy for a space all too brief, the other through long years, in which she was to be to the youngest generation a lamp of wisdom, a flame of warmth and tenderness, a fountain of joy.

Among the memory pictures of this time is one of her sitting at her desk, laboring at her endless correspondence; beside her, on the floor, the baby of the period, equally absorbed in the contents of the waste-paper basket.

Or we see the tall figure of the Doctor, stooping in the doorway between the two houses, a crowing child on his shoulders, old face and young alight with merriment. These were Richards grandbabes; the Hall children were the summer delight of the grandparents, as they and their mother usually spent the summer at Oak Glen.

"*Friday, September 13.* Before I open even my New Testament to-day, I must make record of the joyful birth of Flossy's little son [Samuel Prescott Hall]. . . . God bless this dear little child! May he bring peace and love. . . .

" During the confinement I could not think of anything divine or spiritual. It was Nature's grim, mechanical, traditional task. But now that it is over, my heart remembers that Life is not precious without God, and the living soul just given stands related to the quickening spirit."

". . . I can get little time for study, as I must help

SAMUEL G. HOWE, WITH HIS GRANDCHILD
ALICE RICHARDS, 1873

nurse dear Flossy. My mind is strangely divided between my dear work and my dear child and grandchild. I must try to keep along with both, but on no account to neglect the precious grandchild."

"*October 1.* O year! thou art running low. The last trimester."

"*October 2.* This day, thirty-two years ago, my dearest brother Henry died in my arms, the most agonizing experience. Never again did Death so enter into my heart, until my lovely son of three years departed many years later, leaving a blank as sad and bitter. Henry was a rare and delicate person. . . . His life was a most valuable one to us for help and counsel, as well as for affection. Perhaps no one to-day thinks about his death except me, his junior by two years, wearing now into the decline of life. Dear brother, I look forward to the reunion with you, but wish my record were whiter and brighter."

"*October 5.* Boston. Came up for directors' meeting of New England Woman's Club. Went afterward to Mrs. Cheney's lecture on English literature. . . . A suggestive and interesting essay, which I was glad to hear and have others hear. It gave me a little pain, that, though she pleasantly alluded to me as one who has laid aside the laurel for the olive branch, she said nothing whatever about my writings, which deserve to be spoken of in characterizing the current literature of the day; but she perhaps does not read or like my works, and besides, people think of me nowadays more as an active woman's woman than as a literary character, as the phrase is. All life is full of trial, and when I hear literary performance praised, and remember my own love for it, and for praise, I think a little how much of all this I have sacrificed in these later years for a service that has made me enemies as well as friends. I felt called upon to do this, and I still think that if I made a mistake, it was one of those honest mistakes it is best to make."

She was giving Maud music lessons this autumn, reading Plutarch with her, taking her to parties and giving parties for her. Later, we find her holding mission services at Vineyard Haven; addressing the Saturday Morning Club ("Subject — *Object :* I smile at this antithesis"); delivering a lecture at Albany — with the lecture left behind.

"Got to work at once making abstracts from memory. . . . Spoke more than an hour. . . . Got my money — would rather have paid it than have had such an experience. Felt as if my inner Guide had misled and deserted me. But some good to some one may come of what I said and tried to say."

She returned from this trip very weary, only to find "my lecture advertised, not one line of it written — subject, 'Men's Women and Women's Women.' Set to work at once, almost overpowered by the task, and the shortness of the time."

The lecture was finished in the morning, delivered in the afternoon.

"Warm congratulations at the close. . . . Such a sense of relief!"

On December 19 she notes the departure of "dear

Flossy and her dearest little Boy. . . . House very desolate without them. This boy is especially dear to
Doctor Howe and myself."

"*December 28.* Maria Mitchell's Club lecture to-day
was beautiful exceedingly. I might have envied her
the steady grasp and unbroken advance of scientific
study, did I not feel sure that God gives to each his
own work. Mine, such as it is, would be helped and
beautified by the knowledge which she imparts so
easily, but perhaps all of her that I shall remember
and try to follow is her spirit. Her silver hair seems
lustrous with spiritual brightness, as do her dark eyes.
Her movements are full of womanly grace, not ballroom grace."

From now on the movement is *sempre crescendo.*
Work for peace, work for clubs; lecturing, preaching,
tending the Doctor in his days of illness; taking the
youngest daughter to balls and parties; founding a
club for her, too. She felt that the young girls of
Maud's age needed the onward impulse as much as
their elders; accordingly, in November, 1871, she called
together a meeting of young women, and with their
aid and good-will formed the Saturday Morning Club
of Boston. The energy with which this organization
sprang into being showed that the time was ripe for it.
That energy, handed on through two generations, is no
less lively to-day; the name of the club recalls a hundred beautiful and interesting occasions.

The Journal hurries us on from day to arduous day.
Even the aspiration of New Year's Day, 1873, breathes

the note of hurry: "Dear Lord, let me this year be worthy to call upon thy name!"

February 5 finds her on another quest: "Mem. Never to come by this route again. Had to turn out at Utica at 4 A.M. Three hours in depot. . . ."

"*March 1.* Went to Saturday Morning Club. Found that John Fiske had failed them. Was told to improvise a lecture on the spot. Did so. . . ."

"*March 5.* Went to hear the arguments in favor of rescinding the vote of censure against Charles Sumner. . . ."

[In 1872, Sumner introduced in the Senate of the United States a resolution that the names of battles with fellow-countrymen should not be continued in the Army Register, nor placed on the regimental colors of the United States. This measure was violently opposed; the Legislature of Massachusetts denounced it as "an insult to the loyal soldiery of the Nation, . . . meeting the unqualified condemnation of the Commonwealth." For more than a year Sumner's friends, headed by John G. Whittier, strove to obtain the rescinding of this censure; it was not till 1874 that it was rescinded by a large majority.]

"*March 10.* A morning for work in my own room, so rare a luxury that I hardly know how to use it. Begin with my Greek Testament. . . ."

"*March 17.* Radical Club. . . . It was an interesting sitting, but I felt as if the Club had about done its work. People get to believing that talk turns the world: it is much, but it is nothing without work. . . ."

"*May 27.* Fifty-four years old to-day. Thank God

for what I have had and hope to have. . . . In the afternoon my dear children had a beautiful birthday party for me, including most of my old friends and some of the newer ones. Agassiz came, and his wife; he brought a bouquet and kissed me. I had beautiful flowers. . . . Poor Chev was ill with a frightful headache. I was much touched by the dear children's affectionate device and shall remember this birthday."

This was the first of the Birthday Receptions, which were to be our happiest festivals through many happy years.

Monday, June 2, was the day she had appointed as Mothers' Peace Day, her annual Peace Festival.

"The day of many prayers dawned propitious, and was as bright and clear as I could have wished."

She was up early, and found the hall "beautifully decorated with many fine bouquets, wreaths, and baskets, the white dove of Peace rising above other emblems." There were two services, morning and evening, and many speakers. "Mr. Tilden and Mr. Garrison both did nobly for me. . . . Thank God for so much!"

She had the great joy of hearing that the day was celebrated in other countries besides her own. In London, Geneva, Constantinople, and various other places, services were held, and men and women prayed and sang in behalf of peace: this she counted among the precious things of the year, and of several years to come.

"*June 6.* Quiet at last, and face to face with the eternal Gospel. Weary and confused, anxious to wind up my business well, and begin my polyglot sheet. . . ."

Yet on June 10 she is arriving in New York at 5.40
A.M., bound for a peace meeting.

"*June 11.* I got two bricks from the dear old house
at the corner of Broadway and Bond Street, now all
down and rebuilding. Will have one enamelled for
myself. Ah, Lord, what a bitter lesson is in this tearing-
down! How I was wanting in duty to the noble parent who built this grand home for me! I hope to help
young people to understand something of parental
love and its responsibilities. But parents also must
study children, since each new soul may require a
new method."

"*June 12.* Home very gladly. Helped Maud with
her Latin. At 3.30 to rehearse 'Midsummer-Night's
Dream.' I Hermia and Snout. At 7.30 the reading,
which was the pleasantest we have had."

[These readings were in the vestry of the Church of
the Disciples. Mr. Clarke, our mother, Erving Winslow, and others of the congregation took part: we
remember the late Professor James Mills Pierce as
Orlando in "As You Like It"; his beautiful reading of
the part contrasting oddly with his middle-aged, long-
bearded personality. Our mother's rendering of Maria
in "Twelfth Night" was something to remember.]

"*June 17.* Up at five and to get a boat. Maud and
the Lieutenant [Zalinski] rowed me to Fort Independence and back, a most refreshing excursion. Dear Dr.
Hedge came out to make a morning visit. I kept him
as long as I could. We talked of Bartol, Rubinstein,
Father Taylor, and Margaret Fuller, whom he knew
when she was fourteen years old. He urged me to labor

for dress reform, which he considered much needed. Had preached two sermons on the subject which his dressy parishioners resented, telling him that their husbands approved of their fine clothes. I begged him to unearth these sermons and give them to us at the club. We spoke of marriage, and I unfolded rapidly my military and moral theory of human relations. Thought of a text for a sermon on this subject: 'Arise, take up thy bed and walk.' This because the ills of marriage which are deemed incurable are not. We must meet them with the energetic will which converts evil into good, and without which all good degenerates into evil."

July finds her at Oak Glen. She is full of texts and sermons, but makes time to write to Fanny Perkins,[1] proposing "*Picnics with a Purpose*, sketching, seaside lectures, astronomical evenings." This thought may have been the germ from which grew the Town and Country Club, of which more hereafter.

The writing of sermons seems to have crowded serious poetry out of sight in these days, but the Comic Muse was always at hand with tambourine and flageolet, ready to strike up at a moment's notice. There was much coming and going of young men and maidens at Oak Glen in those days, and much singing of popular songs of a melancholy or desperate cast. The maiden was requested to take back the heart she had given; what was its anguish to her? There were handfuls of earth in a coffin hid, a coffin under the daisies, the

[1] Mrs. Charles C. Perkins.

beautiful, beautiful daisies; and so on, and so on, *ad lachrymam.* She bore all this patiently; but one day she said to Maud, "Come! You and these young persons know nothing whatever of real trouble. I will make you a song about a real trouble!" And she produced, words and tune, the following ditty: —

COOKERY BOOKERY, OH!

My Irish cook has gone away
Upon my dinner-party day;
I don't know what to do or say —
Cookery bookery, oh!

Chorus :

Sing, saucepan, range, and kitchen fire!
Sing, coals are high and always higher!
Sing, crossed and vexed, till you expire!
Cookery bookery, oh!

She could cook every kind of dish,
"Wittles" of meat and "wittles" of fish,
And soup as fancy as you wish —
And she is gone away!

She weighed two hundred pounds of cheek,
She had a voice that made me meek,
I had to listen when she did speak —
Cookery bookery, oh!

My husband comes, a saucy elf,
And eyes the saucepan on the shelf;
Says he, "Why don't you cook yourself?"
Cookery bookery, oh!

Chorus :

Sing, saucepan, range, and kitchen fire!
Sing, coals are high and always higher!
Sing, crossed and vexed, till you expire!
Cookery bookery, oh!

Jocosa Lyra! one chord of its gay music suggests
another. It may have been in this summer that she
wrote "The Newport Song," which also has its own
lilting melody.

> *Non sumus fashionabiles:*
> *Non damus dapes splendides:*
> But in a modest way, you know,
> We like to see our money go;
> *Et gaudeamus igitur,*
> Our soul has nought to fidget her!
>
> We do not care to quadrigate
> On Avenues in gilded state:
> No gold-laced footmen laugh behind
> At our vacuity of mind:
> But in a modest one-horse shay,
> We rumble, tumble as we may,
> *Et gaudeamus igitur,*
> Our soul has nought to fidget her!
>
> When æstivation is at end,
> We've had our fun and seen our friend.
> No thought of payment makes us ill,
> We don't know such a word as "bill":
> *Et gaudeamus igitur,*
> Our soul has nought to fidget her!

She always tried to go at least once in the summer
to see the old people at the Town Farm, a pleasant,
gray old house, not far from Oak Glen.

"In the afternoon visited the poorhouse with J. and
F. and found several of the old people again, old Nancy
who used to make curious patchwork; old Benny, half-
witted; Elsteth, Henrietta, and Harriet, very glad to
see us. Julia read them a Psalm, then Harriet and
Elsteth sang an interminable Methodist hymn, and I
was moved to ask if they would like to have me pray

with them. They assented, and I can only say that my heart was truly lifted up by the sense of the universality of God's power and goodness, to which these forlorn ones could appeal as directly as could the most powerful, rich, or learned people."

Later she writes: —

"The summer seems to me to have been rich in good and in interest as I review it. Sweet, studious days, pleasant intercourse with friends, the joy of preaching, and very much in all this the well-being of my dear family, children and grandchildren, their father and grandfather enjoying them with me. This is much to thank God for."

Some of the family lingered on after most of the household *impedimenta* had been sent up to Boston, and were caught napping.

"Sitting quietly with Chev over the fire after a game of whist with Julia and Paddock, — a hack-driver knocked at the door of our little back parlor, saying that a gentleman was waiting at the front door for admission. I opened the door and found Dr. Alex Voickoff, who had learned in Boston of our being here and had come down to stay over Sunday. The floors of nearly every parlor and bedroom had been newly oiled. We had no spare bedding. I spared what I could from my ill-provided bed — we made the guest as comfortable as we could. The bedding had been sent up to Boston. *Hinc illæ lachrymæ.*"

"*November 26.* Saw Salvini's 'Othello.' As wonderful as people say it is. The large theatre [the Boston] packed, and so quiet that you could have heard a pin

drop. From the serene majesty of the opening scenes
to the agony of the end, all was grand and astounding
even to us to whom the play is familiar. The Italian
version seemed to me very fine, preserving all the literary points of the original. In fact it seemed as if I had
always before heard the play through an English translation, so much did the Italian speech and action light
it up."

She found Salvini's "Hamlet" "not so good for him
as 'Othello,' yet he was wonderful in it, and made a
very strong impression."

She met the great actor, and found his manners "cordial, natural, and high-toned." She gave a dinner-
party for him, and found him to improve more and
more on further acquaintance. He became a valued
friend, always greeted with delight.

In December, 1873, Richard Ward, her last surviv-
ing uncle, died. He had lived on at No. 8 Bond Street
after the death of Uncle John, and had kept up the
traditions of that hospitable house, always receiving
her most affectionately.

"*December 11.* Uncle Richard's funeral. A quiet one,
but on the whole satisfactory and almost pleasant, he
having lived out his life and dying surrounded by his
children and other relatives, and the family gathering
around his remains wearing an aspect of cordiality and
mutual good-will. I put a sprig of white daphne in the
folds of the marble drapery of dear father's bust and
kissed the bust, feeling that it had taken all of these
years to teach me his value and the value of the moral
and spiritual inheritance which I had from him and

could not wholly waste with all the follies which
checker the better intentions of my life. I went to
Greenwood and into the vault, and saw the sacred
names of the dear departed on the slabs which sealed
the deposit of their remains. It was all like a dream
and a sad one."

"*December 12.* No. 8 Bond Street. I came down here
to write the records of yesterday and to-day in this
dear old house, whose thronging memories rise up to
wring my heart, in the prospect of its speedy disman-
tlement and the division of its dear contents. Here I
came on my return from Europe in 1844, bringing my
dear Julia, then an infant of six months. Uncle John
had just bought and fitted it up. Here I came to attend
Sister Louisa's wedding, Uncle John being rather distant to me, supposing that I had favored the marriage.
Here I saw dear Brother Marion for the last time. Here
I came in my most faulty and unhappy period. Here,
after my first publications; here, to see my play acted
at Wallack's. Here, when death had taken my dearest
Sammy from me. Uncle John was so kind and merciful
at that time, and always except that once, when indeed
he did not express *dis*pleasure, but I partly guessed it
and learned it more fully afterwards. God's blessing
rest upon the memory of this hospitable and unstained
house. It seems to me as if neither words nor tears
could express the pain I feel in closing this account
with my father's generation."

The most important episode of 1874, the visit to
Samana, has already been described. Turning the

leaves of the Journal for this year, we feel that the change and break were necessary to her as well as to the Doctor. There were limits even to her strength.

"*January, 1874.* A sort of melancholy of confusion, not knowing how I can possibly get through with the various requisitions made upon my time, strength, thought, and sympathy. Usually I feel, even in these moods, the nearness of divine help. To-day it seems out of my consciousness, but is not on that account out of my belief. . . ."

"The past week one dreadful hurry. Things look colorless when you whirl so fast past them."

"The month ending to-day seems the most hurried of my life. Woman's Club, Saturday Club, Philosophical group, Maud's music, ditto party, and all her dressing and gayety, beside writing for [the Woman's] Journal, . . . two lectures [Salem and Weston], both gratuitous, and the care of getting up and advertising Bishop Ferrette's lectures. And in all these things I seem not to do, rather than to do, the dissipation of effort so calls me away from the quiet, concentrated sort of work which I love."

It was time for the Doctor to say "Come!" and to carry her off to those tropical solitudes they had learned to love so well. Yet the departure was painful, for Maud must be left behind. On March 1 we read: —

"Of to-day I wish to preserve the fact that, waking early in painful perplexity about Maud, Santo Domingo, etc., and praying that the right way might open for me and for all of us, my prayer seemed answered by the very great comfort I had in hearing the prayer and sermon of Henry Powers of New York. The decided spiritual tone of the prayer made me feel that I must try to take, every day, this energetic attitude of moral will and purpose, even if I fail in much that I wish to do."

On May 27 she writes: —

"My birthday. Fifty-five years old. Still face to face with the mercies of God in health and sanity, enjoying all true pleasures more than ever and weaned from some false ones. I feel a great lassitude, probably from my cold and yesterday's fatigue. I have not worked this year as I did the year before, yet I have worked a good deal, too, and perhaps have tried more to fulfil the duty nearest at hand. . . . I thank God for my continued life, health, and comfort. . . . I ask to see Samana free before I go. . . . 'Thy will be done' is the true prayer."

Samana was not to be free, spite of the efforts of its friends, and she was not to see it again.

The record of this year and the next is a chronicle of arduous work, with the added and ever-deepening note of anxiety; it was only for a time that the visit to Samana checked the progress of the Doctor's physical failure. He was able in the summer of 1874 to write the forty-third report of the Perkins Institution: an important one in which he reviewed his whole work among the blind. He felt that this would probably be his last earthly task; yet the following summer found him again taking up the familiar work, laboring with what little strength was left him, and when eyes and hand refused to answer the call of the spirit, dic-

"GREEN PEACE"
From a photograph taken in 1875

tating to his faithful secretary. It has been told elsewhere how in this last summer of his life he labored to make more beautiful and more valuable the summer home which had become very dear to him. Returned to Green Peace, he had some happy days in his garden, but for gardener and garden they were the last days. The city had decided to put a street through Green Peace: already workmen were digging trenches and cutting trees. Our mother went to the authorities, and told them of his feeble condition. The work was stopped at once, and not resumed during his lifetime.

Through these years her time was divided between the invalid and the many public duties which had already taken possession of her life. Little by little these were crowded out: instead of lecture or concert came the ever-shortening walk with the Doctor, the evening game of whist or backgammon which lightened a little his burden of pain and weariness.

Yet she was preparing, on January 4, 1876, to keep a lecture engagement of long standing, when the blow fell. He was stricken down, and lay for some days insensible, waiting the final summons.

There was no hope of his recovery: those around him waited patiently, any violence of grief held in check by the silent rebuke of the serene face on the pillow.

The day after his death she writes: —

"I awoke at 4.30, but lay still to bear the chastening hand of God, laid upon me in severe mercy. . . .

"Some good words came to me: 'Let not your heart be troubled,' etc. 'He doth not willingly afflict,' etc.

"Before breakfast went into Chev's room, so sweet and peaceful. . . . I laid my lace veil, my bridal veil, upon the head of his bedstead. . . . In place of my dear husband I have now my foolish papers. Yet I have often left him for them. God accept the poor endeavor of my life!"

On the day after the funeral she writes: "Began my new life to-day. Prayed God that it might have a greatly added use and earnestness."

And several weeks later, after the memorial meeting in his honor: —

"Yesterday seems to have filled the measure of the past. To-day I must forward in the paths of the future. My dear love is sometimes with me, at least as an energizing and inspiring influence, but how shall I deserve ever to see him again?"

The paths of the future! She was to tread them with cheerful and willing feet through many long years, never wholly losing the sense of companionship with her good comrade.

She devoted the spring of 1876 to the writing of a brief memoir of him, which was printed in pamphlet form and in raised type for the use of the blind. With the latter object in view the memoir was necessarily brief. The labor of condensing into a small space the record of a long and super-active life was severe, but it was the tonic she needed. The days of quiet at Green Peace, the arduous work, with a page of Greek or a chapter of Baur for relaxation, brought mind and nerves back to their normal condition.

The work speaks for itself. As it is little known to-day outside the schools for the blind, we quote the concluding paragraph: —

"In what is said, to-day, concerning the motherhood of the human race, the social and spiritual aspects of this great office are not wholly overlooked. It must be remembered that there is also a fatherhood of human society, a vigilance and forethought of benevolence recognized in the individuals who devote their best energies to the interests of mankind. The man to whose memory the preceding pages are dedicated is one of those who have best filled this relation to their race. Watchful of its necessities, merciful to its short-comings, careful of its dignity, and cognizant of its capacity, may the results of his labor be handed down to future generations, and may his name and example be held in loving and lasting remembrance."

CHAPTER XVII

THE WOMAN'S CAUSE

1868–1910

Women who weave in hope the daily web,
Who leave the deadly depths of passion pure,
Who hold the stormy powers of will attent,
As Heaven directs, to act, or to endure;

No multitude strews branches in their way,
Not in their praise the loud arena strives;
Still as a flameless incense rises up
The costly patience of their offered lives.

J. W. H.

WE have seen that after the Doctor's death our mother felt that another chapter of life had begun for her. It was a changed world without that great and dominant personality. She missed the strength on which she had leaned for so many years, the weakness which through the past months she had tended and cherished. Henceforth she must lead, not follow; must be captain instead of mate.

In another sense, the new life had actually begun for her some years before, when she first took up public activities; to those activities she now turned the more ardently for the great void that was left in heart and home. We must now go back to the later sixties, and speak of her special interests at that time.

Looking back over her long life, we see her in three

aspects, those of the student, the artist, the reformer. First came youth, with its ardent study; then maturity, with its output of poems, plays, essays. So far she had followed the natural course of creative minds, which must absorb and assimilate in order that they may give out. It is in the third phase that we find the aspect of her later life, a clear vision of the needs of humanity, and a profound hospitality which made it imperative for her to give with both hands not only what she had inherited, but what she had earned. Having enjoyed unusual advantages herself, the moment she saw the way to give other women these advantages, she was eager to "help the woman-standard new unfurled."

In the first number of the "Woman's Journal," of which she was one of the founders and first editors, she writes (January 8, 1870): —

"We who stand beside the cradle of this enterprise are not young in years. Our children are speedily preparing to take our place in the ranks of society. Some of us have been looking thoughtfully toward the final summons, not because of ill health or infirmity, but because, after the establishment of our families, no great object intervened between ourselves and that last consummation. But these young undertakings detain us in life. While they need so much care and counsel, we cannot consent to death. And this first year, at least, of our Journal, we are determined to live through."

Again she writes of this new departure: —

"In an unexpected hour a new light came to me,

showing me a world of thought and character. The
new domain was that of true womanhood, woman no
longer in her ancillary relation to man, but in direct
relation to the divine plan and purpose, as a free agent
fully sharing with man every human right and every
human responsibility. This discovery was like the addition of a new continent to the map of the world. It
did not come all at once. In my philosophizing I at
length reached the conclusion that woman must be
the moral and spiritual equivalent of man. How otherwise could she be entrusted with the awful and inevitable responsibilities of maternity? The Civil War
came to an end, leaving the slave not only emancipated but endowed with the full dignity of citizenship.
The women of the North had greatly helped to open
the door which admitted him to freedom and its safeguard, the ballot. Was the door to be shut in their
face?"

When this new world of thought, this new continent
of sympathy was opened to her, she was nearly fifty
years old. "Oh! had I earlier known," she exclaims,
"the power, the nobility, the intelligence which lie
within the range of true womanhood, I had surely
lived more wisely and to better purpose."

Speaking of this new interest in her life, her old
friend Tom Appleton (who had not the least sympathy
with it) once said, "Your mother's great importance to
this cause is that she forms a bridge between the world
of society and the world of reform."

She soon found that she was not alone in her questioning; similar thoughts to hers were germinating

in the minds of many women. In our own and other countries a host of earnest souls were awake, pressing eagerly forward. In quick succession came the women's clubs and colleges, the renewed demand for woman suffrage, the Association for the Advancement of Women, the banding together of women ministers. The hour had come, and the women. In all these varying manifestations of one great forward and upward movement in America, Julia Ward Howe was *pars magna.* Indeed, the story of the latter half of her life is the story of the Advance of Woman and the part she played in it.

The various phases may be taken in order. Oberlin, the first coeducational college, was chartered in 1834. Vassar, the first college for women only, was chartered in 1861, opened in 1865. Smith and Wellesley followed in 1875. Considering this brave showing, it is strange to recall the great fight before the barred doors of the great universities. The women knocked, gently at first, then strongly: our mother, Mrs. Agassiz, and the rest. They were greeted by a storm of protest. Learned books were written, brilliant lectures delivered, to prove that a college education was ruinous to the health of women, perilous to that of future generations. The friends of Higher Education replied in words no less ardent. Blast and counterblast rang forth. Still the patient hands knocked, the earnest voices called: till at length — there being friends as well as foes inside — slowly, with much creaking and many forebodings, the great doors opened; a crack, then a space, till to-day they swing wide, and the

Higher Education of Women now stands firm as the Pyramids.

The idea of woman suffrage had long been repugnant to our mother. The demand for it seemed unreasonable; she was inclined to laugh both at the cause and its advocates; yet when, in November, 1868, Colonel Thomas Wentworth Higginson asked her to give her name to a call for a meeting in behalf of woman suffrage she did not refuse. It would be "a liberal and friendly meeting," the Colonel said, "without bitterness or extravagance."

On the day of the meeting she "strayed into Horticultural Hall" in her "rainy-day suit, with no idea of taking any active part in the proceedings." Indeed, she had hoped to remain unnoticed, until summoned by an urgent message to join those who sat upon the platform; reluctantly she obeyed the summons. With this simple action the old order changed for her. On the platform were gathered the woman suffrage leaders, some of whom she already knew: William Lloyd Garrison, Wendell Phillips, Thomas Wentworth Higginson, James Freeman Clarke; veteran captains of Reform, her husband's old companions-in-arms. Looking in their steadfast faces, she felt that she belonged with them; that she must help to draw the car of progress, not drag like a brake on its wheel.

Beside these were some unknown to her. She saw now for the first time the sweet face of Lucy Stone, heard the silver voice which was to be dear to her through many years. "Here stood the true woman, pure, noble, great-hearted, with the light of her good

life shining in every feature of her face." These men
and women had been the champions of the slave.
They now asked for wives and mothers those civil
rights which had been given to the negro; "that im-
partial justice for which, if for anything, a Republican
Government should stand." Their speech was earnest; she listened as to a new gospel. When she was
asked to speak, she could only say, "I am with you."

With the new vision came the call of a new duty.
"What can I do?" she asked. The answer was ready.
The New England Woman Suffrage Association was
formed, and she was elected its first president. This
office she held, with some interruptions, through life.
It is well to recall the patient, faithful work of the
pioneer suffragists, who, without money or prestige,
spent *themselves* for the cause. Their efforts, compared
to the well-organized and well-financed campaigns of
to-day, are as a "certain upper chamber" compared
with the basilica of St. Peter, yet it was in that quiet
room that the tongues of Pentecost spoke.

"I am glad," she often said, "to have joined the
suffrage movement, because it has brought me into
such high company."

The convert buckled to her new task with all her
might, working for it early and late with an ardor that
counted no cost.

"Oh! dear Mrs. Howe, you are so *full* of inspiration!"
cried a foolish woman. "It enables you to do *so
much!*"

"Inspiration!" said "dear Mrs. Howe," shortly.
"Inspiration means *perspiration!*"

She says of her early work for suffrage: —

"One of the comforts which I found in the new association was the relief which it afforded me from a sense of isolation and eccentricity. For years past I had felt strongly impelled to lend my voice to the convictions of my heart. I had done this in a way, from time to time, always with the feeling that my course in doing so was held to call for apology and explanation by the men and women with whose opinions I had hitherto been familiar. I now found a sphere of action in which this mode of expression no longer appeared singular or eccentric, but simple, natural, and, under the circumstances, inevitable."

It was no small thing for her to take up this burden. The Doctor, although a believer in equal suffrage, was strongly opposed to her taking any active part in public life. He felt as Grandfather Howe had felt forty years before when his son Sam spoke in public for the sake of Greece; it jarred on his traditions. Others of the family also deplored the new departure, and her personal friends almost with one accord held up hands of horror or deprecation. These things were inexpressibly painful to her; she loved approbation; the society and sympathy of "kent folk," whose traditions corresponded with her own; but her hand was on the plough; there was no turning back.

Suffrage worked her hard. The following year the New England Woman Suffrage Association issued a call for the formation of a national body; the names signed were Lucy Stone, Caroline M. Severance, Julia Ward Howe, T. W. Higginson, and G. H. Vibbert.

Representatives from twenty-one States assembled in Cleveland, November 24, 1869, and formed the American Woman Suffrage Association. There was already a "National Woman Suffrage Association," formed a few months earlier; the new organization differed from the other in some points of policy, notably in the fact that men as well as women were recognized among the leaders. Colonel Higginson was its president at one time, Henry Ward Beecher, Bishop Gilbert Haven, and Dudley Foulke at others. The New England Woman's Club also admitted men to membership: it was a point our mother had much at heart. She held that the Quaker organization was the best, with its separate meetings of men and women, supplemented by a joint session of both. She always insisted upon the salutary influence that men and women exercise upon one another.

"The two sexes police each other," she often said. She always maintained the importance of their united action in matters of public as of private interest. She was essentially a humanist in contradistinction to a feminist.

She worked for the American Association during the twenty-one years of its separate existence, first as foreign corresponding secretary, afterward as president, and in various other capacities. When, in 1890, the two societies united to form the National American Woman Suffrage Association, she became and continued through life one of the vice-presidents of that body. From the first, she was recognized as an invaluable leader. The years of philosophical study had made her mind supple, alert, quick to grasp and to respond, even as the study of languages brought her the gift of ready speech and pure diction. Her long practice in singing had given her voice strength, sweetness, and carrying power; above all, she was a natural orator, and speaking was a joy to her. The first time she ever made a speech in public was to a group of soldiers of the Army of the Potomac on the occasion of a visit to Washington during the war. She had driven out to visit the camp outside the Capital. Colonel William B. Greene disconcerted her very much by saying, "Mrs. Howe, you must speak to my men."

She refused, and ran away to hide in an adjacent tent. The Colonel insisted, and finally she managed to make a very creditable little speech to the soldiers.

Now, she no longer ran away when called upon to speak. Wherever the work called her, she went gladly; like St. Paul, she was "in journeyings often, . . . in weariness and painfulness, in watchings often"; the journals are full of incidents picturesque to read, uncomfortable to live through. Occasionally, after some tremendous exertion, we read, "Maud must not know of this!" or, "No one must ever know that I took the wrong train!"

Much of her most important work for woman suffrage was done at the State House, Boston. In Massachusetts, the custom of bringing this subject before the legislature every year long prevailed. She always went to these hearings. She considered it a privilege to take part in them; counted them "among her most valued recollections." They extended over forty years or more.

These occasions were often exasperating as well as fatiguing. She never wearied of presenting the arguments for suffrage; she often suffered vexation of spirit in refuting those brought against it, but she never refused the battle. "If I were mad enough," she said once, "I could speak in Hebrew!"

She was "mad enough" when at a certain hearing woman suffrage was condemned as a "minority cause." Her words, if not in Hebrew, show the fighting spirit of ancient Israel.

We quote from memory:—

The Reverend ———: "The fact that most women are indifferent or opposed is a sufficient proof that woman suffrage is wrong."

Mrs. Howe: "May I ask one question? Were the Twelve Apostles wrong in trying to bring about a better social condition when almost the whole community was opposed to them?"

Dr. ———: "I suppose that question was asked merely for rhetorical effect."

Mrs. Howe (having asked for two minutes to reply, with the whispered comment, "*I shall die* if I am not allowed to speak!"): "I do not know how it is with Dr. ———, but I was not brought up to use the Bible for rhetorical effect. To my mind, the suffragists and their opponents are like the wise and the foolish virgins of the parable, equal in number but not in wisdom. When the Bridegroom cometh, may Dr. ——— have his wedding garment ready!"

She thus recalls some of the scenes in the State House where she was so long a familiar figure: —

"I have again and again been one of a deputation charged with laying before a legislature the injustice of the law which forbids the husband a business contract with his wife, and of that which denies to a married woman the right to be appointed guardian of her children. We reasoned also against what in legal language is termed 'the widow's quarantine,' the ordinance which forbids a widow to remain in her husband's house more than forty days without paying rent, the widower in such case possessing an unlimited right to abide under the roof of his deceased wife. Finally, we dared ask that night-walkers of the male sex should be made liable to the same penalties as women for the same offence. Our bill passed the legislature, and became part of the laws of Massachusetts."

Elsewhere she writes: "In Massachusetts the suffragists worked for fifty-five years before they succeeded in getting a law making mothers equal guardians of their minor children with the fathers. In Colorado, when the women were enfranchised, the next legislature passed such a bill." Of the movement by which women won a right to have a voice in the education of their children, she says: "The proposal to render women eligible for service on the School Board was met at first with derision and with serious disapproval. The late Abby W. May had much to do with the early consideration of this measure, and the work which finally resulted in its adoption had its first beginning in the parlors of the New England Woman's Club, where special meetings were held in its behalf. The extension of the school suffrage to women followed, after much work on the part of men and of women."

"These meetings," she said once, speaking before the Massachusetts Woman Suffrage Association, "show, among other things, the character of those who believe in suffrage with their whole heart. We who are gathered here are not a frantic, shrieking mob. We are not contemners of marriage, nor neglecters of home and offspring. We are individually allowed to be men and women of sound intellect, of reputable life, having the same stake and interest in the well-being of the community that others have. Most of us are persons of moderate competence, earned or inherited. We have had, or hope to have, our holy fireside, our joyful cradle, our decent bank account. Why should any consider us as the enemies of society, we who have everything to gain by its good government?"

It seems fitting to add a few more of her words in behalf of the cause which she served so long, — words spoken at Club meetings, at Conventions before Legislatures.

"But besides the philosophy of woman suffrage, we want its religion. Human questions are not glorified until they are brought into touch with the Divine. . . ."

"The weapon of Christian warfare is the ballot, which represents the peaceable assertion of conviction and will. Adopt it, O you women, with clean hands and a pure heart!"

. . . .

"The religion which makes me a moral agent equally
with my father and brother, gives me my right and
title to the citizenship which I am here to assert. I
ought to share equally with them its privileges and
its duties. No man can have more at stake in the community than I have. Imposition of taxes, laws concerning public health, order, and morality, affect me
precisely as they affect the male members of my
family, and I am bound equally with them to look to
the maintenance of a worthy and proper standard and
status in all of these departments."

. . . .

"God forbid that in this country chivalry and legislation should be set one against the other. I ask you,
gentlemen, to put your chivalry into your legislation.
Let the true Christian knighthood find its stronghold
in your ranks. Arm yourselves with the best reasons,
with the highest resolve, and deliver us poor women from
the injustice which oppresses and defrauds us."

. . . .

"Revere the religion of home. Keep its aitar flame
bright in your heart. . . . The vestals of ancient Rome
were at once guardians of the hearth and custodians
of the archives of the Roman State. So, in every time,
the home conserves the sacred flame of life, and the
destiny of the nation rests with those who keep it."

. . . .

"Go abroad with the majesty and dignity of your
home about you. . . . Let the modest graces of the
fireside adorn you in the great gathering. This is a

new sort of home missionary, one who shall carry the
blessed spirit of home wherever she goes, a spirit of
rest, of healing, of reconciliation and good-will."

.   .   .   .

"One aspect of this [the military argument] would
make the protection which men are supposed to give
to women in time of war the equivalent for the political
rights denied them. But, gentlemen, let me ask what
protection can you give us which shall compare with
the protection we give you when you are born, little
helpless creatures, into the world, without feet to stand
upon, or hands to help yourselves? Without this tender,
this unceasing protection, no man of you would live
to grow up. It may easily happen that no man of a
whole generation shall ever be called upon to defend
the women of his country in the field. But it cannot
happen that the women of any generation shall fail
to give their unwearied and energetic protection to the
infant men born of it. Some of us know how full of
labor and detail this protection is; what anxious days,
what sleepless nights it involves. The mothers are
busy at home, not only building up the bodies of the
little men, but building up their minds too, teaching
them to be gentle, pure and honest, cultivating the
elements of the human will, that great moralizing
power on which the State and the Church depend. A
man is very happy if he can ever repay to his mother
the protection she gave him in his infancy. So, the
plea of protection has two sides."

"If manhood suffrage is unsatisfactory, it does not
at all show that woman suffrage would be. On the con-

trary, we might make it much better by bringing to it the feminine mind, which, in a way, complements the masculine, and so, I think, completes the mind of humanity. We are half of humanity, and I do frankly believe that we have half the intelligence and good sense of humanity, and that it is quite time that we should express not only our sentiments but our determined will, to set our faces as a flint toward justice and right, and to follow these through the difficult path, through the thorny wilderness. Not to the bitter end, but a very sweet end, and I hope it may be before my end comes."

. . . .

Her last service to the cause of woman suffrage was to send a circular letter to all the editors and to all the ministers of four leading denominations in the four oldest suffrage States, Wyoming, Colorado, Utah, and Idaho, asking whether equal suffrage worked well or ill. She received 624 answers, 62 not favorable, 46 in doubt, and 516 in favor. A letter from her to the London "Times," stating these results, appeared on the same day that the news of her death was cabled to Europe.

Thinking of the long years of effort which followed her adoption of the cause of woman suffrage, a word of the Doctor's, spoken in 1875, comes vividly to mind.

"Your cause," said he, "lacks one element of success, and that is opposition. It is so distinctly just that it will slide into popularity." He little thought that the cause was to wait forty years for that slide!

Side by side with the suffrage movement, growing along with it and with the women's clubs, and in time to be absorbed by them, was another movement which was for many years very dear to her, the Association for the Advancement of Women.

This Association had its beginning in 1873, when Sorosis, then a sturdy infant, growing fast and reaching out in every direction, issued a call for a Congress of Women in New York in the autumn of that year. She says of this call: —

"Many names, some known, others unknown to me, were appended to the document first sent forth. My own was asked for. Should I give or withhold it? Among the signatures already obtained, I saw that of Maria Mitchell,[1] and this determined me to give my own."

She went to the Congress, and "viewed its proceedings a little critically at first," its plan appearing to her "rather vast and vague."

Yet she felt the idea of the Association to be a good one; and when it was formed, with the above title, and with Mrs. Livermore as president, she was glad to serve on a sub-committee, charged with selecting topics and speakers for the first annual Congress.

The object of the Association was "to consider and present practical methods for securing to women higher intellectual, moral, and physical conditions, with a view to the improvement of all domestic and social relations."

[1] She had a great regard and admiration for Miss Mitchell. Scientific achievement seemed to her well-nigh miraculous, and roused in her an almost childlike reverence.

At its first Congress she said:

"How can women best associate their efforts for the amelioration of Society? We must come together in a teachable and religious spirit. Women, while building firmly and definitely the fabric they decide to rear, must yet build with an individual tolerance which their combined and corporate wisdom may better explain. The form of the Association should be representative, in a true and wide sense. Deliberation in common, mutual instruction, achievement for the whole better and more valuable than the success of any, — these should be the objects held constantly in view. The good of all the aim of each. The discipline of labor, faith, and sacrifice is necessary. Our growth in harmony of will and in earnestness of purpose will be far more important than in numbers."

One hundred and ninety women formed this Association: a year later there were three hundred. The second Congress was held in Chicago, with an attendance "very respectable in numbers and character from the first, and very full in afternoon and evening."

On the second day, October 16, 1874, the subject considered was "Crime and Reform." The Journal says: —

"Mrs. Ellen Mitchell's paper on fallen women was first-rate throughout. I spoke first after it, saying that we must carry the war into Africa and reform the men. . . ."

The meetings of the Congress grew more and more important to her. That of 1875 found her "much tossed in mind" about going, on account of the

Doctor's ill health. She consulted Mr. Clarke, but felt afterward that this was a mistake.

"My dæmon says: 'Go and say nothing. Nobody can help you bear your own child.'"

She went.

No matter how fatiguing these journeys were, she never failed to find some enjoyment in them; many were the pleasant "fruits of friendship" gathered along the way. Some one of the sisters was sure to have a tiny teapot in her basket; another would produce a spirit-lamp; they drank their tea, shared their sandwiches, and were merry. She loved to travel with her "dear big Livermore," with Lucy Stone, and the faithful Blackwells, father and daughter; perhaps her best-loved companion was Ednah Cheney, her "esteemed friend of many years, excellent in counsel and constant and loyal in regard."

Once she and Mrs. Cheney appeared together at an "A.A.W." meeting in a Southern city, where speaking and singing were to alternate on the programme. It was in their later years: both were silver-haired and white-capped. Our mother was to announce the successive numbers. Glancing over the programme, she saw that Mr. So-and-So was to sing "The Two Grenadiers." With a twinkling glance toward Mrs. Cheney, she announced, "The next number will be 'The Two Granny Dears'!"

The Reverend Antoinette Blackwell, describing one of these journeys, says: —

"As we went onward I was ready to close my eyes and 'loll' or look lazily out to see the flying landscape

seem to be doing the work. When I roused enough to
look at Mrs. Howe she was reading. Later, I looked
again, she was still reading. This went on mile after
mile till I was enough interested to step quietly across
the aisle and peep over Mrs. Howe's shoulder without disturbing her. She was reading a Greek volume,
apparently with as much enjoyment as most of us gain
from reading in plain English when we are not tired.
. . . With apparent unwearied enjoyment, she told us
anecdotes, repeated the little stories and rhymes and
sang the little songs which she had given to her children and grandchildren. . . .

"We lingered at the breakfast table in the morning
and among other things came to comparing social likes
and dislikes. 'I never can bring myself to destroy the
least bit of paper,' said Mrs. Howe, meaning paper
written on, containing the record of human thought
and feeling which might be of worth, and its only record. To her these were the chief values of life."

The following notes are taken from the record
of "A.A.W." journeys in the eighties: —

"*Buffalo, October 22, 1881.* I felt quite distracted
about leaving home when I came this way for the
Congress, but have felt clear about the good of it, ever
since. I rarely have much religious meditation in
these days, except to be very sorry for a very faulty
life. I will therefore record the fact that I have felt
an unusual degree of religious comfort in these last
days. It seemed a severe undertaking to preach to-day
after so busy a week, and with little or no time for
preparation. But my text came to me as it usually

does, and a hope that the sermon would be given to me, which, indeed, it seemed to be. I thought it out in bed last night and this morning. . . ."

"My beautiful, beautiful West,
I clasp thee to my breast!
Or rather down I lie,
Like a little old babe and cry,
A babe to second childhood born,
Astonished at the mighty morn,
And only pleading to be fed,
From Earth's illimitable bread!"

"Left Schenectady yesterday. Drawing-room car. Read Greek a good deal. At Syracuse I took the tumbler of the car and ran out to get some milk, etc., for supper. Spent 25 cents, and took my slender meal in the car, on a table. After this, slept profoundly all the evening; took the sleeper at Rochester, and slept like the dead, having had very insufficient sleep for two nights past. Was awakened early to get out at Cleveland — much detained by a young woman who got into the dressing-room before me, and stayed to make an elaborate toilet, keeping every one else out. When at last she came out, I said to her, 'Well, madam, you have taken your own time, to the inconvenience of everybody else. You are the most selfish woman I ever travelled with.' Could get only a cup of coffee and a roll at Cleveland — much confusion about cars — regained mine, started, and found that I had left my trunk at Cleveland, unchecked. Flew to conductor, who immediately took measures to have it forwarded. Must wait all day at Shelby, in the most forlorn hole I ever saw called a hotel. No parlor, a dark bedroom for me to stay in, a cold hell without the

fire, and a very hot one with it. Dirty bed not made
up, a sinister likeness of Schuyler Colfax hanging high
on the wall, and a print of the managers of Andy Johnson's impeachment. I — in distress about my trunk
— have telegraphed to Mansfield for the title of my
lecture and learn that it is 'Polite Society.' Must give
it without the manuscript, and must borrow a gown to
give it in."

"*Minnesota in Winter*

"The twistings and turnings of a lecture trip have
brought me twice, in the present season, to Minnesota. . . .

"To an Easterner, a daily walk or two is the first
condition of health. Here, the frost seemed to enter
one's very bones, and to make locomotion difficult. . . .
Life at the hotel was mostly an anxious *tête-à-tête*
with an air-tight stove. Sometimes you roasted before
it, sometimes you froze. As you crammed it with wood
at night, you said, 'Will you, oh! will you burn till
morning?' Finally, on the coldest night of all, and at
that night's noon, you bade it farewell, on your way to
the midnight train, and wondered whether you should
be likely to go further and fare worse. . . .

"After the lecture an informal sitting was held in
the parlor of my hostess, at which there was much talk
of the clubs of Boston; 'If I forget thee, O Jerusalem!'
being the predominant tone in the minds of those present. And at noon, away, away, in the caboose of a
freight car, to meet the passenger train at Owatonna,
and so reach Minneapolis by early evening.

"To travel in such a caboose is a somewhat rough experience. The dirt is grimy and of long standing. The pictures nailed up on the boards are not of an edifying description. The railroad employees who have admitted us into their place of refuge wear dirty overalls, and eat their dinner out of tin pails all afloat with hot coffee. One of my own sex keeps me in countenance. . . .

"*Minneapolis*

"Twenty years ago, a small collection of wooden houses, of no particular account, except for the natural beauties of the spot on which they stood. New, a thriving and well-built city, whose manufacturers have settled the controversy between use and beauty, by appropriating the Falls of St. Anthony to the running of their saw- and flour-mills. My first sensation of delight here was at finding myself standing on Hennepin Avenue. To a reader of Parkman's histories, the spot was classic. . . . To refresh my own recollections, I had recourse to the Public Library of the town, where I soon found Parkman's 'Discovery of the Great West.' Armed with this volume, with the aid of a cheap and miserable railroad map, I traced out something of the movements of those hardy French explorers. It was like living part of a romance, to look upon the skies and waters which had seen them wandering, suffering, yet undaunted. . . .

"*St. Paul*

"But I cannot rest so near St. Paul without visiting this famous city also. I contemplate a trip in the cars, but my friendly host leaves his business for a day, and drives me over in an open sleigh. I do not undertake this jaunt without Bostonian fears of death of cold, but Minnesota cold is highly stimulating, and with the aid of a bottle of hot water, I make the journey without a shiver. . . . Numbers of Indian squaws from Mendota walk the streets in groups. I follow three of them into a warehouse. One of them has Asiatic features — the others are rather pretty. They are Sioux. I speak to them, but they do not reply. The owner of the warehouse asks what he can show me. I tell him that I desire to see what the squaws will buy. He says that they buy very little, except beads, and have only come into the store to warm themselves. They smile, and obviously understand English. We dine at the hotel, a very pleasant one. There is no printed bill of fare, but the waiter calls off 'beefsteak, porksteak,' etc., and we make a comfortable meal. I desire to purchase some dried buffalo meat, and find some, not without difficulty, as the season for selling it is nearly over. The crowning romance of the day is a sleighride of five miles on the Mississippi, giving us a near view of its fluted bluffs and numerous islets. We visit also the Falls of Minnehaha, now sheeted in ice, but very beautiful, even in this disguise. We talk of 'Hiawatha,' and my companion says, 'If Mr. Longfellow had ever seen a Sioux Indian, he would not have written "Hiawatha."' The way to the bottom of the falls is so slippery with ice that I conclude not to attempt it. The day, which was one of great exposure, passed in great pleasure, and without chill or fatigue. . . .

"In my days of romance, I remember watching
late one night on board the Mediterranean steamer in
order to be sure of the moment in which we should pass
beyond the boundaries of the Italian shore. Something like such a feeling of interest and regret came
over me when, in the unpoetic *sleeper*, I asked at what
hour of the night the cars would pass out of Minnesota
on the way back to Chicago. This sincere testimony
from a veteran of travel, in all sorts, will perhaps con-
vince those who do not know the young State that she
has a great charm of beauty and of climate, besides a
great promise of future prosperity and eminence."

"*Kansas*

"Travel in Minnesota was living romance. Travel
in Kansas is living history. I could not cross its
borders, new as these are, without unlocking a volume
of the past, written in blood and in prayer, and sealed
with the forfeit of noble lives. A ghostly army of war-
riors seemed to escort me as I entered the fair, broad
territory. John Brown, the captain of them, stretched
his hand to the Capitol, and Sumner, and Andrew, and
Howe were with him. Here was the stand made, here
the good fight begun, which, before it was well under
way, divided the thought and sentiment of Europe, as
well as those of America.

"My tired spirit sought to shake off at this point the
commonplace sense of weariness and annoyance. To
be in Kansas, and that for work, not for pastime. To
bring the woman's word where the man's rough sword
and spade had once wrought together, this was poetry,

not prose. To be cold, and hungry, and worn with journeying, could not efface the great interest and pleasure. . . .

"*Atchison*

"I was soon told that a gentleman was anxious to speak with me concerning my land at Grasshopper, which borders immediately upon his own. Judge Van Winkle accordingly, with due permission, waited upon me, and unfolded his errand. Grasshopper, he said, was a growing place. It possessed already a store and an apothecary. It had now occasion for a schoolhouse, and one corner of my land offered the most convenient place for such an institution. The town did not ask me to give this land — it was willing to pay a fair price for the two acres wanted. Wishing to learn a little more about the township, I asked whether it possessed the requisite variety of creeds.

"'Have you a Baptist, a Methodist, an Episcopalian, and a Universalist church?'

"'No,' said my visitor, 'we have no church at all. People who wish to preach can do so in some private house.' I afterwards learn that Judge Van Winkle is a student of Plato; who knows what may be his Hellenic heresy? He is endorsed, however, by others as a good, solid man, and the proposition for the schoolhouse receives my favorable consideration.

"*Leavenworth*

"My first visit to Leavenworth was a stay of a couple of hours between trains, on my way to southern Kansas. Short as this was, it yet brought to my acquaintance two new friends, and to my remembrance two old ones. Of the new friends, the first seen was Rev. Edward Sanborn, the Unitarian minister of the place. Mr. Sanborn met me at the comfortless depot, and insisted upon taking me to his lodgings, where Friend Number Two, in the shape of his amiable wife, added herself to the list of my well-wishers. Mr. Sanborn had just been burned out. His house took fire while he and his wife were spending Christmas Day with a neighbor, and burned so quickly that no article in it could be saved. He had found in the ashes the charred remains of his manuscript sermons, and had good hope of being able to decipher them. As the pleasant minutes passed in easy conversation, I could not help reflecting on the instinctive hospitality of Western life. This cosy corner in a mere hired bedroom had given me a rest and a shelter which I should have been unwilling to ask for in some streets of palaces which have been familiar to me from my youth up."

The Association for the Advancement of Women was a pioneer society, and did vital work for twenty-five years. During the greater part of that time she was its president. She never missed (save when in Europe) one of its annual congresses, or one of the mid-year conferences (of officers only) which she considered of high moment. She worked for the Association with a loving enthusiasm that never varied or faltered; and it was a real grief to her when the changing of the old order resolved it into its elements, to take new shape in the larger and farther-reaching work of the General Federation of Clubs, and other kindred societies.

Many of these may be called the children of "A.A.W." The greatest service of the latter was in founding women's clubs throughout the country. Wherever they went, to conferences or conventions, its leaders called about them the thoughtful women of the neighborhood, and helped them to plan local associations for study and work.

There was still another aspect of the Woman Question, dearer to her even than "A.A.W."

A woman minister once said: "My conviction that Mrs. Howe was a divinely ordained preacher was gained the first time that she publicly espoused the question of woman suffrage in 1869."

We have seen that little Julia Ward began her ministrations in the nursery. At eight years old she was adjuring her little cousin to love God and he would see death approaching with joy. At eleven she was writing her "Invitation to Youth" : —

> Oh! let thy meditations be of God,
> Who guides thy footsteps with unerring eye;
> And who, until the path of life is trod,
> Will never leave thee by thyself to die.
>
> When morning's rays so joyously do shine,
> And nature brightens at the face of day,
> Oh! think then on the joys that shall be thine
> If thou wilt early walk the narrow way.

We have followed her through the Calvinistic period of religious gloom and fervor; through the intellectual

awakening that followed; through the years when she
could say to Philosophy, —

> ". . . The world its plenitude
> May keep, so I may share thy beggary."

These various phases were like divers-colored shades
covering a lamp: through them all the white flame of
religion burned clear and steady, fostered by a natural piety which was as much a part of her as the
breath she drew.

In the year 1865 came the call to preach. She was
asked to speak before the Parker Fraternity in Boston.
She chose for her discourse a paper on "Ideal Causation," which she had thought "the crown of her
endeavor hitherto."

"To my sorrow, I found that it did not greatly interest my hearers, and that one who was reported to
have wondered 'what Mrs. Howe was driving at' had
spoken the mind of many of those present.

"I laid this lesson much to heart, and, becoming
convinced that metaphysics did not supply the universal solvent for human evils, I determined to find a *pou
sto* nearer to the sympathies of the average community,
from which I might speak for their good and my own.

"From my childhood the Bible had been dear and
familiar to me, and I now began to consider texts and
sermons, in place of the transcendental webs I had
grown so fond of spinning. The passages of Scripture
which now occurred to me filled me with a desire to
emphasize their wisdom by a really spiritual interpretation. From this time on, I became more and more
interested in the religious ministration of women. . . ."

Her first sermon was preached at Harrisburg in 1870. Then followed the sermons in Santo Domingo, and those of the Peace Crusade in London; from this time, the Woman Ministry was one of the causes dearest to her heart. The Journal from now on contains many texts and notes for sermons.

In 1871, "What the lost things are which the Son of Man came to save, lost values, lost jewels, darkened souls, scattered powers, lost opportunities."

A year later: "Preached in the afternoon at the South Portsmouth meetinghouse. Text, 'I will arise and go unto my father.' Subject: 'The Fatherhood of God.' I did as well as usual. . . . In the evening my text was: 'Abide in me and I in you,' etc., but I was at one moment so overcome with fatigue that the whole thread of my discourse escaped me. I paused for a moment, excused myself briefly to the congregation, and was fortunate enough to seize the thread of my discourse again, and got through quite well. I felt this very much, — the fear of failure, I mean. The fatigue was great and my brain felt it much. My dæmon told me beforehand that I could not repeat this sermon and had better read it. I shall believe him next time. This is a difficult point, to know how far to trust the dæmon. He is not to be implicitly trusted, nor yet to be neglected. In these days I am forced to review the folly and shortcomings of my life. My riper reason shows me a sad record of follies and of faults. I seem to sit by and listen sadly; no chastening for the present is joyous but grievous."

"*Sunday, September 29.* Reverend Mrs. Gustine to

dine. I afterwards to church to hear her. A sweet woman, called of God, with a real power. Her voice, manner, and countenance, most sweet and impressive. Intellection not remarkable, I think, but tone, feeling, and effect very remarkable. No one, I think, would doubt the reality of spiritual things after hearing her. I asked myself why I am not jealous of her, as she preaches far more effectively than I do. Well, partly because I believe in my own gift, such as it is, and partly because what she does is natural, genuine, and without pretence or pretension. Her present Society was much disturbed by strife when she was called to its care. No man, she told me, could have united the opposing parties. A true woman could. This shows me a work that women have to do in the Church as well as elsewhere. Where men cannot make peace, they can. Mrs. Gustine says that by my writings and example I have helped her a good deal. I am glad to hear this, but pray to do far better than I have yet done. . . . Thought much about Mrs. Gustine, who, without any of my training and culture, can do what I cannot. I can also do what she cannot — think a subject out. She can only shadow and suggest, yet how powerful is the contact of her soul, and what a good power!"

"*Saturday, October 26.* To Vineyard Haven to help Mr. Stevens with to-morrow's services. . . . Arrival rainy and dismal. Mission house lonely in a storm. Mr. S.'s young niece very capable and pleasant; did the honors and took care of me. I was very hungry before supper, having had nothing since breakfast except a few chestnuts and a biscuit. Wondered a little why I had come."

"*Sunday, 27th.* Found out why I had come. Preached from text: 'Oh, that men would praise the Lord for his goodness and for his wonderful works,' etc. Consider these wonderful works: the world we live in, a human body and brain, a human soul.

"*Evening.* 'The ministry of reconciliation,' how Christianity reconciles man to God, nature to spirit, men to each other.

"I went through the two services entirely alone. I felt supported and held up. I had hoped and prayed this journey might bring some special good to some one. It brought great comfort to me. . . ."

On February 16, 1873, after hearing a powerful sermon, she feels awakened to take up the work over which she has dreamed so much, and talks with her friend, Mary Graves, herself an ordained minister of the Unitarian Church, about "our proposed Woman's Mission here in Boston." A few days later she writes: "Determine that my Sunday services must be held and to see Redpath [1] in this connection."

The result of this determination was the organization of the Woman's Liberal Christian Union, which held Sunday afternoon meetings through the spring. She preached the first sermon, on March 16. "I meant," she says, "to read my London sermon, but found it not suitable. Wrote a new one as well as I could. Had a very good attendance. Was forced to play the hymn

[1] Of the Redpath Bureau.

tunes myself. Am thankful that the occasion seemed
to meet with acceptance."

In 1873, a number of women ministers having come
to Boston to attend the May Anniversaries, she conceived the idea of bringing them together in a meeting
all their own. She issued a call for a Woman Preachers'
Convention, and this convention, the first held in any
country, met on May 29, 1873. She was elected president, the Reverends Mary H. Graves and Olympia
Brown vice-presidents, Mrs. Bruce secretary. The
Journal describes this meeting as "most harmonious
and happy."

In 1893, speaking of this time, she said: —

"I find that it is just twenty years, last spring, since
I made the first effort to gather in one body the women
who intended to devote themselves to the ministry.

"The new liberties of utterance which the discussion
of woman suffrage had brought us seemed at this time
not only to invite, but to urge upon us a participation
in the advocacy of the most vital interests both of the
individual and of the community. With some of us,
this advocacy naturally took the form of preaching.
Pulpits were offered us on all sides, and the charm of
novelty lent itself to such merit and power as Nature
had vouchsafed us. I am so much of a natural church-
woman, I might say an ecclesiast, that I at once began
to dream of a church of true womanhood. I felt how
much the masculine administration of religious doctrine had overridden us women, and I felt how partial
and one-sided a view of these matters had been incul-
cated by men, and handed down by man-revering

mothers. Now, I thought, we have got hold of what is really wanting in the Church universal. We need to have the womanly side of religion represented. Without this representation, we shall not have the fulness of human thought for the things that most deeply concern it. As a first step, I undertook to hold religious services on Sunday afternoons, and to secure for them the assistance of as many woman preachers as I could hear of. I had in this undertaking the assistance of my valued friend, Reverend Mary H. Graves."

The society thus formed was first called "The Woman's Church," later, "The Woman's Ministerial Conference." A second meeting was held, June 1, 1874, but it was not till 1892 that this Conference was finally organized and established, to her great satisfaction. She was elected its president, and held the office till death.

The secretary, Reverend Ada C. Bowles, says of this Conference: "As its main object was to promote a sense of fellowship, rather than to expect associated labor, owing to the scattered membership, meetings were not always regularly held, or possible. But it has held together because Mrs. Howe loved it, and had a secretary as loyal to her as she was to all the women ministers."

She herself has said: "I was impressed with the importance of religious life, and believed in the power of association. I believed that women ministers would be less sectarian than men; and I thought that if those of different denominations could meet occasionally and compare notes, it would be of value."

After the formal conference, she welcomed the members at her own house, talked with them, and heard of their doings. Her eyes kindled as she heard of the Wayside Chapel (of Malden, Massachusetts) built by its pastor, Mrs. E. M. Bruce, who was also its trustee, janitor, choir, and preacher; heard how for thirteen years this lady had rung the bell every evening for vesper service, and had never lacked a congregation: or of the other woman who was asked "very diffidently" if she would conduct the funeral services of an honest and upright man who had died of drink, owing to an inherited tendency.

"They had expected to have it in the undertaker's rooms," said the Reverend Florence Buck, of Wisconsin, "but we had it in my own church. It was packed with people of all sorts, who had been interested in him; and the Bartenders' Union were there in a body. . . . It was an opportunity that I would not have given up to preach to the President and Senate of the United States. Next day . . . they said, 'We expected she'd wallop us to hell; but she talked to us like a mother!'"

Then she turned to the president, and said, "The woman minister is often lonely. I want to thank Mrs. Howe, who welcomed me at the beginning of my ministry. Her hand-clasp has stayed with me ever since."

Our mother was never ordained: it is doubtful whether she ever contemplated such a step; but she felt herself consecrated to the work; wherever she was asked to preach, she went as if on wings, feeling this call more sacred than any other. She preached in all parts of the country, from Maine to California, from Minnesota to Louisiana; but the pulpit in which she felt most truly at home was that of the Church of the Disciples. Mr. Clarke had first welcomed her there: his successor, Charles Gordon Ames, became in turn her valued friend and pastor.

The congregation were all her friends. On Sundays they gathered round her after service, with greetings and kind words. She was ready enough to respond. "Congregationing," as she called this little function, was her delight; after listening devoutly to the sermon, there was always a reaction to her gayest mood. Her spirit came to church with folded hands of prayer, but departed on dancing feet. Sometimes she reproached herself with over-friskiness; but mostly she was too wise for this, and let the sun shine when and where it would.

She preached many times in the Church of the Disciples. The white-clad figure, the clasped hands, the upturned face shining with the inner light, will be remembered by some who read these pages.

END OF VOLUME I

JULIA WARD HOWE
1819–1910

IN TWO VOLUMES
VOLUME II

Julia Ward Howe

Julia Ward Howe
1819-1910

By
LAURA E. RICHARDS
AND MAUDE HOWE ELLIOTT

ASSISTED BY
FLORENCE HOWE HALL

*With Portraits and other
Illustrations*

Volume II

Cherokee Publishing Company
Atlanta, Georgia
1990

Library of Congress Cataloging-in-Publication Data

Richards, Laura Elizabeth Howe, 1850-1943.
  Julia Ward Howe, 1819-1910 / by Laura E. Richards and
Maude Howe Elliott : assisted by Florence Howe Hall
      p.   cm.
  Reprint. Originally published : Boston : Houghton Mifflin, 1915.
  Includes index.
  ISBN: 0-87797-196-X (cloth) : $39.95
    1. Howe, Julia Ward, 1819-1910--Biography.   2. Authors, American-
-19th century--Biography.   3. Feminists--United States--Biography.
    I. Elliott, Maude Howe, 1854-1948.   II. Hall, Florence Howe, 1845-
1922.   III. Title.
  PS2018.R5   1990
  811'.3--dc20   90-47729
                                                                      CIP

This book is printed on acid-free paper which conforms to the American National
Standard Z39.48-1984 *Permanence of Paper for Printed Library Materials.* Paper
that conforms to this standard's requirements for pH, alkaline reserve and
freedom from groundwood is anticipated to last several hundred years without
significant deterioration under normal library use and storage conditions.

Manufactured in the United States of America

ISBN: 0-87797-196-X

94 93 92 91 90   10 9 8 7 6 5 4 3 2 1

Published by arrangement with Houghton Mifflin Company.

 Cherokee Publishing Company is an operating division of
The Larlin Corporation, P O Box 1730, Marietta, Ga 30061

CONTENTS

ILLUSTRATIONS

JULIA WARD HOWE

JULIA WARD HOWE

CHAPTER I

EUROPE REVISITED

1877; *aet.* 58

A MOMENT'S MEDITATION IN COLOGNE CATHEDRAL

> Enter Life's high cathedral
> With reverential heart,
> Its lofty oppositions
> Matched with divinest art.
>
> Thought with its other climbing
> To meet and blend on high;
> Man's mortal and immortal
> Wed for eternity.
>
> When noon's high mass is over,
> Muse in the silent aisles;
> Wait for the coming vespers
> In which new promise smiles.
>
> When from the dome height echoes
> An "*Ite, missa est,*"
> Whisper thy last thanksgiving,
> Depart, and take thy rest.   J. W. H.

FROM the time of the Doctor's death till her marriage in 1887, the youngest daughter was her mother's companion and yoke-fellow. In all records of travel, of cheer, of merriment, she can say thankfully: "*Et ego in Arcadia vixi.*"

The spring of 1877 found the elder comrade weary with much lecturing and presiding, the younger somewhat out of health. Change of air and scene was prescribed, and the two sailed for Europe early in May. Throughout the journeyings which followed, our mother had two objects in view: to see her own kind of people, the seekers, the students, the reformers, and their works; and to give Maud the most vivid first impression of all that would be interesting and valuable to her. These objects were not always easy to combine.

After a few days at Chester (where she laments the "restoration" of the fine old oak of the cathedral, "now shining like new, after a boiling in potash") and a glimpse of Hawarden and Warwick, they proceeded to London and took lodgings in Bloomsbury (a quarter of high fashion when she first knew London, now given over to lodgings). Once settled, she lost no time in establishing relations with friends old and new. The Unitarian Association was holding its annual conference; one of the first entries in the Journal tells of her attending the Unitarian breakfast where she spoke about "the poor children and the Sunday schools."

Among her earliest visitors was Charles Stewart Parnell, of whom she says: —

"Mrs. Delia Stewart Parnell, whom I had known in America, had given me a letter of introduction to her son, Charles, who was already conspicuous as an advocate of Home Rule for Ireland. He called upon me and appointed a day when I should go with him to the House of Commons. He came in his brougham and saw me safely deposited in the ladies' gallery. He was then at the outset of his stormy career, and his sister Fanny told me that he had in Parliament but one supporter of his views, 'a man named Biggar.' He certainly had admirers elsewhere, for I remember having met a disciple of his, O'Connor by name, at a 'rout' given by Mrs. Justin McCarthy. I asked this lady if her husband agreed with Mr. Parnell. She replied with warmth, 'Of course; we are all Home Rulers here.'"

"*May 26.* To Floral Hall concert, where heard Patti — and many others — a good concert. In the evening to Lord Houghton's, where made acquaintance of Augustus Hare, author of 'Memorials of a Quiet Life,' etc., with Mrs. Proctor, Mrs. Singleton [Violet Fane], Dr. and Mrs. Schliemann, and others, among them Edmund Yates. Lord Houghton was most polite and attentive. Robert Browning was there."

Whistler was of the party that evening. His hair was then quite black, and the curious white forelock which he wore combed high like a feather, together with his striking dress, made him one of the most conspicuous figures in the London of that day. Henry Irving came in late: "A rather awkward man, whose performance of 'Hamlet' was much talked of at that time." She met the Schliemanns often, and heard Mrs. Schliemann speak before the Royal Geographical Society, where she made a plea for the modern pronunciation of Greek. In order to help her husband in his work, Mrs. Schliemann told her, she had committed to memory long passages from Homer which proved of great use to him in his researches at Mycenæ and Tiryns.

"*May 27.* . . . Met Mr. and Mrs. Wood — he has excavated the ruins at Ephesus, and has found the site

of the Temple of Diana. His wife has helped him in his
work, and having some practical experience in the use
of remedies, she gave much relief to the sick men and
women of the country."

"*June 2.* Westminster Abbey at 2 P.M. . . . I enjoyed the service, Mendelssohn's 'Hymn of Praise,'
Dean Stanley's sermon, and so on, very unusually.
Edward Twisleton seemed to come back to me, and so
did dear Chev, and a spiritual host of blessed ones who
have passed within the veil. . . ."

"*June 14.* Breakfast with Mr. Gladstone. Grosvenor Gallery with the Seeleys. Prayer meeting at Lady
Gainsborough's.

"We were a little early, for Mrs. Gladstone complained that the flowers ordered from her country seat
had but just arrived. A daughter of the house proceeded to arrange them. Breakfast was served at two
round tables, exactly alike.

"I was glad to find myself seated between the great
man and the Greek minister, John Gennadius. The
talk ran a good deal upon Hellenics, and I spoke of the
influence of the Greek in the formation of the Italian
language, to which Mr. Gladstone did not agree. I
know that scholars differ on the point, but I still retain
the opinion I expressed. I ventured a timid remark
regarding the number of Greek derivatives used in our
common English speech. Mr. Gladstone said very
abruptly, 'How? What? English words derived from
Greek?' and almost

"'Frightened Miss Muffet away.'

"He is said to be habitually disputatious, and I

thought that this must certainly be the case; for he
surely knew better than most people how largely and
familiarly we incorporate the words of Plato, Aristotle,
and Xenophon in our everyday talk." [1]

Mr. Gladstone was still playing the first rôle on the
stage of London life. Our mother notes hearing him
open the discussion that followed Mrs. Schliemann's
address before the Royal Geographical Society. Lord
Rosebery, who was at that time Mr. Gladstone's private secretary, talked much of his chief, for whom he
expressed impassioned devotion. Rosebery, though he
must have been a man past thirty at the time, looked a
mere boy. His affection for "Uncle Sam" Ward was as
loyal as that for his chief, and it was on his account
that he paid our mother some attention when she was
in London.

She always remembered this visit as one of the most
interesting of the many she made to the "province in
brick." She was driving three horses abreast, — her
own life, Maud's life, the life of London. She often
spoke of the great interest of seeing so many different
circles of London society; likening it to a layer cake,
which a fortunate stranger is able to cut through, enjoying a little of each. Her modest Bloomsbury lodgings were often crowded by the leaders of the world of
letters, philanthropy, and art, and some even of the
world of fashion. The little lodging-house "slavey"
was often awed by the titles on the cards she invariably presented between a work-worn thumb and

[1] *Reminiscences*, pp. 411 and 412.

finger. It is curious to contrast the brief record of
these days with that of the Peace Crusade.

"*June 10.* To morning service at the Foundling
Hospital — very touching. To luncheon with M. G. D.
where met the George Howards."

"*June 15.* . . . 'Robert' [opera] with Richard
Mansfield."

"*June 18.* Synagogue."

"*June 19.* Lord Mayor's Mansion House. I am to
speak there concerning Laura Bridgman. Henry James
may come to take me to St. Bart.'s Hospital."

"*June 25.* 'Messiah.' Miss Bryce."

"*June 26.* Dined with Capt. Ward. Theatre. Justin McCarthy."

"*June 28.* Meeting in Lambeth Library."

"*June 29.* Russell Gurney's garden party.

"Miss Marston's, Onslow Sq., 4 P.M. Anti-vivisection. Met Dudley Campbell. A day of rest, indeed. I
wrote out my anti-vivisection argument for to-morrow,
and finished the second letter to the Chicago 'Tribune.'
Was thus alone nearly all day. Dined at Brentini's in
my old fashion, chop, tea, and beer, costing one shilling
and fivepence."

She remembered with pleasure an evening spent
with the Duke and Duchess of Devonshire at Devonshire House. A ball at Mr. Goschen's was another evening of enchantment, as was also the dinner given for
her at Greenwich by Edmund Yates, where she had a
good talk with Mr. Mallock, whose "New Republic"

was one of the books of that season. She managed, too, sometimes to be at home; among her visitors were William Black, John Richard Green, and Mr. Knowles, editor of the "Nineteenth Century."

The London visit lasted nearly two months; as the engagements multiply, its records grow briefer and briefer. There are many entries like the following: —

"Breakfast with Lord Houghton, where met Lord Granville and M. Waddington, late Minister of Education in France. Garden party at Chiswick in the afternoon. Prince of Wales there with his eldest son, Prince Albert Victor. Mrs. Julian Goldsmith's ball in the evening."

It is remembered that she bravely watched the dancers foot it through the livelong night, and drove home by daylight, with her "poor dancing Maud"!

Madame Waddington was formerly Miss King, the granddaughter of Mr. Ward's old partner. Our mother was always interested in meeting any descendants of Prime, Ward & King.

With all this, she was writing letters for the Chicago "Tribune" and the "Woman's Journal." This year of 1877 saw the height of the Æsthetic movement. Mrs. Langtry, the "Jersey Lily," was the beauty and toast of the season. Gilbert and Sullivan's "Patience" was the dramatic hit of the year, and " Greenery yallery, Grosvenor Gallery " the most popular catch of the day.

She found it hard to tear herself away from England; the visit (which she likened to one at the house of an adored grandmother) was over all too soon. But

July was almost gone; and the two travellers finally
left the enchanted island for Holland, recalling Emerson's advice to one going abroad for the first time:
"A year for England, and a year for the rest of the
world!"

The much neglected Journal now takes up the story.
The great Franz Hals pictures delighted her beyond
measure. She always bought the best reproductions
she could afford, and valued highly an etching that
she owned from his Bohémienne. She never waited
for any authority to admire either a work of art or
a person. She had much to say about the influence
of the Dutch blood both in our own family and in our
country, which was to her merely a larger family connection. All through Holland she was constantly not-
ing customs and traditions which we seemed to have
inherited; and she felt a great likeness and sympathy
between herself and some of the Dutch people she
knew.

"*The Hague.* To the old prison where the instruments of torture are preserved. The prison itself is so
dark and bare that to stay therein was a living death.
To this was often added the most cruel torture. The
poor wretch was stretched on a cross, on which revolving wheels, turned by a crank, agonized and destroyed his spinal column — or, by another machine,
his head and feet were drawn in opposite directions —
or, his limbs were stretched out and every bone broken
with an iron bar. Tortures of fire and water were
added. Through all these horrors, I saw the splendors

of faith and conscience which illuminated these dungeons, and which enabled frail humanity to bear these
inflictions without flinching."

She always wanted to see the torture chambers. She
listened to all the detailed explanations and looked at
all the dreadful instruments, buoyed up by the thought
of the splendors she speaks of, when mere shrinking
flesh-and-blood creatures like her companion, who only
thought of the poor tortured bodies, could not bear
the strain of it.

From The Hague they went to Amsterdam, where
they "worked hard at seeing the rich museum, which
contains some of the largest and best of Rembrandt's
pictures, and much else of interest"; thence to Antwerp. Here she writes: —

"To the Museum, where saw the glorious Rubens
and Van Dycks, together with the Quentin Matsys
triptych. Went to the Cathedral, and saw the dear
Rubens pictures — my Christ in the Elevation of the
Cross seemed to me as wonderful as ever. The face
asks, 'Why hast thou forsaken me?' but seems also
to reflect the answer, from the very countenance of
the Father. Education of the Virgin by Rubens —
angels hold a garland above the studious head of the
young Madonna. This would be a good picture for
Vassar."

"*Sunday, July 29.* Up betimes — to high mass at
the Cathedral. Had a seat near the Descent, and saw
it better than ever before. Could not see the Elevation so well, but feasted my eyes on both. Went later
to the church of St. Paul where Rubens's Flagella-

tion is. Found it very beautiful. At 4 P.M. M. Félu[1]
came to take us to the Zoo, which is uncommonly
good. The collection of beasts from Africa is very rich.
They are also successful in raising wild beasts, having
two elephants, a tiger, and three giraffes which have
been born in the cages — some young lions also. The
captive lioness always destroyed her young, and these
were saved by being given to a dog to nurse. . . ."

August found the travellers in Prussia.
"Passed the day in Berlin. . . . At night took railroad for Czerwinsk, travelling second-class. After securing our seats, as we supposed, we left the cars to
get some refreshments, when a man and a woman dis-
placed our effects, and took our places. The woman
refused to give me my place, and annoyed me by push-
ing and crowding me."

The brutality of this couple was almost beyond belief. She was always so gracious to fellow-travellers
that they usually "made haste to be kind" in return.
She made it a point to converse with the intelligent-
looking people she met, either in the train or at the
tables d'hôte then still in vogue. She talked with these
chance acquaintances of their country or their profession. It was never mere idle conversation.

This journey across Europe was undertaken solely
for the pleasure of seeing her sister, always her first
object in visiting Europe. The bond between them
was very strong, spite of the wide difference of their
natures and the dissimilarity of their interests. Mrs.

---

[1] The armless painter. See *ante*, vol. I, chap. XII.

Terry was now visiting her eldest daughter, Annie
Crawford, married to Baron Eric von Rabé and living
at Lesnian in German Poland. Baron Eric had served
in the Franco-Prussian War with distinction, had been
seriously wounded, and obliged to retire from active
service. Here was an entirely new social atmosphere,
the most conservative in Europe. Even before the
travellers arrived, the shadow of formality had fallen
upon them; for Mrs. Terry had written begging that
they would arrive by "first-class"! At that time the
saying was, "Only princes, Americans, and fools travel
first-class," and our mother's rule had been to travel
second. The journey was already a great expense, and
the added cost seemed to her useless. Accordingly,
she bought second-class tickets to a neighboring station and first-class ones from there to Czerwinsk. This
entailed turning out in the middle of the night and
waiting an hour for the splendid express carrying the
stiff and magnificently upholstered first-class carriages,
whose red plush seats and cushions were nothing like
so comfortable as the old grey, cloth-lined, second-
class carriages!

Still, the travellers arrived looking as proud as they
could, wearing their best frocks and bonnets. They
travelled with the Englishwoman's outfit. "Three
suits. Hightum, tightum, and scrub." "Hightum"
was for any chance festivity, "tightum" for the *table
d'hôte*, "scrub" for everyday travelling. The question of the three degrees was anxiously discussed on
this occasion; it was finally decided that only "hightum" would come up to the Von Rabé standard.

"*August 4.* Arrived at Czerwinsk, where sister L. and Baron von Rabé met us. He kissed my hand in a courtly manner. My sister looks well, but has had a hard time. We drove to Lesnian where Annie von R. and her mother-in-law made us welcome."

"*August 9, Lesnian.* A quiet day at home, writing and some work. Tea with Sister L. in the open air. Then went with Baron von Rabé to visit his farm buildings, which are very extensive; not so nicely finished as would be the case in America. We got many fleas in our clothes. . . . In the evening the Baron began to dispute with me concerning the French and the use and excellence of war, etc. . . ."

"*August 12.* Up early — to Czerwinsk and thence by Dirschau to Marienburg to see the famous Ritterschloss of the Teutonic Knights. . . . Marien-Kirch. . . . Angel Michael weighing the souls, a triptych — the good in right wing received by St. Peter and clothed by angels, the wicked in the other wing going down. The beautiful sheen of the Archangel — like peacock brightness — a devil with butterfly wings."

"*August 14.* In the church yesterday we were shown five holes in a flat tombstone. They say that a parricide was buried beneath this stone, and the fingers of his hand forced themselves through these holes. They showed us this hand, dried, and hung up in a chapel. Here also we saw a piece of embroidery in fine pearls, formerly belonging to the Catholic service, and worth thousands of dollars. Some very ancient priests' garments, with Arabic designs, were said to have been

brought from the East by the Crusaders. An astro-
nomic clock is shown in the church. The man who made
it set about making another, but was made blind lest
he should do so. By and by, pretending that he must
repair or regulate something in the clock, he so puts it
out of order that it never goes again.

"The amber-merchant — the felt shoes — views of
America — the lecture — the Baltic."

She was enchanted with Dantzig. The ancient
Polish Jews in their long cloth gabardines, with their
hair dressed in two curls worn in front of the ear and
hanging down on either side of the face, showed her
how Shylock must have looked. She was far more
interested in the relics of the old Polish civilization
than in the crude, brand-new Prussian régime which
was replacing it; but this did not suit her hosts. The
peasants who worked on the estate were all Poles; the
relations between them and their employer smacked
strongly of serfdom. One very intelligent man, who
often drove her, was called Zalinski. It struck her that
this man might be related to her friend Lieutenant
Zalinski, of the United States Army. She asked him if
he had any relatives in America. He replied that a
brother of his had gone to America many years before. He seemed deeply interested in the conversation
and tried once or twice to renew it. One of the family,
who was driving with our mother at the time, managed to prevent any more talk about the American
Zalinski, and when the drive was over she was seriously called to account.

"Can you not see that it would be extremely unfortunate if one of our servants should learn that any
relative of his could possibly be a friend of one of our
guests?"

She was never allowed to see Zalinski again; on inquiring for him, she learned that he had been sent to a
fair with horses to sell. He did not return to Lesnian
during the remainder of her stay.

One of the picturesque features of the visit was the
celebration of Baron Eric's birthday. It was a general
holiday, and no work was done on the estate. After
breakfast family and guests assembled in front of the
old château; the baron, a fine, soldierly-looking man,
his wife, the most graceful of women, and the only
daughter, a lovely little girl with the well-chiselled
Crawford features. The peasants, dressed in their best,
assembled in procession in the driveway; one by one,
in order of their age or position, they came up the steps,
presented the Baroness with a bouquet, bent the knee
and kissed the hand of Baron and Baroness. To most of
the guests the picture was full of Old-World romance
and charm. To one it was an offence. That the granddaughter of her father, the child of her adored sister,
should have been placed by fate in this feudal relationship to the men and women by whose labor she lived
outraged her democratic soul.

The Journal thus describes the days at Lesnian: —

"The Baron talked much last evening, first about
his crops, then about other matters. He believes duelling to be the most efficient agency in promoting a
polite state of society. Would kill any one whom he

suspected of great wrong much sooner than bring him
to justice. The law, he says, is slow and uncertain —
the decision of the sword much more effectual. The
present Government favors duelling. If he should kill
some one in a duel, he would have two months of imprisonment only. He despises the English as a nation
of merchants. The old German knights seem to be his
models. With these barbarous opinions, he seems to
be personally an amiable and estimable man. Despises
University education, in whose course he might have
come in contact with the son of a carpenter, or small
shopkeeper — he himself went to a Gymnase, with
sons of gentlemen. . . ."

"Everything in the Junkerschaft [1] bristles for another war. Oscar von Rabé's room, in which I now
write, contains only books of military drill.

"This day we visited the schoolhouse — session
over, air of the room perfectly fetid. Schoolmaster,
whom we did not see, a Pole — his sister could speak
no German. Tattered primers in German. Visited the
Jew, who keeps the only shop in Lesnian. Found a
regular country assortment. He very civil. *Gasthaus*
opposite, a shanty, with a beer-glass, coffee-cup and
saucer rudely painted on its whitewashed boards.
Shoemaker in a damp hovel, with mahogany furniture,
quite handsome. He made me a salaam with both
hands raised to his head."

"We went to call upon Herr von Rohr, at Schen-
skowkhan — an extensive estate. I had put on my
Cheney silk and my bonnet as a great parade. Our

[1] The Prussian aristocracy.

host showed us his house, his books and engravings —
he has several etchings by Rembrandt. Herr von
Mechlenberg, public librarian of Königsberg, a learned
little old man, trotted round with us. We had coffee
and waffles. Mechlenberg considers the German
tongue a very ancient one, an original language, not
patched up like French and English, of native dialects
mingled with Latin."

In one of her letters to the Chicago "Tribune" is a
significant passage written from Lesnian: —

"Having seen in one of the Dantzig papers the announcement that a certain Professor Blank would soon
deliver a lecture upon America, showing the folly of
headlong emigration thither and the ill fortune which
many have wrought for themselves thereby, one of us
remarked to a Dantziger that in such a lecture many
untruths would probably be uttered. Our friend replied, with a self-gratulatory laugh, 'Ah, Madame!
We Germans know all about the women of America.
A German woman is devoted to her household, its care
and management; but the American women all force
their husbands to live in hotels in order that they may
have no trouble in housekeeping.'"

She was as sensitive to criticism of her country as
some people are to criticism of their friends. Throughout her stay in Germany she suffered from the captious
and provoking tone of the Prussian press about things
American.

Even in the churches she met this note of unfriend-
liness. She took the trouble to transcribe in her Journal
an absurd newspaper story.

" An American Woman of Business

"Some little time since, a man living near Niagara
Falls had the misfortune to fall from the bridge leading
to Goat's Island. [Berlin paper says *Grat* Island.] He
was immediately hurried to the edge of the fearful
precipice. Here, he was able to cling to a ledge of rock,
and to support himself for half an hour, until his un-
avoidable fate overtook him. A compassionate and
excited multitude rushed to the shore, and into the
house, where the unhappy wife was forced to behold
the death struggle of her husband, lost beyond all
rescue, this spot yielding the best view of the scene of
horror. The 'excellent' wife had too much coolness to
allow this opportunity of making money to escape her,
but collected from every person present one dollar for
window rent. (Berliner *Fremdenblatt*, Sunday, August
26, 1877.)"

The stab was from a two-edged sword; she loved
profoundly the great German writers and composers.
She was ever conscious of the debt she owed to Germany's poets, philosophers, and musicians. Goethe
had been one of her earliest sources of inspiration,
Kant her guide through many troublous years; Beethoven was like some great friend whose hand had led
her along the heights, when her feet were bleeding from
the stones of the valley. These were the Germans she
knew; her Germany was theirs. Now she came in contact with this new *Junker* Germany, this harsh, military, unlovely country where Bismarck was the ruling

spirit, and Von Moltke the idol of the hour. It was a rough awakening for one who had lived in the gentler Fatherland of Schiller and of Schubert.

"*August 31, Berlin.* Up early, and with carriage to see the review. . . . A great military display. The Emperor punctual at 10. '*Guten Morgen!*' shouted the troops when he came. The Crown Princess on horseback with a blue badge, Hussar cap. The kettle-drum man had his reins hitched, one on either foot, guiding his horse in this way, and beating his drums with both hands. . . ."

The Crown Princess, later the Empress Frederick, daughter of Queen Victoria, and mother of the present German Emperor, was the honorary colonel of the hussar regiment whose uniform she wore, with the addition of a plain black riding-skirt. Civilization owes this lady a debt that cannot be paid save in grateful remembrance. During the Franco-Prussian War she frequently telegraphed to the German officers commanding in France, urging them to spare the works of art in the conquered country. Through her efforts the studios of Rosa Bonheur and other famous painters escaped destruction.

The early part of September was spent in Switzerland. Chamounix filled the travellers with delight. They walked up the Brevant, rode to the Mer de Glace on muleback. The great feature, however, of this visit to Switzerland was the Geneva Congress, called by Mrs. Josephine Butler to protest against the legalizing of vice in England.

"At the Congress to-day — spoke in French. . . . I spoke of the two sides, active and passive, of human nature, and of the tendency of the education given to women to exaggerate the passive side of their character, whereby they easily fall victims to temptation. Spoke of the exercise of the intellectual faculties as correcting these tendencies — education of women in America — progress made. Coeducation and the worthier relations it induces between young men and women. Said, where society thinks little of women, it teaches them to think little of themselves. Said of marriage, that Milton's doctrine, 'He for God only, she for God in him,' was partial and unjust. '*Ce Dieu, il faut le mettre entre les deux, de manière que chacun des deux appartienne premièrement à Dieu, puis tous les deux l'un à l'autre.*'"

"Wish to take up what Blank said to-day of the superiority of man. Woman being created second. That is no mark of inferiority. Shall say, this doctrine of inequality very dangerous. Inferior position, inferior education, legal status, etc. Doctrine of morality quite opposite. If wife patient and husband not, wife superior — if wife chaste, husband not, wife superior. Each indispensable to each other, and to the whole. Gentlemen, where would you have been if we had not cradled and tended you?"

"*Congress.* . . . Just before the end of the meeting Mr. Stuart came to me and said that Mrs. Butler

wished me to speak for five minutes. After some hesitation I said that I would try. Felt much annoyed at
being asked so late. Went up to the platform and did
pretty well in French. The audience applauded,
laughing a little at some points. In fact, my little
speech was a decided success with the French-speak-
ing part of the audience. Two or three Englishwomen
who understood very little of it found fault with me
for occasioning laughter. To the banquet. . . ."

"*September 23.* This morning Mrs. Sheldon Ames
and her brother came to ask whether I would go to
Germany on a special mission. Miss Bolte also wished
me to go to Baden Baden to see the Empress of Germany."

"*September 24.* A conference of Swiss and English
women at 11 A.M. A sister of John Stuart Mill spoke,
like the other English ladies, in very bad French.
'*Nous femmes*' said she repeatedly. She seemed a
good woman, but travelled far from the subject of the
meeting, which was the work to be done to carry out
what the Congress had suggested. Mrs. Blank, of
Bristol, read a paper in the worst French I ever heard.
'*Ouvrager*' for '*travailler*' was one of her mistakes."

In spite of some slight criticisms on the management of this Congress, she was heart and soul in sympathy with its object; and until the last day of her life,
never ceased to battle for the higher morality which at
all costs protests against the legalizing of vice.

Before leaving Geneva she writes: —

"To Ferney in omnibus. The little church with its

inscription '*Deo erexit Voltaire*,' and the date. . . . I remember visiting Ferney with dear Chev; remember that he did not wish me to see the model [of Madame Du Châtelet's monument] lest it should give me gloomy thoughts about my condition — she died in childbirth, and the design represents her with her infant bursting the tomb."

October found the travellers in Paris, the elder still intent on affairs of study and reform, the younger grasping eagerly at each new wonder or beauty.

There were meetings of the Academy of Fine Arts, the Institute of France, the Court of Assizes: teachers' meetings, too, and dinners with deaconesses (whom she found a pleasant combination of cheerfulness and gravity), and with friends who took her to the theatre.

"To Palais de Justice. Court of Assizes — a young man to be condemned for an offence against a girl of ten or twelve, and then to be tried for attempt to kill his brother and brother-in-law. . . .

"We were obliged to leave before the conclusion of the trial, but learned that its duration was short, ending in a verdict of guilty, and sentence of death. In the days that followed our thoughts often visited this unfortunate man in his cell, so young, apparently without friends — his nearest relatives giving evidence against him, and, in fact, bringing the suit that cost his life. It seems less than Mosaic justice to put a man to death for a murder which, though attempted, was not actually committed. A life for a life is the old doctrine. This is a life for an attempt upon a life."

An essay on Paris, written soon after, recalls further
memories. She visited the French Parliament, and was
surprised at the noise and excitement which prevailed.
"The presiding officer agitates his bell again and
again, to no purpose. He constantly cries, in piteous
tone: 'Gentlemen, a little silence, if you please.'"

She tells how "one of the ushers with great pride
pointed out Victor Hugo in his seat," and says further:
"I have seen this venerable man of letters several
times,—once in his own house. . . . We were first shown
into an anteroom, and presently into a small drawing-
room. The venerable viscount kissed my hand . . .
with the courtesy belonging to other times. He was of
middle height, reasonably stout. His eyes were dark
and expressive, and his hair and beard were snow-
white. Several guests were present. . . . Victor Hugo
seated himself alone upon a sofa, and talked to no one.
While the rest of the company kept up a desultory
conversation, a servant announced M. Louis Blanc,
and our expectations were raised only to be immediately
lowered, for at this announcement Victor Hugo arose
and withdrew into another room, from which we were
able to hear the two voices in earnest conversation. . . ."

"*November 27.* Packing to leave Paris to-night for
Turin. The blanks left in my diary do not mark idle
days. I have been exceedingly busy, . . . have written
at least five newspaper letters, and some other correspondence. Grieved this morning over the time
wasted at shop windows, in desiring foolish articles
which I could not afford to buy, especially diamonds,
which I do not need for my way of life. Yet I have had

more good from my stay in Paris than this empty
Journal would indicate. Have seen many earnest men
and women — have delivered a lecture in French —
have started a club of English and American women
students, for which *Deo gratias!* Farewell, dear Paris,
God keep and save thee!"

She mentions this club in the "Reminiscences." "I
found in Paris a number of young women, students
of art and medicine, who appeared to lead very isolated lives and to have little or no acquaintance with
one another. The need of a point of social union for
these young people appearing to me very great, I invited a few of them to meet me at my lodgings. After
some discussion we succeeded in organizing a small
club, which, I am told, still exists. . . . [If we are not
mistaken, this small club was a mustard seed which in
time grew into the goodly tree of the American Girls'
Club.] I was invited several times to speak while in
Paris. . . . I spoke in French without notes. . . . Before leaving Paris I was invited to take part in a congress of woman's rights. It was deemed proper to elect
two presidents for this occasion, and I had the honor
of being chosen as one of them. . . .

"Somewhat in contrast with these sober doings was
a ball given by the artist Healy at his residence. I had
told Mrs. Healy in jest that I should insist upon dancing with her husband. Soon after my entrance she
said to me, 'Mrs. Howe, your quadrille is ready for
you. See what company you are to have.' I looked
and beheld General Grant and M. Gambetta, who led

out Mrs. Grant, while her husband had Mrs. Healy for his partner in the quadrille of honor. . . . Marshal MacMahon was at this time President of the French Republic. I attended an evening reception given by him in honor of General and Mrs. Grant. Our host was supposed to be at the head of the Bonapartist faction, and I heard some rumors of an intended *coup d'état* which should bring back imperialism and place Plon-Plon [the nickname for Prince Napoleon] on the throne. . . . I remember Marshal MacMahon as a man of medium height, with no very distinguishing feature. He was dressed in uniform and wore many decorations."

During this visit to Paris, our mother consorted largely with the men and women she had met at the Geneva Congress. She takes leave of Paris with these words: "Better than the filled trunk and empty purse, which usually mark a return from Paris, will be a full heart and a hand clasping across the water another hand pure and resolute as itself."

The two comrades journeyed southward by way of Turin, Milan, and Verona. Of the last place the Journal says: —

"Busy in Verona — first, amphitheatre, with its numerous cells, those of the wild beasts wholesomely lighted and aired, those of the prisoners, dark and noisome and often without light of any kind. . . . Then to the tombs of the Scaligers — grim and beautiful. Can Signoria who killed his brother was the last. Can Grande, Dante's host."

In Verona she was full of visions of the great poet whose exile she describes in the poem called, "The Price of the Divina Commedia." One who met her there remembers the extraordinary vividness of her impressions. It was as if she had seen and talked with Dante, had heard from his own lips how hard it was to eat the salt and go up and down the stairs of others.

From Verona to Venice, thence to Bologna. Venice was an old friend always revisited with delight. Bologna was new to her; here she found traces of the notable women of its past. In the University she was shown the recitation room where the beautiful female professor of anatomy is said to have given her lectures from behind a curtain, in order that the students' attention should not be distracted from her words of wisdom by her beauty. In the picture gallery she found out the work of Elisabetta Sirani, one of the good painters of the Bolognese school.

And now, after twenty-seven years, her road led once more to Rome.

CHAPTER II

A ROMAN WINTER

1878–1879; *aet.* 59–60

JANUARY 9, 1878

A voice of sorrow shakes the solemn pines
Within the borders of the Apennines;
A sombre vision veils the evening red,
A shuddering whisper says: the King is dead.

Low lies he near the throne
That strange desert and fortune made his own;
And at his life's completion, from his birth
In one fair record, men recount his worth.

Chief of the Vatican!
Heir of the Peter who his Lord denied,
Not of the faith which that offence might hide,
Boast not, "I live, while he is coldly laid."
Say rather, in the jostling mortal race
He first doth look on the All-father's face.
Life's triple crown absolvèd weareth he,
Clear Past, sad Present, fond Futurity.

J. W. H.

THE travellers arrived in Rome in good time for the Christmas dinner at Palazzo Odescalchi, where they found the Terrys and Marion Crawford. On December 31 our mother writes: —

"The last day of a year whose beginning found me full of work and fatigue. Beginning for me in a Western railway car, it ends in a Roman palace — a long stretch of travel lying between. Let me here record that this year has brought me much good and pleasure, as well as some regrets. My European tour was undertaken for dear Maud's sake. It took me away from the dear ones at home, and from opportunities of work which I should have prized highly. I was President of the Woman's Congress, and to be absent not only from its meeting, but also from its preparatory work, caused me great regret. On the other hand, I saw delightful people in England, and have seen, besides the old remembered delights, many places which I never visited before. . . . I am now with my dear sister, around whom the shadows of existence deepen. I am glad to be with her; though I can do so little for her, she is doing very much for me."

This was a season of extraordinary interest to one who had always loved Italy and pleaded for a generous policy toward her. Early in January it became known that King Victor Emanuel was dying. At the Vatican his life-long adversary Pius IX was wasting away with a mortal disease. It was a time of suspense. The two had fought a long and obstinate duel: which of them, people asked, would yield first to the conqueror on the pale horse? There were those among the "Blacks" of Rome who would have denied the last sacrament to the dying King. "No!" said Pio Nono; "he has always been a good Catholic; he shall not die without the sacrament!" On the 9th of January the King died, and "the ransomed land mourned its sovereign as with one heart." [1]

"*January 12.* Have just been to see the new King [Umberto I] review the troops, and receive the oath

[1] *Reminiscences,* p. 423.

of allegiance from the army. The King's horse was a fine light sorrel — he in full uniform, with light blue trousers. In Piazza del Independenza. We at the American Consulate. Much acclamation and waving of handkerchiefs. Went at 5 in the afternoon to see the dead King lying in state. His body was shown set on an inclined plane, the foreshortening disfigured his poor face dreadfully, making his heavy moustache to look as if it were his eyebrows. Behind him a beautiful ermine canopy reached nearly to the ceiling — below him the crown and sceptre on a cushion. Castellani's beautiful gold crown is to be buried with him."

She says of the funeral: —

"The monarch's remains were borne in a crimson coach of state, drawn by six horses. His own favorite war-horse followed, veiled in crape, the stirrups holding the King's boots and spurs, turned backward. Nobles and servants of great houses in brilliant costumes, bareheaded, carrying in their hands lighted torches of wax. . . . As the cortège swept by, I dropped my tribute of flowers.[1] . . ."

"*January 19.* To Parliament, to see the mutual taking of oaths between the new King and the Parliament. Had difficulty in getting in. Sat on carpeted stair near Mrs. Carson. Queen came at two in the afternoon. Sat in a loggia ornamented with red velvet and gold. Her entrance much applauded. With her the little Prince of Naples,[2] her son; the Queen of Portugal, her sister-in-law; and Prince of Portugal,

---

[1] *Reminiscences*, p. 423.   [2] The present King, Victor Emanuel III.

son of the latter. The King entered soon after two —
he took the oath standing bareheaded, then signed
some record of it. The oath was then administered
to Prince Amadeo and Prince de Carignan, then in
alphabetical order to the Senate and afterwards to the
Deputies."

A month later, Pio Nono laid down the burden of
his years. She says of this: —

"Pope Pius IX had reigned too long to be deeply
mourned by his spiritual subjects, one of whom remarked in answer to condolence, 'I should think he
had lived long enough!'"

The winter passed swift as a dream, though not
without anxieties. Roman fever was then the bane of
American travellers, and while she herself suffered only
from a slight indisposition, Maud was seriously ill.
There was no time for her Journal, but some of the
impressions of that memorable season are recorded in
verse.

> Sea, sky, and moon-crowned mountain, one fair world,
> Past, Present, Future, one Eternity.
> Divine and human and informing soul,
> The mystic Trine thought never can resolve.

One of the great pleasures of this Roman visit was
the presence of her nephew Francis Marion Crawford. He was then twenty-three years old, and extremely handsome; some people thought him like the
famous bas-relief of Antinous at the Villa Albano.
The most genial and companionable of men, he devoted himself to his aunt and was her guide to the *trat-*

toria where Goethe used to dine, to Tasso's Oak, to
the innumerable haunts dedicated to the poets of
every age, who have left their impress on the Eternal
City.

Our mother always loved acting. Her nearest approach to a professional appearance took place this
winter. Madame Ristori was in Rome, and had promised to read at an entertainment in aid of some
charity. She chose for her selection the scene from
"Maria Stuart" where the unhappy Queen of Scots
meets Elizabeth and after a fierce altercation triumphs
over her. At the last moment the lady who was to
impersonate Elizabeth fell ill. What was to be done?
Some one suggested, "Mrs. Howe!" The "Reminiscences" tell how she was "pressed into the service,"
and how the last rehearsal was held while the musical
part of the entertainment was going on. "Madame
Ristori made me repeat my part several times, insisting that my manner was too reserved and would make
hers appear extravagant. I did my best to conform to
her wishes, and the reading was duly applauded." [1]

Another performance was arranged in which Madame Ristori gave the sleep-walking scene from "Macbeth." The question arose as to who should take the
part of the attendant.

"Why not your sister?" said Ristori to Mrs. Terry.
"No one could do it better!"

In the spring, the travellers made a short tour in
southern Italy. One memory of it is given in the
following verses: —

[1] *Reminiscences*, p. 425.

NEAR AMALFI

Hurry, hurry, little town,
With thy labor up and down.
Clang the forge and roll the wheels,
Spring the shuttle, twirl the reels.
    Hunger comes.

Every woman with her hand
Shares the labor of the land;
Every child the burthen bears,
And the soil of labor wears.
    Hunger comes.

In the shops of wine and oil
For the scanty house of toil;
Give just measure, housewife grave,
Thrifty shouldst thou be, and brave.
    Hunger comes.

Only here the blind man lags,
Here the cripple, clothed with rags.
Such a motley Lazarus
Shakes his piteous cap at us.
    Hunger comes.

Oh! could Jesus pass this way
Ye should have no need to pray.
He would go on foot to see
All your depths of misery.
    Succor comes.

He would smooth your frowzled hair,
He would lay your ulcers bare,
He would heal as only can
Soul of God in heart of man.
    Jesus comes.

Ah! my Jesus! still thy breath
Thrills the world untouched of death.
Thy dear doctrine showeth me
Here, God's loved humanity
    Whose kingdom comes.

The summer was spent in France; in November they sailed for Egypt.

"*November 27, Egypt.* Land early this morning — a long flat strip at first visible. Then Arabs in a boat came on board. Then began a scene of unparalleled confusion, in the midst of which Cook's Arabian agent found me and got my baggage — helping us all through quietly, and with great saving of trouble. . . . A drive to see Pompey's Pillar and obelisk. A walk through the bazaar. Heat very oppressive. Delightful drive in the afternoon to the Antonayades garden and villa. . . . Mr. Antonayades was most hospitable, gave us great bouquets, and a basket of fruit."

"*Cairo.* Walked out. A woman swung up and down in a box is brown-washing the wall of the hotel. She was drawn up to the top, quite a height, and gradually let down. Her dress was a dirty blue cotton gown, and under that a breech-cloth of dirty sackcloth. We were to have had an audience from the third Princess [1] this afternoon, and were nearly dressed for the palace when we were informed that the reception would take place to-morrow, when there will be a general reception, it being the first day of Bairam. Visit on donkey-back to the bazaars, and gallop; sunset most beautiful."

"Up early, and all agog for the palace. I wore my black velvet and all my [few] diamonds, also a white bonnet made by Julia McAllister [2] and trimmed with her lace and Miss Irwin's white lilacs. General Stone

---

[1] The favorite wife of the Khedive.
[2] A cousin who was of the party.

sent his carriage with *sais* richly dressed. Reception
was at Abdin Palace — row of black eunuchs outside,
very grimy in aspect. Only women inside — dresses
of bright pink and yellow satin, of orange silk, blue,
lilac, white satin. Lady in waiting in blue silk and
diamonds. In the hall they made us sit down, and
brought us cigarettes in gilt saucers. We took a whiff,
then went to the lady in waiting who took us into the
room where the three princesses were waiting to receive us. They shook hands with us and made us sit
down, seating themselves also. First and second Princesses on a sofa, I at their right in a fauteuil, on my
left the third Princess. First in white brocaded satin,
pattern very bright, pink flowers with green leaves.
Second wore a Worth dress of corn brocade, trimmed
with claret velvet; third in blue silk. All in stupendous
diamonds. Chibouks brought which reached to the
floor. We smoke, I poorly, — mine was badly lighted,
— an attendant in satin brought a fresh coal and then
the third Princess told me it was all right. Coffee in
porcelain cups, the stands all studded with diamonds.
Conversation rather awkward. Carried on by myself
and the third Princess, who interpreted to the others.
Where should we go from Cairo? Up the Nile, in January to Constantinople."

"Achmed took me to see the women dance, in a
house where a wedding is soon to take place. Dancing
done by a one-eyed woman in purple and gold brocade — house large, but grimy with dirt and neglect.
Men all in one room, women in another — several of
them one-eyed, the singer blind — only instruments

the earthenware drum and castanets worn like rings
on the upper joints of the fingers. Arab café — the
story-teller, the one-stringed violin. . . ."
"To the ball at the Abdin Palace. The girls looked
charmingly. Maud danced all the night. The Khedive [1]
made me quite a speech. He is a short, thickset man,
looking about fifty, with grizzled hair and beard. He
wore a fez, Frank dress, and a star on his breast. Tew-
fik Pasha, his son and heir, was similarly dressed. Consul Farman presented me to both of them. The suite
of rooms is very handsome, but this is not the finest of
the Khedive's palaces. Did not get home much before
four in the morning. In the afternoon had visited the
mosque of Sultan Abdul Hassan. . . ."

After Cairo came a trip up the Nile, with all its
glories and discomforts. Between marvel and marvel
she read Herodotus and Mariette Bey assiduously.
"*Christmas Day.* Cool wind. Native *reis* of the
boat has a brown woollen capote over his blue cotton
gown, the hood drawn over his turban. A Christmas
service. Rev. Mr. Stovin, English, read the lessons for
the day and the litany. We sang 'Nearer, my God, to
Thee,' and 'Hark, the herald angels sing.' It was a
good little time. My thoughts flew back to Theodore
Parker, who loved this [first] hymn, and in whose
'meeting' I first heard it. Upper deck dressed with
palms — waiters in their best clothes. . . ."
"To-day visited Assiout, where we arrived soon
after ten in the morning. Donkey-ride delightful,

[1] Ismail Pasha.

visit to the bazaar. Two very nice youths found us
out, pupils of the American Mission. One of these
said, 'I also am Christianity.' Christian pupils more
than one hundred. Several Moslem pupils have embraced Christianity. . . . This morning had a very
sober season, lying awake before dawn, and thinking
over this extravagant journey, which threatens to
cause me serious embarrassment."

And again: —

"The last day of a year in which I have enjoyed
many things, wonderful new sights and impressions,
new friends. I have not been able to do much useful
work, but hope to do better work hereafter for what
this year has shown me. Still, I have spoken four times
in public, each time with labor and preparation — and
have advocated the causes of woman's education, equal
rights and equal laws for men and women. My heart
greatly regrets that I have not done better, during these
twelve months. Must always hope for the new year."

The record of the new year (1879) begins with the
usual aspirations: —

"May every minute of this year be improved by
me! This is too much to hope, but not too much to
pray for. And I determine this year to pass no day
without actual prayer, the want of which I have felt
during the year just past. Busy all day, writing, washing handkerchiefs, and reading Herodotus."

On January 2, she "visited Blind School with General Stone — Osny Effendi, Principal. Many trades
and handicrafts — straw matting, boys — boys and
girls weaving at hand loom — girls spinning wool and

flax, crochet and knitting — a lesson in geography.
Turning lathe — bought a cup of rhinoceros horn."

On January 4 she is "sad to leave Egypt — dear
beautiful country!"

"*Jerusalem, January 5.* I write in view of the
Mount of Olives, which glows in the softest sunset
light, the pale moon showing high in the sky. Christ
has been here — here — has looked with his bodily
eyes on this fair prospect. The thought ought to be
overpowering — *is* inconceivable."

"*January 9.* In the saddle by half past eight in the
morning. Rode two hours, to Bethlehem. Convent —
Catholic. Children at the school. Boy with a fine head,
Abib. In the afternoon mounted again and rode in
sight of the Dead Sea. Mountains inexpressibly desolate and grand. Route very rough, and in some places
rather dangerous. . . . Grotto of the Nativity — place
of the birth — manger where the little Christ was laid.
Tomb of St. Jerome. Tombs of two ladies who were
friends of the Saint. Later the plains of Boaz, which
also [is] that where the shepherds heard the angels.
Encamped at Marsaba. Greek convent near by receives men only. An old monk brought some of the
handiwork of the brethren for sale. I bought a stamp
for flat cakes, curiously cut in wood. We dined luxuri-
ously, having a saloon tent and an excellent cook. . . .
Good beds, but I lay awake a good deal with visions of
death from the morrow's ride."

"*January 10.* [In camp in the desert near Jericho.]
'Shoo-fly' [1] waked us at half past five banging on a

---

[1] A negro attendant.

tin pan and singing 'Shoo-fly.' We rose at once and
I felt my terrors subside. Felt that only prayer and
trust in God could carry me through. We were in the
saddle by seven o'clock and began our perilous crossing
of the hills which lead to the Dead Sea. Scenery inexpressibly grand and desolate. Some frightful bits of
way — narrow bridle paths up and down very steep
places, in one place a very narrow ridge to cross, with
precipices on either side. I prayed constantly and so
felt uplifted from the abjectness of animal fear. After
a while we began to have glimpses of the Dead Sea,
which is beautifully situated, shut in by high hills,
quite blue in color. After much mental suffering and
bodily fatigue on my part we arrived at the shores of
the sea. Here we rested for half an hour, and I lay
stretched on the sands which were very clean and
warm! Remounted and rode to Jordan. Here, I had
to be assisted by two men [they lifted her bodily out
of the saddle and laid her on the ground] and lay on
my shawl, eating my luncheon in this attitude. Fell
asleep here. Could not stop long enough to touch the
water. We rested in the shade of a clump of bushes,
near the place where the baptism of Christ is supposed
to have taken place. Our cans were filled with water
from this sacred stream, and I picked up a little bit of
hollow reed, the only souvenir I could find. Remounted
and rode to Jericho. Near the banks of the Jordan we
met a storm of locusts, four-winged creatures which
annoyed our horses and flew in our faces. John the
Baptist probably ate such creatures. Afternoon ride
much better as to safety, but very fatiguing. Reached

Jericho just after sunset, a beautiful camping-ground. After dinner, a Bedouin dance, very strange and fierce. Men and women stood in a semicircle, lighted by a fire of dry thorns. They clapped their hands and sang, or rather murmured, in a rhythm which changed from time to time. A chief danced before them, very gracefully, threatening them with his sword, with which he played very skilfully. They sometimes went on their knees as if imploring him to spare them. He came twice to our tent and waved the sword close to our heads, saying, '*Taih backsheesh.*' The dance was like an Indian war-dance — the chief made a noise just like the war-whoop of our Indians. The dance lasted half an hour. The chief got his backsheesh and the whole troop departed. Lay down and rested in peace, knowing that the dangerous part of our journey was over."

"*In Camp in the Desert. January 11.* In the saddle by half past seven. Rode round the site of ancient Jericho, of which nothing remains but some portions of the king's highway. Ruins of a caravanserai, which is said to be the inn where the good Samaritan lodged his patient. Stopped for rest and luncheon, at Beth — and proceeded to Bethany, where we visited the tomb of Lazarus. I did not go in — then rode round the Mount of Olives and round the walls of Jerusalem, arriving at half past three in the afternoon. I became very stiff in my knees, could hardly be mounted on my horse, and suffered much pain from my knee and abrasions of the skin caused by the saddle. Did not get down at the tomb of Lazarus because I could not have

descended the steps which led to it, and could not have
got on my horse again. When we reached our hotel,
I could not step without help, and my strength was
quite exhausted. I say to all tourists, avoid Cook's
dreadful hurry, and to all women, avoid Marsaba!
This last day, we often met little troops of Bedouins
travelling on donkeys — sometimes carrying with
them their cattle and household goods. I saw a beautiful white and black lamb carried on a donkey. Met
three Bedouin horsemen with long spears. One of
these stretched his spear across the way almost touching my face, for a joke."

"*Jerusalem. Sunday, January 12.* English service.
Communion, interesting here where the rite was instituted. I was very thankful for this interesting
opportunity."

"*January 15.* Mission hospital and schools in the
morning. Also Saladin's horse. Wailing place of the
Jews and some ancient synagogues. In the afternoon
walked to Gethsemane and ascended the Mount of
Olives. In the first-named place, sang one verse of our
hymn, 'Go to dark Gethsemane.' Got some flowers
and olive leaves. . . ."

After Jerusalem came Jaffa, where she delivered an
address to a "circle" at a private house. She says: —
"In Jaffa of the Crusaders, Joppa of Peter and Paul,
I find an American Mission School, kept by a worthy
lady from Rhode Island. Prominent among its points
of discipline is the clean-washed face, which is so en-
throned in the prejudices of Western civilization. One

of her scholars, a youth of unusual intelligence, finding himself clean, observes himself to be in strong contrast with his mother's hovel, in which filth is just kept clear of fever point. 'Why this dirt?' quoth he; 'that which has made me clean will cleanse this also.' So without more ado, the process of scrubbing is applied to the floor, without regard to the danger of so great a novelty. This simple fact has its own significance, for if the innovation of soap and water can find its way to a Jaffa hut, where can the ancient, respectable, conservative dirt-devil feel himself secure?"

Apropos of mission work (in which she was a firm believer), she loved to tell how one day in Jerusalem she was surrounded by a mob of beggars, unwashed and unsavory, clamoring for money, till she was well-nigh bewildered. Suddenly there appeared a beautiful youth in spotless white, who scattered the mob, took her horse's bridle, and in good English offered to lead her to her hotel. It was as if an angel had stepped into the narrow street.

"Who are you, dear youth?" she cried.

"I am a Christian!" was the reply.

In parting she says, "Farewell, Holy Land! Thank God that I have seen and felt it! All good come to it!"

From Palestine the way led to Cyprus ("the town very muddy and bare of all interest") and Smyrna, thence to Constantinople. Here she visited Robert College with great delight. Returning, she saw the "Sultan going to Friday's prayers. A melancholy, frightened-looking man, pale, with a large, face-absorbing nose. ..."

"*February 3.* Early at Piræus. Kalopothakis [1] met us there, coming on board. . . . To Athens by carriage. Acropolis as beautiful as ever. It looks small after the Egyptian temples, and of course more modern — still very impressive. ..."

Athens, with its welcoming faces of friends, seemed almost homelike after the Eastern journeyings. The Journal tells of sight-seeing for the benefit of the younger traveller, and of other things beside.

"Called on the *Grande Maîtresse* at the Palace in order to have cards for the ball. Saw the Schliemann relics from Mycenæ, and the wonderful marbles gathered in the Museum. Have been writing something about these. To ball at the palace in my usual sober rig, black velvet and so forth. Queen very gracious to us. . . . Home by three in the morning."

"*February 12.* At ten in the morning came a committee of Cretan officers of the late insurrection, presenting a letter through Mr. Rainieri, himself a Cretan, expressing the gratitude of the Cretans to dear Papa for his efforts in their behalf. . . . Mr. Rainieri made a suitable address in French — to which I replied in the same tongue. Coffee and cordial were served. The occasion was of great interest. . . . In the afternoon spoke at Mrs. Felton's of the Advancement of Women as promoted by association. An American dinner of perhaps forty, nearly all women, Greek, but under-

[1] A Greek Protestant minister.

standing English. A good occasion. To party at
Madame Schliemann's."

"*February 15*. Miserable with a cold. A confused day
in which nothing seemed to go right. Kept losing sight
of papers and other things. Felt as if God could not
have made so bad a day — my day after all; I made it."

"*February 18*. To ball at the Palace. King took
Maud out in the German."

"*February 21*. The day for eating the roast lamb
with the Cretan chiefs. Went down to the Piræus
warmly wrapped up. . . . Occasion most interesting.
Much speech-making and toasting. I mentioned
Felton."

"*February 22*. Dreadful day of departure. Packed
steadily but with constant interruptions. The Cretans
called upon me to present their photographs and take
leave. Tried a poem, failed. Had black coffee — tried
another — succeeded. . . ."

"*February 23*. Sir Henry Layard, late English minister to the Porte, is on board. Talked Greek at dinner
— beautiful evening — night as rough as it could well
be. Little sleep for any of us. Glad to see that Lord
Hartington has spoken in favor of the Greeks, censur-
ing the English Government."

"*February 26*. . . . Sir Henry Layard and I *tête-à-
tête* on deck, looking at the prospect — he coveting it,
no doubt, for his rapacious country, I coveting it for
liberty and true civilization."

The spring was spent in Italy. In May they came
to London.

"*May 29.* Met Mr. William Speare.... He told me of his son's death, and of that of William Lloyd Garrison. Gallant old man, unique and enviable in reputation and character. Who, oh! who can take his place? 'Show us the Father.'"

The last weeks of the London visit were again too full for any adequate account of them to find its way into her letters or journals. She visited London once more in later years, but this was her last long stay. She never forgot the friends she made there, and it was one of the many day-dreams she enjoyed that she should return for another London season. Sometimes after reading the account of the gay doings chronicled in the London "World," which Edmund Yates sent her as long as he lived, she would cry out, "O! for a whiff of London!" or, "My dear, we must have another London season before I die!"

CHAPTER III

NEWPORT

1879–1882; *aet.* 60–63

A THOUGHT FOR WASHING DAY

The clothes-line is a Rosary
Of household help and care;
Each little saint the Mother loves
Is represented there.

And when across her garden plot
She walks, with thoughtful heed,
I should not wonder if she told
Each garment for a bead.

. . . .

A stranger passing, I salute
The Household in its wear,
And smile to think how near of kin
Are love and toil and prayer.

J. W. H.

JULY, 1879, found our mother at home at Oak Glen, unpacking trunks and reading a book on the Talmud. She had met the three married daughters in Boston ("We talked incessantly for seven hours," says the Journal), and Florence and Maud accompanied her to Newport, where Florence had established her summer nursery. There were three Hall grandchildren now, and they became an important factor in the life at Oak Glen. All through the records of these summer days runs the patter of children's feet.

She kept only one corner of the house for her private use; a room with the north light which she then thought essential. This was at once bedroom and workroom: she never had a separate study or library.

HALL FOUR GENERATIONS
MRS. HOWE, MRS. HALL, HENRY MARION HALL,
JULIA WARD HOWE HALL
From a photograph, 1903

Here, as in Green Peace days, she worked quietly and steadily. Children and grandchildren might fill the house, might have everything it contained: she asked only for her "precious time." When she could not have an hour she took half an hour, a quarter, ten minutes. No fragment of time was too small for her to save, to invest in study or in work; and as her mind concentrated instantly on the subject in hand, no such fragment was wasted. The rule of mind over body was relentless: sick or well, she must finish her stint before the day closed.

This summer of 1879 was a happy one. After the feverish months of travel and pleasure, her delight in the soft Newport climate was deeper than ever. She always felt the change from the air of the mainland to that of the island, and never crossed the bridge from Tiverton to Bristol Ferry without an exclamation of pleasure. She used to say that the soft, cool air of Newport smoothed out the tired, tangled nerves "like a silver comb"!

"*July 29.* To my Club, where, better than any ovation, an affectionate greeting awaited me. . . . Thucydides is very difficult."

This was the Town and Country Club, for some years a great interest to her. In her "Reminiscences" she tells how in a summer of the late sixties or early seventies, when Bret Harte and Dr. J. G. Holland, Professors Lane and Goodwin of Harvard were spending the season at Newport: "A little band of us combined to improve the beautiful summer season by picnics, sailing parties, and household soirées, in all of which these brilliant literary lights took part. Helen Hunt and Kate Field were often of our company, and Colonel Higginson was always with us."

.   .   .   .

Among the frolics of that summer was the mock Commencement, arranged by her and Professor Lane.

"I acted as President, Colonel Higginson as my aide; we both marched up the aisle in Oxford caps and gowns. I opened the proceedings by an address in Latin, Greek, and English; and when I turned to Colonel Higginson and called him '*fili mihi dilectissime*,' he wickedly replied with three bows of such comic gravity that I almost gave way to unbecoming laughter. Not long before this he had published a paper on the Greek goddesses. I therefore assigned as his theme the problem, 'How to sacrifice an Irish bull to a Greek goddess.' Colonel George Waring, the well-known engineer, being at that time in charge of a valuable farm in the neighborhood, was invited to discuss 'Social small potatoes: how to enlarge their eyes.' An essay on rhinoscopy was given by Fanny Fern, the which I, chalk in hand, illustrated on the blackboard by the following equation: —

"Nose+nose+nose=proboscis.
Nose−nose−nose=snub.

"A class was called upon for recitations from Mother Goose in seven different languages. At the head of this Professor Goodwin honored us with a Greek version of the 'Man in the Moon.' A recent Harvard graduate,

Dr. Gorham Bacon, recited the following, also of her
composition: —

> "'Heu iterum didulum,
> Felis cum fidulum,
> Vacca transiluit lunam,
> Caniculus ridet,
> Quum tale videt,
> Et dish ambulavit cum spoonam.'

"The question being asked whether this last line was
in strict accordance with grammar, the scholar gave
the following rule: 'The conditions of grammar should
always give way to the exigencies of rhyme.'

"The delicious fooling of that unique summer was
never repeated. Out of it came, however, the more
serious and permanent association known as the Town
and Country Club of Newport. I felt the need of upholding the higher social ideals and of not leaving true
culture unrepresented, even in a summer watering-
place."

With the help and advice of Professor and Mrs. William B. Rogers, Colonel Higginson and Mr. Samuel
Powell, a number of friends were called together in the
early summer of 1874 and she laid before them the plan
of the proposed club. After speaking of the growing
predominance of the gay and fashionable element in
Newport society, she said: —

"But some things can be done as well as others.
Newport . . . has also treasures which are still unexplored. . . .

"The milliner and the mantua-maker bring here
their costly goods and tempt the eye with forms and
colors. But the great artist, Nature, has here mer-

chandise far more precious, whose value and beauty
are understood by few of us. I remember once meeting a philosopher in a jeweller's shop. The master of
the establishment exhibited to us his choicest wares,
among others a costly diamond ornament. The philosopher [we think it was Emerson] said, 'A violet is more
beautiful.' I cannot forget the disgust expressed in the
jeweller's face at this remark."

She then outlined the course laid out by the "Friends
in Council," lectures on astronomy, botany, natural
history, all by eminent persons. They would not expect
the Club to meet them on their own ground. They
would come to that of their hearers, and would un-
fold to them what they were able to understand.

Accordingly, Weir Mitchell discoursed to them on
the Poison of Serpents, John La Farge on the South
Sea Islands, Alexander Agassiz on Deep-Sea Dredg-
ing and the Panama Canal; while Mark Twain and
"Hans Breitmann" made merry, each in his own
inimitable fashion.

The Town and Country Club had a long and happy
career. No matter what heavy work she might have
on hand for the summer, no sooner arrived at Newport
than our mother called together her Governing Committee and planned out the season's meetings.

It may have been for this Club that she wrote her
"Parlor Macbeth," an extravaganza in which she appeared as "the impersonation of the whole Macbeth
family."

In the prologue she says: —

"As it is often said and supposed that a woman is at

the bottom of all the mischief that is done under the
sun, I appear and say that I am she, that woman, the
female fate of the Macbeth family."

In the monologue that follows, Lady Macbeth
fairly lives before the audience, and in amazing trav-
esty relates the course of the drama.

She thus describes the visit of the weird sisters (the
three Misses Macbeth) who have been asked to con-
tribute some of "their excellent hell-broth and devilled
articles" for her party.

"At 12 м., a rushing and bustling was heard, and
down the kitchen chimney tumbled the three weird
sisters, finding everything ready for their midnight
operations. . . . 'That hussy of a Macbeth's wife leaves
us nothing to work with,' cried one. 'She makes double
trouble for us.' 'Double trouble, double trouble,'
they all cried and groaned in chorus, and presently fell
into a sort of trilogy of mingled prose and verse which
was enough to drive one mad.

> "'Where hast thou been?
> Sticking pigs.
> And where hast thou?
> Why, curling wigs
> Fit for a shake in German jigs
> And hoo! carew! carew!'

·   ·   ·   ·   ·   ·

"'We must have Hecate now, can't do without her.
Throw the beans over the broomstick and say boo!'
And lo, Hecate comes, much like the others, only
rather more so. . . .

"Now they began to work in good earnest. And
they had brought with them whole bottles of *sun-*

ophon, and *sozodont,* and *rypophagon,* and *hyperbolism*
and *consternaculum,* and a few others. And in the
whole went. And one stirred the great pot over the
fire, while the others danced around and sang —

> "'Black pepper and red,
> White pepper and grey,
> Tingle, tingle, tingle, tingle,
> Till it smarts all day.'

"'Here's dyspepsia! Here's your racking headache
of a morning. Here's podagra, and jaundice, and a few
fits. And now it's done to a turn, and the weird sisters
have done what they could for the family.'

"A rumbling and tumbling and foaming was now
heard in the chimney — the bricks opened, and He-cat
and She-cat and all the rest of them went up. And I
knew that my supper would be first-rate."

The time came when some of the other officers of
the Town and Country Club felt unable to keep the
pace set by her. She would still press forward, but
they hung back, feeling the burden of the advancing
years which sat so lightly on her shoulders. The Club
was disbanded; its fund of one thousand dollars, so
honorably earned, was given to the Redwood Library,
one of the old institutions of Newport.

The Town and Country Club was succeeded by the
Papéterie, a smaller club of ladies only, more intimate
in its character. The exchange of "paper novels"
furnished its name and its *raison d'être.* The members
were expected to describe the books taken home from
the previous meeting. "What have you to tell us of

the novel you have been reading?" the president would demand. Then followed a report, serious or comic, as the character of the volume or the mood of the meeting suggested. A series of abbreviated criticisms was made and a glossary prepared: for example, —

"B. P. — By the pound.
M. A. S. — May amuse somebody.
P. B. — Pot-boiler.
F. W. B. — For waste-basket.
U. I. — Uplifting influence.
W. D. — Wholly delightful.
U. T. — Utter trash."

The officers consisted of the Glossarian, the Penologist, whose duty it was to invent penalties for delinquents, the Cor. Sec. and the Rec. Sec. (corresponding and recording secretaries) and the Archivist, who had charge of the archives. During its early years a novel was written by the Club, each member writing one chapter. It still exists, and part of the initiation of a new member consists in reading the manuscript. The "delicious fooling" that marked the first year of the Town and Country Club's existence was the animating spirit of the Papéterie. A friend christened it "Mrs. Howe's Vaudeville." Merrymaking was her safety-valve. Brain fag and nervous prostration were practically unknown to her. When she had worked to the point of exhaustion, she turned to play. Fun and frolic went along with labor and prayer; the power of combining these kept her steadily at her task till the end of her life. The last time she left her house, six days before her death, it was to preside at the Papéterie, where she was as usual the life of the meeting! The

Club still lives, and, like the New England Woman's Club, seems still pervaded by her spirit.

The Clubs did not have all the fun. The Newport "Evening Express " of September 2, 1881, says: "Mrs. Julia Ward Howe has astonished Newport by her acting in 'False Colors.' But she always was a surprising woman."

Another newspaper says: "The interest of the Newport world has been divided this week between the amateur theatricals at the Casino and the lawn tennis tournament. Two representations of the comedy of 'False Colors' were given on Tuesday and Wednesday evenings. . . . The stars were undoubtedly Mrs. Julia Ward Howe and Mr. Peter Marié, who brought down the house by their brightness and originality. . . . Mr. Peter Marié gave a supper on the last night of the performance, during which he proposed the health of Mrs. Julia Ward Howe and the thanks of the company for her valuable assistance. Mrs. Howe's reply was very bright and apt, and her playful warnings of the dangers of sailing under false colors were fully appreciated."

It is remembered that of all the gay company she was the only one who was letter-perfect in her part.

To return to 1879. She preached many times this summer in and around Newport.

" *Sunday, September 28.* Hard at work. Could not look at my sermon until this day. Corrected my reply to Parkman.[1] Had a very large audience for the place — all seats full and benches put in."

[1] Francis Parkman had written an article opposing woman suffrage.

"My sermon at the Unitarian Church in Newport.
A most unexpected crowd to hear me."

"*September 29.* Busy with preparing the dialogue
in 'Alice in Wonderland' for the Town and Country
Club occasion. . . . ."

Many entries begin with "hard at work," or "very
busy all day."

This summer was made delightful by a visit from
her sister Louisa, with her husband [1] and daughter.
Music formed a large part of the summer's pleasure.
The Journal tells of a visit from Timothée Adamowski
which was greatly enjoyed.

"*October 11.* Much delightful music. Adamowski
has made a pleasant impression upon all of us."

"*October 12, Sunday.* Sorry to say we made music all
day. Looked hard for Uncle Sam, who came not."

"*October 13.* Our delightful matinée. Adamowski
and Daisy played finely, he making a great sensation.
I had the pleasure of accompanying Adamowski in a
Nocturne of Chopin's for violin and piano. All went
well. Our pleasure and fatigue were both great. The
house looked charming."

In the autumn came a lecture tour, designed to re-
coup the heavy expenses of the Eastern trip. Never
skilful in matters of money-making, this tour was
undertaken with less preparation than the modern
lecturer could well imagine. She corresponded with

---

[1] Luther Terry, an American painter who had lived long in Rome, and
had been a close friend of Thomas Crawford. He survived his wife by
some years.

one and another Unitarian clergyman and arranged her
lectures largely through them. Though she did not
bring back so much money as many less popular
speakers, she was, after all, her own mistress, and was
not rushed through the country like a letter by ambitious managers.

The Journal gives some glimpses of this trip.

"Twenty minutes to dress, sup, and get to the hall.
Swallowed a cup of tea and nibbled a biscuit as I
dressed myself."

"Found the miserablest railroad hotel, where I
waited all day for trunk, in distress! . . . Had to lecture without either dress or manuscript. Mrs. Blank
hastily arrayed me in her black silk, and I had fortunately a few notes."

She never forgot this lesson, and in all the thirty-
odd years of speaking and lecturing that remained,
made it an invariable rule to travel with her lecture and
her cap and laces in her handbag. As she grew older,
the satchel grew lighter. She disliked all personal service, and always wanted to carry her hand-luggage herself. The light palm-leaf knapsack she brought from
Santo Domingo was at the end replaced by a net, the
lightest thing she could find.

The Unitarian Church in Newport was second in her
heart only to the Church of the Disciples. The Reverend Charles T. Brooks, the pastor, was her dear
friend. In the spring of 1880 a Channing memorial
celebration was held in Newport, for which she wrote
a poem. She sat on the platform near Mr. Emerson,

heard Dr. Bellows's discourse on Channing, "which was exhaustive, and as it lasted two hours, exhausting." The exercises, W. H. Channing's eulogium, etc., etc., lasted through the day and evening, and in the intervals between addresses she was "still retouching" her poem, which came last of all. "A great day!" says the Journal.

"*July 23.* Very busy all day. Rainy weather. In the evening I had a mock meeting, with burlesque papers, etc. I lectured on *Ism- Is-not-m,* on *Asm-spasm-plasm.*"

"*July 24.* Working hard, as usual. Marionettes at home in the evening. Laura had written the text. Maud was Julius Cæsar; Flossy, Cassius; Daisy, Brutus."

"*July 28.* Read my lecture on 'Modern Society' in the Hillside Chapel at Concord. . . . The comments of Messrs. Alcott and W. H. Channing were quite enough to turn a sober head."

"To the poorhouse and to Jacob Chase's with Joseph Coggeshall. Old Elsteth, whom I remember these many years, died a few weeks ago. One of the pauper women who has been there a long time told me that Elsteth cried out that she was going to Heaven, and that she gave her, as a last gift, a red handkerchief. Mrs. Anna Brown, whom I saw last year, died recently. Her relatives are people in good position and ought to have provided for her in her declining years. They came, in force, to her funeral and had a very nice coffin for her. Took her body away for burial. Such meanness needs no comment.

"Jacob was glad to see me. Asked after Maud and

doubted whether she was as handsome as I was when he first saw me (thirty or more years ago). His wife said to me in those days: 'Jacob thinks thee's the only good-looking woman in these parts.' She was herself a handsome woman and a very sweet one. I wish I had known I was so good-looking."

Of the writing of letters there was no end. Correspondence was rather a burden than a delight to her; yet, when all the "duty letters" were written, she loved to take a fresh sheet and frolic with some one of her absent children. Laura, being the furthest removed, received perhaps more than her share of these letters; yet, as will appear from them, she never had enough.

To Laura

OAK GLEN, October 10, 1880.

DEAREST, DEAREST L. E. R., —

How I wonder how you R! Cause of silence not hardness of heart, but the given necessity of scribbling for dear life, to finish a promised paper for the Woman's Congress, *sedebit* next week. I in Boston Wed., Thurs., and Fri. — day being understood. Mowski [Adamowski] left us yesterday morning. . . . We had him here a fortnight, and enjoyed his visit extremely. At table, between the courses, he played on every instrument of the orchestra. I asked once for the bass drum, which he imitated, adding thereunto the cymbals. We had a lunch party last week, for the bride, Maud Appleton, and "invited quite fashionable," and after

all she did n't come. "Sick in bed with diphtheria."
May by some be considered an excuse, but then,
it's very rude to be sick, and it's very troublesome
to other people. (This to make you feel badly about
your own shortcomings.) We had a little dance,
too, on Friday evening. An omnibus party came out
and a few others. I pounded the Lancers and some
ancient waltzes and polkas, ending with the Virginia
reel, in which last I thought my floor would give way,
the young men stamped so. I have no paper left
except some newspaper wrappers, so can't write any
more. Got up and found this scrap, then hunted for
my pen, which, after some search, I found in my mouth.
This is what it is to be lit'ry. Oh, my! I sometimes
wish I was n't! . . .

In October, while visiting Julia at the Institution,
she missed her footing and fell down the two steps leading to the dining-room, breaking the ligaments of her
knee. A letter to Laura makes the first mention of this
serious accident, whose effects she felt all her life.

OAK GLEN, November 9, 1880.
DEAREST LAURA CHILD, —
    Behold the mum-jacket, sitting clothed and in her
chair, confronting you after long silence, with comforting words of recovery. I am now in the fourth week
of my infirmity, and I really think that the offending,
or rather offended, muscles have almost recovered
their natural power of contraction. My exercise is
still restricted to a daily walk from my bed in the small

parlor to my chair in the large parlor, and back again. But this walk, which at first was an impotent limp, with bones clicking loosely, is now a very respectable performance, not on the tight rope, indeed, but, let us say, on the tight garter. . . . The only break in the general uniformity of my life was dear Uncle Sam's arrival on Sunday last. He remained with us a couple of hours, and was as delightful as ever. Oh! more news. With his kind help, I have taken Mrs. Lodge's small house for the winter and this opens to me a comfortable prospect, though, even with his help, the two ends will have to be pulled a little in order to meet. . . .

The furnished house in lower Mount Vernon Street proved a pleasant habitat. It was nine years since she had had a house in Boston; in spite of her lameness, perhaps partly because of it, she enjoyed entertaining her family and friends. Mrs. Terry and her daughter spent part of the winter with them.

The year 1880 was marked by the publication of her first book since "Later Lyrics": a tiny volume entitled "Modern Society," containing, beside the title essay, a kindred one on "Changes in American Society." The Journal makes little or no mention of this booklet, but Thomas Wentworth Higginson says of it: "It would be hard to find a book in American literature better worth reprinting and distributing. . . . In wit, in wisdom, in anecdote, I know few books so racy."

"*January 1, 1881.* I have now been lame for twelve weeks, in consequence of a bad fall which I had on

October 17. I am still on crutches with my left knee
in a splint. Have had much valuable leisure in consequence of this, but have suffered much inconvenience and privation of preaching, social intercourse, etc.
Very little pain since the first ten days. Farewell, Old
Year! Thank the Heavenly Father for many joys,
comforts and opportunities."

Her physician insisted upon her keeping quiet, but
she could not obey him, and continued to travel about
on crutches to keep her many engagements. Her faithful coachman, Frank McCarthy, was her companion
on these journeys.

"*January 26.* Busy most of the day with my lecture. Had a visit from H. P. B.,[1] who advised me to
keep still and go nowhere until my lameness shall be
much better. Took 4.30 train for Concord, Massachusetts. Maud would go with me, which grieved me,
as she thereby lost a brilliant ball. . . . We went to
Mr. Cheney's, where we found Frank Barlow, a little
older, but quite unchanged as to character, etc. He
has the endearing coquetry of a woman. Dear Mr.
Emerson and Mrs. came to my lecture. Mr. E. said
that he liked it. The audience was very attentive
throughout. Stepped only once on my lame foot in
getting into the sleigh. . . ."

"*January 28.* Busy all day with my address for
woman's suffrage meeting in the evening. . . . When
I entered with my crutches the audience applauded
quite generally. . . . Wendell Phillips made the concluding speech of the evening. He was less brilliant

[1] Dr. H. P. Beach.

than usual, and kept referring to what I had said. I thanked him for this afterwards, and he said that my speech had spoiled his own; that I had taken up the very points upon which he had intended to dwell."

"*February 11.* Lecture at Groton, Massachusetts. As I went down the steps to the carriage, one of my crutches slipped and the careless hackman on my right let me fall, Frank catching me, but not until I had given my knee a severe wrench which gave me great pain. I suffered much in my travel, but got through, Frank helping me. . . . My knee seemed much inflamed and kept me awake much of the night. My lecture on 'Polite Society' was well received. The good people of the house brought me their new ledger, that my name might be the first recorded in it."

"*February 12.* Dinner of Merchants' Club. Edward Atkinson invites me. Got back by early train, 7.50 A.M., feeling poorly. Did not let Maud know of my hurt. Went to the dinner mentioned above, which was at the Vendôme. . . . Was taken in to dinner by the President, Mr. Fitz. Robert Collyer had the place on my right. He was delightful as ever. Edward Everett Hale sat near me and talked with me from time to time. Of course my speech afflicted me. I got through it, however, but had to lose the other speeches, the hour being so late and the night so inclement, very rainy."

"*February 20.* Very lame this morning. No courage to try to go out. Have been busy with Kant and Miss Cobbe's new book, 'Duties of Women,' which I am reviewing for the 'Christian Register.' . . ."

To Laura

129 MOUNT VERNON STREET,
February 27, 1881.

MY DEAREST LAURA, —

. . . Mr. Longfellow came to see us yesterday, and told us his curious dreams. In one of them, he went to London and found James Russell Lowell *keeping a grocery*. In another, people were vituperating the bad weather, and dear Papa said: "Remember, gentlemen, who makes it!" This impressed us as very characteristic of our dear one. My lameness is decreasing very slowly, and I have now been a week without the splint. The knee, however, still swells if I attempt to use it, and my life is still much restricted as to movement. . . .

"*February 28*. . . . A cloud seems to lift itself from that part of my mind which concerns, or should concern, itself with spiritual things. Sometimes a strong *unwillen* seizes me in this direction. I feel in myself no capacity to comprehend any features of the unseen world. My belief in it does not change, but my imagination refuses to act upon the basis of the 'things not seen.'"

"*March 5*. Longfellow to dine."

"*March 30*. In the evening to the ever-pleasing Hasty-Pudding Theatrical Play, a burlesque of Victor Hugo's 'Notre Dame de Paris,' with many saucy interjections. The fun and spirits of the young men were very contagious, and must have cheered all present who needed cheering. . . ."

To Laura

129 MOUNT VERNON STREET,
March 24, 1881.

MY DARLING LAURA, —

The March wind blows, and gives me the spleen. I don't care about anything, don't want my books, nor my friends, nor nothing. But you, poor child, may not be in this wicked, not caring condition, and so I will write you, having oughted to for a considerable time. Nothing stays put, not even put-ty. Letters don't stay answered, faces don't stay washed, clothes don't stay either clean or new. Children won't stay the youngest. The world won't stay anywhere, anyhow. Forty years ago was good enough for me. Why could n't it stay? Now, I see you undertaking to comfort me in good earnest, and know just how you would begin by saying: "Well, it should!"... Nunc Richard[1] here yesterday. Remarked nothing in particular, I replying in like manner. Kept his arm very dark, under a sort of cloak. We condoled [with] each other upon our mental stupidity, and parted with no particular views or sentiments. I have been to-day at a worldly fashionable lunch. Nobody cared for anything but what they had on and had to eat. "He! he!" said one: "ho! ho! ho!" the other. "Is your uncle dead yet?" "No, but my aunt is." "Grandfather Wobblestick used to say"—"Why, of course he did!" Which is all that I remember of the conversation. Now, darling, this is perfectly hateful of me to turn and snarl at the hand which has just been putting good morsels into my

[1] The late Richard Sullivan.

mouth. But you see, this is a March wind in Boston,
and I can't help it. And I hobbled greatly up the big
staircase, also down. That's all. Auntie and Daisy
and Maud lunched, too, munchingly. D. made a new
capote for Maud. Nobody made nothing new for me.
I had no lace bow under my chin, and looked so neglected! Maud and Daisy always on the wing, concerts, theatres, lunches, etc., etc. Auntie and I have
some good evenings at home, in which we refresh the
venerable intelligence with the modern publication,
we do, to wit, "Early Life of Charles James Fox." We
also play Russian backgammon. Big Frank Crawford
has enlargement of 's liver. This P.M. late Mrs. C. C.
Perkins has recep. for Miss Carl Schurz. Girls going,
but going first to X.'s weekly weak tea and weaker
talk. Here again, you spleeny devil, get thee behind
me! I love my fellow-creatures, but, bless you, not in
this month. . . . Julia Nagnos takes tea round generally, and finds that it agrees with her. . . . I regard
you, on the whole, with feeling. Farewell, Laura, I am
your poor old mad March hare Mamma. Love to
Skip and the little ones.

"*April 7.* Finished Carlyle's 'Reminiscences' to-
day. Perhaps nothing that he has left shows more
clearly what he was, and was not. A loyal, fervent,
witty, keen man. . . . His characterizations of individuals are keenly hit off with graphic humor. But he
could make sad mistakes, and could not find them out,
as in the case of what he calls our 'beautiful Nigger
Agony'!!"

"I went out to the Cambridge Club, having had chills and fever all the night before. Read my lecture on Paris, which was well received, and followed by a good discussion with plenty of differences of opinion. Evening at home; another chill and fever."

To Laura

129 MOUNT VERNON STREET,
April 24, 1881.

Bad old party, is and was. Badness mostly of heart, though head has a decided crack in it. Unfeeling old Beast! Left Laura so long without a word. Guess 't is n't worth while for her to write anything more.

My poor dear little Laura, how miserably you must have been feeling, I know well by your long silence. Oh! posterity! posterity! how much you cost, and how little you come to! Did I not cost as much as another? And what do I come to? By Jingo!

Darling, I have got some little miserable mean excuses. Want 'em? Have had much writing to do, many words for little money. For " Critic " (N.Y.) and for " Youth's Companion " and other things. Then, have kept up great correspondence with Uncle Sam, who has given me a house in Beacon Street! *oh gonniac!* [1]

We had lit'ry party last week. Dr. Holmes and William Dean Howells read original things. James Freeman Clarke recited and we had ices and punch.

---

[1] Welsh for " glory " : a favorite exclamation of hers, learned in childhood from a Welsh servant.

Maud thought it frumpy, but others liked it very
much. Have been to church to-day, heard J. F. C.
'Most off crutches now and hobble about the house
with a cane. Use crutches to go up and down stairs
and to walk in the street. . . . Have heard much music
and have seen Salvini once, in the "Gladiator," and
hope to see him on Thursday, in "Macbeth." How are
the dear children? I do want to see them, 'specially
July Ward. . . .

"*May 27.* Soon after 7 A.M. arrived Uncle Sam with
my dear sister Annie Mailliard from California; the
whole intended as a birthday surprise. My sister is
very little changed; always a most tender, sensitive
woman. Sister Louisa did n't know of this and came
at 11 A.M. to bring my greetings and gifts, with Mr.
Terry, Daisy, and Uncle Sam. When Sister Annie
appeared, Sister Louisa almost fainted with delight
and astonishment."

"*June 20, Oak Glen.* Dear Flossy suffering at 6 A.M.
— about all day. Her child, a fine boy, born at 3 P.M.
We are all very happy and thankful. It was touching
to see the surprise and joy of the little children when
they were admitted to a sight of their new relative.
There was something reverent in the aspect of the
little creatures, as if they partly felt the mystery of
this new life which they could not understand. Some
one told them that it came from Heaven. Harry, four
years old, said: 'No, it did n't come from Heaven, for
it has n't any wings.'"

To Laura (who, as usual, wanted a letter)

OAK GLEN, July 10, 1881.

Yes, she was a little injured, but not so bad as she pretends. Feelings hurt dreadful? Self-esteem bruised and swollen? Spleen a little touched? Well, she has had the doctor, and the doctor said: " Her mother is a public character, what can we do about it? "

> Could my ink forever flow,
> Could my pen no respite know.

Well, my darling, it was too bad, so we'll make up, and kiss and be friends. But now you look here. Besides all my lit'ry work, which seems to be heaviest in summer time, I had an awful deal to do in taking care of Flossy's children and the new baby. The babe is of the crying sort! When anything is to be done for his Ma, the nurse expects some one to hold him. . . . I returned last night from a journey to Vermont, where I read a paper before the American Institute of Education, and also spoke at a suffrage meeting and also at an outdoor mass meeting, and also at a suffrage meeting in Montpelier, and came back, after four days' absence, very tired. (Chorus, Don't tell Maud.) . . .

"*August 30.* My first performance at the Casino Theatre. It went off very successfully, and I was much applauded, as were most of the others. Supper afterwards at Mrs. Richard Hunt's, where I had to appear in 'plain clothes,' having been unable to accomplish evening dress after the play. Dear Flossy went with me."

Another "performance" of that summer is not noted in the Journal; an impromptu rendering of "Horatius at the Bridge," in the "green parlor" at Oak Glen, with the following cast: —

Horatius..................F. Marion Crawford.
Spurius Lartius.......................J. W. H.
Herminius.......................Maud Howe.

The green parlor was an oval grass plot, thickly screened by tall cedars. Laura recited the ballad, keeping her voice as she could while the heroes waged desperate combat, but breaking down entirely when Horatius "plunged headlong in the tide," and swam with magnificent action across — the greensward!

"*September 18.* Preached in Tiverton to-day. Text: 'The fashion of this world passeth away.' Subject: Fashion, an intense but transient power; in contra-distinction, the eternal things of God."

"*September 25.* Spent much of this day in compos-ing a poem in commemoration of President Garfield's death. Spared no pains with this and succeeded better than I had expected."

"*September 26.* The President's funeral. Services held in most cities of the United States, I should judge. Solemn services also in London and Liverpool."

To Samuel Ward

241 BEACON STREET,
December 22, 1881.

DEAREST BROTHER, —

... *Your* house, darling, was bright and lovely, yes-terday. I had my old pet, Edwin Booth, to lunch —

we were nine at table, the poet Aldrich disappointing
us. From three to four we had a reception for Mr.
Booth, quite the *crème de la crème*, I assure you.
Among others, Dr. Holmes came. The rooms and furniture were much admired. We gave only tea at the
levee, but had some of your good wine at the luncheon.
P.S. Mr. Booth in "Lear" last night was sublime!

To the same

Edwin Booth had sent us his box for the evening.
The play was "Hamlet," the performance masterly.
People's tastes about plays differ, but I am sure that
no one on the boards can begin to do what Booth does.
I saw him for a moment after the play, and he told me
that he had done his best for me. Somehow, I thought
that he was doing his very best, but did not suppose
that he was thinking of me particularly. . . .

"*January 29, 1882.* Frank [Marion Crawford] had
met Oscar Wilde the evening before at Dr. Chadwick's;
said that he expressed a desire to make my acquaintance. Wrote before I went to church to invite him to
lunch. He accepted and Maud and Frank, or rather
Marion, flew about to get together friends and viands.
Returning from a lifting and delightful sermon of
J. F. C.'s, I met Maud at the door. She cried: 'Oscar
is coming.' Mrs. Jack Gardner, Madame Braggiotti,
and Julia completed our lunch party. Perhaps ten or
twelve friends came after lunch. We had what I might
call a 'lovely toss-up,' *i.e.*, a social dish quickly com-
pounded and tossed up like an omelet."

During this year and the next, Crawford made his home at 241 Beacon Street. Here he wrote his first three books, "Mr. Isaacs," "Dr. Claudius," and "A Roman Singer." He was a delightful inmate, and the months he spent under our mother's roof were happy ones. A tender *camaraderie* existed between aunt and nephew. During his first winter in Boston he thought of going on the stage as a singer, and studied singing with Georg Henschel. He had a fine voice, a dramatic manner, full of fire, but an imperfect ear. This fault Henschel at first thought could be remedied: for months they labored together, trying to overcome it. Crawford delighted in singing, and "Auntie" in playing his accompaniments. At dusk the two would repair to the old Chickering grand to make music — Schubert, Brahms, and arias from the oratorios they both loved. In the evening the three guitars would be brought out, and aunt and nephew, with Maud or Brother Harry, would sing and play German students' songs, or the folk-songs of Italy, Ireland, and Scotland. Our mother was sure to be asked for Matthias Claudius's "*Als Noah aus dem Kasten war*": Crawford would respond with "*Im schwarzen Wallfisch zu Ascalon.*"

This was the first of thirty happy years passed at 241 Beacon Street, the house Uncle Sam bought for her. The day she moved in, a friend asked her the number of her new house.

"241," she answered. "You can remember it because I'm the two-forty one."

Oscar Wilde was at this time making a lecture tour through the United States. This was the heyday of

his popularity; he had been heralded as the apostle
of the æsthetic movement. At his first lecture, given
at the old Boston Music Hall, he appeared in a black
velvet court suit with ruffles, and black silk stockings,
his hair long and curling on his shoulders. A few moments after he had taken his place on the platform, a
string of Harvard students filed into the hall, dressed
in caricature of the lecturer's costume, each with a sun-
flower in his coat and a peacock feather in his hand.
Our mother, who was in the audience, recognized near
the head of the procession her favorite grand-nephew,
Winthrop Chanler. Wilde took this interruption in
good part, welcoming the lads and turning the laugh
against them. "Imitation is the sincerest flattery,"
he said, "though this is a case where I might say,
'Save me from my friends.'"

Wilde came several times to the house in Boston;
later Uncle Sam brought him to spend a day or two
at Oak Glen, where the household was thrown into a
flutter by the advent of his valet. It was one thing to
entertain the æsthete, another to put up the gentleman's gentleman. In spite of all the affectation of
the æsthetic pose, Wilde proved a rarely entertaining
guest. He talked amazingly well; in that company
all that was best in the man came to the surface.
He recited his noble poem, "The Ode to Albion,"
under the trees of Oak Glen, and told endless stories
of Swinburne, Whistler, and other celebrities of the
day. The dreadful tragedy came later; at this time
he was one of the most brilliant figures in the literary
world.

"*March 4.* To Saturday Morning Club with Mrs. [John] Sherwood; very busy; then with her to Blind Asylum in a carriage. Drove up to front entrance and alighted, when the gale took me off my feet and threw me down, spraining my left knee so badly as to render me quite helpless. I managed to hobble into the Institution and to get through Julia's lunch, after which I was driven home. Sent for Dr. Beach and was convicted of a bad sprain, and sentenced to six weeks of (solitary) confinement."

"*March 5.* In bed all day."

"*March 6.* On the lounge; able to work."

"*March 8.* Day of mid-year conference of A.A.W. Business meeting at the N.E.W.C., where I, of course, could not be present. Afternoon meeting was in my room. On the whole satisfactory."

To Laura

241 BEACON STREET,
March 18, 1882.

Whereupon, my dearest, let there be no further pribbles and prabbles, which I conjugate thus: I pribble, thou prabblest, he, she, or it pribble prabbles. Maud leaveth on a Tuesday, come thou on that same Tuesday, taking care to keep thy nose in front of thy countenance, and not otherwisely, which were neither wisely nor too well. I hope thou wilt not fail to come on Tuesday. And pray don't forget the baby, as the nurse might find it lonesome to be here without her. During the period of thy visit, I will change my name to *Jinkins,* we will have such high Jinks! . . . Beacon

Street looks as though it wanted something. I think thou beest it. . . .

Am ever thy lame game MOTHER.

"*March 24.* Longfellow died at about 3.30 P.M. today. He will be much and deservedly lamented. The last of dear Chev's old set, the Five of Clubs, nicknamed by Mary Dwight the 'Mutual Admiration Society.' On hearing of this event, I put off my reception for the Zuñi chiefs, which should have been on Monday, when the funeral will probably take place."

"*March 26.* Dear Brother Sam came on very unexpectedly to attend the funeral service held at the Longfellow [house] for relatives and intimates. I also was bidden to this, but thought it impossible for me to go, lame as I am. Sent word out to Julia Anagnos, who came in, and went in my place with Uncle Sam. The dear old fellow dined with us. I got downstairs with great difficulty and fatigue. We had a delightful evening with him, but he would go back to New York by the night train."

"*March 30.* To-day the Zuñi chiefs and Mr. Cushing, their interpreter and adopted son, came to luncheon at 1.45. There were twelve Indian chiefs in full Indian dress. Reception afterwards."

The Zuñi Indians live in Arizona. Once in the year they make a pilgrimage to the seashore, and wading into the ocean at sunrise, offer prayer to the Great Spirit, and fill their vessels of woven grass with water to be used through the year in their religious exercises.

This pilgrimage had always been made to the Pacific; but in the hearts of the tribe lingered a tradition that once in a hundred years the "Water of Sunrise" should be visited, and they dreamed of the Eastern ocean. The tradition was now confirmed, the dream fulfilled, through the friendly offices of Mr. Cushing.

The ceremony was one of touching interest; hundreds of people gathered at City Point to watch it. Most of the spectators felt the beauty and solemnity of the service (for such it was), but a few were inclined to jeer, till they were sternly rebuked by Phillips Brooks.

As our mother could not go to see the Zuñis, they must come to see her, and Mr. Cushing gladly brought them. They were grave, stalwart men, with a beautiful dignity of carriage and demeanor. A picture not to be forgotten is that of her in her white dress, bending eagerly forward to listen while the chiefs, sitting in a circle on the floor, told stories, Mr. Cushing interpreting for her benefit. At parting, each man took her hand, and raised it to his forehead with a gesture of perfect grace. The eldest chief, before this salute, held her hand a moment, and blew across the palm, east and west. "Daughter," he said, "our paths have crossed here. May yours be bright hereafter!"

"*April 1.* To-day Edward [Everett] Hale brought me a parting memento of the Zuñis — the basket with which they had dipped up the water from the 'ocean of sunrise.' Mr. Cushing sent this. E. E. H. also spoke about five hymns which should be written corresponding to the five great hymns of the Catholic mass. He asked me to write one of these and I promised to try."

"*April 16.* Splint off to-day. Waited for Dr. Beach, so could not go to church. Had an interesting talk with the Doctor on the Immortality of the Soul, in which he is a believer."

"*April 27.* Made to-day a good start in writing about Margaret Fuller. This night at 8.50 P.M. died Ralph Waldo Emerson, *i.e.*, all of him that could die. I think of him as a father gone — father of so much beauty, of so much modern thought."

"*May 7.* To church, going out for the first time without a crutch, using only my cane.

"J. F. C.'s sermon was about Emerson, and was very interesting and delicately appreciative. I think that he exaggerated Emerson's solid and practical effect in the promotion of modern liberalism. The change was in the air and was to come. It was in many minds quite independently of Mr. Emerson. He was the foremost literary man of his day in America, philosopher, poet, reformer, all in one. But he did not make his age, which was an age of great men and of great things."

"*May 14.* Had a sudden thought in church of a minister preaching in a pulpit and a fiend waiting to carry him off to hell. Made some verses out of this.

"This is Whitsunday. . . . I do hope and pray for a fresh outpouring this year. While I listened to Dr. Furness, two points grew clear to me: one was, that I would hold my Peace Meeting, if I should hold it alone, as a priest sometimes serves his mass. The second was, that I could preach from the text: 'As ye have borne the image of the earthy, so shall ye bear the image of the heavenly,' and this sermon I think I could preach to the prisoners, as I once tried to do years ago when dear Chev found the idea so intolerable that I had to give it up. I am twenty years older now, and the Woman Ministry is a recognized fact.

"Still Sunday afternoon. I am now full of courage for this week's heavy work."

"*May 30.* Alas! alas! dear Professor Rogers dropped dead to-day after some exercise at the Institute of Technology. How he had helped me in the Town and Country Club! Without his aid and that of his wife, I doubt whether I could have started it at all: he was always vice-president as I was president. I cannot think how I can do without him."

"*July 22.* Commemoration of Mr. Emerson at Concord Town Hall. Several portraits of him and very effective floral decorations; no music. Prayer by Rev. Dr. Holland; introductory remarks by F. B. Sanborn in which he quoted a good part of a poem by W. E. Channing, R. W. E. its theme. Then came an unmercifully long paper by Dr. X., much of which was interesting and some of which was irrelevant. He insisted upon Mr. Emerson's having been an evolutionist, and unfolded a good deal of his own tablecloth along with the mortuary napkin."

"*July 29.* Had a studious and quiet day. Was in good time for the performance [at the Casino]. . . ."

In a letter to "Uncle Sam" she speaks of "the labor
and fatigue of preparing for the theatricals, which are
happily over. We had rehearsals every day last week.
My part was a short one, but I took great pains to
make it as good as I could. Some points which I
thought of on the spur of the moment added greatly
to the fun of the impersonation. We had a fine
house, and an enthusiastic reception. I had a floral
tribute — only think of it! — a basket of beautiful
roses. . . ."

"*September 18.* Left Newport to attend Saratoga
Convention, being appointed a delegate from the
Channing Memorial Church, with its pastor, Reverend
C. W. Wendte."

"*November 8.* Cousin Nancy Greene, my father's
cousin, enters to-day upon her ninety-ninth year. I
called to see her, going first to town to buy her some
little gift. . . . Had a very interesting talk with her.
She was nicely dressed in black, with a fresh cap and
lilac ribbon, and a little silk handkerchief. For her
this was quite an unusual toilette. I wished her a good
year to come, but she said: 'Why should I want to live
another year? I can do nothing.' I suggested that
she should dictate her reminiscences to the girl who
waits upon her and who writes, she says, a good hand."

"*November 11.* I went to see the old Seventh Day
Baptist Church, now occupied by the Newport Historical Society, in which my great-grandfather, Governor Samuel Ward, used to attend service. . . ."

"*December 24, Boston.* Spoke at the Home for Intemperate Women at 6 P.M. I did my best. Text:

'Of whom the whole family in heaven and earth are named.' Subject: The Christian family; God, its father, all mankind brothers and sisters. . . . Afterwards went to the Christmas 'Messiah.' Felt more sure than ever that no music so beautiful as this has ever been written."

CHAPTER IV

241 BEACON STREET: THE NEW ORLEANS EXPOSITION

1883–1885; *aet.* 64–66

The full outpouring of power that stops at no frontier,
But follows *I would* with *I can*, and *I can* with *I do it!*

J. W. H.

THE winter of 1882–83 found her once more with a family of some size, her son and his wife joining forces with her at 241 Beacon Street. In Harry's college days, mother and son had made much music together; now the old music books were unearthed, and the house resounded with the melodies of Rossini and Handel. It was a gay household, with Crawford living in the reception room on the ground floor; play was the order of the evening, as work was of the day.

The new inmates brought new friends to the circle, men of science, the colleagues of her beloved "Bunko," now Professor Howe of the Institute of Technology, Italians, and other Europeans introduced by Crawford. There was need of these new friends, for old ones were growing fewer. Side by side in the Journal with the mention of this one or that comes more and more frequently the record of the passing of some dear companion on life's journey. Those who were left of the great band that made New England glorious in the nineteenth century held closely to each other, and the bond between them had a touching significance. Across the street lived Oliver Wendell Holmes; in

MRS. HOWE'S BOSTON HOUSE, 241 BEACON STREET

Cambridge was Thomas Wentworth Higginson; in Dorchester, Edward Everett Hale.

In a letter to her brother she speaks of "the constant 'tear and trot' of my Boston life, in which I try to make all ends meet, domestic, social, artistic, and reformatory, and go about, I sometimes think, like a poor spider who spins no web. . . . Marion has been very industrious, and is full of good work and of cheer. His book ["Mr. Isaacs"] has been such a success as to give him at once a recognized position, of which the best feature, economically, is that it enables him to command adequate and congenial employment at fairly remunerative prices. . . ."

To Laura

My darling Child, —

Your letter makes me say that I don't know anything, whether I have written or not, or ought to write, or not. Mammy's poor old head is very much worse than ever, and I don't get time even to read letters, some days. I can't tell why, except that there are many points and people to be reached, in one way and another, and I rush hither and thither, accomplishing, I fear, very little, but stirring many stews with my own spoon. It seems to me that I could not bear another winter of this stress and strain, which is difficult to analyze or account for, as "she need n't have done it, you know." Why she must do it, notwithstanding, is hard to tell, or what it is in doing it which so exhausts all nervous energy and muscular strength. Now, darling, after this prelude in a minor

key, let me thank heaven that, after all, I am well in
health, and comfortable.

Wednesday, 10th, 2.20 P.M. I wrote the above at
noon, yesterday, expecting Salvini to lunch. . . . Mrs.
Appleton came in, and kept me, until 2 minus 20
minutes, at which time, nearly beside myself with
anxiety, I tumbled upstairs, out of one garment and
into another. Such was my dressing. Salvini came
and was charming. After luncheon came a reception.
Your little girls were there, looking delightfully. Porter was pleased to say that the little ones, hanging
around the (old) grandmother made a pleasing picture. . . . No more from 'fection

MAR.

In later January she has "a peaceful day at Vassar
College. . . . In the afternoon met the teachers and
read some poems, to wit, all of the Egyptian ones, and
the poem on the Vestal dug up in Rome. At bedtime
last night I had a thought of ghosts. I spoke of this
to Maria Mitchell to-day. She told me that Mr. Matthew Vassar's body had been laid in this room and
those of various persons since, which, had I known,
I had been less comfortable than I was."

"*February 18.* Young Salvini [Alessandro] and Ventura to luncheon, also Lizzie Boott and Mrs. Jack
[Gardner]. Salvini is beautiful to look at, having
a finely chiselled Greek head. He is frank, cordial,
and intelligent, and speaks very appreciatively of his
parts, especially of Romeo."

"To the Intemperate Women's Home where I spoke from the text, 'Repent, for the kingdom of heaven is at hand.'"

To Laura

March 17, 1883.

DARLING CHILD, —

Just let drop everything, and take me up on your lap. I'se very tired, writing, tugging at all sorts of things. Long silence b'tween us. Growing estrangement, eh? Richardses are better, eh? Which nobody can deny. . . . Have been hard at work upon a memoir of Maria Mitchell, which is well-nigh finished. . . . Am spleeny to-day: the weather being according. . . .

To "Uncle Sam"

March 28, 1883.

MY DARLING BROTHER, —

I owe you two good long letters, and am ashamed to think how long it is since you have seen my crabbed chirography. Of course, it is the old story. I have been dreadfully busy with all sorts of work, in all of which I take delight, while yet to quote St. Paul, "The good that I would I do not." To give you a few items, I have just finished a short memoir of Maria Mitchell, Professor of Astronomy at Vassar College. This was an interesting task, but had to be very carefully done. At the same time, I had to correct Maud's memoir of me, which is to be published in the same collection of biographies of *eminent* women! I think I am eminent for undertaking ten times more than I can do, and doing about one tenth of it. Well — I have given three Sunday preachments at a sort of Woman's church which they have here. My themes were: "The Order of the Natural and the Spiritual," "Tares and Wheat," and "The Power of Religion in the Life." I was in New York last Wednesday, to preside over the mid-year Conference of the Woman's Congress. . . . I had a visit from Salvini the other day. He was most charming, and sent me a box for last evening's performance of "The Outlaw," in Italian: "Morte Civile." I went, with my Harry and Laura, I in my best attire. I had received some very beautiful roses, which I threw upon the stage, at the recall after the third Act. To-day I met Wendell Phillips in the street, and made him come in to see Marion, whose letter on English rule in India, printed in the New York "Tribune," he had liked very much. Phillips asked me how I came to live in this part of the city, and I told him about your gift of the house. . . . Marion is sitting by my fire, with Browning's "Jocoseria" in his hands, from which he has been reading passages. It sounds strange and silly. . . .

To the same

Oak Glen, May 10, 1883.

. . . — I have been here alone all these days, with many gentle ghosts of past companionship, and with a task at which I work steadily every day. This is a life of Margaret Fuller, rewritten mostly from the memoirs already published, but also recast in my own thought. The publisher is in a hurry for it, and

I have to work without intermission, *i.e.*, as long as I can, every day; but with all the diligence in my power, I cannot get along very rapidly. When I have finished my stint, I refresh myself with a little Greek, and also with an Italian novel which I have brought with me. The place looks lovely, and I sat, this afternoon, on the western piazza, near that angle where you and I used to sit, last summer, and enjoyed a bath of sunshine. . . .

To Laura

Oak Glen, August 21, 1883.

My Much Neglected Darling, —

I give you to-day my first hour, or half-hour, as the case may be, feeling that my long silence has been abominable, and must be broken, even if you should feel it to be your duty to throw an inkstand at my head, in return for my letter. It is partly Backbone's fault. Backbone has been so scrouged and put upon by the summer's work that he sometimes cuts up amazing. Said work is pretty well out of hand at this moment, the last chapters of "Margaret Fuller" being ready for the press. . . . I have so much felt the shocking uncharity of things in the way of diaries and letters which have been published within the last few years. Not the least bad exhibition in this kind has been made by Carlyle and his wife. I have just finished reading the three volumes of her letters and memorials, which were indeed interesting to me by the mention in them of persons whom I myself have known. Still, the spirit of the book is painful. It is sad to see how she adopted, at times, her husband's harsh creed. I should think Froude, the editor, must be wanting in common taste and decency, to have allowed the letters to appear in all this crudeness. I am so glad that I never went near them, after that one tea-drink, a very bad one, forty years ago. Is this enough about the Carlyles? And is it strictly charitable? I dunno; I'm getting very old to know anything. . . .

The "Life of Margaret Fuller" (in Roberts Brothers' series of "Famous Women") was a small book, yet it stood for much careful work, and was so recognized and received. The recognition sometimes took a singular form, *e.g.*, a letter from a gentleman styling himself "Prof. Nat. & Geol.," who desires two copies of the "Margaret Fuller," and asks her to "accept for them a choice selection of '*Lithological*,' Cabinet of Geological Mineral specimens, representing the Glacial, and Emptus period, also the Crystalline formation of the Earth's Strata, in Coolings, Rubbings, and Scratchings of the Drift Age."

The exchange was not effected.

To "Uncle Sam"

December 15, 1883.

DARLING BRO' SAM, —

I must write you at once, or my silence will expand into a broad ocean which I shall be afraid to cross. . . . I have had a very laborious year, now screwed to my desk, and working at *timed* tasks, now travelling

widely, and scattering my spoken words. . . . Well,
so much for desk-work, now for the witch broomstick
on which I fly. The Congress was held in Chicago,
in mid-October. From this place, I went to Minneapolis. . . . Harry and his wife are here, paying handsomely their share of our running expenses. The little
house looks friendly and comfortable, and I hope,
after a few more flights, to enjoy it very much. These
will now be very short. . . . Boston is all alive with
Irving's acting, Matthew Arnold's lectures, Cable's
readings, and the coming opera. *Père* Hyacinthe also
has been here, and a very eminent Hindoo, named
Mozumdar. I have lost many of these doings by my
journeys, but heard Arnold's lecture on Emerson last
evening. I have also heard one of Cable's readings.
Arnold does not in the least understand Emerson, I
think. He has a positive, square-jawed English mind,
with no super-sensible *aperçûs*. His elocution is piti-
able, and when, after his lecture, Wendell Phillips
stepped forward and said a few graceful words of farewell to him, it was like the Rose complimenting the
Cabbage. . . .

The year 1883 closed with a climax of triumphant
fatigue in the Merchants' and Mechanics' Fair, in
which she was president of the Woman's Department.
This was to lead to a far more serious undertaking in
the autumn of 1884, that of the Woman's Department
of the New Orleans Exposition. The Journal may
bridge the interval between the two.

"*February 3, 1884.* Wendell Phillips is dead.

"To speak at the meeting in memory of Cheshub Chunder Sen at Parker Memorial Hall. Heard T. W. Higginson and Mrs. Cheney. H. spoke at length of Phillips and said too much about his later mistakes, I thought, saying nothing about his suffrage work, of which I took care to speak, when it was my turn: Several persons thanked me for my words, which treated very briefly of Phillips's splendid services to humanity."

[She spoke of him as "the most finished orator of our time," and as "the Chrysostom of modern reform."]

"*February 6.* Wendell Phillips's funeral. I am invited to attend memorial services at Faneuil Hall on Friday evening. I accept."

"*February 9.* .... I was very glad that I had come to this, the People's meeting, and had been able to be heard in Faneuil Hall, the place of all others where the *People* should commemorate Wendell Phillips. My task was to speak of his services to the cause of Woman. Others spoke of him in connection with Labor Reform, Anti-Slavery, Ireland, and Temperance."

To Laura

Just so, knowed you'd take advantage of my silence to write su'thin saucy. Until I got your kammunikation I felt kind o' penitent like — had n't thanked for no Xmas nor nothing. Felt self to be shabby and piglike in conduct, though perfectly angelic in intention. Pop comes your letter — pop goes my repentance. "She's got even with me," I said: "If she went into a tailor's shop to get a cabbage leaf, to make an apple pie, what does it matter by what initials she calls herself? Who's going to distress themselves about the set of her cloak? And she do boast about it preposterous, and that are a fact."

Here endeth the first meditation, and I will now fall back upon the "Dearly beloved," for the rest of the service. . . .

To the same

241 BEACON STREET, February 11, 1884.

Oh, thou, who art not quite a Satan!

Question is, dost thou not come very near it? . . .

I have been very busy, and have *orated* tremendous, this winter. I did n't go for to do it, you know, but I cou'n' avoin it. [A household expression, dating back to her childhood, when a gentleman with a defect of speech, speaking of some trouble incurred by her father, said, "Poor Mr. Warn! he cou'n' avoin it!" This gentleman was a clergyman, and was once heard to assure his congregation that "their hens [heads] wou'n be crownen with glory!"]

"*February 12.* Hearing at State House, Committee of Probate, etc., on the petition of Julia Ward Howe and others that the laws concerning married women may be amended in three respects. We had prepared three separate bills, one providing that the mother shall have equal rights with the father in their children, especially in determining their residence and their education. A second ruling that on the wife's death, the husband, who now gets all her real estate, may

have one half, and the children the other, and that
the widow shall have the same right to half the husband's real estate after his death. A third bill was
devised to enable husband and wife to contract valid
money obligations toward each other."

Through the untiring efforts of the Suffragists these
bills were all passed.

"*March 27.* . . . I heard with dismay of the injury
done to my Newport place by the breaking of Norman's dam. Was very much troubled about this."

To Laura

March 29, 1884.

MY DEAREST DARLING, —

Dunno why I hain't wrote you, 'cept that, while I
was lame, the attitude of reclining with my foot extended was very fatiguing to me. The injury was very
slight. I only knocked my left foot pretty hard (*an-
glicé*, stubbed my toe) hurrying upstairs, but the weak
left knee gave way, and turned, letting me down, and
feloniously puffing itself up, which Charity never does.
It could not be concealed from Maud, and so Beach
was sent for, and a fortnight of *stay still* ordered and
enforced. On Tuesday last I broke bounds and railed
it to Buffalo, New York, with my crutches, which
were no longer needed. This was for the mid-year
Conference of our Congress. Before I say more under
this head, let me tell you that I returned from Buffalo
this morning, much the better for my trip. I had a

lovely visit there, in a most friendly and comfortable house, with carriages at my disposition. A beautiful luncheon was given to us Congressers and I gave a lecture on Thursday evening, price $50, and sat in a high chair, thinking it not prudent to stand so long. . . .

"*April 4.* In the latter part of the eighteenth century a Christian missionary, Chinese, but disguised as a Portuguese, penetrated into Corea, and was much aided in his work by the courageous piety of Columba Kang, wife of one of the lesser nobles. She and the missionary suffered torture and death. . . . Merchants, not diplomatists, are the true apostles of civilization. "Questions for A.A.W. [*i.e.*, for the annual Conference of the Association for the Advancement of Women]: How far does the business of this country fulfil the conditions of honest and honorable traffic? "What is the ideal of a mercantile aristocracy?"

"*April 7.* General Armstrong called last evening. He spoke of the negroes as individually quick-witted and capable, but powerless in association and deficient in organizing power. This struck me as the natural consequence of their long subjection to despotic power. The exigencies of slavery quickened their individual perceptions, and sharpened their wits, but left them little opportunity for concerted action. Freedom allows men to learn how to coöperate widely and strongly for ends of mutual good. Despotism heightens personal consciousness through fear of danger, but itself fears nothing so much as association among men, which it first prohibits and in time renders impossible."

"*April 15*. A delightful Easter. I felt this day that, in my difficulties with the Anti-Suffragists, the general spread of Christian feeling gives me ground to stand upon. The charity of Christendom will not persist in calumniating the Suffragists, nor will its sense of justice long refuse to admit their claims."

"*April 17*. Sam Eliot was in a horse-car, and told me that Tom Appleton had died of pneumonia in New York. The last time I spoke with him was in one of these very cars. He asked me if I had been to the funeral, meaning that of Wendell Phillips. I was sure that he had been much impressed by it. I saw him once more, on Commonwealth Avenue on a bitter day. He walked feebly and was much bent. I did not stop to speak with him which I now regret. He was very friendly to me, yet the sight of me seemed to rouse some curious vein of combativeness in him. He had many precious qualities, and had high views of character, although he was sometimes unjust in his judgments of other people, particularly of the come-outer reformers."

"*April 19*. To get some flowers to take to T. G. A.'s house. Saw him lying placid in his coffin, robed in soft white cashmere, with his palette and brushes in his hands. . . ."

To Florence

April 20, 1884.

. . . I went yesterday to poor Tom Appleton's funeral. It is very sad to lose him, and every one says that a great piece of the old Boston goes with him. . . .

I dined with George William Curtis yesterday at Mrs. Harry Williams's. George William was one of Tom Appleton's pall-bearers, — so were Dr. Holmes and Mr. Winthrop. . . .
Curtis's oration on Wendell Phillips was very fine.

"*April 20.* Thought sadly of errors and shortcomings. At church a penitential psalm helped me much, and the sermon more. I felt assured that, whatever may be my fate beyond this life, I should always seek, love, and rejoice in the good. Thus, even in hell, one might share by sympathy the heavenly victory."

"*May 5.* I begin in great infirmity of spirit a week which brings many tasks. First, I must proceed in the matter of Norman's injury to my estate, either to a suit or a settlement by arbitration unless I can previously come to an understanding with N."

A heavy affliction was soon to drive all other thoughts from her mind. On May 19, a telegram arrived from Italy saying, "Samuel Ward expired peacefully."

She writes: "Nothing could be more unexpected than this blow. Dear Bro' Sam had long since been pronounced out of danger. . . . Latterly we have heard of him as feeble, and have felt renewed anxiety, but were entirely unprepared for his death."

"*May 20.* Dark days of nothingness these, to-day and yesterday. Nothing to do but be patient and explore the past."

"*May 21.* Had a sitting all alone with dear Uncle Sam's picture this afternoon. I thought it might be the time of his funeral. I read the beautiful 90th Psalm and a number of his bright, sweet lyrics. A sympathetic visit from Winthrop Chanler."

"*May 27.* . . . Dear Brother Sam's death has brought me well in sight of the farther shore. May I be ready when it is my turn to cross."

To her sister Louisa

DEAREST SISTER, —

I was already in debt to you for one good letter when this later one arrived, giving me the full, desired particulars of our dear one's last days on earth. You and Annie both write as though the loss were heaviest to me, and I only feel that I cannot feel it half enough. The pathos of a life of such wonderful vicissitudes! I cannot half take it in. What must he not have suffered in those lonely days of wandering and privation, while I was comfortable in my household! . . . God knows, I had every reason to love him, for he was heroically faithful to his affection for me. Now, I feel how little I appreciated his devotion, and how many chimeras, in my foolish wool-gathering head, crowded upon this most precious affection, which was worthy of a much larger place in my thoughts. His death is a severe loss to Maud and me. . . . We were always hoping to rejoin him, and to pass some happy years with him. A great object is withdrawn from our two lives. Nothing can take his place to either of us. . . . As I write, the tears come. Like you,

I long to sit and talk it all over with the two who are all I have left of my own generation. To our children, the event cannot be at all what it is to us. They are made for the future, and our day is not theirs. I was comforted, in your first letter, in reading of that pleasant, quiet talk you had with him, when, among other things, you read to him the lovely verses from St. John's Gospel, which have become a classic of consolation among Christian people. I believe that he is in the heaven accorded to those who have loved their fellow-men, for who ever coined pure kindness into acts as he did? One of the lessons I learn from his life is that it is very hard for us to judge rightly the merits and demerits of others. Here was a man with many faults on the surface, and a heart of pure gold beneath. . . . The thought of his lonely funeral and solitary grave has wrung my heart at times, but sometimes I think of it as a place where one might be glad to be at rest. . . . But now, dear, I have had all the heart-break I can bear, writing this letter. Let me now speak of the living and tell you where and how we are. . . . I left very unwillingly to come down here, and try to get my poor wrecked place in order. You know, of course, that the dam which was built to cut off my water, and against which I obtained an injunction, burst this spring, and destroyed my two ponds, my carriage, and a good part of my barn. I have tried, in a lumbering way, to get justice, but have not yet succeeded. I have had, too, a great deal of trouble in my presidency of the Woman's Congress, this year. Almost as soon as I open my eyes in the morning, these black dogs of worry spring upon me. I long to be free from them. . . .

"*June 28.* Senator Bayard to William A. Duncan about dear Bro' Sam: 'It is just one of those little kindnesses of which his life was so full. There is no doubt, as you say, that his later years were his best! The wine of life fined itself. . . . He was readily sympathetic, and did in Rome as Romans did, and kept time and tune to a great variety of instruments. But the kind good heart *always beat truly*, and the array of good deeds to his credit in the great book of account is delightful to think of.' "

To Laura

NEWPORT, August 15, 1884.

Have n't I written to you? I have an idea of some long letter of mine not answered by you. But this may be one of those imaginary good actions which help to puff me up. Life, you see, gallops on to such a degree with me that I don't know much difference between what I have intended to do and what I have done. . . .

I think novels is humbug. What you think? They don't leave you anything but a sort of bad taste. . . .

"*August 27.* Simply good for nothing, but to amuse the little Hall children. A strange dead level of indifference. Do not see any difference between one thing and another. This, I should think, must come from a vagary of the liver. Worst sort of nervous pros-

INTERIOR, 241 BEACON STREET

tration — to prostrate one's self before one's nerves. To town in the afternoon, when the dead indifference and lassitude went off somewhat."

"*August 29.* We dined at the Booths' to-day, meeting Mr. and Mrs. Joseph Jefferson and William Warren. A rare and delightful occasion. Jefferson talked much about art. He, Booth, and Warren all told little anecdotes of forgetfulness on the stage. Jefferson had told a love-story twice, Booth had twice given the advice to the players [in "Hamlet"], Warren, in 'Our American Cousin,' should have tried to light a match which would not light. He inadvertently turned the ignitable side, which took fire, and so disconcerted him that he forgot where he was in the play and had to ask some one what he had last said, which being told him enabled him to go on."

"*September 25.* Finished to-day my Congress paper. I have written this paper this week instead of going to the Unitarian Convention, which I wished much to attend. . . . I did not go because I thought I ought neither to leave home unnecessarily, to spend so much money, nor to put off the writing of the A.A.W. paper.

"I shall look a little to see whether circumstances hereafter will not show that it was best for me to follow this course. My Dæmon did not say 'go,' but he sometimes plays me false. I have certainly had the most wonderful ease in writing this paper which, I thought, would occupy a number of weary days, and lo! it has all written itself, *currente calamo.*"

"*October 5.* Is the law of progress one of harmony

or of discord? Do the various kinds of progress, moral,
intellectual, political, and economic or industrial,
agree or disagree? Do they help or hinder each
other? "

To Laura

NEWPORT, RHODE ISLAND, October 9, 1884.

MY DARLING LAURA, —

My poor wits, in these days, are like bits of sewing
silk wound on a card. You unwind a little and straightway come to an end. The wonder is, there are so
many ends. Here is a precise picture of our days as
passed at present. Morning, I wake early, lie and
think over my past life, with little satisfaction.
Bathe. Breakfast. Walk with Maud, Sonny [1] tugging alongside. Maud goes much further than I do.
Sonny and I return, take a basket and gather dry
twigs to brighten the evening fire. I visit my mare in
her stable — a good custom, as my man is not over-
careful of her stall. Maud comes back, I *exercise* her
voice. I go to books, she to desk. Study Greek a good
deal, reading Thucydides and Aristophanes. Dinner,
coffee, more reading and writing, unless we go to
town. Evening, music, reading or cards, worrying
about ——, bed. I have not mentioned my own much
writing, because you will understand it. I am trying
to compass a story, but have my fears about it. My
paper for the Woman's Congress is entitled "How to
broaden the Views of Society Women." Darling dear,
what more can I tell you? Is n't this too much al-

---

[1] John Howe Hall.

ready? Now, do spunk up and have some style about
you. . . . Be cheerful and resolute, my love, life comes
but once, and is soon over. . . .

"*October 13.* To New Bedford, for the Suffrage
meeting; trains did not connect at Myricks, where,
after some delay and negotiation, I with difficulty persuaded the conductor of a freight train to take me to
New Bedford in his caboose. This saved me time
enough to go to the Delano Mansion, restore my
strength with food, and put on my cap and ruche. The
Delanos were very kind. I read my Congress paper on
'Benefits of Suffrage to Women.' "

"*November 23.* To Louisburg Square to my old
friend's funeral [Hamilton Wilde]. . . . Around and
before me were the friends and associates of the golden
time in which his delightful humor and *bonhomie* so
often helped me in charades and other high times. It
was ghostly — there were Lizzie Homans and Jerry
Abbott, who took part with him and William Hunt in
the wonderful charade in which the two artists rode a
tilt with theatre hobbies. The gray heads which I had
once seen black, brown, or blond, heightened the effect
of the picture. It was indeed a *sic transit.* I said to
Charles Perkins — 'For some of us, it is the dressing
bell!' Oh! this mystery! So intense, so immense a
fact and force as human life, tapering to this little
point of a final leave-taking and brief remembrance!"

Now came the New Orleans Exposition, in which
she was to be chief of the Woman's Department.

It was already late when she received the appointment, but she lost no time. Establishing her headquarters at No. 5 Park Street (for many years the
home of the "Woman's Journal" and the New England Woman's Club), she sent out circulars to every
State in the Union, asking for exhibits, and appealed
to the editors of newspapers all over the country to
send women correspondents for a month or more to
the Exposition. She called meetings in Boston, New
York, Providence, Philadelphia, and Hartford, at all
of which she spoke, imploring the women to bestir
themselves, and, late as it was, to make an effort to get
together a proper showing of women's work for the
great Fair.

Beside all this, she kept up through the autumn
an active correspondence with the Exposition authorities at New Orleans.

The Exposition was scheduled to open on the 1st
of December: it did actually open on the 16th. She
writes: —

"A steamer had been chartered to convey thither
the officers of the Exposition and their invited guests.
Seated on the deck, the chief of the Woman's Department and her fellow-workers watched the arrival of
the high dignitaries of the State and city, escorted by
members of the military, and by two bands of music;
one, the famous Mexican Band. All the craft on the
river were adorned with flags and streamers. The
Crescent, which gives the city its familiar designation,
was pointed out, and the 'Father of Waters' was
looked upon with admiring eyes. The steamer brought

us to the Exposition grounds, and here a procession was formed in which the ladies of the Woman's Department were assigned a place which they had some difficulty in keeping. The march led to the Main Building. The opening prayer was made by the Reverend De Witt Talmage. At a given moment a telegram was received from the President of the United States, Chester A. Arthur, declaring the Exposition to be formally open. Immediately after, the son of the Director-General, a fine lad of twelve years, touched the electric button by which the machinery of the Exposition was set in motion.

"Returning by land, we found the streets gay with decorations, in which the colors of the orthodox flag were conspicuous."

Maud was with her, and shared her labors, as did her devoted friend Isabel Greeley. At this time the floor of the gallery destined for the women's exhibit was not laid. By December 29 the officers of the department were able to hold a meeting in "an enclosure without doors or suitable furniture." When all was supposed to be ready for the exhibits, it was found that the roof leaked badly, the timber having so shrunk under the action of the sun as to tear away the waterproof felting. Moreover, there was not enough money to carry on the business of the Department. Funds had been promised by the Board of Management, but these funds were not forthcoming, the Board itself being in difficulties. Our mother had foreseen this contingency.

"Ladies," she said, "we must remember that women

have sometimes built churches with no better instruments than thimbles and a teapot! If the worst comes to the worst, we must come before the public and endeavor with its aid to earn the money necessary to complete our enterprise."

This foreboding soon became a fact, and early in January she found herself in rather a " tight corner." She had sent out the call for exhibits to every State in the Union ; with great effort the women of the country had responded most generously. She now felt herself personally responsible for these exhibits, and determined that, *coûte que coûte*, they should be well displayed and the Woman's Department properly installed.

There was no money: very well! she would earn some. She arranged a series of entertainments, beginning with a lecture by herself. There followed a time of great stress and anxiety, which taxed to the utmost her mother-wit and power of invention. Faculties hitherto dormant awoke to meet the task; she devised practical, hard, common-sense methods, far removed from her life habit of intellectual labor. She had moved into a new apartment in the house of life, one nearer the earth and not quite so near the stars. She often quoted during these months Napoleon's saying, on being told that something he wished to do was impossible, *"Ne me dîtes pas ce bête de mot !"*

In spite of endless vexations, it was a time of tremendous enjoyment; every nerve was strained, every gift exercised; the cup of life was brimming over, even if it was not all filled with honey.

" *January 13, 1885.* Preparing for my lecture this
evening. Subject, 'Is Polite Society Polite?' Place,
Werlein Hall. I was very anxious — the lecture appeared to me very homely for a Southern audience
accustomed to rhetorical productions. My reception
was most gratifying. The house was packed and many
were sent away. Judge Gayarré introduced me. Joa-
quin Miller came first, reciting his 'Fortunate Isles.'
I said in opening that even if my voice should not fill
the hall, my good-will embraced them all. Every point
in the lecture was perceived and applauded, and I felt
more than usually in sympathy with my audience."

"The second entertainment devised for the relief
of the Woman's Department was a '*Soirée Créole*,'
the third and last a 'grand musical *matinée*' at the
French Opera House, for which we were indebted to
the great kindness of Colonel Mapleson, who granted
us the use of the house, and by whose permission several of his most distinguished artists gave their services. Monsignor Gillow, Commissioner for Mexico,
also allowed his band to perform."

The difficulty of persuading the different artists to
sing, of pacifying their separate agents in the matter
of place on the programme and size of the letters in
which names were advertised, of bringing harmony
out of all the petty rivalries and cabals between the
different members of the troupe, required a patience
worthy of a better cause. Meanwhile there were other
troubles. Most of the women commissioners appointed
by the different States proved loyal comrades to their

chief in her great and distressful labor; but there were
others who gave her endless trouble.

"*February 6.* Our concert. The weather was favorable. Lieutenant Doyle came to escort me to the
theatre. My box was made quite gay by the uniforms
of several navy officers. The house was packed. We
took $1500 and hope to have more. I particularly en-
joyed the *Semiramide* overture, which the band gave
grandly. Rossini's soul seemed to me to blossom out
of it like an immortal flower."

These entertainments brought in over two thousand
dollars. This money enabled the women to install such
exhibits as were ready, to pay for a time the necessary
workmen, and to engage a special police force for the
protection of their goods. The United States ships in
the harbor also espoused the cause, Admiral Jouett,
of the flagship Tennessee, and Captain Kane, of the
Galena, sending experienced craftsmen whose ready
and skilful work soon changed the somewhat desolate
aspect of the gallery.

The arrangements were as simple as might be, the
greatest expense being the purchase of showcases. The
tables were of rough pine boards covered with cam-
brics and flannels, the draperies of the simplest and
cheapest, the luxury of a carpet was enjoyed only here
and there; but the excellence of the exhibits, and the
taste with which they were displayed, made the department a pleasant place. The winter was cold; the
wooden walls of the Government Building let in many

a chilling blast; but there was a stove in the office of the chief of installation, and with its help the daily cup of tea was made which kept the workers alive.

Each State and Territory had a separate opening day for its exhibit. These days were marked by public meetings at which compliments were exchanged, addresses made, and the exhibits turned over to the management. It was considered obligatory for all the commissioners to attend these meetings, and the women spent many weary hours trying to hear the addresses of distinguished individuals whose voices contended in vain with the din of the machinery. The Mexican Band played, and relieved the tedium of the long sittings; but the women commissioners were upheld chiefly by the feeling that they were drawn together from all parts of the country, and were taking an honored part in a great industrial and peaceful pageant, whose results would be important to the country and to mankind at large.

The Journal tells in February of the "opening of the colored people's department; very interesting. A numerous assemblage of them showed a wide range of types. Music, military, drumming especially good. Saw in their exhibit a portrait of John A. Andrew which looked like a greeting from the old heroic time."

The Woman's Department was formally opened on March 3, though it had really been open to the public since early January. The day was one of the gayest in the history of the Exposition. The gallery of the Government Building was bright with flowers and gay with flags. Admiral Jouett had sent the ship's band as a special compliment; the music was delightful, the speeches excellent. We quote from Mrs. Howe's address: —

"I wish to speak of the importance, in an industrial point of view, of a distinct showing of women's work in the great industrial exhibits. There are few manufactures in which the hand and brain of woman have not their appointed part. So long, however, as this work is shown merely in conjunction with that of men, it is dimly recognized, and makes no distinct impression. The world remains very imperfectly educated concerning its women. They are liable to be regarded as a non-producing class, supported by those to whom, in the order of nature, their life is a necessary condition of existence itself. . . . Exhibits like the present, then, are useful in summing up much of this undervalued work of women. A greater moral use they have in raising the standard of usefulness and activity for the sex in general. Good work, when recognized, acts as a spur to human energy. Those who show how women can excel are examples to shame those who do not try. They lay upon their sex an obligation to stronger endeavor and better action, and society gains thereby.

"Still more have I at heart the association, in these enterprises, of women who are not bound to each other by alliance of blood, or affinity of neighborhood. Greater and more important than the acquisition of skill is the cultivation of public spirit. 'Pro bono publico' is a motto whose meaning men should learn from their infancy, and at their firesides. How shall they learn it unless the women, the guardian spirits of the household, shall hold and teach, beyond all other doctrines, that of devotion and loyalty to the public good?

"I value, then, for the sake of both men and women, the disinterested association of women for the promotion of the great interests of society. . . .

"You were stirred the other day by the bringing back of a battle-flag whose rents had been carefully mended. I tell you, sisters, we have all one flag now, broad and bright enough to cover us all. Let us see that no rent is made in it.

"All that the best and wisest men can imagine for the good of the human race can be wrought if the best women will only help the best men."

One of her most arduous tasks was the arranging of a course of twenty-four "Twelve-o'Clock Talks," which were given every Saturday from the middle of February till the close of the Exposition. How she labored over them her companion daughter well remembers: remembers too what success crowned the effort. The subjects varied widely. Captain Bedford Pym, R.N., discoursed on Arctic explorations; Charles Dudley Warner told the story of the Elmira Reformatory; the Japanese Commissioner spoke of woman's work in Japanese literature. These talks were free to the public, and proved so popular that eight years later the same plan was carried out in the Woman's Department of the Chicago World's Fair, and again proved its excellence and value.

As if all this were not enough, she must found a Literary Association among the young people of New Orleans. She named them the Pans, and among their number were several whose names have since become well known in literature. Grace King, Elizabeth Bisland, and others will remember those evenings, when their bright youth flashed responsive to the call of the elder woman of letters.

In all the stress and hurry, we find this entry: —

"My dear father's birthday. I left the Exposition early and walked to visit dear Marion's grave in Girard Street Cemetery. A lovely place it was. He is buried above ground in a sort of edifice formed of brick, the rows of coffins being laid on stone floors, each single one divided from those on either side of it by a stone partition. 'Francis Marion Ward, died September 3rd, 1847.' Erected by William Morse, dear Marion's friend."

"*May 16.* Gave my talk to the colored people, soon after two in the afternoon in their department. A pretty hexagonal platform had been arranged. Behind this was a fine portrait of Abraham Lincoln, with a vase of beautiful flowers [gladiolus and white lilies] at its base. I spoke of Dr. Channing, Garrison, Theodore Parker, Charles Sumner, John A. Andrew, Lucretia Mott, and Wendell Phillips, occupying about an hour. They gave me a fine basket of flowers and sang my 'Battle Hymn.' Afterwards the Alabama cadets visited us. We gave them tea, cake and biscuits and I made a little speech for them."

Winter and spring passed rapidly, each season bringing fresh interest. The picturesqueness of New Orleans, the many friends she made among its people, the men and women gathered from every corner of the world, well made up to her for the vexations which inevitably attended her position. Looking back on these days, she said of them: "It was like having a big, big Nursery to administer, with children good, bad, and middling. The good prevailed in the end, as it usually or always does, and yet I used to say that Satan had a fresh flower for me every morning, when I came to my office, and took account of the state of things."

The difficulties with which the unfortunate managers were struggling made it impossible for them to keep their promises of financial support to the Woman's Department. Things went from bad to worse. Finally she realized that she herself must find the money to pay the debts of her department and to return the exhibits to the various States. She wrote a letter to John M. Forbes, of Boston, urging him to help her and her assistants out of their alarming predicament. Through Mr. Forbes, the Honorable George F. Hoar, Senator from Massachusetts, learned the state of the case. The sum of $15,000 had been named as that necessary to pay all just claims and wind up the affairs of the Department. At this time a bill was before Congress for an appropriation to aid the Exposition. Thanks to the efforts of Mr. Hoar, a sum of $15,000 was added to this bill with the express clause, "For the Relief of the Woman's Department." The

bill was passed without discussion. The news was
received with great rejoicing in New Orleans, especially in the Woman's Department, "where our need
was the sorest." The promise brought new life to the
weary workers; but they were to be far more weary
before the end. The Exposition closed on the last day
of May. Summer was upon them; the Northern women, unused to the great heats of New Orleans,
longed to close up their business and depart, but the
money had not come from Congress, and they could
not leave their post. Days dragged on; days of torrid,
relentless heat. Our mother must borrow money for
the Department here and there to bridge over the gap
between promise and fulfilment. Worn out by fatigue,
anxiety, and the great heat, she fell seriously ill. Those
nearest her begged her to go home and leave to others
the final settlement of affairs, but she would not hear
of this. She would get well: she *must* get well! Rally-
ing her forces, mental and physical, she did get well,
though her illness for a time seemed desperate.

At long last, when June was nearly half over, the
money came, and with it the end of her long task.
Accounts were audited, checks drawn, exhibits de-
spatched; and with farewell greetings and congratulations, "the whole weary matter ended." Her report as
President of the Woman's Department tells the story:

"The business of the Woman's Department having
thus been brought successfully to a close, it only remains for its President to resign the office she has
filled, with some pain and much pleasure, for more
than six months, — to thank the officers of her staff

for their able and faithful services, the vice-presidents, and the lady commissioners in general, for the friendly support she has had from them almost without exception. . . .

"The classification by States she considers to have justified itself, partly through the more distinct knowledge thus gained of the work of women in localities widely distant from each other, partly in the good acquaintance and good-will developed by this method of work. The friendly relations growing out of it still bind together those who are now thousands of miles apart, but who, we may hope, will ever remain united in a common zeal for promoting the industrial interests of women.

"Finally, she would say that she considers herself happy in having taken part in an Exposition of so high and useful a character as that which has latterly made New Orleans a centre of interest in the civilized world. She takes leave with regret of a city in which she has enjoyed much friendly intercourse and hospitality; a city in whose renewed prosperity she must henceforth feel a deep and lasting interest."

To Laura

Oak Glen, July 19, 1885.

How I left New Orleans, how I came North, how I let myself down here, is no doubt known to you thro' inference. How hot New Orleans was before I left it, you cannot know, nor how sick I was once upon a time, nor how I came up upon iced champagne and recovered myself, and became strong again. Ever since

I came home, I have slaved at my report of the Woman's Department. Weary pages have I written. Life seems at last to consist in putting a pen into an inkstand, and taking it out again, scribble, scribble, nibble, nibble (meal-times), and go to bed between whiles. . . .

So ended one of the most interesting and arduous experiences of her life. She always held in affectionate remembrance the city where she had enjoyed and suffered so much, and the friends she made there.

To Laura

OAK GLEN, November 4, 1885.

YOU LITTLE HATEFUL THING!

Herewith returned is the letter you wrote for. I had a mind to send it to you, beast that you are, without one word, just to pay you for that postal. Of course, I meant to write you immediately afterward in a separate envelope, telling you that I still love you. But there! I reflected that you could have a bad feeling if you opened the envelope and found no greeting from me. For the sake of posterity, Madam, I declined to give you this bad feeling. I do also retain some proprietorship in a certain pair of eyes which are like Sapphira's. Oh! I mean sapphires, and I don't want to dim them with any tear diamonds. "You flatter yourself," replies the Good-Natured One,[1] "to think of my shedding tears about anything that you could

---

[1] Laura had once been told that she "would not amount to much without her good nature."

say or do, or leave unsaid or undone." Just so. All right. I have got beefsteak for dinner to-day. What do you think of the weather, and does your husband know when your blacking is out?

Now, my sweet darling, your old Mammy is just back from a *tremendous* jaunt. I had a beautiful time in Iowa, and am as well as possible. Only think, travelling and at work for one calendar month, and not a finger ache, 'cept one day, when I had a slight headache. And I brought home over $200 earned by lectures. . . .

To the same

THE BERKELEY NUISANCE,[1] NEW YORK,
December 26, 1885.

. . . What have I been doing for the last eight weeks? Never you mind, my little dear. Mostly putting a girdle round the earth by correspondence, and some-ly worrying about my poor relations. Don't you flatter yourself that I ever thought of you under this head. But the ———, and the ———, and the ———, taken together, are enough to give one a turn at the worry-cat system. Well 'm, I had also to see the distribution of the whole edition of my New Orleans Report, and I can only compare this to the process of taking down a house, and of sending each individual brick somewhere, labelled with your compliments; supposing the bricks to be one thousand in number, it would take some time to distribute them, Harry Richards will be able to tell you how much time, and how many

---

[1] Berkeley Chambers, where she and Maud spent this winter.

masculine oaths would go to each hundred of the articles. Well, that's enough about that. You have had one of my bricks sent you, and hang me if I believe you have read it. Sweetison (a new little 'spression which I have this minute invented), I stayed at Oak Glen until Monday last, which was the 21st. Then I came here by the way of Boston, and arrove on Tuesday evening. Our quarters, or rather eighths, are small, considering my papers and Maud's clothes. The food is fine, the style first-rate, the rigs imposing to a degree, but, ah! I kind of hate it all. New York is too frightfully dirty! and then so stereotyped and commonplace. Boston losing its prestige? Not as I am at present advised. . . .

CHAPTER V

MORE CHANGES

1886–1888; *aet.* 67–69

GIULIA ROMANA ANAGNOS

Giulia Romana! how thy trembling beauty,
    That oft would shudder at one breath of praise,
Comes back to me! before the trump of duty
    Had marshalled thee in life's laborious ways.

We used to wonder at thy blush in hearing
    Thy parents praised. We now know what it meant:
A consciousness of their gifts reappearing
    Perchance in thine — to consummation blent.

Oh, she was beautiful, beyond all magic
    Of sculptor's hand, or pencil to portray!
Something angelical, divinely tragic,
    Tempered the smile that round her lips would play.

Dear first-born daughter of a hero's heart!
    Pass to perfection, all but perfect here!
We weep not much, remembering where thou art,
    Yet, child of Poesy! receive a tear.

                                    T. W. PARSONS.

THE years 1886 and 1887 were marked by two events which changed materially the course of her private life: the death of Julia, the beloved eldest daughter, and the marriage of Maud, the house-mate and comrade.

During the winter of 1885–86 she made her headquarters in New York. Lecture engagements, conferences, and sermons took her hither and thither, and much of the time that should have been "precious" was passed in trains and boats.

In the last days of February, Julia was stricken with

rheumatic fever, which soon developed into typhoid. The weather was "direful: bitter cold and furious wind." Our mother went at once to South Boston, where "arriving, found my dear child seriously but not dangerously ill. Her joy at my coming was very pathetic."

On the 28th she writes: —

"I cannot be sure whether it was on this day that she said to me: 'Mamma, don't you remember the dream you had when Flossy and I were little children, and you were in Europe? You dreamed that you saw us in a boat and that the tide was carrying us away from you. Now the dream has come true, and the tide is bearing me away from you.'

"This saying was very sad to me; but my mind was possessed with the determination that death was not to be thought of."

For a time conditions seemed to improve, and she hastened to New York, where her presence was imperative; but a telegram summoned her back: Julia was not so well, and "a pain as of death" fell on the anxious mother.

"Saw by Katie's face when she opened the door that things were worse. I flew up the stairs and found my darling little changed, except that her breathing seemed rather worse. She was so glad to see me! . . . About this time I noticed a change come over her sweet face. . . . I felt, but would not believe, that it was the beginning of the end. Julia was presently very happy, with Michael on one side of her and myself on the other. Each of us held a hand. She said: 'I am

JULIA ROMANA ANAGNOS

very happy now: if one has one's parents and one's
husband, what more can one want?' And presently,
'The angels have charge of me now, mamma and
Mimy.'[1] She said to me: 'What does the Lord want to
kill me for? I am dying.' I said, 'No, my darling, you
are going to get well.' She said: 'Remember, if anything happens to me, you two must stay together.' . . .
A little later Michael and I were alone with her. She
began to wander, and talk as if with reference to her
club or some such thing. 'If this is not the right thing,'
she said, 'call another priestess'; then, very emphati-
cally: 'Truth, truth.' These were her last words.

"My darling should have been forty-two years old
this day. . . ."

A few days later she writes to Mary Graves: —

"I am not wild, nor melancholy, nor inconsolable,
but I feel as America might if some great, fair State
were blotted from its map, leaving only a void for the
salt and bitter sea to overwhelm. I cannot, so far, get
any comfort from other worldly imaginings. If God
says anything to me now, he says, 'Thou fool.' The
truth is that we have no notion of the value and beauty
of God's gifts until they are taken from us. Then He
may well say: 'Thou fool,' and we can only answer
to our name."

The Journal says: —

"This is the last day of this sorrowful March which
took my dear one from me. I seem to myself only dull,
hard, and confused under this affliction. I pray God
to give me comfort by raising me up that I may be

[1] Michael.

nearer to the higher life into which she and her dear
father have passed. And thou? *eleison.* . . ."

"Have had an uplifting of soul to-day. Have written to Mary Graves: 'I am at last getting to stand
where I can have some spiritual outlook.' The confusion of 'is not' is giving place to the steadfastness of
'is.' Have embodied my thoughts in a poem to my
dear Julia and in some pages which I may read at the
meeting intended to commemorate her by the New
England Woman's Club."

The Journal of this spring is full of tender allusions
to the beloved daughter. The dreams of night often
brought back the gracious figure; these visions are
accurately described, each detail dwelt on with loving
care.

In the "Reminiscences" she tells of Julia's consecrated life, of her devotion to her father, and to the
blind pupils; describes, too, her pleasure in speaking
at the Concord School of Philosophy (where her "mind
seemed to have found its true level") and in a Meta-
physical Club of her own founding.

"It was beautiful to see her seated in the midst of
this thoughtful circle, which she seemed to rule with
a staff of lilies. The club was one in which diversity
of opinion sometimes brought individuals into sharp
contrast with each other; but her gentle government
was able to bring harmony out of discord, and to subdue alike the crudeness of scepticism and the fierce-
ness of intolerance."

In the "Reminiscences" we find also the record of
Julia's parting injunction to her husband: "Be kind

to the little blind children, for they are papa's children."

"These parting words," our mother adds, "are inscribed on the wall of the Kindergarten for the Blind at Jamaica Plain. Beautiful in life, and most beautiful in death, her sainted memory has a glory beyond that of worldly fame."

She considered Julia the most gifted of her children. The "Reminiscences" speak of her at some length, making mention of her beneficent life, and of her published works, a volume of poems entitled "Stray Chords," and "Philosophiæ Quæstor," a slender volume in which she described the Concord School of Philosophy and her pleasure therein.

In our mother's house of life, each child had its special room, though no door was locked to any. In all things pertaining to philosophy, Julia was her special intimate. For help and sympathy in suffrage and club doings, she turned naturally to Florence, an ardent worker in these fields; with Harry she would specially enjoy music; with Laura would talk of books; while Maud was the "Prime Minister" in social and household matters. So, till the very last, we gray-haired children leaned on her, clung to her, as in the days when we were children indeed.

A few years before Julia's death, our mother wrote to Mrs. Cheney, who had lost her only daughter: "This combat of the soul with deadly sorrow is a single-handed one, so far as human help is concerned. I do believe that God's sweet angels are with us when we contend against the extreme of calamity."

Heavy as this affliction was, it brought none of the paralysis of grief caused by Sammy's death: rather, as after the passing of the Chevalier, she was urged by the thought of her dead child to more and higher efforts.

In the quiet of Oak Glen she wrote this summer a careful study of Dante and Beatrice, for the Concord School of Philosophy.[1] July 20 found her at Concord, where she and Julia had been wont to go together. She says, "I cannot think of the sittings of the School without a vision of the rapt expression of her face as she sat and listened to the various speakers." [2]

Spite of her grief in missing this sweet companionship she found the sessions of the School deeply interesting. She was "much more nervous than usual" about her lecture; which "really sounded a good deal better than it had looked to me. It was wonderfully well received."

We are told by the last living representative of the School of Philosophy, Mr. F. B. Sanborn, that she was the most attractive, and sometimes the most profound, of its lecturers; "had the largest audiences, and gave the most pleasure; especially when she joined delicate personal criticism or epigrammatic wit with high philosophy."

The meetings of the School were always a delight to her; the papers written for it were among her most valuable essays; indeed, we may look upon them as

---

[1] This was a summer school of ten years (1879–88) in which Emerson, Alcott, and W. T. Harris took part.

[2] *Reminiscences*, p. 440.

the flowering of all her deep and painful toil in the field of philosophy.[1]

September finds her planning an "industrial circle" in each State; a woman's industrial convention hereafter; and attending a Suffrage Convention at Providence.

"Spoke of the divine right, not of kings or people, but of righteousness. Spoke of Ouida's article in the 'North American Review.' It had been reported that I declined to answer it. I said: 'You cannot mend a stocking which is *all* holes. If you hold it up it will fall to pieces of itself.'

"In the afternoon spoke about the Marthas, male and female, who see only the trouble and inconvenience of reform: of the Marys who rely upon principle."

After this we have "a day of dreadful hurry, preparing to go West and also to shut up this house. Had to work *tight* every minute. . . ."

This Western lecture trip was like many others, yet it had its own peculiar pleasures and mishaps.

"*October 12.* Dunkirk, lecture. . . . No one must know that I got off at the wrong station — Perrysburg, a forlorn hamlet. No train that would bring me to Dunkirk before 6.30 P.M. Ought to have arrived at 1.30. Went to the 'hotel,' persuaded the landlord to lend his buggy and a kindly old fellow to harness his horses to it, and drove twenty miles or more over the mountains, reaching Dunkirk by 5.10 P.M. When the buggy was brought to the door of the hotel, I said:

[1] These essays were published in a volume entitled *Is Polite Society Polite?*

'How am I to get in?' 'Take it slow and learn to
pedal,' said my old driver. Presently he said, 'I guess
you ain't so old as I be.' I replied, 'I am pretty well
on toward seventy.' 'Well, I am five years beyond,'
said he. He drives an accommodation wagon between
Perrysburg and Versailles, a small town where a man
once wanted to set up a mill, and to buy land and
water power, and they would n't sell either. Whereupon he went to Tonawanda and made the place.
'Guess they'd have done better to gin him the land
and water, and to set up his mill for him,' said my
man, Hinds."

On this trip she saw the Mammoth Cave of Ken-
tucky, taking the seven-mile walk; went as far as
Kansas City; was received everywhere with delightful warmth.

To Laura

December 1, 1886.

You see, I was waiting for the winter to begin, in
order to write you, and that you ought to have known.
But bless you, in Gardiner, Maine, you don't know
when real *Winter* begins, 'cause you have so much sham
winter. Well, better late than never. Here's thanking
you very much for the delightful [tea] cozy. Maud
said, "What are you going to do with it?" sarcastic-
like. I replied, "Put it on my head"; to which she
inquit, "Most natural thing for you to do." The sight
of the monogram gave me real satisfaction and a sense
of inborn dignity. You boil down to your monogram,
after all, and this one was beyond my highest expec-

tations. I am only thinking, dear, whether you would not have shown more respect by putting the crimson satin bow on the monogram side, and thus, as it were, calling attention to the distinguished initials. . . . I am grinding now in all of my mills, of which one is a paper for the "Woman Suffrage Bazaar," which paper I am doing my best to edit. I cannot in conscience ask you to send me anything for its columns, because, poor dear, you have to do so much work on your own account. At the same time, a trifling overflow into the hat would be very welcome. . . .

Winter brought another grave anxiety. Florence in her turn developed rheumatic fever and became alarmingly ill. The mother-bird flew to her in terror. On the way she met Henry Ward Beecher and told him of her deep distress, made still more poignant by the thought of the little children who might be left motherless. She was scarcely comforted by his assurance that he "had known stepmothers who were very good to their stepchildren"!

It was Christmas time, and she divided her time between the beloved patient and the children who must not lack their holiday cheer.

"*December 27.* The day was a very distressing one to me. I sat much of the time beside Flossy with a strange feeling that I could keep her alive by some effort of my will. I seemed to contend with God, saying, 'I gave up Julia, I can't give up Flossy — she has children.' . . ."

"*December 28.* Most of the day with dear Flossy,

who seems a little better. I sat up with her until 1.30
A.M., and made a great effort of will to put her to
sleep. I succeeded — she slept well for more than an
hour and slept again for a good while without any
narcotic."

Throughout the illness she fought against the use
of narcotics.

The cloud of danger and anxiety passed, and the
year closed in happiness and deep thankfulness. The
last entry reads: —

"God bless all my dear people, sisters, children,
grandchildren, and cousins. God grant me also to serve
while I live, and not to fail of the high and holy life.
Amen!"

To Laura

Monday, January 31, 1887.

Now, you just look here.

Daughter began her school and music to-day. Nobody's a-neglecting of her. What you mean? Grandma took her to Clarke church, prouder than a peacock, — Grandma, I mean.

Congregation *inquit:* "Whose child is that?"

"Laura's," *responsa sum.*

"*Id cogitavi*" was the general answer. And she's
pop'lar, she is. Little fourteen-year-olds keep a-coming and a-coming. And I draws her bath, and tucks her
up in bed. And she's having a splendid time. And
I want some more of this paper. And my feelings
won't allow me to say any more. No — my dearest
sweetest pug pie, your darling won't be forgotten for a

moment. We could n't get at the lessons before, and
last week, like strong drink, was raging.

'Fectionate

MA.

Maud was now engaged to John Elliott, a young
Scottish painter, whose acquaintance they had made
in Europe in 1878. The marriage took place on February 7, 1887. Though there were many periods of
separation, the Elliotts, when in this country, made
their home for the most part with our mother. The
affection between her and her son-in-law was deep;
his devotion to her constant. Through the years that
were to follow, the comradeship of the three was hardly
less intimate than that of the two had been.

The Journal carries us swiftly onward. In place of
the long meditations on philosophy and metaphysics,
we have brief notes of comings and goings, of speaking
and preaching, writing and reading. She works hard
to finish her paper on "Women in the Three Professions, Law, Medicine, and Theology," for the "Chau-
tauquan." "Very tired afterwards."

She speaks at the Newport Opera House with Mrs.
Livermore (who said she did not know Mrs. Howe
could speak so well); she takes part in the Authors'
Reading for the Longfellow Memorial in the Boston
Museum, reciting "Our Orders" and the "Battle
Hymn," with her lines to Longfellow recently composed.

"I wore my velvet gown, my mother's lace, Uncle
Sam's *Saint Esprit*, and did my best, as did all the
others."

The next day she speaks at a suffrage meeting in Providence, and makes this comment: —

"Woman suffrage represents individual right, integral humanity, ideal justice. I spoke of the attitude and action of Minerva in the 'Eumenides'; [1] her resistance to the Furies, who I said personified popular passion fortified by ancient tradition; her firm stand for a just trial, and her casting the decisive ballot. I hoped that this would prefigure a great life-drama in which this gracious prophecy would be realized."

In a "good talk with Miss Eddy," [2] she devises a correspondence and circular to obtain information concerning art clubs throughout the country. "I am to draft the circular."

She makes an address at the Unitarian Club in Providence.

"The keynote to this was given me yesterday, by the sight of the people who thronged the popular churches, attracted, in a great measure no doubt, by the Easter decoration and music. I thought: 'What a pity that everybody cannot hear Phillips Brooks.' I also thought: 'They can all hear the lesson of heavenly truth in the great Church of All Souls and of All Saints; *there* is room enough and to spare.'"

She writes a poem for the Blind Kindergarten at Jamaica Plain.

"I worked at my poem until the last moment and even changed it from the manuscript as I recited it. The occasion was most interesting. Sam Eliot pre-

[1] Cf. Æschylus.
[2] Miss Sarah J. Eddy, then of Providence, a granddaughter of Francis Jackson.

sided, and made a fine opening address, in which he
spoke beautifully of dear Julia and her service to the
blind; also of her father. I was joined by Drs. Peabody and Bartol, Brooke Herford and Phillips Brooks.
They all spoke delightfully and were delightful to be
with. I recited my poem as well as I could. I think it
was well liked, and I was glad of the work I bestowed
on it."

She preaches at Parker Fraternity [1] on "The Ignorant Classes."

Small wonder that at the Club Tea she finds herself
"not over-bright." Still, she had a "flash or two. The
state of Karma [calmer], orchestral conversation, and
solo speaking."

She hears the Reverend William Rounceville Alger's
paper on the "Blessed Life." "Very spiritual and in
a way edifying; but marred by what I should call
'mixed metaphysic.' One goes beyond his paper to feel
a deep sympathy with him, a man of intense intellectual impulse, in following which he undergoes a sort
of martyrdom; while yet he does not seem to me to hit
the plain, practical truth so much as one might wish.
He is an estray between Western and Eastern thought,
inclining a good deal, though not exclusively, to the
latter."

She goes to conferences of women preachers, to
peace meetings; to jubilee meetings, in honor of Queen
Victoria; she conducts services at the Home for Intemperate Women, and thinks it was a good time.

She "bites into" her paper on Aristophanes, "with

[1] Boston.

a very aching head"; finishes it, delivers it at Concord before the School of Philosophy.

"Before I began, I sent this one word to Davidson,[1] *eleison*. This because it seemed as if he might resent my assuming to speak at all of the great comedian. He seemed, however, to like what I said, and in the discussion which followed, he took part with me, against Sanborn, who accuses Aristophanes of having always lent his wit to the service of the old aristocratic party. Returned to Boston and took train for Weirs, New Hampshire, where arrived more dead than alive."

She is at Newport now, and there are tender notes of pleasure with the Hall grandchildren, of "reading and prayers" with them on Sunday, of picnics and sailing parties.

Still, in dreams, she calls back the lost daughter; still records with anxious care each visionary word and gesture.

"Dreamed this morning of Charles Sumner and dearest Julia. She was talking to me; part of the time reclining on a sort of lounge. I said to some one, 'This is our own dear Julia, feel how warm she is.' . . . I think I said something about our wanting to see her oftener. She said pathetically, 'Can't you talk of me?' I said, 'We do, darling.' 'Not very often,' I think was her reply. Then she seemed to come very near me, and I said to her, 'Darling, do they let you come here as often as you want to?' She said, 'Not quite.' I asked

---

[1] Thomas Davidson, founder of the "New Fellowship" (London and New York) and of the "Breadwinners' College."

why, and she answered almost inaudibly, 'They are afraid of my troubling people.' I stirred and woke; but the dear vision remains with me, almost calling me across the silent sea."

She writes innumerable letters; date and address of each is carefully noted, and now and then an abstract of her words.

"The bane of all representative action is that the spur of personal ambition will carry people further than larger and more generous considerations of good are apt to do. So the mean-hearted and ambitious are always forward in politics; while those who believe in great principles are perhaps too much inclined to let the principles do all the work. . . ."

The following extracts hurry the year to its close: —

"*November 7.* Left for Boston by 10.20 A.M. train, to attend the celebration of Michael's [Anagnos] fiftieth birthday at the Institution, and the opening meeting of the N.E.W.C. . . . Arriving in Boston, I ran about somewhat, fatiguing myself dreadfully. Reached the Institution by 4.30 P.M., when, throwing myself on the bed for necessary rest, the desired rhymes for Anagnos's birthday flashed upon me, 'all of a sudden,' and instead of napping, I called for pen and ink and wrote them. The meeting was very good; I presided. Dwight and Rodocanachi made speeches, the latter presenting the beautiful chain given to Michael by the teachers of the Institution. Michael was much moved and could not but be much gratified. I proposed three cheers at the end."

"I stole half an hour to attend a meeting in memory

of Hannah Stephenson [the friend and house-mate of Theodore Parker] of whom much good was said that I did not know of. I reproached myself for having always been repelled by her ugliness of countenance and tart manner, and having thus failed to come within the sphere of her really noble influence. The occasion recalled a whole vision of the early and painful struggle in Boston; of the martyrdom of feeling endured by friends of the slave — of Parker's heroic house and pulpit. It seemed, as it often does, great to have known these things, little to have done so little in consequence."

"*November 27.* Finished my lecture on 'Woman in the Greek Drama.' It was high time, as my head and eyes are tired with the persistent strain. . . . All the past week has been hard work. No pleasure reading except a very little in the evening."

"*December 1.* . . . Took 2.30 train for Melrose. . . . I read my new lecture — 'Woman as shown by the Greek Dramatists': of whom I quoted from Æschylus, Sophocles, and Aristophanes. A Club Tea followed: a pleasant one. I asked the mothers present whether they educated their daughters in hygiene and housekeeping. The response was not enthusiastic, and people were more disposed to talk of the outer world, careers of women, business or profession, than to speak of the home business. One young girl, however, told us that she was a housekeeping girl; a very pleasant lady, Mrs. Burr, had been trained by her mother, to her own great advantage."

"*December 18.* For the [Parker] Fraternity a text

occurs to me, 'Upon this rock I will build my church.'
Will speak of the simple religious element in human
nature, the loss of which no critical skill or insight
could replace. Will quote some of the acts and expressions of the true religious zeal of other days, and ask
why this means nothing for us of to-day."

Her first act of 1888 was to preach this sermon before
the Parker Fraternity. It was one of those best liked
by herself and others.

The great event of this year was her visit to California. She had never seen the Pacific Coast; the Elliotts were going to Chicago for an indefinite stay; her
sister Annie, whom she had not seen in many years,
begged earnestly for a visit from the "Old Bird."

She decided to make the journey, and arranged a
lecture tour to cover its expenses.

The expedition was throughout one of deepest interest. It began with "a day of frightful hurry and
fatigue. I had been preparing for this departure for
some time past; yet when the time came, it seemed as
if I could hardly get off. Maud worked hard to help
me. She insisted upon arranging matters for me; went
to the bank; got my ticket. We parted cheerfully,
yet I felt the wrench. God knows whether she will
ever be in my house again, as my partner in care and
responsibility. . . ."

After an "A.A.W." conference in Boston, and a
Woman's Council in Washington, she took the road.
Her first stop was at Chicago. Here she was "very
busy and not quite well. Divided the day between
Maud and some necessary business. At 3.15 P.M. the

dreadful wrench took place. Maud was very brave,
but I know that she felt it as I did. . . ."

To Maud

MERCHANTS' HOTEL,
ST. PAUL, MINNESOTA, April 10.

So far, so good, my dear sweet child. I got me off
as well as possible, though we had many complica-
tions and delays as to the ticket. My section was very
comfortable. I had supper in the dining-car, and slept
well, no theatre-troupe nor D. T. being aboard. I
have now got my ticket all straight to 'Frisco, and
won't I frisk oh! when I get there!

The next stop was at Spokane Falls. Here she had
"a bronchial attack; very hoarse and sore in my throat
and chest. Went over my lecture carefully, leaving
out some pages. Felt absolute need of tea-stimulant,
and went downtown, finding some in a grocer's shop.
The good servant Dora made me a hot cup which
refreshed me greatly. Very hoarse at my lecture.
Opera House a good one enough; for a desk, a box
mounted on a barrel, all covered with a colored paper; decent enough. Lecture: 'Polite Society'; well
received." The Spokane of to-day may smile at the
small things of yesterday; yet our mother always
spoke with pleasure of her cordial reception there.

Walla Walla, Walula, Paser. In the last-named
place she "found a tavern with many claimants for
beds. Mrs. Isaacs, who came with me from Walla
Walla for a little change of air, could not have a sep-

arate room, and we were glad to share not only a small room but also a three-quarters bed. I was cramped and slept miserably. She was very quiet and amiable."

At Tacoma again (on the way whither she felt as if her life hung by a thread while crossing the Notch), there was but one room for the two ladies, but they occupied it "very peacefully."

After church at Tacoma "we heard singing in one of the parlors, and went in quest of it. In the great parlor of the hotel where hops take place, we found an assemblage of men and women, mostly young, singing Gospel hymns, with an accompaniment of grand piano. The Bishop of New Zealand stood in the middle of the apartment singing with gusto. Presently he took his place at the instrument, his wife joining him as if she thought his situation dangerous for a 'lone hand.' A little later, some one, who appeared to act as master of ceremonies, asked me to come over and be introduced to the Bishop, to which I consented. His first question was: 'Are you going to New Zealand immediately?' He is a Londoner. 'Ah, come; with all your States, you can show nothing like London.' Being asked for a brief address, he spoke very readily, with a frank, honest face, and in a genial, offhand manner. A good specimen of his sort, not fine-brained, nor over-brained, but believing in religion and glad to devote his life to it. The Bishop has blue eyes and a shaggy head of grizzled hair."

After Tacoma came "hospitable Seattle"; where she lectured and attended a meeting of the Seattle Emerson Club; then to Olympia, by a small Sound steamer.

"A queer old bachelor on board, hearing me say
that I should like to live in Washington Territory, said
he would give me a handsome house and lot if I would
live in Olympia, at which several Olympians present
laughed."

She left Olympia by train, *en route* for Portland.
The conductor, "Brown by name," saw the name on
her valise, and claimed acquaintance, remembering
her when she lived in Boylston Place. Soon after,
passing a lovely little mill-stream, with a few houses
near it, by name Tumwater, she consulted him as to
the value of land there, with the result that she bought
several acres of "good bottom land."

This was one of several small purchases of land made
during her various journeyings. She always hoped
that they would bring about large results: the Tumwater property was specially valued by her, though
she never set foot in the place. The pioneer was strong
in her, as it was in the Doctor; the romance of travel
never failed to thrill her. Speeding hither and thither
by rail, her eye caught beauty and desirableness in a
flash; the settler stirred in her blood, and she longed to
possess and to develop. Tumwater she fondly hoped
was to bring wealth to the two eldest grandchildren,
to whom she bequeathed it.

In Portland she spent several days, lectured three
times, and was most hospitably entertained. On her
one disengaged evening she went down into the hotel
parlor, played for the guests to dance, played accompaniments for them to sing. She spoke to the school
children; "she made slight acquaintance with various

people," most of whom told her the story of their lives. Briefly, she touched life at every point.

Finally, on May 5, she reached San Francisco, and a few hours later the ranch of San Geronimo, where the Mailliards had been living for some years.

"Situation very beautiful," she says; "a cup in the mountains." Here she found her beloved sister Annie, the "little Hitter" of her early letters; here she spent happy days, warm with outer and inner sunshine.

California was a-tiptoe with eagerness to see and hear the author of the "Battle Hymn"; many lectures were planned, in San Francisco and elsewhere. The Journal gives but brief glimpses of this California visit, which she always recalled with delight as one of the best of all her "great good times." In the newspaper clippings, preserved in a scrapbook, we find the adjectives piled mountain high in praise and appreciation. Though not yet seventy, she was already, in the eye of the youthful reporter, "aged"; her silver hair was dwelt on lovingly; people were amazed at her activity. One of the great occasions was the celebration of Decoration Day by the Grand Army of the Republic in the Grand Opera House, at which she was the guest of honor. The house was packed; the stage brilliant with flowers and emblems. Her name was cheered to the echo. She spoke a few words of acknowledgment.

"I join in this celebration with thrilled and uplifted heart. I remember those camp-fires, I remember those dreadful battles. It was a question with us women,

'Will our men prevail? Until they do they will not come home.' How we blessed them when they did; how we blessed them with our prayers when they were in the battlefield. Those were times of sorrow; this is one of joy. Let us thank God, who has given us these victories."

The audience rose *en masse*, and stood while the "Battle Hymn" was sung, author and audience joining in the chorus.

After her second lecture in Santa Barbara, she "sauntered a little, and spent a little money. Bought some imperfect pearls which will look well when set. Wanted a handsome brooch which I saw; thought I had best conquer my desire, and did so."

At Ventura: "Got so tired that I could hardly dress for lecture." The next day she proposed to Mrs. S. at dinner (1 P.M.) to invite some young people for the evening, promising to play for them to dance. "She [Mrs. S.] ordered a buggy and drove about the village. Her son stretched a burlap on the straw matting and waxed it. About thirty came. We had some sweet music, singers with good voices, and among others a pupil of Perabo, who was really interesting and remarkable."

At one of the hospitable cities, a gentleman asked her to drive with him, drove her about for a couple of hours, descanting upon the beauties of the place, and afterwards proclaimed that Mrs. Howe was the most agreeable woman he had ever met. "And I never once opened my lips!" she said.

On June 10 she preached in Oakland: "the one ser-

mon which I have felt like preaching in these parts:
'Thou art Peter, and upon this rock.' The house was
well filled. . . . After service as I leaned over to speak
to those who stopped to greet me, I saw one of our
old church-members, who told me, with eyes full of
tears, that our dear James Freeman Clarke is no
more. This was like an ice-bolt; I could not realize it
at first.

> " 'A very tender history
> Did in your passing fall.'

"Years of sweet converse, of following and depend-
ence, end with this event."

So we come to the last day at the ranch, the parting
with the dear sister; the departure for San Francisco,
laden with roses and good wishes.

On the way eastward she stopped at Salt Lake City,
and went to the Mormon Tabernacle; "an enormous
building with a roof like the back of a turtle; many
tourists present. The Mormons mostly an ill-looking
and ill-smelling crowd. Bishop Whitney, a young man,
preached a cosmopolite sermon, quoting Milton and
Emerson. He spoke of the Christian Church with pat-
ronizing indulgence; insisted upon the doctrine of
immediate and personal revelation, and censured the
Mormons for sometimes considering their families before their church. Communion, bread in silver baskets
and water in silver cups, handed to every one, children partaking with the rest; no solemnity."

"*June 26.* To visit the penitentiary, where thirty
Mormon bishops are imprisoned for polygamy. Spoke

with one, Bishop of Provo, a rather canny-looking
man, whom we found in the prison library, reading.
The librarian (four years' term for forgery) told me it
was the result of liquor and bad company. I said a
few motherly words to him and presently proposed
to speak to the prisoners, to which the jailer gladly
assented. I began by saying, 'I feel to speak to you,
my brothers.' Said that all of us make mistakes and
many of us do wrong at times. Exhorted them to
give, in future, obedience to the laws upon which the
existence of society depends. The convict Montrose
sent to me a little chain and ornaments of his own
making. I promised to send one or two books for the
library. . . ."

So, through "bowery and breezy Nebraska; such a
relief to eyes and nerves!" to Chicago, where Maud
kept and comforted her as long as might be, and sent
her refreshed on her way; finally to Boston, where she
arrived half-starved, and so to Newport.

To Maud

July 8, 1888.

Grumble, grumble — tumble, tumble,
For something to eat,
Fast-y fast-y nasty, nasty,
At last, at last-y,
Ma's dead beat!

"Oh! the dust of it, and the swirl, in which the black
porter and the white babies all seemed mixed up together. A few dried and withered old women, like myself, were thrown in, an occasional smoky gent, and
the gruel 'thick and slab,' was what is called Human

Nature! This is the spleeny vein, and I indulge it to make you laugh, but really, my journey was as comfortable as heat and speed would allow. Imagine my feelings on learning that there was no dining or buffet car! Do not grieve about this, the biscuits and bananas which you put up carried me quite a way. We got a tolerable breakfast at Cleveland, and a bad dinner at Buffalo, but dry your eyes, the strawberry shortcake was uncommonly good. And think how good it is that I have got through with it all and can now rest good and handsome.

The summer entries in the Journal are varied and picturesque. "My cow, of which I was fond, was found dead this morning. . . . My neighbor Almy was very kind. . . . I feel this a good deal, but complaining will not help matters."

"Mr. Bancroft [George], historian, brought Dr. Hedge to call after dinner. Mr. B. kissed me on both cheeks for the first time in his life. We had a very pleasant and rather brilliant talk, as might have been expected where such men meet."

She writes to Maud: —

"Mr. Alger seized upon my left ear metaphorically and emptied into it all the five-syllable words that he knew, and the result was a mingling of active and passive lunacy, for I almost went mad and he had not far to go in that direction."

And again; apropos of ———— : "How the great world does use up a man! It is not merely the growing older, for that is a natural and simple process; but it is

the coating of worldliness which seems to varnish the
life out of a man; dead eyes, dead smile, and (worst
of all) dead breath."

"*September 23.* To church in Newport. A suggestive sermon from Mr. Alger on 'Watching,' *i.e.*, upon
all the agencies that watch us, children, foes, friends,
critics, authorities, spirits, God himself.

"As we drove into town [Newport] I had one of
those momentary glimpses which in things spiritual
are so infinitely precious. The idea became clear and
present to my mind that God, an actual presence,
takes note of our actions and intentions. I thought
how helpful it would be to us to pass our lives in a
sense of this divine supervision. After this inward
experience I was almost startled by the theme of Alger's sermon. I spoke to him of the coincidence, and
he said it must have been a thought wave. The thought
is one to which I have need to cling. I have at this
moment mental troubles, obsessions of imagination,
from which I pray to be delivered. While this idea
of the divine presence was clear to me, I felt myself lifted above these things. May this lifting continue."

"*November 4.* In my prayer this morning I thanked
God that I have come to grieve more over my moral
disappointments than over my intellectual ones.
With my natural talents I had nothing to do: with
my use or abuse of them, everything.

"I have thought, too, lately, of a reason why we
should not neglect our duty to others for our real or
supposed duty to ourselves. It is this: ourselves we

have always with us; our fellows flit from our company, or pass away and we must help them when and while we can."

On December 5 she hears "the bitter news of Abby May's death. Alas! and alas! for the community, for her many friends, and for the Club and the Congress in which she did such great silent service. God rest her in His sweet peace!"

On Christmas Day she went to "Trinity Church, where I enjoyed Phillips Brooks's sermon. Felt much drawn to go to communion with the rest; but thought it might occasion surprise and annoyance. Going into a remote upper gallery I was present at the scene, and felt that I had my communion without partaking of the 'elements.' These lines also suggested themselves as I walked home: —

"The Universal bread,
The sacrificial wine,
The glory of the thorn-crowned head,
Humanity divine."

"The last day of the year dawned upon me, bringing solemn thoughts of the uncertainty of life, and sorrow for such misuse of its great gifts and opportunities as I am well conscious of. This has been a good year to me. It carried me to the Pacific slope, and showed me indeed a land of promise. It gave me an unexpected joy in the harmonious feelings toward me and the members of A.A.W. at the Detroit Congress. It has, alas! taken from me my dear pastor, most precious to me for help and instruction, and other dear and valued friends, notably Sarah Shaw Russell,[1] Abby W.

[1] Mrs. George Russell, widow of the Doctor's friend and college chum.

May and Carrie Tappan.[1] I desire to set my house in order, and be ready for my departure; thankful to live, or willing to cease from my mortal life when God so wills. . . ."

[1] Caroline Tappan was Caroline Sturgis, daughter of Captain William Sturgis, and sister of Ellen (Sturgis) Hooper, — member of the inmost Transcendentalist circle, and friend of Emerson, Ellery Channing, and Margaret Fuller.

CHAPTER VI

SEVENTY YEARS YOUNG

1889–1890; *aet.* 70–71

The seven decades of my years
I figure like those Pleiad spheres
Which, thro' the heaven's soft impulse moved,
Still seek a sister star beloved.

Thro' many sorrows, more delight,
Thro' miracles in sound and sight,
Thro' battles lost and battles won,
These star-spaced years have led me on.

Though long behind me shows the path,
The future still its promise hath,
For tho' the past be fair and fond,
The perfect number lies beyond.

J. W. H.

SHE was dissatisfied with herself in these days.

"*January 1, 1889.* In my prayer this night I asked for weight and earnestness of purpose. I am too frivolous and frisky."

"On waking I said, 'If God does not help me this day, I shall not be able to finish my address' [for a Washington's Birthday celebration at Newport]."

She thinks He did help her, as she found the vein of what she wished to say, and finished it to her "tolerable satisfaction."

"As I entered the hall in the evening, the thought of Cinderella struck me, and I used it by comparing the fashion, of which we make so much account, to Cinderella with her rat horses and pumpkin carriage, so resplendent until her hour came; then the horses would

not carry her, the golden coach would not hold her,
her illusory grandeur was at an end. Our cause of truth
and justice I compared to the Princess in her enchanted
sleep, who lies spellbound until the true champion
comes to rescue her, and the two go forth together,
to return to sleep and diversion, oh, never more."

This is the note throughout the Journal; the record
of work, the prayer for strength. Yet the friskiness was
there; no one but herself would have had less of it.

She had already entered the happy estate of grandmotherhood, and enjoyed it to the full. New songs
must be made for the little new people, new games invented. We see her taking a grandchild's hands in
hers, and improvising thus: —

> " We have two hands,
>   To buckle bands!
> We have ten fingers,
>   To make clotheswringers!
> We have two thumbs,
>   To pick up crumbs!
> We have two heels,
>   To bob for eels!
> We have ten toes,
>   To match our nose!"

If the child be tired or fretful, "Hush!" says the
grandmother. "Be good, and I will play you the 'Canarybird's Funeral.' " Off they go to the piano, and the
"Canarybird's Funeral" is improvised, and must be
played over and over, for this and succeeding grandchildren. For them, too, she composed the musical
drama of "Flibbertigibbet," which she was to play
and recite for so many happy children, and grown folks

too. Flibbertigibbet was a black imp who appeared one day in the market-place, and playing a jig on his fiddle, set all the people dancing whether they would or no. She played the jig, and one did not wonder at the people. Next came Flibbertigibbet's march, which he played on his way to prison; his melancholy, as he sat in durance; the cats on the roof of his prison; finally, entrance of the benevolent fairy, who whisks him off in a balloon to fairyland. All these, voice and piano gave together: nobody who heard "Flibbertigibbet" ever forgot it. She set Mother Goose to music for the grandchildren; singing of Little Boy Blue, and the Man in the Moon. She thought these nursery melodies among her best compositions; from time to time, however, other and graver airs came to her, dreamed over the piano on summer evenings, or in twilight walks among the Newport meadows. Some of these airs were gathered and published in later years.[1]

In May of this year she notes the closing of a life long associated with hers.

"*May 24.* Laura Bridgman died to-day at about 12 M. This event brings with it solemn suggestions, which my overcrowded brain cannot adequately follow. Her training was a beautiful out-blossoming from the romance of my husband's philanthropy. She has taught a great lesson in her time, and unfortunates of her sort are now trained, without question of the result. This was to S. G. H. an undiscovered country in the first instance. I cannot help imagining him as stand-

[1] *Song Album.* Published by G. Schirmer & Co.

ing before the face of the Highest and pointing to his work: happy, thrice happy man, with all his sorrow!"

The close of her seventieth year was a notable milestone on the long road. May found her still carrying full sail; a little more tired after each exertion, a little puzzled at the occasional rebellion of "Sister Body," her hard-worked "A.B.,"; but not yet dreaming of taking in a reef.

The seventieth birthday was a great festival. Maud, inviting Oliver Wendell Holmes to the party, had written, "Mamma will be *seventy years young* on the 27th. Come and play with her!"

The Doctor in his reply said, "It is better to be seventy years young than forty years old!"

Dr. Holmes himself was now eighty years old. It was in these days that she went with Laura to call on him, and found him in his library, a big, bright room, looking out on the Charles River, books lining the walls, a prevailing impression of atlases and dictionaries open on stands. The greeting between the two was pleasant to see, their talk something to remember. "Ah, Mrs. Howe," said the Autocrat, "you at seventy have much to learn about life. At eighty you will find new vistas opening in every direction!"

Ten years later she was reminded of this. "It is true!" she said.

At parting he kissed her, which touched her deeply.

He was in another mood when they met at a reception shortly after this. "Ah! Mrs. Howe," he said, "you see I still hang on as one of the old wrecks!"

"Yes, you are indeed *Rex!*" was the reply.

"Then, Madam," he cried with a flash, "you are *Regina!*"

To return to the birthday! Here are a few of the letters received: —

From George William Curtis

WEST NEW BRIGHTON, STATEN ISLAND, N.Y.,
May 9, 1889.

MY DEAR MRS. ELLIOTT, —

I shall still be too lame to venture so far away from home as your kind invitation tempts me to stray, but no words of my regard and admiration for Mrs. Howe will ever limp and linger. I doubt if among the hosts who will offer their homage upon her accession to the years of a ripe youth there will be many earlier friends than I, and certainly there will be none who have watched her career with more sympathy in her varied and humane activities. Poet, scholar, philanthropist, and advocate of true Democracy, her crown is more than triple, and it is her praise as it may well be her pride to have added fresh lustre to the married name she bears.

I am sincerely sorry that only in this inadequate way can I join my voice to the chorus of friendly rejoicing and congratulation on the happy day, which reminds us only of the perpetual youth of the warm heart and the sound mind.

Very truly yours,
GEORGE WILLIAM CURTIS.

From W. W. Story

My dear Julia, —

(I suppose I may still call you so — we are both so young and inexperienced) I cannot let this anniversary of your birth go by, without stretching out my hands to you across the ocean, and throwing to you all they can hold of good wishes, and affectionate thought, and delightful memories. Though years have gone by since I have seen you, you are still fresh, joyous, and amusing, and charming as ever. Of this I am fully persuaded, and often I look into that anxious mirror of my mind, and see you and wander with you, and jest with you and sing with you, as I used in the olden days; and never will I be so faithless as to believe that you are any older than you were — and I hope earnestly you are no wiser and that a great deal of folly is still left in you — as it is, I am happy to say, in me.

For, after all, what is life worth when its folly is all departed? When we have grown wise and sad as well as old — it is time to say Good-bye. But that time has not come for us yet. So let us still shout *Evviva!*

I do not mention the fact of your age, — I don't know it, — but if I should guess, from what I know I should say twenty-five. I was twenty-eight when I left America — and that is such a few months ago — and I know you were born somewhat about the same time.

You will receive a great many congratulations and

expressions of friendship, but none more sincere than those of

Your old friend — I mean

Your young friend,

W. W. STORY.

ROME, PALAZZO BARBERINI,
May 10, 1889.

From James Russell Lowell

68 BEACON STREET,
13th May, 1889.

DEAR MRS. HOWE, —

I should n't have suspected it, but if you say so, I am bound to believe this improbability, as absurd as Leporello's Catalogue for its numerals. If it be so — I beg pardon — since it is so, I am glad that you are going to take it cheerfully as who should say to Time, "Another turn of the glass, please, my young friend, I'm writing." But alas, I can't be there to take a glass with you. You say, "if there be no obstacle." No less than a couple of thousand miles of water, harder to get over than the years themselves, which indeed get behind more swiftly than they ought. I can at least wish you many happy returns of the day and will drink to your health on the 27th. I sail on the 18th.

Pray accept my thanks and regrets and make them acceptable to your children.

Faithfully yours,

JAMES RUSSELL LOWELL.

The Journal thus notes the occasion.

"My seventieth birthday. A very busy day for all of us. . . . My head was dressed at eleven. All my children were here, with daughter- and sons-in-law. I had many lovely gifts. The house was like a garden of costly flowers. Breakfast was at 12.30; was in very good style. Guests: General Walker, John S. Dwight, E. E. Hale, Mrs. Jack Gardner, Mmes. Bell, Pratt, and Agassiz. Walker made the first speech at the table, H. M. H.[1] being toastmaster. Walker seemed to speak very feelingly, calling me the first citizeness of the country; stood silent a little and sat down. Dwight read a delightful poem; Hale left too soon to do anything. H. introduced J. S. D. thus: 'Sweetness and light, your name is Dwight.' While we sat at table, baskets and bouquets of wonderful flowers kept constantly arriving; the sweet granddaughters brought them in, in a sort of procession lovely to see. It rained in the afternoon, but the house was thronged with visitors, all the same."

A sober entry, written the next day, when she was "very tired, with a delightful fatigue": but on the day itself she was gay, enjoying her "party" to the full, treasuring every flower, wondering why people were so good to her.

The festivities lasted several days, for every one wanted to "play Birthday" with her. The New England Woman's Club gave her a luncheon, which she valued next to the home celebration; the blind children of the Perkins Institution must hear her speak, and in return sing some of her songs, and give her

---

[1] Henry Marion Howe.

flowers, clustering round her with tender, groping fingers that sought to clasp hers. Moreover, the last week of May is Anniversary Week in Boston. Suffragists, women ministers, Unitarians, "uplifters" of every description, held their meetings (traditionally in a pouring rain) and one and all wanted Mrs. Howe.

"I have said to God on every morning of these busy days: 'Give me this day,' and He has given them all: *i.e.*, He has given me power to fulfil the task appointed for each."

When she finally got to Newport, she was "dazed with the quiet after the strain of heart and fatigue."

The ministry was much in her mind this summer.

"I take for my guidance a new motto: 'I will ascend'; not in my ambition, but in my thoughts and aims."

"A dry Sunday, *i.e.*, no church, it being the women's turn to go. I shelled peas for dinner. Began Rambaud's 'History of Russia.' . . . I think of two sermons to write, one, 'A spirit of Power'; one, 'Behold, I show you a more excellent way.' "

Suffrage had its meed too in these summer days.

"Have copied my Call for the Congress. In my coming suffrage talks will invite women to study the history of their sex in the past, and its destiny in the future; inertia and ignorance are the great dangers of society. The old condition of women largely increased instead of diminishing these sources of evil. The women were purposely kept ignorant, in order that they might be enslaved and degraded. Inertia is largely fostered by the paralysis of independent action. . . ."

"I feel just now that we ought to try hard to have all the Far West represented at the Denver Congress."

"Thought a book or article about 'Fooleries' would be entertaining and instructive. The need of this element in human society is shown by the ancient jesters and court fools. . . . In Bible times Samson made sport for the Philistines. People now do their own dancing and their own fooling: some of it very dull. Query: What ancient jests have been preserved? 'The Fools of old and of all time' would not be a bad title."

In October came the Woman's Congress in Denver; she was there, "attending all meetings and sessions."

"Mrs. ———'s paper on 'The Redemptive Power of Art' was very so-so, and did not touch my conception of the theme, viz., art made valuable for the reform of criminals. I spoke of this with warmth."

After the Congress "the visiting ladies enjoyed a drive about the city of Denver. I went early to the High School with A. A. B.[1] Found Mrs. Cheney speaking to the pupils assembled. She did not notice our entrance and spoke of me very warmly. Presently, turning round, she saw us and we all laughed. I spoke to them of my 'drink of youth'; compared the spirits of youth to steam given to carry them on a celestial railroad; compared youth to wine in a beautiful vase; spoke of ancient libations to the gods; our libation to be poured to the true Divine; urged them not to starve their studies in order to feed their amusements. 'Two ways of study, one mean, the other generous.' Told

[1] The Reverend Antoinette Blackwell.

them not to imitate savages, who will barter valuable land for worthless baubles; not so to barter their opportunities for barren pleasures."

She preached at Unity Church Sunday morning.

"At Grace Church [Methodist] in the afternoon. Spoke to the text, 'God hath not left himself without a witness.' This witness is in every human heart; which, with all its intense desires, desires most of all, law, order, religion. . . . I applied my text to the coming out into the new territories; a rough Exodus stimulated by the love of gold; but with the army of fortune-seekers go faithful souls, and instead of passing out of civilization, they extend its bounds. 'Praise waiteth for thee in Zion' — yes, but the Prophet says: 'The solitary places shall be glad for them,' et cetera. I set this down for future use."

The Denver people were most friendly, and she enjoyed the visit greatly. Thence she stepped westward once more, lecturing and preaching as she went, everywhere welcomed with cordial warmth, everywhere carrying her ministry with her.

"A sweet young mother was dreadfully plagued with two babies; I helped her as much as I could."

"A delicate young woman was travelling with her father, a boy of five years, and a semi-friend, semi-help, not much of either. This party sat opposite me in the Pullman, and soon made acquaintance. She is going for her health from Tacoma to California. An odd-looking genius, something like —— in his youth, got in somewhere and attracted my attention by his restless manner. I took him for no good; a gambler, perhaps. He seemed to notice me a good deal. . . . "Made acquaintance with the odd-looking young man. He is a timber-land broker. He had noticed me because I reminded him of his mother. We became friends. He told me his story. He brought another gentleman, a man more of society than himself, and we and Mrs. Campbell played whist. We were quite gay all day. In the evening a sad, elderly man whom I had observed, came over and showed me his wife's photograph as she had looked in health, and then a photograph of her in her last illness; he holding her up in his arms. He said he was travelling to help his sorrow.

"At Reading my two whist gentlemen cried out, '*Tamales!*' and rushed out. They presently returned, bringing some curious Mexican eatables, corn meal with chicken and red peppers rolled in corn leaves. These folk all left at Sacramento at three in the morning."

California was once more her goal. This second visit was brief and hurried.

"Hurry, scurry to dress for the Forefathers' Day celebration. Oakley was my squire. I was taken down to dinner by Professor Moore, President of the occasion. . . . I was suddenly and unexpectedly called for, and all were requested to rise, which was a great honor done me. I spoke of two Congregationalists whom I had known, Antoinette Blackwell, of whose ordination I told; then of Theodore Parker, of whom

I said, 'Nothing that I have heard here is more Christian than what I heard from him.' I told of his first having brought into notice the hymn, 'Nearer, My God, to Thee,' and said that I had sung it with him; said that in advising with all women's clubs, I always urged them to include in their programmes pressing questions of the day. Was much applauded. . . . They then sang the 'Battle Hymn' and we adjourned."

She spent Christmas with Sister Annie, in great contentment; her last word before starting for home is, "Thank God for much good!"

To Maud

BOSTON.

I reached Boston very comfortably on Monday night about eleven o'clock. I was slower than usual [on the journey] in making friends with those around me, but finally thought I would speak to the pleasant-looking woman on my left. She had made acquaintance with the people who had the two sections behind mine. I had observed a gaunt young man going back and forth, with a look on his face which made me say to my friend in Number Nine: "That man must have committed a murder." Who do you think he turned out to be? Lieutenant Ripley, of the Vandalia, U.S.N., the great ship which went to pieces on the Samoan reef. I, of course, determined to hear about it from his own lips, and we had a most interesting talk. He is very slight, but must be all nerve and muscle. All the sailors in the top in which he was clinging for his life fell off and were drowned. He held on till the Trenton came down upon them, when, with the others who were saved in other parts of the rigging, he crept along a hawser and somehow reached the Trenton. Fearing that she would go to pieces, he started with fifteen sailors to swim ashore — he alone was saved — he says he is much practised in swimming. I spoke of this all as a dreadful experience. "Yes," said he, with a twinkle in his eye, "but the storm cleared out the Germans for us." He was thrown ashore insensible, but soon recovered consciousness — had been naked and without food for thirty-six hours. Took a cup of coffee in one hand, and a cup of brandy in the other, and swallowed a little from each alternately, his refection lasting from nine in the evening till one o'clock at night. . . .

To the same

We have not seen the sun in some days. I hope that he has shined upon you. Item, I have almost finished my anxious piece of work for the N.Y. "Evening Post," after which I shall say, "Now, frolic, soul, with thy coat off!"

In January, 1890, she "heard young Cram [1] explain 'Tristram and Iseult,' and young Prescott execute some of the music. It seemed to me like *broken china*, no complete chord; no perfect result; no architectonic."

She never learned to like what was in those days "the new music." Wagner and Brahms were anathema to her, as to many another music-lover of her time,

[1] Ralph Adams Cram, architect and *littérateur*.

notably John Sullivan Dwight, long-time Boston's
chief musical critic. Many a sympathetic talk they
had together; one can see him now, his eyes burning
gentle fire, head nodding, hands waving, as he denounced what seemed to him wanton cacophony. She
avoided the Symphony Concerts at which "the new
music" was exploited; but it was positive pain to
her to miss a symphony of Beethoven or Schubert.

In March of this year the Saturday Morning Club
of Boston gave a performance of the "Antigone" of
Sophocles.

"In afternoon to the second representation of the
'Antigone.' . . . On the whole very pathetic and powerful. Mrs. Tilden full of dramatic fire; Sally Fairchild
ideally beautiful in dress, attitude, and expression.
The whole a high feast of beauty and of poetry. The
male parts wonderfully illusive, especially that of
Tiresias, the seer. . . ."

To Laura

241 BEACON STREET, BOSTON,
April 26, 1890.

I'se very sorry for unhandsome neglect complained
of in your last. What are we going to do about it? I
have now and then made efforts to reclaim the old
Party, but have long considered her incorrigible.
What shall we say, then? "Where sin doth abound,
Grace shall much more abound," or words to that
effect, are recorded of one Paul, of whom I have no
mean opinion. So, there's Scripture for you, do you
see? As I wrote you yes'day or day before, things

have been *hoppy* here since my return. The elder
Agassiz used to mention in his lectures the *Lepidoptera*,
and I think that's the creature (insect, I b'lieve) which
infests Boston. What I have hopped for, and whither
to, I cannot in the least remember. Flossy was here,
as you know, and I hop't for her. I also 'tended two
of the festival Oratorios, which were fine, but to me
very fatiguing. I find that I must take public amusements, when I do take them, in the afternoon, as in
the evening bodily fatigue overmasters even the æsthetic sense, and it is not worth while to pay a large
price for the pleasure of wishing one's self at home. . . .
The benefit at Boston Museum for the Vincent Hospital netted over $1600. It was a brilliant success,
but I caught there the first cold I have had since my
return from the Far West. Maud is very busy with
the flower table, which she has undertaken, *having
nothing to do*. This is for the Vincent Fair, which
will take place on Tuesday, 29th. . . . Have got a few
lovely books from Libbie's sale of the Hart collection
— among other things, a fine French edition of "Les
Misérables," which I am at last glad never to have
read, as I shall enjoy it, *D.V.*, in some of the long
reading days of summer. . . .

Your ownty donty

Ma.

P.S. Before the Libbie sale I wickedly bid $25 upon
a small but very precious missal. It brought $825!!

When she reached Oak Glen in mid-June, she felt a
"constant discouragement"; was lonely, and missed

the cheerful converse of her club and suffrage friends. "My work seems to me to amount to nothing at all." She soon revived, and "determined to fulfil in due order all the tasks undertaken for this summer; so attacked the Kappa poem and wrote at a stretch twenty-two verses, of four lines each, which was pretty much my day's work. Read in Martineau, in J. F. C., a little Greek, and the miserable ' Les Misé-rables.' "

She decided to hold some conversations in the Unitarian parsonage, and wrote out the following topics for them: —

"Useful undertakings in this city as existing and needed."

"How to promote public spirit in American men and women."

"How to attain a just average estimate of our own people."

"How far is it wise to adopt the plan of universal reading for ourselves and our young people?"

"In what respects do the foreign civilizations retard, in what do they promote the progress of our own civilization?"

In August she preached to the women in Sherborn Prison, choosing a "text of cheer and uplifting: 'Thine is the kingdom, and the power, and the glory.' Read part of Isaiah 40th. Said that I had wished to bring them some word of comfort and exhilaration. Pointed out how the Lord's Prayer begins with solemn worship and ascription, aspiring to God's Kingdom, praying for daily bread and for deliverance from temptation and all evil; at the close it rises into this joyous strain, 'Thine is the kingdom,' et cetera. Tried to show how the kingdom is God, the great providential order, before and beyond all earthly government; then the power, that of perfect wisdom and goodness, the power to know and rule all things, to be everywhere and ever present, to regulate the mighty sweep of stars and planets, and, at the same time, to take note of the poorest and smallest of us; the glory first of the visible universe, glory of the day and night, of the seasons, glory of the redeeming power of truth, glory of the inexhaustible patience, of boundless compassion and love."

She enjoyed the visit to the prison and was thankful for it.

A few days later, at a meeting in Newport, she heard a lady demand that the children of genius should be set apart from others for special education and encouragement, receiving a pension even in their early years. She demanded colleges of genius, and a retreat for people of genius. By thus fostering juvenile promise, we should produce giants and demigods.

"I, being called upon, gave the card house a tolerable shaking, and, I think, brought it down, for which several people thanked me."

Vividly as she lived in the present, the past was never far from her.

"Had in the morning at first waking a very vivid mind-picture of my sweet young mother lying dead, with two or three of us little ones standing about her. My brother Henry, two years my senior, laid his little hand upon her forehead and said: 'It is as cold as a

stone,' or some such comparison. I felt strangely, this
morning, the very pain and agony of that moment,
preceding the tragical vision of a life in which that
central point of nurture, a mother's affection and wisdom, has been wanting. The scene in my mind was
only a vivid reminiscence of what actually took place,
which I never forgot, but I had not felt it as I did
to-day in many years."

Perhaps at heart she was always the little child
who used to say to herself at night, "Now I will
stretch out and make myself as long as I can, so that
the robbers will think I am a grown-up person, and
perhaps then they will not touch me!" "Then," she
told us, "I would stretch myself out at full length,
and go to sleep."

She was reading Martineau's "Study of Religion"
this summer with close attention and deep interest.
His writings gave her unfailing delight. His portrait
hung in her room; on her desk lay always a slender
volume of his "Prayers," her favorite passages marked
in pencil. When Louise Chandler Moulton lay dying,
the best comfort she could devise for her was the loan
of this precious little volume.

The "Study of Religion" is not light reading. We
find now and then: "Head threatening. Will not
tackle Martineau to-day"; and again: "My head is
possessed with my study of Martineau. Had a moment's realizing sense this morning of the universe as
created and constantly re-created by the thought of
the will of God. The phrase is common enough: the
thought, vast beyond human conception."

When her head was clear, she studied the great theologian eagerly, copying many passages for more complete assimilation.

September brought "alarums and excursions." "Awoke and sprang at once into the worry saddle." Another Congress was coming, another "A.A.W." paper to be written, beside an opening address for the Mechanics' Fair, and "1500 words for Bok," on some aspect of the American woman.

She went to Boston for the opening of the Mechanics' Fair, and sat beside Phillips Brooks in the great hall. "They will not hear us!" she said. "No," replied Brooks. "This is the place where little children are *seen* and not *heard.*"

"Mayor Hart backed up the Tariff while I praised Free Trade. My text was two words of God: 'Use and Beauty.' My brief address was written carefully though hastily."

There was no neighborly electric road in Rhode Island in those days, and the comings and goings were fatiguing.

"A hard day. . . . The rain was pitiless, and I in my best clothes, and without rubbers. Embraced a chance of driving to the Perry House, where . . . it was cold and dark. I found a disconsolate couple from Schenectady who had come to Newport for a day's pleasuring. Did my best to entertain them, walking about the while to keep warm."

She got home finally, and the day ends with her ordering a warm mash for the horse.

This horse, Ha'pence, a good and faithful beast,

ran a great danger this summer. The coachman, leaving in dudgeon, poisoned the oats with Paris green, a diabolical act which the Journal chronicles with indignation. Fortunately the deed was discovered in time.

She was always thoughtful of animals. During the reign at 241 Beacon Street of the little fox-terrier Patch, it often fell to her lot to take him out to walk, and she felt this a grave responsibility.

One day Patch ran away on Beacon Street, and would not come back when she called him. At this instant Dr. Holmes, passing, paused for a friendly greeting.

"Mrs. Howe," he said, "I trust this fine morning —"

"*Catch the dog!*" cried Mrs. Howe. One author flew one way, one the other; between the two Patch was caught and brought in triumph home.

One dog story recalls another. She was in the North Station one day, about to start for Gardiner, as was also the setter Diana, crated and very unhappy.

"Here, Auntie!" said the baggage-master; "you set here and be company for the dog, and I'll get your check!"

She complied meekly, and was found somewhat later by her escort, "being company" for a much-comforted Diana.

CHAPTER VII

A SUMMER ABROAD

1892–1893; *aet.* 73–74

Methinks my friends grow beauteous in my sight,
As the years make their havoc of sweet things;
Like the intenser glory of the light
When the sad bird of Autumn sits and sings.
Ah! woe is me! ah! Memory,
Be cheerful, thanking God for things that be.

J. W. H.

THE longing to revisit England and enjoy another "whiff" of a London season was gratified in the summer of 1892. Accompanied by the Elliotts and a granddaughter, she sailed for Liverpool on the 4th of June; "a day of almost inconceivable pressure and labor. I could not waste one minute, yet could not do some of the simplest things which I intended to do. Our departure was tolerably decorous and comfortable."

"*June 13. At sea.* Have enjoyed some good reading, and have read one book, 'Bel Ami,' by Guy de Maupassant, which I found so objectionable that I had to skip whole passages of mere sensual description. My loathing of the book and its personages will keep me from encountering again the filth of this author. . . ."

"*June 16. Chester.* Attended service in the Cathedral. I first came to Chester as a bride, forty-nine years ago; then in 1867 with dear Chev, Julia, and Laura; in 1877 with dear Maud; and now with Maud and her husband and my dear grandchild, Alice Richards. These three periods in my woman's life gave me much to think of."

June 18 found the party established in pleasant lodgings in Albion Street, Hyde Park, where they were soon surrounded by friends old and new.

"*June 21.* . . . In the afternoon Lady Aberdeen, Arthur Mills, and Henry Harland visited me. A. M.'s hair is quite white. It was only iron grey when we last met, thirteen years ago."

"*June 22.* Mrs. Brooke Herford wrote to ask me to come out this afternoon to meet Mrs. Humphry Ward. The Albert Hall performance very interesting. Lord Aberdeen sent his carriage for us. My seat was next to that of the Countess, who appeared in a very fine dress of peach-blossom corded silk, with white lace draperies — on my left was Lord Brooke. Lady Aberdeen introduced me to Lord Kenmare and Dr. Barnardo. The singing of the children, a band of rescued waifs, moved me to tears. The military drill of the boys and the Maypole dance of the girls were very finely done. There are more than 4000 of these children in Barnardo Homes."

"*June 23.* To the first view of the Society of English Portrait Painters. Portraits on the whole well worth seeing — Herkomers *very* good, also Mrs. Anna Lea Merritt's and others. A superb portrait of Cardinal Manning, in full red and ermine. In the evening Lady Aberdeen sent her carriage for me and I went with her to a meeting of the Liberal League, at which

she spoke with a pleasant playfulness, dwelling somewhat upon the position that Home Rule, if given to
Ireland, would do away with the ill-feeling of the Irish
in America towards England. To lunch with Lady
Aberdeen. Lief Jones came into the meeting while
Lady Aberdeen was speaking, and with him Lady
Carlisle. She shook hands with me very cordially.
Presently Lief Jones began his address, which was
quite lengthy, presenting the full platform of the Liberal Party. He is a brisk, adroit speaker, and made
points in favor of Woman Suffrage, of Home Rule, of
the disestablishment of the Anglican Church in Wales
and Scotland, of the eight-hour labor law, of the purchase of the waterworks, now owned by eight com-
panies in the city."

"*June 24.* The lunch at Lady Aberdeen's was very
pleasant. Mrs. Eva McLaren [1] talked with me, as
did Miss Ferguson. The American Minister, Robert
Lincoln,[2] was introduced to me and was very friendly."

"*June 25.* Went to Toynbee Hall by Whitechapel
'bus. Had received a note, which I supposed to be
from a lady, offering to show me over the institution.
We were shown into a large room, bare of carpet, but
with some pictures and bric-à-brac. After waiting
half an hour, a young gentleman made his appearance,
a Mr. Ames — the letter had been from him. He
showed me Mr. Charles [not General] Booth's map
of gradations of wealth and poverty in London. The
distinctions are marked by colors and shades of color
— criminal centres designated by black. In the after-

---

[1] Author of *Civil Rights of Women.*   [2] Son of Abraham Lincoln.

noon to Sarasate's concert, all violin and piano-forte, but very fine."

"*June 26.* To hear Stopford Brooke in the morning, an interesting sermon. . . . He called the Agnostics and Nirvanists a type found in many classes, but not a class. . . ."

"*June 27.* To lunch with Mrs. Harland. *Very* pleasant. Edmund Gosse was the guest invited to meet me. He was vivacious, easy, and agreeable. Also the composer Marzials. . . ."

"*June 28.* To Westminster Abbey. To Alice, its interest seemed inexhaustible. It is so, indeed, had one time to be 'strewing violets all the time,' as E. B. B. said. Longfellow's bust has been placed there since my last visit; the likeness is good. I wandered about as long as my feet would carry me, thinking sometimes of Gray's question, 'Can storied urn,' etc. The Harlands came later and brought the composer of 'Twickenham Ferry.' With Alice to dine at Toynbee Hall. A pleasant dinner. A bright young man, Bruce by name, related to Abyssinian Bruce, took Alice in to dinner — sitting afterwards in Ames's room, where we met an alderman, a bricklayer, a trades' unionist; later, we heard a lecture from Commander Gladstone, on the Norman-Breton churches, with fine stereoscopic plates. A violent storm came on, but we managed to ' 'bus it' home, taking a cab only at Marble Arch."

"*June 29.* To dine with the Greek Minister at eight o'clock, and to the *soirée* of the Academy.

"To Chelsea, to call upon Mrs. Oscar Wilde. . . .

He showed me with pride a fine boy of five years. We had some talk of old times, of his visit to America; I reminded him of the *ver*milion balcony at which he laughed." [Wilde had complained that the usual pronunciation of these words was prosaic.]

"*June 30.* . . . Mrs. Oscar Wilde asks us to take tea on Thursday; she has invited Walter Pater. . . . Have writ to James Bryce."

"*July 2.* To see Oscar Wilde's play, 'Lady Windermere's Fan,' at St. James's Theatre. We went by invitation to his box, where were Lady Wilde and Mrs. Oscar. The play was perfectly acted, and is excellent of its kind, the *motif* not new, but the *dénouement* original in treatment. After the play to call on Lady Rothschild, then to Constance Flower,[1] who showed us her superb house full of treasures of art."

"*July 4.* Mrs. [Edmund] Gosse came and took us to Alma-Tadema's beautiful house and garden. He met us very cordially. Mrs. Smalley came. She was Wendell Phillips's adopted daughter. I had a pleasant talk with her and with Mr. and Mrs. Hughes, whom I charged with a friendly message to Thomas himself. After this to Minister Lincoln's Fourth of July reception. Harry White, Daisy Rutherford's husband, was introduced."

Elsewhere she says of this visit to Alma-Tadema: —

"His charming wife, once seen, explains some of the features of his works. She has yellow hair of the richest color; her eyes also have a primrose tint, while her complexion has a pale bloom of its own, most re-

[1] Lady Battersea.

sembling that of a white rose. She gave us tea from lozenge-shaped cups, with saucers to match. In the anteroom below we admired a painting by her own hand, of yellow jonquils and a yellow fan, on a dark background. Her husband seemed pleased when we praised this picture. So these two artists occupy their golden nest peaceably, and do not tear each other's laurels.

"Let me say here that the passion for the golden color still prevails. In dress, in furniture, in porcelain, it is the prevailing favorite. Long banished from the social rainbow, it now avenges itself for years of neglect, and, as every dog must have his day, we will say that the yellow dog is now to have his, and that the dog-star of this coming August will certainly be of his color."

"*July 6*. With Maud to Liberty's, where she beguiled me, alas! into buying a fine black silk mantle for six guineas. To Nutt's in the Strand for my Greek books. He had only the 'Nicomathean Ethics,' a fine edition which I bought for twelve shillings. Then to Poole's in Hallowell Street, where bought two editions of Aristotle's 'Government,' with English notes. At Poole's found a copy of Schiller's 'Robbers,' which I bought for threepence."

"*July 7*. Afternoon tea with Mrs. Oscar, meeting an aunt of Mrs. Wilde's, and Mrs. Burne-Jones. The aunt had been in Japan — she had known Fenollosa and Professor Morse. Then to Mrs. Louise Chandler Moulton, who introduced a number of people, among them William Sharp, a poet."

"*July 8.* I had rashly promised to lunch with the Brooke Herfords at Hampstead, and to take five-o'clock tea with Mrs. Rebecca Moore at Bedford Place. The Herfords were delightful, and Hampstead is a charming suburb. We saw the outside of Mrs. Barbauld's house. Herford said much good of Cookson, a farmer's son whom he had known in England from his beginnings, a dignified, able, excellent man in his esteem. From this a long distance to Mrs. Moore. We reached her in good time, however. Found her alone, in a pleasant little dwelling. Three ladies came to tea, which was served quite in state — Stepniak [1] came also."

"*July 9.* To lunch with Lady Henry Somerset. Some talk with Lady H. about Mrs. Fawcett, *et al.*: also concerning Mrs. Martin's intended candidacy for the presidency of the United States, which, however futile in itself, we deplore as tending to throw ridicule upon the Woman's Cause. She thought that the Conservatives would give women the Parliamentary Suffrage in England on account of the great number of women who have joined the Primrose League."

"*July 10.* To the Temple Church. The organ voluntaries, strangely, I thought, were first Chopin's 'Funeral March,' second the 'Dead March' in 'Saul.' A notable sermon from Dr. Vaughan. The discourse was really concerned with the political situation of the moment: the strong division of feeling throughout the country, and the fears of many lest the doctrine in

[1] Sergius Stepniak, a Russian author, then a political exile living in England.

which they believe should be overthrown. He said that the real Ark of God was the Church Universal, which has been defined as the whole company of believing Christian people throughout the world. Many changes would occur, but the vital principle of religion would prove itself steadfast — a truly noble sermon, worthy of Phillips Brooks."

"*July 12.* To the New Gallery in which were two fine portraits by Herkomer, a superb one of Paderewski by Tadema, and one of Walter Crane by Watts, also of distinguished excellence. Later, called upon the Duchess of Bedford, a handsome woman, sister to Lady Henry Somerset. We talked of her sister's visit to the United States. I was well able to praise her eloquence and her general charm. She has known Lowell well. We talked of the old London, the old Boston, both past their palmiest literary days. She had heard Phillips Brooks at Westminster Abbey; admired him much, but thought him optimistic."

"*July 14.* Was engaged to spend the afternoon at Mrs. Moulton's reception and to dine with Sebastian Schlesinger. . . . Many people introduced to me — Jerome, author of 'Three Men in a Boat'; Molloy, songwriter; Theodore Watts, poetical critic of the 'Athenæum.' . . . At the dinner I met Mrs. O'Connor, who turned out to be a Texan, pretty and very pleasant, an Abolitionist at the age of six. . . ."

"*July 15.* . . . To the Harlands', where met Theodore Watts again, and had some good talk with him about Browning and other friends. Also Walter Besant, whom I greeted very warmly as 'our best friend.'"

"*July 17.* A sermon of surpassing beauty and power from the dear Bishop of Massachusetts [Phillips Brooks]. . . . The power and spirit of the discourse carried me quite away. We waited to speak with him. I had a dear grasp of the hand from him. I shook my finger at him and said, 'Is this resting?' He laughed and said, 'This is the last time. I shall not speak again until I reach Massachusetts.' I wrote some lines on coming home, only half expressing my thought, which was that the mother of so brave a son could not have had one coward drop of blood in her veins — another little scrap, too, about the seven devils that Christianity can cast out. General Walker in the afternoon and the Harlands to dinner."

They left London to join Mrs. Terry at Schwalbach, lingering for a little on the way in Holland and Belgium.

"*July 27. The Hague.* To see Mesdag and his pictures. Found Mesdag a hale man of perhaps fifty years — perhaps less; a fine house, and, besides his own paintings of which we saw a number, a wonderful collection of pictures, mostly modern French, Troyon, Corot, Rousseau, Daubigny. Some good things by a Roman artist, Mancini, whom Mesdag praised highly — he is very poor, but has some excellent qualities. A picture of a little girl reclining on a pillow with a few flowers in her hand, pleased me very much — he also praised it. Much fine tapestry, china, etc., etc. He was gruffly pleasant and hospitable."

"*July 28. Antwerp.* Visited Cathedral and *Musée.*

Saw my picture, Rubens's Elevation of the Cross,
but felt that my eyesight has dimmed since I last saw
it. Found Félu, the armless artist, in the *Musée* copying a picture of Godiva. He was very glad to see us.
Much talk with him about Flemish art. A little ramble
after dinner and a nibble at a bric-à-brac shop, which,
however, did not become a bite."

"*July 31. Cologne.* A great concourse of people
awaited the arrival of a steamer with the Arion Musical Society of New York. Köln choral societies were
represented by fine banners and by members in medi-
æval costumes, very picturesque. The steamer came
alongside with many flags, foremost among them our
own dear 'Stars and Stripes.' We waved handkerchiefs vigorously as these last passed by, and were
saluted by their bearers."

"*August 2.* Left Cologne by Rhine steamer. I remember these boats as crowded, dirty, and very comfortless, but I found this one as well appointed as need
be. Spent the day mostly on deck enjoying the great
beauty and romance of the trip. . . . I chilled myself
pretty badly on deck, but stayed up until perhaps
half-past seven. A very young Westphalian on board
astonished us all by his powers of drinking and of
smoking. He talked with me; said, '*Sie sind deutsch,*'
which I denied."

"*August 3.* Reached Schwalbach at three. My dear
sister [Mrs. Terry] came out to greet us. The meeting was a little tearful, but also cheerful. Much has
passed and passed away in these eventful years. . . .
Presently Louisa and I were as though we had not

been parted at all. She is little changed, and retains
her old grace and charm of manner."

"*August 4.* Out early with my sister. We have a
regular and restful plan of living. Meet after dinner,
coffee with my sister at half-past four, supper at half-
past seven, in the evening reading aloud and conversation. I am miserable with pain, probably rheumatic,
in my left hip. Think I must have got a chill on the
Rhine boat. I say nothing about this. Daisy and
Wintie [Mr. and Mrs. Winthrop Chanler] came this
afternoon."

"*August 7.* To Anglican service with my dear sister.
A dull sermon. The service indifferently read — just
the stereotyped Church of England article. My dreadful hip joint does not ache to-day, and I am ready to
skip about with joy at the relief even if it prove but
temporary. The pain has been pretty severe and I
have said nought about it, fearing treatment."

"*August 9.* Read Aristotle, as I have done all these
days. Took up St. Paul's Epistle to the Romans,
with a more distinct view than heretofore of his attitude relative to them, and theirs to him. Walked out
with my sister, and saw at the bric-à-brac booth near
the Stahlbrunnen a ring composed of a fine garnet,
set with fine diamonds, wonderfully cheap, 136 marks
— I foolishly wanted it."

"*August 16. Heidelberg.* To the Castle — an endless walk and climb. I was here in 1843, a bride, with
dear Chev, my dearest brother Marion, and my cousin, Henry Hall Ward. We went to the Wolfbrunnen
to breakfast — went on ponies to the Castle, where

we wandered at will, and saw the mighty tun. Some French people were wandering there also, and one of them, a lady with a sweet soprano voice, sang a song of which the refrain was: '*Comme une étoile au firmament.*' H. H. Ward long after found this song somewhere. His voice has now been silent for twenty years, dear Marion's for forty-six, and here I come to-day, with my grown-up granddaughter, whom dear Chev only knew as a baby. How long the time seems, and yet how short! Two generations have grown up since then in our family. My sister Louisa, then a young beauty, is here with me, a grandmother with grandchildren nearly grown. 'So teach us to number our days.'"

It seemed to the second and third generations that the two sisters could hardly have been lovelier in that far-off springtime than now in the mellow beauty of their autumn. It was a delight to see them together, a high privilege to sit by and listen to the interchange of precious memories: —

"Do you remember —"

"And do you remember again —"

"*August 24. Sonnenberg.* . . . At breakfast an elderly lady seemed to look at me and to smile. I supposed her to be one of my Club ladies, or some one who had entertained me, so presently I asked her if she were 'one of my acquaintances.' She replied that she was not, but would be pleased to make my acquaintance. We met soon after in one of the corridors; having

incautiously mentioned my name, I asked for hers,
she replied, 'Sforza — Duchess Sforza Cesarini.' She
had been attracted by my Breton caps, and especially
by Daisy's beautiful version of this simple adornment.
She is a reader of Rosmini." [1]

The Duchess confessed afterward that she had requested her maid to observe and copy the cap, and
had been somewhat troubled in mind lest she had been
guilty of a constructive discourtesy.

"*September 3.* Received and answered a letter from
Jenkin Lloyd Jones, informing me of my election to
an Advisory Board to hold a World's Unitarian Congress at Chicago in September, 1893. I have accepted
this."

"*September 4.* My last day at Sonnenberg. . . . Gave
my sister my little old Greek Lexicon, long a cherished
companion. I had thought of reading the family one
of my sermons, but my throat was troublesome and
no one asked me to do anything of the kind. They
wished to hear 'Pickwick,' and a long reading was held
in my room, the fire in the grate helping to cheer us."

"*September 15.* Left Montreux for Paris. Reed
brought me a beautiful yellow rose, half-blown, upon
which I needs must exercise my old trick of versification. Paper I had none — the back of a pasteboard
box held one stanza, the cover of a Tauchnitz the
others."

[1] Rosmini-Serbati, a noted philosopher and founder of the order of
the Brothers of Charity.

"*September 18.* Heard to-day of the noble poet, Whittier's death. What a great heart is gone with him!"

"*September 22. Liverpool.* Embarked at about ten in the morning. Edward Atkinson, wife and daughter on board, a valuable addition to our resources."

"*September 29. At sea.* I said in my mind: 'There is nothing in me which can redeem me from despair over my poor life and wasted opportunities. That redemption which I seek must be in Thee. There is no progress in the mere sense of ill-desert. I must pass on from it to better effort beyond, self-reproach is negative: woe is me that I was born! Amendment must have positive ground.' I wrote some lines in which a bit of sea-weed shining in the sun seemed as an illustration of the light which I hope to gain."

"*September 30.* A performance of Jarley's Waxworks in the evening was much enjoyed. Edward Atkinson as Mrs. Partington in my witch hat recited some merry nonsense of Hood's about European travel."

"*October 2. Boston.* In the early morning John M. Forbes's yacht, the Wild Duck, hovered around us, hoping to take off his daughter, Mrs. Russell. . . . Quite a number of us embraced this opportunity with gratitude. . . ."

"*October 3.* All seems like a dream."

"*October 7. Newport.* I begin my life here with a prayer that the prolongation of my days on earth may be for good to myself and others, that I may not sink into senile folly or grossness, nor yet wander into æsthetic conceit, but carry the weight of my experience in humility, in all charity, and in a loving and serviceable spirit."

The last entry in the Journal for 1892 strikes the keynote of what was to prove the most absorbing interest of the coming year.

"*December 31.* Farewell, dear 1892. You were the real *quattro* centenary of Columbus's discovery, although we have been so behind time as not to be ready to celebrate this before 1893. 1492 was indeed a year momentous to humanity."

To her many cares was added now work for the Columbian Exhibition at Chicago. The Woman's Department of the World's Fair was ably administered by Mrs. Potter Palmer, who consulted her frequently, her experiences in the New Orleans Cotton Centennial proving useful in the Columbian Exhibition. The "Twelve-o'Clock Talks," so successful in the Crescent City, were, at her suggestion, repeated at Chicago, and proved most valuable. The Association for the Advancement of Women and many other associations were to meet in Chicago this year. She writes to the Reverend Jenkin Lloyd Jones concerning the Parliament of Religions and the Unitarian Congress; to Aaron Powell touching the Congress on Social Purity. There are letters, too, about the Alliance of Unitarian Women, the Congress of Representative Women, and the Association of Women Ministers and Preachers.

"*January 7*. [*Boston*.] To speak to the Daughters of the American Revolution at the house of Miss Rebecca W. Brown. I had dreaded the meeting, feeling that I must speak of suffrage in connection with the new womanhood, and anticipating a cold or angry reception. What was my surprise at finding my words, which were not many, warmly welcomed! Truly, the hour is at hand!"

"*January 8*. To speak for Dr. Clisby at Women's Educational and Industrial Union. I had dreaded this, too, fearing not to interest my audience. The occasion was very pleasant to me, and, I think, to them; Mrs. Waters endorsed my estimate of Phillips Brooks as a perfectly disinterested worker. Mrs. Catlin of New York agreed in my praise of Bishop Henry C. Potter on the same grounds; both also spoke well in relation to my most prominent point — emancipation from the slavery of self."

"*January 23*. Oh! and alas! dear Phillips Brooks died suddenly this morning at half-past six. Alas! for Christendom, which he did so much to unite by redeeming his domain in it from superstition, formalism, and uncharity. Oh! to have such a reputation, and *deserve it!*"

"*March 4*. To-day have been allowed to visit the study of the late dear Bishop of Massachusetts. I took this pin from his pincushion, to keep for a souvenir. Made Rosalind write down the names of a number of the books. The library is a very generous one, comprising a large sweep of study and opinion. A charming frieze over the large window had been painted by

Mrs. Whitman. We entered with a reverent feeling, as if in a sacred place. . . . The dining-room, and his seat thereat, with portraits of his parents and grandfather. The mother was of his color, dark of eyes and hair, strong temperament, otherwise no special resemblance. His father looked substantial but not remarkable."

In mid-May she went to Chicago, to take part in the World's Congress of Representative Women, and in many of the other congresses and conferences of that notable year.

"*May 16. Chicago.* Was appointed to preside today over a Report Convention [of the above Congress]; went to Room 6 of the Art Palace and found no one. Mrs. Kennard came presently, and Mrs. Clara B. Colby, who stood by me bravely — when about a dozen had gathered I opened the meeting. Mrs. Colby read reports for two associations, British, I think. A German delegate had a long report written in German, which it would have been useless for her to read. She accordingly reported as she was able, in very funny English, I helping her when she was at a loss for a word. Her evident earnestness made a good impression. I reported for A.A.W., partly in writing, partly *extempore*. In the evening read my paper on the Moral Initiative as regards Women. The hall [of Washington] was frightfully cold."

"*May 17.* Going to the Art Palace this afternoon I found an audience waiting in one of the small halls with no speaker. Madame C. had engaged to speak on musical education. I was requested to fill the breach, which I did, telling of the Boston Conservatory of Music, early music in Boston, and down to our time. Had an ovation afterwards of friendly handshaking."

"*May 19.* Meeting of National Alliance of Unitarian Women."

"*May 27.* My seventy-fourth birthday. Thank God for my continued life, health, and bodily and mental powers. My prayer to Him is that, whether I am to have a year, a month, a week, or a day more, it may be for good to myself and others.

"Went to the Columbian Exhibition. Thomas's Orchestra playing for Mrs. Potter Palmer's reception given to the women of the Press Association. Later I went into the model kitchen where tea was served by the Cingalese. Mrs. Palmer asked me to follow her brief address with a few words. I did this and told of its being my birthday, at which Mrs. Palmer gave me her bouquet of carnations, and the ladies present rose and waved handkerchiefs. Read my sermon for tomorrow twice and feared it might not strike a keynote here."

"*May 28.* Rather nervous about getting to town in time for my service at the Unitarian Church, — we were in good time. My mind was much exercised about my prayer, I having decided to offer the longer one, which I did, I hope, acceptably. I don't think that the sermon *told* as it did in Boston. The church is not easy to speak in. Mr. Fenn said a few words very tenderly about his pleasure in receiving me into his pulpit. The pulpit roses were given me."

"*May 29.* Went to the Exposition, where met Mrs. Charlotte Emerson Brown. Went with her to her space in the Organization Room. She will receive and care for my exhibits. Saw the very fine collection of club manuals, histories, etc." [1]

"*May 30.* Made a little spurt to begin my screed for Aaron Powell's meeting on Sunday. Went with dear Maud and Helen Gardner to the Fair. Side-shows as follows: Cairo Street, Cairo Theatre, Soudanese dancers (very black savages wearing top tufts of black hair or wool, clothed in strips of dirty white cotton cloth), old Vienna, dinner at Vienna restaurant. . . .

"The Cairo dancing was simply horrid, no touch of grace in it, only a most deforming movement of the whole abdominal and lumbar region. We thought it indecent. The savages were much better, though they only stamp their bare feet and clap their hands in rhythm without music. One had a curious smooth lyre, which seemed to give no sound. Their teeth were beautifully white and regular. One of them came up to me and said, 'Mamma,' as if to indicate my age. Then into a bark hut, to see the Soudanese baby dance — a dear little child that danced very funnily to a tumtum."

Early June found her back in Boston and hard at work.

"*June 8.* Finished my screed for the July 'Forum.' Subject, 'A Proper Observance of the Fourth of July.' I have prayed over this piece of work as over all the

[1] Mrs. Charlotte Emerson Brown was at this time president of the General Federation of Women's Clubs, and had prepared this exhibit, the first of its kind in club history.

others which have been strung, one after another, in this busiest of years for me. I have also despaired of it, and am not yet sure of its acceptance."

Next day she felt that she "must see the last of dear Edwin Booth." The Journal describes his funeral at length; "the sun perfectly golden behind the trees." She brought away a bit of evergreen from the grave, and at church, two days later, "had the sexton slide it in among the pulpit flowers; afterward brought it home. Perhaps a silly fancy, but an affectionate one." She wrote a poem in memory of Mr. Booth, "not altogether to my satisfaction." She felt his death as a real loss; he remained always to her a beautiful and heroic figure, connected with a great time.

"*June 15*. 'Thus far the Lord has led me on.' I have had many pieces of work to accomplish, and when almost despairing, seemed to have been uplifted right into my working seat, and so have fulfilled my tasks as well as I was able. Have still my Fourth of July poem to write, and wish to write a poem in memory of Edwin Booth. I'm hungry, oh! how hungry, for rest and reading. Must work very hard for A.A.W. this season. . . ."

She went to Harvard Class Day this summer, her eldest grandson, Samuel Prescott Hall, being of the graduating class; drove out to Cambridge in a pouring rain, and enjoyed the occasion. "I saw my Boy march with his fellows; when they cheered Weld, I waved a napkin."

The summer sped by on wings of study and work;

she was lame, but that gave her the more time for writing. The Journal records many letters; among other things, "a short screed for the man who asks to be convinced that there is such a thing as soul." In September she spread other wings and flew back to Chicago for the Parliament of Religions, and some last Impressions of the Dream City of the World's Fair.

"*September 23.* Went to the Parliament of Religions where Jenkin Lloyd Jones put me on the platform. Heard Dr. Momery, who gave a pleasant, liberal, and spirited address, a little *elementary*, as he closed by reciting 'Abou Ben Adhem,' which is as familiar to Americans as A B C. In the evening went to meet, or rather find, the women ministers. Miss Chapin excused herself from attending and asked me to run the meeting. . . . I read my short screed, briefly narrating my own efforts to found an association of women ministers. Miss Putnam and Mary Graves were appointed as a committee to consult with me as to a plan of organization."

"*September 26.* Up early. . . . Visited the German village, castle and museum, the mining, agricultural, shoe and leather buildings for a brief space. Made a turn in the Ferris Wheel. . . . Mary Graves came for me, and we started for the Parliament in good time. The first speaker was intolerably narrow and out of place, insisting upon the hostility of Christ to all ethnic religions. I could not refrain from taking him up a little, very mildly. I was received with applause and the Chautauqua salute, and my brief speech (fourteen minutes without notes) was much applauded. I was very thankful for this opportunity."

This impromptu speech made a deep impression. In the newspaper reports great stress was laid on it, with singular result. She was amazed next day to hear her name roared out in the Midway Plaisance by a touter who stood at the gateway of one of the sideshows where some Orientals were at prayer.

"Come in, all ye Christian people," the man cried. "Come in and see these devout Mohammedans at their devotions. Julia Ward Howe has knocked the orthodoxy into a cocked hat."

The quiet little figure, passing in the motley throng, paused for a moment and looked with astonishment into the touter's face, which gave no sign of recognition.

"This," said a friend, who happened to come up at the moment, — "this is fame!"

CHAPTER VIII

"DIVERS GOOD CAUSES"

1890–1896; *aet.* 71–77

A DREAM OF THE HEARTHSTONE

A figure by my fireside stayed,
Plain was her garb, and veiled her face;
A presence mystical she made,
Nor changed her attitude, nor place.

Did I neglect my household ways
For pleasure, wrought of pen or book?
She sighed a murmur of dispraise,
At which, methought, the rafters shook.

. . . .

"Now, who art thou that didst not smile
When I my maddest jest devised?
Who art thou, stark and grim the while
That men my time and measure prized?"

Without her pilgrim staff she rose,
Her weeds of darkness cast aside;
More dazzling than Olympian snows
The beauty that those weeds did hide.

Most like a solemn symphony
That lifts the heart from lowly things,
The voice with which she spake to me
Did loose contrition at its springs.

"Oh, Duty! Visitor Divine,
Take all the wealth my house affords,
But make thy holy methods mine;
Speak to me thy surpassing words!

"Neglected once and undiscerned,
I pour my homage at thy feet.
Till I thy sacred law have learned
Nor joy, nor life can be complete."

J. W. H.

IN the closing decade of the nineteenth century a
new growth of "causes" claimed her time and sym-

pathy. The year 1891 saw the birth of the Society
of American Friends of Russian Freedom; modelled
on a similar society which, with "Free Russia" as its
organ, was doing good work in England.

The object of the American society was "to aid by
all moral and legal means the Russian patriots in their
efforts to obtain for their country political freedom
and self-government." Its circular was signed by
Thomas Wentworth Higginson, Julia Ward Howe,
John Greenleaf Whittier, James Russell Lowell, George
Kennan, William Lloyd Garrison, Henry I. Bowditch,
F. W. Bird, Alice Freeman Palmer, Charles G. Ames,
Edward L. Pierce, Frank B. Sanborn, Annie Fields,
E. Benjamin Andrews, Lillie B. Chace Wyman, Sam-
uel L. Clemens, and Joseph H. Twitchell.

James Russell Lowell, writing to Francis J. Garrison
in 1891, says: "Between mote and beam, I think *this*
time Russia has the latter in her eye, though God
knows we have motes enough in ours. So you may take
my name even if it be in vain, as I think it will be."

It was through this society that she made the
acquaintance of Mme. Breschkovskaya,[1] the Russian
patriot whose sufferings and sacrifices have endeared
her to all lovers of freedom. The two women felt
instant sympathy with each other. Mme. Breschkovskaya came to 241 Beacon Street more than once,
and they had much talk together. On one of these
occasions our mother was asked to play some of her
own compositions. Her fingers strayed from one thing

---

[1] Now (1915) a political prisoner in Siberia: she escaped, but was
recaptured and later removed to a more remote place of imprisonment.

to another; finally, on a sudden impulse, she struck the opening chords of the Russian National Hymn. Mme. Breschkovskaya started forward. "Ah, madame!" she cried, "do not play that! You cannot know what that air means to us Russians!"

At a great meeting in Faneuil Hall the two spoke, in English and Russian respectively, while other addresses were in Yiddish and Polish. All were frantically applauded by the polyglot audience which filled the hall to overflowing. William Dudley Foulke presided at this meeting. Speaking with our mother several years later, he reminded her of the occasion, which he thought might have been of a somewhat anarchistic tendency. He was not sure, he said, that they had not made fools of themselves. "One can afford," she replied, "to make a very great fool of one's self in such a cause as that of Russian liberty!"

The year 1891 saw the birth of another society in which she was deeply interested, the Women's Rest Tour Association, whose object was "simply to make it easier for women who need a trip abroad to take one."

It was proved "that the sum of $250 was sufficient to enable a woman of simple tastes to enjoy a summer's vacation in Europe"; a travelling fund was established from which women could borrow, or — in certain cases — receive gifts; a handbook was issued, etc., etc.

In an unobtrusive way, the Women's Rest Tour Association did and continues to do much good. She was its president to the close of her life, and in silent and lovely tribute to her memory the office has since then remained vacant.

In the early nineties all Christendom was aroused by the outrages committed by the Turks in Armenia. From almost every Christian country rose a cry of horror: indignation meetings were called; protest, denunciation, and appeal were the order of the day. In Boston a meeting was held at Faneuil Hall (November 26, 1894), called together by the Boston Armenian Relief Committee. She was on the platform, and spoke from her heart.

"I could not," she says, "stay away from this meeting. My heart was here, and I came, not so much to speak, as to hear what is to be done about this dreadful trouble. For something must be done. I have to pray God night and morning that He would find some way to stay this terrible tide of slaughter. . . .

"I recall the first action of Florence Nightingale when she went to take care of the sick and wounded in the Crimean War. She found many things wanting for the comfort of the soldiers in the hospitals, but she could not get at them. Some seal or mandate was waited for. 'The men are suffering,' Florence Nightingale said. 'Break in the doors — open the boxes—give me the blankets and medicines. I must have them!' — and so she did. Now, the fleets of the Western nations are waiting for some diplomatic development which shall open the way for action. I think that we, the United States of America, are now called upon to play the part of Florence Nightingale; to take our stand and insist upon it that the slaughter shall cease. Oh!

let us give money, let us give life, but let us stand by our principles of civil and religious liberty. I am sure that if we do so, we shall have behind us, and with us, that great spirit which has been in the world for nineteen centuries past, with ever-increasing power. Let us set up in these distant lands the shelter of the blessed Cross, and of all that it stands for, and let us make it availing once and forever."

Soon after this the Friends of Armenia organized as a society, she being its president. Among its members were William Lloyd Garrison, Henry Blackwell and his devoted daughter Alice, and M. H. Gulesian. Singly or in company they went about, through Massachusetts, holding meetings, rousing the people to aid in the protest of Christendom against heathendom, of mercy against cruelty. "Spoke for Armenia," is a frequent entry in the Journal of these days.

In one of these addresses she said: —

"It may be asked, where is the good of our assembling here? what can a handful of us effect against this wicked and remorseless power, so far beyond our reach, so entrenched in the selfishness of European nations who are the creditors of the bankrupt state, and who keep her alive in the hope of recovering the debt which she owes them? The walls of this old hall should answer this question. They saw the dawn of our own larger liberties. They heard the first indignant plea of Wendell Phillips when, in the splendor of his youth, he took the field for the emancipation of a despised race which had no friends. So, on this sacred arena, I throw down the glove which challenges the Turkish

Government to its dread account. What have we for us in this contest? The spirit of civilization, the sense of Christendom, the heart of humanity. All of these plead for justice, all cry out against barbarous warfare of which the victims are helpless men, tender women and children. We invoke here the higher powers of humanity against the rude instincts in which the brute element survives and rules.

"Aid us, paper, aid us, pen,
Aid us, hearts of noble men!

Aid us, shades of champions who have led the world's progress! Aid us, thou who hast made royal the scourge and crown of thorns!"

After hearing these words, Frederick Greenhalge, then Governor of Massachusetts, said to her, "Ah, Mrs. Howe, you have given us a prose Battle Hymn!"

The Friends of Armenia did active and zealous service through a number of years, laboring not only for the saving of life, but for the support and education of the thousands of women and orphans left desolate. Schools and hospitals were established in Armenia, and many children were placed in American homes, where they grew up happily, to citizenship.

Nearly ten years later, a new outbreak of Turkish ferocity roused the "Friends" to new fervor, and once again her voice was lifted up in protest and appeal. She wrote to President Roosevelt, imploring him to send some one from some neighboring American consulate to investigate conditions. He did so, and his action prevented an impending massacre.

In 1909, fresh persecutions brought the organization

once more together. The Armenians of Boston reminded her of the help she had given before, and asked
her to write to President Taft. This she promptly did.
Briefly, this cause with so many others was to be
relinquished only with life itself.

On the fly-leaf of the Journal for 1894 is written:
"I take possession of the New Year in the name of
Faith, Hope, and Charity. J. W. Howe."

"Head bewildered with correspondence, bills, etc.
Must get out of this or die."

"A threatening head, and a week before me full of
functions. I feel weak in mind and dazed with confu-
sions, but will trust in God and keep my powder dry."

"Hearing on Suffrage, Green Room, 10 A.M. My
mind was unusually clear for this speaking. I determined to speak of the two sorts of people, those
who naturally wish to keep the best things for themselves, and those whose appreciation of these things
is such that they cannot refrain from spreading them
abroad, giving freely as they have received. I was able
to follow and apply this tolerably in my ten-minute
speech. . . ."

"Annual meeting of Rest Tour Association; a delightful meeting, full of good suggestions. I made
one concerning pilgrimages in groups. . . . I had a
sudden glimpse to-day of the unfailing goodness of
God. This and not our merits brings the pardon of
our sins."

"To hear Irving in 'Louis XI'; a strong play and a
good part for him. Left after Act Fourth to attend
Mrs. Gardner's musicale, at which Busoni pounded

fearfully. I said, 'He ought to play with his boots on his hands.' He played two curious compositions of Liszt's: St. Francis's Sermon to the Birds and to the Fishes — much roaring as of old ocean in the second."

" *Boston.* Attended Mrs. Mary Hemenway's funeral in the morning. . . . A great loss she is, but her life has been a great gain. Would that more rich men had such daughters! That more rich women had such a heart! . . ."

" C. G. A. preached a funeral sermon on Mrs. Hemenway. As he opened his lips, I said to myself, ' What can he teach us that her life has not taught us? ' The sermon, however, was most instructive. Such a life makes an epoch, and should establish a precedent. If one woman can be so disinterested and so wise, others can emulate her example. I, for one, feel that I shall not forget this forcible presentation of the aspect of such a character, of such a history. God send that her mantle may fall upon this whole community, stimulating each to do what he or she can for humanity."

To Maud

241 BEACON STREET, April 21, 1894.

MY DEAREST DEAR CHILD, —

. . . Let me tell you of the abolition of the old Fast Day and of the new holiday, April 19, ordained in its stead. This, you may remember, is the anniversary of the Battle of Lexington. The celebration here was quite on a grand scale. The bells of the old North Church were rung and the lanterns hung out. A horseman, personating Paul Revere, rode out to rouse the farmers of Concord and Lexington, and a sham fight, imitating the real one, actually came off with an immense concourse of spectators. The Daughters of the American Revolution had made me promise to go to their celebration at the Old South, where I sat upon the platform with Mrs. Sam Eliot, Regent, and with the two orators of the day, Professor Channing and Edward Hale. I wore the changeable silk that Jenny Nelson made, the Gardner cashmere, and the *bonnet* which little you made for me last summer. McAlvin refreshed it a little, and it looked most proud. Sam Eliot, who presided, said to me, " Why, Julia, you look like the queen that I said you were, long ago. If I could do so, I would introduce you as the Queen." I tell you all this in order that you may know that I was all right as to appearance. I was to read a poem, but had not managed to compose one, so I copied out "Our Country" from "Later Lyrics," and read it as I was never able to read it before. For the first time, it *told* upon the audience. This was because it was especially appropriate to the occasion. . . .

" *May 11.* Opposed the dispensing with the reading of State Reports. The maker of the motion said that we could read these at home. I said, 'Yes, and we can read the Bible at home, but we like to go to church and hear it read.' Finished my screed for this evening and licked my Columbus poem into shape, the dear Lord helping me."   .

To Maud

PLAINFIELD, N.J., May 16, 1894.

MY DEAREST MAUD, —

. . . First place, I had a visit from Laura. We threw the ball daily, and had lunches and punches. We went to hear de Koven's "Robin Hood," the music of which is strongly *reminiscent*, and also saw Mounet-Sully's "Hamlet," a very wonderful piece of acting. Flossy and I had three days of conventioning in Philadelphia, last week. Flossy's little speech was one of the best at the convention, and was much applauded. I was received on all hands with affectionate goodwill. . . . There seemed to be, among the Eastern women, a desire to make *me* president [of the General Federation of Women's Clubs]. This I immediately put out of the question and Mrs. Cheney stood by me, saying that Massachusetts would not see me killed with work. It would indeed have been out of the question, as the position is probably one of great labor and responsibility. . . .

YOUR MOTHEREST MOTHER.

The Seventy-fifth Birthday brought the customary festivities. The newspapers sent reporters; she had a word for each. To the representative of the "Advertiser," she said, "I think that I enjoy the coming of old age with its peacefulness, like the going down of the sun. It is very lovely! I am so glad to be remembered by so many. The twilight of life is indeed a pleasant season!"

To Maud

241 BEACON STREET, May 31, 1894.

MY DEAREST CHILD, —

I send you a budget of tributes to my birthday. The "Springfield Republican" has a bit about it, with a good and gratifying poem from Sanborn. *Really*, dear, between you and me what a old humbug it is! But no matter — if people will take me for much better than I am, I can't help it, and must only try to live up to my reputation. . . . I received a good letter from you, "a little scolding at first," but "soft rebukes with blessings ended," as Longfellow describes the admonitions of his first wife. . . . At the Suffrage Festival, Governor Long presided, and in introducing me waved a branch of lilies, saying, "In the beauty of the lilies she is still, at seventy-five." Now that I call handsome, don't you? . . .

Flossy had a very successful afternoon tea while I was with her. She had three ladies of the *Civitas* Club and invited about one hundred of her neighbors to hear them read papers. It was n't suffrage, but it was good government, which is about the same thing. The parlors looked very pretty. I should think seventy or eighty came and 'all were delighted. Did I write you that at Philadelphia she made the most admired speech of the occasion? She wore the brocade, finely made over, with big black velvet top sleeves and rhinestone comb, and they 'plauded and 'plauded, and I sat, grinning like a chessy cat, oh! so welly pleased.

" *July 1.* [*Oak Glen.*] Despite my severe fatigue went in town to church; desired in my mind to have some good abiding thought given me to work for and live by. The best thought that came to me was something like this: we are careful of our fortune and of our reputation. We are not careful enough of our lives. Society is built of these lives in which each should fit his or her place, like a stone fitly joined by the builder. We die, but *the life we have lived remains,* and helps to build society well or ill. Later on I thought that it sometimes seems as if a rope or chain of mercy would be let down to pull some of us out of sin and degradation, out of the Hell of passion. If we have taken hold of it and have been rescued, shall we not work to have others drawn up with us? At such moments, I remember my old wish to speak to the prisoners, never fully realized."

"*August 13.* Finished my poem for the Bryant Centenary, of which I have despaired; my mind has seemed dull of late, and I have had a hard time with this poem, writing what appeared to me bald-doggerel, with no uniting thought. In these last three days, I have hammered upon it, and bettered it, coming in sight of a better vein and to-day, not without prayerful effort, I got it about ready, *D.G.*"

To Maud

OAK GLEN, August 27, 1894.

. . . An interesting French gentleman has been giving readings at Mrs. Coleman's. He read us Corneille's "Cid" last evening with much dash and spirit. It is a famous play, but the sentiment is very stilted, like going up a ladder to shave one's self. I was at Providence on Friday to meet a literary club of ladies. I read to them the greater part of my play, "Hippolytus," written the summer before Sammy was born, for Edwin Booth. It seemed very ghostly to go back to the ambitions of that time, but the audience, a parlor one, expressed great satisfaction. . . . I 'fesses that I did attend the Bryant Centenary Festival at Cummington, Mass. I read a poem written for the occasion. Charles Dudley Warner and Charles Eliot Norton were there, and Parke Godwin presided.

"*August 31.* To Newport with Flossy, taking my screed with me, to the meeting of Colonial Dames, at the rooms of the Historical Society, one of which is the old Seventh-Day Baptist Church, which my great grandfather, Governor Samuel Ward, used to attend. . . . Bishop Clarke made the closing address, full of good sense, sentiment and wit — a wonderful man for eighty-two years of age."

To Laura

Oak Glen, September 6, 1894.

Q. What has been your mother's treatment of you latterly?

Ans. Quite devilish, thank you.

Q. Has her conduct this past season been worse than usual?

Ans. Much as usual. I regret to say, could n't be worse.

(Family Catechism for 1894.)

SNAPSHOT IN THE OAK GLEN PARLOR
Taken by Major Dudley Mills

Oh! I've got a day to myself, and I've got some chillen, and I'm going to write to 'em, you bet.

You see, Laura E., of the plural name of Dick, there warn't no summer, only one of those patent, boiled-down contrivances, all shrivelled up, which if you puts them in water, they swells out, but there warn't no water (Encycl. Brit., Article "Drought"); and so the dried-up thing did n't swell, and there warn't no summer, and that is why you have n't heard from me. ... I'm sorry, anyhow, that I can't allow you the luxury of one moment's grievance against me, but I can't; I may, *now and then*, forget to write ("! ! ! !" says L. E. R.), but I 'dores you all the same. I carry the sweet cheer of your household through all my life. Am drefful glad that you have been to camp this season; wish I could go myself. Only think of Celia Thaxter's death! I can hardly believe it, she always seemed so full of life. . . .

"*September 28.* Here begins for me a new period. I have fulfilled as well as I could the tasks of the summer, and must now have a little rest, a day or so, and then begin in good earnest to prepare for the autumn and winter work, in which A.A.W. comes first, and endless correspondence."

To Maud

241 BEACON STREET, December 19, 1894.

Last Sunday evening I spoke in Trinity Church, having been invited to do so by the rector, Dr. Donald. Wonders will never cease. The meeting was in behalf

of the colored school at Tuskegee, which we A.A.W.'s
visited after our Congress. I dressed myself with unusual care. Dr. Donald gave me the place of honor
and took me in and upon the platform in the chancel
where we all sat. Governor Greenhalge was the first
speaker. I came about fourth, and to my surprise was
distinctly heard all over the house. You may easily
imagine that I enjoyed this very much, although it
was rather an anxious moment when I stepped forward
to speak. . . . We are all much shocked at the death
of dear Robert Louis Stevenson of which you will
have heard before this reaches you. What a loss to
literature!

"*January 1, 1895.* I was awake very early and
made the prayer that during this year I might not say
one uncharitable word, or be guilty of one ungenerous
action."

"*January 6.* . . . My afternoon service at the Women's Educational and Industrial Union. . . . The day
was very stormy and Mrs. Lee met me at the carriage,
offering to excuse me from speaking to the five persons
who were in attendance. I felt not to disappoint those
five, and presently twenty-three were present, and we
had a pleasant talk, after the reading of the short
sermon."

"*January 8.* . . . Felt much discouraged at waking,
the long vista of work opening out before me, each
task calling for some original brain-work, I mean for
some special thought worth presenting to an audience.
While I puzzled, a thought came to me for this day's

suffrage speech: 'The kingdom cometh not with observation.' The silent, gradual, wonderful growth of
public sentiment regarding woman suffrage, the
spreading sense of the great universal harmony which
Christ delivered to us in the words and acts of a few
years, and which, it seems to me, is only now beginning to make itself generally felt and to shape the
world's councils increasingly."

"*January 25.* I awoke this morning overwhelmed
by the thought of my lecture at Salem, which I have
not written. Suddenly a line of my own came to me,
'Had I one of thy words, my Master,' and this brought
me the train of thought, which I shall endeavor to
present. The one word which we all have is 'charity.'
I wrote quite a screed and with that and some speaking shall get through, I hope. . . . Got a good lead of
thought and felt that I could supply *extempore* what
I had not time to write. Harry and Fanny had a
beautiful dinner for Lady Henry Somerset."

"*January 26.* Lunch and lecture in Salem. A dreadful storm; I felt that I must go. The hackman and I
rolled down the steps of the house, he, fortunately for
me, undermost and quite stout of person; otherwise
the shock would have been severe and even dangerous. . . ."

[N.B. The terrified hackman, picking himself up,
found her already on her feet.

"Oh! Mrs. Howe," he cried, "let me help you into
the house!"

"Nonsense!" was the reply. "I have just time to
catch my train!"]

To Maud

241 BEACON STREET, February 24, 1895.

I lost a good lecture engagement at Poughkeepsie through a blizzard. Did not start, finding that roads were badly blocked. My engagement at Brooklyn was a good one — a hundred dollars. I stayed at Chanler house, which was Chanleresque as usual. Peter Marié gave me a fine dinner. Margaret went with me, in white satin. I wore my black and white which you remember well. It still looks well enough. I wore some beautiful lace which I got, through dear sister Annie, from some distressed lace woman in England. I went to New York by a *five*-hour train, Godkin of the "Nation" taking care of me. He remembers your kind attentions to him when you met him in the Pullman with a broken ankle.

"*March 30.* . . . I awoke very early this morning, with a head so confused that I thought my brain had given out, at least from the recent overstrain. . . . Twice I knelt and prayed that God would give me the use of my mind. An hour in sleep did something towards this and a good cup of tea put me quite on my feet. . . ."

"*April 8.* In the late afternoon Harry, my son, came, and after some little preparation told me of the death of my dear sister Annie. I have been toiling and moiling to keep the engagements of this week, but here comes the great silence, and I must keep it for some days at least. . . ."

"*April 10.* .... It suddenly occurred to me that this might be the hour, as this would surely be the day of dear Annie's funeral. So I found the 90th Psalm and the chapter in Corinthians, and sat and read them before her picture, remembering also Tennyson's lines: —

"'And *Ave, Ave, Ave* said
Adieu, adieu, forever more.'"

To Laura

241 BEACON STREET, April 14, 1895.

BUONA PASQUA, DEAR CHILD! —

.... I feel thankful that my darling died in her own home, apparently without suffering, and in the bosom of her beloved family. She has lived out her sweet life, and while the loss to all who loved her is great, we must be willing to commit our dear ones to God, as we commit ourselves. The chill of age, no doubt, prevents my feeling as I should once have done, and the feeling that she has only passed in a little before me, lessens the sense of separation.

12.25. I have been to our Easter service, which I found very comforting and elevating, though it brought some tears, of which I have not shed many, being now past the age at which they flow freely. I thought a good deal of the desolate Easter at the ranch. For them, too, let us hope that the blessed season has brought comforting thoughts. .... I went too to a Good Friday service at the new Old South, at which Dr. Donald of Trinity, Cuckson of Arlington [Unitarian] and Gordon, orthodox [Congregational], each took part. It was such an earnest, a reconciled and

unified Christendom as I am thankful to have lived
to see.

Love and blessings to you and yours, dear child.

Affect.,

MOTHER.

"*May 20*. Have writ a brief letter to Mary G. Hen-
nessey, Dixon, Illinois. She intends to speak of me in
her graduation address and wanted me to send her
'a vivid history of my life,' with my 'ideas of literary
work.' I declined the first, but sent a bit under the
last head."

"*May 27*. . . . Suffrage meeting in the evening. I
presided and began with, 'Sixty years ago to-day I was
sixteen years old. If I only knew now what I thought
I knew then'!"

"*June 2*. . . . To communion in afternoon. The
minister asked whether I would speak. I told what I
had felt as I entered the church that afternoon, 'a sort
of realization of the scene in that upper chamber, its
gloom and its glory. What was in that great heart
whose pulsations have made themselves felt down to
our own time, and all over the world? What are its
sorrows? It bore the burthen of the sorrows and dis-
tresses of humanity, and we who pledge him here in
this cup are bound to bear our part of that burthen.
Only thus shall we attain to share in that festival
of joy and of revealed power which followed the days
of doubt and despair.'

"All this came to me like a flash. I have written it
down from memory because I value the thought."

"*June 15.* Attended the funeral of my old friend and helper, Dr. Williams, the oculist. . . . Six stalwart sons carried the coffin. . . . I thought this: 'I am glad that I have at last found out that the battle of life is an unending fight against the evil tendencies, evil mostly because exceeding right measure, which we find in ourselves. Strange that it should take so long to find this out. This is the victory which God gives us when we have fought well and faithfully. Might I at least share it with the saints whom I have known.' "

"*July 14.* . . . When I lay down to my rest before dinner, I had a momentary sense of the sweetness and relief of the last lying down. This was a new experience to me, as I have been averse to any thought of death as opposed to the activity which I love. I now saw it as the termination of all fight and struggle, and prayed that in the life beyond I might pay some of the debts of affection and recompense which I have failed to make good in this life. Feeling a little like my old self to-day, I realize how far from well I have been for days past."

"*July 27.* Woke with an aching head. . . . Prayed that even in suffering I might still have 'work and worship.' Alliteration is, I know, one of my weaknesses. I thought afterwards of a third W—, work, worship, welcome. These three words will do for a motto of the life which I now lead, in which these words stand for my ruling objects, 'welcome' denoting 'hospitality' in which I should be glad to be more forward than I have been of late. . . ."

"*July 28.* Reading Mr. Hedge's review of Historic
Christianity to-day, I felt puzzled by his showing of
the usefulness of human errors and delusion in the
great order of Providence. Lying down for my midday
rest, it became more clear to me that there is truth of
sentiment and also intellectual truth. In Dr. Hedge's
view, the inevitable mistakes of human intellect in its
early unfolding were helpful to the development of
true sentiment. Higher than this, however, must be
the agreement of the two, prefigured perhaps in such
sentences as 'Mercy and truth have kissed each other.'
This thought also came to me: 'Oh, God, no kingdom is worth praying for but thine.' "

To Laura

OAK GLEN, August 2, 1895.

DEAREST PIDGE, ALSO MIDGE, —

. . . I will condescend to inform you that I am well,
that Flossy is very faithful in taking care of me, and
that we are reading Bulwer's "Pelham," the stupidest
of novels. We are two thirds through with it, and how
the author of "Rienzi" could have offered the public
so dull a dish, even in his unripe youth, passes my
understanding.

You must not get too tired. Remember that no one
will have mercy upon you unless you will have mercy
upon yourself. We sit out a good deal, and enjoy our
books, all but "Pelham," our trees, birds, and butterflies.

Affectionate

MA.

"*September 30.* My dearest Maud left me this morning for another long absence; she is to sail for Europe. She had forbidden me to see her off, but I could not obey her in this and sat with her at breakfast, and had a last kiss and greeting. My last words called after her were: 'Do not forget to say your prayers.' May God keep my dearest child and permit us to meet again, if it is best that I should live until her return, of which at present the prospect seems very good. . . ."

The Association for the Advancement of Women met in New Orleans this year, but first she must go with Florence to the Council of the General Federation of Women's Clubs at Atlanta, Georgia, where a great exposition was also being held. The expedition began with disaster.

"*October 31.* Left Boston by Colonial train at 9 A.M. Rolled down my front steps, striking my forehead and bruising myself generally, in getting to the carriage. . . ."

After taking her part in the Council and visiting the Exposition, she proceeded to New Orleans, where a warm welcome awaited her. A few days after her arrival, she was driving to some function when a trolley car ran into the carriage, shaking her up badly and bruising her lame knee severely. It seemed imperative that she should rest for a few days, and hostess and daughter pleaded with her. Florence begged in particular that she would cancel her engagement to preach in the Unitarian Church; begged a little too

insistently. "I *would n't*, dear mother!" "Flossy,"
was the reply, "you are you, and I am I! I shall
preach on Sunday!"

To Maud

241 BEACON STREET, November 17, 1895.

MY DARLING CHILD, —

. . . I had a confused and weary time moving up
from Newport, and my Southern journey followed
"hard upon." Mrs. Cheney, Eva Channing, Mrs.
Bethune, and I started on October 31. Flossy joined
us in New York. We reached Atlanta on Friday. Our
meetings were held in the Woman's Building of the
Atlanta Exposition, and were very pleasant, the Exposition being also well worth visiting. I spoke in the
Unitarian Church on the Sunday following, and on
November 4 we started for New Orleans which we
reached the next morning. We were all to be entertained, and Mrs. King, our old friend, had written me
a cordial invitation to stay with her. The whole family
turned out to receive us, and we were made at home
at once. . . . Mrs. King had always been most kind and
loyal to me. Our days in New Orleans, only six in
number, were delightful. I saw most of the old friends.
. . . After the accident to Mrs. King and myself, I
felt much like seeking my own hearth. You will have
seen or heard that a trolley car upset our carriage. . . .
All said that it was a wonderful escape. My bruises
are nearly well now, and I am able to go about as
usual. New Orleans has improved much since we
were there. The old mule cars have disappeared, and

much of the mud. People feel very glad that the Lottery has been got rid of, but they are bitter against the sugar trust. Mrs. Walmsley received our A.A.W. ladies very cordially at her fine house and sent me beautiful flowers. . . . I spoke in the Unitarian Church on Sunday, so I had my heart's desire fulfilled. . . .

To Laura

241 BEACON STREET, BOSTON,
December 18, 1895.

'Pon my word and honor, could n't come at it before! . . . Last week I spoke straight along, every day until Saturday; was dreadfully tired. This week have n't spoken at all. Oh, I forgot, lecture on "Race Problems in Europe," before my own Club. Have sent the Armenians the money for a lecture given at Nahant last week, $10. Oh! the difficult dollars! . . .

"*December 28.* . . . Mrs. Barrows dined *tête-à-tête* with me, and we had much talk about Armenia. I said: 'If we two should go to England, would it do any good?' I spoke only half in earnest. She said: 'If you would only go, I would go with you as your henchman.' This set me thinking of a voyage to England and a crusade such as I made for Peace in 1872. I am, however, held forcibly here by engagements, and at my age, my bodily presence might be, as St. Paul says, 'contemptible.' I must try to work in some other way."

To Laura

241 BEACON STREET, December 29, 1895.

. . . The mince pie was in the grand style, and has
been faithfully devoured, a profound sense of duty
forbidding me to neglect it. . . . I went to a fine musical party at Mrs. Montie Sears's on Thursday evening, 26th. Paderewski played, at first with strings a
Septet or Septuor of Brahms', and then many things
by himself. Somehow, I could not enjoy him much; he
played miraculously, but did not seem to be *in it.*

I am more than ever stirred up about the Armenians. The horrible massacres go on, just the same,
and Christendom stands still. Oh! a curse on human
selfishness! . . . We are to have a dramatic entertainment for the Red Cross on Jan. 7th at Boston
Theatre. . . .

"*December 29.* . . . I determined to-day to try to
work more systematically for the Armenians. Think
I will write to Clara Barton and Senator Hoar, also to
Lady Henry Somerset, an arraignment of Christendom
for its supineness towards the Turks, an allusion to
Cœur de Lion and the ancient Crusaders. . . ."

"*December 30.* . . . Clara Barton held a meeting for
the Red Cross. . . . I was the last speaker and I think
that, as sometimes happens, my few words brought
things to a crisis, for the moment only, indeed, but
even that may help."

"*December 31.* Rising early and with a mind somewhat confused and clouded, I went to my window.

As I looked out, the gray clouds parted, giving me a moment's sight of a star high up in the heavens. This little glimpse gave me hope for the day and great comfort. It was like an answering glance to my many troubled questions. . . ."

"We have stood for that which was known to be right in theory, and for that which has proved to be right in practice. (From my suffrage address at State House in 1894)."

In December, 1895, appeared her first volume since "Margaret Fuller," a collection of essays, published under the title of the opening one, "Is Polite Society Polite?" In the preface she says: —

"I remember, that quite late in the fifties, I mentioned to Theodore Parker the desire which I began to feel to give living expression to my thoughts, and to lend to my written words the interpretation of my voice.

"Parker, who had taken a friendly interest in the publication of my first volumes, 'Passion Flowers' and 'Words for the Hour,' gave his approval also to this new project. 'The great desire of the age,' he said, 'is for vocal expression. People are scarcely satisfied with the printed page alone: they crave for their instruction the living voice and the living presence.' . . ."

Of the title essay she says: —

"I remember that I was once invited to read this essay to a village audience in one of the New England States. My theme was probably one quite remote from the general thought of my hearers. As I went on, their indifference began to affect me, and my thought was that I might as well have appealed to a set of wooden tenpins as to those who were present on that occasion.

"In this, I afterwards learned that I was mistaken. After the conclusion of the evening's exercise, a young man, well known in the community, was heard to inquire urgently where he could find the lecturer. Friends asked, what did he want of her? He replied: 'Well, I did put my brother in the poorhouse, and now that I have heard Mrs. Howe, I suppose that I must take him out.' "

Another personal reminiscence goes back to her childhood days: —

"I had a nursery governess when I was a small child. She came from some country town, and probably regarded her position in my father's family as a promotion. One evening, while we little folks gathered about her in our nursery, she wept bitterly. 'What is the matter?' we asked; and she took me up in her lap, and said: 'My poor old father came here to see me to-day, and I would not see him. I bade them tell him that he had mistaken the house, and he went away, and as he went I saw him looking up at the windows so wistfully!' Poor woman! We wept with her, feeling that this was indeed a tragical event, and not knowing what she could do to make it better.

"But could I see that woman now, I would say to her: 'If you were serving the king at his table, and held his wine-cup in your hand, and your father stood without, asking for you, you should set down the cup,

and go out from the royal presence to honor your
father, so much the more if he is poor, so much the
more if he is old.' And all that is really polite in polite
society would say so too."

On the same page is a memory of later years: —

"I once heard a lady, herself quite new in society,
say of a Parisian dame who had shown her some attention: 'Ah! the trouble with Madame ——— is that
she is too good-natured. She entertains everybody.'
'Indeed,' thought I, 'if she had been less good-natured,
is it certain that she would have entertained you?'"

CHAPTER IX

IN THE HOUSE OF LABOR

1896–1897; aet. 77–78

THE HOUSE OF REST

I will build a house of rest,
Square the corners every one:
At each angle on his breast
Shall a cherub take the sun;
Rising, risen, sinking, down,
Weaving day's unequal crown.

. . . .

With a free, unmeasured tread
Shall we pace the cloisters through:
Rest, enfranchised, like the Dead;
Rest till Love be born anew.
Weary Thought shall take his time,
Free of task-work, loosed from rhyme.

. . . .

Measured bread shall build us up
At the hospitable board;
In Contentment's golden cup
Is the guileless liquor poured.
May the beggar pledge the king
In that spirit gathering.

Oh! My house is far away;
Yet it sometimes shuts me in.
Imperfection mars each day
While the perfect works begin.
In the house of labor best
Can I build the house of rest.

J. W. H.

On the fly-leaf of the Journal for 1896 is written: —
"That it may please Thee, to have mercy upon all
men, we beseech Thee to hear us, Good Lord."

"*January 1.* I ask for this year, or for so much of
it as God may grant me, that I may do some service in

the war of civilization against barbarism, in my own country and elsewhere."

"*January 18.* . . . Re-wrote and finished my Easter poem, for which *gratias Deo!* I have had so much small business that I almost despaired of accomplishing this poem, of which the conception is good, but the execution very faulty. I took it all to pieces to-day, kept the thoughts and altered the arrangement."

"*January 23.* Dinner of Sorosis at the Waldorf, at 7 o'clock.

"Reached New York at 3 P.M. Elizabeth [Mrs. John Jay Chapman] had sent maid and carriage for me, which was most kind. Had a good rest and a short walk and went to Sorosis dinner, which was very brilliant and fine. I was asked to speak and took for my topic, 'The Day of Small Things'; the beginning of Sorosis and the New England Woman's Club, considered so trifling a matter, yet very important because it had behind it a very important principle; the fact that the time had come in which women were bound to study, assist, and stand by each other. I quoted Christ's saying about the mustard seed. Miss Barton's mission to Armenia I called a mustard seed, and one which would have very important results."

"*January 27.* . . . Wrote a few lines to Mrs. Charles A. Babcock, Oil City, Pennsylvania, for a woman's issue of a paper called the 'Derrick.' She wishes me to say what I thought would be the result of the 'women's edition' fad. I said that one result would be to drive to desperation those who receive letters, asking contributions to these issues."

"*February 9.* Another inspired sermon from C. G. Ames. Miss Page asked, 'Why is he so earnest? What does it mean?' I replied, 'He is in one of those waves of inspiration which come sometimes. The angel has certainly troubled the pool and we can go to it for healing.' Returning home, I wrote some lines about my sister Annie's picture. I had in church a momentary glimpse of the meaning of Christ's saying, 'I am the vine and ye are the branches.' I felt how the source of our spiritual love is in the heavenly fatherhood, and how departing from our sense of this we become empty and barren. It was a moment of great comfort. . . ."

"*February 10.* . . . Gulesian last evening said that the Armenians want me to go to England, as a leader in advocacy of their cause. The thought brought me a new feeling of energy and enthusiasm. I think I must first help the cause in Washington, D.C."

"*February 26.* Hearing at State House on Suffrage. Worked at it [her address] somewhat in the early morning. Was tolerably successful in making my points. Was rather disappointed because no one applauded me. Considered that this was a lesson that we must learn, to do without praise. It comforted me to take it in this way. Soon the interest of what the others said put my own matters quite out of my mind. The hearing was a good one, all except a dreadful woman, calling herself a Socialist, full of insufferable conceit and affectation of knowledge. An English labor man spoke well."

"*March 22.* . . . As I left church, Mrs. James Free-

man Clarke stopped me, took both of my hands in
hers and said she was sure that the world was better
for my having been in it. This from so undemonstra-
tive a person moved me a good deal and consoled me
somewhat for my poor deserts and performances in the
past — a burden which often weighs heavily upon
me. . . ."

"*April 2.* Conservatory of Music, 3 P. M. I went in
fear and trembling with a violent bronchial cold and
cough, in a miserable storm. I prayed all the way
there that I might be pleasant in my demeanor, and
I think that I was, for my trouble at having to run
such a risk soon went out of my mind, and I enjoyed
the occasion very much; especially meeting pupils from
so many distant States, and one or two from Canada."

"*April 8.* . . . I asked in my prayer this morning,
feeling miserably dull and weak, that some deed of
help and love might be given me to accomplish to-day.
At noon came three gentlemen, Hagop Bogigian, Mr.
Blanchard, and Mr. Breed, of Lynn, praying me to
make an appeal to the women of America for their
Armenian sisters, who are destroying themselves in
many instances to avoid Turkish outrage. The funds
subscribed for relief are exhausted and some new stimulus to rouse the public is much needed. . . . I felt that
I had had an answer to my prayer. . . ."

To Maud

241 BEACON STREET, April 18, 1896.

. . . Let me tell you now, lest you should hear of it in
some other way, that I was urged to go to England

this summer to intercede with Queen Victoria for the Armenians. I thought of it, but the plan seemed to me chimerical and futile. I still have them and the Cretans greatly at heart, but I don't think I could do any good in the way just mentioned. I should have been glad to make a great sacrifice for these persecuted people, but common sense must be adhered to, in all circumstances. . . .

To the same

241 BEACON STREET, April 18, 1896.

. . . If you go to Russia, be careful to go as Mrs. John Elliott, not as Maud Howe Elliott. Your name is probably known there as one of the friends of "Free Russia," and you might be subjected to some annoyance in consequence. You had better make acquaintance with our minister, whoever he may be. The Russians seem now to have joined hands with the Turks. If the American missionaries can only be got rid of, Russia, it is said, will take Armenia under her so-called protection, and will compel all Christians to join the Greek Church. There is so much spying in Russia that you will have to be very careful what you talk about. I rather hope you will not go, for a dynamite country is especially dangerous in times of great public excitement, which the time of the coronation cannot fail to be. . . .

"*April 20.* F. J. Garrison called and made me an offer, on the part of Houghton, Mifflin & Company, that they should publish my 'Reminiscences.' . . . I accepted, but named a year as the shortest time possible for me to get such a book ready. . . ."

As a matter of fact, it took three years for her to complete the "Reminiscences." During these years, while she made it her principal literary work, it still had to take its chance with the rest, to be laid down at the call of the hour and taken up again when the insistence of "screed" or poem was removed: this while in Boston or Newport. During the Roman winter, soon to be described, she wrote steadily day by day; but here she must still work at disadvantage, having no access to journals or papers, depending on memory alone.

"*May 7.* Question: Cannot we follow up the Parliament of Religions by a Pan-Christian Association? I will try to write about this."

"*May 19.* Had sought much for light, or a leading thought about what I ought to do for Armenia. . . . Wrote fully to Senator Hoar, asking his opinion about my going abroad and whether I could have any official support."

"*May 28.* Moral Education Association, 10 A.M., Tremont Temple.

"I wish to record this thought which came to me on my birthday: As for individuals, no bettering of fortunes compares in importance with the bettering of character; so among nations, no extension of territory or aggregation of wealth equals in importance the fact of moral growth. So no national loss is to be deplored in comparison with loss of moral earnestness."

"*Oak Glen, June 30.* . . . Finished this afternoon my perusal of the 'Memoir' of Mr. John Pickering. Felt myself really uplifted by it into an atmosphere of culture and scholarship, rarely attained even by the intelligent people whom we all know. . . ."

"*July 12.* . . . I pray this morning for courage to undertake and fervor to accomplish something in behalf of Christian civilization against the tide of barbarism, which threatens to over-sweep it. This may be a magazine article; something, at any rate, which I shall try to write.

"1 P.M. Have made a pretty good beginning in this task, having writ nine pages of a screed under the heading: 'Shall the frontier of Christendom be maintained and its domain extended?'"

To Maud

OAK GLEN, July 18, 1896.

MY DARLING WANDERER, —

Here I am comfortably settled for the summer, bathed in greenery and good air. I had barely unpacked my books and papers when Daisy came out on horseback to insist upon my paying her a visit. I did this, and went to her on Wednesday, returning home on the following Monday. On the 4th of July I attended, by invitation, the meeting of the Cincinnati in the Old State House here. Cousin Nathanael Greene presided. Charles Howland Russell read aloud the Declaration of Independence. Governor

Lippitt made an address in which he mentioned Governor Samuel Ward, my great-grandfather. . . . I have a good piano this year. We went on Monday last to see the furniture at Malbone, all of which has just been sold at auction. A good deal of it was very costly and some of it very handsome. . . . Apropos of worldly goods, Cornelius Vanderbilt has had a stroke.

To Laura

OAK GLEN, July 25, 1896.

Oh, yes! you now and then do lend me a daughter, and so you'd ought to. Which, did n't I profit by Alice's visit? My good woman (as poor, dear ———— used to say when she was in wrath), I should think so. Clear comfort the wretch was to me, wretch because she had such an old miserable to look after. I sometimes catch myself thinking that, however it may be with other families, your family, madam, came into this world for my especial pleasure and comfort. What do you think of this view? No matter what you think, dear, it won't make any difference as to facts. . . . I miss even the youth in Alice's voice. I would like, mum, if you please, mum, to enjoy about sixty years more of grandmotherhood, with fresh crops of grandchildren coming up at reasonable intervals. Our life here, this summer, is even unusually quiet. We have few visitors. . . . I am, as usual, well content with my books, and busy with my papers. Flossy reads aloud Green's "History of the English People" about half an hour daily, after breakfast. The boys reluctantly submit to listen, fidgeting a good deal. It is less readable for youth than I supposed it to be. We play whist in the evening, and had a wood fire last evening, the weather being suddenly cold. I learned yesterday, from the " 'Tiser," the death of Adolphe Mailliard [her brother-in-law] which has brought me many sober thoughts, despite the trifling tone of this letter. I had waked the day before, thinking that some one said to me " Mailliard is dying." I recorded it in my Diary, but had no idea that I should so soon hear of it as a reality. What a chapter ends with him!

"*August 15.* To-day is mercifully cool. I have about finished my A.A.W. screed, *D.G.* The great heats have affected me very much; my brain has been full of fever fancies and of nonsense. I prayed earnestly this morning that I might not survive my wits. I have great hope that I shall not. . . ."

"*August 17.* Have read in Minot J. Savage's 'Four Great Questions,' and in the long biography of my uncle, Rev. B. C. Cutler. His piety and faithfulness appear to me most edifying. His theology at the present time seems impossible. I am sorry that I saw so very little of him after my marriage, but he was disposed to consider me as one of the lost, and I could not have met him on any religious ground. I could do this better now, having learned something of the value which very erroneous opinions may have, when they serve, as in his case, to stimulate right effort and true feeling."

THE SIX RICHARDS GRANDCHILDREN

From a photograph by R. H. Richards

To Laura

OAK GLEN, August 21, 1896.

Being in a spleeny and uncomfortable mood to-day, what resource so legitimate as to betake myself to my own family? No particular reason for growling, growly so much the more. If I only had a good grievance now, how I would improve it! Well, you see, trouble is some of us have not any money to speak of, and in consequence we ain't nobody, and so on. There I hear the voice of my little mother Laura, saying: "Well, well!" in her soothing way. The truth is, darling, that first I was roasted out, and then it "friz horrid," and my poor old "conshushion" could n't quite stand it. . . . D' ye see? "Well, no," says Laura: "I don't exactly see." Well, s'pose you don't — what then? You sweetheart, this is just the way this old, unthankful sinner was taken, just now. But I've got bravely over it, and I submit to health, comfort, delightful books, young company and good friends. Edifying, ain't it? . . .

"*September 15*. In the cars, reading the Duke of Argyll's fine opuscule, 'Our [England's] Responsibilities for Turkey,' my heart was lifted up in agonized prayer. I said, 'O God! give me a handwriting on the wall, that I may truly know what I can do for these people.' And I resolved not to go back from the purpose which prompted this prayer.

"Arrived at St. John [New Brunswick] and was made very welcome. Reception in the evening by the ladies of the Council. Speeches: Rev. Mr. De Wars, Anglican minister, spoke of our taking A.A.W. to England. I wondered if this was my handwriting on the wall."

"*October 10.* Wheaton Seminary Club, Vendôme. Reminiscences of Longfellow and Emerson. . . . As I was leaving one lady said to me, 'Mrs. Howe, you have shocked me very much, and I think that when you go to the other world, you will be sorry that you did not stay as you were,' *i.e.,* Orthodox instead of Unitarian. Miss Emerson apologized to me for this rather uncivil greeting. I feel sure that the lady misunderstood something in my lecture. What, I could not tell."

"*November 1.* The Communion service was very delightful. I prayed quite earnestly this morning that the dimness of sight, which has lately troubled me, might disappear. My eyes are really better to-day. I seemed at one moment during the service to see myself as a little child in the Heavenly Father's Nursery, having played my naughty pranks (alas!) and left my tasks unperformed, but coming, as bedtime draws near, to kiss and be forgiven."

To Maud

ROKEBY, BARRYTOWN, N.Y., December 25, 1896.

MY OWN DEAREST, —

I am here according to promise to spend Christmas with Daisy.[1] I occupy Elizabeth Chanler's room, beautifully adorned with hangings of poppy-colored silk.

[1] Mrs. Winthrop Chanler.

. . . All of us helped to dress the tree, which was really beautiful. The farm people came in at about six o'clock, also the old tutor, Bostwick, and the Armstrong cousins. After dinner, we had a fiddler in the hall. Alida danced an Irish jig very prettily, and we had a Virginia reel, which I danced, if you please, with Mr. Bostwick. Then we snuggled up to the fire in the library and Wintie read aloud from Mark Twain's "Huckleberry Finn.". . .

The year 1897 brought new activities. The Lodge Immigration Bill roused her to indignation and protest; there were "screeds" and letters to the powers that were.

In the early spring came another crisis in the East, Greece and Crete bearing this time the brunt of Turkish violence. Thirty years had passed since Crete made her first stand for independence; years of dumb suffering and misery. Now her people rose again in revolt against their brutal masters, and this time Greece felt strong enough to stand openly by her Cretan brothers.

Our mother was deeply moved by this new need, which recalled so many precious memories. The record of the spring of 1897 is much concerned with it.

Written on the fly-leaf of the Journal: "The good God make me grateful for this new year, of which I am allowed to see the beginning. Thy kingdom come! I have many wishes, but this prayer will carry them all. January 1, 1897.

"Oh, dear!"

"*January 4.* ... Went in the evening to see the Smith College girls, Class of '95, play 'Midsummer Night's Dream.' A most lovely and ideal performance. Their representation of the Athenian clowns was incredibly good, especially of Nick Bottom."

"*January 5.* ... Was grieved and shocked to learn early this morning that my brilliant neighbor, General Francis A. Walker, had died during the night. He always greeted me with chivalrous courtesy, and has more than once given me his arm to help me homeward, when he has found me battling with the high winds in or near Beacon Street. ..."

To Maud

241 BEACON STREET, BOSTON, January 18, 1897.

About the life "*à deux seulement*," I agree with you in thinking that it is not good for either party. It is certainly very narrowing both to the mind and to the affections, and is therefore to be avoided. A reasonable amount of outside intercourse is a vital condition of good living, even in the most sympathetic and intimate marriages, and the knowledge of this is one of the strong points in the character of women generally, who do nine tenths of what is done to keep up social intercourse. ...

"*April 2.* Evening; celebration of twenty-fifth year of Saturday Morning Club. Have writ draft of an open letter regarding Greek matters; also finished a very short screed for this evening. ..."

"*April 18.* ... I determined to work more for the

Greeks and to try and write something about the craze prevailing just now for the Eastern religions, which are rather systems of speculation than of practical religion."

To Maud

April 18, 1897.

. . . Mrs. Berdan made a visit here, and I gave a reception for her, and took her to the great occasion of the Saturday Morning Club, celebrating their twenty-fifth anniversary. The whole thing was very beautiful — the reception was in the tapestry room of the Art Museum. I was placed in a sort of throne chair, with the president and ex-presidents in a line at my left, and the cream of Boston was all brought up and presented to me. In another of the large rooms a stage had been arranged, and from this I made my little speech. Then came some beautiful singing by Mrs. Tebbets, with a small orchestral accompaniment, and then was given one act of Tennyson's "Princess" and Browning's "In a Balcony." The place, the performances, and the guests made this a very distinguished occasion. I had gone just before this to see Louisa Cushing's wonderful acting in a French play of the Commune. She possesses great tragic power and reminds one of Duse and of Sarah Bernhardt. I suppose that H. M. H. has written you of his appointment as Professor of Metallurgy, etc., at Columbia College, New York. He and Fannie are much pleased with this, and it is considered a very important step for him. I shall miss him a good deal, but am glad of it for his sake. Michael[1] and I went yesterday to the annual breakfast of the Charity Club. Greece had been made the topic of the day. Michael made a splendid speech, and sang three stanzas of the Greek National Hymn, albeit he cannot sing at all — he intoned it. I also made a little speech, and some money was given to aid the Greek cause. Hezekiah Butterworth was present, and I offered the following conundrum: "What's butter worth?" Answer, "The cream of everything." Adieu, my dearest.

Ever your loving

MOTHER.

"*April 26.* Received permission to use Faneuil Hall for a Woman's Meeting of Aid and Sympathy for Greece. . . ."

"*May 3.* Working at sending out notices of the Faneuil Hall meeting."

"*May 4.* The day was auspicious for our meeting. Although very tired with the preparations, I wrote my little screed, dressed, and went betimes to the Hall, where I was expected to preside. I found it prettily arranged, though at very small expense. I wore as a badge a tiny Greek flag made of blue and white ribbon, and brought badges of these colors for the young ladies who were to take up the collection. Many whom I had requested to come were present. Sarah Whitman, Lizzie Agassiz, Mrs. Cornelius Felton, Mrs. Fields, Mrs. Whitney, besides our Committee and Mrs. Barrows. M. Anagnos gave us the band of the In-

[1] Anagnos.

stitution, which was a great help. They played several times. I introduced C. G. Ames, who made a prayer. My opening address followed. Mmes. Livermore and Woolson, and Anagnos made the most important addresses. As the band played 'America,' a young Greek came in, bearing the Greek flag, which had quite a dramatic effect. The meeting was enthusiastic and the contribution unusual for such a meeting, three hundred and ninety-seven dollars and odd cents. Thank God for this success."

"*May 13.* . . . *Head desperately bad in the morning.* . . . Have done no good work to-day, brain being unserviceable. Did, however, begin a short screed for my speech at Unitarian Festival.

"The Round Table was most interesting. Rev. S. J. Barrows read a carefully studied monograph of the Greek struggle for liberty. Mr. Robinson, of the Art Museum, spoke mostly of the present desperate need. I think I was called next. I characterized the Turks as almost '*ferae naturae.*' Spoke of the low level of European diplomacy. Said that we must fall back upon the ethical people, but hope for a general world-movement making necessary the adoption of a higher level of international relation — look to the religious world to uphold the principle that no religion can henceforth be allowed to propagate itself by bloodshed."

"*May 18.* A lecture at Westerly, Rhode Island. . . . My lameness made the ascent of steps and stairs very painful. . . ."

"*May 22.* Heard a delightful French Conference

and reading from M. Louis. Had a fit of timidity about the stairs, which were high and many; finally got down. Had a worse one at home, where could not get up the staircase on my feet, and had to execute some curious gymnastics to get up at all."

"*May 25.* My knee was very painful in the night, and almost intolerable in the morning, so sent for Wesselhoeft, who examined it and found the trouble to proceed from an irritation of a muscle, probably rheumatic in character. He prescribed entire rest and threatened to use a splint if it should not soon be better. I must give up some of my many engagements, and cannot profit by the doings of this week, alas!"

"*May 27.* I am to speak at the Unitarian Festival; dinner at 5 P.M.

"This is my seventy-eighth birthday. If the good God sees fit to grant me another year, may He help me to fill it with good work. I am still very lame, but perhaps a little better for yesterday's *massage*. Gifts of flowers from many friends began early to arrive, and continued till late in the evening. The house was resplendent and fragrant with them. I worried somewhat about the evening's programme and what I should say, but everything went well. Kind Dr. Baker Flynt helped me, cushion and all, into Music Hall, and several gentlemen assisted me to the platform, where I was seated between the Chairman of the Festival Committee and Robert Collyer. . . . I desired much to have the word for the occasion, but I am not sure whether I had."

"*June 2.* My first day of 'solitary confinement.'. . ."

To Laura

241 BEACON STREET, June 2, 1897.

As poor Susan Bigelow once wrote me: —

"The Buffalo lies in his lonely lair,
No friend nor agent visits him there."

She was lame at the time, and I had once called her, by mistake, "Mrs. Buffalo." Well, perfidious William,[1] rivalling in tyranny the Sultan of Turkey, has forbidden me to leave this floor. So here I sit, growly and bad, but obliged to acquiescence in W.'s sentence. . . .

Affect.,

MUZ-WUZ.

To Maud

241 BEACON STREET, June 4, 1897.

DEAREST DEAR CHILD, —

First place, darling, dismiss from your mind the idea that reasonable people to-day believe that the souls of men in the pre-Christian world were condemned and lost. The old religions are generally considered to-day as necessary steps in the religion of the human race, and therefore as part of the plan of a beneficent Providence. The Jews were people of especial religious genius, producing a wonderful religious literature, and Christianity, which came out of Judaism, is, to my belief, the culmination of the religious sense of mankind. But Paul himself says, speaking to the Athenians, that "God hath not left himself without a witness," at any time. I was brought up, of course, in

[1] Dr. Wesselhoeft.

the old belief, which I soon dismissed as irreconcilable with any idea of a beneficent Deity. As for the doctrine of regeneration, I think that by being born again the dear Lord meant that we cannot apprehend spiritual truths unless our minds are earnestly set upon understanding them. To any one who has led a simple, material life, without aspiration or moral reflection, the change by which his attention becomes fastened upon the nobler aspect of character and of life is really like a new birth. We may say the same of the love of high art and great literature. Some people turn very suddenly from a frivolous or immoral life to a better and more thoughtful way. They remember this as a sudden conversion. In most of us, I think the change is more gradual and natural. The better influences win us from the evil things to which most of us are in some way disposed. We have to seek the one and to shun the other. I, for example, am very thankful that my views of many things are unlike what they were twenty or thirty or forty years ago. I attribute this change mostly to good influences, reading, hearing sermons and high conversation. These things often begin in an effort of will to "move up higher." If I write more about this, I shall muddle myself and you. Only don't distress yourself about regeneration. I think it mostly comes insensibly, like a child's growth. . . .

I attended the memorial meeting at the unveiling of the Shaw Monument. You can't think how beautiful the work is. The ceremonies took place Monday, beginning with a procession which came through

Beacon Street. Governor Wolcott, in a barouche and four, distinctly bowed to me. The New York Seventh Regiment came on and marched beautifully; our Cadets marched about as well. There was also a squad from our battleships, two of which were in the harbor. At twelve o'clock we all went to Music Hall where they sang my "Battle Hymn." The Governor and Mayor and Colonel Harry Lee spoke. Willie James gave the oration and Booker Washington really made *the* address of the day, simple, balanced, and very eloquent. I had a visit yesterday from Larz and Isabel [Anderson]. He told me much about you. Darling, this is a very poor letter, but much love goes with it.

Affectionate

MOTHER.

"*June 6.* . . . Have writ a note to little John Jeffries, *aet.* six years, who sent me a note in his own writing, with a dollar saved out of five cents per week, for the 'poor Armenians.' He writes: 'I don't like the Turks one bit. I think they are horrid.' Have sent note and dollar to A. S. B. for the Armenian orphans."

"*June 27, Oak Glen.* My first writing in this dear place. Carrie Hall yesterday moved me down into dear Chev's bedroom on the first floor, Wesselhoeft having forbidden me to go up and down stairs. I rebelled inwardly against this, but am compelled to acknowledge that it is best so. Carrie showed great energy in moving down all the small objects to which she supposed me to be attached. I have now had an exquisite sitting in my green parlor, reading a sermon of dear James Freeman Clarke's."

"*June 28.* Wrote my stint of 'Reminiscences' in the morning. . . . At bedtime had very sober thoughts of the limitation of life. It seemed to me that the end might be near. My lameness and the painful condition of my feet appear like warnings of a decline of physical power, which could only lead one way. My great anxiety is to see Maud before I depart."

"*July 10.* I dreamed last night, or rather this morning, that I was walking as of old, lightly and without pain. I cried in my joy: 'Oh, some one has been mind-curing me. My lameness has disappeared.' Have writ a pretty good screed about John Brown."

"*July 22.* . . . Dearest Maud and Jack arrived in the evening. So welcome! I had not seen Jack in two years. I had begun to fear that I was never to see Maud again."

"*July 26.* Had a little time of quiet thought this morning, in which I seemed to see how the intensity of individual desire would make chaos in the world of men and women if there were not a conquering and reconciling principle of harmony above them all. This to my mind can be no other than the infinite wisdom and infinite love which we call God."

"*August 18.* I prayed this morning for some direct and definite service which I might render. At noon a reporter from the 'New York Journal' arrived, beseeching me to write something to help the young Cuban girl, who is in danger of being sent to the Spanish Penal Colony [Ceuta] in Africa. I wrote an appeal in her behalf and suggested a cable to the Pope.

This I have already written. The Hearsts will send it. This was an answer to my prayer. Our dear H. M. H. arrived at 3 P.M. . . ."

"*August 29.* Had a little service for my own people, Flossy and her four children. Spoke of the importance of religious culture. Read the parable of the wise and foolish virgins. Flossy thought the wise ones unkind not to be willing to share with the foolish. I suggested that the oil pictured something which could not be given in a minute. Cited Beecher's saying, which I have so long remembered, that we cannot get religion as we order a suit of clothes. If we live without it, when some overwhelming distress or temptation meets us, we shall not find either the consolation or the strength which true faith gives."

"*September 23.* Have just learned by cable from Rome that my dearest sister Louisa died yesterday morning. Let me rather hope that she awoke from painful weakness and infirmity into a new glory of spiritual life. Her life here has been most blameless, as well as most beautiful. Transplanted to Rome in her early youth and beauty, she became there a centre of disinterested hospitality, of love and of charity. She was as rare a person in her way as my sweet sister Annie. Alas! I, of less desert than either, am left, the last of my dear father's and mother's children. God grant that my remaining may be for good! And God help me to use faithfully my little remnant of life in setting my house in order, and in giving such completeness as I can to my life-work, or rather, to its poor efforts."

"*September 25.* Was sad as death at waking, pon-

dering my many difficulties. The day is most lovely. I
have read two of Dr. Hedge's sermons and feel much
better. One is called 'The Comforter,' and was probably written in view of the loss of friends by death.
It speaks of the spirit of a true life, which does not
pass away when the life is ended, but becomes more
and more dear and precious to loving survivors. The
text, from John XVI, 7: 'It is expedient for you that
I go away.' Have writ a good screed about the Rome
of 1843–44."

To Laura
OAK GLEN, September 27, 1897.

. . . My dear sister and I have lived so long far apart,
that it is difficult for me to have a *realizing sense* of
her departure. It is only at moments that I can feel
that we shall meet on earth no more. I grieve most
of all that my life has been so far removed from hers.
She has been a joy, a comfort, a delight to so many
people, and I have had so little of all this! The remembrance of what I have had is indeed most precious, but
alas! for the long and wide separation. What an enviable memory she leaves! No shadows to dim its beauty.

I send you, dear, a statement regarding my relations
with Lee and Shepard. I am much disheartened about
my poems and almost feel like giving up. *But I won't.*
Affect.,
MOTHER.

In November, 1897, she sailed for Italy with the
Elliotts.

CHAPTER X

THE LAST ROMAN WINTER

1897–1898; *aet.* 78

THE CITY OF MY LOVE

She sits among th' eternal hills,
Their crown, thrice glorious and dear;
Her voice is as a thousand tongues
Of silver fountains, gurgling clear.

Her breath is prayer, her life is love,
And worship of all lovely things;
Her children have a gracious port,
Her beggars show the blood of kings.

By old Tradition guarded close,
None doubt the grandeur she has seen;
Upon her venerable front
Is written: "I was born a Queen!"

She rules the age by Beauty's power,
As once she ruled by armèd might;
The Southern sun doth treasure her
Deep in his golden heart of light.

Awe strikes the traveller when he sees
The vision of her distant dome,
And a strange spasm wrings his heart
As the guide whispers: "There is Rome!"

.   .   .   .

And, though it seem a childish prayer,
I've breathed it oft, that when I die,
As thy remembrance dear in it,
That heart in thee might buried lie.

J. W. H.

THE closing verse of her early poem, "The City of My Love," expresses the longing that, like Shelley's, her heart "might buried lie" in Rome. Some memory of this wish, some foreboding that the wish might be

granted, possibly darkened the first days of her last
Roman winter. In late November of the year 1897
she arrived in Rome with the Elliotts to pass the
winter at their apartment in the ancient Palazzo
Rusticucci of the old Leonine City across the Tiber;
in the shadow of St. Peter's, next door to the Vatican.
The visit had been planned partly in the hope that she
might once more see her sister Louisa. In this we know
she was disappointed. They reached Rome at the beginning of the rainy season, which fell late that year.
All these causes taken together account for an unfamiliar depression that creeps into the Journal. She
missed, too, the thousand interests of her Boston life;
her church, her club, her meetings, all the happy business of keeping a grandmother's house where three
generations and their friends were made welcome. At
home every hour of time was planned for, every ounce
of power well invested in some " labor worthy of her
metal." In Rome her only work at first was the writing
of her " Reminiscences" for the "Atlantic Monthly."
Happily, the depression was short-lived. Gradually
the ancient spell of the Great Enchantress once more
enthralled her, but it was not until she had founded a
club, helped to found a Woman's Council, begun to
receive invitations to lecture and to preach, that the
accustomed *joie de vivre* pulses through the record.
The sower is at work again, the ground is fertile, the
seed quickening.

"*December 1*. The first day of this winter, which
God help me to live through! Dearest Maud is all

kindness and devotion to me, and so is Jack, but I have Rome *en grippe;* nothing in it pleases me."

"*December 6.* Something, perhaps it is the bright weather, moves me to activity so strongly that I hasten to take up my pen, hoping not to lapse into the mood of passive depression which has possessed me ever since my arrival in Rome."

"*December 7.* We visited the [William J.] Stillmans — S. and I had not met in thirty years, not since '67 in Athens. Went to afternoon tea at Miss Leigh Smith's. She is a cousin of Florence Nightingale, whom she resembles in appearance. Mme. Helbig was there, overflowing as ever with geniality and kindness."

Mr. Stillman was then the Roman correspondent of the London "Times," a position only second in importance to that of the British Ambassador. His tall, lean figure, stooping shoulders, — where a pet squirrel often perched, — his long grey beard and keen eyes were familiar to the Romans of that day. His house was a meeting-place for artists and *litterati.* Mrs. Stillman our mother had formerly known as the beautiful Marie Spartali, the friend of Rossetti and Du Maurier, the idol of literary and artistic London. A warm friendship grew up between them. Together they frequented the antiquaries, gleaning small treasures of ancient lace and peasant jewels.

"I bought this by the Muse Stillman's advice": this explanation guaranteed the wisdom of purchasing the small rose diamond ring set in black enamel.

"*December 9.* Dined with Daisy Chanler. We met there one Brewster and Hendrik Anderson. After dinner came Palmer [son of Courtland] and his sister. He is a pianist of real power and charm — made me think of Paderewski, when I first heard him. . . ."

"*December 10.* Drove past the Trevi Fountain and to the Coliseum, where we walked awhile. Ladies came to hear me talk about Women's Clubs. This talk, which I had rather dreaded to give, passed off pleasantly. . . . Most of the ladies present expressed the desire to have a small and select club of women in Rome. Maud volunteered to make the first effort, with Mme. DesGrange and Jessie Cochrane to help her."

"*December 12.* Bessie Crawford brought her children to see me. Very fine little creatures, the eldest boy [1] handsome, dark like his mother, the others blond and a good deal like Marion in his early life."

"*December 14.* In the afternoon drove with Jack to visit Villegas. Found a splendid house with absolutely no fire — the cold of the studio was tomb-like. A fire was lighted in a stove and cakes were served, with some excellent Amontillado wine, which I think saved my life."

"*December 18.* When I lay down to take my nap before dinner, I had a sudden thought-vision of the glory of God in the face of Jesus Christ. I seemed to see how the human could in a way reflect the glory of the divine, giving not a mechanical, but an affec-

[1] Harold Crawford, who was killed in the present war (1915), fighting for the Allies.

tional and spiritual re-showing of the great unfathom-
able glory. I need not say that I had no sleep — I
wish the glimpse then given me might remain in my
mind."

"*December 21.* Feeling much better in health, I
determined to take up my 'Reminiscences' again.
Mme. Rose passed the evening with me. She told me
that Pio Nono had endorsed the Rosminian philosophy, which had had quite a following in the Church,
Cardinal Hohenlohe having been very prominent in
this. When Leo XIII was elected, the Jesuits came
to him and promised that he should have a Jubilee if
he would take part against the Rosminian ideas, and
put the books on the Index Expurgatorius, the which
he promptly did. Hohenlohe is supposed to have been
the real hero of the poisoning described in Zola's
'Rome' — his servant died after having eaten of something which had been sent from the Vatican."

"*December 25.* Blessed Christmas Day! Maud and
I went to St. Peter's to get, as she said, a whiff of the
mass. We did not profit much by this, but met Edward
Jackson, of Boston, and Monsignor Stanley, whom I
had not seen in many years. We had a pleasant fore-
gathering with him.

"In St. Peter's my mind became impressed with
the immense intellectual force pledged to the upbuild-
ing and upholding of the Church of Rome. As this
thought almost overpowered me, I remembered our
dear Christ visiting the superb temple at Jerusalem
and foretelling its destruction and the indestructi-
bility of his own doctrine."

On fair days she took her walk on the terrace, feasting her eyes on the splendid view. In the distance the Alban and the Sabine Hills, Mount Soracte and the Leonessa; close at hand the Tiber, Rome's towers and domes, St. Peter's with the colonnade, the Piazza, and the sparkling fountains. She delighted in the flowers of the terrace, which she called her "hanging garden"; she had her own little watering-pot, and faithfully tended the white rose which she claimed as her special charge. From the terrace she looked across to the windows of the Pope's private apartment. Opposed as she was to the Pontiff's policy, she still felt a sympathy with the old man, whose splendid prison she often passed on her way to St. Peter's, where in bad weather she always took her walk.

"*December 31.* I am sorry to take leave of this year, which has given me many good things, some blessings in disguise, as my lameness proved, compelling me to pass many quiet days, good for study and for my 'Reminiscences,' which I only began in earnest after Wesselhoeft condemned me to remain on one floor for a month."

"*January 3, 1898.* I feel that my 'Reminiscences' will be disappointing to the world in general, if it ever troubles itself to read them, — I feel quite sure that it has neglected some good writing of mine, in verse and in prose. I cannot help anticipating for this book the same neglect, and this discourages me somewhat.

"In the afternoon drove to Monte Janiculo and saw the wonderful view of Rome, and the equestrian statue of Garibaldi crowning the height. We also drove through the Villa Pamfili Doria, which is very beautiful."

"*January 6.* To visit Countess Catucci at Villino Catucci. She was a Miss Mary Stearns, of Springfield, Massachusetts. Her husband has been an officer of the King's bersaglieri. Before the unification of Italy, he was sent to Perugia to reclaim deserters from among the recruits for the Italian army. Cardinal Pecci was then living near Perugia. Count Catucci called to assure him with great politeness that he would take his word and not search his premises. The Cardinal treated him with equal politeness, but declined to continue the acquaintance after his removal to Rome, when he became Pope in 1878."

"*January 12.* The first meeting of our little circle — at Miss Leigh Smith's, 17 Trinità dei Monti. I presided and introduced Richard Norton, who gave an interesting account of the American School of Archæology at Athens, and of the excavations at Athens. . . . Anderson to dine. He took a paper outline of my profile, wishing to model a bust of me."

The Winthrop Chanlers were passing the winter in Rome; this added much to her pleasure. The depression gradually disappeared, and she found herself once more at home there. She met many people who interested her: Hall Caine, Björnstjerne Björnson, many artists too. Don José Villegas, the great Spanish painter (now Director of the Prado Museum at Madrid), who was living in his famous Moorish villa on the Monte Parioli, made a brilliant, realistic portrait of her, and Hendrik Anderson, the Norwegian-American sculptor, modelled an interesting terra-cotta bust. While the sittings for these portraits were going on, her niece said to her: —

"My aunt, I can expect almost anything of you, but I had hardly expected a *succès de beauté.*"

Among the diplomats who play so prominent a part in Roman society, the Jonkheer John Loudon, Secretary of the Netherlands Legation, was one of her favorite visitors; there are frequent mentions of his singing, which she took pleasure in accompanying.

"*January 15.* We had a pleasant drive to Villa Madama where we bought fresh eggs from a peasant. Cola cut much greenery for us with which Maud had our rooms decorated. Attended Mrs. Heywood's reception, where met some pleasant people — the Scudder party; an English Catholic named Christmas, who visits the poor, and reports the misery among them as very great; a young priest from Boston, Monsignor O'Connell; [1] a Mr. and Mrs. Mulhorn, Irish, — he strong on statistics, she a writer on Celtic antiquities, — has published a paper on the Celtic origin of the 'Divina Commedia,' and has written one on the discovery of America by Irish Danes, five hundred years before Columbus."

Mr. and Mrs. J. C. Heywood lived a few doors from the Rusticucci in the Palazzo Giraud Torlonia, one of the finest Roman palaces. Mr. Heywood held an office in the Papal Court, and had a papal title which

[1] Now Cardinal O'Connell.

he was wise enough not to use in general society. He was an American, a Harvard graduate of the class of 1855. His chief occupation, outside of his duties at the Vatican, was the collection of a fine library. His house was a rendezvous of Black[1] society. He lived in much state and entertained with brilliant formality. Among the great social events of that winter was his reception given for Cardinal Satolli, who arrived dressed in splendid vestments, escorted by his suite. The hostess courtesied to the ground and kissed the ring on his finger. All the other Catholic ladies followed suit. Sitting very straight in her chair, our mother bided her time; finally the Cardinal was brought to her. He was a genial, courteous man and very soon they were deep in friendly talk. Though she disliked the Roman hierarchy as an institution, she counted many friends among the priests of Rome.

"*January 18.* To St. Peter's. The Festival of St. Peter's Chair. Vespers in the usual side chapel. Music on the whole good, some sopranos rather ragged, but parts beautifully sung. Was impressed as usual by the heterogeneous attendance — tourists with campstools and without, ecclesiastics of various grades, students, friars; one splendid working-man in his corduroys stood like a statue, in an attitude of fixed attention. Lowly fathers and mothers carrying small children. One lady, seated high at the base of a column, put her feet on the seat of my stool behind me. Saw the gorgeous ring on the finger of the statue of St. Peter."

"*January 19.* Have composed a letter to Professor

[1] *I.e.*, Clerical.

Lanciani, asking for a talk on the afternoon of February 9, proposing 'Houses and Housekeeping in Ancient Rome,' and 'The Sibyls of Italy.' Mr. Baddeley came in, and we had an interesting talk, mostly about the ancient Cæsars, Mrs. Hollins asking, 'Why did the Romans put up with the bad Cæsars?' He thought the increase of wealth under Augustus was the beginning of a great deterioration of the people and the officials."

"*January 21.* Went in the afternoon to call upon Baroness Giacchetti. Had a pleasant talk with her husband, an enlightened man. He recognizes the present status of Rome as greatly superior to the ancient order of things — but laments the ignorance and superstition of the common people in general, and the peasantry in particular. A sick woman, restored to health by much trouble taken at his instance, instead of thanking him for his benefactions, told him that she intended to make a pilgrimage to the shrine of a certain Madonna, feeling sure that it was to her that she owed her cure."

"*January 26.* The day of my reading before the Club, at Jessie Cochrane's rooms. I read my lecture over very carefully in the forenoon and got into the spirit of it. The gathering was a large one, very attentive, and mostly very appreciative. The paper was 'Woman in the Greek Drama.' "

"*January 31.* Have made a special prayer that my mind may be less occupied with my own shortcomings, and more with all that keeps our best hope alive. Felt little able to write, but produced a good page on the principle '*nulla dies sine linea.*' "

"*February 4.* Hard sledding for words to-day — made out something about Theodore Parker."

"*February 7.* Wrote some pages of introduction for the Symposium — played a rubber of whist with L. Terry; then to afternoon tea with Mrs. Thorndike, where I met the first Monsignor [Dennis] O'Connell, with whom I had a long talk on the woman question, in which he seems much interested. He tells me of a friend, Zahm by name, now gone to a place in Indiana, who has biographies of the historical women of Bologna."

"*February 9.* Club at Mrs. Broadwood's. I read my 'Plea for Humor,' which seemed to please the audience very much, especially Princess Talleyrand and Princess Poggia-Suasa."

"*February 11.* Read over my paper on 'Optimism and Pessimism' and have got into the spirit of it. Maud's friends came at 3 P.M., among them Christian Ross, the painter, with Björnstjerne Björnson."

"*February 16.* To Mrs. Hurlburt's reception. — Talked with Countess Blank, an American married to a Pole. She had much to say of the piety of her Arab servant, who, she says, swallows fire, cuts himself with sharp things, etc., as acts of devotion !! Met Mr. Trench, son of the late Archbishop, Rev. Chevenix Trench. He has been Tennyson's publisher. Did not like T. personally — said he was often rude — read his own poems aloud constantly and very badly; said, 'No man is a hero to his publisher.' Told about his sale of Henry George's book, a cheap edition, one hundred and fifty thousand copies sold in England."

"*February 18.* Have done a good morning's work
and read in the 'Nineteenth Century' an article on
Nelson, and one on the new astronomy. St. Thomas
Aquinas's advice regarding the election of an abbot
from three candidates: —

"'What manner of man is the first?'

"'*Doctissimus.*'

"'*Doceat,*' says St. Thomas. 'And the second?'

"'*Sanctissimus.*'

"'*Oret!* and the third?'

"'*Prudentissimus!*'

"'*Regat!* Let him rule!' says the Saint."

"*February 20.* To Methodist Church of Rev. Mr.
Burt. A sensible short discourse — seems a very sincere man: has an earlier service for Italians, well
attended. On my way home, stopped at Gargiulo's
and bought a ragged but very good copy of the
'Divina Commedia,' unbound, with Doré's illustrations."

"*February 26.* To tea at Mrs. Hazeltine's where met
William Allen Butler, author of 'Nothing to Wear' —
a bright-eyed, conversable man. Have a sitting to
Anderson. When I returned from Mrs. Hazeltine's I
found Hall Caine. . . . He told much about Gabriel
Rossetti, with whom he had much to do. Rossetti was
a victim of chloral, and Caine was set to keep him
from it, except in discreet doses."

"*March 4.* Went to see the King and Queen, returning from the review of troops. They were coldly
received. She wore crimson velvet — he was on horseback and in uniform. . . ."

"*March 9.* Club at Jessie Cochrane's; young Loyson, son of Père Hyacinthe, gave an interesting lecture on the religion of Ancient Rome, which he traced back to its rude Latin beginning; the Sabines, he thought, introduced into it one element of spirituality. Its mythology was borrowed from Greece and from the Etruscans — later from Egypt and the East. The Primitive Aryan religion was the worship of ancestors. This also we see in Rome. A belief in immortality appears in the true Aryan faith. Man, finding himself human, and related to the divine, felt that he could not die."

"*March 15.* . . . Mme. Helbig gave us an account of the Russian pilgrimage which came here lately. Many of the pilgrims were peasants. They travelled from Russia on foot, wearing bark shoes, which are very yielding and soft. These Russian ladies deprecated the action of Peter the Great in building St. Petersburg, and in forcing European civilization upon his nation, when still unprepared for it."

"*March 18.* . . . Drove with Maud, to get white thorn from Villa Madama. Went afterwards to Mrs. Waldo Story's reception, where met Mrs. McTavish, youngest daughter of General Winfield Scott. I was at school with one of her older sisters, Virginia, who became a nun."

As the winter wore away and the early Roman spring broke, the last vestige of the discomfort of the first weeks vanished. The daily drives to the country in search of wild flowers were an endless delight, as well as the trips to the older quarters of the city. She

found that, while during the first weeks she had lost
the habit of looking keenly about at the sights, the old
joy soon came back to her, and now she was quick to
see every picturesque figure in the crowd, every classic
fragment in the architecture. "The power of seeing
beautiful things, like all other powers, must be exercised to be preserved," she once said.

"*March 19.* I have not dared to work to-day, as I
am to read this afternoon. The reading was well attended and was more than well received. Hall Caine
came afterwards, and talked long about the Bible. He
does not appear to be familiar with the most recent
criticism of either Old or New Testament."

"*March 24.* 'There is a third silent party to all our
bargains.' [Emerson.]

"I find this passage in his essay on 'Compensation'
to-day for the first time, having written my essay on
'Moral Triangulation of the Third Party' some thirty
years ago."

"*March 26.* Dined with Mrs. McCreary — the Duke
of San Martino took me in to dinner — Monsignor
Dennis O'Connell sat on the other side of me. I had
an interesting talk with him. Mrs. McCreary sang my
'Battle Hymn.' They begged me to recite 'The Flag,'
which I did. Mrs. Pearse, daughter of Mario and
Grisi, sang delightfully."

"*March 30.* A fine luncheon party given by Mrs.
Iddings, wife of the American Secretary of Embassy
at the Grand Hotel. Mme. Ristori was there; I had
some glimpses of reminiscence with her. I met her
with 'La terribil' Medea,' which I so well remember

hearing from her. I presently quoted her toast in 'La Locandiera,' of which she repeated the last two lines. Maud had arranged to have Mrs. Hurlburt help me home. Contessa Spinola also offered, but I got off alone, came home in time to hear most of Professor Pansotti's lecture on the Gregorian music, which, though technical, was interesting."

"*March 31.* I woke up at one, after vividly dreaming of my father and Dr. Francis. My father came in, and said to me that he wished to speak to Miss Julia alone. I trembled, as I so often did, lest I was about to receive some well-merited rebuke. He said that he wished my sister and me to stay at home more. I saw the two faces very clearly. My father's I had not seen for fifty-nine years."

"*April 6.* Went in the afternoon with Mrs. Stillman to the Campo dei Fiori, where bought two pieces of lace for twenty *lire* each, and a little cap-pin for five *lire*. Saw a small ruby and diamond ring which I very much fancied."

"*April 10.* Easter Sunday, passed quietly at home. Had an early walk on the terrace. . . . A good talk with Hamilton Aïdé, who told me of the Spartali family. In the afternoon to Lady Kenmare's reception and later to dine with the Lindall Winthrops."

"*April 11.* In the afternoon Harriet Monroe, of Chicago, came and read her play — a parlor drama, ingenious and well written. The audience were much pleased with it."

"*April 13.* . . . In the evening dined with Theodore Davis and Mrs. Andrews. Davis showed us his treasures gathered on the Nile shore and gave me a scarab."

"*April 18.* . . . Went to hear Canon Farrar on the 'Inferno' of Dante — the lecture very scholarly and good."

"*April 22.* With Anderson to the Vatican, to see the Pinturicchio frescoes, which are very interesting. He designed the tiling for the floors, which is beautiful in color, matching well with the frescoes — these represent scenes in the life of the Virgin and of St. Catherine. . . ."

"*April 24.* To Miss Leigh Smith's, where I read my sermon on the 'Still Small Voice' to a small company of friends, explaining that it was written in the first instance for the Concord Prison, and that I read it there to the convicts. I prefaced the sermon by reading one of the parables in my 'Later Lyrics,' 'Once, where men of high pretension,' etc. . . ."

This was one of several occasions when she read a sermon at the house of Miss Leigh Smith, a stanch Unitarian, who lived at the Trinità de' Monti in the house near the top of the Spanish Steps, held by generations of English and American residents the most advantageous dwelling in Rome. On Sunday mornings, when the bells of Rome thrilled the air with the call to prayer, a group of exiles from many lands gathered in the pleasant English-looking drawing-room. From the windows they could look down upon the flower-decked Piazza di Spagna, hear the song of the nightingales in the Villa Medici, breathe the perfume of violets and almond blossoms from the Pincio. This morning, or another, Paul Sabatier was among the listeners, a grave, gracious man, a Savoyard pastor, whose "Life of Saint Francis of Assisi" had set all Rome talking.

"*April 25.* To lunch with the Drapers. Had some good talk with Mr. D. [the American Ambassador]. He was brought up at Hopedale in the Community, of which his father was a member, his mother not altogether acquiescing. He went into our Civil War when only twenty years of age, having the day before married a wife. He was badly wounded in the battle of the Wilderness. Mosby [guerilla] met the wounded train, and stripped them of money and watches, taking also the horses of their conveyances. A young Irish lad of fourteen saved Draper's life by running to Bull Plain for aid."

"*April 26.* Lunch at Daisy Chanler's, to meet Mrs. Sanford, of Hamilton, Canada, who is here in the interests of the International Council of Women. She seems a nice, whole-souled woman. . . . I have promised to preside at a meeting, called at Daisy's rooms for Thursday, to carry forward such measures as we can and to introduce Mrs. Sanford and interpret for her."

"*April 27.* Devoted the forenoon to a composition in French, setting forth the objects of the meeting. . . ."

"*April 28.* Went carefully over my French address. In the afternoon attended the meeting at Daisy's where I presided."

This was the first time the Italian women had taken part in the International Council.

"*April 30.* To Contessa di Taverna at Palazzo

Gabrielli, where I met the little knot of newly elected officers of the Council of Italian Women that is to be. Read them my report of our first meeting — they chattered a great deal. Mrs. Sanford was present. She seemed grateful for the help I had tried to give to her plan of a National Council of Italian Women. I induced the ladies present to subscribe a few *lire* each, for the purchase of a book for the secretary, for postage and for the printing of their small circular. Hope to help them more further on. . . ."

"*May 1.* . . . I gave my 'Rest' sermon at Miss Leigh Smith's. . . . Afterwards to lunch with the dear Stillman Muse. Lady Airlie and the Thynne sisters were there. Had a pleasant talk with Lady Beatrice. . . . Wrote a letter to be read at the Suffrage Festival in Boston on May 17. . . ."

Lady Beatrice and Lady Katherine Thynne; the latter was married later to Lord Cromer, Viceroy of Egypt. The Ladies Thynne were passing the winter with their cousin, the Countess of Kenmare, at her pleasant apartment in the Via Gregoriana. Among the guests one met at Lady Kenmare's was a dark, handsome Monsignore who spoke English like an Oxford Don, and looked like a Torquemada. Later he became Papal Secretary of State and Cardinal Merry del Val.

"*May 2.* Have worked as usual. A pleasant late drive. Dined with Eleutherio,[1] Daisy Chanler, and Dr. Bull; whist afterwards; news of an engagement and victory for us off Manila."

[1] Her brother-in-law, Luther Terry.

"*May 4.* . . . We dined with Marchese and Marchesa de Viti de Marco at Palazzo Orsini. Their rooms are very fine, one hung with beautiful crimson damask. An author, Pascarello, was present, who has written comic poems in the Romanesque dialect, the principal one a mock narrative of the discovery of America by Columbus. Our host is a very intelligent man, much occupied with questions of political economy, of which science he is professor at the Collegio Romano. His wife, an American, is altogether pleasing. He spoke of the present Spanish War, of which foreigners understand but little."

"*May 5.* A visit from Contessa di Taverna to confer with me about the new departure [the International Council of Women]. She says that the ladies will not promise to pay the stipulated contribution, five hundred *lire* once in five years, to the parent association. . . ."

"*May 8.* An exquisite hour with dear Maud on the terrace — the roses in their glory, red, white, and yellow; honeysuckle out, brilliant. We sat in a sheltered spot, talked of things present and to come. Robert Collyer to lunch. I asked him to say grace, which he did in his lovely manner. He enjoyed Maud's terrace with views of St. Peter's and the mountains. In the afternoon took a little drive.

"Several visitors called, among them Louisa Broadwood, from whom I learned that the little Committee for a Woman's Council is going on. The ladies have decided not to join the International at present, but to try and form an Italian Council first. Some good

results are already beginning to appear in the coöperation of two separate charities in some part of their
work."

"*May 9.* I must now give all diligence to my preparation for departure. Cannot write more on 'Reminiscences' until I reach home. Maud made a dead set
against my going to Countess Resse's where a number
of ladies had been invited to meet me. I most unwillingly gave up this one opportunity of helping the
Woman's Cause; I mean this one remaining occasion,
as I have already spoken twice to women and have
given two sermons and read lectures five times. It
is true that there might have been some exposure in
going to Mme. R.'s, especially in coming out after
speaking."

A few years after this, the Association which she
did so much to found, held the first Woman's Congress
ever given in Italy, at the Palace of Justice in Rome.
It was an important and admirably conducted convention. The work for the uplift of the sex is going
on steadily and well in Italy to-day.

"*May 12.* Sat to Villegas all forenoon. Had a little
time on the terrace. Thought I would christen it the
'Praise God.' The flowers seem to me to hold their
silent high mass, swinging their own censers of sweet
incense. Went to Jack's studio and saw his splendid
work.[1] In the afternoon went with my brother-in-law
to the cemetery to visit dear Louisa's grave. Jack had
cut for me many fine roses from the terrace. We

[1] Elliott was at work upon his Triumph of Time, a ceiling decoration
for the Boston Public Library.

dropped many on this dear resting-place of one much and justly beloved. . . . Dear old Majesty of Rome, this is my last writing here. I thank God most earnestly for so much."

CHAPTER XI

EIGHTY YEARS

1899–1900; *aet.* 80–81

HUMANITY

Methought a moment that I stood
Where hung the Christ upon the Cross,
Just when mankind had writ in blood
The record of its dearest loss.

The bitter drink men offered him
His kingly gesture did decline,
And my heart sought, in musing dim,
Some cordial for those lips divine.

When lo! a cup of purest gold
My trembling fingers did uphold;
Within it glowed a wine as red
As hearts, not grapes, its drops had shed.
Drink deep, my Christ, I offer thee
The ransom of Humanity.

J. W. H.

Though Jesus, alas! is as little understood in doctrine as followed in example. For he has hitherto been like a beautiful figure set to point out a certain way, and people at large have been so entranced with worshipping the figure, that they have neglected to follow the direction it indicates.

J. W. H.

THE winter of 1898–99 saw the publication of "From Sunset Ridge; Poems Old and New." This volume contained many of the poems from "Later Lyrics" (long out of print), and also much of her later work. It met with a warm recognition which gave her much pleasure.

Late in 1899 appeared the "Reminiscences," on which she had been so long at work. These were even

more warmly received, though many people thought
them too short. Colonel Higginson said the work
might have been "spread out into three or four interesting octavos; but in her hurried grasp it is squeezed
into one volume, where groups of delightful interviews
with heroes at home and abroad are crowded into
some single sentence."

The book was written mostly from memory, with
little use of the Journals, and none of the family letters
and papers, which she had carefully preserved through
many years; she needed none of these things. Her past
was always alive, and she went hand in hand with its
dear and gracious figures.

But we have outstripped the Journals and must go
back to the beginning of 1899.

"[Boston.] *January 1, 1899.* I begin this year with
an anxious mind. I am fighting the Wolf, hand to
hand. I am also confused between the work already
done on my 'Reminiscences,' and that still wanting
to give them some completeness. May the All-Father
help me!"

"*January 9.* Dined with the Massachusetts Press
Club Association. I made a little speech partly
thought out beforehand. The best bit in it — 'Why
should we fear to pass from the Old Testament of our
own liberties, to the New Testament of liberty for all
the world?' — came to me on the spur of the moment. . . ."

"*January 16.* . . . Dickens Party at the New England Woman's Club. I despaired of being able to go,
but did manage to get up a costume and take part.

Many very comical travesties, those of Pickwick and
Captain Cuttle remarkably good; also Lucia M. Peabody as Martin Chuzzlewit, and Mrs. Godding in full
male dress suit. I played a Virginia reel and finally
danced myself."

The part she herself took on this occasion was that
of Mrs. Jellyby, a character she professed to resemble.
At another club party she impersonated Mrs. Jarley,
with a fine collection of celebrities, which she exhibited proudly. She always put on her best motley
for her "dear Club"; and in those days its fooling
was no less notable than its wisdom. Among other
things, she instituted the Poetical Picnics, picnic suppers to which every member must bring an original
poem: some of her best nonsense was recited at these
suppers.

It has been said that she had the gift of the word
in season. This was often shown at the Club; especially when, as sometimes happened, a question of
the hour threatened to become "burning." It is remembered how one day a zealous sister thundered so
loud against corporal punishment that some mothers
and grandames were roused to equally ardent rejoin-
der. The President was appealed to.

"*Dear* Mrs. Howe, I am sure that *you* never laid a
hand on *your* children!"

"Oh, yes," said dear Mrs. Howe. "I cuffed 'em a
bit when I thought they needed it!"

Even "militancy" could be touched lightly by her.
Talk was running high on the subject one day; eyes
began to flash ominously, voices took on "a wire

edge," as she expressed it. Again the appeal was made.

"Can you imagine, Mrs. Howe, under *any* circumstances — "

The twinkle came into the gray eyes. "Well!" she said. " I am pretty old, but I *think* I could manage a broomstick!"

The tension broke in laughter, and the sisters were sisters once more.

"*January 23*. Worked as usual. Attended the meeting in favor of the Abolition of the Death Penalty, which was interesting. . . . I spoke on the ground of hope."

"*February 7*. . . . I hope to take life more easily now than for some time past, and to have rest from the slavery of pen and ink."

"*February 28*. . . . Was interviewed by a Miss X, who has persevered in trying to see me, and at last brought a note from ———. She is part editor of a magazine named 'Success,' and, having effected an entrance, proceeded to interview me, taking down my words for her magazine, thus getting my ideas without payment, a very mean proceeding. . . ."

"*March 21*. Tuskegee benefit, Hollis Street Theatre.

"This meeting scored a triumph, not only for the performers, but for the race. Bishop Lawrence presided with much good grace and appreciation. Paul Dunbar was the least distinct. Professor Dubois, of Atlanta University, read a fine and finished discourse. Booker Washington was eloquent as usual, and the Hampton quartet was delightful. At the tea which followed at Mrs. Whitman's studio, I spoke with these men and with Dunbar's wife, a nearly white woman of refined appearance. I asked Dubois about the negro vote in the South. He thought it better to have it legally taken away than legally nullified."

"*April 17.* Kindergarten for the Blind. . . . I hoped for a good word to say, but could only think of Shakespeare's 'The evil that men do lives after them; the good is oft interréd with their bones,' intending to say that this does not commend itself to me as true. Mr. Eels spoke before me and gave me an occasion to use this with more point than I had hoped. He made a rather flowery discourse, and eulogized Annie Sullivan and Helen Keller as a new experience in human society. In order to show how the good that men do survives them, I referred to Dr. Howe's first efforts for the blind and to his teaching of Laura Bridgman, upon whom I dwelt somewhat. . . ."

"*April 23.* . . . Had a sort of dream-vision of the dear Christ going through Beacon Street in shadow, and then in his glory. It was only a flash of a moment's thought. . . ."

"*April 25.* To Alliance, the last meeting of the season. Mrs. —— spoke, laying the greatest emphasis on women acting so as to *express themselves in freedom.* This ideal of self-expression appears to me insufficient and dangerous, if taken by itself. I mentioned its insufficiency, while recognizing its importance. I compared feminine action under the old limitations to the touching of an electric eel, which immediately gives one a paralyzing shock. I spoke also

of the new woman world as at present constituted, as
like the rising up from the sea of a new continent. In
my own youth women were isolated from each other
by the very intensity of their personal consciousness.
I thought of myself and of other women in this way.
We thought that superior women ought to have been
born men. A blessed change is that which we have
witnessed."

As her eightieth birthday drew nigh, her friends
vied with one another in loving observance of the
time. The festivities began May 17 with a meeting of
the New England Women's Press Association, where
she gave a lecture on "Patriotism in Literature" and
received "eighty beautiful pink roses for my eighty
years."

Next came the "annual meeting and lunch of the
New England Woman's Club. This took the character of a pre-celebration of my eightieth birthday,
and was highly honorific. I can only say that I do
not think of myself as the speakers seemed to think
of me. Too deeply do I regret my seasons of rebellion,
and my shortcomings in many duties. Yet am I
thankful for so much good-will. I only deserve it
because I return it."

Between this and the day itself came a memorial
meeting in honor of the ninety-sixth anniversary of
Emerson's birth. Here she spoke "mostly of the ladies
of his family" — Emerson's mother and his wife. Said
also, "Emerson was as great in what he did not say as
in what he said. Second-class talent tells the whole

story, reasons everything out; great genius suggests
even more than it says."

She was already what she used to call "Boston's
old spoiled child!" All through the birthday flowers,
letters, and telegrams poured into the house. From
among the tokens of love and reverence may be chosen
the quatrain sent by Richard Watson Gilder: —

> "How few have rounded out so full a life!
> Priestess of righteous war and holy peace,
> Poet and sage, friend, sister, mother, wife,
> Long be it ere that noble heart shall cease!"

The "Woman's Journal" issued a special Birthday
number. It was a lovely and heart-warming anniversary, the pleasure of which long remained with
her.

Among the guests was the beloved physician of many
years, William P. Wesselhoeft. Looking round on the
thronged and flower-decked rooms, he said, "This is
all very fine, Mrs. Howe; but on your ninetieth birthday I shall come, and *nobody else!*" Alas! before
that day the lion voice was silent, the cordial presence gone.

Three days later came an occasion which stirred
patriotic Boston to its depths. The veterans of the
Grand Army of the Republic had invited Major-
General Joseph Wheeler to deliver the Memorial Day
oration in Boston Theatre. Our mother was the second
guest of honor. She has nothing to say of this occasion
beyond the fact that she "had a great time in the
morning," and that in the open carriage with her
sat "General Wheeler's two daughters — *very* pleas-

ing girls"; but pasted in the Journal is the following clipping from the "Philadelphia Press": —

BOSTON WARMED UP

The Major has just returned from Boston, where he was present at the Memorial Day services held in Boston Theatre.

It was the real thing. I never imagined possible such a genuine sweeping emotion as when that audience began to sing the "Battle Hymn." If Boston was cold, it was thawed by the demonstration on Tuesday. Myron W. Whitney started to sing. He bowed to a box, in which we first recognized Mrs. Howe, sitting with the Misses Wheeler. You should have heard the yell. We could see the splendid white head trembling; then her voice joined in, as Whitney sang, "In the beauty of the lilies," and by the time he had reached the words, —

"As He died to make men holy, let us die to make men free," —

the whole vast audience was on its feet, sobbing and singing at the top of its thousands of lungs. If volunteers were really needed for the Philippines, McKinley could have had us all right there.

The same evening she went "to Unitarian meeting in Tremont Temple, where read my screed about Governor Andrew, which has cost me some work and more anxiety. Rev. S. A. Eliot, whom I saw for the first time, was charmingly handsome and friendly. I was introduced as 'Saint Julia' and the whole audience rose when I came forward to read. Item: I had dropped my bag with my manuscript in the carriage, but Charles Fox telephoned to the stable and got it for me."

The spring of this year saw an epidemic of negro-

lynching, which roused deep indignation throughout the country. On May 20 the Journal records
"a wonderful meeting at Chickering Hall, called by
the colored women of Boston, to protest against the
lynching of negroes in the South. Mrs. Butler M.
Wilson presided, an octoroon and a woman of education. Her opening address was excellent in spirit and
in execution. A daughter of Mrs. Ruffin also wrote
an excellent address: Mrs. Cheney's was very earnest
and impressive. Alice Freeman Palmer spoke as I
have never before heard her. My rather brief speech
was much applauded, as were indeed all of the others.
Mrs. Richard Hallowell was on the platform and
introduced Mrs. Wilson."

This brief speech brought upon her a shower of
letters, mostly anonymous, from persons who saw
only the anti-negro side of this matter, so dreadful in
every aspect. These letters were often denunciatory,
sometimes furious in tone, especially one addressed to

Mrs. Howe, Negro Sympathizer,
Boston.

This grieved her, but she did not cease to lift up her
voice against the evil thing whenever occasion offered.

"*July 7. Oak Glen. . . .* My son and his wife came
over from Bristol to pass the day. He looks as young
as my grandsons do. At fifty, his hair is blond, without
gray, and his forehead unwrinkled."

"*July 16. . . .* While in church I had a new thought
of the energy and influence of Christ's teaching. 'Ask
and ye shall receive,' etc. These little series of com-

mands all incite the hearers to action: Ask, seek, knock. I should love to write a sermon on this, but fear my sermonizing days are over, alas!"

"*August 7.* Determined to do more literary work daily than I have been doing lately. Began a screed about dear Bro' Sam, feeling that he deserved a fuller mention than I have already given him. . . ."

"*September 4.* Discouraged over the confusion of my papers, the failure of printers to get on with my book, and my many bills. Have almost had an attack of the moral sickness which the Italians call *Achidia.* I suppose it to mean indifference and indolence. . . ."

To Laura

Oak Glen, September 6, 1899.

. . . Here's a question. Houghton and Mifflin desire to print [1] the rough draft of my "Battle Hymn," which they borrowed, with some difficulty, from Charlotte Whipple, who begged it of me, years ago. I hesitate to allow it, because it contains a verse which I discarded, as not up to the rest of the poem. It will undoubtedly be an additional attraction for the volume. . . .

"*September 7.* Have attacked my proofs fiercely. . . ."

To Laura

Oak Glen, September 16, 1899.

Yours received, *très chère.* Why not consult Hays Gardiner [2] about printing the original draft of the

---

[1] In the *Reminiscences.*

[2] The late John Hays Gardiner, author of *The Bible as Literature,* *The Forms of Prose Literature,* and *Harvard.*

"Hymn"? Win's[1] opinion would be worth having, also. I think I shall consult E. E. Hale, albeit the two just named would be more fastidious.[2]

"*October 21.* My last moments in this dear place. The past season appears to me like a gift of perfect jewels. I pray that the winter may have in store for me some good work and much dear and profitable companionship. I must remember that this may be my last summer here, or anywhere on earth, but must bear in mind that it is best to act with a view to prolonged life, since without this outlook, it is very hard for us to endeavor or to do our best. Peace be with you, beautiful summer and autumn. Amen."

She was never ready to leave Oak Glen; the town house always seemed at first like a prison.

"*October 23. Boston.* A drizzly, dark day. I struggled out twice, saying to myself: 'It is for your life.' . . ."

"*October 24.* Have had two days of chaos and discouragement. . . ."

"*October 27.* A delightful and encouraging conference of A.A.W. held in my parlors. The prevailing feeling was that we should not disband, but should hold on to our association and lie by, hoping to find new innings for work. Florida was spoken of as good ground for us. I felt much cheered and quickened by the renewal of old friendships. . . ."

A Western lecture trip had been planned for this

---

[1] Edwin Arlington Robinson, author of *Captain Craig*, etc.

[2] The facsimile printed in the *Reminiscences* contains the discarded stanza.

autumn, but certain untoward symptoms developed and Dr. Wesselhoeft said, "No! no! not even if you had not had vertigo." She gave it up most reluctantly, confiding only to the Journal the hope that she might be able to go later.

"*November 9.* Celebration of dear Chev's birthday at the Institution. I spoke of the New Testament word about the mustard seed, so small but producing such a stately tree. I compared this little seed to a benevolent impulse in the mind of S. G. H. and the Institution to a tree. 'What is smaller than a human heart? What seems weaker than a good intention? Yet the good intention, followed by the faithful heart, has produced this great refuge in which many generations have already found the way to a life of educated usefulness.' . . ."

"*November 19.* . . . Before the sermon I had prayed for some good thought of God. This came to me in the shape of a sudden perception to this effect: 'I am in the Father's house already.' . . ."

"*November 30.* . . . In giving thanks to-day, I made my only personal petitions, which were first, that some of my dear granddaughters might find suitable husbands, . . . and lastly, that I might *serve* in some way until the last breath leaves my body. . . ."

"*December 16.* I had greatly desired to see the 'Barber.' Kind Mrs. [Alfred] Batcheller made it possible by inviting me to go with her. The performance was almost if not quite *bouffe.* Sembrich's singing marvellous, the acting of the other characters excellent, and singing very good, especially that of De Reszke and Campanari. I heard the opera in New York more than seventy years ago, when Malibran, then Signorina Garcia, took the part of Rosina."

"*December 31.* . . . 'Advertiser' man came with a query: 'What event in 1899 will have the greatest influence in the world's history?' I replied, 'The Czar's Peace Manifesto, leading to the Conference at The Hague.' "

November, 1899, saw the birth of another institution from which she was to derive much pleasure, the Boston Authors' Club. Miss Helen M. Winslow first evolved the idea of such a club. After talking with Mmes. May Alden Ward and Mabel Loomis Todd, who urged her to carry out the project, she went to see the "Queen of Clubs." "Go ahead!" said our mother. "Call some people together here, at my house, and we will form a club, and it will be a good one too."

The Journal of November 23 says: —

"Received word from Helen Winslow of a meeting of literary folks called for to-morrow morning at my house."

This meeting was "very pleasant: Mrs. Ward, Miss Winslow, Jacob Strauss, and Hezekiah Butterworth attended — later Herbert Ward came in."

It was voted to form the Boston Authors' Club, and at a second meeting in December the club was duly organized.

In January the Authors' Club made its first public appearance in a meeting and dinner at Hotel Vendôme,

Mrs. Howe presiding, Colonel Higginson (whom she described as her "chief Vice") beside her.

The brilliant and successful course of the Authors' Club need not be dwelt on here. Her connection with it was to continue through life, and its monthly meetings and annual dinners were among her pet pleasures. She was always ready to "drop into rhyme" in its service, the Muse in cap and bells being oftenest invoked: *e.g.*, the verses written for the five hundredth anniversary of Chaucer's death: —

> Poet Chaucer had a sister,
> He, the wondrous melodister.
> She did n't write no poems, oh, no!
> Brother Geoffrey trained her so.
> Honored by the poet's crown,
> Her posterity came down.
>
> . . . .
>
> Ages of ancestral birth
> Went for all that they were worth.
> Hence derives the Wentworth name
> Which heraldic ranks may claim.
> That same herald has contrived
> How the Higginson arrived.
>
> He was gran-ther to the knight
> In whose honor I indite
> Burning strophes of the soul
> 'propriate to the flowing bowl.
>
> Oft the worth I have defended
> Of the Laureate-descended,
> But while here he sits and winks
> I can tell you what he thinks.
>
> "Never, whether old or young,
> Will that woman hold her tongue!
> Fifty years in Boston schooled,
> Still I find her rhyme-befooled.

Oft in earnest, oft in jest,
We have met and tried our best.
Nought I dread an open field,
I can conquer, I can yield,
Self from foes I can defend,
But Heav'n preserve us from our friend!"

She and her "chief Vice" were always making merry together; when their flint and steel struck, the flash was laughter. It may have been at the Authors' Club that the two, with Edward Everett Hale and Dr. Holmes, were receiving compliments and tributes one afternoon.

"At least," she cried, "no one can say that Boston drops its *H's!*"

This was in the winter of 1900. It was the time of the Boer War, and all Christendom was sorrowing over the conflict. On January 3 the Journal says: —

"This morning before rising, I had a sudden thought of the Christ-Babe standing between the two armies, Boers and Britons, on Christmas Day. I have devoted the morning to an effort to overtake the heavenly vision with but a mediocre result."

These lines are published in "At Sunset."

On the 11th the cap and bells are assumed once more.

" . . . To reception of the College Club, where I was to preside over the literary exercises and to introduce the readers. I was rather at a loss how to do this, but suddenly I thought of Mother Goose's 'When the pie was opened, the birds began to sing.' So when Edward Everett Hale came forward with me and introduced me as 'the youngest person in the hall,' I said, 'Ladies and Gentlemen, I shall prove the truth of what our reverend friend has just said, by citing a quotation from Mother Goose ['When the pie was opened,' etc.], and the first bird that I shall introduce will be Rev. E. E. Hale.' Beginning thus, I introduced T. W. Higginson as the great American Eagle; Judge [Robert] Grant as a mocking-bird; C. F. Adams as the trained German canary who sings all the songs of Yawcob Strauss; C. G. Ames said, 'You must n't call me an owl.' I brought him forward and said, 'My dear minister says that I must not call him an owl, and I will not; only the owl is the bird of wisdom and he is very wise.' I introduced Mrs. Moulton as a nightingale. For Trowbridge I could think of nothing and said, 'This bird will speak for himself.' Introduced N. H. Dole as 'a bird rarely seen, the phœnix.' At the close E. E. H. said, 'You have an admirable power of introducing.' This little device pleased me foolishly."

"*February 4.* Wrote a careful letter to W. F. Savage. He had written, asking an explanation of some old manuscript copy of my 'Battle Hymn' and of the theft perpetrated of three of its verses in 'Pen Pictures of the War,' only lately brought to my notice. He evidently thought these matters implied doubt at least of my having composed the 'Hymn.' To this suspicion I did not allude, but showed him how the verses stolen had been altered, probably to avoid detection. . . ."

"*March 3.* Count di Campello's lecture, on the religious life in Italy, was most interesting. His uncle's movement in founding a National Italian Catholic Church seemed to me to present the first solution I have met with, of the absolute opposition between Catholic and Protestant. A Catholicism without spiritual tyranny, without ignorant superstition, would bridge over the interval between the two opposites and bring about the unification of the world-church. . . ."

"*March 13.* . . . Passed the whole morning at State House, with remonstrants against petition forbidding Sunday evening concerts. T. W. H. spoke remarkably well. . . ."

"*March 30.* . . . Had a special good moment this morning before rising. Felt that God had granted me a good deal of heaven, while yet on earth. So the veil lifts sometimes, not for long."

April found her in Minneapolis and St. Paul, lecturing and being "delightfully entertained."

"*May 8. Minneapolis.* Spoke at the University, which I found delightfully situated and richly endowed. Was received with great distinction. Spoke, I think, on the fact that it takes the whole of life to learn the lessons of life. Dwelt a little on the fact that fools are not necessarily underwitted. Nay, may be people of genius, the trouble being that they do not learn from experience. . . ."

On leaving she exclaims: —

"Farewell, dear St. Paul. I shall never forget you, nor this delightful visit, which has renewed (almost)

the dreams of youth. In the car a kind old grandmother, with two fine little boy grands. . . .

"The dear old grandmother and her boys got out
at the Soo. Other ladies in the Pullman were *very*
kind to me, especially a lady from St. Paul, with her
son, who I thought might be a young husband. She
laughed much at this when I mentioned it to her.
Had an argument with her, regarding hypnotism, I
insisting that it is demoralizing when used by a strong
will to subdue a weak one."

"*May 25.* [*Boston.*] Went in the afternoon to Unitarian meeting at Tremont Temple. S. A. Eliot made
me come up on the platform. He asked if I would give
a word of benediction. I did so, thanking God earnestly in my heart for granting me this sweet office,
which seemed to lift my soul above much which has
disturbed it of late. Why is He so good to me? Surely
not to destroy me at last."

"*June 3.* . . . Before church had a thought of some
sweet spirit asking to go to hell to preach to the people
there. Thought that if he truly fulfilled his office, he
would not leave even that forlorn pastorate. . . ."

"*June 10.* . . . Could not find the key to my money
bag, which distressed me much. Promised St. Anthony
of Padua that if he would help me, I would take pains
to find out who he was. Found the key immediately. . . ."

"*June 18.* . . . The little lump in my right breast
hurts me a little to-day. Have written Wesselhoeft
about it. 4.50 P.M. He has seen it and says that it is
probably cancerous; forbids me to think of an opera-

tion; thinks he can stop it with medicine. When he told me that it was in all probability a cancer, I felt at first much unsettled in mind. I feared that the thought of it would occupy my mind and injure my health by inducing sleeplessness and nervous excitement. Indeed, I had some sad and rather vacant hours, but dinner and Julia's [1] company put my dark thought to flight and I lay down to sleep as tranquilly as usual."

[Whatever this trouble was, it evidently brought much suffering, but finally disappeared. We learn of it for the first time in this record; she never spoke of it to any of her family.]

"*Oak Glen. June 21.* Here I am seated once more at my old table, beginning another *villeggiatura*, which may easily be my last. Have read a little Greek and a long article in the 'New World.' I pray the dear Heavenly Father to help me pass a profitable season here, improving it as if it were my last, whether it turns out to be so or not."

[She was not in her usual spirits this summer. She felt the heat and the burden of years. The Journal is mostly in a minor key.]

"*July 16.* Took up a poem at which I have been working for some days, on the victims in Pekin; a strange theme, but one on which I feel I have a word to say. Wrote it all over. . . ."

"*July 19.* Was much worn out with the heat. In afternoon my head gave out and would not serve me for anything but to sit still and observe the flight of birds and the freaks of yellow butterflies. . . ."

[1] Julia Ward Richards.

MRS. HOWE
From a photograph by John Elliott

"*July 26.* Have prayed to-day that I may not find life dull. This prolongation of my days on earth is so precious that I ought not to cease for one moment to thank God for it. I enjoy my reading as much as ever, but I do feel very much the narrowing of my personal relations by death. How rich was I in sisters, brothers, elders! It seems to me now as if I had not at all appreciated these treasures of affection. . . ."

"*July 31.* Have writ notes of condolence to Mrs. Barthold Schlesinger and to M. E. Powel. I remember the coming of Mrs. Powel's family to Newport sixty-five years ago. The elders used to entertain in the simple ways of those days, and my brother Henry and I used to sing one duet from the 'Matrimonio Segreto,' at some of their evening parties. In the afternoon came the ladies of the Papéterie; had our tea in the green parlor, which was pretty and pleasant. . . ."

To Laura

OAK GLEN, August 3, 1900.

. . . I grieve for the death of King Umberto, as any one must who has followed the fortunes of Italy and knows the indebtedness of the country to the House of Savoy. Thus, the horror of this anarchy, thriving among Italians in our own country. I am so thankful that the better class among them have come out so strongly against it! I was present when King Umberto took the oaths of office, after the death of his father. He was a faithful man, not quite up to the times, perhaps, but his reign was beset with problems and difficulties. I am sure that the Queen greatly respected and honored him, although I believe that she was first betrothed to his brother Amadeo, whom, it is said, she loved. Alas, for the tyranny of dynastic necessity. Their only child was very delicate, and has no child, or had not, when I was in Rome. As to the Chinese horror, it is unspeakably dreadful. Even if the ministers are safe, hundreds of foreigners and thousands of native Christians have been cruelly massacred. I cannot help hoping that punishment will be swift and severe. . . .

A letter from H. M. H. yesterday, in great spirits. At a great public dinner recently, the president of the association cried: "*Honneur à Howe!*"

Affect.,
                    MOTHER.

"*August 17.* . . . In the evening I was seized with an attack of verse and at bedtime wrote a rough draft of a *Te Deum* for the rescue of the ministers in Pekin."

"*August 20.* . . . Got my poem smooth at some expense of force, perhaps. I like the poem. I think that it has been *given* me."

This *Te Deum* was printed in the "Christian Herald" in September, 1900.

"*Sunday, September 2.* . . . I had, before service began, a clear thought that *self* is death, and deliverance from its narrow limitations the truest emancipation. In my heart I gave thanks to God for all measure in which I have attained, or tried to attain, this liberation. It seems to me that the one moment of this which we could perfectly attain, would be an immortal joy."

A week later, she went to New York to attend a reception given to the Medal of Honor Legion at Brooklyn Academy. She writes: —

"Last evening's occasion was to me eminently worth the trouble I had taken in coming on. To meet these veterans, face to face, and to receive their hearty greeting, was a precious boon vouchsafed to me so late in life. Their reception to me was cordial in the extreme. The audience and chorus gave me the Chautauqua salute, and as I left the platform, the girl chorus sang the last verse of my 'Hymn' over again, in a subdued tone, as if for me alone. The point which I made, and wished to make, was that, 'our flag should only go forth on errands of justice, mercy, etc., and that once sent forth, it should not be recalled until the work whereunto it had been pledged was accomplished.' This with a view to Pekin. . . ."

"*September 13.* . . . The Galveston horror [1] was much in my mind yesterday. I could not help asking why the dear Lord allowed such dreadful loss of life. . . ."

"*October 25.* My last writing at this time in this dear place. The season, a very busy one, has also been a very blessed one. I cannot be thankful enough for so much calm delight — my children and grandchildren, my books and my work, although this last has caused me many anxieties. I cannot but feel as old John Forbes did when he left Naushon for the last time and went about in his blindness, touching his writing materials, etc., and saying to himself, 'Never again, perhaps.' If it should turn out so in my case,

[1] A terrible storm and tidal wave which had nearly destroyed the city.

God's will be done. He knows best when we should
depart and how long we should stay. . . ."

"On the way home and afterwards, these lines of
an old hymn ran in my mind: —

> " 'Fear not, I am with thee, oh, be not afraid.
> I, I am thy God, and will still give thee aid.'

This comforted me much in the forlorn exchange of
my lovely surroundings at Oak Glen for the imprisonment of a town house."

"*November 4. 241 Beacon Street.* The dear minister
preached on 'All Saints and All Souls,' the double
festival of last week. At Communion he said: 'Dear
Sister Howe, remember that if you are moved to speak,
you have freedom to do so.' I had not thought of
speaking, but presently rose and spoke of the two
consecrated days. I said: 'As I entered this church to-
day, I thought of a beautiful cathedral in which one
after another the saints whom I have known and
loved, appeared on either side; first, the saints of my
own happy childhood, then the excellent people whom
I have known all my life long. The picture of one of
them hangs on these walls.[1] His memory is fresh in
all our hearts. Surely it is a divine glory which we
have seen in the faces of these friends, and they seem
to lead us up to that dearest and divinest one, whom
we call Master'; and so on. I record this to preserve
this vision of the cathedral of heart saints. . . ."

"*December 25.* I was awake soon after five this
morning, and a voice, felt, not heard, seemed to give
me a friendly warning to set my house in order for

[1] James Freeman Clarke.

my last departure from it. This seems to bring in view my age, already long past the scriptural limit, suggesting also that I have some symptoms of an ailment which does not trouble me much, but which would naturally tend to shorten my life. In my mind I promised that I would heed the warning given. I only prayed God to make the parting easy for me and my dear ones, of whom dear Maud would be the most to be pitied, as she has been most with me and has no child to draw her thoughts to the future. After this, I fell asleep.

"We had a merry time at breakfast, examining the Christmas gifts, which were numerous and gratifying. . . ."

"*December 31.* . . . Here ends a year of mercies, of more than my usual health, of power to speak and to write. It has been a year of work. God be thanked for it."

CHAPTER XII

STEPPING WESTWARD

1901–1902; *aet.* 82–83

But here the device of the spiral can save us. We must make the round, but we may make it with an upward inclination. "Let there be light!" is sometimes said in accents so emphatic, that the universe remembers and cannot forget it. We carry our problems slowly forward. With all the ups and downs of every age, humanity constantly rises. Individuals may preserve all its early delusions, commit all its primitive crimes; but to the body of civilized mankind, the return to barbarism is impossible.

J. W. H.

"*January 7.* I have had a morning of visioning, lying in bed. 'Be still and know that I am God,' seemed to be my sentence. I thought of the Magdalen's box of spikenard, whose odor, when the box was broken, filled the house. The separate religious convictions of the sects seemed to me like so many boxes of ointment, exceedingly precious while shut up, but I thought also that the dear Lord would one day break these separate boxes, and that then their fragrance would fill the whole earth, which is His house.

"This is my first writing in this book. From this thought and the 'Be still,' I may try to make two sermons.

"In afternoon came William Wesselhoeft, Sr., and prescribed entire quiet and rest for some days to come. Oh! I do long to be at work."

"*January 9.* To-day for the first time since January 3, I have opened a Greek book. I read in my Æschylus ["Eumenides"] how Apollo orders the Furies to leave his shrine, to go where deeds of barbarity, tortures, and mutilations are practised."

At this time she heard of her son's receiving from the Czar the cross of the Order of St. Stanislas. She writes to him:— ₡

"Goodness gracious me!

"Are you sure it is n't by mistake? Do you remember that you are my naughty little imp? . . . Well, well, it takes away my breath! Dearest Boy, my heart is lifted up with gratitude. If your father were only here, to share our great rejoicing! Joy! joy! . . ."

She had always taken a deep interest in Queen Victoria, whose age was within three days of her own. Many people fancied a resemblance between the two; indeed, when in England as a bride, she was told more than once: " You look like our young Queen!" It is remembered how one of her daughters, knocking at the door of a Maine farmhouse to inquire the way, was met by a smiling, "I know who you are! You are the daughter of the Queen of America!"

The Queen's death, coming as it did during her own illness, gave her a painful shock.

"*January 23.* The news of Queen Victoria's death quite overcame me for a moment this morning. Instead of settling to my work, I wrote a very tiny ' bust of feeling' about her, which I carried to the 'Woman's Journal' office, where I found a suffrage meeting in progress. I could only show myself and say that I was not well enough to remain. . . ."

" Bust of feeling" was a favorite expression of hers.

Old Bostonians will recall its origin. "A certain rich man," seeing a poor girl injured in a street accident, offered to pay her doctor's bill. This being presented in due time, he disclaimed all responsibility in the affair; and when reminded of his offer, exclaimed, "Oh, that was a bust of feeling!"

On January 31, she was "in distress of mind all day lest Maud should absolutely refuse to let me give my lecture at Phillips Church this evening." Later she writes: "Maud was very kind and did nothing to hinder my going to South Boston." She went and enjoyed the evening, but was not so well after it.

"*February 10.* A Sunday at home; unable to venture out. Wesselhoeft, Jr., called, left medicine, and forbade my going out before the cough has ceased. Have read in Cheyne's 'Jewish Religious Life after the Exile,' finding the places of reference in the Bible. Afterwards read in 'L'Aiglon,' which is very interesting but not praiseworthy, as it endeavors to recall the false glory of Napoleon."

"*February 18.* Have been out, first time since February 3, when I went to church and was physically the worse for it. . . . Last night had a time of lying awake with a sort of calm comfort. Woke in the morning full of invalid melancholy, intending to keep my bed. Felt much better when in motion. Must make a vigorous effort now to get entirely well."

These days of seclusion were hard for her, and every effort was made to bring the "mountains" to her, since she could not go to them.

A club was formed among her friends in Boston for the study and speaking of Italian: this became one of her great pleasures, and she looked forward eagerly to the meetings, delighted to hear and to use the beautiful speech she had loved since childhood.

"*February 22.* The new club, *Il Circolo Italiano,* met at our house. Count Campello had asked me to say a few words, so I prepared a very little screed in Italian, not daring to trust myself to speak *extempore* in this language. We had a large attendance; I thought one hundred were present. My bit was well received, and the lecture by Professor Speranza, of New York, was very interesting, though rather difficult to follow. The theme was D'Annunzio's dramas, from which he gave some quotations and many characterizations. He relegates D'Annunzio to the Renaissance when *Virtù* had no real *moral significance.* Compared him with Ibsen. The occasion was exceedingly pleasant."

To Laura

I had hoped to go to church to-day, but my Maud and your Julia decided against it, and so I am having the day at home. It is just noon by my dial, and Maud is stretched in my Gardiner chair, comfortably shawled, and reading Lombroso's book on "The Man of Genius," with steadfast attention. Lombroso's theory seems to be that genius, almost equally with insanity, is a result of degeneration. . . .

"*March 1.* The first day of spring, though in this climate this is a *wintry* month. I am thankful to have got on so far in this, my eighty-second year. My greatest trouble is that I use so poorly the precious time spared to me. Latterly I have been saying to myself, 'Can you not see that the drama is played out?' This partly because my children wish me to give up public speaking."

"*March 4.* . . . To New England Woman's Club; first time this year, to my great regret and loss. I was cordially welcomed. . . . A thought suddenly came to me, namely, that the liberal education of women would give the death-blow to superstition. I said, 'We women have been the depositaries of religious sensibility, but we have also furnished the impregnable storehouse of superstition, sometimes gracious, sometimes desperately cruel and hurtful to our race.' No one noticed this, but I hold fast to it. . . ."

"*March 8.* . . . To Symphony Concert in afternoon, which I enjoyed but little, the music being of the multi-muddle order so much in vogue just now. An air of Haydn's sounded like a sentence of revelation in a chatter. . . ."

It may have been after this concert that she wrote these lines, found in one of her notebooks: —

> Such ugly noises never in my life
> My ears endured, such hideous fiddle-strife.
> A dozen street bands playing different tunes,
> A choir of chimney sweeps with various runes,
> The horn that doth to farmer's dinner call,
> The Chinese gong that serves in wealthier hall,
> The hammer, scrub brush, and beseeching broom,
> While here and there the guns of freedom boom,
> "Tzing! bang! this soul is saved!" "Clang! clang! it is n't!"
> And *mich* and *dich* and *ich* and *sich* and *sisn't!*

Five dollar bills the nauseous treat secured,
But what can pay the public that endured?

"*March 17.* Before lying down for a needed rest, I must record the wonderful reception given to-day to Jack Elliott's ceiling.[1] The day was fine, clear sunlight. Many friends congratulated me, and some strangers. Vinton, the artist, Annie Blake, Ellen Dixey were enthusiastic in their commendation of the work, as were many others. I saw my old friend, Lizzie Agassiz, my cousin Mary Robeson and her daughter, and others too numerous to mention. . . . This I consider a day of great honor for my family. . . . *Deo gratias* for this as well as for my son's decoration."

"*March 31.* . . . Had a sort of vision in church of Moses and Christ, the mighty breath of the prophets reaching over many and dark ages to our own time, with power growing instead of diminishing. When I say a vision, I mean a vivid thought and mind picture."

"*April 3.* Have writ to Larz Anderson, telling him where to find the quotation from Horace which I gave him for a motto to his automobile, 'Ocior Euro.' Sanborn found it for me and sent it by postal. It must have been more than thirty years since dear Brother Sam showed it to me. . . ."

"*April 7.* A really inspired sermon from C. G. A., 'The power of an unending life.' . . . The Communion which followed was to me almost miraculous. Mr. Ames called it a festival of commemoration, and it brought me a mind vision of the many departed dear

[1] The Triumph of Time, at the Public Library.

ones. One after another the dear forms seemed to paint themselves on my inner vision: first, the nearer in point of time, last my brother Henry and Samuel Eliot. I felt that this experience ought to pledge me to new and more active efforts to help others. In my mind I said, the obstacle to this is my natural inertia, my indolence; then the thought, God can overcome this indolence and give me increased power of service and zeal for it. Those present, I think, all considered the sermon and Communion as of special power and interest. It almost made me fear lest it should prove a swan song from the dear minister. Perhaps it is I, not he, who may soon depart."

Later in April she was able to fulfil some lecture engagements in New York State with much enjoyment, but also much fatigue. After her return she felt for a little while "as if it was about time for her to go," but her mind soon recovered its tone.

Being gently reproved for giving a lecture and holding a reception on the same day, she said, "That is perfectly proper: I gave and I received: I was scriptural and I was blessed."

Asked on another occasion if it did not tire her to lecture, — "Why, no! it is they [the audience] who are tired, not I!"

On April 27 she writes: —

"I have had a great gratification to-day. Mrs. Fiske Warren had invited us to afternoon tea and to hear Coquelin deliver some monologues. I bethought me of my poem entitled 'After Hearing Coquelin.' Maud wrote to ask Mrs. Warren whether she would like to have me read it and she assented. I procured a fresh copy of the volume in which it is published, and took it with me to this party, which was large and *very* representative of Boston's most recognized people. Miss Shedlock first made a charming recitation in French, which she speaks perfectly. Then Coquelin gave three delightful monologues. The company then broke up for tea and I thought my chance was lost, but after a while order was restored. M. Coquelin was placed where I could see him, and I read the poem as well as I could. He seemed much touched with the homage, and I gave him the book. People in general were pleased with the poem and I was very glad and thankful for so pleasant an experience. Learned with joy of the birth of a son to my dear niece, Elizabeth Chapman."

Another happy birthday came and passed. After recording its friendly festivities, she writes: —

"I am *very* grateful for all this loving kindness. Solemn thoughts must come to me of the long past and of the dim, uncertain future. I trust God for His grace. My life has been poor in merit, in comparison to what it should have been, but I am thankful that to some it has brought comfort and encouragement, and that I have been permitted to champion some good causes and to see a goodly number of my descendants, all well endowed physically and mentally, and starting in life with good principles and intentions; my children all esteemed and honored for honorable service in their day and generation."

"*May 30. Decoration Day.* . . . In the afternoon

Maud and I drove out to Mount Auburn to visit the dear graves. We took with us the best of the birthday flowers, beautiful roses and lilies. I could not have much sense of the presence of our dear ones. Indeed, they are not there, but where they are, God only knows."

"*May 31.* Free Religious meeting. . . . The fears which the bold programme had naturally aroused in me, fears lest the dear Christ should be spoken of in a manner to wound those who love him — these fears were at once dissipated by the reverent tone of the several speakers. . . ."

"*June 1.* . . . To the Free Religious festival. . . . I found something to say about the beautiful morning meeting and specially of the truth which comes down to us, mixed with so much rubbish of tradition. I spoke of the power of truth 'which burns all this accumulation of superstition and shines out firm and clear, so we may say that "the myth crumbles but the majesty remains."' . . ."

She managed to do a good deal of writing this summer: wrote a number of "screeds," some to order, some from inward leading: *e.g.*, a paper on "Girlhood Seventy Years Ago," a poem on the death of President McKinley.

"*October 5.* A package came to-day from McClure's Syndicate. I thought it was my manuscript returned and rejected, and said, 'God give me strength not to cry.' I opened it and found a typewritten copy of my paper on 'Girlhood,' sent to me for correction in lieu of printer's proof. Wrote a little on my screed about

'Anarchy.' Had a sudden thought that the sense and spirit of government is responsibility."

"*October 6*. . . . Wrote a poem on 'The Dead Century,' which has in it some good lines, I hope."

"*October 8*. The cook ill with rheumatism. I made my bed, turning the mattress, and put my room generally to rights. When I lay down to take my usual *obligato* rest, a fit of verse came upon me, and I had to abbreviate my lie-down to write out my *inspiration*."

The "*obligato* rest"! How she did detest it! She recognized the necessity of relaxing the tired nerves and muscles; she yielded, but never willingly. The noon hour would find her bending over her desk, writing "for dear life," or plunged fathoms deep in Grote's "Greece," or some other light and playful work. Daughter or granddaughter would appear, watch in hand, countenance steeled against persuasion. "Time for your rest, dearest!"

The rapt face looks up, breaks into sunshine, melts into entreaty. "Let me finish this note, this page; then I will go!" Or it may be the sprite that looks out of the gray eyes. "Get out!" she says. "Leave the room! I never saw you before!"

Finally she submits to the indignity of being tucked in for her nap; but even then her watch is beside her on the bed, ticking away the minutes till the half-hour is over, and she springs to her task.

"*November 3. 241 Beacon Street*. My room here has been nicely cleaned, but I bring into it a great heap of books and papers. I am going to try *hard* to be less disorderly than in the past."

How hard she did try, we well remember. The book trunk was a necessity of the summer flitting. It carried a full load from one book-ridden house to the other, and there were certain books — the four-volume Oxford Bible, the big-print Horace, the Greek classics, shabby of dress, splendid of type and margin — which could surely have found their way to and from Newport unaided.

One book she never asked for — the English dictionary! Once Maud, recently returned from Europe, apologized for having inadvertently taken the dictionary from 241 Beacon Street.

"How dreadful it was of me to take your dictionary! What have you done? Did you buy a new one?"

"I did not know you had taken it!"

"But — how did you get along without a dictionary?"

The elder looked her surprise.

"I never use a word whose meaning I do not know!"

"But the spelling?"

There was no answer to this, save a whimsical shrug of the shoulders.

"*November 11.* The day of the celebration of dear Chev's one hundredth birthday. Before starting for the Temple I received three beautiful gifts of flowers, a great bunch of white roses from Lizzie Agassiz, a lovely bouquet of violets from Mrs. Frank Batcheller, and some superb chrysanthemums from Mrs. George H. Perkins. The occasion was to me one of solemn joy and thankfulness. Senator Hoar presided with beautiful grace, preluding with some lovely reminiscences of

Dr. Howe's visit to his office in Worcester, Massachusetts, when he, Hoar, was a young lawyer. Sanborn
and Manatt excelled themselves, Humphreys did very
well. Hoar requested me to stand up and say a few
words, which I did, he introducing me in a very felici-
tous manner. I was glad to say my word, for my heart
was deeply touched. With me on the platform were
my dear children and Jack Hall and Julia Richards;
Anagnos, of course; the music very good."

Senator Hoar's words come back to us to-day, and
we see his radiant smile as he led her forward.

"It is only the older ones among us," he said, "who
have seen Dr. Howe, but there are hundreds here who
will want to tell their children that they have seen
the author of the 'Battle Hymn of the Republic.'"

Part of her "word" was as follows: —

"We have listened to-day to very heroic memories;
it almost took away our breath to think that such
things were done in the last century. I feel very grateful to the pupils and graduates of the Perkins Institution for the Blind who have planned this service in
honor of my husband. It is a story that should be
told from age to age to show what one good resolute
believer in humanity was able to accomplish for the
benefit of his race. . . . The path by which he led
Laura Bridgman to the light has become one of the
highways of education, and a number of children similarly afflicted are following it, to their endless enlargement and comfort. What an encouragement does this
story give to the undertaking of good deeds!

"I thank those who are with us to-day for their

sympathy and attention. I do this, not in the name
of a handful of dust, dear and reverend as it is, that
now rests in Mount Auburn, but in the name of a
great heart which is with us to-day and which will
still abide with those who work in its spirit."

"*November 26. Thursday.* A day of pleasant agitation from beginning to end. I tried to recognize in
thought the many mercies of the year. My fortunate
recoveries from illness, the great pleasures of study,
friendly intercourse, thought and life generally. Our
Thanksgiving dinner was at about 1.30 P.M., and was
embellished by the traditional turkey, a fine one, to
which David, Flossy, Maud, and I did justice. The
Richards girls, Julia and Betty, and Chug[1] and Jack
Hall, flitted in and out, full of preparation for the
evening event, the marriage of my dear Harry Hall to
Alice Haskell. I found time to go over my screed for
Maynard very carefully, rewriting a little of it and
mailing it in the afternoon.

" In the late afternoon came Harry Hall and his best
man, Tom McCready, to dine here and dress for the
ceremony. Maud improvised a pleasant supper: we
were eight at table. Went to the church in two carriages. Bride looked very pretty, simple white satin
dress and tulle veil. Six bridesmaids in pink, carrying
white chrysanthemums. H. M. H.[2] seemed very boyish, but looked charmingly. . . ."

"*December 31.* The last day of a blessed year in
which I have experienced some physical suffering, but

---

[1] Dr. Lawrence J. Henderson.
[2] The bridegroom, Henry Marion Hall.

also many comforts and satisfactions. I have had
grippe and bronchitis in the winter and bad malarial
jaundice in the summer, but I have been constantly
employed in writing on themes of great interest and
have had much of the society of children and grandchildren. Of these last, two are happily married, *i.e.*,
in great affection. My dear Maud and her husband
have been with me constantly, and I have had little
or no sense of loneliness. . . ."

The beginning of 1902 found her in better health
than the previous year.

She records a luncheon with a distinguished company, at which all agreed that "the 'Atlantic' to-day
would not accept Milton's 'L' Allegro,' nor would any
other magazine."

At the Symphony Concert "the Tschaikowsky
Symphony seemed to me to have in it more noise than
music. Felt that I am too old to enjoy new music."

"*January 24*. Suffrage and Anti-Suffrage at the
State House. I went there with all of my old interest
in the Cause. The Antis were there in force: Mrs.
Charles Guild as their leader; Lawyer Russell as their
manager. I had to open. I felt so warm in my faith
that for once I thought I might convert our opponents.
I said much less than I had intended, as is usually the
case with me when I speak *extempore*."

"*February 7*. . . . I went to see Leoni's wonderful
illuminated representation of leading events in our
history; a very remarkable work, and one which ought
to remain in this country."

"*February 11.* Dreamed of an interview with a female pope. I had to go to Alliance Meeting to speak about Wordsworth. I hunted up some verses written about him in my early enthusiasm, probably in 1840 or 1841. This I read and then told of my visit to him with Dr. Howe and the unpleasantness of the experience. Spoke also of the reaction in England against the morbid discontent which is so prominent and powerful in much of Byron's poetry. . . ."

"*February 12.* . . . In my dream of yesterday morning the woman pope and I were on very friendly terms. I asked on leaving whether I might kiss her hand. She said, 'You may kiss my hand.' I found it fat and far from beautiful. As I left her, methought that her countenance relaxed and she looked like a tired old woman. In my dream I thought, 'How like this is to what Pope Leo would do.'"

"*February 13.* . . . Felt greatly discouraged at first waking. It seemed impossible for me to make a first move under so many responsibilities. A sudden light came into my soul at the thought that God will help me in any good undertaking, and with this there came an inkling of first steps to be taken with regard to Sig. Leoni's parchment.[1] I went to work again on my prize poem, with better success than hitherto. . . ."

"*February 14.* Philosophy at Mrs. Bullard's. . . . Sent off my prize poem with scarcely any hope of its obtaining or indeed deserving the prize, but Mar [2] has promised to pay me something for it in any case, and I was bound to try for the object, namely, a good civic poem. . . ."

---

[1] That is, to have it bought by some public society.   [2] An editor.

"*February 15.* . . . A day of great pleasure, profit and fatigue. . . . Griggs's lecture. . . . The address on 'Erasmus and Luther' was very inspiring. Griggs is in the full tide of youthful inspiration and gives himself to his audience without stint. He did not quite do justice to the wonderful emancipation of thought which Protestantism has brought to the world, but his illustration of the two characters was masterly. I said afterwards to Fanny Ames: 'He will burn himself out.' She thinks that he is wisely conservative of his physical strength. I said, 'He bleeds at every pore.' I used to say this of myself with regard to ordinary social life. Went to the Club, where was made to preside. Todd and Todkinee[1] both spoke excellently. Then to Symphony Concert to hear Kreisler and the 'Pastoral Symphony.' "

"*February 16.* . . . The Philosophy meeting and Griggs's lecture revived in me the remembrance of my philosophic studies and attempts of thirty-five years ago, and I determined to endeavor to revise them and to publish them in some shape. Have thought a good deal this morning of this cream of genius in which the fervent heat of youth fuses conviction and imagination and gives the world its great masters and masterpieces. It cannot outlast the length of human life of which it is the poetry. Age follows it with slow philosophy, but can only strengthen the outposts which youth has gained with daring flight. Both are divinely ordained and most blessed. Of the dear Christ the world had only this transcendent efflorescence. I said

---

[1] Professor Todd, of Amherst, and his wife, Mabel Loomis Todd.

to Ames yesterday, 'I find in the Hebrew prophets
all the doctrine which I find in Christ's teaching.' He
said, 'Yes, it is there seminally.' We agreed that it
was the life which made the difference."

"*February 21.* . . . My dearest Maud left by 1 P.M.
train to sail for Europe to-morrow. I could not go to
the hearing. Was on hand to think of small details
which might have been overlooked. Gave them my
fountain pen, to Jack's great pleasure. Julia Richards
came to take care of me. I suffered extreme depression
in coming back to the empty house, every corner of
which is so identified with Maud's sweet and powerful
presence. The pain of losing her, even for a short
time, seemed intolerable. I was better in the evening.
Chug amused me with a game of picquet."

Her spirits soon rallied, and the granddaughters
did their best to fill the great void. She writes to
Laura about this time: —

> Not a sign was made, not a note was wrote,
> Not a telegram was wired,
> Not a rooster sent up his warning note,
> When the eggs from your larder were fired.

> We swallow them darkly at break of fast,
> Each one to the other winking,
> And "woe is me if this be the last"
> Is what we are sadly thinking.

> The egg on missile errand sent
> Some time has been maturing,
> And, with whate'er endearment blent,
> Is rarely reassuring.

> But yours, which in their freshness came
> Just when they might be wanted,
> A message brought without a name,
> "'Love," we will take for granted.   [*Copyrighted.*]

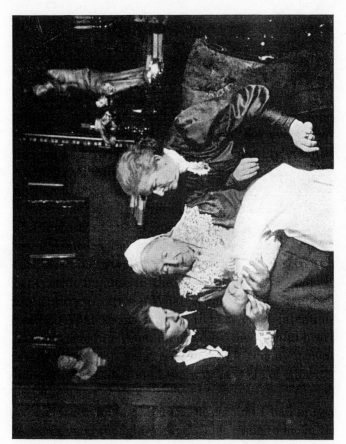

RICHARDS FOUR GENERATIONS

MRS. HOWE, MRS. RICHARDS, MRS. SHAW, HENRY SHAW

From a photograph by C. A. Shaw, 1907

Julia is rather strict with me, but very good, considering whose grandchild she is.

Affect.,

MOTHER.

"*March 25.* I received in one day three notes asking me regarding the 'Life of Margaret Shepard,' and 'Secret Confessions of a Priest.' One writer had seen in some paper that she could have the books by applying to me; Miss ——— wrote to the same intent; Miss ——— wrote and enclosed forty cents' worth of stamps for one of the books. I have replied to all that I know nothing of the books in question, and that I am neither agent nor bookseller."

"*March 30.* Lunch with Mrs. Fields after church. Heard a very inspiring sermon from Samuel A. Eliot. This young man has a very noble bearing and a stringent way of presenting truth. He has that *vital* religious power which is rare and most precious. Before he had spoken I had been asking in my mind, how can we make the *past present to us?* The Easter service and Lent also seem intended to do this, but our imaginations droop and lag behind our desires. . . ."

"*April 2.* . . . Went in the evening to see 'Ben-Hur' with kind Sarah Jewett — her treat, as was my attendance at the opera. The play was altogether spectacular, but very good in that line. . . ."

"*April 3.* . . . Went to the celebration of E. E. Hale's eightieth birthday, in which the community largely participated. Senator Hoar was the orator and spoke finely. . . . Hale's response was manly, cheery,

and devout. He has certainly done much good work,
and has suggested many good things."

"*April 12.* Lunch with Mrs. Wheelwright. I found
Agnes Repplier very agreeable. She had known the
wife of Green, the historian, 'very, almost too brilliant.' Told me something about his life. I enjoyed
meeting her."

To Laura

Yes, I likes my chilluns better 'n other folkses' chilluns. P'raps 't is as well sometimes to let them know
that I do. . . .

What you write about my little Memoir of your
dear Papa touches me a good deal. I did my best to
make it as satisfactory as the limits imposed upon me
would allow. I don't think that I ever had a word of
commendation for it. Michael killed it as a book by
printing it entire in his Report for the year. Now I am
much gratified by your notice of it. You are most
welcome to use it in connection with the letters.[1]

"*May 16.* In the evening the Italian supper at the
Hotel Piscopo, North End. I recited Goldoni's toast
from the 'Locandiera,' and also made a little speech
at the end of the banquet. Padre Roberto, a Venetian
priest, young and handsome, sat near me. . . ."

"*May 18.* . . . I had prayed that this might be a
real Whitsunday to me and I felt that it was. Notice
was given of a meeting at which Catholic, Jew, Epis-

[1] *Letters and Journals of Samuel Gridley Howe.*

copalian, and Unitarian are to speak regarding the
Filipinos. This seemed like the Millennium. It is the
enlargement of religious sympathy; not, as some may
think, the progress of critical indifferentism.

"During this morning's service my desire to speak
to prisoners reasserted itself strongly; also my thought
of one of my sermons which I wish to write. One
should be to the text: 'The glory of God in the face
of Jesus Christ,' the reflection of divine glory in God's
saints, like the reflection of the sun's light in the
planets. Another about Adam being placed in Eden
to tend the flowers and water them. This should concern our office in the land of our birth, into which we
are born to love and serve our country. Will speak of
the self-banished Americans, Hale's 'Man without a
Country,' etc. This day has been so full of thought
and suggestion that I hardly know how to let it go.
I pray that it may bear some fruit in my life, what is
left of it."

"*May 24.* The annual Club luncheon in honor of
my birthday. I felt almost overwhelmed by the great
attention shown me and by the constant talk of
speakers with reference to myself. ... I don't find in
myself this charm, this goodness, attributed to me by
such speakers, but I know that I love the Club and
love the world of my own time, so far as I know it.
They called me Queen and kissed my hand. When I
came home I fell in spirit before the feet of the dear
God, thanking Him for the regard shown me, and praying that it might not for one moment make me vain. I
read my translation of Horace's ode, 'Quis Desiderio,'

and it really seemed to suit the mention made by Mrs.
Cheney of our departed members, *praecipuë*, Dr. Zack;
Dr. Hoder [?] of England was there, and ex-Governor
Long and T. W. Higginson, also Agnes Irwin. It was
a great time."

"*July 5.* . . . I wrote to Ethel V. Partridge, Omaha,
a high-school student: 'Get all the education that you
can. Cultivate habits of studious thought with all
that books can teach. The fulfilment of the nearest
duty gives the best education.' I fear that I have
come to know this by doing the exact opposite, *i.e.*,
neglecting much of the nearest duty in the pursuit of
an intellectual wisdom which I have not attained. . . ."

Maud and Florence were both away in the early
part of this summer, and various grandchildren kept
her company at Oak Glen. There were other visitors,
among them Count Salome di Campello, a cheery
guest who cooked spaghetti for her, and helped the
granddaughter to set off the Fourth of July fire-
works, to her equal pleasure and terror. During his
visit she invited the Italian Ambassador [1] to spend a
couple of days at Oak Glen. On July 14 she writes: —

"Not having heard from the Italian Ambassador,
the Count and I supposed that he was not coming. In
the late afternoon came a letter saying that he would
arrive to-morrow. We were troubled at this late intelligence, which gave me no time to invite people to
meet the guest. I lay down for my afternoon rest with
a very uneasy mind. Remembering St. Paul's words

[1] Count Mayer des Planches.

about 'Angels unawares,' I felt comforted, thinking
that the Angel of Hospitality would certainly visit
me, whether the guest proved congenial or not."

"*July 15.* . . . The Ambassador arrived as previously announced. He proved a most genial and
charming person; a man still in the prime of life, with
exquisite manners, as much at home in our simplicity
as he doubtless is in scenes of luxury and magnificence.
Daisy Chanler drove out for afternoon tea, at my
request, and made herself charming. After her came
Emily Ladenberg, who also made a pleasing impression. Our guest played on the piano and joined in
our evening whist. We were all delighted with
him."

After the Ambassador's departure she writes: —

"He gave me an interesting account of King Charles
Albert of Savoia. He is a man of powerful temperament, which we all felt; has had to do with Bismarck
and Salisbury and all the great European politicians
of his time. We were all sorry to see him depart."

The Journal tells of many pleasures, among them
"a delightful morning in the green parlor with Margaret Deland and dear Maud."

On August 24 she writes: —

"This day has been devoted to a family function of
great interest, namely, the christening of Daisy and
Wintie's boy baby, Theodore Ward, the President [1]
himself standing godfather. Jack Elliott and I were
on hand in good time, both of us in our best attire.

[1] Theodore Roosevelt.

We found a very chosen company, the Sydney Websters, Owen Wister, Senator Lodge and wife, the latter standing as godmother. Mr. Diman, of the School,[1] officiated, Parson Stone being ill. The President made his response quite audibly. The Chanler children looked lovely, and the baby as dear as a baby can look. His godfather gave him a beautiful silver bowl lined with gold. I gave a silver porringer, Maud a rattle with silver bells; lunch followed. President Roosevelt took me in to the table and seated me on his right. This was a very distinguished honor. The conversation was rather literary. The President admires Emerson's poems, and also Longfellow and Sienkiewicz. He paid me the compliment of saying that Kipling alone had understood the meaning of my 'Battle Hymn,' and that he admired him therefor. Wister proposed the baby's health, and I recited a quatrain which came to me early this morning. Here it is: —

> "Roses are the gift of God,
> Laurels are the gift of fame;
> Add the beauty of thy life
> To the glory of thy name."

"I said, 'Two lines for the President and two for the baby'; the two first naturally for the President. As I sat waiting for the ceremony, I called the dear roll of memory, Uncle Sam and so on back to Grandpa Ward. I was very thankful to participate in this beautiful occasion. But the service and talk about the baby's being born in sin, etc., etc., seemed to me very inconsistent with Christ's saying that he who

[1] St. George's, Newport.

would enter into the Kingdom of Heaven must become
'as a little child.' He also said, 'of such is the kingdom
of heaven.' "

She had a high admiration for Colonel Roosevelt,
and a regard so warm that she would never allow any
adverse criticism of him in her presence. The following verses express this feeling: —

> Here 's to Teddy,
> Blythe and ready,
> Fit for each occasion!
> Who as he
> Acceptably
> Can represent the Nation?
>
> Neither ocean
> Binds his motion,
> Undismayed explorer;
> Challenge dares him,
> Pullman bears him
> Swifter than Aurora.
>
> Here 's to Teddy!
> Let no eddy
> Block the onward current.
> Him we trust,
> And guard we must
> From schemes to sight abhorrent.
>
> When the tuba
> Called to Cuba
> Where the fight was raging,
> Rough and ready
> Riders led he,
> Valorous warfare waging.
>
> Here 's to Teddy!
> Safe and steady,
> Loved by every section!

South and North
Will hurry forth
To hasten his election.
                    1904.

On September 12, a notice of the death of William
Allen Butler is pasted in the Diary. Below it she
writes: —

"A pleasant man. I met him at the Hazeltines' in
Rome in 1898 and 1899. His poem ["Nothing to
Wear"] was claimed by one or two people. I met his
father [a Cabinet Minister] at a dinner at the Ban-
crofts' in New York, at which ex-President Van Buren
was also present, and W. M. Thackeray, who said to
me across the table that Browning's 'How They
Brought the Good News' was a 'good jingle.' "

On the 29th she spoke at a meeting of the New
England Woman's Club in memory of Dr. Zakrzewska,
and records her final words: —

"I pray God earnestly that we women may never
go back from the ground which has been gained for
us by our noble pioneers and leaders. I pray that
these bright stars of merit, set in our human firmament, may shine upon us and lead us to better and
better love and service for God and man."

"In the afternoon to hear reports of delegates to
Biennial at Los Angeles. These were very interesting,
but the activity shown made me feel my age, and its
one great infirmity, loss of power of locomotion. I felt
somehow the truth of the line which Mr. Robert C.
Winthrop once quoted to me: —

"'Superfluous lags the veteran on the stage.' "

Yet a few days later she writes: —

"I had this morning so strong a feeling of the goodness of the divine Parent in the experience of my life, especially of its most trying period, that I had to cry out, 'What shall I, who have received so much, give in return?' I felt that I must only show that forbearance and forgiveness to others which the ever blessed One has shown to me. My own family does not call for this. I am cherished by its members with great tenderness and regard. I thought later in the day of a sermon to prisoners which would brighten their thoughts of the love of God. Text from St. John's Epistle, 'Behold what manner of love is this that we should be called the sons of God.'"

This was the year of the coal strike in Pennsylvania, which made much trouble in Boston. She notes one Sunday that service at the Church of the Disciples was held in the church parlors "on account of the shortage of coal." This recalls vivid pictures of the time; distracted coal merchants dealing out promises, with nothing else to deal; portly magnates and stately dames driving down Beacon Street in triumph with coals in a paper bag to replenish the parlor fire: darker pictures, too, of poverty and suffering.

At 241 Beacon Street the supply was running low, and the coal dealer was summoned by telephone. "A load of coal? Impossible, madam! We have no — I beg your pardon! Mrs. Julia Ward Howe? *Mrs. Howe's house is cold?* You shall have some within the hour!"

CHAPTER XIII

LOOKING TOWARD SUNSET

1903–1905; aet. 84–86

IN MUSIC HALL

Looking down upon the white heads of my contemporaries

Beneath what mound of snow
Are hid my springtime roses?
How shall Remembrance know
Where buried Hope reposes?

In what forgetful heart
As in a cañon darkling,
Slumbers the blissful art
That set my heaven sparkling?

What sense shall never know,
Soul shall remember;
Roses beneath the snow,
June in November.

J. W. H.

THE year 1903 began with the celebration at Faneuil Hall of the fortieth anniversary of Lincoln's Emancipation Proclamation. She was one of the speakers. "I felt much the spirit of the occasion, and spoke, I thought, better than usual, going back to the heroic times before and during the war, and to the first celebration forty years ago, at which I was present."

Work of all kinds poured in, the usual steady stream.

"*January 6.* Wrote a new circular for Countess."

Who the Countess was, or what the circular was about, is not known. By this time it had become the custom (or so it seemed to exasperated daughters and granddaughters) for any one who wanted anything in the literary line, from a proverb to a pamphlet, to ask her for it.

It is remembered how on a certain evening, when she was resting after a weary day, a "special delivery" note was received from a person whom she scarcely knew, asking for "her thoughts on the personality of God, by return mail." This was one of the few requests she ever denied. People asked her to give them material for their club papers (sometimes to write them!), to put them through college, to read their manuscripts, to pay the funeral expenses of their relatives. A volume of the letters conveying these requests would be curious reading.

The petition for a "little verse" was rarely refused. Her notebooks are full of occasional poems, only a small proportion of which ever appeared in print. Many of them are "autographs." She always meant to honor every request of this kind; the country must be full of volumes inscribed by her. Here are a few of them.

For Francis C. Stokes, Westtown School, Pennsylvania

> Auspicious be the rule
> Of love at Westtown School,
> And happy, mid his youthful folks
> The daily task of Master Stokes!

[When this gentleman's note came, she was "tired to death." The granddaughter said, "You *can't* do it. Let me write a friendly note, and you shall sign it!"

"You're right," she said, "I can't: I am too tired to think!" But when she saw the note taken away, "No, no!" she cried, "I can! He is probably a most

hard-working man, and a little word may cheer him.
Here, I have a line already! "]

Wealth is good, health is better, character is best.

> Citizens of the new world,
> Children of the promise,
> So let us live!

Love to learn, and learn to love.

Remember to forget your troubles, but don't forget to remember your blessings.

For Mr. Charles Gallup, who had written to her several times without receiving a reply, she wrote —

> If one by name Gallup
> Desires to wallop
> A friend who too slowly responds,
> She will plead that her age
> Has attained such a stage
> She is held hand and foot in its bonds.

Here, again, are a few sentences, gathered from various calendars.

The little girls on the school bench, using or misusing their weekly allowance, are learning to build their future house, or pluck it down.

No gift can make rich those who are poor in wisdom.

In whatever you may undertake, never sacrifice quality for quantity, even when quantity pays and quality does not.

For so long, the body can perform its functions and hold together, but what term is set for the soul? Nothing in its make-up foretokens a limited existence. Its sentence would seem to be, "Once and always."

The verses in the notebooks are by no means all "by request." The rhyming fit might seize her anywhere, at any time. She wrote the rough draft on whatever was at hand, often on the back of note, circular, or newspaper wrapper. She could never forget the wartime days when paper cost half a dollar a pound.

Nor were people content with writing: they came singly, in pairs, in groups, to proffer requests, to pay respects, to ask counsel. The only people she met unwillingly were those who came to bewail their lot and demand her sympathy.

No one will ever know the number of her benefactions. They were mostly, of necessity, small, yet we must think they went a long way. At the New England Woman's Club, whenever a good new cause came up, she would say, "I will start the subscription with a dollar!" Many noble and enduring things began with the "President's dollar." If she had had a hundred dollars to give, it would have been joyfully given: if she had had but ten cents, it would not have been withheld. She had none of the false pride which shrinks from giving a small sum.

Beggars and tramps were tenderly dealt with. A discharged criminal in particular must never be refused help. Work must be found for him if possible; if not, it is to be feared that he got a dollar, "to help him find work"!

"*January 10.* At 11.30 received message from 'New York World' that it would pay for an article sent at once on 'Gambling among Society People.' Wrote this in a little more than an hour."

"*January 20.* . . . Some little agitation about my appearance at the Artists' Festival to-night, as one of the patronesses. I had already a white woollen dress quite suitable for the prescribed costume. Some benevolent person or persons ordered for me and sent a cloak of fine white cloth, beautiful to look at but heavy to wear. A headdress was improvised out of one of my Breton caps, with a long veil of lawn. Jack Elliott made me a lovely coronet out of a bit of gold braid with one jewel of dear Maud's. Arriving, to my surprise, I found the Queen's chair waiting for me. I sat thereon very still, the other patronesses being most kind and cordial, and saw the motley throng and the curious pageants. Costumes most beautiful, but the hall too small for much individual effect. Adèle Thayer wore the famous Thayer diamonds."

"*January 27*. Woke early and began to worry about the hearing. . . . Dressed with more care than usual and went betimes to State House. Had a good deliverance of my paper. The opposition harped upon our bill as an effort to obtain class legislation, saying also that they knew it to be an entering wedge to obtain suffrage for all women; the two positions being evidently irreconcilable. When our turn for rebuttal came, I said: 'Many years ago John Quincy Adams presented in Congress a petition for the abolition of slavery in the District of Columbia, but none of the Southerners imagined that this petition was intended to keep the other negroes of the South in slavery! Are we, who, for thirty years past, and more, have been coming here to ask for full suffrage for all women, to be accused of coming here now with a view to the exclusion of our former clients from suffrage? How can we be said to contemplate this and at the same time to be putting in an entering wedge for universal suffrage?'

"I thank God for what I did say at the hearing and for what I did not say. Two of the opposing speakers were rude in their remarks; all were absurd, hunting an issue which they knew to be false, namely, our seeking for class legislation."

"*January 28.* Although very tired after yesterday's meeting, I went in the evening to see 'Julius Cæsar' in Richard Mansfield's interpretation. The play was beautifully staged; Mansfield very good in the tent scene; parts generally well filled. . . ."

"*March 3.* My dear Maud returned this evening from New York. She has been asked to speak at to-morrow's suffrage hearing. I advised her to reflect before embarking upon this new voyage. . . . When she told me what she had in mind to say, I felt that a *real word* had been given her. I said: 'Go and say that!' . . ."

"*April 1.* . . . A telegram announced the birth of my first great-grandchild, Harry Hall's infant daughter.[1] . . ."

"*April 11.* To Mrs. Bigelow Lawrence's, Parker House, to hear music. Mrs. [Henry] Whitman called for me.

"Delightful music; two quartettes of Beethoven's, a quintette of Mozart's, which I heard at Joseph Coolidge's some thirty or more years ago. I recognized it by the first movement, which Bellini borrowed in a sextette which I studied in my youth from 'La Straniera,' an opera never given in these days. . . ."

"*April 17.* Winchendon lecture. . . . A day of an-

[1] Julia Ward Howe Hall.

"*June 9.* My first preaching in London. Worked pretty much all day at sermon, intending, not to read, but to talk it — for me, a difficult procedure. At 4.30 P.M. left off, but brain so tired that nothing in it. Subject, the kingdom of heaven. . . . Got a bad cup of tea — dressed (in my well-worn black silk) and went to the Drawing-Room at Freemasons' Tavern. God knows how I felt. 'Cast down but not forsaken.' . . . I got through better than I feared I might. Felt the method to be the right one, speaking face to face and heart to heart."

"*June 10.* Small beer going out of fashion leaves women one occupation the less. Fools are still an institution; and will remain such." [1]

"*June 16.* . . . A good attendance in spite of the heat. . . . Agonized over my failure to come up to what I had designed to do in the discourse."

"*June 18.* . . . Saw the last of my dear friend E. Twisleton, who took me to the National Gallery, where we saw many precious gems of art. . . . At parting, he said: 'The good Father above does not often give so great a pleasure as I have had in these meetings with you.' Let me enshrine this charming and sincere word in my most precious recollection, from the man of sixty-three to the woman of fifty-three."

"*June 27.* Left Leeds at 7 A.M., rising at 4.30. . . . To Miss [Frances Power] Cobbe's, where met Lady Lyall, Miss Clough, Mrs. Gorton, Jacob Bright, *et al.* Then to dinner with the dear Seeleys. An unceremonious and delightful meal. Heart of calf. Then to John

---

[1] "To suckle fools and chronicle small beer." *Othello.*

kept saying, 'I found it out immediately,' to those around me. . . ."

"*May 28.* My prayer for the new year of my life beginning to-day is, that in some work that I shall undertake I may help to make clear the goodness of God to some who need to know more of it than they do. . . ."

"*June 22.* Mabel Loomis Todd wrote asking me for a word to enclose in the corner-stone of the new observatory building at Amherst [Massachusetts]. I have just sent her the following: —

> The stars against the tyrant fought
> In famous days of old;
> The stars in freedom's banner wrought
> Shall the wide earth enfold.

"*June 23.* Kept within doors by the damp weather. Read in William James's book, 'Varieties of Religious Experience.'. . . Had a strange fatigue — a restlessness in my brain."

"*June 25.* . . . The James book which I finished yesterday left in my mind a painful impression of doubt; a God who should be only my better self, or an impersonal pervading influence. These were suggestions which left me very lonely and forlorn. To-day, as I thought it all over, the God of Abraham, Isaac, and Jacob seemed to come back to me; the God of Christ, and his saints and martyrs. I said to myself: 'Let me be steeped in the devotion of the Psalms, and of Paul's Epistles!' I took up Coquerel's sermons on the Lord's Prayer, simple, beautiful, positive. . . ."

"*July 30. Oak Glen.* Rose at 6.15 A.M. and had good

these things than for the opera, with Grisi, Mario, and
Lablache: she might even have written some funny
verses about the windmill-tilting of her Don Quixote.
Now, she stood in the place that failing health forbade
him to fill, with a depth of interest, an earnestness of
purpose, equal to his own. She, too, now heard the
sorrowful sighing of the prisoners.

At one of the meetings of this congress, a jailer of the
old school spoke in defence of the system of flogging
refractory prisoners, and described in brutal fashion a
brutal incident. Her blood was on fire: she asked leave
to speak.

"It is related," she said, "of the famous Beau
Brummel that a gentleman who called upon him one
morning met a valet carrying away a tray of neck-
cloths, more or less disordered. 'What are these?'
asked the visitor; and the servant replied, 'These are
our failures!' When I see the dark coach which in our
country carries the criminal to his place of detention,
I say, 'Society, here are your failures.'"

Her words were loudly applauded, and the punishment was voted down.

The Journal gives her further speech on this occasion: "Spoke of justice to women. They had talked of
fallen women. I prayed them to leave that hopeless
phrase. Every fallen woman represents a man as
guilty as herself, who escapes human detection, but
whose soul lies open before God. Speak of vicious, dissolute women, but don't speak of fallen women unless
you recognize the fall of man, the old doctrine."

Two days before this she had preached her last ser-

"*November 1. South Berwick.* A delightful drive.
Mary Jewett, Annie Fields, and I to visit Mrs. Tyson
in the Hamilton House described by Sarah in her
'Tory Lover.' . . . Most interesting. Mrs. Tyson very
cordial and delightful. . . . She came over later to dinner and we had such a pleasant time! In afternoon
copied most of my screed for the 'Boston Globe.'"

It surely was not on this occasion that she described
dinner as "a thing of courses and remorses!"

"*November 2.* Took reluctant leave of the Jewett
house and the trio, Sarah, Mary, and Annie Fields.
We had a wonderful dish of pigeons for lunch. . . ."

It was delightful to see our mother and Miss Jewett
together. They were the best of playmates, having a
lovely intimacy of understanding. Their talk rippled
with light and laughter. Such stories as they told!
such songs as they sang! who that heard will ever
forget our mother's story of Edward Everett in his
youth? He was to take three young ladies to drive,
and had but the one horse; he wished to please them
all equally. To the first he said, "The horse is perfectly fresh now; you have him in his best condition."
To the second he said, "The horse was a little antic
at first, so you will have the safer drive." To the
third he said, "Now that the other two have had
their turn, we need not hasten back. You can have
the longest drive."

It is recalled that during this visit, when Laura
felt bound to remonstrate in the matter of fruitcake,
"Sarah" took sides with ardor. "You shall have all
you want, Mrs. Howe, and a good big piece to take

divine will and standard which can help us to mould our lives aright without running from one extreme to another. My heart's wish would now be to devote myself to some sort of religious ministration. God can open a way for this in which the spirit of my desire may receive the form of his will. I must lecture this winter to earn some money and spread, I hope, some good doctrine. . . ."

Such was the beginning of her work for peace, which was to end only with her life. Disappointed in her hope of a world congress, she turned the current of her effort in a new direction. She would have a festival, a day which should be called Mothers' Day, and be devoted to the advocacy of peace doctrines. She chose the second day of June; for many years she and her friends and followers kept this day religiously, with sweet and tender observances which were unspeakably dear to her.

In 1876 there was a great peace meeting in Philadelphia. The occasion is thus described by the Reverend Ada C. Bowles: "There were delegates from France, Italy, and Germany, each with a burning desire to be heard, and all worth hearing, but none able to speak English. The audience looked to the anxious face of the President with sympathy; then a voice was heard, 'Call for Mrs. Howe.' Those present will never forget how her presence changed the meeting from a threatened failure to a noble success. The German, Frenchman, and Italian stood in turn by her side. At the proper moment she lifted a finger, and then gave in

We are reminded of a contemporary of hers who, being gently rebuked for giving rich food to a delicate grandchild, replied with lofty scorn, "Stuff and nonsense! *Teach his stomach!*"

"*November 8.* . . . In late afternoon some visioning, *i.e.*, lying down to rest and asking and answering questions in my mind: —

"Question: Can anything exceed the delight of the first mutual understanding of two lovers?

"Answer: This has its sacredness and its place, but even better is the large affection which embraces things human and divine, God and man.

"Question: Are Saviour and Saints alive now?

"Answer: If you believe that God is just, they must be. They gave all for His truth: He owes them immortality."

"*November 16.* Dear Auntie Francis's wedding day. I think it was in 1828. My sisters and I were bridesmaids, my brothers groomsmen. Dear father, very lame, walked up with a cane to give her away. Grandma Cutler looked much discontented with the match. Father sent the pair off in his own carriage, with four horses, their manes and tails braided with white ribbons. They drove part of the way to Philadelphia."

"*November 28.* . . . To Wellesley College. . . . William Butler Yeats lectured on the revival of letters in Ireland. We dined with him afterwards at Miss Hazard's house. He is a man of fiery temperament, with a slight, boyish figure: has deep-set blue eyes and dark hair; reminds me of John O'Sullivan [1] in his tempera-

---

[1] Hawthorne's friend of the *Democratic Review.*

ment; is certainly, as Grandpa Ward said of the Red Revolutionists, with whom he dined in the days of the French Revolution, 'very warm.'"

"*November 29.* . . . This came into my mind, apropos of reformers generally: 'Dost thou so carry thy light as to throw it upon *thyself*, or upon thy *theme?*' This appears to me a legitimate question. . . ."

"*December 21.* Put the last touches to my verses for Colonel Higginson's eightieth birthday. Maud went with me to the celebration held by the Boston Authors' Club at the Colonial Club, Cambridge. T. W. H. seemed in excellent condition; I presided as usual. Bliss Perry, first speaker, came rather late, but made a very good address. Crothers and Dean Hodges followed, also Clement. Judge Grant read a simple, strong poem, *very good*, I thought. Then came my jingle, intended to relieve the strain of the occasion, which I think it did. Maud says that I hit the bull's eye; perhaps I did. Then came a pretty invasion of mummers, bearing the gifts of the Club, a fine gold watch and a handsome bronze lamp. I presented these without much talk, having said my say in the verses, to which, by the bye, Colonel H. responded with some comic personal couplets, addressed to myself."

Here is the "jingle."

> Friends! I would not ask to mingle
> This, my very foolish jingle,
> With the tributes more decorous of the feast we hold to-day;
> But the rhymes came, thick and swarming
> Just like bees when honey's forming,
> And I could not find a countersign to order them away.

For around this sixteenth lustre
Of our friend's, such memories cluster
Of the days that lie behind it, full of glories and regrets,
Days that brought their toils and troubles,
Lit by some irradiant bubbles
Which became prismatic opals in the sun that never sets.

Picnics have we held together
Sailing in the summer weather,
Sitting low to taste the chowder on the sands of Newport Bay,
And that wonderful charade, sir,
You know well, sir, that you made, sir,
When so many years of earnest did invite an hour of play.

. . . .

He shall rank now with the sages
Who survive in classic pages,
English, German, French and Latin, Greek, so weary to construe;
Did he con his Epictetus
Ere he came to-night to greet us?
He, *àoristos* in reverence, among the learned few.

He may climb no more the mountain,
But he still employs the fountain
Pen from whose incisive point pure Helicon may flow,
And his "Yesterdays" so cheerful
Charm the world so wild and tearful,
And the Devil calls for copy, and he never answers "No."

Do I speak for everybody,
When I utter this rhapsòdy,
To induce our friend to keep his pace in following Life's incline;
Never slacken, but come on, sir,
Eighty-four years I have won, sir;
Still the olive branch shall bless you, still the laurel wreath entwine!

So, you scribbling youths and lasses,
Elders, too, fill high your glasses!
Let the toast be Wentworth Higginson, of fourscore years possest;
If the Man was good at twenty,
He is four times that now, ain't he?
We declare him four times excellent, and better than his best.

This time our mother went with him, together with Maud and a party of friends. She had been loth to go, for she had already planned her peace crusade in England, but finding how much he desired it, she compromised on part of the time.

They sailed from New York early in February, 1872, in the steamer Tybee. The voyage was rough and stormy. The companion daughter of the time remembers how the wretched little Tybee pitched and heaved; even more vividly she recalls the way in which our mother from the first made society out of the strangely assorted company on board. She was the magnet, and drew them all to her: the group of conventional ladies who had never before been at sea, the knot of naval officers going to join their ship, — among them George W. De Long, the hero of the ill-fated Jeannette expedition; a colonel, and a judge, the former interested in the Samana Bay Company. She made out of this odd company and the gruff old captain a sort of court which she ruled in a curious way. She did not seem to compel their admiration so much as to compel each to give his best.

The Tybee cast anchor in the harbor of Puerto Plata, and the voyagers saw Mont Isabel towering above them, its foot in the clear beryl water where the palms grew down to the very edge of the yellow sea sand, its head wrapped in the clouds. The Doctor came to the stateroom, crying, "Come up and see the great glory!"

Our mother's delight can be imagined when they sailed into the harbor of Santo Domingo and landed mentary mental vision of myself in the Valley of the Shadow, with a splendid champion in full armor walking beside me, a champion sent by God to make the dread passage easy and safe. . . ."

"*April 2*. . . . Learned the deaths of X. and Abby Morton Diaz. Poor X., her conduct made her impossible, but I always thought she would send flowers to my funeral. Mrs. Diaz is a loss — a high-strung, public-spirited woman with an heroic history."

"*April 4*. To the carriage-drivers' ball. They sent a carriage for me and I took Mary, the maid. . . . Mr. Dan was waiting outside for me, as was another of the committee who troubled me much, pulling and hauling me by one arm, very superfluous. My entrance was greeted with applause, and I was led to the high seats, where were two aides of the Governor, Dewey and White, the latter of whom remembers Governor Andrew. The opening march was very good. I was taken in to supper, as were the two officers just mentioned. We had a cozy little talk. I came away at about 10.30."

"*April 14*. Mr. Butcher came to breakfast at nine o'clock. He told me about the man Toynbee, whom he had known well. He talked also about Greeks and Hebrews, the animosity of race which kept them apart until the flourishing of the Alexandrian school, when the Jews greedily absorbed the philosophy of the Greeks."

This was Mr. S. H. Butcher, the well-known Greek scholar. She enjoyed his visit greatly, and they talked "high and disposedly" of things classical and modern.

"*May 28*. My meeting of Women Ministers. They

the shade of heavy mango trees. Or we explore the
country on this side the river. The great thing to
guard against is the danger of rain. This we encountered one afternoon in some severity. Suddenly one of
the party cried '*Llava!*' and down came the waters.
We were somewhat heated with our ride, and the penetrating rain fell chill upon us. A large tree gave us
shelter for a few moments, but we were soon forced to
seek more effectual protection. This we found, after
some delay, in a *boio*, or hut, into which horses and
riders were dragged pell-mell. The night was closing
in, the Chief at home, and presumably anxious, the
rain unabating. Which of the tropical spasms would
end our far-spent life? Would it be lockjaw, a common
result of severe chill in these regions? Would it be
a burning, delirious fever with a touch of yellow; or
should we get off with croup and diphtheria?

"The rain presently stopped, and we returned to
the saddle, and then, by easy stages, to the city. On
reaching home, we were advised to bathe the chilled
surfaces with rum, not the wicked New England article, but the milder product of the country. Of all the
evil consequences spoken of as sure to follow such an
exposure, fever, lockjaw, and sore throat, we have so
far not seen the earliest symptom."

It was Carnival. All the cabinet officers and their
wives devoted themselves to the entertainment of the
party. The Minister of War, Señor Curiel, a little
twinkling fiery man, devoted himself especially to our
mother, and was her right hand in the many expeditions she arranged. The Secretary of State, Señor

"*June 29.* Heard to my sorrow of the death of delightful Sarah Whitman. Wrote a little screed for 'Woman's Journal' which I sent. . . ."

In early July, she went to Concord for a memorial meeting in honor of Nathaniel Hawthorne.

"*July 11.* . . . Alice Blackwell, some days ago, wrote beseeching me to write to President Roosevelt, begging him to do something for the Armenians. I said to myself, 'No, I won't; I am too tired and have done enough.' Yesterday's sermon gave me a spur, and this morning I have writ the President a long letter, to the effect desired. God grant that it may have some result!"

"*July 17.* I despaired of being able to write a poem as requested for the Kansas semi-centennial celebration in October, but one line came to me: 'Sing us a song of the grand old time!' and the rest followed. . . ."

This poem is printed in "At Sunset."

"*July 21.* Writ . . . to Mrs. Martha J. Hosmer, of Rock Point, Oregon, who wrote me a kindly meant letter, exhorting me to 'seek the truth and live,' and to write to a Mrs. Helen Wilman, eighty-five years old and the possessor of some wonderful knowledge which will help me to renew my youth. . . ."

"*September 25.* I could not go to church to-day, fearing to increase my cold, and not wishing to leave my dear family, so rarely united now. Have been reading Abbé Loisy's 'Autour d'un petit Livre,' which is an apologetic vindication of his work 'L'Évangile et l'Église,' which has been put upon the Index [Expurgatorius]. I feel sensibly all differences between dollars' worth of sweet cake and a bottled ocean of weak beer formed the principal items of the bill, as brought to us. The friends came at 5 P.M., to decorate the room with flowers, also to arrange two tables, on one of which *las dulces* were arrayed, while the other was made to display a suspicious-looking group of glasses. A band, we were told, would be indispensable. We demurred at this, having intended to musicate upon our own grand piano. Hearing, however, that the band could be had for the sum of twelve dollars, we gave in on this point.

"One long room runs the whole length of one side of the palace, and serves us at once for dining and reception room. A long corridor encounters this room at right angles, entirely open to the weather, on one side. These two spaces constitute all our resources for receiving company. We lit them with Downer's best [kerosene] and ranged rows of rocking-chairs, opposite to each other, after the manner of this country, and also of Cuba.

"The company began to arrive at 8 P.M. The young ladies were mostly attired in colored tarlatans, prettily trimmed with lace and flowers. Some of them were not over fourteen years of age. All were quite youthful in their appearance, and unaffected in their manners. The young men, mostly employed in the various shops of the city, were well-dressed and polite. The band was somewhat barbaric in its aspect. A violin, a 'cello, a tambourine, and a clarinet. The clarinet-player was of uncommon size, with wild, dark eyes, which seemed to dilate as he played. . . .

"The dancing continued with little interruption until nearly 2 A.M. We were told that it is often continued till daylight. From time to time an attack was made upon the two tables. But the enjoyment of the good things provided was quite moderate compared with the cramming of a first-class party in Boston or New York. The guests were of many shades, as to color, although the greater number would have passed for white people, anywhere. Some of the handsomest among them were very dark. One young man reminded us of Edwin Booth in "Othello." . . . None of these people look like the mulattoes in the North. The features and the fibre appear finer, and the jet-black hair often suggests an admixture of Indian blood. The difference of social position shows itself in the manners of these people. The cruel colorphobia has never proscribed them. They have no artificial sense of inferiority, but take themselves as God made them, and think that if He is content with their complexions, mankind at large may be so.

"We were much pleased with our party, and with the simple and unaffected gayety of our guests. It was really a party in the open air, one whole side of our ballroom being unenclosed, save by the infrequent colonnade. We looked from the dancers to the stars, and back again to the dancers. It was all fairylike and dreamlike. The favorite '*dansa*' much resembles, not a ballet, but a stage dance, such as is introduced in the course of the drama. The beer flowed, and the couples flew. One innovation we introduced, a Virginia reel, which the clever clarinet-player caught and accom-

Richards son-in-law, when in the late afternoon Rosalind told me that dear noble Ednah Cheney had died. This caused me much distress. My first word was: 'The house of God is closed! Such a friend is indeed a sanctuary to which one might retire for refuge from all mean and unworthy things.'

"A luminous intellect, unusual powers of judgment and of sympathy as well. She has been a tower of strength to me. I sent word by telephone to Charles G. Ames, begging that *her* hymn might be sung at church to-morrow. . . ."

"*November 21.* Dear E. D. C.'s funeral. . . . I spoke of her faith in immortality, which I remember as unwavering. I said: 'No, that lustrous soul is not gone down into darkness. It has ascended to a higher light, to which our best affections and inspirations may aspire.'"

"*December 25.* . . . Got out my dearest little Sammy's picture and placed it on my mantelshelf. [He was a Christmas child.] Maud and I went to the Oratorio, which we enjoyed. . . . I wondered whether the heavenly ones could not enjoy the beautiful music."

"*December 31.* A little festivity. . . . At supper I was called upon for a toast, and after a moment's thought, responded thus: —

> "God grant us all to thrive,
> And for a twelvemonth to be alive,
> And every bachelor to wive;
> And many blessings on the head
> Of our dear Presidential Ted.

"We saw the year out; a year of grace to me, if ever I had one."

elevation of the Host a perfect Babel. Music, 'Ernani,' 'Fra Diavolo,' with some similar things. A single trumpet shrieked at some high moments. The bells rang like a thousand tin pans. Orchestra and chorus not together and both out of tune. The ceremony otherwise perhaps as well as usual. A priest made a brief address in Spanish, praising the day and complimenting the President. . . ."

"Studied Baur, Aristophanes, and '*Etudes sur la Bible.*' Music lesson to Maud. O'Sullivan to dine. . . . Baez sent word that he would visit us between 5 and 6 P.M. We accordingly put things in the best order possible under the circumstances. *Ung puo de tualetta* for the ladies seemed proper. At dinner received Baez' card with a great dish of fine sapotes. Baez arrived. He speaks French quite tolerably, is affable, and has an intelligent face; in fact looks like a person of marked talent. We talked of things in the United States. He has made fourteen voyages to Europe. . . . I sang '*Una Barchetta*' for him. He came with one servant, who stayed outside — no ceremony and no escort. . . ."

After the beauty of the place — indeed possibly before it — she valued the opportunity that came to her of preaching. On the voyage to Santo Domingo she had learned of a shepherdless flock of colored Protestants, their minister dead, their "elder" disabled by lameness. Here was an opportunity not to be lost. She engaged to hold Sunday evening services in their church, a small wooden building with a mud floor and a mahogany pulpit. The "Reminiscences" describe these services; the tattered hymn-books whose leaves

Tom's Cabin," and worked hard over it. The pace began to tell.

She spoke for the friends of Russian freedom, "a warm speech, almost without preparation. I knew that I should find my inspiration in the occasion itself. I had almost a spasm of thankfulness to Almighty God for the opportunity to speak for such a cause at such a time."

At the suffrage hearing soon after, she "spoke of the force of inertia as divinely ordained and necessary, but ordained, too, to be overcome by the onward impulse which creates worlds, life, and civilization. Said it was this inertia which opposed suffrage, the *dread* of change inherent in masses, material or moral, etc., etc."

Among her winter delights were the "Longy" concerts of instrumental music. She writes of one: —

"Was carried away by the delight of the music — all wind instruments.. A trio of Handel for bassoon and two oboes was most solid and beautiful. . . . I could think of nothing but Shakespeare's 'Tempest' and 'Midsummer Night's Dream.' The thought that God had set all human life and work to music over-powered me, and coming home I had a rhapsody of thanksgiving for the wonderful gift. . . ."

The next day came an entertainment in aid of Atlanta University and Calhoun School; she "enjoyed this exceedingly, especially the plantation songs, which are of profoundest pathos, mixed with overpowering humor. It was pleasant, too, to see the audience in which descendants of the old anti-slavery folk formed quite a feature. I had worked hard at the screed which

MRS. HOWE
From a photograph by Underwood, 1905

out its difficulties, is so much better to me in remembrance than anything else I have done here that I must make a little break and pause before I speak of other things.

"In this pause I remember my prayer at Puerto Plata, that I and mine might come to this new region with a reverent and teachable spirit. That prayer was an earnest one to me. I hope it has, as all prayers should, accomplished its own fulfilment. I have been here among dear people. I find all the human varieties in this society, not digested and harmonized by noble culture, but existing and asking for the centralizing and discriminating agencies which in civilization sort out the different tastes, characters, and capacities, and assign to each its task, giving devotion its wings and crime its treadmill. This little population in a great country, a country in which Nature allows no one to starve, has lived and so shown its right to live and maintain itself. It has accomplished its political division from a state antipathetic to it, having its dark face turned fixedly towards barbarism [Hayti].

"I stood in a little church in the city and island of Santo Domingo, to preach the glad tidings of the gospel of Peace. It was a humble little temple, with a mud floor, and plastered walls, and a roof which scarcely kept out the rain, but it was a place full of comfort to me and to others. The seats and spaces were all filled, for it had no aisles. The small windows and doors were cushioned, so to speak, with human countenances, wearing an expression of curiosity or attention. The way to the church was lined on both sides with the presented me with a fine bouquet of white carnations with blue and white ribbons, the colors of Greece. Sanborn read from dear Chev's letters of 1825. Michael spoke at great length, with great vehemence and gesticulation. I understood many words, but could only guess at the general drift. I imagine that it was very eloquent, as he was much applauded."

"*April 30.* Lorin Deland called to talk about the verses which I am to write and read at his theatre. The thought of Cassandra seized me. She, coming to the house of the Atridæ, had a vision of its horrors; I, coming to this good theatre, have a vision of the good things which have been enjoyed there and which shall still be enjoyed. Wrote down some five or six lines, 'lest I forget.'"

Mr. and Mrs. Deland were among her best friends of the second generation. Indeed, there was such a sympathy and comprehension between her and "Margaret" that the latter playfully declared herself a daughter abandoned in infancy, and was wont to sign herself, "Your doorstep Brat"!

"*May 5.* . . . 'Without religion you will never know the real beauty and glory of life; you will perceive the discords, but miss the harmony; will see the defects, but miss the good in all things.'"

In these years an added burden was laid upon her, in the general and affectionate desire for her presence on all manner of occasions. The firemen must have her at their ball, the Shoe and Leather Trade at their banquet, the Paint and Oils Association at their din-

wretched baby of six months, he in a muslin gown and
nothing else, crying with cold. I got out a cotton flannel dressing-sack, and wrapped him up in it and tended
him a good deal. . . .

"May the purpose for which I undertake this painful and solitary journey be ever strong enough in my
thoughts to render every step of it pure, blameless and
worthy. Great God, do not let me desert thee! For
that is the trouble. Thou dost not desert us. I dread
unspeakably these dark days of suffering and confusion. To go is like being hanged. . . ."

"Captain said something about my preaching on
Sunday, so I have been laying out some points for a
sermon. . . . But it is not very likely that the Captain
will really ask me to hold service.

"Talk with purser about Homer. He has a vivacious
mind, and might easily learn Greek, or anything else he
would have a mind to."

"*Sunday.* It turned out that the Captain and passengers did wish me to hold a little service to-day, so
at 10.30 A.M. I met them in the dining-saloon. I had a
Bible, from which I read the 116th Psalm — a prayer
followed — then the missionary hymn, 'From Green-
land's icy mountains' — then my little sermon, of
which I have the headings. I am so very glad to have
been able and enabled to do this.

"Began to teach the purser to read from notes with
a leaf of music out of some periodical. Copied Baur a
little — talked and heard much talk."

"*April 17.* . . . Expect to get in to-morrow, not very
late, unless another contrary gale. Frigate birds and

used the words 'tasks' and 'erect' as if they rhymed. This troubled me a good deal. My prayer was, 'God help the fool.'"

"*May 20.* My trouble of mind about the deficient verse woke me at 6.30 A.M. I tossed about and wondered how I could lie still until 7.30, my usual time for rising. The time passed somehow. I could not think of any correction to make in my verse. Hoped that I should find that I had not written it as I feared. When I came to look at it, there it was. Instantly a line with a proper rhyme presented itself to my mind. To add to my trouble I had lost the address to which I had sent the poem. My granddaughter, Julia Richards, undertook to interview the Syndicate by long-distance telephone, and, failing this, to telegraph the new line for me. So I left all in her hands. When I returned, she met me with a smile and said, 'It is all right, Grandmother.' She had gone out, found a New York directory, guessed at the Syndicate, got the correspondent, and put her in possession of the new line. I was greatly relieved. I have been living lately with work running after me all the time. Must now have a breathing spell. Have still my 'Simplicity' screed to complete."

The Authors' Club celebrated her eighty-sixth birthday by a charming festival, modelled on the Welsh Eistedfodd, "at which every bard of that nation brought four lines of verse — a sort of four-leaved clover — to his chief." [1] Sixty quatrains made what

[1] T. W. Higginson, *The Outlook*, January 26, 1907.

besetting sin, as it shows one must have had an ancestor from whom it was inherited!" She enjoyed a jewel as she did a flower or a song: she loved to deck her dear ones and herself with trinkets; a jeweller's window was a thing of delight to her, not to be passed without the tribute of a pause and a glance at its treasures. Yet a purchase of this kind seldom failed to bring its retributive pang the day after.

"Was sorry to have made so foolish a use of the money. Resolve never to do so again, unless some new light should make it seem right. God will not have my mind occupied with such nonsense. . . . Have written my sermon for to-morrow evening."

They spent two months in Samana in almost absolute retirement. The Doctor read "Don Quixote" in Spanish, she Aristotle in Greek and Baur in German. The former "was early and late in the saddle, and dashed up and down the steep hillsides of Samana with all his old fearlessness." The latter followed as she might, "in perils and dangers, in terrors often."

"I had never been a bold rider, and I must confess that I suffered agonies of fear in following him on these expeditions. If I lagged behind, he would cry, 'Come on! it's as bad as going to a funeral to ride with you.' And so, I suppose, it was. I remember one day when a great palm branch had fallen across our path. I thought that my horse would certainly slip on it, sending me to the depths below. That very day, while Dr. Howe took his siesta, I went to the place where this impediment lay, and with a great effort threw it over the steep mountain-side. The whole neighborhood

MRS. HOWE'S REPLY

Why, bless you, I ain't nothing, nor nobody, nor much,
If you look in your Directory, you'll find a thousand such;
I walk upon the level ground, I breathe upon the air,
I study at a table, and reflect upon a chair.

I know a casual mixture of the Latin and the Greek,
I know the Frenchman's *parlez-vous*, and how the Germans speak;
Well can I add, and well subtract, and say twice two is four,
But of those direful sums and proofs remember nothing more.

I wrote a pretty book one time, and then I wrote a play,
And a friend who went to see it said she fainted right away.
Then I got up high to speculate upon the Universe,
And folks who heard me found themselves no better and no worse.

Yes, I've had a lot of birthdays and I'm growing very old,
That's why they make so much of me, if once the truth were told.
And I love the shade in summer, and in winter love the sun,
And I'm just learning how to live, my wisdom's just begun.

Don't trouble more to celebrate this natal day of mine,
But keep the grasp of fellowship which warms us more than wine.
Let us thank the lavish hand that gives world beauty to our eyes,
And bless the days that saw us young, and years that make us wise.

"*May 27.* My eighty-sixth birthday. I slept rather late, yesterday having been eminently a 'boot-and-saddle' day. . . . The Greeks, mostly working-people, sent me a superb leash of roses with a satin ribbon bearing a Greek inscription. My visitors were numerous, many of them the best friends that time has left me. T. W. H. was very dear. My dear ones of the household bestirred themselves to send flowers, according to my wishes, to the Children's Hospital and to Charles Street Jail."

"*May 28.* . . . A great box of my birthday flowers ornamented the pulpit of the church. They were to be

board the Dominican war schooner. I went in the boat
and found Chev in the custom-house with the commission seated around. A good many of our people present. Chev read his protest, which was strong and
simple. . . . We then went out of the building; the
employés of our Company marched up in their best
clothes, their hats stuck full of roses, and stood in order
on either side the flagstaff. The man ordered by the
commission lowered the flag. Just before, Chev got
our people to stand in a circle around him, made a
lovely little address. The old Crusader never appeared
nobler or better than on this occasion, when his beautiful chivalry stood in the greatest contrast to the barbarism and ingratitude which dictated this act. My
mind was full of cursing rather than blessing. Yet finding myself presently alone with the superseded flag I
laid my hand upon it and prayed that if I had power to
bless anything, my prayers might bless the good effort
which has been made here."

On April 2 she adds: "The blacks here say that the
taking down of our flag was like the crucifixion of our
Lord. We are assured that they would have offered
forcible resistance, if we had authorized their so doing."

"*May 9*. The last day of our last week in Samana.
. . . God knows when I shall have so much restful leisure again. My rides on horseback, too, are ended for
the present, though I may mount once more to-day or
to-morrow. All these pleasures have been mixed with
pains — my fear on horseback . . . but far more than
all, my anxiety about the dearest ones at home. The
affairs of the Company, too, have given me many sad

"*July 1. Oak Glen.* . . . . Found a typed copy of my 'Rest' sermon, delivered in our own church, twelve years ago. Surely preaching has been my greatest privilege and in it I have done some of my best work."

"*July 2.* Unusually depressed at waking. Feared that I might be visited by 'senile melancholia' against which I shall pray with all my might. . . . Began Plato's 'Laws.'"

Plato seems to have acted as a tonic, for on the same day she writes to her daughter-in-law, expressing her joy in "Harry's" latest honor, the degree of Doctor of Laws conferred by Harvard College: —

To Mrs. Henry Marion Howe

OAK GLEN, July 2, 1905.

Thanks very much for your good letter, giving me such a gratifying account of the doings at Harvard on Commencement Day. I feel quite moved at the thought of my dear son's receiving this well-merited honor from his *alma mater*. It shows, among other things, how amply he has retrieved his days of boyish mischief. This is just what his dear father did. I think you must both have had a delightful time. How did our H. M. H. look sitting up in such grave company? I hope he has not lost his old twinkle. I am very proud and glad. . . .

She was indeed proud of all her son's honors; of any success of child or grandchild; yet she would pretend to furious jealousy. "I see your book is praised, Sir!" (or, "Madam!") "It probably does not deserve it.

H'm! nobody praises *my* books!" etc., etc. And all the
time her face so shining with pleasure and tenderness
under the sternly bended brows that the happy child
needed no other praise from any one.

"*July 23.* . . . I feel to-day the isolation consequent
upon my long survival of the threescore and ten ap-
portioned as the term of human life. Brothers and
sisters, friends and fellow-workers, many are now in
the silent land. I am praying for some good work, paying work, so that I may efficiently help relatives who
need help, and good causes whose demand for aid is
constant. . . ."

"*July 24.* To-day Harry and Alice Hall have left
me with their two dear children. I have had much delight with baby Frances, four months old. . . . I pray
that I may be able to help these children. I looked forward to their visit as a kindness to them and their
parents, but it has been a great kindness to me. . . ."

"*September 5.* Some bright moments to-day. At
my prayer a thought of the divine hand reaching down
over the abyss of evil to rescue despairing souls! . . ."

"*September 19.* Dear Flossy and Harry left. I shall
miss them dreadfully. She has taken care of me these
many weeks and has been most companionable and
affectionate. My dear boy was as ever very sweet
and kind. . . ."

" *September 22.* Have puzzled much about my promised screed for the 'Cosmopolitan' on 'What would be
the Best Gift to the People of the Country?' As I got
out of bed it suddenly occurred to me as 'the glory of
having promoted recognition of human brotherhood.'

This must include 'Justice to Women.' I meant to tackle the theme at once, but after breakfast a poem came to me in the almost vulgar question, 'Does your Mother know you're out?' I had to write this, also a verse or two in commemoration of Frederic L. Knowles, a member of our Authors' Club, who has just passed away."

"*September 25.* . . . I must have got badly chilled this morning, for my right hand almost refuses to guide the pen. I tried several times to begin a short note to David Hall, but could not make distinct letters. Then I forced myself to pen some rough draft and now the pen goes better, but not yet quite right. I had the same experience last winter once. I suppose that I have overtired my brain; it is a warning. . . ."

"*October 5.* . . . I had a moment of visioning, in which I seemed to see Christ on the cross refusing to drink the vinegar and gall, and myself to reach up a golden cup containing 'the love pledge of humanity.' Coming home I scrawled the verses before lying down to rest." [1]

"*October 9.* After a week of painful anxiety I learn to-day that my screed for the 'Cosmopolitan' is accepted. I felt so persuaded to the contrary that I delayed to open the envelope until I had read all my other letters. . . ."

"*October 25.* Meeting of Boston Authors' Club. . . . Worked all the morning at sorting my letters and papers. . . . Laura, Maud, and I drove out to Cam-

---

[1] These verses are printed in *At Sunset*, under the title of "Humanity," and at the head of chapter xi of this volume.   2

nurse dear Flossy. My mind is strangely divided between my dear work and my dear child and grandchild.
I must try to keep along with both, but on no account
to neglect the precious grandchild."

"*October 1.* O year! thou art running low. The last
trimester."

"*October 2.* This day, thirty-two years ago, my dearest brother Henry died in my arms, the most agonizing
experience. Never again did Death so enter into my
heart, until my lovely son of three years departed many
years later, leaving a blank as sad and bitter. Henry
was a rare and delicate person. . . . His life was a most
valuable one to us for help and counsel, as well as
for affection. Perhaps no one to-day thinks about his
death except me, his junior by two years, wearing now
into the decline of life. Dear brother, I look forward
to the reunion with you, but wish my record were
whiter and brighter."

"*October 5.* Boston. Came up for directors' meeting
of New England Woman's Club. Went afterward to
Mrs. Cheney's lecture on English literature. . . . A
suggestive and interesting essay, which I was glad to
hear and have others hear. It gave me a little pain,
that, though she pleasantly alluded to me as one who
has laid aside the laurel for the olive branch, she said
nothing whatever about my writings, which deserve
to be spoken of in characterizing the current literature
of the day; but she perhaps does not read or like my
works, and besides, people think of me nowadays more
as an active woman's woman than as a literary character, as the phrase is. All life is full of trial, and when I

CHAPTER XIV

"THE SUNDOWN SPLENDID AND SERENE"

1906–1907; *aet.* 87–88

HYMN FOR THE INTERNATIONAL CONGRESS OF RELIGIOUS LIBERALS

Held in Boston, 1907

Hail! Mount of God, whereon with reverent feet
The messengers of many nations meet;
Diverse in feature, argument, and creed,
One in their errand, brothers in their need.

Not in unwisdom are the limits drawn
That give far lands opposing dusk and dawn;
One sun makes bright the all-pervading air,
One fostering spirit hovers everywhere.

So with one breath may fervent souls aspire,
With one high purpose wait the answering fire.
Be this the prayer that other prayers controls, —
That light divine may visit human souls.

The worm that clothes the monarch spins no flaw,
The coral builder works by heavenly law;
Who would to Conscience rear a temple pure
Must prove each stone and seal it, sound and sure.

Upon one steadfast base of truth we stand,
Love lifts her sheltering walls on either hand;
Arched o'er our head is Hope's transcendent dome,
And in the Father's heart of hearts our home.

J. W. H.

"I PRAY for many things this year. For myself, I ask continued health of mind and body, work, useful, honorable, remunerative, as it shall please God to send; for my dear family, work of the same description with comfortable wages, faith in God, and love to each other; for my country, that she may keep her high promise to mankind; for Christendom, that it may become more Christ-like; for the struggling nationalities, that they may attain to peace and justice."

"Such a wonderful dream in the early morning. I was in some rural region alone; the clear blue sky was over my head. I looked up and said, 'I am fed from God's table. I am sheltered under His roof.' While I still felt this joy, a lone man, passing by, broke into a complaint on the hardness of things. I wanted in my dream to call him back, but he passed too rapidly. I still see in my 'mind's eye' that blue sky and the lone man passing by, I still recall the thrill of that meditation, literally in Dreamland, as I was quite asleep when it visited me. . . ."

The great event of this winter was a trip to Baltimore for a Woman Suffrage Convention.

"*February 4.* I had not been able to think of anything to say in Baltimore, but this morning it seemed to come to me. I have just written out my screed, . . . taking a point of view which I do not think I have presented before, viz.: that inferior education and restricted activity made women the inferiors of men, as naturally as training, education, and free agency make civilized men the superior of the savage. I think that the dear Lord gave me this screed, which is short and simple enough, but, I think, convincing. . . ."

This Convention came near being her last. Tonsillitis was epidemic in the city; the halls were draughty; at one meeting a woman with a severe cold, a stranger,

kissed her effusively. She took the infection, was prostrated for some days, and made the return journey
while still too weak to travel. Florence, who was with
her, protested in vain. "I would go," she said, "*if the
hearse was at the door!*" A serious illness followed on
her return. A month and more passed before she
began to regain strength and spirits.[1]

"*March 31.* Had a happy lighting up when I lay
down for afternoon rest. Felt the immensity of God's
goodness and took heart for the future."

In April she records "a delightful visit from Robert
Collyer, accompanied by Annie Fields. I asked him:
'Robert, what is religion?' He replied, 'To love God
with all one's heart, Christ helping us.' He began his
prayer last Sunday thus: 'Our Father who art in
heaven, on earth, and in hell!'"

On April 13, she was "out for the first time since
February 14, when I returned sick from Baltimore. . . ."

Another week and she was at her church, for the first
time since January 18.

It had been a long and weary time, yet one remembers not so much the suffering and confinement as the
gayety of it. There was a sigh for the Journal, but for
the family, and the faithful nurse, —

"Quips and cranks, and wanton wiles,
Nods and becks, and wreathéd smiles."

This nurse was known to others as Lucy Voshell,
but her patient promptly named her "Wollapuk."

[1] It may be noted that this epidemic of tonsillitis was actually fatal to
Miss Susan B. Anthony, who never recovered from the illness contracted
in Baltimore.

She was as merry as she was skillful, and the two made much fun together. Even when the patient could not speak, she could twinkle. As strength gradually returned, the ministrations of Wollapuk became positively scenes of revelry; and the anxious guardian below, warding off would-be interviewers or suppliants, might be embarrassed to hear peals of laughter ringing down the stair.

Early in May she has "young J. W. Hurlburt to dine; a pleasant young playwright, grandson to General Hurlburt of the Civil War. . . ."

"I had lent my play of 'Hippolytus' to young Hurlburt to read. He brought it back yesterday with so much praise of parts of it as to revive the pang which I felt when, Charlotte Cushman and Edwin Booth having promised to fill the principal parts, the manager's wife suddenly refused to fill her part, and the whole fell through. This with much other of my best literary work has remained a dead letter on my own shelves. I am glad as well as sad to feel that it deserved better treatment."

She had a wheel-chair, and on pleasant days it was her delight to be wheeled through the Public Garden, now in full May beauty, to see the flowers and the children. She was able to attend several meetings, and to write several papers.

"*May 18.* Have read part of the recital of Anna Ticknor's achievement in her society to encourage studies at home. Her work is really heroic. I wish that I had better understood it. Still I did admire it a great deal, but had little idea of the great benevolence and sympathy developed in her work, which was a godsend to thousands of women."

"*May 26.* My dear son arrived in the evening to celebrate my birthday. He seems well and happy. I was thankful to see him. Flowers kept arriving all day."

"*May 27.* Attended church and carried some of my birthday flowers for the pulpit. . . . In the afternoon a beautiful reception which the rain kept from being the over-crowd which I had rather feared. Colonel Higginson came and gave me some lovely verses written for the occasion. William R. Thayer did likewise. Arthur Upson had already sent me some. I enjoyed it all very much; dined downstairs with my dear family, who drank my health standing. H. M. H., being called upon for a word, said, 'The dear old girl!' and could not have said better. I thanked and blessed them all. We passed the evening together. The Greeks of Boston sent splendid red roses and ribbons with motto. The Italians sent flowers."

After this she wrote an essay on "How to Keep Young," in which she says: —

"Try to keep in touch with the best spirits of your time, with those who are raising instead of lowering the tone of the atmosphere in which they live.

"Avoid the companionship of those who deride sacred things and are inclined to ignore the limits of refinement and good taste.

"Remember that ignoble amusements react upon character.

"Never forget that we grow like to that we contemplate.

"Keep it always in mind that it must be through our own efforts that our progress through life shall bring with it the fulfilment of the best promise of our youth."

"*July 2. Oak Glen.* Nurse Voshell, nicknamed by me Wollapuk, left this morning. I have become so dependent upon her that I shall miss her very much. I have been impatient of having her so long, but now see how very helpful she has been to me.

"I began to write a retrospect of my essay on 'Distinctions between Philosophy and Religion,' but feel that this will be of little value. Oh! that I had taken Dr. Hedge's advice and published these papers soon after they were written. As it is I have lost two of the best of them, viz.: this one just mentioned and 'Moral Triangulation of the Third Party,' in obligations and contrasts."

In these days she met with a grave loss in the death of Michael Anagnos.

"I am deeply grieved at his death, which is a real loss to me and my family, and almost irreparable to the Institution which he has served nobly with entire devotion and disinterest and has enriched by his great and constant efforts. He built three Kindergartens for the blind. God rest his soul!

"I pray that my great pain at the death of my son-in-law may inspire me to help the blind as I never have helped them!"

"My strength has failed so much of late that my strong love of life begins to waver. I should be glad to live to print some of my studies in Philosophy, and to have some of my musical compositions taken down by dictation."

"*August 31.* . . . The last day of a summer which brought a serious grief in the death of Michael Anagnos, who, ever since my visit to Greece in 1867, has been an important factor in my life. I am much troubled in the effort to compose a poem to be read at the memorial services to be held for him in late October. . . ."

A photograph taken at this time shows her sitting in her hooded chair on the piazza, her Greek books and her canary beside her, a serene and lovely picture. It was so she used to sit every morning. First she read her Testament, and a prayer of James Martineau, or some other good saint; this she called "taking the altitude"; then she turned to her Æschylus or Aristotle.

Before thus settling down, there would be a walk on the piazza, or along the highway. Sheltered by a broad hat, the friend of many years, wrapped in the "passionate pilgrim," as she named a certain ancient purple cloak, leaning on her ebony stick — who that passed that way has not seen her? Bits of her talk, as we strolled together, come back to us; as when the clouds parted suddenly at the close of a gray day, then shutting in again. "Oh!" she cried, "it is like being engaged to the man you love, for five minutes!"

"*September 16.* . . . I had had much hesitation about

undertaking to speak at Shiloh Baptist Church [colored] this afternoon; but it came to me as something which I ought to do, and so I gave the promise, and, with some studying, wrote the sermon. The result fully justified the effort. I spoke to a large and very attentive congregation, in which a number of white outsiders were mingled in with the people of the church. . . . Mrs. Jeter sang my 'Battle Hymn,' the congregation joining in the 'Glory Hallelujah.' I then read my screed, which was heard with profound attention, one and another crying out at intervals, 'Amen!' and 'Glory be to God!' . . . I was very thankful for the good issue of what had seemed an almost wild undertaking at eighty-seven years of age."

"*October 23.* Have prayed and worked over the poem for Michael's memorial services — think that I have made it as good as I can, but not good enough. Alas! I am too old."

She went up to Boston for this meeting in Tremont Temple, which was a most impressive one, Greeks and Americans uniting to do honor to a good man.

"*October 24.* . . . I read my verse, my voice serving me very well. Bishop Lawrence helped me both to rise and to return to my seat. He made a most touching allusion to my dearest dear Julia's devotion to the blind, and said where a man was engaged in a noble work there usually rose up a noble woman to help him."

"*October 26.* Had a sudden blessed thought this morning, viz.: that the 'Tabernacle eternal in the heavens' is the eternity of truth and right. I naturally desire life after death, but if it is not granted me, I have yet a part in the eternal glory of this tabernacle."

"*October 29.* Dear H. M. H. left us this morning, after a short but very pleasant visit. He brought here his decorations of his Russian order to show us; they are quite splendid. He is the same dear old simple music- and mischief-loving fellow, very sensitive for others, very modest for himself, and very dear."

"*November 7.* . . . Prayed *hard* this morning that my strength fail not."

During this summer, an electric elevator had been put into the Boston house, and life was made much easier for her. From this time we became familiar with the vision of her that still abides, flitting up or down in her gilded car. Watching her ascent, clad in white, a smile on her lips, her hand waving farewell, one could only think of "The chariot of Israel and the horsemen thereof."

Another good gift was a Victor machine. When the after-dinner reading was over, she would say, "Now bring my opera-box!"

The white armchair was wheeled into the passage between the two parlors. Here she sat in state, while the great singers poured out their treasures before her, while violinist and pianist gave her their best. She listened with keen and critical enjoyment, recalling how Malibran gave this note, how Grisi and Mario sang that duet. Then she would go to the piano and play from memory airs from "Tancredi," "Il Pirata," "Richard Cœur de Lion," and other operas known to us only through her. Or she would — always without notes — play the "Barber of Seville" almost from beginning to end, with fingers still deft and nimble.

She loved the older operas best. After an air from "Don Giovanni," she would say, "Mozart must be in heaven: they could never get on without him!" She thought Handel's "Messiah" the most divine point reached by earthly music. Beethoven awed and swayed her deeply, and she often quoted his utterance while composing, "*Ich trat in der Nähe Gottes!*" She thrilled with tender pleasure over Verdi's "*Non ti scordar,*" or "*Ai nostri monti,*" and over "Martha." She enjoyed Chopin "almost too much." "He is exquisite," she would say, "but somehow — rotten!"

Among the pleasures of this winter was a visit to New York. She writes after it: —

"My last day in my dear son's house. He and Fannie have been devotedly kind to me. They made me occupy their room, much to my bodily comfort, but to the great disquiet of my mind, as I hated much to inconvenience them. My son has now a very eminent position. . . . God bless the house and all in it."

"*December 17.* The Old South Chapter of D.A.R.'s met in the real Old South Church; there was much good speaking. I recited my 'Battle Hymn' and boasted my descent from General Marion, the Swamp Fox, saying also, 'When, eluding the vigilance of children and grandchildren, I come to such a meeting as this, without a previous promise not to open my lips, I think that I show some of the dexterity of my illustrious relative.' I also had to spring up and tell them that my grandmother, niece to General Marion, gave

her flannel petticoat to make cartridges for the soldiers of the Revolution."

The path of the guardian (or jailer, as she sometimes put it) was not always plain. The wayfaring
woman might easily err therein.

After some severe fatigue, convention or banquet,
she might say, "This is the last time. Never let me do
this again!"

Thereupon a promise would be exacted and made.
The fatigue would pass and be forgotten, and the next
occasion be joyously prepared for.

"You told me not to let you go!" the poor jailer
would say.

"Oh, I did n't mean it!"

"But you promised!"

"That was two weeks ago. Two weeks is a long
time for me to keep a promise!"

If the jailer still persisted, she played her last card
and took the trick.

"I can't talk about it. You tire my head!"

Now and then Greek met Greek. One snowy afternoon she encountered the resident granddaughter,
cloaked and hooded, preparing to brave the storm.

"Dear child," said the grandmother, "I do not
often use authority with you young people, but this
time I must. I cannot allow you to go out in this
blizzard!"

"Dearest grandmother," replied the maiden, "*where
are you going yourself?*"

There was no reply. The two generations dissolved
in laughter, and started out together.

She bids farewell to 1906 as "dear Year that hast brought me so many comforts and pleasures!" and thus hails the New Year: —

"I earnestly pray for God's blessing on this year! . . . I might possibly like one more European journey to see the Gallery at Madrid, and the châteaux of Touraine, but I do not ask it, as I may have more important occupation for my time and money. . . . *Du reste*, the dear Father has done so much better for me, in many ways, than I have ingenuity to wish, that I can only say, 'Thy will be done, only desert me not.'"

She determines "at last to be more prompt in response to letters and bills. I am now apt to lose sight of them, to my great inconvenience and that of other people."

It was pain to her to destroy even a scrap of paper that bore writing: the drifts of notes and letters grew higher and higher among the piles of books, new and old. The books were not all her own choice. Many a firstling of verse found its way to her, inscribed with reverent or loving words by the author. Would Mrs. Howe send a few lines of appreciation or criticism? She would; mostly she did. She wrote in the autograph albums, and on the pieces of silk and cotton for "autograph quilts": she signed the photographs: she *tried* to do everything they asked.

"*January 11*. Having hammered at some verses for General Lee, when I lay down to rest a perfect flood of rhymes seized me. Nonsense verses for to-morrow's festival; there seemed to be no end to them. I scrawled some of them down as it was late and dark. Sanborn to dine — unexpected, but always welcome."

"*January 12.* Copied and completed my lines for the evening. Found a large assemblage of members and invited guests [of the Authors' Club]; a dais and chair prepared for me, Colonel Higginson standing on my right. Many presentations — Gilder and Clyde Fitch, Owen Wister, Norman Hapgood. Aldrich [T. B.] took me in to dinner and sat on my right, Hon. John D. Long on my left; next beyond A. sat Homans Womans.[1] I despaired of making my jingle tell in so large and unfamiliar a company. At last I took courage and read it, bad as I thought it. To my surprise, it told, and created the merriment which had been my object so far as I had any. My 'Battle Hymn' was sung finely by a male quartette. Colonel Higginson and I were praised almost out of our senses. A calendar, got up with much labor, was presented to each of us."

"*January 13.* To church, to take down my vanity after last evening's laudations. . . ."

"*January 15.* Made a final copy of my lines on Robert E. Lee, — read them to Rosalind — the last line drew a tear from each of us, so I concluded that it would do and sent it.

"To Tuesday Club, where the effort which I made to hear speakers tired my head badly. Themes: 'Whether and how to teach Ethics in Public Schools'; also, 'The English Education Bill.' Socrates having been mentioned as an exemplar, I suddenly cried out

---

[1] Mrs. Charles Homans.

that I thought he did wrong to stay and suffer by
unjust laws and popular superstition. A first-class
American would have got away and would have
fought those people to the bitter death. This fiery
little episode provoked laughter, and several privately
told me they were glad of it."

"*January 25.* . . . Read Colonel Higginson's account
of me in the 'Outlook.' Wrote him a note of thanks,
saying that he has written beautifully, with much tact
and kindness. It remains true that he has not much
acquaintance with the serious side of my life and character, my studies of philosophy, etc. He has described
what he has seen of me and has certainly done it with
skill and with a most kind intention."

She said of the Colonel's paper, " He does not realize that my *life* has been here, the four walls of my
room."

"*February 5.* . . . Began a sermon on the text, 'I
saw Satan like lightning fall from heaven.' . . ."

"*February 6.* Wrote a good bit on the sermon begun
yesterday — the theme attracts me much. If I give
it, I will have Whittier's hymn sung: 'Oh! sometimes
gleams upon our sight —'

"Wrote to thank Higginson for sending me word
that I am the first woman member of the society of
American Authors. . . ."

"*February 14.* Luncheon at 3 Joy Street. . . . My
seat was between T. W. H. and President Eliot, with
whom I had not spoken in many years. He spoke to
me at once and we shook hands and conversed very
cordially. I had known his father quite well — a lover

of music, who had much to do with the early productions of Beethoven's Symphonies in Boston, collecting
money in aid of the undertaking. President Eliot made
a good speech for Berea; others followed. . . . When
my name was called, I had already a good thought to
express."

"*February 18.* To N.E.W.C., where Colonel Higginson and I spoke of Longfellow; I from long and intimate acquaintance, he from a literary point of view.
He said, I thought rightly, that we are too near him
to be able to judge his merits as a poet; time must test
them."

"*February 27.* . . . In evening went with the Jewett
sisters to the celebration of Longfellow's Centennial.
I had copied my verses written for the first Authors'
Reading *in re* Longfellow, rather hoping that I might
be invited to read them. This did not happen. I had
had no reason to suppose that it would, not having
been thereunto invited. Had a seat on the platform
among the poet's friends, myself one of the oldest of
them. It seemed as if I could hardly hold my tongue,
which, however, I did. I remembered that God has
given me many opportunities of speaking my thoughts.
If He withheld this one I am bound to suppose it was
for the best. I sat on the platform, where Sarah Jewett
and I were the only women in the charmed circle.

"Item. The audience rose and greeted me as I
ascended to the platform at Sanders Theatre."

She could not bear to be "left out"; indeed, she
rarely was. In this one respect she was, perhaps, the
"spoiled child" that she sometimes called herself.

March brought a new pleasure, in seeing and meeting Novelli, the great Italian actor.

"*March 14.* The banquet of the Circolo at Lombardy Inn. . . . My seat was at the head of the table with Novelli on my right and Tosti, the consul, on my left. Had some pleasant talk with each. Then I had a good inspiration for part of my speech, in which I mentioned the egg used by Columbus, and made to stand, to show that things held to be impossible often proved possible. I said that out of this egg 'was hatched the American Eagle.' Madame Novelli shed tears at this, and Novelli kissed my hand. The Italian servants listened eagerly to all the speaking, and participated in the applause. President Geddes, Secretary Jocelyn, and others spoke well and rather briefly. Dear Padre Roberto was really eloquent."

"*March 16.* . . . In the evening to see Novelli in 'Morte Civile'; his personation wonderfully fine, surpassing even Salvini in the part. . . ."

"*March 17.* . . . Went to South Boston to say a word at the presentation of dear Michael's portrait to the Perkins Institution by the Howe Memorial Club. . . . Also had a wonderful fit of verse — wrote two sonnets to Dante and a versification of my conceit about the hatching of the American Eagle from the egg of Columbus."

"*March 23.* A 'boot-and-saddle' day. . . . I found that my Authors' Club will meet to-day in Cambridge. Higginson telephoned, asking me to speak of Aldrich; I asked permission to leave the College Club after the speaking. Ordered a carriage at 4.30, sprang into it,

and reached the Authors' meeting in good time to say
something about Aldrich. . . . Found a man who has
studied the Berber races in Africa. Had a good talk
with him. Came home dreadfully tired. To bed by
9.30. At the College Club I said that to give women
the vote in this State would not double the illiterate
vote — proposed a census of comparative illiteracy of
the sexes in Massachusetts at least."

We had long besought her to have her musical
compositions written down, and now this was done in
part. Once or twice a week Mr. John M. Loud came
to the house and took down her melodies, she singing
and playing them to him. She always enjoyed the
hour with the young composer. A number of the
melodies thus preserved were published in a "Song
Album" by G. Schirmer some months later.

"*April 8*. Great trouble of mind about attending the
Peace Convention in New York, which I have promised to do. Laura dead against it, reinforced by Wesselhoeft, Sr., who pronounces it dangerous for me. I at
last wrote to ask my dear minister about it."

"*April 9*. . . . A violent snowstorm keeps me at
home. Minister and wife write, 'Don't go to Peace
Convention.' I asked God in my prayer this morning
to make going possible or impossible for me. I took
C. G. A.'s letter as making it impossible, as I had
decided to abide by his decision. Wrote a letter of explanation to Anna Garlin Spencer. I am much disappointed, but it is a relief not to cause Laura such painful anxiety as she would have felt if I had decided to

go. She wept with joy when I gave it up. We had a very pleasant dinner party for the Barrett Wendells with their friends, Professor Ames, of Berkeley University, California, 'Waddy' Longfellow, Charles Gibson, Laura, Betty, and I."

She sent a letter to the Convention, which was read by Florence. In this, after recalling her Peace Crusade of 1872, she said: —

"Here and there, a sisterly voice responded to my appeal, but the greater number said: 'We have neither time nor money that we can call our own. We cannot travel, we cannot meet together.' And so my intended Peace Congress of Women melted away like a dream, and my final meeting, held in the world's great metropolis, did not promise to lead to any important result.

"What has made the difference between that time and this? New things, so far as women are concerned, viz.: the higher education conceded to them, and the discipline of associated action, with which later years have made them familiar. Who shall say how great an element of progress has existed in this last clause? Who shall say what fretting of personal ambition has become merged in the higher ideal of service to the State and to the world? The noble army of women which I saw as a dream, and to which I made my appeal, has now come into being. On the wide field where the world's great citizens band together to uphold the highest interests of society, women of the same type employ their gifts and graces to the same end. Oh, happy change! Oh, glorious metamorphosis! In less than half a century the conscience of mankind has made its greatest stride toward the control of human affairs. The women's colleges and the women's clubs have had everything to do with the great advance which we see in the moral efficiency of our sex. These two agencies have been derided and decried, but they have done their work.

"If a word of elderly counsel may become me at this moment, let me say to the women here assembled: Do not let us go back from what we have gained. Let us, on the contrary, press ever forward in the light of the new knowledge, of the new experience. If we have rocked the cradle, if we have soothed the slumbers of mankind, let us be on hand at their great awakening. to make steadfast the peace of the world!"

She was glad afterward that she had not gone; but a significant corollary to the matter appears on April 25: —

"Providence — a pleasant trip, made possible by dear Laura's departure."

(That is, "dear Laura" knew nothing about it till afterward. How often we recalled the old Quaker's saying to her, "It was borne in upon me at an early period that if I told no one what I intended to do, I should be enabled to do it!")

In the last week of April ("dear Laura" being still absent) she spoke four times in public, on four successive days. These addresses were at the Kindergarten for the Blind ("I missed the snap which Michael's presence was wont to give; I spoke praise of him to the children, as one to be held in dear remembrance; to the visitors, as having left the public a sacred

legacy in these schools, which he created with so much
labor"), at Faneuil Hall, a meeting about Old Home
Week, at the West Newton High School, and at Providence. On the fifth day she was at the Wintergreen
Club, answering the question, "What is the Greatest
Evil of the Present Day?"—"False estimates of
values, vehement striving for what hinders rather than
helps our spiritual development."

After this bout she was glad to rest a day or two,
but in another week was ready for the Woman Suffrage
Festival. "I to open it, evening, Faneuil Hall. A day
of rushing. Lady Mary and Professor Gilbert Murray
to breakfast 9 A.M., which I much enjoyed. Then my
little music man, who took three tunes; then a snatch
at preparation for the evening's exercises. Jack and
Elizabeth Chapman in the afternoon. At 4.45 got a
little rest and sleep. At 5.40 drove to Faneuil Hall,
which I found not so full as sometimes. Thought miserably of my speech. Light to read it very dim. I
called to order, introduced Mr. White and the ladies'
quartette, then read my poor little scribble. . . . I was
thankful to get through my part, and my speech in
print was n't bad at all."

In May she preached at the Church of the Disciples.

"A culmination of anxiety for this day, desired
and yet dreaded. My head growled a little at waking,
but not badly. My voice seemed all right, but how
about the matter of my sermon? Was it all worth
while, and on Whitsunday too? I wore my white cashmere dress. Laura went with me to church. C. G. A.
was there. As he led me to the pulpit, the congregation

rose. The service was very congenial and calming to my anxiety. I read the sermon quite audibly from beginning to end. It was listened to with profound attention, if I may say so."

"*May 20. . . .* Marion Crawford arrived soon after three for a little visit. He looks greatly improved in health since I last saw him. He must have passed through some crisis and come out conqueror. He has all his old charm. . . ."

She was lamenting the death of her cousin and childhood playfellow, Dr. Valentine Mott Francis, when "a much greater affliction" fell upon her in the death of her son-in-law, David Prescott Hall. "This hurts me," she writes, "like a physical pain."

To Florence

OAK GLEN, July 3, 1907.

MY DEAREST DEAR FLOSSY, —

You are quite right in saying that we greatly need the consoling belief in a future life to help us bear the painful separation which death brings. Surely, the dear Christ believed in immortality, and promised it to faithful souls. I have myself derived great comfort from this belief, although I must confess that I know nothing about it. You may remember what [Downer] said to your dear father: "I don't know anything about it, but Jesus Christ certainly believed in immortality, and I pin my faith on him, and *run for luck*." . . . Alice and her trio of babes came safe to hand this morning. Frances at once began to spread the gravel from outdoors on the best staircase, but desisted when forbid-

den to do so. . . . Farewell, dearest child. You have
had a grievous loss, and will feel it more and more.
We must trust in God, and take our sorrows believing
in the loving fatherhood. Maud writes me that she
suffers an *irreparable* loss in dear David's death. . . .

Your loving
MOTHER.

Much work was on hand this summer: a poem for
Old Home Week in Boston, another for the Coopers-
town Centennial, a paper on the "Elegant Literature
of Fifty Years Since," one for the "Delineator" on
"The Three Greatest Men I Have Known." These
were Ralph Waldo Emerson, Theodore Parker, and
Dr. Howe. She spent much time and pains on this
article. She read Elliot Cabot's "Life of Emerson,"
which she thought "certainly a good piece of work,
but deficient, it seems to me, in the romantic sympathy
which is the true interpretation of Emerson and of all
his kind."

She "hammered" hard on the two poems, with good
results.

"*July 14.* I can hardly believe it, but my miserable
verses, re-read to-day, seemed quite possible, if I can
have grace to fill out their sketchiness. Last word to-
night: I think I have got a poem. *Nil desperandum!*"

"*July 24.* Difficult to exaggerate the record of my
worry this morning. I feel a painful uncertainty about
going to Boston to read my poem for Old Home
Week. Worse than this is my trouble about two
poems sent me while in Boston, with original music,

to be presented to the committee for Home Week, which I have entirely forgotten and neglected. To do this was far from my intention, but my old head fairly gave out in the confusion of the various occasions in which I was obliged to take an active part."

She yielded to entreaty and stayed at home, and was rewarded by "a most gratifying letter from Edward Everett Hale, telling me that Josiah Quincy read my poem with real feeling, and that it was warmly received."

"My prayer is answered. I have lived to see my dear girl again. . . . I give thanks earnestly and heartily, but seem for a time paralyzed by her presence."

With the early autumn came a great pleasure in a visit to the new "Green Peace," the house which her son had built at Bedford Hills, New York. She was delighted with the house and garden; the Journal tells of all manner of pleasant gayeties.

"*September 12.* Fannie had a luncheon party even pleasanter than yesterday's. Rev. Mr. Luquer is a grandson of Dominick Lynch, who used to come to my father's house in my childhood and break my heart by singing 'Lord Ullin's Daughter.' I remember creeping under the piano once to hide my tears. He sang all the Moore melodies with great expression. . . . This, his descendant, looks a good deal like him. Was bred a lawyer. My good Uncle Cutler twice asked him whether he would study for the ministry. He said, 'No.' My uncle said the second time, 'What shall it profit a man if he gain the whole world and lose his own soul?' This word, he told me, came back to him.

. . . Worked a good deal on my poem. At least thought and thought much, and altered a little."

This was the poem which prefaces this chapter and which was written for the forthcoming Unitarian Convention in Boston. She had been at work on it for some time, first "*trying to try for it,*" and later "hammering" and polishing with great care. "It came to me like a flash," she says, "but had to be much thought over and corrected." And again, "It was given to me something as was my 'Battle Hymn.' . . ."

"*October 25.* Wrote to a very bumptious child, thirteen years old, who proffers me her friendship and correspondence, claiming to have written poems and magazine contributions praised by 'noted authors.' I sent her back her letter, with three or four corrections and a little advice, kindly meant, but which may not be so taken. . . . She will probably turn and rend me, but I really felt it might do her good."

"*November 14. Gardiner.* A good meditation. The sense of God in the universe seems to be an attribute of normal humanity. We cannot think of our own personal identity without at the same time imagining a greater self from which we derive. This idea may be crude and barbarous, great minds have done much to make it otherwise; Christ most of all with His doctrine of divine love, providence, and forgiveness. The idea of a life beyond this one seems also to appertain to normal humanity. We had best accept this great endowment which philosophy seeks to analyze much as a boy will take a watch to pieces, but cannot put it together again so that it will work."

"*November 15.* Another long sitting and meditation. What have individual philosophers done for religion? As I recall what I could learn of the Kantian philosophy, I think that it principally taught the limitations of human knowledge, correcting thereby the assumptions of systems of thought and belief to *absolute* authority over the thinker and believer. He calls conscience 'the categorical imperative'; but that term in no wise explains either the origin or authority of the moral law. His rule of testing the rectitude of the act by the way in which, if it were made universal, it would affect the well-being of society, is useful, but simply pragmatic, not in William James's sense. The German idealism, the theory by which we evolve or create all that occupies our senses and our mind, appears to me a monstrous expanse of egotism. No doubt, dialectics serve as mental athletics, and speculative thought may be useful as an exercise of the mental powers; but processes which may be useful in this way might be very unfit to be held as permanent possessions of persuasion. It occurs to me that it might be more blessed to help the souls in hell than to luxuriate with saints in heaven."

"*November 20. Boston.* Began my screed on the 'Joys of Motherhood' for the 'Delineator.' Wrote *currente calamo.* . . ."

"*November 23.* Rather an off day. Found T. W. Higginson's little volume of verses, presented to me on my seventieth birthday, and read a good deal in it. When the Colonel gave it to me, he read a little poem, 'Sixty and Six,' very charmingly. Seems to me that I

ought to have read this little book through long before
this time. One of the sweetest poems in it is about
the blue-eyed baby that they lost after some six weeks'
happy possession. I sent a pretty little baby wreath
for it, feeling very sorry for them both."

"*November 28.* Much troubled about my Whittier
poem."

"*December 3.* Thanks be to God! I have written
my Whittier rhyme. It has cost me much labor, for I
have felt that I could not treat a memory so reverend
with cheap and easy verses. I have tried to take his
measure, and to present a picture of him which shall
deserve to live." [1]

Mr. and Mrs. Cobden-Sanderson, the English suffragists, were in Boston this winter. They dined with
her, and proved "very agreeable. Mrs. Sanderson's
visit ought to help suffrage mightily, she is in such
dead earnest for it. After dinner I proposed that
each one should name his favorite Browning poem.
I named 'Pippa,' Mrs. Sanderson 'Paracelsus,' Mr. S.,
'The Grammarian's Funeral,' etc., etc. The talk was
so good that we could not stop it to hear the Victor,
which I regretted."

Another delightful dinner of this winter was one
given in her honor by her niece, Mrs. Richard Aldrich
(Margaret Chanler), in New York. Among the guests
were Kneisel, the violinist, and Schelling, the pianist.
Mrs. Aldrich demanded "Flibbertigibbet," and our
mother played and recited it in such a manner that the

---

[1] This poem appears in *At Sunset.*

two musicians were inspired to play, as the people in
the story were to dance. Kneisel flew home for his
violin, Schelling sat down at the piano, and the two
played Bach for her and to her delight.

"The occasion was memorable!" she says.

Returning from New York, she was able to attend
the Whittier Centennial at Haverhill.

"*December 17.* ... Sanborn came to take me. ... I
have been praying to be well for this occasion, my
last public engagement for some weeks. I am thankful
to have been able, at my advanced age, to read this
poem at the Whittier Celebration and to be assured
by one present that I had never been in better voice,
and by others that I was generally heard without difficulty by the large audience."

"*December 31.* Oh, blessed year 1907! It has been
granted me to write four poems for public occasions,
all of which have proved acceptable; also three fatiguing magazine articles, which have for the time
bettered my finances. I have lived in peace and good-
will with all men, and in great contentment with my
own family, to which this year added a promising
little great-grandson, taking away, alas! my dear son-
in-law, David Prescott Hall. I found a very compe-
tent and friendly young musician who has taken down
nearly all my songs. ... A word was given me to
speak, namely, 'Thanks for the blessed, wonderful
year just past.'"

CHAPTER XV

SANTO DOMINGO

1872–1874; *aet.* 53–56

A PARABLE

"I sent a child of mine to-day;
    I hope you used him well."
"Now, Lord, no visitor of yours
    Has waited at my bell.

"The children of the Millionnaire
    Run up and down our street;
I glory in their well-combed hair,
    Their dress and trim complete.

"But yours would in a chariot come
    With thoroughbreds so gay;
And little merry maids and men
    To cheer him on his way."

"Stood, then, no child before your door?"
    The Lord, persistent, said.
"Only a ragged beggar-boy,
    With rough and frowzy head.

"The dirt was crusted on his skin,
    His muddy feet were bare;
The cook gave victuals from within;
    I cursed his coming there."

What sorrow, silvered with a smile,
    Slides o'er the face divine?
What tenderest whisper thrills rebuke?
    "The beggar-boy was mine!"

J. W. H.

WE must go back a little to tell another story.

In the winter of 1870–71 the Republic of Santo Domingo sent through its president an urgent request for annexation to the United States. President Grant our hearts. When she entered a room, all faces lighted up, as if she carried a lamp in her hand.

Day in, day out, she was the *Guter Camerad.* The desire *not to irritate* had become so much a second nature that she was the easiest person in the world to live with. If the domestic calm were disturbed, "*Don't say anything !*" was her word. "*Wait a little !*"

She might wake with the deep depression so often mentioned in the Journal. Pausing at her door to listen, one might hear a deep sigh, a plaintive ejaculation; but all this was put out of sight before she left her room, and she came down, as one of the grandchildren put it, "bubbling like a silver tea-kettle."

Then came the daily festival of breakfast, never to be hurried or "scamped." The talk, the letters, some of which we might read to her, together with the newspaper. We see her pressing some tidbit on a child, watching intently the eating of it, then, as the last mouthful disappeared, exclaiming with tragic emphasis, "*I wanted it !*" Then, at the startled face, would come peals of laughter; she would throw herself back in her chair, cover her face with her hands, and tap the floor with her feet.

"Look at her!" cried Maud. "*Rippling with sin !*"

How she loved to laugh!

"One day," says a granddaughter, "the house was overflowing with guests, and she asked me to take my nap on her sofa, while she took hers on the bed. We both lay down in peace and tranquillity, but after a while, when she thought I was asleep, I heard her laughing, until she almost wept. Presently she fell asleep, and slept her usual twenty minutes, to wake in the same gales of mirth. She laughed until the bed shook, but softly, trying to choke her laughter, lest I should wake.

"'What is it about?' I asked. 'What is so wonderful and funny?'

"'Oh, my dear,' she said, breaking again into laughter, 'it is nothing! It is the most ridiculous thing! I was only trying to translate " fiddle-de-dee " into Greek!'"

This was in her ninety-second year.

But we are still at the breakfast table. Sometimes there were guests at breakfast, a famous actor, a travelling scholar, caught between other engagements for this one leisure hour.

It was a good deal, perhaps, to ask people to leave a warm hotel on a January morning; but it was warm enough by the soft-coal blaze of the dining-room fire. Over the coffee and rolls, sausages and buckwheat cakes, leisure reigned supreme; not the poet's "retired leisure," but a friendly and laughter-loving deity. Everybody was full of engagements, harried with work, pursued by business and pleasure: no matter! the talk ranged high and far, and the morning was half gone before they separated.

Soon after breakfast came the game of ball, played *à deux* with daughter or grandchild; the ball was tossed back and forth, the players counting meanwhile up to ten in various languages. She delighted in adding to her vocabulary of numerals, and it was a good day when she mastered those of the Kutch-Kutch Esquimaux.

Then came the walk, gallantly taken in every weather save the very worst. She battled with the west wind, getting the matter over as quickly as might be. "*It is for my life!*" she would say. But on quiet, sunny days she loved to linger along Commonwealth Avenue, watching the parade of babies and little children, stopping to admire this one or chat with that.

This function accomplished, she went straight to her desk, and "P. T." reigned till noon. It was a less rigorous "P. T." than that of our childhood. She could break off in a moment now, give herself entirely, joyously, to the question of dinner for the expected guest, of dress for the afternoon reception, then drop back into Aristotle or Æschylus with a happy sigh. It was less easy to break off when she was writing; we might be begged for "half a moment," as if our time were fully as precious as her own; but there was none of the distress that interruption brought in earlier years. Perhaps she took her writing less seriously. She often said, "Oh, my dear, I am beginning to realize at last that I shall never write my book now, my Magnum Opus, that was to be so great!"

She practised her scales faithfully every day, through the later years. Then she would play snatches of forgotten operas, and the granddaughter would hear her — if she thought no one was near — singing the brilliant *arias* in "a sweet thread of a voice."

After her practising, if she were alone, she would sit at the window and play her Twilight Game: counting the "passing," one for a biped, two for a quadruped, ten for a white horse, and so on.

In the evening, before the "Victor" concert, came the reading aloud: this was one of her great pleasures. No history or philosophy for the evening reading; she must have a novel (not a "problem novel"; these she detested!) — a good stirring tale, with plenty of action in it. She thrilled over "With Fire and Sword," "Kim," "The Master of Ballantrae." She could not bear to hear of financial anxieties or of physical suffering. "It gives me a pain in my knee!"

We see her now, sitting a little forward in her straight-backed chair, holding the hand of the reading granddaughter, alert and tense. When a catastrophe appears imminent, "Stop a minute!" she cries. "I cannot bear it!" — and the reader must pause while she gathers courage to face disaster with the hero, or dash with him through peril to safety.

She would almost be sorry when the doorbell announced a visitor; almost, not quite, for flesh and blood were better than fiction. If the caller were a familiar friend, how her face lighted up!

"Oh! now we can have whist!"

The table is brought out, the mother-of-pearl counters (a Cutler relic: we remember that Mr. Ward did not allow cards in his house!), and the order for the rest of the evening is "A clear fire, a clean hearth, and the rigor of the game!" —

It was a happy day when, as chanced once or twice, Mr. Ernest Schelling, coming on from New York to play with the Boston Symphony Orchestra, offered to come and play to her, "all by herself, whatever she wanted, and for as long as she liked." She never forgot this pleasure, nor the warm kindness of the giver.

One day Mr. Abel Lefranc, the French lecturer of the year at Harvard, came to lunch with her. He apologized for only being able to stay for the luncheon hour, owing to a press of engagements and work that had grown overpowering. He stayed for two hours and a half after luncheon was over, and during all that time the flow of poignant, brilliant talk, *à deux*, held the third in the little company absorbed. She was entirely at home in French, and the Frenchman talked over the problems of his country as if to a compatriot.

A few days afterwards a Baptist minister from Texas, a powerfully built and handsome man, came to wait on her. He also stayed two hours: and we heard his "Amen!" and "Bless the Lord for that!" and her gentler "Bless the Lord, indeed, my brother!" as their voices, fervent and grave, mingled in talk.

She never tried to be interested in people. She *was* interested, with every fibre of her being. Little household doings: the economies and efforts of brave young people, she thrilled to them all. Indeed, all *human facts* roused in her the same absorbed and reverent interest.

These are Boston memories, but those of Oak Glen are no less tender and vivid. There, too, the meals were festivals, the midday dinner being now the chief one, with its following hour on the piazza; "Grandmother" in her hooded chair, with her cross-stitch embroidery or "hooked" rug, daughters and grandchildren gathered round her. Horace and Xenophon were on the little table beside her, but they must wait till she had mixed and enjoyed her "social salad."

At Oak Glen, too, she had her novel and her whist, bézique or dominoes, as the family was larger or smaller. She never stooped to solitaire; a game must be an affair of companionship, of the "social tie" in defence of which "Bro' Sam," in his youth, had professed himself ready to die. Instead of the "Victor" concert, she now made music herself, playing four-hand pieces with Florence, the "music daughter," trained in childhood by Otto Dresel. This was another great pleasure. (Did any one, we wonder, ever *enjoy* pleasures as she did?) These duets were for the afternoon; she almost never used her eyes in the evening. They were perfectly good, strong eyes; in the latter years she rarely used glasses; but the habit dated back to the early fifties, and might not be shaken.

We see her, therefore, in the summer afternoons, sitting at the piano with Florence, playing, "Galatea, dry thy tears!" "Handel's old tie-wig music," as she called his operas. Or, if her son were there, she would play accompaniments from the "Messiah" or "Elijah"; rippling through the difficult music, transposing it, if necessary to suit the singer's voice, with ease and accuracy. Musicians said that she was the ideal accompanist, never asserting herself, but giving perfect sympathy and support to the singer.

We return to the Journal.

"*January, 1908.* I had prayed the dear Father to give me this one more poem, a verse for this year's Decoration Day, asked for by Amos Wells, of Christian Endeavor belonging. I took my pen and the poem came quite spontaneously. It seemed an answer to my prayer, but I hold fast the thought that the great Christ asked *no sign* from God and needed none, so deeply did he enter into life divine. I also thought, regarding Christ and Moses, that we must be content that a certain mystery should envelop these heroic figures of human history. Our small measuring tape or rod is not for them. If they were not exactly in fact what we take them to be, let us deeply reverence the human mind which has conceived and built up such splendid and immortal ideals. Was not Christ thinking of something like this when he made the sin against the Holy Ghost and its manifestations the only unpardonable error? He surely did not mean to say that it was beyond the repentance which is the earnest of forgiveness to every sin."

A day or two after this she met at luncheon "a young Reverend Mr. Fitch. . . . He is earnest and clear-minded, and should do much good. I spoke of the cup [of life], but advised him to use the spoon for stirring up his congregation."

She was asked for a "long and exhaustive paper on Marion Crawford in about a week. I wrote, saying that I could furnish an interesting paper on the elder and younger Crawford, but without any literary estimate of Marion's work, saying that family praise was too much akin to self-praise; also the time allotted much too short."

One night she woke "suddenly and something seemed to say, 'They are on the right tack now.'

MRS. HOWE
From a painting by John Elliott, 1908

This microscopic and detailed study of the causes of evil on society will be much forwarded by the direct agency of women. They too will supply that inexhaustible element of hopefulness, without which reforms are a mere working back and forth of machinery. These two things will overcome the evil of the world by prevention first, and then by the optimistic anticipation of good. This is a great work given to Woman now to do. Then I caught at various couplets of a possible millennial poem, but feared I should not write it. Have scrawled these on a large pad. This line kept coming back to me, 'Living, not dying, Christ redeemed mankind.'. . . This my first day at my desk since Saturday, March 28. I may try some prose about the present patient analysis of the evil of society, the patient intelligent women associated in all this work. To reclaim waste earth is a glory. Why not a greater to reclaim the moral wastes of humanity?"

This midnight vision impressed her deeply, and through the succeeding days she wrote it out in full, bit by bit. On the envelope containing it is written, "An account of my vision of the world regenerated by the combined labor and love of Men and Women." In it she saw "men and women of every clime working like bees to unwrap the evils of society and to discover the whole web of vice and misery and to apply the remedies, and also to find the influences that should best counteract the evil and its attendant suffering.

"There seemed to be a new, a wondrous, ever-

permeating light, the glory of which I cannot attempt
to put into human words — the light of the newborn
hope and sympathy — blazing. The source of this
light was born of human endeavor. . . ."

She saw "the men and the women, standing side
by side, shoulder to shoulder, a common lofty and indomitable purpose lighting every face with a glory
not of this earth. All were advancing with one end
in view, one foe to trample, one everlasting goal to
gain. . . .

"And then I saw the victory. All of evil was gone
from the earth. Misery was blotted out. Mankind
was emancipated and ready to march forward in a
new Era of human understanding, all-encompassing
sympathy and ever-present help, the Era of perfect
love, of peace passing understanding."

Mrs. Humphry Ward was in Boston this spring, and
there were many pleasant festivities in her honor.

A "luncheon with Mrs. Humphry Ward at Annie
Fields'; very pleasant. Edward Emerson there, easy
and delightful. . . ."

A fine reception at the Vendôme, where she and
Mrs. Ward stood under "a beautiful arch of roses"
and exchanged greetings.

"A delightful call from Mrs. Humphry Ward. We
had much talk of persons admired in England and
America. She has great personal attraction, is not
handsome, but very '*simpatica*' and is evidently whole-
souled and sincere, with much 'good-fellowship.' We
embraced at parting."

In strong contrast to this is her comment on a writer whose work did not appeal to her. "But she has merit; yes, she certainly has merit. In fact —" with a flash — "she is meret-ricious!"

May brought the Free Religious Banquet, at which she "compared the difference of sect to the rainbow which divides into its beauty the white light of truth"; and the State Federation of Women's Clubs, where another apt comparison occurred to her.

"I compared the old order among women to the juxtaposition of squares set cornerwise to each other; the intensity of personal feeling and interest infusing an insensible antagonism into our relations with each other. 'Now,' I said, 'the comparison being removed, we no longer stand cornerwise to each other, but so that we can fit into line, and stand and act in concert.'..."

"*Newport.* I begin to feel something of the 'labor and sorrow' of living so long. I don't even enjoy my books as I used to. My efforts to find a fit word for the Biennial [of the General Federation of Women's Clubs, to meet in Boston, June 22 and 23] are not successful...."

She soon revived under her green trees, and enjoyed her books as much as ever: "got hold of" her screed, wrote it, went up to Boston to deliver it, came back to meet an excursion party of "Biennial" ladies visiting Newport. (N.B. She was late for the reception, and her neighbor, Bradford Norman, drove her into Newport in his automobile "at a terrific clip." On alighting, "Braddie," she said, "if I were ten years

younger, I would set up one of these hell-wagons myself!")

She enjoyed all this hugely, but the fatigue was followed by distress so great that the next morning she
"thought she should die with her door locked." (She
would lock her door: no prayers of ours availed against
this. In Boston, an elaborate arrangement of keys
made it possible for her room to be entered; at Oak
Glen there was but the one stout door. On this occasion, after lying helpless and despairing for some time,
she managed to unlock the door and call the faithful
maid.)

On June 30 she writes: —

"Oh, beautiful last day of June! Perhaps my last
June on earth. . . . I shall be thankful to live as long
as I can be of comfort or help to any one. . . ."

"*July 12.* . . . Sherman to Corse [Civil War], 'Can
you hold out till I arrive?' Corse to Sherman, 'I have
lost an arm, my cheekbone, and am minus one ear,
but I can lick *all hell* yet.'"

"*July 30.* Have felt so much energy to-day that
thought I must begin upon my old philosophizing
essays. . . . Could find only 'Duality of Character.'
What is the lesson of this two-foldness? This, that the
most excellent person should remember the dual member of his or her firm, the evil possibility; and the most
persistent offender should also remember the better
personality which is bound up with its opposite, and
which can come into activity, if invited to do so."

"*August 28.* Wrote an immediate reply to a Mrs.
———, who had written to ask leave to use a part

of my 'Battle Hymn' with some verses of her own. I replied, refusing this permission, but saying that she should rewrite her own part sufficiently to leave mine out, and should not call it the 'Battle Hymn of the Republic.' The metre and tune, of course, she might use, as they are not mine in any special sense, but my phrases *not*."

After writing an article for the "Delineator," on "What I should like to give my Country for a Christmas Gift," she dreads a failure of her productive power, but is reassured by Maud's verdict. "I took much pains with it, but think she overpraises it a little to raise my spirits." The gift she would choose was "a more vigilant national conscience." The little essay counts but seventy lines, but every word tells.

In early September she performed a "very small public service," unveiling in Newport a bronze tablet in honor of Count de Rochambeau. She would have been glad to speak, but an anxious daughter had demurred, and at the moment she "only thought of pulling the string the right way."

"*September 21. Green Peace, New York.* A delightful drive with Mr. Seth Low in his auto. A good talk with him about the multi-millionnaires and the Hague Conferences which he has attended. We reached Green Peace in time for Mr. Frank Potter to sing about half of my songs. He has a fine tenor voice, well cultivated, and is very kind about my small compositions. I had not counted upon this pleasure. I dreaded this visit, for the troublesome journey, but it has been delightful. I am charmed to see my son so handsomely and com-

fortably established, and with a very devoted wife.
Potter brought me some flowers and a curious orchid
from Panama."

"*November 3. Oak Glen.* Yesterday and to-day have
had most exquisite sittings in front of my house in the
warm sunshine; very closely wrapped up by the dear
care of my daughters."

These sittings were on what she called her boulevard,
a grassy space in front of the house, bordering on the
road, and taking the full strength of the morning sun.
Here, with the tall screen of cedars behind her, and a
nut tree spreading its golden canopy over her head, she
would sit for hours, drinking in the sweet air that was
like no other to her.

A companion picture to this is that of the twilight
hour, when she would sit alone in the long parlor,
looking out on the sunset. Black against the glowing
sky rose the pines of the tiny forgotten graveyard,
where long-ago neighbors slept, with the white rose
tree drooping over the little child's grave; a spot of
tender and melancholy beauty. All about were the
fields she loved, fragrant with clover and wormwood,
vocal with time-keeping crickets. Here she would sit
for an hour, meditating, or repeating to herself the
Odes of Horace, or some familiar hymn. Horace was
one of her best friends, all her life long. She knew
many of the Odes by heart, and was constantly memorizing new ones. They filled and brightened many
a sleepless or weary hour. Here, when the children
came back from their walk, they would find her, quiet
and serene, but ready instantly to break into laughter

with them, to give herself, as always, entirely and joyously. Now and then she wrote down a meditation; here is one: —

"A thought comes to me to-day which gives me great comfort. This is that, while the transitory incidentals of our life, important for the moment, pass out of it, the steadfast divine life which is in our earthly experience, perseveres, and can never die nor diminish. I feel content that much of me should die. I interpret for myself Christ's parable of the tares sown in the wheat field. As regards the individual, these tares are our personal and selfish traits and limitations. We must restrain and often resist them, but we cannot and must not seek to eradicate them, for they are important agents not only in preserving, but also in energizing our bodily life. Yet they are, compared with our higher life, as the tares compared with the wheat, and we must be well content to feel that, when the death harvest comes, these tares will fall from us and perish, while the wheat will be gathered into the granary of God.

"I do not desire ecstatic, disembodied sainthood, because I do not wish to abdicate any one of the attributes of my humanity. I cherish even the infirmities that bind me to my kind. I would be human, and American, and a woman. Paul of Tarsus had one or two ecstasies, but I feel sure that he lived in his humanity, strenuously and energetically. Indeed, the list he gives us of his trials and persecutions may show us how much he lived as a man among men, even though he did once cry out for deliverance from the body of

death, whose wants and pains were a sore hindrance
to him in his unceasing labors. That deliverance he
found daily in the service of Truth, and finally once
for all, when God took him.

"Another thought upholds me. With the recurrence
of the cycle, I feel the steady tramp and tread of the
world's progress. This Spring is not identical with last
Spring, this year is not last year. The predominant
fact of the Universe is not the mechanical round and
working of its forces, but their advance as moral life
develops out of and above material life. Mysterious
as the chain of causation is, we know one thing about
it, viz.: that we cannot reverse its sequence. Whatever
may change or pass away, my father remains my
father, my child, my child. The way before us is open
— the way behind us is blocked with solid building
which cannot be removed. And in this great onward
order, life turns not back to death, but goes forward
to other life, which we may call immortality. If I
would turn backward, I stand still in paralyzed opposition to the mighty sweep of heavenly law. It must go
on, and if I could resist and refuse to go with it, I
should die a moral death, having isolated myself from
the movement which is life. But, do what I will, I
cannot resist it. I am carried on perforce, as inanimate
rocks and trees are swept away in the course of a
resistless torrent. Shall I then abdicate my human
privilege which makes the forces of nature Angels to
help and minister to me? Let me, instead, take hold
of the guiding cords of life with resolute hands and
press onward, following the illustrious army whose

crowned chiefs have gone before. They too had their weakness, their sorrow, their sin. But they are set as stars in the firmament of God, and their torches flash heavenly light upon our doubtful way, ay, even upon the mysterious bridge whose toll is silence. Beyond that silence reigns the perfect harmony."

"*November 6.* Expecting to leave this dear place to-morrow before noon, I write one last record in this diary to say that I am very thankful for the season just at end, which has been busy and yet restful. I have seen old friends and new ones, all with pleasure, and mostly with profit of a social and spiritual kind. I have seen dear little Eleanor Hall, the sweetest of babies. Have had all of my dear children with me, some of my grandchildren, and four of my great-grands.

"Our Papéterie has had pleasant meetings. . . . I am full of hope for the winter. Have had a long season of fresh air, delightful and very invigorating. . . . *Utinam! Gott in Himmel sei Dank!*"

"*November 28. Boston.* Have been much troubled of late by uncertainties about life beyond the present. Quite suddenly, very recently, it occurred to me to consider that Christ understood that spiritual life would not end with death, and that His expressed certainty as to the future life was founded upon His discernment of spiritual things. So, in so far as I am a Christian, I must believe in the immortality of the soul, as our Master surely did. I cannot understand why I have not thought of that before. I think now that I shall nevermore lose sight of it. . . . Had a very fine call from Mr. Locke, author of the 'Beloved Vagabond,' a book which I have enjoyed."

"*December* 5. . . . I learned to-day that my dear friend of many years [the Reverend Mary H. Graves] passed away last night very peacefully. . . . This is a heart sorrow for me. She has been a most faithful, affectionate and helpful friend. I scarcely know whether any one, outside of my family, would have pained me more by their departure. . . ."

This was indeed a loss. "Saint Mouse," as we called her, was a familiar friend of the household: a little gray figure, with the face of a plain angel. For many years she had been the only person who was allowed to touch our mother's papers. She often came for a day or two and straightened out the tangle. She was the only approach to a secretary ever tolerated.

We used to grieve because our mother had no first-rate "Crutch"; it seemed a waste of power. Now, we see that it was partly the instinct of self-preservation, — keeping the "doing" muscles tense and strong, because action was vital and necessary to her — partly the still deeper instinct of giving her *self*, body and mind. She seldom failed in any important thing she undertook; the "chores" of life she often left for others to attend to or neglect.

The Christmas services, the Christmas oratorio, brought her the usual serene joy and comfort. She insists that Handel wrote parts of the "Messiah" in heaven itself. "Where else could he have got 'Comfort ye,' 'Thy rebuke,' 'Thou shalt break them,' and much besides?"

Late in December, 1908, came the horror of the Sicilian earthquake. She felt at first that it was impossible to reconcile omnipotence and perfect benevolence with this catastrophe.

"We must hold judgment in suspense and say, 'We don't and we can't understand.'"

She had several tasks on hand this winter, among them a poem for the Centenary of Lincoln's birth. On February 7 she writes: —

"After a time of despair about the poem for the Lincoln Centenary some lines came to me in the early morning. I arose, wrapped myself warmly, and wrote what I could, making quite a beginning."

She finished the poem next day, and on the 12th she went "with three handsome grandchildren" to deliver it at Symphony Hall before the Grand Army of the Republic and their friends.

"The police had to make an entrance for us. I was presently conducted to my seat on the platform. The hall was crammed to its utmost capacity. I had felt doubts of the power of my voice to reach so large a company, but strength seemed to be given to me at once, and I believe that I was heard very well. T. W. H. [Colonel Higginson] came to me soon after my reading and said, 'You have been a good girl and behaved yourself well.'"

The next task was an essay on "Immortality," which cost her much labor and anxious thought.

"*March 3.* . . . Got at last some solid ground for my screed on 'Immortality.' Our experience of the goodness of God in our daily life assures us of His mercy hereafter, and seeing God everywhere, we shall dwell in the house of the Lord forever."

"*March 27.* I am succeeding better with my 'Immortality' paper. Had to-day a little bit of visioning with which I think that I would willingly depart, when my time comes. The dreadful fear of being buried alive disappeared for a time, and I saw only the goodness of God, to which it seemed that I could trust all question of the future life. I said to myself — 'The best will be for thee and me.'"

It was in this mood that she wrote: —

"I, for one, feel that my indebtedness grows with my years. And it occurred to me the other day that when I should depart from this earthly scene, 'God's poor Debtor' might be the fittest inscription for my gravestone, if I should have one. So much have I received from the great Giver, so little have I been able to return."

"*April 5.* . . . Heard May Alden Ward, N.E.W.C., on 'Current Events.' *Praecipuë* tariff reform. Proposed a small group to study the question from the point of view of the consumer. What to protect and how? American goods cheaper in Europe than here. Blank tells me of pencils made here for a foreign market and sold in Germany and England at a price impossible here. I said that the real bottomless pit is the depth of infamous slander with which people will assail our public servants, especially when they are faithful and incorruptible, apropos of aspersions cast on Roosevelt and Taft. Mrs. Ward read a very violent attack upon some public man of a hundred or more years ago.

He was quoted as a monster of tyranny and injustice. His name was George Washington."

"*April 8*. . . . My prayer for this Easter is that I may not waste the inspiration of spring. . . ."

In these days came another real sorrow to her.

"*April 10*. To-day brings the sad news of Marion Crawford's death at Sorrento. His departure seems to have been a peaceful one. He comforted his family and had his daughter Eleanor read Plato's 'Dialogues' to him. Was unconscious at the last. Poor dear Marion! The end, in his case, comes early. His father was, I think, in the early forties when he died of a cancer behind the eye which caused blindness. He, Thomas Crawford, had a long and very distressing illness."

Crawford had been very dear to her, ever since the days when, a radiant schoolboy, he came and went in his vacations. There was a complete sympathy and understanding between them, and there were few people whom she enjoyed more.

"I wrote a letter to be read, if approved, to-morrow evening at the Faneuil Hall meeting held to advocate the revision of our extradition treaty with the Russian Government, which at present seems to allow that government too much latitude of incrimination, whereby political and civil offences can too easily be confused and a revolutionist surrendered as a criminal, which he may or may not be."

Later in the month she writes: —

"In the early morning I began to feel that I must attempt some sort of tribute to my dear friend of many years, Dr. Holmes, the centenary of whose birth is to be celebrated on Tuesday next. I stayed at home from church to follow some random rhymes which came to me in connection with my remembrance of my ever affectionate friend. I love to think of his beautiful service to his age and to future ages. I fear that my rhymes will fail to crystallize, but sometimes a bad beginning leads to something better. . . ."

The poem was finished, more or less to her satisfaction, but she was weary with working over it, and with "reading heavy books, Max Müller on metaphysics, Blanqui on political economy."

"*May 10.* I began this day the screed of 'Values' which I mentioned the other day. I have great hopes of accomplishing something useful, remembering, as I do, with sore indignation, my own mistakes, and desiring to help young people to avoid similar ones."

The ninetieth birthday was a festival, indeed. Letters and telegrams poured in, rose in toppling piles which almost — not quite — daunted her; she would hear every one, would answer as many as flesh and blood could compass. Here is one of them: —

Most hearty congratulations on your ninetieth birthday from the boy you picked up somewhere in New York and placed in the New York Orphan Asylum on April 6th, 1841. Sorry I have never been able to meet you in all that time. You [were] one of the Board of Trustees at that time.

Respectfully and Thankfully,
Wм. Davidson.

I was then about five years old, now seventy-three.

Writing to her friend of many years, Mrs. Ellen Mitchell, she says: —

"Your birthday letter was and is much valued by me. Its tone of earnest affection is an element in the new inspiration recently given me by such a wonderful testimony of public and private esteem and goodwill as has been granted me in connection with my attainment of ninety years. It all points to the future. I must work to deserve what I have received. My dearest wish would be to take up some thread of our A.A.W. work, and continue it. I rather hope that I may find the way to do this in the study of Economics which I am just starting with a small group. . . ."

To Mrs. Harriet Prescott Spofford

DEAR MRS. SPOFFORD, —

You wrote me a lovely letter on my ninetieth birthday. I cannot help feeling as if the impression expressed by you and so many other kind friends of my personal merits must refer to some good work which I have yet to do. What I have done looks small to me, but I have tried a good deal for the best I have known. This is all I can say. I am much touched by your letter, and encouraged to go on trying. Don't you think that the best things are already in view? The opportunities for women, the growing toleration and sympathy in religion, the sacred cause of peace? I have lived, like Moses, to see the entrance into the Promised Land. How much is this to be thankful for! My crabbed hand shows how Time abridges my working powers, but I march to the brave music still, as you and many of the juniors do.

Wishing that I might sometimes see you, believe me

Yours with affectionate regard,

JULIA WARD HOWE.

Close upon the Birthday came another occasion of the kind which we — in these later years — at once welcomed and deplored. She enjoyed nothing so much as a "function," and nothing tired her so much.

On June 16, Brown University, her husband's *alma mater* and her grandfather's, conferred upon her the degree of Doctor of Laws. She went to Providence to receive it in person, and thus describes the commencement exercises to Mrs. Mitchell: —

"The ordeal of the Doctorate was rather trying, but was made as easy as possible for me. The venerable old church was well filled, and was quite beautiful. I sat in one of the front pews — two learned people led me to the foot of the platform from which President Faunce, with some laudatory remarks, handed me my diploma, while some third party placed a picturesque hood upon my shoulders. The band played the air of my 'Battle Hymn,' and applause followed me as I went back to my seat. So there!"

Her companion on that occasion writes: —

"She sat listening quietly to the addresses, watched each girl and boy just starting on the voyage of life as they marched to the platform and received from the President's hand the scrap of paper, the parchment diploma, reward of all their studies. Her name was called last. With the deliberate step of age, she walked forward, wearing her son's college gown over her white dress, his mortar-board cap over her lace veil. She seemed less moved than any person present; she could not see what we saw, the tiny gallant figure bent with fourscore and ten years of study and hard labor. As she moved between the girl students who stood up to let her pass, she whispered, 'How tall they are! It seems to me the girls are much taller than they used to be.' Did she realize how much shorter she was than she once had been? I think not.

"Then, her eyes sparkling with fun while all other eyes were wet, she shook her hard-earned diploma with a gay gesture in the faces of those girls, cast on them a keen glance that somehow was a challenge, 'Catch up with me if you can!'

"She had labored long for the higher education of women, suffered estrangement, borne ridicule for it — the sight of those girl graduates, starting on their life voyage equipped with a good education, was like a sudden realization of a life-long dream; uplifted her, gave her strength for the fatigues of the day. At the dinner given for her and the college dignitaries by Mrs. William Goddard, she was at her best."

She was asked for a Fourth of July message to the Sunday-School children of the Congregational Church, and wrote: —

"I want them to build up character in themselves and in the community, to give to the country just so many men and women who will be incapable of meanness or dishonesty, who will look upon life as a sacred trust, given to them for honorable service to their fellow men and women. I would have them feel that, whether rich or poor, they are bound to be of use in their day and generation, and to be mindful of the Scripture saying that 'no man liveth unto himself.' We all have our part to do in keeping up the character and credit of our country. For her sake we should study to become good and useful citizens."

In the summer of 1909 the Cretan question came up again. Once more Turkey attempted to regain active possession of Crete; once more the voice of Christendom was raised in protest. She had no thought this time of being "too old." Being called upon for help, she wrote at once to President Taft, "praying him to find some way to help the Cretans in the terrible prospect of their being delivered over, bound hand and foot, to Turkish misrule." She was soon gladdened by a reply from the President, saying that he had not considered the Cretans as he should, but promising to send her letter to the Secretary of State. "I thank God most earnestly," she writes, "for even thus much. To-day, I feel that I must write all pressing letters, as my time may be short."

Accordingly she composed an open letter on the Cretan question. "It is rather crude, but it is from my heart of hearts. I had to write it."

Suffrage, too, had its share of her attention this summer. There were meetings at "Marble House" [Newport] in which she was deeply interested. She attended one in person; to the next she sent the second and third generations, staying at home herself to amuse and care for the fourth.

On the last day of August she records once more her sorrow at the departure of the summer. She adds, "God grant me to be prepared to live or die, as He shall decree. It is best, I think, to anticipate life, and to cultivate forethought. . . . I think it may have been to-day that I read the last pages of Martineau's 'Seat of Authority in Religion,' an extremely valuable book, yet a painful one to read, so entirely does it do away with the old-time divinity of the dear Christ. But it leaves Him the divinity of character — no theory or discovery can take that away."

Late September brought an occasion to which she had looked forward with mingled pleasure and dread; the celebration of the Hudson-Fulton Centennial in New York. She had been asked for a poem, and had taken great pains with it, writing and re-writing it, hammering and polishing. She thought it finished in July, yet two days before the celebration she was still re-touching it.

"I have been much dissatisfied with my Fulton poem. Lying down to rest this afternoon, instead of sleep, of which I felt no need, I began to try for some new lines which should waken it up a little, and think that I succeeded. I had brought no manuscript paper, so had to scrawl my amendments on Sanborn's old long envelope."

Later in the day two more lines came to her, and again two the day after. Finally, on the morning of the day itself, on awakening, she cried out, —

"I have got my last verse!"

The occasion was a notable one. The stage of the Metropolitan Opera House was filled with dignitaries, delegates from other States, foreign diplomats in brilliant uniforms. The only woman among them was the little figure in white, to greet whom, as she came forward on her son's arm, the whole great assembly rose and stood. They remained standing while she read her poem in clear unfaltering tones; the applause that rang out showed that she had once more touched the heart of the public.

This poem was printed in "Collier's Weekly," unfortunately from a copy made before the "last verse" was finished to her mind. This distressed her. "Let this be a lesson!" she said. "Never print a poem or speech till it has been delivered; always give the eleventh hour its chance!"

This eleventh hour brought a very special chance; a few days before, the world had been electrified by the news of Peary's discovery of the North Pole: it was the general voice that cried through her lips, —

The Flag of Freedom crowns the Pole!

The following letter was written while she was at work on the poem: —

To Laura

OAK GLEN, July 9, 1909.

Why, yes, I'm doing the best I know how. Have written a poem for the Hudson and Fulton celebration, September 28. Worked hard at it. Guess it's only pretty good, if even that. Maud takes me out every day under the pine tree, makes me sit while she reads aloud Freeman's shorter work on Sicily. I enjoy this. ... I have just read Froude's "Cæsar," which Sanborn says he hates, but which I found as readable as a novel. Am also reading a work of Kuno Fischer on "Philosophy," especially relating to Descartes. Now you know, Miss, or should know, that *same* had great *fame*, and sometimes *blame*, as a philosopher. But he don't make no impression on my mind. I never doubted that I was, so don't need no "*cogito, ergo sum*," which is what Carty, old Boy, amounts to. Your letter, dear, was a very proper attention under the circumstances. Should n't object to another. Lemme see! objects cannot be subjects, nor *vice versa*. How do you know that you washed your face this morning? You don't know it, and I don't believe that you did. You might consult H. Richards about some of these particulars. He is a man of some sense. You are, bless you, not much wiser than your affectionate

MA.

Returned to Oak Glen, after the celebration, she writes: —

To her son and his wife

OAK GLEN, October 1, 1909.

... I found my trees still green, and everything comfortable. I did not dare to write to any one yesterday, my head was so full of nonsense. Reaction from brain-fatigue takes this shape with me, and everything goes "higgle-wiggledy, hi-cockalorum," or

words to that effect. . . . We had a delightful visit with
you, dear F. G. and H. M. I miss you both, and miss
the lovely panorama of the hills, and the beauteous
flower parterres. Well, here's for next year in early
Autumn, and I hope I may see you both before that
time. With thanks for kindest entertainment, and
best of love,

Your very affectionate

MOTHER AND DITTO-IN-LAW.

To George H. Richards [1]

OAK GLEN, October 1, 1909.

DEAR UNCLE GEORGE, —

I got through all right, in spite of prospective views,
of fainting fits, apoplexy, what not? Trouble is now
that I cannot keep calling up some thousands of people,
and saying: "Admire me, do. I wrote it all my little
own self." Seriously, there is a little reaction from so
much excitement. But I hope to recover my senses in
time. I improved the last two stanzas much when I
recited the poem. The last line read

The Flag of Freedom crowns the Pole!

I tell you, I brought it out with a will, and they all
[the audience] made a great noise. . . .

We doubt if any of the compliments pleased her so
much as that of the Irish charwoman who, mop in
hand, had been listening at one of the side doors of

---

[1] Her man of business and faithful friend. Though of her children's
generation, she had adopted him as an "uncle."

the theatre. "Oh, you dear little old lady!" she cried. "You speaked your piece *real* good!"

Late October finds her preparing for the move to Boston.

"I have had what I may call a spasm of gratitude to God for His great goodness to me, sitting in my pleasant little parlor, with the lovely golden trees in near view, and the devotion of my children and great kindness of my friends well in mind. Oh! help me, divine Father, to merit even a very little of Thy kindness!"

In this autumn she was elected a member of the American Academy of Arts and Letters, and in December she wrote for its first meeting a poem called "The Capitol." She greatly desired to read this poem before the association, and Maud, albeit with many misgivings, agreed to take her on to Washington. This was not to be. On learning of her intention, three officers of the association, William Dean Howells, Robert Underwood Johnson, and Thomas Nelson Page, sent her a "round-robin" telegram, begging her not to run the risk of the long winter journey. The kindly suggestion was not altogether well taken. "Ha!" she flashed out. "They think I am too old, but there's a little ginger left in the old blue jar!"

She soon realized the wisdom as well as the friendliness of the round robin, and confided to the Journal that she had been in two minds about it.

On Christmas Day she writes: —

"Thanks to God who gave us the blessed Christ. What a birth was this! Two thousand years have only

increased our gratitude for it. How it has consecrated
Babyhood and Maternity! Two infants, grown to
man's estate, govern the civilized world to-day, Christ
and Moses. I am still thankful to be here in the flesh,
as they were once, and oh! that I may never pass
where they are not!"

The winter of 1909–10 was a severe one, and she
was more or less housed; yet the days were full and
bright for her. "Life," she cried one day, "is like a
cup of tea; all the sugar is at the bottom!" and again,
"Oh! I must go so soon, and I am only just ready to
go to college!"

When it was too cold for her to go out, she took her
walk in the house, with the windows open, pacing
resolutely up and down her room and the room opposite. She sat long hours at her desk, in patient toil.
She was always picking up dropped stitches, trying to
keep every promise, answer every note.

"Went through waste-paper basket, redeeming some
bits torn to fragments, which either should be answered
or recorded. Wrote an autograph for Mr. Blank. It
was asked for in 1905. Had been *put away* and forgotten."

She got too tired that morning, and could not fully
enjoy the Authors' Club in the afternoon.

"Colonel Higginson and I sat like two superannu-
ated old idols. Each of us said a little say when the
business was finished."

It is not recalled that they presented any such
appearance to others.

She went to the opera, a mingled pleasure and pain.

"It was the 'Huguenots,' much of which was known to me in early youth, when I used to sing the 'Rataplan' chorus with my brothers. I sang also Valentine's prayer, '*Parmi les fleurs mon rêve se ranime,*' with obligato bassoon accompaniment, using the 'cello instead. I know that I sang much better that night than usual, for dear Uncle John said to me, 'You singed good!' Poor Huti played the 'cello. Now, I listened for the familiar bits, and recognized the drinking chorus in Act 1st, the 'Rataplan' in Act 2d. Valentine's prayer, if given, was so overlaid with *fioritura* that I did not feel sure of it. The page's pretty song was all right, but I suffered great fatigue, and the reminiscences were sad."

Through the winter she continued the study of economics with some fifteen members of the New England Woman's Club. She read Bergson too, and now and then "got completely bogged" in him, finding no "central point that led anywhere."

About this time she wrote: —

"*Some Rules for Everyday Life*

"1. Begin every day with a few minutes of retired meditation, tending to prayer, in order to feel within yourself the spiritual power which will enable you to answer the demands of practical life.

"2. Cultivate systematic employment and learn to estimate correctly the time required to accomplish whatever you may undertake.

"3. Try to occupy both your mind and your muscles, since each of these will help the other, and both deteriorate without sufficient exercise.

"4. Remember that there is great inherent selfishness in human nature, and train yourself to consider adequately the advantage and pleasure of others.

"5. Be thankful to be useful.

"6. Try to ascertain what are real uses, and to follow such maxims and methods as will stand the test of time, and not fail with the passing away of a transient enthusiasm.

"7. Be neither over distant nor over familiar in your intercourse; friendly rather than confidential; not courting responsibility, but not declining it when it of right belongs to you.

"8. Be careful not to falsify true principles by a thoughtless and insufficient application of them.

"9. Though actions of high morality ensure in the end the greatest success, yet view them in the light of obligation, not in that of policy.

"10. Whatever your talents may be, consider yourself as belonging to the average of humanity, since, even if superior to many in some respects, you will be likely to fall below them in others.

"11. Remember the Christian triad of virtues. Have faith in principles, hope in God, charity with and for all mankind."

A windy March found her "rather miserably ailing." Dr. Langmaid came, and pronounced her lungs "sound as a bass drum"; nothing amiss save a throat irritated by wind and dust. Thereupon she girded herself and buckled to her next task, a poem for the centenary of James Freeman Clarke.

"I have despaired of a poem which people seem to expect from me for the dear James Freeman's centennial. To-day the rhymes suddenly flowed, but the thought is difficult to convey — the reflection of heaven in his soul is what he gave, and what he left us."

"*April 1.* Very much tossed up and down about my poem. . . ."

"*April 2.* Was able at last, *D.G.*, to make the poem explain itself. Rosalind, my incorruptible critic, was satisfied with it. I think and hope that all my trouble has been worth while. I bestowed it most unwillingly, having had little hope that I could make my figure of speech intelligible. I am very thankful for this poem, cannot be thankful enough."

This was her third tribute to the beloved Minister, and is, perhaps, the best of the three. The thought which she found so difficult of conveyance is thus expressed: —

> Lifting from the Past its veil,
> What of his does now avail?
> Just a mirror in his breast
> That revealed a heavenly guest,
> And the love that made us free
> Of the same high company.
> These he brought us, these he left,
> When we were of him bereft.
> . . . .

She thus describes the occasion: —

"Coughed in the night, and at waking suffered much in mind, fearing that a wild fit of coughing might make my reading unacceptable and even ridiculous. Imagine my joy when I found my voice clear and strong, and read the whole poem [forty-four lines] without the slightest inclination to cough. This really was the granting of my prayer, and my first thought about it was, 'What shall I render to the Lord for all His goodness to me?' I thought, 'I will interest myself more efficiently in the great questions which concern Life and Society at large.' If I have 'the word for the moment,' as some think, I will take more pains to speak it."

A little later came a centenary which — alas! — she did not enjoy. It was that of Margaret Fuller, and was held in Cambridge. She was asked to attend it, and was assured that she "would not be expected to speak." This kindly wish to spare fatigue to a woman of ninety-one was the last thing she desired. She could hardly believe that she would be left out — she, who had known Margaret, had talked and corresponded with her.

"They have not asked me to speak!" she said more than once as the time drew near.

She was reassured; of course they would ask her when they saw her!

"I have a poem on Margaret!"

"Take it with you! Of course you will be asked to say something, and then you will be all ready with your poem in your pocket."

Thus Maud, in all confidence. Indeed, if one of her own had gone with her, the matter would have been easily arranged; unfortunately, the companion was a friend who could make no motion in the matter. She returned tired and depressed. "They did not ask me to speak," she said, "and I was the only person present who had known Margaret and remembered her."

For a little while this incident weighed on her. She felt that she was "out of the running"; but a winning race was close at hand.

The question of pure milk was before the Massachusetts Legislature, and was being hotly argued. An urgent message came by telephone; would Mrs. Howe say a word for the good cause? Maud went to her room, and found her at her desk, the morning's campaign already begun.

"There is to be a hearing at the State House on the milk question; they want you dreadfully to speak. What do you say?"

"Give me half an hour!" she said.

Before the half-hour was over she had sketched out her speech and dressed herself in her best flowered silk cloak and her new lilac hood, a birthday gift from a poor seamstress. Arrived at the State House, she sat patiently through many speeches. Finally she was called on to speak; it was noticed that no oath was required of her. As she rose and came forward on her daughter's arm, — "You may remain seated, Mrs. Howe," said the benevolent chairman.

"I prefer to stand!" was the reply.

She had left her notes behind; she did not need them. Standing in the place where, year after year, she had stood to ask for the full rights of citizenship, she made her last thrilling appeal for justice.

"We have heard," she said, "a great deal about the farmers' and the dealers' side of this case. We want

the matter settled on the ground of justice and mercy;
it ought not to take long to settle what is just to all
parties. Justice to all! Let us stand on that. There
is one deeply interested party, however, of whom we
have heard nothing. He cannot speak for himself; I
am here to speak for him: the infant!"

The effect was electrical. In an instant the tired audience, the dull or dogged or angry debaters, woke to
a new interest, a new spirit. No farmer so rough, no
middle-man so keen, no legislator so apathetic, but
felt the thrill. In a silence charged with deepest feeling
all listened as to a prophetess, as, step by step, she
unfolded the case of the infant as against farmers and
dealers.

As Arthur Dehon Hill, counsel for the Pure Milk
Association, led her from the room, he said, "Mrs.
Howe, you have saved the day!"

This incident was still in her mind on her ninety-
first birthday, a few days later.

"My parlors are full of beautiful flowers and other
gifts, interpreted by notes expressive of much affection, and telegrams of the same sort. What dare I ask
for more? Only that I may do something in the future
to deserve all this love and gratitude. I have intended
to deserve it all and more. Yet, when in thought I
review my life, I feel the waste and loss of power thro'
want of outlook. Like many another young person,
I did not know what my really available gifts were.
Perhaps the best was a feeling of what I may call 'the
sense of the moment,' which led a French friend to say
of me: '*Mme. Howe possède le mot à un dégré remar-*

quable.' I was often praised for saying ' just the right word,' and I usually did this with a strong feeling that it ought to be said."

Early in June, just as she was preparing for the summer flitting, she had a bad fall, breaking a rib. This delayed the move for a week, no more, the bone knitting easily. She was soon happy among her green trees, her birds singing around her.

The memories of this last summer come flocking in, themselves like bright birds. She was so well, so joyous, giving her lilies with such full hands; it was a golden time.

As the body failed, the mind — or so it seemed to us — grew ever clearer, the veil that shrouds the spirit ever more transparent. She " saw things hidden."

One day a summer neighbor came, bringing her son, a handsome, athletic fellow, smartly dressed, a fine figure of gilded youth. She looked at him a good deal: presently she said suddenly, —

"You write poetry!"

The lad turned crimson: his mother looked dumfounded. It proved that he had lately written a prize poem, and that literature was the goal of his ambition. Another day she found a philosopher hidden in what seemed to the rest of the family merely "a callow boy in pretty white duck clothes." So she plucked out the heart of each man's mystery, but so tenderly that it was yielded gladly, young and old alike feeling themselves understood.

Among the visitors of this summer none was more welcome than her great-grandson, Christopher Birckhead,[1] then an infant in arms. She loved to hold and watch the child, brooding over him with grave tenderness: it was a beautiful and gracious picture of Past and Future.

Maud had just written a book on Sicily, and, as always, our mother read and corrected the galley proofs. She did this with exquisite care and thoughtfulness, never making her suggestions on the proof itself, but on a separate sheet of paper, with the number of the galley, the phrase, and her suggested emendations. This was her invariable custom: the writer must be perfectly free to retain her own phrase, if she preferred it.

Walking tired her that summer, but she was very faithful about it.

"Zacko," she would command John Elliott, "take me for a walk."

The day before she took to her bed, he remembers that she clung to him more than usual and said, —

"It tires me very much." (This after walking twice round the piazza.)

"Once more!" he encouraged.

"No — I have walked all I can to-day."

"Let me take you back to your room this way," he said, leading her back by the piazza. "That makes five times each way!"

She laughed and was pleased to have done this, but he thinks she had a great sense of weakness too.

Her favorite piece on the "Victor" that summer was "The Artillerist's Oath." The music had a gallant ring to it, and there was something heroic about the

[1] Son of Caroline Minturn (Hall) and the Reverend Hugh Birckhead.

whole thing, something that suggested the Forlorn Hope — how many of them she had led! When nine o'clock came, she would ask for this piece by the nickname she had given it, taken from one of its odd lines, —

"I'll wed thee in the battle's front!"

While the song was being given, she was all alert and alive, even if she may have been sleepy earlier in the evening. She would get up with a little gesture of courage, and take leave of us, always with a certain ceremony, that was like the withdrawing of royalty. The evening was then over, and we too went to bed!

As we gather up our treasures of this last summer, we remember that several things might have prepared us for what was coming, had not our eyes been holden. She spoke a great deal of old times, the figures of her childhood and girlhood being evidently very near to her. She quoted them often; "My grandma used to say — " She spoke as naturally as the boy in the next room might speak of her.

She would not look in the glass; "I don't like to see my old face!" she said. She could not see the beauty that every one else saw. Yet she kept to the very last a certain tender coquetry. She loved her white dresses, and the flowered silk cloak of that last summer. She chose with care the jewels suited to each costume, the topaz cross for the white, the amethysts for the lilac. She had a great dread of old people's being untidy or unprepossessing in appearance, and never grudged the moments spent in adjusting the right cap and lace collar.

There was an almost unearthly light in her face, a transparency and sweetness that spoke to others more plainly than to us: Hugh Birckhead saw and recognized it as a look he had seen in other faces of saintly age, as their translation approached. But we said joyously to her and to each other, "She will round out the century; we shall all keep the Hundredth Birthday together!" And we and she partly believed it.

The doctor had insisted strongly that she should keep, through the summer at least, the trained nurse who had ministered to her after her fall. She "heard what he said, but it made no difference." In early August she records "a passage at arms with Maud, in which I clearly announced my intention of dispensing with the services of a trained nurse, my good health and simple habits rendering it entirely unnecessary."

She threatened to write to her man of business.

"*I would rather die*," she said, "than be an old woman with a nurse!"

Maud and Florence wept, argued, implored, but the nurse was dismissed. The Journal acknowledges that "her ministrations and Dr. Cobb's diagnosis have been very beneficial to my bodily health." On the same day she records the visit of a Persian Prince, who had come to this country chiefly to see two persons, the President of the United States and Mrs. Julia Ward Howe. "He also claims to be a reincarnation of some remarkable philosopher; and to be so greatly interested in the cause of Peace that he declines to visit our ships now in the harbor here, to which he has been invited."

Reading Theodore Parker's sermon on "Wisdom and Intellect," she found it so full of notable sayings that she thought "a little familiar book of daily inspiration and aspiration" might be made from his writings: she wrote to Mr. Francis J. Garrison suggesting this, and suggesting also, what had been long in her mind, the collecting and publishing of her "Occasional Poems."

In late September, she was "moved to write one or more open letters on what religion really is, for some one of the women's papers"; and the next day began upon "What is Religion?" or rather, "What Sort of Religion makes Religious Liberty possible?"

A day or two later, she was giving an "offhand talk" on the early recollections of Newport at the Papéterie, and going to an afternoon tea at a musical house, where, after listening to Schumann Romances and Chopin waltzes, and to the "Battle Hymn" on the 'cello, she was moved to give a performance of "Flibbertigibbet." This occasion reminded her happily of her father's house, of Henry "playing tolerably on the 'cello, Marion studying the violin, Bro' Sam's lovely tenor voice."

Now came the early October days when she was to receive the degree of Doctor of Laws from Smith College. She hesitated about making the tiresome journey, but finally, "Grudging the trouble and expense, I decide to go to Smith College, for my degree, but think I won't do so any more."

She started accordingly with daughter and maid, for Northampton, Massachusetts. It was golden weather, and she was in high spirits. Various college dignitaries met her at the station; one of these had given up a suite of rooms for her use; she was soon established in much peace and comfort.

Wednesday, October 5, was a day of perfect autumn beauty. She was early dressed in her white dress, with the college gown of rich black silk over it, the "mortarboard" covering in like manner her white lace cap. Thus arrayed, a wheeled chair conveyed her to the great hall, already packed with visitors and graduates, as was the deep platform with college officials and guests of honor. Opposite the platform, as if hung in air, a curving gallery was filled with white-clad girls, some two thousand of them; as she entered they rose like a flock of doves, and with them the whole audience. They rose once more when her name was called, last in the list of those honored with degrees; and as she came forward, the organ pealed, and the great chorus of fresh young voices broke out with

"Mine eyes have seen the glory of the coming of the Lord —"

It was the last time.

Later in the day the students of Chapin House brought their guest-book, begging for her autograph. She looked at Laura with a twinkle.

"Do you think they would like me to write something?"

Assured on that point, she waited a moment, and then wrote after her signature, —

Wandered to Smith College
In pursuit of knowledge;
Leaves so much the wiser,
Nothing can surprise her!

She reached home apparently without undue fatigue. "She will be more tired to-morrow!" we said; but she was not. Her son came for the week-end, and his presence was always a cordial. Sunday was a happy day. In the evening we gathered round the piano, she playing, son and daughters singing the old German student songs brought by "Uncle Sam" from Heidelberg seventy years before.

On the Tuesday she went to the Papéterie, and was the life and soul of the party, sparkling with merriment. Driving home, it was so warm that she begged to have the top of the carriage put back, and so she enjoyed the crowning pageant of the autumn, the full hunter's moon and the crimson ball of the sun both visible at once.

Wednesday found her busy at her desk, confessing to a slight cold, but making nothing of it. The next day bronchitis developed, followed by pneumonia. For several days the issue seemed doubtful, the strong constitution fighting for life. Two devoted physicians were beside her, one the friend of many years, the other a young assistant. The presence of the latter puzzled her, but his youth and strength seemed tonic to her, and she would rest quietly with her hand in his strong hand.

On Sunday evening the younger physician thought her convalescent; the elder said, "If she pulls through the next twenty-four hours, she will recover."

But she was too weary. That night they heard her say, "God will help me!" and again, toward morning, "I am so tired!"

Being alone for a moment with Maud, she spoke one word: a little word that had meant "good-bye" between them in the nursery days.

So, in the morning of Monday, October 17, her spirit passed quietly on to God's keeping.

Those who were present at her funeral will not forget it. The flower-decked church, the mourning multitude, the white coffin borne high on the shoulders of eight stalwart grandsons, the words of age-long wisdom and beauty gathered into a parting tribute, the bugle sounding Taps, as she passed out in her last earthly triumph, the blind children singing round the grave on which the autumn sun shone with a final golden greeting.

We have told the story of our mother's life, possibly at too great length; but she herself told it in eight words.

"Tell me," Maud asked her once, "what is the ideal aim of life?"

She paused a moment, and replied, dwelling thoughtfully on each word, —

"To learn, to teach, to serve, to enjoy!"

THE END

INDEX

INDEX

Abbott, J., i, 214, 215; ii, 99.
Abdin Palace, ii, 35, 36.
Abdul Hamid II, ii, 42.
Abdul Hassan, mosque of, ii, 36.
Aberdeen, Countess of, ii, 165, 166.
Aberdeen, J. C. H. Gordon, Earl of, ii, 165.
Abolitionists, i, 177, 305; ii, 171.
Academy of Fine Arts, French, ii, 23.
Acroceraunian Mountains, i, 272.
Acropolis, ii, 43.
Adamowski, Timothée, ii, 55, 58.
Adams, Charles Follen, ii, 270, 273; verse by, ii, 335.
Adams, Mrs. C. F., i, 266.
Adams, John, i, 4.
Adams, John Quincy, ii, 312.
Adams, Nehemiah, i, 168.
Advertiser, Boston, ii, 195, 222.
Ægina, i, 73.
Æschylus, ii, 130, 282, 348, 372.
Agassiz, Alexander, ii, 50.
Agassiz, Elizabeth Cary, i, 124, 345, 361; ii, 228, 287, 292.
Agassiz, Louis, i, 124, 151, 251, 345; ii, 150, 158.
Aïdé, Hamilton, ii, 251.
Airlie, Lady, ii, 254.
Alabama, ii, 108.
Albania, i, 272.
Albany, i, 342.
Albert of Savoy, ii, 303.
Albert Victor, ii, 9.
Albinola, Sig., i, 94.
Alboni, Marietta, i, 87.
Alcott, A. Bronson, i, 285, 290; ii, 57, 120.
Aldrich, Mrs. Richard, ii, 367.
Aldrich, T. B., i, 244, 262; ii, 70, 354, 357, 358.
Aldrich, Mrs. T. B., i, 245.
Alger, Wm. R., i, 207, 244, 245; ii, 127, 139, 140.
Allston, John, i, 12.
Alma-Tadema, Lady, ii, 168, 169.
Alma-Tadema, Laurence, ii, 168, 169, 171.
Almy, Mr., ii, 139.
Amadeo, ii, 31, 278.
Amalfi, ii, 33.
Amberley, Lady, i, 266.
Amélie, Queen, ii, 30.
America, i, 7, 11, 207, 247, 267, 273, 320, 344; ii, 18, 21, 189.

American Academy of Arts and Letters, ii, 399.
American Academy of Science, i, 251, 259.
American Authors, Society of, ii, 355.
American Branch, International Peace Society, i, 306.
American Civil War, i, 176, 186, 219–22; ii, 253.
American Institute of Education, ii, 68.
American Notes, i, 81.
American Peace Society, i, 303.
American Revolution, i, 6.
American School of Archæology, Athens, ii, 243.
American Woman Suffrage Association, i, 365.
Ames, Mr., ii, 166, 167.
Ames, Charles Gordon, i, 392; ii, 187, 193, 216, 229, 273, 280, 287, 288, 298, 324, 328, 358, 361.
Ames, Fanny, ii, 297.
Ames, Mrs. Sheldon, ii, 22.
Amsterdam, ii, 11.
Anacreon, i, 289.
Anagnos, Julia R., i, 96, 104, 106, 114, 115, 116, 119, 122, 126, 128, 133, 159–63, 172, 181, 216, 249–51, 264, 265, 267, 297, 349, 350, 352; ii, 46, 59, 65, 70, 73, 74, 115–20, 123, 127, 128, 129, 164, 349.
Anagnos, Michael, i, 273, 281, 288–90, 297, 331, 332; ii, 116–18, 129, 228, 229, 293, 300, 347, 348, 349, 357, 360.
Ancient and Honorable Artillery Company, i, 232.
Anderson, Hendrik, ii, 240, 243, 244, 248, 252.
Anderson, Isabel, ii, 233.
Anderson, Larz, i, 169; ii, 233, 287.
Andrew, John A., i, 150, 151, 186, 189, 195, 220, 231, 233, 238, 239, 246, 261, 283, 381; ii, 105, 265, 323.
Andrew, Mrs. J. A., i, 186, 231.
Andrews, E. B., ii, 187.
Anniversary Week, i, 389; ii, 151.
Anthony, Susan, ii, 344.
Antioch College, i, 169.
Antonayades, Mr., ii, 34.
Antwerp, i, 279; ii, 11, 172.
Antwerp Cathedral, ii, 11, 172.
Antwerp Musée, ii, 11, 172, 173.
Ap Thomas, Mr., i, 266.

Ventura, II, 136.
Ventura, Sig., II, 82.
Vergniaud, P. V., I, 7.
Vermont, I, 118; II, 68.
Verona, I, 278; II, 26, 27.
Versailles, I, 8, 309.
Vibbert, G. H., I, 364.
Victor Emanuel I, II, 28–30.
Victor Emanuel II, II, 30, 278.
Victoria, Queen, I, 267; II, 20, 127, 218, 283.
Victoria, Empress (Frederick), II, 20.
Victory, Temple of, I, 274.
Vienna, I, 94; II, 182.
Villegas, José, II, 240, 243, 256.
Vincent Hospital, II, 158.
Vineyard Haven, I, 342, 387.
Vinton, Mr., II, 287.
Virginia, I, 29.
Viti de Marco, Marchesa de, II, 255.
Viti de Marco, Marchese de, II, 255.
Voickoff, Alex, I, 350.
Voshell, Lucy, II, 344, 345, 347.

Waddington, Mary K., II, 9.
Waddington, William, II, 9.
Wade, Benjamin, I, 321.
Wadsworth, William, I, 86.
Wagner, Richard, II, 156.
Wales, I, 88; II, 166.
Walker, Francis, II, 150, 172, 226.
Wallace, H. B., I, 134, 271.
Wallack's Theatre, I, 143, 352.
Walmsley, Mrs., II, 209.
Ward, name of, I, 4.
Ward, Capt., II, 8.
Ward, Anne, I, 19, 22.
Ward, Annie. See Mailliard.
Ward, Emily A., I, 50, 57, 60, 64.
Ward, F. Marion, I, 17, 22, 30, 46–48, 58, 130, 352; II, 108, 174, 175, 411.
Ward, Henry, I, 22, 60.
Ward, Henry, I, 31, 60; II, 174, 175.
Ward, Henry, I, 17, 46–48, 58, 65, 66, 74, 341; II, 160, 277, 288, 411.
Ward, Herbert D., II, 270.
Ward, Mrs. Humphry, II, 165, 378.
Ward, John, I, 4.
Ward, John, I, 22, 28, 64–66, 72, 107, 129, 238, 242–45, 258, 351, 352; II, 401.
Ward, Julia, I, 17, 18.
Ward, Julia Rush, I, 17–22, 28, 61; II, 160, 235.
Ward, Louisa. See Crawford and Terry.
Ward, Mary. See Dorr.
Ward, Mary, I, 238.
Ward, May Alden, II, 270, 388.
Ward, Phœbe, I, 19.
Ward, Gov. Richard, I, 4.
Ward, Richard, I, 242, 351.
Ward, Gov. Samuel, I, 4; II, 78, 198, 221.

Ward, Col. Samuel, I, 5–9, 15, 16, 19, 21, 22, 37–39; II, 304, 320.
Ward, Samuel, I, 16–18, 21, 22, 25, 28, 29, 33–42, 46–52, 58–64, 68, 243, 272, 289, 351; II, 9, 16, 78, 89, 108, 235, 251, 319, 373.
Ward, Samuel, I, 17, 30, 42, 46, 48, 51, 56–58, 62, 64, 65, 72, 77, 78, 143, 147, 153, 154, 219, 242; II, 7, 55, 60, 66, 67, 71, 72, 74, 78, 93–96, 125, 267, 287, 304, 369, 375, 411, 413. Letters to, 69, 70, 78, 81, 83, 84, 86.
Ward, Thomas, I, 4.
Ward, W. G., I, 238, 242.
Ward, Mrs. W. G., I, 238.
Waring, George, II, 48.
Warner, C. D., II, 107, 198.
Warner, H. P., I, 265.
Warren, Mrs. Fiske, I, 288.
Warren, William, II, 97.
Warwick, R. I., I, 9, 16.
Washington, II, 134.
Washington, D.C., I, 186, 187, 189, 192, 200, 206, 238, 240, 246, 258, 259, 366; II, 131.
Washington, Booker, II, 233, 261.
Washington, George, I, 4–6, 12, 13, 111, 189; II, 143, 389.
Washington Heights, I, 111.
Wasson, Mr., I, 285, 290.
Waters, Mrs., II, 179.
Watts, Theodore, II, 171.
Webster, Dr., I, 132.
Webster, Sydney, II, 304.
Weiss, John, I, 284–86.
Wells, Amos R., II, 375.
Wendell, Barrett, II, 359.
Wendte, C. W., II, 78.
Wesselhoeft, William, Sr., II, 230, 231, 242, 264, 269, 275, 282.
Wesselhoeft, William, Jr., II, 284, 333.
Westminster Abbey, II, 6, 167, 171.
Wheeler, Joseph, II, 264.
Wheeling, I, 169.
Wheelwright, Mrs., II, 300.
Whipple, Charlotte, II, 267.
Whipple, E. P., I, 210, 222, 262.
Whistler, J. McN., II, 5, 72.
White, Mr., II, 323, 361.
White, A. D., I, 321.
White, Daisy R., II, 168.
White, Harry, II, 168.
Whitehouse, Fitzhugh, II, 326.
Whitman, Mrs. Henry, II, 313.
Whitman, Sarah, II, 180, 228, 262, 325.
Whitney, Bishop, II, 137.
Whitney, Mrs., II, 228.
Whitney, M. W., II, 265.
Whittier, J. G., I, 138, 152, 153, 210, 344; II, 177, 187, 355, 367, 368. Letter of, I, 138.
Wild, Hamilton, I, 201; II, 99.